Tennis
in the
NORTHLAND

A HISTORY OF
BOYS' HIGH SCHOOL TENNIS
IN MINNESOTA

(1929–2003)

by JIM HOLDEN

Beaver's Pond Press, Inc.

Front cover photos: (Top Left to Bottom Right of Front Flap) Jack Thommen, 1946 doubles champion from Minneapolis Southwest. David Wheaton, 1984 singles champion from Minnetonka. Paul Odland, two-time Class AA singles champion from Edina. Peg Brenden—won lawsuit to play on the St. Cloud Tech boys' team in 1972. Chuck Darley, three-time singles champion from Rochester. Erik Nelson, 1987 Class A singles champion from New London-Spicer. Inside Front Flap: Greenway of Coleraine doubles team of John Wirtanen (left) and Jim Miller (right) and coach Paul Bouchard (center). Eric Butorac, 1999 Class AA singles champion from Rochester John Marshall. Back Cover Photo: Brace Helgeson, member of St. Cloud Tech 1976 state championship team.

Answer to question on inside flap—*What do all of the following individuals have in common?*
All were Minnesota state champions.

ISBN 10: 1-59298-218-2
ISBN 13: 978-1-59298-218-9

Library of Congress Catalog Number: 2008921097

Printed in the United States of America

First Printing: 2008

12 11 10 09 08   5 4 3 2 1

Beaver's Pond Press, Inc.

7104 Ohms Lane, Suite 101
Edina, MN 55439
(952) 829-8818
www.BeaversPondPress.com

to order, visit www.BookHouseFulfillment.com
or call 1-800-901-3480. Reseller discounts available.

To John Mueller, for his lifetime of service to Minnesota tennis and his invaluable assistance in the writing of this book.

Contents

Foreword

I first knew Jim Holden as the boy's high school coach who built a winning program in Northfield, MN. His impressive record and meritorious service to the Minnesota Coaches Association brought him Hall of Fame recognition. His most important legacy, however, lay in his dedication to the youngsters and the life lessons he taught them. Whenever I asked his players about Jim or the Northfield program, they always responded with praise and appreciation.

Next Jim became my colleague at Gustavus Adolphus College, preparing students to become effective high school teachers. He developed a special interest in Mark Ensrud, a gifted English and secondary education major who also played on the varsity tennis team and taught at Tennis and Life Camps. Northfield needed an English teacher and a dynamic tennis coach who could keep the Northfield program strong, and Mark was the perfect man for the job.

Now I know Jim as a researcher and author, past retirement age, still passionate about Minnesota high school tennis. *Tennis in the Northland* is a labor of love that celebrates the accomplishments of Minnesota's best high school boys' tennis players and the service of Minnesota's most dedicated high school coaches. Anyone with an interest in Minnesota tennis will enjoy Jim's book immensely.

Tennis in the Northland is a comprehensive history of Minnesota boys' high school tennis. It contains all the records and facts that one would expect a good historian to gather. All of the state champions and the Hall of Fame coaches—and so many more—are featured here. Holden's book is special because he took the time to interview many, many people. Their stories and insights offer rare perspectives that show the hopes, values, humor, and lives of the Minnesota boys' tennis community.

Most of the featured people are not famous. Their accomplishments would not attract national attention. But Jim has molded their stories into a beautiful mosaic that captures the reader's attention and expresses the essence of Minnesota boys' high school tennis. Already some of the people that he interviewed have died, but their memories recorded here will continue to live, reminding us of an interesting era that otherwise could have escaped our attention.

Minnesota tennis enthusiasts owe a deep debt to Jim Holden. *Tennis in the Northland* took years to write; and the history it captures is priceless. Jim will never be reimbursed monetarily for his long hours of labor, but his reward will be great. He will be remembered as a Hall of Fame coach with an asterisk after his name, designating years of meritorious service to Minnesota boys' high school tennis long after he retired from coaching.

—Steve Wilkinson, Gustavus Men's Tennis Coach

Acknowledgements

Attempting to give credit to those who assisted in the creation of this book is a bit like the Academy Award winning actor trying to remember to thank everyone who helped him/her win the award. You're nervous about it and you don't want to leave anyone out; on the other hand, you don't want to ramble on and on. It's an impossible task, and you know you can't please everyone; but you carry on.

So that's what I will do, carry on, with the understanding that I will slight some who deserve credit. I begin with an apology to those who might have reason to ask, "Why didn't he mention my name?"

At the top of the list of people to thank is my long-suffering wife, Caroline, who encouraged me from the get-go, put up with having the phone out of commission when I was on the computer, and read the manuscript with interest and a keen eye. Next, I offer a heartfelt thank you to all who read chapters and provided valuable suggestions: Wayne Kivell, longtime Northfield girls' tennis coach and for many years my doubles partner; Scott Nesbit, 1975 State doubles champion, St. Olaf College men's and women's tennis coach, and one of my flyfishing buddies; Bob Phelps, a friend who is also a trained journalist with a keen sense of what looks good and what doesn't; and all of the players and coaches who read e-mail drafts or listened patiently while I read their profiles to them over the phone.

I'd also like to thank three of Minnesota's tennis oldtimers, some of the first individuals I interviewed for this book: Marv Hanenberger, Jack Thommen, and Bernie Gunderson. Marv, my oldest living "contact" from the first years of high school tennis in Minnesota (he played in the third State Tournament in 1932), gave me a wealth of information about Rochester tennis. (There is more about Marv scattered throughout the book, but there is a profile on him in Chapter Nine.) Jack has taken a keen interest in my project right from the start, and he often calls and gives me encouragement with words to this effect,

"How's your book going, Jim?" You'll read about Jack in chapters six and eight. Bernie, a former Minneapolis Washburn High School, U of M Gopher, and top-ranked senior player and a great supporter of local tennis, has also provided moral support. Bernie and Jack, by the way, were inducted into the Northern Section Hall of Fame in 2007.

Next, I'm most grateful to Hall of Fame coach Steve Wilkinson for writing the Foreword, for providing a treasury of resources (especially information about Minnesota high school champions who played tennis at Gustavus), and for his insightful suggestions.

In addition, I am grateful to the staff at Beaver's Pond Press, but especially Milt and Dara, for all their help and to the graphic designer of *Tennis in the Northland*, Jay Monroe of James Monroe Design.

Thanks also to the staff at the MSHSL who allowed me to snoop through the *ANNUALS* and tennis tournament programs to find scores of matches and other information I really needed. Special kudos to Director of Information Howard Voigt who burned a CD of photos I selected from old *ANNUALS* and gave me permission to use these photos in the book.

While I'm on the topic of permissions, I'm also grateful to the USTA Northern Section folks for allowing me to use photos from their *Yearbooks*. Special thanks to former Marketing/Communications Director David Shama and his successor, Lisa Mushett, for dredging up information about NWTA Hall of Fame members and for answering my many questions. Thanks also to Northfield friend Ardy Koehler for scanning photos for me.

John Mueller and the President's Award

Finally, this book could not have been written without the inestimable help I received from John Mueller. John was a three-year star at Robbinsdale High School and a standout college tennis player who played No. 1 singles and doubles for three years at Augsburg and one year at St. Cloud State. After graduation and a stint in the Service, John went on to become a very successful USPTA pro in area clubs such as the Golden Valley Country Club, Oakdale, and North Star, and a high school coach. But I know him best as the official historian of Minnesota tennis, and in that role he provided me with information which laid the foundation for this book: all the results from every boys' high school tournament from 1929-2001, results from the girls' tournaments from 1974 (the first year) to 2001, the Interscholastic Tournament results from 1903 to 1949 (the last year), results from the private/parochial school tournaments, and answers to my thorniest questions.

John has given his life to tennis in Minnesota, not only through his coaching but also through his work in various capacities for the Northern Section. For example, he has chaired the Hall of Fame Committee, headed up the Awards Committee, helped rate players for USTA League tennis, and served on the board of directors. As a result of these efforts, he has earned praise from those he taught (Apple Valley coach Denise Remak called him "the brightest tennis man I know") and two coveted awards from the Section: Frank Voigt Pro of the Year in 1979 and the President's Award in 1997.

Throughout the years he has had a passion for preserving Minnesota's rich tennis history, and he has done a great deal of reading, researching, and recording in order to preserve this history. I'm betting a new tennis racket that he knows more about Minnesota tennis history than anyone in the state (well, maybe Bob Larson can challenge him to a Tennis Trivial Pursuit battle).

So, John, this book's for you; and I proudly dedicate it in gratitude for all you have done to help it become a reality.

Notes to Readers

1. I have used quotations from **Shakespeare's works** to introduce each chapter because I find Shakespeare's observations about human nature relevant even to the sport of tennis.

2. With respect to **dates**, you will note that I concluded the narratives of the singles and doubles champions with the 2003 spring season, the actual 75th year of authorized state high school tournament play. However, when it seemed logical to do so, I included information as recent as 2007 in some of the other chapters.

3. Therefore, as you read the book, you will note that I have provided personal information about individuals that reflects their current life status.

4. Finally, I saw the following **poem** in the 1931 MSHSL *ANNUAL* and thought it appropriate for the book because so many of the individuals I spoke to talked about the friendships they developed from their time in tennis.

Did you lose the match?

Did his shots go past?

Were his serves too speedy?

His volleys too fast?

Did your lobs fly out, your slams hit the net?

Were you beaten so badly you didn't get a set?

Did you do your best, call everything right?

Play hard to the end, not lose your fight?

Praise his good shots, and not get sore?

Then you made a friend,

That's more than the score—

And you had a good time,

That's what the game's for.

—Daniel Chase

Introduction

It is in the spirit of this remark, made by Elizabeth (King Henry IV's queen) to King Richard, that I commend this book to all who have an interest in Minnesota boys' high school tennis. Of course I hope it is compelling and so will speed you along, but I also hope the stories are plainly and simply told. This is a book of stories about tennis players, coaches, teams, professional coaches, fans, and others who have contributed to the game here in the northland. It is an attempt to preserve an important part of Minnesota high school sports history in order to overcome what novelist Milan Kundera, in *The Book of Laughter and Forgetting*, calls "the struggle of memory against forgetting." I remember glancing at the obituary column in the *Star Tribune* on January 15, 2004, and seeing the headline "Charles Britzius, Engineer, Dies at 92," and kicking myself for not interviewing this first state doubles champion and singles runner-up before he passed away. Lest we forget the stories of Minnesota tennis players such as Britzius, I have interviewed perhaps 300 people and invited them to share their memories, their stories.

"An honest tale speeds best being plainly told."
—Richard III

There are of course pitfalls in telling stories in this manner, for memory is fallible, subjective, capricious. So reader beware. And no doubt there are some errors of fact contained in these pages, perhaps even a few unintended exaggerations. For these I apologize, but I do not apologize for making first-person stories a central focus of the book, for stories are the lifeblood of a culture, including that of tennis. An Indian proverb captures this idea so well: "Tell me a fact and I'll learn. Tell me a truth and I'll believe. But tell me a story and it will live in my heart forever."

Because I had coached tennis during its growth years of the 1970s and '80s, I suppose I fancied myself something of a custodian of the past for boys' high school tennis. So of the many memorable stories I recounted in this book, readers will discover (1) what it was like to play in the 1932 tournament from the words of nonagenerian Marv Hanenberger; (2)

how flip cards helped 1939 singles champion Christie Geanakoplos learn to play tennis; (3) how a small school like St. James managed to upset mighty Rochester in the 1954 tournament; (4) which players are considered the best in state history and why; (4) how the sleepy farm community of Blue Earth developed into a tennis power; (5) information about the role of professional coaches such as Frank Voigt on the high school tennis scene; (6) why Edina has been able to maintain its dominance of boys' tennis; (7) who were and are the preeminent coaches; and, (8) some of the compelling stories resulting from our unpredictable spring weather.

In addition to these narratives, there is an appendix which includes information about teams, players, coaches, and even media personalities. I decided to include this information because there is no one place where it can be found and because I have always had a passion for sports data. When I was a young boy growing up in Sherburn, MN, I was a baseball statistics junkie who could name the position players on most major league teams and especially those of my favorite team, the St. Louis Cardinals. But I could also recite the batting averages, number of home runs, runs batted in, stolen bases, errors, and fielding percentages of my favorite Cardinals' players. When I started coaching tennis in 1971, I found a new outlet for this mania and began keeping records for my new sport, compiling a year-end record book which included individual players' wins and losses, team dual-meet records, the team record against other schools, individual honors won by players during the season, etc. I also found myself turning to the high school results section of the *Star Tribune* every day during the season to check tennis match scores. This "obsession" led me to pore over the rankings list, the prize money winners' list, and even Grand Slam results in my monthly tennis magazines as well. And I suppose it's one reason I eventually served for many years as the coaches' rankings representative for Region I.

In doing research for this book, I had some difficulty tracking down Minnesota high school tennis data. To be sure, the *ANNUALS* in the MSHSL office were important resources and Minnesota tennis historian John Mueller provided a great deal of information, but there is no one book or central location one can consult to find much of the data included here.

More important than the statistics listed in the appendix, however, are the tales told by Minnesota tennis players, coaches, and others involved in the game. But because human memory is idiosyncratic and often uncertain, I also relied on stories in back issues of Bob Larson's *Tennis Midwest* magazine, articles in the *Star Tribune* and other newspapers, more recent editions of the MSHSL *ANNUALS*, and old high school yearbooks stored at the Minnesota Historical Society library. But for the most part I wanted to honor the subjects I interviewed by giving them a chance to tell their stories in their own words.

My search was a delightful journey that gave me the privilege of talking to many extraordinary individuals who have given so much to the great game of tennis. And each interviewee in turn led me to someone else I should contact: "Oh, you should talk to so and so," they would say. I was like my two-year-old grandson discovering things on a walk to the park: first a pine cone, then a manhole cover, then a boxelder bug crawling on the sidewalk. At other times I was a detective tracking down clues.

Alas, I could not track down some clues and I could not talk to every former singles and doubles champion or coach (some are deceased and others I could not locate). So some stories are incomplete snapshots, but I believe those which I have developed more fully are representative. And though these stories have not played out on the bright lights of Broadway stages, there have been many dramatic performances on "off-Broadway" tennis stages all over the state of Minnesota. So while the actors on these stages may not have gotten as much ink as their big stage football or basketball brethren, many of their performances were truly memorable to those of us who were privileged enough to see them.

What follows is the result of my search for stories about people who play and coach tennis, watch tennis, and love tennis. So I hope former players, former and current coaches, and all tennis lovers will take pleasure in reading this book. I hope you'll also make some new discoveries about Minnesota boys' high school tennis, but above all I hope you enjoy the stories.

Foul Weather
in the Northland

I can't think of a better expression than Shakespeare's to describe those who play or coach tennis in Minnesota in the early spring. We must all be fools to endure the indignities heaped on us by our cruel spring weather. Californians and Floridians, you have no clue. I vividly recall one such indignity my friend Wayne Kivell (the former Northfield girls' tennis coach) and I endured in early May of 2002. We had driven to Red Wing to watch the Northfield boys' team play the Wingers on a day most people would not have let their dogs out of the house. Coach Mark Ensrud of Northfield had persuaded the Red Wing coach to play the match because there weren't many makeup days left before the conference and region tournaments. It was one of those alternately miserable but at times marginally playable spring days that give those of us who live in Minnesota false hope. At best the temperature was barely above freezing , so we were dressed appropriately in layers of clothes (t-shirts, woolen shirts, sweatshirts, down jackets, jeans), but when we arrived at the courts it started to mist and the wind was blowing. So we traipsed back to the car for our rain jackets. As soon as the match started the sun came out, but only to tease, for within seconds it started to sleet. This was followed by a few light snowflakes, more sporadic wind gusts, the sun peaking through gray clouds again, more light sprinkles, and even a brief burst of hail. And still the boys played on—it was Minnesota after all. Numbed by the cold, buffeted by the wind, and chilled by the rain, we finally retreated to the comfort of our heated

> *"Lord, what fools these mortals be. "*
> —A Midsummer Night's Dream

car and drove back to Northfield before the match was completed.

But even in late May or early June the weather here can play havoc with the best-laid plans. For example, in the district tournament finals at Waseca in 1975 it began to rain hard and the coaches were advised that there were tornado warnings for the area. So we packed up our gear and drove to nearby Owatonna to finish the tournament sans rain and tornado warnings. And many years the State Tournament is bedeviled by foul weather. Perhaps the best example to illustrate is one from the 1980 team final. According to *Star Tribune* writer Howard Sinker, the tournament "started beneath a bright sun and ended up beneath an air-conditioned bubble after a heavy thunderstorm at the 98th Street Racquet Club in Bloomington. The rain pounding down on the bubble caused enough racket—the noisy kind—to mess with attention spans and mute judges' calls. It was hot inside, too. There was more. A power failure suspended the 1980 final for about twenty minutes and, about three hours after the first serve, Edina West escaped with a 3-2 win [over Anoka]" (June 4, 1980).

Coach Tom Vining of Roseville talked about how coaches learned to adapt to the weather as they grew older. "It took a number of spring seasons until you finally learned how to dress for the weather. In your 20s you wore the sport coat you taught in that day; but in your 40s you had boots over your wing tips, long johns under your Dockers, and an Arctic parka slung over your shoulder."

Changeable weather is typical of spring days in Minnesota, for spring can be as capricious as a two-year old who can't decide what she wants, an unpredictable wild animal in captivity, or a restless sleeper who tosses and turns all night. Choose what metaphor you will, the truth is that playing tennis here in the northland in the spring is a tremendous challenge. So what follows are some selected stories from Minnesota coaches and players, stories reflecting the challenges (and the humor) of playing tennis in the state in the spring.

Let's begin with a "four elements" comparison. Remember these: earth, air, wind, and fire? The Greeks described them as making up the basic structure of the cosmos. Well, we have our own four cosmic elements that plague those who try to play tennis in the spring in Minnesota. First there's *snow and ice*, then there's *rain*, then *cold*, and finally *wind*—one of the four original elements.

The first of these elements, a hindrance of monumental proportions, is *snow* (and its companion *ice*), the last vestige of winter which sometimes hangs on even into May. Almost everyone I spoke with talked of shoveling this white menace in the early season or even blowing it off with snowblowers to make the courts playable. In addition, many spoke of shoveling snow even in mid-April or early May in order to play a match. For instance, on April 15, 1983, a storm dumped sixteen inches of snow on the courts in Northfield and over much of the state, forcing 400 schools to close, halting mail deliveries, closing the Minneapolis airport for five hours, causing numerous power outages, and deflating the Metrodome. This unexpected calamity gave my players a chance to perform four days of unpaid community service while shoveling off the courts. When they were done shoveling, our five courts were a tiny island in the midst of a vast snowfield.

Even a week later, during a match we played in Simley, snow banks surrounded the courts there. That year we were also scheduled to play a tournament in Coon Rapids, but it was snowed out twice and eventually canceled. This sixteen-inch storm was of course an anomaly (a record snowfall for that date and the most snow that late in the spring), but snow showers sometimes bedevil Minnesota tennis players well into May.

For example, Coach Bud Schmid of Brainerd remembers one year in May when a foot of snow fell the night before a scheduled match. I would have been inspired by the words of the legendary early twentieth century Mayor Curley of Boston who said, after a great snowfall in the city, "God put it [the snow] there and God will take it away." I would have done the sensible thing and postponed the meet. But Bud, the intrepid Minnesota coach, was not deterred. In the true pioneering spirit of Minnesota tennis coaches, he rousted his players up early and, according to Bud, "they shoveled off the courts—eight of them, enough to have the snow melt and we did play the match that PM."

To be fair, storms of this magnitude in May are relatively rare. It was April, dubbed "the cruelest month" by T. S. Eliot in *The Waste Land*, that often blew snow on the courts and in the faces of players. Here is a story, told by Coach Tom Vining of Alexander Ramsey, that perhaps best exemplifies this "only-in-Minnesota-in-the-spring" experience.

> We were playing in a four-team round robin tournament at Blue Earth on an extremely ugly April Saturday. Somehow we managed to defeat each team under circumstances that I can only describe as incredible. At one point during our final match with Hal's squad [Blue Earth, coached by Hal Schroeder], nearing the end of this brutal day, I called my captain over to the fence to say a few words. After chatting for but a few seconds, I noticed that his eyeglasses became completely covered over with driving snow. All I saw were those two white disks where his eyes should have been and I started laughing. It was absurd. It symbolized for me Minnesota tennis in the spring.

The match (and day) mercifully ended and Vining and his players headed home. But the saga continued, as Vining noted:

> We were slowed to a crawl by a snowstorm on the way home, and, to top it off, the school van ran out of gas in the middle of nowhere. Kids hiked to a farmhouse and returned with enough gas to get us to the nearest town. One kid had the presence of mind to call his folks and get them to call others to tell them we were OK but that we'd be home late. Some time around one AM, as I crawled into bed, I had a fleeting vision of looking into my captain's whited-out eyes and I laughed quietly to myself. Minnesota tennis, sometimes it makes no sense. I'm still laughing.

Coach Whitey Olson of Thief River Falls has a similar, if less dramatic, story about an April tournament in St. Cloud: "On the way to St. Cloud we ran into about three inches of snow. Ten miles north of Detroit Lakes we ended up forty yards into a plowed field. I called Coach Bill Ritchie and he agreed to rearrange our team's early round match. We won the tournament." And 1986 singles champion Jason Hall of Minnehaha Academy told about the time he "played a match wearing gloves and a hat, with snow falling."

These are just stories about playing in the snow. What about getting the snow and ice off the courts in early April to clear them for practice? In most cases the school custodians would not perform this job, so it was left to the players and coaches to clear the courts. For instance, Coach Jolly Carlson of Madison said, "Our courts were used as a multiple play center for elementary students, so the ice always packed down." His sons Jeff, 1978 state doubles champion, and Barry, recall with no little amusement those days of clearing the courts. Jeff said, "We were always so excited to get out there we would be chipping ice and hauling it off the courts in wheelbarrows." Barry remembers even using hair dryers to melt the ice, but he especially recalls the ice-chipping: "We would 'recapture' one court at a time [there were three black top courts] with just enough room behind the baseline and sidelines to do groundstrokes. . . any type of angle shot or deep lob took you into a skating adventure." Two-time state doubles champion Dave Mathews of Edina (1967-68) also recalls that coach John Matlon, ever the taskmaster, " would get us out on Saturday with ice chippers and shovels and wheelbarrows to get ice off the courts." And only in Minnesota would a coach (Tom Osborn of Mound) jokingly remark that "every year we continue to order shovels along with tennis balls."

To my knowledge no one has been killed playing or practicing in such conditions and on such icy surfaces; in truth the courts were the ones that suffered most, sustaining damage each year from all that shoveling, scraping, and chipping. But what could one do? In some of the far northern towns, teams might not have been playing outside until late May if they hadn't helped nature along.

The second element, *rain*, is of course not unique to Minnesota, for April showers bring misery to coaches and players alike no matter where the rain falls. But coupled with cold temperatures, our spring rains have more of a bite to them than those in Florida or California, for example. And for those who coach, rain becomes a literal (or figurative) bleak cloud over their heads. I remember my obsession with weather reports and my frustration when rain forced us into the gym for practice and "chalk talks," or caused meets to be canceled. Other times we squeegeed the courts, sent the boys out to play, then cursed silently when another cloudburst descended and washed out all our good efforts. I also recall one fateful year when we twice drove all the way to Austin (seventy miles), only to be rained out both times. Particularly in the years before indoor courts were available as backups, such rainouts often created a backlog of rescheduled meets. Still, in keeping with the toughness of Minnesotans, sometimes the show went on in spite of the rain. John Desmond, 1958 doubles champion, recalls with pride his days of playing in the rain: "We used to play at the U of M courts when it was raining, using old metal rackets [excellent lightning attractors, by the way] with wire strings. I still remember the nice noise when you hit with them."

Class A singles champion Gregg Anderson (1980) from Blue Earth, at the time playing No. 2 doubles for Robbinsdale Cooper, recalled one of his matches: "I remember playing in the rain at the Stillwater tournament and winning the match after my dad (Coach Chuck Anderson) 'forced' us to stay on the court." 1978 doubles champion Greg Carlson of Madison also recalls playing in the rain at a Saturday invitational tournament: "My brother Gary, playing No. 1 singles against Dean Niehus of Pipestone in 1976, hit a water puddle three times and won a third set tiebreaker 5-4." Today matches like this would not likely be played, for we have become much more concerned about the potential for injury on slick, wet courts. But perhaps the most unusual rain story is one told by former Edina boys' coach Steve Paulsen. "One Saturday morning at the Edina Invitational Tournament, we had to dry the courts; so we went to the country club to get squeegies and gas-powered leaf blowers. Some parents got frustrated, so one of them called a friend who flew a

helicopter. Unfortunately, he couldn't make it so we cancelled the matches."

The next element is *cold*, something that high school players in warm weather states rarely have to contend with. We did not have courts at Northfield High School my first two years, so we practiced on the Carleton College courts at 6:30 AM. My rule of thumb was that if the air temperature was thirty-two degrees or above, we practiced. We could usually do that, in part because there was rarely a wind that early in the morning. One of the players, Northfield's No. 1 singles player from 1972-74, Stan Hunter, memorialized this experience in music. An excellent musician and singer, he created a tennis theme song—to be sung at 6:30 AM when the temperature was thirty-six degrees or lower. Here are the lyrics as Stan recalled them, sung, as he said, "in a low monotone voice, as if one were very cold, and had gotten up too early."

Playin' in the mornin' with three dead balls,
Playin' in the mornin' with three dead balls,
Playin' in the mornin' with three dead balls,
'n' it's colder than hell.

And anyone who played in Minnesota surely remembers bundling up in sweats, gloves, hats, and maybe even long underwear to practice or compete in some of those numbingly cold early season days. 1988 Class A singles champion Roger Anderson of Blue Earth tells about "searching our sock drawers hoping to find one with a hole in the toe so we could slide the racket handle through the hole and wear the sock over our hand to keep warm." Owatonna coach Tom Byrne said, "It was so cold and windy one day I had to stay in the van and the players wore gloves." Kent Helgeson of St. Cloud Tech recalls playing when the air temperature was below freezing, and his brother Grant remembers a match he played with Billy Nolen of Litchfield. "The match went three sets and ended up being 16-18 in the third set with gusty winds, intermittent snowflakes. Colder than hell but great fun even in losing." Only in Minnesota would a player say it was great fun to play in such conditions.

In the spirit of Nordic Minnesota stoicism, Farmington coach Jack Olwell recalls one year, in the early 1980s, when it did not snow in January and February. During those two months he and one of his valiant players played regularly even on days as cold as eight degrees above zero. About these experiences, Olwell said, "You would be surprised how little difference there was in the ball and racket response. If it was windy we couldn't play because our eyes would water too much. Sometimes, however, the cold defeated us." Coach Ken Peterson of Anoka added, "In 1974 we didn't get outside until our first match on April 17th."

Ah, *wind*! The last of these four devilish elements so common in a Minnesota spring. I like what 1965 singles champion Bob Gray of Rochester had to say about this "bete noire" of Minnesota tennis players: "You couldn't be a successful tennis player in Minnesota if you couldn't play in the wind because in the spring after you shoveled off the courts, you had to know how to play in the wind." For some players the wind positively unhinged them, and they were beaten as soon as they got out of bed and noticed a stiff breeze from the north. Others took the view that the conditions were the same for both players and made the wind their ally, hitting hard topspin shots with the wind at their backs, employing occasional drop shots into the wind, spinning in a high percentage of first serves with the wind, cranking harder first serves into the wind, and hitting crisp topspin lobs into the wind.

Still, even these strategies often failed in the fierce nor'easters that sometimes blew in. 1981 singles champion Bob Bateman of Edina talked about a tournament in Austin in which the wind was blowing at forty mph. "I hit lobs as hard as I could into the wind that came back on my side of the court. . . I loved to lob and I wasn't the smartest guy. It was crazy windy." These were straight south-to-north winds, but the cross winds were nearly impossible to deal with. As an example, 1975-76 singles champion Mark Wheaton of Minnetonka said, "I remember matches when the wind was blowing sideways with gale force and I had to hit the ball into the next court in order for it to go in."

Many high school courts (such as those at Rosemount) were located on treeless plateaus, offering greater opportunities for wind to work its mischief. 1969 singles runner-up Ted Warner of Edina recollects an experience on such courts: "Cooper [Robbinsdale] was out in the middle of nowhere with no trees or protection, so when the Cooper guys took their racket covers off, they peeled back and stuck to the fence." Also, if you played or coached in even one spring season in Minnesota, you surely remember empty tennis ball cans doing erratic conga dances across the courts in the middle of points, or every ball in every hopper rolling to the east (or west) end of the courts depending on the direction of the wind. Coach Jane Kjos of Benson shared this unusual wind story. "We were headed home after a match in Fergus Falls. It was so windy that the van door blew open and it bent so much we couldn't get it shut. So we found a rope at a service station and tied the door shut and drove seventy-five miles home."

To try and combat this nemesis coaches counseled their fragile-minded charges about staying positive on windy days, told them to elect to play with the wind (or against it) for the first game if they won the spin so they could play with (or against) the wind for the next two games, decided who should serve with or against the wind, etc. Anything to make them think they had an advantage. In addition, we planted fast-growing trees like poplars and, of course, bought windscreens and installed them on the fences. Unfortunately, even windscreens were of no use in the occasional spring "tornadoes." Remember those downed tennis fences you'd see after a big storm? Often the windscreens had pulled them down. Or the windscreen fasteners would pull loose and the screens would flap in the breeze like the mainsail on a schooner helplessly adrift in an angry sea.

But mostly, stalwart coaches opted to play, even in near typhoon-like winds. Chuck Anderson's rule was that you played if the temperature was forty degrees and the wind was blowing at forty mph or less. Sure, there were the occasional postponements; but mostly you played the matches when they were scheduled. Coach George Beske of Minneapolis South cites an exception when South had a match with Coach Dave Loo's Fridley team one spring. It was "canceled by the wind and flying sand that somehow showed up on occasion on the Fridley courts." And playing in the wind forced coaches to bring their tennis rule books along to meets, especially to clarify what to do when the ball bounced on the opponent's side and blew back onto your court. Some players didn't know that this was one time you could reach over the net (provided you didn't touch it) and hit the ball. 1982 and 1985 state doubles champion Myles Anderson of Blue Earth described one such experience. Again, in a match at the infamous Austin courts and on the "windiest day I have ever played in," Myles said, "I had one shot into the wind that I hit so hard it blew back and landed just in front of the net and bounced on my side for the point—game and match."

One of my former players, Paul Jenkins, shared some additional wind stories from his years of playing on Northfield's windswept courts. Paul's first story was about a makeshift wind gauge: "Remember Eric Olson's [Paul's teammate] 'wind gauge'? He'd hold his racket head down and the wind would blow the suspended, covered racket from its original 180-degree angle back to 125 degrees." My own wind gauge, chucking leaves or grass into the air to determine the wind direction, was more primitive. Jenkins also said, "I remember hitting a desperation lob on one of the end courts that began its flight outside the fence but was blown back in, thanks to the gale-force zephyr. My befuddled opponent was too surprised to manage a winning reply. That's a home court advantage." His final tale might be apocryphal, but maybe not. According to Paul, "I also swear I recall Andy [Ringlien-1976 doubles champion from Northfield] hitting a kick serve that bounced over the fence. This sounds improbable, but I remember it clearly. His poor opponent was flabbergasted."

What could one do except make the most of these deplorable conditions, as most players and coaches did? Coach Bill Ritchie of St. Cloud Tech, speaking, I suspect, for most of his colleagues, said, "We practiced in bad weather so the players would not let weather conditions affect their games." But before you could even confront the elements, you usually had to endure days and even weeks of practice on slick and fast indoor gym surfaces. John Matlon (and many other coaches) had players hit targets on the gym walls. Mark Wheaton remembers "running in the school halls and getting shin splints," and Roger Anderson recalls hitting sponge balls against the walls of the Blue Earth gym. I had my players run the balcony steps, and we always did conditioning drills and ran wind sprints in the gym.

Coach Bud Schmid of Brainerd put it best: "It was always a race to get the kids ready for competition... so you developed indoor wall drills and became a master at circuit drills to keep all players active and interested. This usually meant early AM hours or late evening hours when the gym was available." Tennis was too often accorded "minor sport" status, so it was difficult to wrest court time away from the so-called major sports such as baseball and, after 1974, softball. Imagine, with only one to maybe three courts in the gym, the chaos that also ensued in the crowded conditions indoors. Coach Mike Remington (now at Eagan) tells this story about one spring when he coached at Rosemount. "With fifty-four tennis players hitting in a small auxiliary gym, the first lesson I learned was to trust my instinct when ducking flying balls; i. e., shadows, watching people around you, etc. You don't need to necessarily see the flying missile approaching to get out of the way."

Sometimes, in a break from the monotony of spending day after day in the gym, coaches let up and gave players a chance to play basketball or other gym games (Bob Bateman recalls playing a basketball game with his Edina teammates against his good friend Todd Ward and his SPA teammates after their match had been rained out, describing it "as the most fun I had in the early season.").

Finally, even before gym practice began, coaches had to go to great lengths to jury-rig gyms and make them tennis-ready. For example, my first year I asked the metal shop teacher to create two standards (made of inflated car tires with metal poles welded into the middle) and two steel hooks that could be inserted in the pulled-up bleachers at each end of the gym. The two tires served as net posts for three courts and the hooks were used to fasten the two outside nets into the bleachers at the proper height. In addition, I painstakingly measured out the courts each year and applied tape as lines so we could hit on an almost-regulation-size court.

One last story illustrates yet another problem for Minnesota tennis players and coaches in the spring: the gathering darkness. Again, here's coach Bud Schmid. "Another funny but typical problem was to try and get the full match in before dark and it always seemed to involve the No. 3 singles player, often a younger competitor. One time we were finishing a match by car lights. It went on forever, so I eventually forfeited the match so we could at least get home by midnight."

With the growth of indoor courts and a new breed of coaches who may be less willing to set up indoor courts in the gym, shovel snow, turn on car lights to finish matches, or sweep and wash the courts, there will probably be fewer and fewer stories such as these, which represent what so many coaches had to do in order to launch their seasons in the often erratic Minnesota spring climate. What to those of us who coached and played in the decades of the 1930s-70s and even early '80s seemed normal, today must seem primitive, quaint, and maybe even a bit obsessive. But it helped us, fools though we were, to cope with the cruel and fickle spring weather that made it so difficult to play tennis in Minnesota in the spring.

Hall of Fame
Coaches

To be sure it is an exclusive group, twenty-eight "fathers unto many sons" (and two "mothers") who represent the hundreds of boys' tennis coaches since 1929 who have struggled with gale-force spring winds and bone-chilling thirty-three degree days, unco-operative athletic directors, unhelpful school maintenance personnel, parents who think they know more than coaches, players who break training rules—and coaches' hearts—and the occasional coach who stacks his/her lineup. Despite such impediments, these coaches persevered—some for almost forty years, happily coaching young men (and a few young women) for very little monetary reward, and sometimes even less acclaim, from a culture that placed a higher value on so-called major sports such as football, basketball, and baseball. Critics might call them "dedicated masochists," for who in his/her right mind would choose to spend up to forty hours a week on top of a full teaching load hitting hundreds of tennis balls in practice each day, shouting instructions into the wind, and driving sweaty adolescents home from tennis meets for a few hundred dollars. What was it that motivated them? Certainly a love for the game of tennis—which many, but not all, of them played as young men and women—and certainly the joy of working with teenagers during those still-impressionable ages of thirteen-eighteen; but it had to be much more than that.

"'Tis a happy thing to be father unto many sons."

—*King Henry VI*

First of all, these coaches came from all parts of the state: the far north, Thief River Falls; the far west, Madison; the far south, Blue Earth; the far east, Hastings; other out-state places; and the Twin Cities and suburbs. Some have coached teams that won State

Tournaments, some have not; some have coached other sports, some have not; some were tennis players in their youth, some were not; some coached girls' tennis, some did not; some were strict disciplinarians, some were not; some were sticklers for conditioning, some focused more on tactics; some were outspoken, some were not. You get the idea—just as every human being is different, so were and are successful tennis coaches.

But enough of this; let's meet these dynamic coaches. In order of their induction into the Minnesota (MN) Boys' Tennis Coaches Association Hall of Fame, they are John Adams of Robbinsdale, Mac Doane of St. Cloud, John Matlon of Edina, Reg Mead of Wadena, and Hal Schroeder of Blue Earth (1993); Jolly Carlson of Madison and Bud Schmid of Brainerd (1994); Whitey Olson of Thief River Falls, Keith Paulson of Austin, and Ed Sewell of North St. Paul (1995); Jerry Sales of St. Cloud Tech and Steve Wilkinson of Gustavus Adolphus College—the only non-high school coach (1996); Jim Holden of Northfield (1997); John Hatch of Blake, Len McGuire of Stillwater, and Lyle Steffenson of Hastings (2000); Henry Dison of Lake City and Ollie Guest of Robbinsdale Cooper (2001); Ted Greer of Edina (2002); Bruce Getchell of White Bear Lake (2003); Cliff Caine of St. Paul Academy, Dallas Hagen of United South Central/Wells—the first woman elected, and Bill Ritchie of St. Cloud Tech (2004); John Eberhart of Pine City, Cheryl King of Anoka, and Mike Premo of Foley (2006); and George Beske of Minneapolis South and Bob Pivec of Coon Rapids (2007).

When we think of a hall of fame, perhaps we think of questions such as the following: What are the qualifications for membership? Who decides? How does one get nominated? These and other questions were addressed by a dedicated group of coaches, led by coach Ken Peterson of Anoka, who wrote a proposal and submitted it for approval to the tennis coaches at the spring 1987 Coaches Association Clinic. The proposal established (1) the *purpose* of the Hall of Fame, (2) the *nominating process*, (3) the *selection committee membership*, (4) the *selection process*, (5) the *criteria for selection*, and (6) the *awards* to be given.

The nominating form to be submitted for potential new members of the Hall of Fame included the usual personal information such as name, address, birthplace, marriage status, children and their ages, and spouse's name; the nominating person or group; rationale for the nomination; personal and coaching history; coaching awards, honors, and highlights; present status; organizations and honors other than coaching; Coaches Association involvement and present status; other highlights and experiences; and the name of the nominator.

It is unfortunate that we have not enshrined some of the coaches from the early years—the 1930s and '40s—but we just don't know much about them. However, this book pays homage to some of them in Chapter Three. The purpose of this particular chapter is to tell the stories of our twenty-eight current inductees, so we begin with the inaugural class of 1993. If longevity was a prerequisite for induction into the Hall of Fame, these first five would have qualified on that measure alone. Here is what an article in the December 1992 *Prep Coach* (titled "Five to Be Inducted into Inaugural Tennis Hall of Fame") says about them: "One hundred and forty-four years in coaching tennis. Done by one person, they would have started in 1849—which was well before the Civil War!"

Reg Mead
Wadena (1993)

In terms of years of service, Reg Mead had one of the longest runs of our Hall of Fame coaches, thirty-six years; and he was one of the true pioneers of Minnesota tennis—particularly in west central Minnesota. Reg, or "Reggie," as Bud Schmid fondly called him, reminded me more of an English country gentleman than a tennis coach, for he never raised his voice, never had an unkind word to say about anyone, and always expected his players to behave on court. When I interviewed Reg, he commented about the opening remarks he always made to the players at an annual Saturday tournament he directed in Wadena: "We're here to improve our tennis and to have fun, but we need to be gentlemen. Now if you want to throw your racket, throw it toward your [school] car because that's where you're going to be." Not surprisingly, he rarely had a problem with racket throwing.

This gentleman's gentleman grew up in Proctor, MN, a small town located on the west edge of what is today greater Duluth. Here, just a short distance from Lake Superior and amidst northern pines, Reg played tennis on courts built by the Duluth, Mesabi, and Iron Range Railroad Company, which made its money by hauling iron ore to Proctor. In high school Reg played doubles his junior and senior years, then after graduation in 1937 attended Duluth State Teachers College (now UMD), where he majored in geography and history and where he also played tennis for two years. After graduating from college in 1941, Reg taught for just one year at Indus, MN, before joining the Service. During his forty-one months in the Service he played a bit of regimental tennis at Camp Lee, Virginia; but for thirty-one months he served with the Quartermaster Corps, servicing army trucks in North Africa, Sicily, Italy, and France. After he was discharged, he took a job in tiny Peterson, MN, for one year (1946-47), leaving to find a job in a bigger town, in part because of a backbreaking schedule of seven different classes and coaching duties at Peterson.

So he landed in Wadena in 1947, the place he would call home for over fifty years and a place where he would teach (mostly in junior high) geography, history, health, and reading, and serve as an audio-visual coordinator. During his thirty-seven years of teaching in this town of 4,274 people, he also coached junior high football and basketball. And it was here that he made his mark as a tennis coach, starting Wadena's first tennis program in 1952 and guiding it with a steady hand until 1987.

Men like Reg were true pioneers of the game in Minnesota, for not only did they have to start their programs from scratch, they also had to keep them going on a wing and a prayer. Here is how Reg described an episode from his first year: "I went in to the superintendent [in those days teachers had to beg superintendents for almost everything—even their individual salaries] the first year and asked for tennis balls and he gave me four cans. They gave me $100 for coaching tennis, so I went down and bought $100 worth of tennis balls. The next spring we used balls from the last year. I took the balls in to a garage, put them in a tire, blew the tire up to thirty pounds, left them [the balls] for two weeks, then took them out and used them. They didn't last more than a week."

Like so many other coaches in that era, he also had to fight for gym time in the early spring, and that was with no court lines marked out in the gym. Reg taped the height of the net on the wall and his players learned to hit flat, backspin, and topspin shots by bouncing the balls and blasting them over the counterfeit net. Later he had one court, so players could add serving to their early spring repertoire. And of course there was the inevitable and necessary snow shoveling of courts that characterized spring tennis all over the state, but especially in northern places such as Wadena.

It is a credit to Reg's coaching ability that, in such a small community, isolated from the hotbeds of tennis, and without indoor courts, he was able to produce so many competitive teams in a region that included bigger schools such as St. Cloud and Brainerd. His "team" won region titles once each in the 1950s and '60s and, with the advent of True Team competition in 1973, Wadena participated in Class A State Tournaments in 1980, '81, and '82—finishing second those last two years. These years, beginning in 1979 and extending to 1983, were the Chris Grabrian years. Grabrian was Reg's great money player who led those three state tournament teams and also made five appearances in the singles tournament, taking fourth in his ninth- and tenth-grade years and third in his junior year, 1982. Grabrian would go on to play two years at Gustavus and two years of Division 1 tennis at the U of Nebraska. Another player Mead coached in the summer but never played for Wadena was Casey Merickel, who transferred to St. Cloud Apollo when his father died and eventually had a successful college tennis career at the U of M. Of course he coached other good players (for example, brothers Brian and John Paulson who took third in the Class A doubles tournament two years in a row, in 1981 and '82); and like so many who coached tennis, he also had the pleasure of coaching his two sons.

His was a simple yet profound approach to the game, "Tennis is something people can learn to do well enough and be able to enjoy playing the rest of their lives." Winning wasn't the be-all and end-all for Reg, though of course his teams were very successful, for he was more interested in helping young boys become good men: "The greatest satisfaction as a teacher [and coach] is to see your students go out and make a good life for themselves." In Reg we see the perfect expression of Shakespeare's adage "'Tis a happy thing to be a father unto many sons."

He also used team meetings to create an attitude of cooperation, and he wanted his "boys" to have fun playing the game. His players felt comfortable coming to him if they had problems, and he had a genuine desire to give them chances to play even if they weren't good players. "I had some kids playing tennis that would get lost on their way to the courts," he remarked. His motto was that tennis "makes good kids into men." One of his former players, Stephen Paper, said of his former coach on the eve of Reg's induction into the Hall, "He taught us to win and lose gracefully. You cannot find a better man."

Reg has many fond memories of his years coaching boys' tennis, including one in which one of his players, Larry Gedde, developed heat stroke on the U of M courts during a state tournament match and Reg had to take him back to the hotel room and put him in a tub of ice water to cool him down.

For his coaching prowess he was voted MN Tennis Coach of the Year in 1982 and District Tennis Coach of the Year in 1984, the same year he was selected as one of eight finalists for National Tennis Coach of the Year. A lifetime member of the MN State High School Coaches Association (MSHSCA) who also served one term as vice president of the Tennis Coaches Association, Mead was honored for thirty years of outstanding contributions to Minnesota high school tennis. For his teaching ability he was given a Freedom Foundations Award from Valley Forge, and he also served his community as a member of several organizations. In addition, he served as a lay leader in his church. In retirement Reg lived for some time in an apartment in Maplewood to be near his daughter, but he passed away in 2005 at age eighty-five.

Hal Schroeder
Blue Earth (1993)

Two hundred miles south of the Twin Cities is some of the richest farm land in the world and the home of coach Hal Schroeder, the small town of Blue Earth (population 3,642). Another of Minnesota's pioneer coaches,

Schroeder amassed one of the most extraordinary records in state tennis history. When he came to this small prairie town to teach mathematics in the fall of 1954, there was no tennis program and only two barely-playable, dilapidated courts in such poor condition that at least one team, Albert Lea, refused to play on them. Blue Earth High's principal, Alice Paulson, noticed that Schroeder had been captain of the Mankato State tennis team and so asked him to start a program for interested boys in the spring of 1955. It would have been hard to imagine that such a modest debut season (in which eight novice players lost all four matches played) would launch a tennis program and tennis teams that would one day be both admired and feared statewide in coming years. This Minnesota "Hoosiers" tennis team would win its first state title in 1977, defeating three much larger schools; and in subsequent years this "little giant" would dominate the competition in Region 2 and win two more state titles in Class A competition.

The man behind this successful program grew up in the tennis hotbed of Rochester where, ironically, he played baseball, excelling as a right fielder on a team that took third place in the 1950 State Tournament. And while he did not play on the Rochester high

Hal Schroeder

school tennis team, he often hit with future state doubles champions Henry Dison and Ron Trondson during the summer. After graduating from high school in 1950, he attended Rochester Junior College for two years and, because they had no baseball program, he joined his friend Trondson on the tennis team. At Rochester he played No. 1 singles his first year and No. 2 singles his second year and paired with Trondson to win the conference doubles championship his second year. Then it was on to Mankato State Teachers College, again to play tennis but this time with both of his Rochester friends. In his two years at Mankato the team lost only to Carleton, qualifying for nationals his senior year, the year in which he also served as captain. In 1954 Hal graduated with a major in mathematics education.

The first spring Hal coached tennis was a year in which Tony Trabert won Wimbledon, the U.S. Open, and the French championships. It was also the year that Disneyland opened, Churchill resigned, and Rosa Parks refused to sit in the back of the bus. Hal remembers 1955 and many of his early years as challenging, to say the least. For example, he recalls how difficult it was to maintain the nets on those two dilapidated courts: "We tried 'wire' or 'fencing' for nets but as people would sit on them they would sag in the middle so we put a post in the middle and then had two smaller sags between the net posts and the middle posts." Five new courts were built in 1960, but because they were tilted for drainage, players either found themselves hitting uphill or downhill; and because there were only "openings" but no doors, players often had to "chase" balls outside the courts. Even when nylon nets were installed, children often broke the weak cables by sitting or swinging on them, so Hal spent two to three hours nearly every Sunday afternoon repairing the nets and cables.

Like the village blacksmiths of old, coaches in Minnesota often had to use a good deal of ingenuity in order to keep their programs going, and Schroeder was a master improviser. Because the five Blue Earth courts were arranged side by side, it was difficult for fans (and coaches) to keep track of match scores; so Hal built his own scorecards, perhaps the first to be used in Minnesota high school tennis meets. In fact, at one of the state

tournaments in the 1960s, Blue Earth fans asked Hal why there were no scorecards being used. Hal made his scorecards from a large sheet of one-fourth-inch thick white plastic, painting black letters on one-foot high by nine-inch wide letters for the opponents' set of scorecards and painting another set blue (for *Blue* Earth, of course) with white letters. His "set" scorecards were hooked into large rings that fit around the cable. Another example of Hal's ingenuity resulted from his experience playing and practicing in cold weather. One cold day in October, during the girls' tennis season, Hal thought of a way to keep the girls' hands warm. "I had my girls cut a hole in an old sock and slip that part over the racket handle and then slip their hand in the ankle and leg part of the sock to keep the hand warm. The boys also kept a sock in their tennis covers for use if needed."

In good weather Schroeder organized station drills, giving his players opportunities to hit hundreds of balls as they worked on all strokes. So, for example, at one station players worked on their forehands, then rotated to the next court after ten minutes to work on another stroke. One court might also include a ball machine drill for the better players.

And on rainy days when the team didn't have the gym for practice, Hal took his players indoors for a four-station workout in which they (1) did sit ups, wrist rolls, and practiced ball tosses and the serve motion in a *hallway*, (2) jumped rope, lifted weights, and stretched in the *study hall room*; (3) stretched some more and hit forehands and backhands into a wall in the *library area*; and (4) practiced serving in the *racketball court*.

Another problem in the earlier years at Blue Earth was that his players had to travel to Rochester or to Norm McDonald's Twin Cities Tennis Supply in Minneapolis to get their rackets restrung. Norm and Marv Hanenberger encouraged Hal to buy a used stringing machine in order to meet his players' needs. So he did and what began as a modest attempt to meet a local need became a seven-day-a-week job in the spring, summer, and fall. Eventually Hal (and his daughter Sharon and sons Mark and Paul) sold and strung rackets for customers in thirty-four states, six countries, and most of Minnesota.

If one coached in small outstate comunities, it was

a given that some schools would have only two or three courts—as Blue Earth did in the 1950s. Matches (especially if there were extra "B" squad or "JV" matches) would often last until dark, so there were many late-night trips home. In addition, Hal faced the daunting task of finding ways to prepare players by having them do drills in the gym. For example, he put tape up for a "net" in the balcony and charted how many times players could hit above this faux net, giving them one point for each successful hit. He also set up a rubber mat (the width of the service box) on the floor and had players serve, giving them two points if they hit the serve on to the mat. His players also hit lobs, then ducked behind a mat while teammates hit overheads back at them. One year he recalls that his team did not practice outside at all before its first match.

Hal remembers a speech he gave in Tulsa, Oklahoma, during the National Coaches Convention in 1978, about the things he did "while inside using gyms in preparation for outside play." After he completed his speech, a coach from California came up to him and said, "If I had to do all of those things I wouldn't be coaching tennis."

As tennis expanded in the 1970s, more courts were built and more spring clinics and summer camps became available; so Hal got on board by moving north during June and August to help his good friend Bud Schmid set up the first tennis camp at Grand View Lodge. And for ten years he worked alongside Bud, Chuck Anderson, Bruce Getchell, and other coaching friends at Camp Lincoln/ Camp Lake Hubert summer camps. Hal also taught tennis one week each summer for several years at a church camp (Chi Rho) in northern Minnesota and conducted one-day clinics in various southern Minnesota communities such as Winnebago, Delavan, Fairmont, Wells, Albert Lea, Austin, and Owatonna. In addition, at home in Blue Earth he ran summer tennis programs for about thirty years.

All of this helps us know the man better, but it is his success as a coach that distinguishes his career. In thirty-seven years as the head boys' coach at Blue Earth, Hal's boys' teams won three state team championships, fourteen Region 2 titles from 1973-1988, and twenty-six South Central Conference titles. In addition, he coached two Class A singles champions, five Class A doubles champions, one doubles team which won the single class

title in 1985, and three doubles runners-up. His overall coaching record was an astonishing 641 dual match wins (about seventeen a year), a state record that may never be broken. During Hal's tenure his boys' teams racked up regular season dual match winning streaks of 111, seventy-nine, and thirty-nine, further evidence of Blue Earth's domination during the Schroeder years. He also started the girls' tennis program and coached it for seventeen years (during which time his teams won one state title and advanced to State sixteen times).

For his efforts Hal was (1) voted MN Boys' Tennis Coach of the Year three times-1976, '77, and '89, (2) inducted into the inaugural MSHSL Tennis Coaches Hall of Fame in 1993, (3) honored with membership in the MN State Coaches Association Hall of Fame in 2000, (4) awarded the Prince National High School Tennis All-American Honorable Mention coaching award in 1986, and (5) given the "Ward C. Burton Tennis Memorial Award for Inspiration to Youth" by the Northwest Tennis Association in 1989 (just the second high school coach to be so honored). This last award, given for developing outstanding junior tennis programs, also put him in the company of such other Minnesota tennis luminaries as Marv Hanenberger, Norm McDonald, Frank Voigt, and Jerry Noyce. In addition, Hal served the MN State High School Boys' Tennis Coaches Association as treasurer and served on the Coaches Advisory Board as well.

One of the highlights of Schroeder's career took place in 1978, when a new complex of six lighted tennis courts was constructed in Blue Earth and named after him. After more than twenty years of struggling to get quality practice and playing time on four deteriorating courts (two of which were used only for serving and volleying practice because they were unplayable), Hal finally had a facility to rival the best in the state. And in 1996 the school and city jointly financed eleven new courts which were dedicated, once again in Hal's name, during a girls' match with Waseca. He was especially proud of having lighted courts, which gave many who could not play tennis during the day a chance to swat balls after dark. Hal said, "Some young people often finished work at the Green Giant plant around midnight and would come to the courts and play for an hour or so."

While tennis kept him busy most of the year, Schroeder was not a "Johnny One-Note," for he also found time to coach junior high and B-squad football before he took the reins of girls' tennis in 1974; varsity and B-squad baseball in the 1950s; and varsity golf—a program which he also started at Blue Earth. In the '50s and even the '60s coaches sometimes supervised two sports teams in a season. Schroeder said, "For several years I coached boys' tennis and golf in the spring at the same time (three days a week with each team plus instructions for the team I was not with that day)." He remembers with some uneasiness the time Blue Earth played a golf meet at home and a tennis meet at Albert Lea on the same day. "One of the tennis players drove the team, which consisted at the time of three singles players and one doubles team, in his car to Albert Lea, and then brought them back after the match." In addition to these many coaching duties, Hal was an active member of the local Lions Club and his church. He also served the mathematics teaching profession with distinction, giving many talks and demonstrations to area, state, and national groups; writing curriculum guides; and for thirty-eight years helping the young people of Blue Earth overcome math anxiety.

In a truly remarkable coaching career spanning five decades (the 1950s-90s), Hal left an indelible mark on the tennis landscape of the state. His success was well earned and well deserved, but he is quick to credit others as well, particularly coaches Chuck Anderson and Steve Wilkinson, supportive Blue Earth administrators, his outstanding assistant coaches, and of course his family.

Anderson, father of the four boys who would help put Blue Earth tennis on the map, said of Hal, "Coach Schroeder has been a very positive influence on our four sons and has contributed immensely to their success by stressing the values of hard work." Others who know Hal speak of his positive attitude, genuine interest in helping young people succeed, and his use of positive reinforcement to instill self-confidence in his players and students. Coach Wilkinson, of Gustavus Adolphus College, whom Hal considers the most influential person in organizing tennis clinics for coaches and players, had this to say of Hal, "It is easy for me to say that Hal has done more for the development of individuals under his teaching

and coaching, for community tennis growth, and for the promotion of tennis instruction throughout the state, than any other coach with whom I have worked."

Today this Prince Hal of Minnesota tennis enjoys retirement in Blue Earth, and though no longer playing tennis—in part because of injuries suffered in a serious car accident—he indulges another of his passions, golf, and still keeps an eye on the Minnesota tennis scene. His sainted wife Elaine and Hal have raised four tennis-playing children who also experienced a great deal of success on Minnesota tennis courts. Oldest son Mark (Blue Earth's No. 1 player on its first two state tournament teams, 1973 and '74) has also coached tennis off and on for a number of years and today lives in Rochester where he manages rental properties. Daughter Laurie topped her brothers by winning a Class A state doubles title (with Kris Fering in 1978), and all, including daughter Sharon, played on Blue Earth state tournament teams. Youngest son Paul, who played No. 2 doubles on the 1988 Class A championship team, also placed third in doubles in 1988 (with Layne McCleary) and fourth in 1989 (again with McCleary). (For more about Schroeder and the Blue Earth program, see Chapter Nine.)

Mac Doane
St. Cloud (1993)

Dubbed the George Washington of St. Cloud tennis by fellow Hall of Fame member Jerry Sales, Mac Doane was truly a father unto many tennis-playing sons and daughters in this central Minnesota city. Sales, one of these "sons," said of Doane, "He taught me the finer points of coaching." Perhaps his most famous "daughter" was girls' tennis pioneer Peg Brenden, who took her first tennis lessons from Doane and his wife Harriet in the summer program they ran. (For more on Brenden, see Chapter Seven.)

There are many more who credit Doane for inspiring their love for tennis, including Bud Schmid, so who was this state tennis legend? Mac Doane was present at the formation of our Minnesota high school tennis universe, playing on the first tennis team at St. Cloud High School in 1929; and after graduation in 1930 he played on the first tennis team at St. Cloud State Teachers College. Though it seems improbable to us today, Doane earned letters in four sports in college: basketball, football, baseball, and yes, tennis. When he graduated in 1934, he accepted a position as an industrial arts and physical education teacher at Central Junior High School in St. Cloud. Soon thereafter, in 1940, he assumed the reins as head tennis coach at the high school, where he served with distinction for thirty-one years. After leaving St. Cloud Tech in 1970, he coached three more years at St. Cloud Apollo, capping his successful thirty-four-year career on the eve of a new tennis revolution in Minnesota, the year of the first True Team tournament. And for twenty-three summers he and his wife donned their tennis shorts and taught the children and

team, made up of Dave Woodward and Larry Nielsen, finished third in the individual competition in 1967; and from 1965-67 his teams featured other outstanding players, including Dave Stearns, arguably one of his best players on the strength of a fifth place doubles showing in 1965 (with Woodward as his partner) and a third place finish in the state singles tournament in 1966. Today Stearns, one of Doane's "sons," coaches the Minnetonka boys' and girls' teams. And though Mac was not his coach in high school, Grant Helgeson, who finished second in the state doubles tournament in 1973, was also one of his proteges. "Mac Doane actually was my first tennis coach... I am ambidex-

Mac Doane (Center), Bill Ritchie (Left), and Jerry Sales (Right)

adults of St. Cloud how to play the game they devoted their lives to. In fact, they started the summer recreational tennis program at St. Cloud.

Though his teams did not win any state titles, Doane's 1967 boys were undefeated in dual meets and ranked No. 1 during the season. That year they earned 11 points at the State Tournament and finished fourth behind champion Edina (20 points), runner-up Minnetonka (15 points), and third place Rochester Mayo (13 points). Doane's doubles

trous and he encouraged me to have two forehands," said Helgeson. In the aforementioned article from the *MN Prep Coach* about the first Tennis Hall of Fame inductees, it was said that Doane "brought top quality tennis to St. Cloud and set the stage for the Tech champions of the 1980s" (December 1992).

As with so many of these early pioneers, Doane was a crafty fellow who devised innovative teaching methods. For instance, *St. Cloud MN Times* writer Tom Larson noted that "he [Doane] developed 'hand tennis,' a game kids played without rackets to teach them how to count the score and hone their fundamentals. 'Wall tennis' was also his invention, a sort of handball game kids could play against a wall when the weather outside prevented them from playing" (July 16, 1992). He also used his considerable powers of persuasion to convince the school board to paint tennis lines on gym floors so the public could play year-round.

In addition, he was a superb coach and a real gentleman. Angelo Pugol, a former assistant principal at St. Cloud Tech, said Doane "had great knowledge of the game, patience, and enthusiasm." Because of his knowledge of the game, he was often called upon to consult on the construction of new tennis courts in St. Cloud and in central Minnesota. In that July 16, 1992, article by Larson, Jerry Sales weighed in again with this observation about Doane: "He doesn't have an egocentric bone in his body. He's a gentleman's gentleman."

In addition to these coaching accomplishments, for thirty-nine years he refereed football and basketball games; and he also became a member of the Professional Tennis Council Coaches Registry in 1965. His playing skills and his coaching service earned him induction into three athletic Halls of Fame, those of St. Cloud State Teachers College, St. Cloud Tech High School, and the MN Tennis Coaches. In ill health for a number of years, Doane passed away in 2006 at age ninety-four.

John Adams
Robbinsdale (1993)

The next member of this extraordinary Hall of Fame class is John Adams, who started the tennis program at Robbinsdale High School in 1949, the year that Pancho Gonzalez defeated Ted Schroeder to win the U.S. Open singles title in an epic five-set thriller 16-18, 2-6, 6-1, 6-2, 6-4. Adams coached tennis until 1975, retiring after twenty-seven years at the helm of the Robbinsdale boys' team. And though he coached many outstanding teams and individuals during his lengthy tenure, it would be unfair to measure Adams' success by any state team and individual titles Robbinsdale earned, for he coached during the years that teams such as Rochester and Edina dominated state

high school tennis. Nevertheless, his teams and players always competed well in the very tough Region 5 and many of his players advanced to the State Tournament, particularly from 1956-66 when Robbinsdale qualified at least one player for State and several times the maximum of two singles players and one doubles team. His most successful team took fourth place in the 1958 tournament, and several of his singles players and doubles teams acquitted themselves well at State. In 1958, for instance, his son, John Adams, Jr., placed fourth and Ken Franco took fifth in the singles tournament; Art Johnson earned a fifth place singles medal in 1961; and Malcolm McCauley and Ric

John Adams

Picard placed fourth in the 1969 doubles competition. In addition, John's teams won several Region 5 titles, District 18 crowns, and four Lake Conference championships.

But it is perhaps for Adams' service during the formative years of tennis in the west Metro suburbs that he will be most remembered. There were very few teams in the suburbs before he arrived at Robbinsdale in 1949; Deephaven was the only other west suburban school that had a tennis program then. The powers in tennis were all located in the city high schools of Minneapolis and St. Paul. From 1934 to 1948 teams from the Twin Cities finished first in unofficial state team standings every year but one, and the singles and doubles champions were nearly all products of city park tennis programs who played for city schools. So it was Adams' good fortune to be present at the birth of a new tennis conference (the Lake) which would by the mid-1960s begin to dominate state tennis. A list of his coaching competitors reads like a veritable Who's Who of Minnesota boys' high school tennis: George Henke of Deephaven (later Minnetonka), Roger Thompson of St. Louis Park, Ted Greer and John Matlon of Edina, Joe White of Bloomington, and Joe Michel of Richfield, for example.

Adams tried to schedule as many teams as he could and remembers that "the St. John's Tournament held each spring at Collegeville was generally a good chance to compete against many of the good players in the central part of the state." In addition to starting up and coaching the high school boys' program, Adams coached a very successful girls' Wightman Cup team from Robbinsdale in the summers for two years. And for many years he served as the Region 5 tournament director when play was held on the U of M courts.

Like most of his contemporaries, coaching as they did in the days before indoor courts and organized summer tennis programs, Adams realized that "if we at Robbinsdale were going to compete at all successfully with teams whose members were country club players, we had to start a summer program for boys and girls ages 6-12." So, in the summer of 1954, he launched Robbinsdale's Park and Recreation Tennis Program for boys and girls, a program he would direct until 1964. During these years he also scheduled dual match competitions with ten other suburban recreational tennis programs and one at Nicollet Park, in which his top youngsters played weekly matches against players from these other teams. Said Adams about these matches, "Boys and girls were on the same team and they had to be in our summer program to participate. There were seven on a team and they were ranked 1-7 in order of ability."

At the end of the season all these recreational association teams competed in a tournament at Nicollet Park. "At the same time," according to Northern Section tennis historian and former Adams' pupil John Mueller, "he [Adams] started a summer high school league that played weekly matches using the 5-point scoring system. Teams

from Edina, Minnetonka, Elk River, Richfield, St. Louis Park, Bloomington, and Minneapolis had teams playing. All the good players were on those teams."

To prepare his summer students, Adams believed in grounding them in the fundamentals of tennis. "My instruction consisted of fifty strokes each of the forehand, backhand, and serve—all facing the instructor and moving together to a rhythmic count. Their next exercise was to take their one tennis ball and move to within six or eight feet of the screen around the court, drop the ball and hit one forehand shot, retrieve the ball, and then hit it again 100 times. Do the same with the backhand and the serve. They absolutely hated this because they wanted to 'play tennis' and didn't realize this was the fastest way for 100 beginners to learn to hit the ball." Out of this program came many top junior and college players and some of the future teaching professionals in the Metro area such as Johnny Adams, Jr.; Jim McGee; the aforementioned John Mueller; Wayne Pearson; Ric Picard; and Don Thaemert.

A fine player himself, Adams won the City of Robbinsdale Men's Singles Tournament for many years; and he and his son John, Jr. (who played tennis at the U of M), formed one of the top father and son doubles teams in the Northwestern Section, often finishing as runner-up to the Stamps of Minnetonka (Adams and his son were ranked No. 2 for five years). Always the promoter, he also organized two men's tennis groups that met for many years on Tuesday nights and Saturday mornings. It was selfless actions such as these that characterized the man, actions that produced players from other communities whose teams were in direct competition with his Robbinsdale boys. For these efforts on behalf of tennis in Minnesota and for his coaching prowess he was recognized by his peers as a member of this first Hall of Fame coaches class and by the Northern Section as Tennis Person of the Year in 1963.

A resident of Faribault, Adams learned to play tennis on his own, often hitting with Lloyd Halsinger, the Faribault Shattuck athletic director, in the summer on the Shattuck courts (at that time there was no high school tennis program at Faribault High School). After graduation in 1935, he enrolled at Mankato State College, where he played No. 1 doubles and No. 2 singles for the tennis team.

In 1939, with a degree in choral music, Adams took his first teaching job at Big Stone Lake, SD. During his two years there he got married (in 1940) and received a deferment from service to continue teaching. He then taught high school music for seven more years in South Dakota, first for just one year at Hecla, for two years at Highmore, and for four years in the capital city of Pierre. During those last two postings he also taught social studies and served as principal.

Finally, he came to Robbinsdale in 1948 where, in addition to his tennis teaching, coaching, and playing, Adams taught music at the high school, directing the choir from 1948-78 and winning many awards. He also directed the five-time national champion City of Robbinsdale Choir and Civic Men's Choir which appeared at and won Aquatennial singing contests and Chicagoland Music Festival contests. Adams died in 2007 at age 90.

John Matlon
Edina (1993)

The last member of this illustrious first group of Hall of Fame coaches is John Matlon, whose eight team championships trumps John Hatch's seven and makes him the boys' coach with the most state titles.

A successful collegiate wrestler at the U of M, Matlon began his tennis coaching career as a relative novice. As with so many coaches of his era, he was trained to coach but he was not a tennis player. He overcame this deficiency by emphasizing fundamentals, tactics, and conditioning. Matlon's longtime assistant, Les Szendrey, who later succeeded him, said of his former head coach, "John was a very disciplined coach—there was no foolishness." From the first days of practice Matlon instilled in his players the importance of

John Matlon

hard work and conditioning the body. For example, Scott Nesbit, current St. Olaf men's and women's tennis coach and a former Edina player, said Matlon required players to run a mile in under seven minutes in order to be on the team. Influenced by the successful Australian Davis Cup tennis teams coached by the indomitable Harry Hopman, Matlon modeled his teams after them, placing the utmost emphasis on working hard and playing hard.

Ted Warner, current Blake coach and one of Matlon's "boys," mentioned how Matlon "was ahead of his time in getting guys in shape." Warner especially remembers one rainy day when Matlon, attired in "his green warmup jumping suit that had to be fifty years old, gave us a workout on the dip bars to strengthen our chest muscles. Then we jumped rope—four minutes and a minute rest, four more minutes and a minute rest, and on and on like that." Nesbit also remembers that Matlon organized practices even in the early morning hours: "We played at Northstar Racket Club at 6 but got up at 5. I threw pine cones at Swendseen's [Greg] window to wake him up."

Matlon was also a stickler for details, according to Nesbit: "He was always recording everything—he had these manila folders for each of us and recorded stuff like hitting ball cans on serves, hitting towels, hitting areas on the court. We did a lot of charting." In addition, according to Nesbit, Matlon taped towels on the gym wall and set up competitions in which players earned points for hitting the towels. 1971 singles champion Bob Amis talked about how Matlon "couldn't teach us a lot about stroke production but always prepared us so well—he prepared us mentally." Amis also mentioned that Matlon "didn't put up with much and that he was respected by all the players, or feared, but ultimately respected and liked."

Another of his former players, 1967 doubles champion Dave Mathews, called Matlon "a very caring, loyal, coach and friend." One incident revealed this softer side of the hardnosed "Mr. Matlon." When Bill Arnold's stepfather died in March 1975, shortly before he and Nesbit won the doubles title, Matlon had the whole Edina team dress up in ties and sit together at the funeral. This softer side of Matlon was revealed in another incident involving the final state tournament match with Madison in 1975. Again, it's Nesbit who tells the story: "We [Edina] were probably nine-ten times larger than Madison, and the number of people who went out for tennis for us was way larger than their graduating class. Coach Matlon took us aside before the match and had us take some time to think about this match and how special it was." Former U of M coach Jerry Noyce added, "Matlon had an absolute drive to make sure that his kids had the opportunity to play and work hard. I never heard him speak negatively about his players."

And opposing coaches, though most often on the losing side, respected Matlon as a coach. Tom Vining of Roseville said of him, "He was an engaging and thoroughly charming liberal intellect. His players were all so well conditioned and well prepared."

All this effort and commitment, during a career that began in 1958 and ended in 1977, produced stunning results: eight state team championships—including the first True Team title in 1973, four team runner-up finishes, four individual state singles champions, and seven individual state doubles champions. In the ultra-competitive Lake Conference, his teams won fifteen team championships, racking up an incredible sixty-three straight dual meet victories between 1962-69. During this period Edina's only losses were to Rochester John Marshall and St. Cloud Tech. (There is more about Matlon and his Edina teams in Chapter Nine.)

In addition to these on-court coaching accomplishments, Matlon earned numerous Lake Conference Coach of the Year awards and the

Northwestern Lawn Tennis Association (NWLTA) President's Award in 1976; served for eight years on the NWLTA Board of Directors; served as chair of the boys' junior development program; and served as NWLTA Junior Davis Cup coach, traveling for many years with the Section's top juniors to national championship tournaments.

Though he admitted on the eve of his retirement in 1977, in a *Minneapolis Tribune* article by Bruce Brothers, that coaching at times was nerve-wracking and stressful, he also said that "working with kids is what keeps a person young" (June 10, 1977) and that coaching was a great joy. In addition to his tennis-coaching duties, Matlon coached wrestling and taught American history at Edina High School.

After retirement Matlon kept his hand in tennis (he became a successful adult tournament player, earning four No. 3 rankings in the Men's 55-and-Over division, for instance) and became an ordained Roman Catholic deacon. Matlon, who died in 1996, is survived by two sons, both of whom played tennis at St. Thomas Academy.

Lloyd "Bud" Schmid
Brainerd (1994)

Suppose we consider Reg Mead and Bud Schmid to be the pioneers of central Minnesota tennis. If Mead was William Clark, the second billing and perhaps less flamboyant of the two famous explorers of the Louisiana Purchase, then Lloyd "Bud" Schmid had to be his Meriweather Lewis. As Schmid and Mead, together they blazed many new trails for future coaches and players in their part of the state and even statewide. Bud lived just forty-five minutes down U.S. Highway 10 from Reg, in the resort town of Brainerd, and they began their careers at roughly the same time—Reg in 1952 and Bud in 1953. Over the years their friendship developed, despite a fierce rivalry that saw their teams meet often in

Reg Mead (Left) & Bud Schmid

scrimmages, season matches, and regional competition. Both had to build programs, in Reg's case from the ground up, in a part of the state where there weren't many tennis programs and where long road trips to meets in places such as Moorhead were the norm. In an April 20, 1983, article by Jim Wallace in the *Brainerd Dalily Dispatch*, Bud talks about hosting the region tournament in 1954 when "we had two WPA courts then. We started playing in the morning and went all day long." He also recalls one early year when "Reggie and I wiped off the Wadena courts with towels" and "it took a lot of them to get rid of the water." Schmid said of the changes he has seen, "the difference in coaching today and from when we started is that today's coaches are pretty much stepping into solid programs. It's not something they had to build" (April 20, 1983).

A St. Cloud native, Schmid remembers beginning his tennis-playing days by standing in his parents' driveway and "hitting targets and playing imaginary games against the barn wall near the home across from us." Though he did not play high school tennis and did not take lessons, he played in a summer recreation program in which he was encouraged by Hall of Fame coach Mac Doane. After graduation from high school in 1943, Bud attended the U of M for one year where he played quarterback and punted on the freshman football team. He then entered the U.S. Air Force for a two-year stint (1944-46).

After serving his country at the tail end of WWII, Bud transferred to what was then called St. Cloud State Teachers' College, graduating in 1949 with a major in physical education and a minor in business. He also played three sports: football, baseball, and tennis. He lettered in all three, playing quarterback on the football team for three years, catcher on the baseball team for two years, and tennis his senior year.

His first teaching jobs were in smaller Minnesota communities, first in Cleveland—near St. Peter—from 1949-50, in Montgomery (1950-51), and then in Lake City (1951-52). In each of these schools he coached, but at Cleveland that first year he remembers doing everything: teaching social science, math, physical education, and history (six preparations) and coaching all three sports (football, basketball, and baseball). Bud said, "You helped construct and line the fields and you drove the

farm boys home every night after practice so they could do their chores. These early years of coaching taught me that in order to get things done and done right you had to do it yourself."

In 1953 he moved north to Brainerd, Paul Bunyan's "stomping grounds," the place he would call home for thirty years and the place where he made his mark in Minnesota sports history. Here he taught junior high biology and physical education, started aquatic swim programs for the community and schools, and taught physical education at the high school in his later years and ran the aquatic program.

While coaching nearly every boys' sport in the school, Bud made his greatest impact on the shape and direction of high school tennis in Minnesota. He admits that he was fortunate to be coaching tennis when the game was ripe for change (particularly in the boom time in the 1970s), a time he dubbed the "Rising of the Tennis Phoenix." In the earliest years of the tennis coaches' association, Bud stepped in and assumed a leadership role. For example, he served as the organization's president in 1972-73, spearheading efforts to develop clinics for state coaches (many of whom were not tennis players but were primarily coaches of other sports, or took the jobs because no one else wanted them); working tirelessly as president of the coaches' association and as a regional rep to the MSHSL for more participation and a True Team state tennis tournament; and writing—with the help of his wife Sue—a tennis coaches handbook which helped coaches understand such important things as MSHSL rules and legislative procedures, the structure of the tennis coaches association, the USTA Code, tournament formats, and coaching ethics—particularly problems associated with lineup "stacking."

In addition to his twenty-eight years as head boys' tennis coach, Bud coached many other sports such as basketball, baseball, football, swimming, track, and wrestling for varying lengths of time. For example, he was head swimming coach for thirteen years and head wrestling coach for five years. Also, this "Energizer Bud(die)" refereed football, basketball, swimming, and wrestling; started both swimming and wrestling as high school sports in Brainerd; ran regional meets in swimming, wrestling, and tennis; and held traveling clinics for area schools new to swimming, tennis, and wrestling.

Like Reg Mead, Bud struggled to find gym time in the first weeks of the season when snow and ice still covered the courts—usually settling for early AM or late evening practices when the gym was not being used by other sports teams. Fortunately, he received encouragement from the Brainerd superintendents and principals, so the "Indoor Palace," as he termed the basketball gym, became an indoor facility every off hour it was available. This gave him the impetus to launch the first winter clinic for coaches in 1973, using his "Palace" (with its four courts) and two courts at Brainerd Community College. Billed in part as a participation clinic ("put on your tennies and let's go"), it provided coaches with access to a variety of exhibits, films, and sessions on all sorts of topics led by outstanding pros and coaches. Still later, Bud helped organize, with Steve Wilkinson, the very successful Tennis and Life clinics for for men, women, coaches, pros, and others interested in the game, "big-time clinics" which brought in big name pros such as Vic Braden and Nick Bollettieri.

During his first summers in Brainerd Bud's motor kept running in fifth gear, as he organized tennis and football programs, then, in 1973, he and Sue helped establish what was to become a highly successful tennis program at Camp Lincoln-Camp Lake Hubert (CL/CLH). The first year, armed only with a ball machine and his outgoing personality, Bud asked owners Fred and Mary Boos if he could teach tennis to guests at the one tennis court in front of the lodge. Eventually new courts were built and, using the facilities at Lake Hubert, at the old Bud Wilkinson football camp, this Bud (Schmid) organized a program of tennis drills and games for young campers and potential tennis stars.

One of the unique features of the camp was that tennis coaches who taught at the camp were paid with a free one-week vacation for their families. Speaking of his experiences at CL/CLH, Bud said, "Ours was a true coaches and family camp in which great friendships started and continue to this day. Many coaches' sons and daughters continued on in tennis, playing on their parents' teams and some even becoming teaching professionals later in life." Following Bud's seven years as director, longtime camp coaches Bruce Getchell and Todd Ruediseli took

over, and CL/CLH still offers this "specialty" camp for youngsters who want to improve their tennis games and have an enjoyable summer camp experience.

In addition to his work at CL/CLH, Bud served as the tennis director at Grand View Lodge on Gull Lake for a number of years in a summer program that ran for six days a week, ten hours a day, and that provided instruction for both children and adults. He also started evening tennis leagues and classes at the four new Brainerd Community College indoor courts and served area schools and resorts as a design consultant for facilities and swimming and tennis programs. By this time Bud had become a certified USPTA teaching pro, passing a test, which he called one of the biggest challenges of his life, with the help of Dave Yorks, and his eyes began to scan the broader vistas of the West.

After several more good years in Brainerd, he and Sue somewhat reluctantly packed their tennis rackets and headed to New Mexico in 1983, intending to "find out what was out there in the growing resort tennis field." What they found was a job at Bishop's Lodge in the mountain resort community of Santa Fe, NM. About this move Bud said, "It was very traumatic for me, but we wanted to get away from shoveling snow and freezing every winter [he was then fifty-nine years old] and we liked the Southwest; but leaving so much of myself behind was pretty rough." Bud served as tennis director and head pro at the Lodge for the next six years, employing innovative teaching techniques such as an aerobic tennis workout to add what his wife, Sue, called "pizzazz to your tennis." He and Sue also offered a class, called "Trouble on the Court," designed to teach spouses, children, and significant others to play and practice with each other without "bloodshed or hard feelings." During these years, in part because heavy snows and cold weather closed tennis down in the winter, the couple took other jobs—Bud as a ski instructor and Sue as a paralegal.

Following successful careers at Bishop's Lodge, they spent four years at the upscale Quail Run Resort in Santa Fe, where Bud served as assistant athletic director and head tennis pro from 1989-93 until health problems forced his retirement. Despite this setback, he still kept busy, helping run the club's tennis tournaments and teaching tennis two or three days a week in the summer and teaching billiards the rest of the year.

Perhaps the most versatile of all the Hall of Fame coaches (look at how many different sports he has coached), Bud has received numerous well-deserved awards for the many hours he has given to tennis and other sports. In addition to membership in this hall of fame, he was voted MN High School Tennis Coaches Association Coach of the Year in 1974, he was inducted into the Brainerd Sports Hall of Fame and the MSHSL Coaches Association Hall of Fame in 1986, and his name is attached to an annual award given to the most promising Brainerd assistant coach. This last award is Bud's most treasured one because it is given for initiative, tenacity, and imagination combined with a devotion to the principles of teamwork, all qualities that Bud possessed.

Truly a man with a giving spirit, Schmid has devoted a lifetime to teaching and coaching a sport which is "fun without the drudgery other sports have, is fun to play and coach, and which gives high school players a sport they can play for a lifetime." And while it's true that he was our Meriweather Lewis, helping to map out a tennis landscape for which coaches and players today should thank him, he is also a humble and modest man. He does not boast of these accomplishments; in fact, he could not even tell me what his coaching record at Brainerd was. But we know that Bud coached a team in 1975 that advanced to the State Tournament through a difficult region that included perennial powerhouse St. Cloud Tech. In addition, he coached some very fine players such as Bob and Merle Speed; Sandy Ruttger and Dave Shanks, quarterfinalists in the 1971 doubles who lost to champions Ted Taney and Chris Barden; Tracy Kennedy, who led Brainerd to State in 1975; and Russ Hampson and Bruce Weiss, doubles entries in 1983.

Schmid's philosophy of coaching was simple, "Keep it active, make it fun, and include everybody that wants to play." When he recalls those early years, he talks of how difficult it was to find information, books, or tapes on tennis instruction and how difficult it was for small, outstate schools to compete with schools in the Twin Cities and others which had access to indoor facilities and coaching from USPTA professionals. Perhaps this tennis isolation drove Bud to become a teaching pro and to campaign for indoor facilities in his community. Or perhaps he became motivated because of an unfortunate incident in his first year of coaching. "It involved my two best players, Bob and Merle Speed [the former a future Twin Cities teaching pro]. I drove them and the golf players to the regional tournament; and while I drove the golf players to their tournament, the director of the tennis tournament and other coaches paired my No. 1 and No. 2 players [the Speed brothers], the best in the tournament, against each other in the first round. I blew my stack and then and there decided I would learn as much as I could about tournament play and vowed to run them fairly."

As with so many coaches, for Bud the best thing about coaching was the wonderful relationships he developed with players and coaches alike. He speaks affectionately of early season scrimmages—often lasting until late in the evening—pizza and pop contests, overnights at that other team's facility, and lots of traveling. Not surprisingly, he mentions many of his fellow Hall of Fame mates, as well as CL/CLH coaches, as his great friends in tennis—Hal Schroeder, Bruce Getchell, Jolly Carlson, Ed Sewell, Bill Ritchie, Whitey Olson, Chuck Anderson and Hal Miller of Willmar. One might argue convincingly that Lloyd "Bud" Schmid had more to do with the growth and improvement in Minnesota high school tennis than any other individual.

In 2007 Bud and Sue returned to Minnesota to live closer to their children and grandchildren.

Robert "Jolly" Carlson
Madison (1994)

Just thirteen miles east of the South Dakota border on U.S. Highway 75, not far from Big Stone Lake and Big Stone National Wildlife Refuge, on what was at one time a vast sea of grass we called the prairie, lies the sleepy little town of Madison, population 1,886. Perhaps its greatest claim to fame is that for many years it was the home of celebrated Minnesota writers Robert and Carol Bly. Located 110 miles from the nearest city, Sioux Falls, SD, and 170 miles from the Twin Cities, it's hard to imagine that this small village could be a hotbed of high school tennis; but indeed it was. And it became a hotbed through the Herculean efforts of one man who believed it was possible to change the world, even if it was only this smaller world of Madison, MN.

This second 1994 inductee was Robert "Jolly" Carlson, a small child from a poor family whose father died when he was only two years old. Despite the loss of his father and the privations of the Great Depression, Carlson was always a smiling, happy child, hence the nickname "Jolly" given him by the local baseball team on which he served as batboy. Later, his paper route customers would say, "Here comes Jolly" when he came to collect money. (Son Gary claims a different origin: "He was a varsity cheerleader for the Augustana football team and at parties he was a talkative, 'Jolly' person.") Carlson was an extraordinary coach and teacher who not only "fathered" tennis in his community but also fathered four sons and one daughter, each of whom learned the game from him and became accomplished players. In fact, in keeping with the theme of fathering players and future coaches, his son Jeff noted that Jolly was called "the father of tennis west of the Chippewa River" by a local sports writer. (For more on Carlson and this tennis family, see Chapter Ten.)

An all-around athlete who played five sports in high school, Jolly Carlson grew up in neighboring Watertown, SD, where he became a tennis legend by winning three straight state singles titles from 1939-41 in tournaments played in the fall. Perhaps most remarkable about his success was that he was a David among Goliaths, a little giant, if you'll excuse the oxymoron. His slight stature was even noted in an October 1940 article in the *New York Times* by Eddie Brietz: "Diminutive 'Jolly' Carlson is believed to be the smallest and youngest prep high school tennis champion in the U.S. A sophomore, he has to stand on a book, 1" thick, to be 5 ft. tall, and drink a gallon of water to be 100 lbs."

Even more noteworthy is the path Carlson trod to become a skilled tennis player. Born in 1924, he grew up

Robert "Jolly" Carlson

during the Depression when drought ruined the lives of many on the Dakota prairie. "I can remember as a boy, in the '30s, when I started playing tennis, if we didn't have a racket we made one out of wood and spent all day playing, or waiting for the one court to open—playing with balls so worn the covers were worn completely off and black." In fact, his mother bought him his first racket for twenty-five cents when he was ten. There were no free rackets and shoes, lessons with pros, or travel to tournaments in those days, as Carlson recalled: "We had no money to buy rackets, balls, or outfits—and no car to travel. When I was a teenager there were few and far between 15-and-under tourneys and no 10-12-14-16-18 divisions like today. I only played in one, the Red River Valley at Fargo, and lost in the finals when I was 14." Despite all these deprivations, and despite the fact that he had never been given a formal lesson, as a seventh grader Jolly was able to defeat all comers in his high school. Unfortunately, South Dakota high school rules didn't allow athletes to play on varsity teams until their ninth-grade year; so Carlson had to wait two years before he got his chance. And he made the most of it, reaching the semifinals of the state singles tournament his first year of competition and then claiming those three straight titles.

After graduation in 1942 and just one semester at Augustana College in Sioux Falls, he joined the Army Air Corps for three years. Following his stint in the service, he returned to Augustana where he continued his tennis-playing career and helped the Vikings win three North Central Conference championships. During those four years (1946-49) he helped coach the team and also won four singles championships and two doubles titles, in 1946 winning all his matches in both singles and doubles. He played No. 1 singles and doubles, sometimes with fellow South Dakota Hall of Famer "Lefty" Johnson. From the very first day he held a racket in his hand, he had a passion for the game of tennis, a passion he would indulge by directing programs in Watertown and Sioux Falls even during the summers of his college years.

After graduating from Augustana in 1949 with a BA in earth science and health education, Carlson earned a masters in education from the U of M in earth science, then took a teaching and coaching job at Carthage College in Illinois, serving as an assistant coach in basketball and as a head tennis coach. Unfortunately, injuries sustained in a bad car accident forced him to leave Carthage after only one year, so he took a job as a youth and Christian education director at Como Park Lutheran Church in St. Paul. Finally, after six years in St. Paul, he was able to return to his first love—coaching—settling in the prairie community he would call home for forty-one years. It was 1957, and Jolly was hired to teach science and physical education. In addition, because he had also played basketball in high school and college, he signed on to coach that sport in Madison, MN. But it was as the first tennis coach at Madison (he started both the boys' and girls' programs there) that he made his mark. His first contract paid him $4,000 a year for teaching and $400 total for his jobs as head basketball and tennis coach and assistant football coach.

This patriarch of western Minnesota tennis coached in Madison for thirty-three years, retiring in 1990 after leading his boys' teams to over 400 wins, seventeen district titles, and ten Region 3 titles. Remarkably, this small school, competing in the one-class tournament against schools 10-25 times its size, won the consolation championship in 1974 and finished runner-up to perennial power Edina in 1975. Carlson remembered with particular affection these two teams in which his four boys played key roles, teams which established a record for number of siblings participating on a state tournament team. And as the girls' tennis coach in Madison, he also led the lady Dragons to nearly 200 wins and seven state tournament berths—including two fourth-place finishes.

As a former coach I know how difficult it is to put your shorts on and pick up your racket to continue teaching tennis in the hot summer months after spending twenty or more hours a week with sweaty high school boys

during the spring, yet Jolly did just that for over thirty-five years, shepherding the summer program he started in 1957. Only failing health eventually kept him off the court. His commitment to the game he loved also extended beyond the fenced-in asphalt courts on which his high school players and summer students labored. For fifteen years he wrote a column, called "'Jolly's' Tennis Shots" in the Madison newspaper. Former players and readers of his column will no doubt recall this advice, dispensed as the ACDs of tennis: A=appearance, attitude, attitude with ability; C=commitment, concentration, and consistency; D=dedication, determination, and discipline. In addition, he organized a Wimbledon week "Family Mixed Doubles Tourney," with strawberries and cream at his house following play; chauffered Madison tennis players to towns in South Dakota such as Watertown and Brookings for friendly competitions; and organized what he called a "Summerfest Tennis-a-Rama" to inaugurate the newly finished tennis courts in Madison.

For his efforts on behalf of boys' tennis in Minnesota he was voted MN Boys' High School Coach of the Year in 1980 and elected to this hall of fame in 1994. In addition, he was elected to the Augustana Sports Hall of Fame in 1982, the SD Tennis Hall of Fame in 1992, and posthumously to the Watertown High School Hall of Fame in 1998. A final honor bestowed on him must have made him extremely proud, for in 1979, in part because his four boys (and later his daughter) played tennis there, St. Olaf College named its new tennis courts the "Carlson Courts." St. Olaf officials, in an article in the Madison *Western Guard* titled "The Carlson Courts," said at the dedication, "the courts were named for Carlson because of his eminence as a tennis player, his promotion of the sport and his influence on young people as a teacher and coach and as a church youth worker" (December 26, 1979).

An old-school disciplinarian, he was described by a rival player as "intense but friendly"; and an opponent from Montevideo admired Jolly's players because they were always "tough, dedicated, and well-drilled." Carlson admitted that "today maybe I couldn't do what we expected years ago when we coached; for example, no shorts under shorts, no bandanas—or baseball hats turned around backward, wear uniform of the day to school, etc." He was a particularly good coach of doubles teams; for example, his sons Greg and Jeff demonstrated what they learned from him by winning the 1978 state doubles title. And like so many coaches living in outstate communities far from the Minnesota tennis centers, Carlson realized that he needed to expose his players to the best competition in order to "shape us into a better team." This often meant long Saturday rides in "Jolly's Rover," an old orange International van, to tournaments and matches in places such as Moorhead, St. Cloud, and the Twin Cities—even 200 miles one-way to White Bear Lake. Carlson proudly reflected that "we did so well in many of these tournaments that sometimes the bigger schools would not play us again or invite us back."

There are of course many reasons why his teams were so successful (his excellent coaching, good tennis genes in his five children, his strong summer programs—often with as many as 150 kids participating, his willingness to put in extra hours on weekends, his dedication and love of the sport), but he was quick to credit his wife, Carol, as well. One year she served as an official assistant when Jolly was ill and she spent many an hour driving her children to and from tennis matches. In addition, she drove junior high kids to meets and chaperoned them. She was a great fan and continues her interest in tennis by watching her grandchildren play.

Regrettably, the car accident in his early adult life restricted Jolly's tennis playing, and his failing kidneys forced him to give up summer teaching in 1992. After struggling with ill health for six years, he received a kidney transplant in August 1993. This "gift" gave him nearly five more years of life, but he passed away March 24, 1998. (For more about Carlson ad his children, see Chapter Ten.)

Ed Sewell
North St. Paul (1995)

The next Hall of Fame coach lived and worked at the eastern end of the state near the Wisconsin border, in a St. Paul suburb. Ed Sewell took a job teaching art and filmmaking at North St. Paul in 1954 and stayed there until he retired in 1985. And except for one year in which he taught art at a college in Darlington, England, on a Fulbright Scholarship, he also coached the Polars boys' tennis team those

thirty-two years.

An imposing man who is as tall (six feet four inches) as Jolly Carlson was short, Ed was another of the many coaches who did not play competitive tennis in high school (though he began playing recreationally at age eight on Minneapolis Park Board courts). Instead he competed in track at Minneapolis North, running the 440, 220, low hurdles, and high hurdles for a team that won the State Tournament his senior year (1943). After graduating from the U of M with an art major and then an MA in art education, he took a teaching job at Ferndale, Michigan, in 1951. At Ferndale he also coached football, basketball, and baseball. And it was there that he took up tennis again, with the help of his very accomplished tennis-playing cousin, Betsy Hiatt, who hit with him on a regular basis.

Once re-introduced to the game, he took to it like a bear to a blueberry patch and soon parlayed his interest into coaching upon his arrival in North St. Paul in 1954. His Polars were always competitive in the Suburban Conference and his 1966 team, on the strength of a runner-up doubles finish by Jerry Burnham and Dwight Dahlen, tied with Edina for the state team championship. In addition, Sewell's Polars won six district and three region titles and 71 dual matches in a row and many of Ed's singles players and doubles teams advanced to the State Tournament over the years. And though none would claim an individual title, several acquitted themselves well. For example, Kim Gustafson finished fourth in the 1969 singles competition and Sewell's doubles teams of Jim LeMire and Ed Anderson took third in 1963, Burnham and Dahlen captured second place in 1966, and Dahlin and Dave Kubes placed fifth in 1967.

Along with Hall of Fame coach Len McGuire of Stillwater, Sewell helped organize a very successful eight-team invitational tournament called the Pony-Polar which attracted many of the best teams in the state. One year it was played at North St. Paul (Polar) and the next at Stillwater (Pony). But McGuire retired in 1961, so, Sewell said, "I talked it over with Tom Byrne from Owatonna High School and it became the Indian-Polar Tourney. The visiting coach would stay with the home coach and the players would stay in the homes of the home-team players."

Always an innovator, Ed taught his doubles teams to

use a formation mostly discredited by those who believed in the conventional "get to net" style. Instead, in part because he didn't believe the "both up" method worked very well, his teams employed the "one up, one back" formation. Ed explained, "In doubles I kept my tallest boy in the ad court and best righthanded stroker in the forehand court and invited teams to hit to our forehand side. We left our forehand side open so we could hit forehands and protect our backhands. This way we won most of the time." Sewell was also not above using a bit of psychology to get what he wanted. One year he persuaded Superintendent Walter Richardson to attend a meet and the night before told his players to wear rags for their uniform of the day. So when the superintendent arrived, he said, "Geez, Sewell, those uniforms are pretty bad." Ed noted with a chuckle that "within a week we had money for new uniforms." Once in a while, when his teams were good, he would use tangible reinforcers to inspire his players as well: "I would buy a milk shake for each player if no one lost. One loss, no milk shake."

Ed Sewell (Back row—Left) North St. Paul Team

Coach Tom Vining of Roseville remembers Sewell as "burly and gruff on the outside but soft-hearted and kind on the inside." Vining added, "He didn't know so much about tennis, but he was a master of organization and intimidation. He also knew how to pick an assistant. Gary Teewinkel was one of the most astute tennis men I've ever seen. They complemented one another perfectly and throughout the 1960s, North's Polars were very competitive."

As so many tennis coaches found, struggling to get gym court time in the early season was a major concern for Sewell. Not only did he have to combat the prevailing notion that tennis was a minor sport and demands for prime gym time from baseball and softball coaches, but he even had to fight for time with the basketball coach whose season had already ended and who wanted to practice for the next year. In spite of these difficulties, Ed made the most of the gym time he had, even scheduling regular matches ("which we called scrimmages") on the one singles and one doubles court available.

With respect to his coaching style, Sewell felt comfortable in the old school brotherhood of those who believed in setting rules and establishing discipline. For instance, he was not pleased when players missed practice, so truant team members had to play a challenge match with the player below them at practice the next day. He firmly believed that players had to earn their positions on the team by defeating teammates in challenge matches. Here's what he had to say about his challenge ladder: "I ranked the boys one through whatever number we had at the start of the year. Every player had to beat the guy behind him to hold his place. I placed no one; the boys placed themselves by playing each other."

Sewell also took this system to another level by requiring players or doubles teams who lost in a match (if the player or team below won) to have a challenge match in the next practice. In addition, the No. 8 B-squad player was permitted to challenge a member of the No. 2 doubles team if they lost their varsity match. And though he was strict about some things, Ed was no martinet. He believed in limiting practices to two hours in order to keep his players fresh, and he scheduled teams he felt the Polars could beat early in the season to give his players confidence for the difficult upcoming competition. His good people skills helped him motivate his players and finagle favors from the school custodians as well. One custodian even painted the singles and doubles lines on the two gym floor courts at the high school as a favor to Ed.

Serving the MN Boys' Tennis Coaches Association as president in 1971-72, Ed worked very hard with Bud

Schmid and others in the organization to persuade the MSHSL to change to a team tournament format—which it did in 1973. In fact, it was Ed who presented the plan to the League when it was approved in 1972. In Ed's first years it made sense that matches consisted of only three singles and one (later, of course, two) doubles matches, for many schools only had two or three courts. Often a school may have had two courts at one site and three at another—as was the case at North St. Paul, so coaches had to send players out to separate sites to play. But in the early 1970s more and more schools had five, eight, or even sixteen (as Coon Rapids did) courts at one site, and the tennis boom produced more players. So Ed recognized a need and pushed for this dramatic and very important change as well.

Finally, Ed was one of those young men who served his country in WWII, fighting at the Battle of the Bulge. Viewing tennis as a great lifetime sport, he himself continued playing for many years after his retirement and into his 70s. He said, "I tried to play a set of tennis every day year-round to stay in shape." In retirement he also tries to sit down at his easel for at least two hours a day to create one painting a month. As a young boy he painted fish for a taxidermist, and today he does realistic paintings such as a series on the life of Teddy Roosevelt and a painting of a sparrow (which he called "Mother's Work Never Ends"). He has also written a history tracing his family's roots back to Samuel Sewell, the famous judge who presided over the Salem witch trials. Today he makes his home in the university town of Lawrence, KS.

Windfield "Whitey" Olson
Thief River Falls (1995)

In far northwestern Minnesota, about sixty miles from the Canadian border and roughly forty miles from North Dakota, sits the town of Thief River Falls, home of the next 1995 inductee, Windfield "Whitey" Olson. Given its location, 300 miles from the Twin Cities and farther north than any other school coached by a Hall of Fame member, it is hard to believe that quality tennis teams could come from there. How could anyone play tennis in April on land that used to be Glacial Lake Agassiz (the name itself

brings a shudder) in average temperatures of 41 degrees? Perhaps it's because so many residents claim northern European ancestry (50 percent are of Norwegian descent and 15 percent are Swedish) that tennis could flourish in the cold and blustery weather so common on this prairie landscape in the spring.

With such a good Scandinavian name as Olson, it seemed fitting that Whitey should be the coach to lead these northland tennis players to fame. Like so many coaches of his era, Olson came to tennis late—in early adulthood. There was no tennis program in his high school (Forest Lake), and he was introduced to the sport in an "Individual Sports" class at Moorhead State U. This first contact with tennis was something of an epiphany for Olson, and he describes it in these words: "I thought it was neat that I didn't have to depend on other team members to be successful, except in doubles, and then there was only one other player. I think that aspect of the sport was what I really liked. Play off for a position and then do the job without anyone to blame."

So when he arrived in Thief River Falls after graduating from Moorhead in 1957 and after teaching one year at Bertha-Hewitt and seven years at Littlefork-Big Falls, he relished the opportunity to coach the sport he fell in love with in college. For a time he coached basketball at Thief River Falls, then in 1969 he assumed the reins as head boys' tennis coach, a position he would hold until 1988. And in 1974 he also started the girls' program, serving as head coach in 1974 and then again from 1979-1988.

During his years as the boys' coach, Olson's teams advanced to the State Tournament from Region 8 and 8AA in 1975, '78, '79, and '80; finished second in the region seven times; and won many invitational team tournament championships. In addition, he coached twenty-seven individuals who advanced to the State Tournament. His top players were Bill Jury (who advanced to State in singles in 1978 and '79), Mitch Rustad (who made three straight appearances at State in singles and, as a senior, placed fourth in the 1980 singles tournament), and the doubles team of Brian Waale and Keith Breiland (third-place doubles finishers in 1975). Olson remembers the late 1970s and early '80s as excellent years with "outstanding boys' tennis players—good students—and supportive parents."

The 1980 team, ranked No. 1 in the state by the coaches association at the beginning of the year, was particularly successful, losing to eventual AA team champion Edina West 3-2 in the first round of the State Tournament and winning three top-eight invitational tournaments during the regular season. Olson remembers this latter experience well: "We drove to St. Paul on a Thursday evening, won the tournament at Stillwater on Friday, then drove to Hibbing Friday night and won the Hibbing Tournament on Saturday. The following Saturday starting at 5 AM we drove to St. Cloud and won that tournament."

There were many other memorable moments in his coaching career (including watching his daughter Michelle play in the state girls' tournament), but some reflected the difficulties often encountered by coaches and teams from the northern part of the state. For example, almost every year that cruel mistress, the weather, kept his players indoors on the gym floor well into spring. In his twenty years of coaching the boys, Olson recalls that "there were only two years that we hit outside on tennis courts before our first meet." In addition to bad weather, sometimes his teams had to contend with what seemed to him a lack of respect for his and other northern teams. Once, in 1978, his individual entries in the State Tournament showed up at the U of M courts only to find a note attached to a gate saying the meet had been moved to indoor courts. No one had notified him of this change of venue. And in 1979 the MSHSL decided to hold quarterfinal state team play at different sites, so Thief River Falls was scheduled to play Region 7 champion Virginia on May 29 at Bemidji. However, it rained in Bemidji so the teams drove seventy miles to Sugar Hills in Grand Rapids to play indoors. After losing a hard-fought match 3-2, he and his boys got home at 2 AM and had to leave right away for the individual State Tournament which was to begin at 9 AM in Minneapolis the same day. Olson recalls with some amusement that the next year, when a Twin Cities team was scheduled to play a quarterfinal match up north, the League changed back to the old method of holding all state matches in Minneapolis.

Despite these and other impediments associated with coaching "up north" (no access to indoor courts being another one), Olson had no regrets. He was a longtime member of the Tennis Coaches Association who served for many years as Region 8 rankings representative and also as the region representative to the MSHSL for basketball and tennis. Retired from coaching in 1988 and from his last position as a counselor at the high school in 1996, he has finally beaten old man weather, for he now spends the winters living in an RV in Edinburg, TX.

Keith Paulson
Austin (1995)

Austin, MN, is home of the George A. Hormel & Co. Meat Packing plant (now called Hormel Foods), Spam luncheon meat, and some of the richest farmland in the world. In addition, it produced powerhouse high school football and basketball teams in the 1950s and '60s. A prairie town located 100 miles from Minneapolis and almost forty miles from the nearest indoor courts at Owatonna, it's nonetheless the home of a very successful boys' tennis program, a program guided for twenty-seven years by coach Keith Paulson. Thanks to his untiring efforts, Austin became one of the premier tennis teams in Region I and the state.

Born and raised in Ames, IA, Paulson learned to play tennis on park and recreation courts in Ames and, after honing his game as a youngster, he competed for his high school team. He graduated from Ames High School in 1952 and then enrolled at Luther College in Decorah, IA. His college career was interrupted for two years of army service (eighteen months of it spent in Berlin, Germany), but he returned to Luther and graduated in 1958 with a social science degree. At Luther he won the Iowa Intercollegiate Athletic Conference No. 1 singles and doubles titles in 1958.

In the fall of 1958 Keith took a teaching job at Charles City High School in his home state, where he started the tennis program and coached until 1964. Moving to Austin in 1964 (where he taught social studies, history, and geography at Ellis Junior High School), he took the boys' tennis coaching job and continued in that role until 1991. During his years at Austin, his team was always one of the best in one of the most competitive conferences in the state, the Big Nine. His teams won seven conference titles, including one in 1978 that his wife, Lois, describes as the

Keith Paulson (back row center) & 1982 Championship Team

most thrilling: "I was teaching and not at the tournament, but I got a phone message saying that the finals were being played at that moment and 'there's an Austin guy in every court.' Austin won the Big Nine that year with 38 points."

After just five years at the helm, Keith led his 1969 boys' team to the first of its two state tournament titles, a victory in which the Packers earned 12 points on the strength of four doubles wins by state doubles champions Steve Runtsch and Greg Knutson, edging out Edina by one point. Ironically, Steve and Greg defeated arch rivals Steve Yoss and Tony Bianco from Rochester Mayo in the finals 4-6, 6-3, 6-4. This was in the era before True Team competition, when each doubles win was worth three points and a singles win was worth just two points. During the season Steve and Greg played singles, but Keith wisely paired them up for tournament competition and doing so paid huge dividends. In an article by Gregg Wong in the June 8, 1969, *St. Paul Pioneer Press*, Keith lauded them as unselfish players and said of their coupling, "Both are good in singles, but for the betterment of the team they elected to team up in doubles and look how it paid off. They lacked experience and a little cohesiveness at first, but I wasn't worried because they are both good tennis players. They

improved rapidly and reached their peak in the State." Keith early on learned what so many astute coaches know: putting one's best singles players (the best players on the team) in doubles was usually a prescription for success. One has only to look at the names of state doubles champions to know that more often than not this pairing of top singles players produced double(s) pleasure.

One could argue that a team championship secured by just two players was in some ways a tainted title; however, it was fairly won under the rules and Keith proved that it was no fluke by coaching teams that advanced to the True Team tournament four more times: 1974, 1980, 1981, and 1982. In 1974 the Packers took third and in 1982 they steamrolled all competition to win the class AA tournament, beating Fridley 5-0, St. Thomas Academy 4-1, and St. Cloud Tech 5-0 in the finals. Led by No. 1 singles player Scott Barber, who also advanced to the quarterfinals of the singles tournament, and singles players Kevin Arnold and Steve Gardner (who paired up for state doubles competition and finished second), Paulson's undefeated Packers had one of the most dominant seasons in Minnesota tennis history. This was also the third straight Region I title for the Austin netters, a run that ended in 1983 with a second place finish to Rochester Mayo.

Though he only coached one individual tournament champion, the doubles team of Runtsch and Knutson in 1969, Keith coached many other singles players and doubles teams that advanced to the State Tournament over the years (for example, singles players Mark Jordahl, Dan Anderson, and Tommy Tauchnitz—who finished fourth in the 1989 Class AA singles tournament). But he was also justly proud of the success enjoyed by his own three children. His oldest son Dan advanced to the state singles tournament two years in a row (1979-80) and upset eighth-grade phenom Casey Merickel from St. Cloud Apollo in the first round before falling to eventual champion Chris Combs in the 1980 tournament. His son Tom played doubles on Keith's 1980-82 state tournament teams. In addition, his daughter Sarah, the No. 1 player on the Austin girls' team for three years, often sought out boys on Keith's team in order to get good competition.

On a personal note, the teams I coached at Northfield met Keith's teams 18 times in 17 years (Austin holding a 10-8 advantage) and I found him to be a perfect gentleman who was always calm and in control of his emotions. He was steady as a stately oak tree, a low-key, even-keel kind of guy. One of Keith's former No. 1 players, Dan Kallman, said of him, "He was a very quiet coach who never raised his voice."

Perhaps this equanimity resulted from confidence in his own tennis ability (he was a very controlled player) and in his tennis knowledge. As mentioned earlier, Keith was a successful high school and college player; and he continued to compete well as an adult, mostly in NWTA tournaments. He and his partner, Dick Kleber from Northfield, were a very competitive doubles team in their age group for many years, achieving a No. 1 ranking in Mens' 45 Doubles in both 1978 and 1979, a No. 1 ranking in Mens' 50 Doubles in 1983, and a No. 1 ranking in 55 doubles in 1988. According to Kleber, a strong backcourt player, "Keith and I complemented each other because he was a very good net player."

For his coaching achievements and for his longtime service as treasurer of the MN Boys' High School Tennis Coaches Association, Paulson was twice named MN State High School Boys' Tennis Coach of the Year—in 1980 and

'82. And in 1990 Keith was also inducted into the Luther College Athletic Hall of Fame.

Sadly, a massive stroke he suffered in 1991 when he was just fifty-eight years old made it impossible for Keith to continue teaching and coaching. However, though he was paralyzed on his right side and had difficulty speaking, these impediments did not keep him away from the tennis courts, for he became Austin's biggest fan in those difficult years before his death in 2002.

Like many Hall of Fame coaches, Paulson began his career in a simpler era, a time when players had only one racket and borrowed a friend's when they broke a string. Then they had to drive sixty miles to Blue Earth (to Hal Schroeder) for restringing. It was a time when players genuinely enjoyed hitting a few balls on wooden gym floors on a Friday night before the season officially opened and a time when players and coaches alike repaired their sneakers with Shoe-goo. Keith's wife, Lois, remembers many nights when three or four pairs of shoes were lined up, drying in the mudroom. It was also a time when a coach had to make do with the courts he had—in Keith's case six cement courts with steel nets located at a windy spot by the Austin athletic field. Though they were not the best courts, they provided a nice home court advantage; and Lois recalls a story to illustrate this advantage: "The suburban schools hated to come to Austin. But once in a while those schools did come. One Saturday in the mid-seventies I particularly remember it was extremely windy. Austin was playing Edina, I think, and should have lost. But the Austin boys knew how to 'play the wind' (they had lots of practice with that) and the Edina guys were used to better conditions. Austin won and it was a very sweet victory for them."

Now there are new courts in Austin, located at the recently restored Wescott Field complex and named after Keith. It is only fitting that his name should grace these courts, for he did so much to develop tennis in Austin, both at the high school and recreational level. Paulson was, for instance, maybe one of the first coaches to hire his own players as instructors in a summer tennis program. In addition to sharing his tennis knowledge with the citizens of Austin, he generously shared it with other coaches. For example, I remember phoning him in 1971 and asking for advice about how to establish a summer tennis program in Northfield; he promptly sent information that would serve as the foundation for our first program.

So I remember Keith Paulson as a generous and caring man who truly loved tennis and wanted to share his experience with others. Kallman, a successful composer and musician who lives in Northfield, recalls another quality he admired in his former coach. "I really appreciated that he was very mindful of other people's interests—we could miss tennis for rehearsals. He didn't insist that tennis be your whole life." Thus, while we honor him as a successful tennis coach, we also remember Paulson as someone who realized that there was more to life than trying to beat the brains out of one's opponents.

Jerry Sales
St. Cloud Tech (1996)

Of the coaches thus far enshrined in the Hall of Fame, Jerry Sales is the first with the title of varsity assistant coach. However, it would not be fair to liken him to Sherlock Holmes' Dr. Watson, for Jerry's powers of deduction were as keen as those of St. Cloud Tech's Sherlock, Bill Ritchie. In fact, Tech's Sherlock thought so much of Watson's (Sales') abilities that he gave him the title of co-coach; and together they solved tennis problems for twenty-three years (from 1971-1993). This dynamic duo guided the St. Cloud Tech Tigers to three state championships (1976, '83, '85), six runner-up finishes, and two third place finishes among the twelve team state tournament appearances they made during those halcyon years. (For more about these Tech teams, see Chapter Nine.)

Jerry's story begins in the west central Minnesota community of Clarissa, where he played basketball and football (captaining the team his senior year, 1952, and bedeviling opponents by running and passing from his halfback position). Though he did not play tennis in high school (there was no tennis program in Clarissa), as a freshman in a tennis class at St. Cloud State Teacher's College he first played the game on courts made of packed granite pieces. Jerry immediately fell in love with the game, so much so that he joined the tennis team for two

years, playing, as he said, "the lowest possible spot on the team... really I was very inexperienced. I guess I won half of my matches."

And like his mentor, Mac Doane, Sales parlayed this interest into a long and successful career as one of the pioneers of tennis in St. Cloud. Following service with the 7th Infantry Division during the Korean War and some time off to work, he graduated from St. Cloud State in 1961 with a BA in social studies and began teaching history at South Junior High School. At South he promptly volunteered to start the first junior high tennis team in St. Cloud. Perhaps most importantly, he was privileged to work there under the guidance of Doane, who was still coaching the high school tennis team. In an article by Tom Larson in the June 2, 1993, *St. Cloud Daily Times*, Sales volunteered to coach in 1962 for nothing and joked that "I always tell people I probably was paid what I was worth." Reflecting on Sales' early career at South Junior High, coach Bill Ritchie said, "Sales' position in the junior high, among budding tennis players, helped keep the varsity team strong... He encouraged good athletes to try tennis." Jerry was a stickler for fundamentals and conditioning, emphasizing what he called a "non-stop work ethic" (June 2, 1993) which employed leg-strengthening exercises such as jumping rope and running.

When he moved to the high school to become Ritchie's assistant in 1971, he partnered with a coach who shared his belief in hard work and conditioning. "I think Tech worked harder on conditioning than any team in the state when Bill and I were together. It was our belief that we would never lose due to a conditioning factor." In the aforementioned article by Larson, former Tech player Jay Schlorf recalls with grudging admiration, "I remember running and running and running and running. And I remember hating it. But you don't appreciate it until after you're gone. In a three-set match, when you need it, you're going to have the legs and it might help you win it" (June 2, 1993).

Throughout his career Jerry also kept his coaching togs on the remainder of the year to serve the game he had learned to love as a young adult. He and other local players started the first mens' leagues in St. Cloud in the early

1960s; and as a city employee in the summer he instituted the first youth leagues in the '70s. These efforts would be but the tip of the iceberg, for Sales also founded the very successful Blazer Tennis Camps at the College of St. Benedict and served as director for fourteen years. In addition, he became a USPTA pro and employed his knowledge as a teacher at the St. Cloud Tennis Center. In that capacity he worked with beginners, adults, and nationally ranked juniors such as Kevin Whipple (a future NCAA Division 3 doubles champion at Gustavus), Tony Larson from Long Prairie (2000 Class A singles champion), and Kerry Snow of Sartell (2002 girls Class AA singles champion).

Beyond the Granite City, Jerry served as president of the MN Boys' Tennis Coaches Association in 1987-88, as an advisory member to the MSHSL for many years, as a member of the Wilson Advisory Staff, and at times as an invited advisor and helper for area tennis teams. For his efforts on behalf of tennis Jerry was elected by his peers as 1989 MN Boys' Tennis Coach of the Year and as a member of this coaches' hall of fame.

Though he sometimes struggled to deal with parents who "pushed instead of supported" their kids, this minor vexation did not stop him from keeping his eye on the prize—helping kids and being a positive role model for them. He derived special satisfaction from "seeing a kid hang in there and be able to contribute" and from making connections with kids and families. One example, that of former Tech player Brian Boland, serves to illustrate the influence Jerry had on his players. Sales said of Boland, "I gave him support and some advice when he applied for and got the tennis coaching job at Indiana State U. He was very successful there and caught the eyes of several schools. He then interviewed and got the U of Virginia job and is currently in his sixth year. We continue to talk to each other every two or three weeks."

On the eve of Coach Sales' retirement, former player Schlorf said this about Jerry: "He taught you how to win. He's a straight shooter; he'll tell you what is what. He's kind of the embodiment of Tech tennis. He's the heart and soul. He's going to be tough to replace" (*St. Cloud Daily Times*, June 2, 1993). Though his reputation for honesty and toughness in part defines his legacy, Jerry also had many other qualities that helped him be successful. For

instance, he had a good moral compass, pointing kids in the right direction. "We expected kids to be responsible and decent people," he said. And while he truly believed in and modeled a strong work ethic, he also recognized the importance of making tennis enjoyable for the players. For example, he said, "Sometimes we would give them an unexpected day off or play basketball or things not directly tennis related. Sometimes we would jog to the Dairy Queen for treats." In addition, his sense of humor served him well over the years, as revealed in his response to a question I posed about the tennis epitaph he would write for himself: "He cared and worked hard and had a lousy backhand."

In the end he will be remembered best as one of the true pioneers of St. Cloud tennis, a link between Mac Doane and Bill Ritchie and even to the present Tech program. Speaking about this legacy, Jerry said, "If I have been helpful in maintaining the Tech tradition, it has been its own reward. The school and tennis program have been deep loves of mine." A lover of travel and reading; father of two grown sons and one daughter; and proud grandfather of four; Bill still resides in St. Cloud where he exercises regularly and volunteers at First United Methodist Church

Steve Wilkinson
Gustavus Adolphus College (1996)

Though Steve Wilkinson is the only person enshrined in the Hall of Fame who did not coach a high school team, no one is more deserving. His is no honorary membership, no Order of the British Empire (O.B.E.) without the title of Sir, it is a membership earned for significant and meritorious service to high school players and coaches for over thirty years. Through his Tennis and Life Coaching Clinics (renamed Tennis and Life Clinics in 1982) and his summer Tennis and Life Camps, he and his clinicians and coaches helped shape the playing and coaching of tennis in Minnesota and neighboring states in ways too numerous to mention. His influence on high school tennis in Minnesota resulted in large part from his efforts in organizing and promoting these clinics and camps. He threw his pebble in the pond in 1973 and it made a small splash in Brainerd, but over the years it has become a giant wave which has reached all corners of the Upper Midwest and beyond.

Wilkinson is also one of the most successful NWTA adult male amateur players from Minnesota in the past thirty years, at least in terms of his accomplishments in national tournaments, but it might have been difficult to predict that a young man growing up in Sioux City, IA, a town that didn't even have a high school tennis program, could become so accomplished.

So how did he learn to play tennis, let alone hone his game? God-given talent figures in the mix, but Steve said he learned the game by following his parents around to tennis courts. He recalls his early tennis memories in these words: "At four years of age we [his brother John and sister Ann] used to accompany my parents to a playground. I rode my scooter and my parents played mixed doubles. I threw a tantrum if they didn't hit me some balls after they were done playing." Steve assumes that his father must have given him some rudimentary instructions, but he doesn't remember that very well and he took only a few city recreation group lessons ("I learned pretty much on my own"). By the time he was ten he began playing tournaments in South Dakota, Iowa, and Nebraska; and at age fourteen he started teaching tennis in the summer program in Sioux City. In addition, there were Sunday afternoon matches involving both adults and kids and intercity matches with Sioux Falls and Omaha.

When he entered high school, he was resigned to the fact that there was no organized tennis program. Nonetheless, he and his father persuaded a high school biology teacher, Harold Asmusen, to fill out the necessary paperwork required by the Iowa State High School League so that he could participate in the State Tournament. And though he doubled as a track performer in the spring, he

Steve Wilkinson

excelled at the State Tennis Tournament, finishing second his junior and senior years to Bob Boysen, a nationally ranked player. And he accomplished this despite the fact that he focused on basketball in the winter and had no indoor courts on which to play. Still, he did hit off the gymnasium wall during the winter; and whenever he could play outside he hit against the wall, served a bucket of balls, or played against anyone who would play.

After graduating from Central High School in 1959, Steve's tennis-playing career blossomed under the tutelage of legendary U of IA coach Don Klotz. Playing No. 1 singles his sophomore, junior, and senior years (freshmen were not yet eligible for varsity competition), Steve reached the Big Ten finals in doubles his senior year and regrets that he didn't quite reach the finals in singles. "I was two points away from beating Marty Riessen of Northwestern in the semis [Riessen and Clark Graebner were at the time playing Davis Cup doubles for the U.S.], leading 6-5, 30-love in the final set before he rallied to beat me."

Unlike many top-level tennis players, such as Jimmy Connors, for whom the game was an obsession, Steve was also a cerebral person for whom the life of the mind was as important or even more important. So, armed with a BA from the U of IA in 1963 (with a major in accounting and a minor in religion), Steve continued his studies at Iowa for six more years, completing his MBA with an emphasis on International Finance in 1965 and a PhD in 1970 in the history of religions—with a focus on Japan—and a specialty in international finance. During the 1965-66 school year he taught accounting and humanities at Western Washington U in Bellingham and, in the most serendipitous event of his life, he met his future wife, Barbara, a native of Germany who was learning English while working as a dental assistant. Steve said, "We met by chance when we both went skiing on Mt. Baker the same day."

And though his mind was working overtime all these years, he was not neglecting his tennis. For several years (1963-65 and 1966-70) he served as an assistant coach at Iowa and for one year as a summer tennis instructor at the Rochester Outdoor Club (1970). In the summer of 1965 Steve played doubles with his former pupil Chuck Darley (whom he had coached occasionally in Iowa City between 1959-62) in "pro" tournaments. Chuck, a three-time MN state singles champion, had just completed his first year at the U of CA-Berkeley, so it must have been a thrill for him to play with his older and more experienced coach against the likes of Arthur Ashe and other top U.S. players. Steve recalls that he and Chuck played (and lost to) Ashe and his UCLA doubles partner, Tom Edlefson, in the U.S. National Clay Court Tournament that summer.

In the fall of 1970 Steve headed north to St. Peter, MN, to take a job as a world religions professor and, of course, men's tennis coach at Gustavus Adolphus College (GAC). Ironically, Wilkinson said, "coaching tennis was not part of my contract, but I volunteered when the previous coach left in the spring of 1970." For seven years he was a successful teacher in the religion department, but it was as a tennis coach that he was to make his mark at GAC. In his thirty-six years at the helm of the men's team the Gusties have won 885 matches and lost just 253 against the toughest national competition. He is only the fourth college coach to reach 800 victories, but perhaps most astonishing, his teams have lost just one MIAC dual meet in thirty-six years, a loss to St. Thomas in 1985. Think about it—one meet! However, since conference titles were based on flighted tournaments and not dual meets, the Gusties did lose conference championships three times: in 1976 to Concordia and in 1985 and '88 to St. Thomas. Their overall conference record, through 2006, is 325-1.

Cutting their competitive teeth on matches against the top teams in the country, Steve's teams traveled to California each spring to play highly ranked Division 3 teams, and the Gusties have participated in the national NAIA and now NCAA Division 3 tournaments in all but three years. In addition, in his early years Gustavus scheduled many Division 1 teams and on occasion even defeated the likes of the U of IA and once lost just 5-4 to the U of M. A master recruiter who persuaded top players from neighboring states such as Iowa (his home state and thus fruitful ground), Illinois, and the Dakotas to enroll at GAC, he also snagged his share of Minnesota's top players over the years, including recent singles champions Todd Bowlby and Eric Butorac. Unlike most college coaches, he made room for nearly all players who came out for tennis, always scheduling dual matches for at least eighteen players (three varsity teams—most of which could defeat any MIAC team). His were true teams in the best sense, and his top teams and individuals always acquitted themselves well on the national stage. Two of his teams won national NCAA spring titles (in 1980 and '82) and three won national indoor titles (2002, '03, '06) and four singles players and six doubles teams won national championships.

In his early years at GAC Steve began to develop a coaching and playing philosophy that would evolve into what he came to call "Tennis and Life," a philosophy that would become the foundation of his own coaching, the coaching clinics, and his summer camps. It focuses on the important things, what he calls the "3 crowns of the Gustavus tennis program: full effort, a positive attitude, and good sportsmanship." And it has roots in some of the greatest religious thoughts and teachings, most notably the Serenity Prayer but also Jesus' great commandment to love God and your neighbor as yourself, the Psalms, and the Prayer of St. Francis. He also gives players or campers who request it a handout listing suggestions for reaching goals without focusing on winning or losing.

Steve considers it a privilege to have had "the opportunity to influence lives, to impart moral values that will positively impact my players—not only in tennis but in all other areas of their lives." In the end, the Serenity Prayer seems appropriate in defining a coach whose grace under pressure and calm demeanor have characterized his interactions with his players, fellow coaches, and summer students: "God, grant me the serenity to accept the things I cannot change, the courage to change the things I can, and the wisdom to know the difference."

For those who have coached tennis in the Upper Midwest and in Minnesota in particular, Steve's generous and selfless efforts in organizing and presenting clinics for players, coaches, and other tennis aficionados put us in his debt. From 1973, when he was asked by then president of the MN High School Tennis Coaches Association and Hall of Famer Bud Schmid to form a clinic for coaches, until 1997, this spring clinic became the most important tennis workshop for groups all over the Northwestern Section. Held in February in the central Minnesota resort town of Brainerd, on Tartan surfaces at three sites, the first clinics were modest, three-day affairs. Many of the coaches came to Brainerd with their families and stayed at the Holiday Inn for an enjoyable midwinter break. The first clinicians were Steve, his mentor and coach Dr. Klotz, Dr. Pat Sherman (a Winona State U physical education professor then teaching at GAC), St. Paul tennis pro Steve Ehlers, girls' program advocate and tennis teacher Jo Warner, and then Wayzata Country Club pro Dave Yorks. Billed as the "first such clinic for men and women of the Upper Midwest" (perhaps a bit of hyperbole considering that there had already been clinics at the U of M in previous years), it was directed toward college and high school coaches, college and high school physical education instructors, and tennis enthusiasts. Emphasis was on helping men and women become competent tennis instructors and coaches, the execution and evaluation of stroke mechanics, strategy, and the exchange of ideas among participants. Recognizing the need for some positive reward for attendance, Steve and former U of M coach Joe Walsh arranged for participants to receive both graduate and undergraduate college credit from Mankato State (where Walsh was then teaching). Another attractive feature of this clinic was that participants had a chance to play tennis during free time. There were also exhibition matches featuring the presenters; individual stroke analysis by the instructors and video tape; lots of handouts; special displays of rackets, clothing, and gadgets; and numerous sessions on coaching and teaching methods and playing strategies.

This first successful clinic would grow into one of the premier coaching/teaching clinics in the U.S., and for over twenty years Steve's name would be associated with it; for he was the prime mover and organizer. In 1978 the clinic was called the Tennis and Life Coaching Clinic (perhaps because Steve had begun to call his summer camps by the name Tennis and Life) and it was held mainly at GAC until 1983, mostly in February or March but for three years in August as well. From 1983 to '88 it was held at Mound-Westonka High School, from 1989-91 at Robbinsdale Armstrong High School, and from 1992-97 at Eagan High School. During these years the presenters and participants included a veritable Who's Who of professional tennis players, internationally known coaches, local pro coaches, Minnesota Hall of Fame coaches, and top state high school and college players from GAC and the U of M. For example, Arthur Ashe, then captain of the U.S. Davis Cup team, came in 1984 to do a session on strategy and mental skills and to speak at the first midwinter banquet to promote national Junior Tennis League play in Minnesota. Other pro players who came were Pete Sampras's coach Paul Annacone; Minnesota's own Ann Henricksson, Ginger Helgeson, John Mattke, and David Wheaton; Tom and Tim Gullickson; Tim Mayotte; Jose Higueras; Dick Stockton; Stan Smith; JoAnne Russell; Sherwood Stewart; Rodney Harmon; and, in the last year, Hall of Fame great Chris Evert. Some of the nationally known coaches and teaching pros were Alice Tym of Yale, Allen Fox of Pepperdine, Peter Burwash, Dennis Van DerMeer, Nick Saviano, Vic Braden, and Nick Bollettieri. And many local pros shared their expertise at these clinics, among them the legendary Frank Voigt, Dave Yorks, Brian Mahin, Chuck Darley, Steve Ehlers, Greg Lappin, Tim Burke, Jack Roach, Dave Pettingill, Ron York, Sue Oertel, Paul Muesing, Connie Custodio, Brian McCoy, Greg Wicklund, Steve Paulsen, Ernie Greene, and Gopher coaches Jerry Noyce and Dave Geatz. Throughout the years Steve's good friends Joe Walsh and Roger Boyer were constants, and of course many of Steve's former players who have now become teaching pros, Kevin Ylinen, Marc Miller, Dick Schneider, Rajan Keswani, Mattke, among others, were also presenters.

As the clinic evolved from its initial focus on stroke mechanics, drills and practice, and coaching strategy, beginning in 1977 specialized sessions were added to address such topics as nutrition, sports psychology, yoga and tennis, fitness, wheelchair tennis, the inner game, sportsmanship. For example, an annual presenter has been former Owatonna and St. Olaf tennis player Dr. Dan Halvorsen, a nutritionist/exercise physiologist. There have also been sessions on wheelchair tennis led by national wheelchair champion Brad Parks; sessions on sports psychology led by Joe Walsh and top national experts such as Jim Loehr and Minnesota's Chris Barden; presentations by sports scientists such as Jack Groppel; sessions on NWTA matters led by Minnesotans Jack Dow (Senior Tennis Players Club), Bob Larson (publisher of *Tennis Midwest* and other tennis magazines), Pat Colbert (MN Regional Schools Program Director), Dave McGill, Patty Mraz (NWTA Directors of Player Development), and Rosemary Langley (NWTA Tennis and Life Clinic coordinator).

In fact, according to a February 1994 article in *Tennis USTA* titled "Beyond Your Average Clinic," the clinic became, in Steve's words, "a tennis happening, where there's almost a carnival atmosphere." Successfully combining entertainment with education, it was able to attract not only coaches but their players. It was a clinic ahead of its time, a pacesetter in promoting other aspects of sport such as nutrition, sportsmanship, sport science, and sports philosophy. Hence the name Tennis and Life. Steve's many connections in tennis have enabled the clinic to attract "some of the people who are recognized [to be] at the forefront of the game and give them a format in which they can do more than just hit tennis balls but share their philosophy of the game (February 1994).

Each clinic began at 9 AM with a session in the gymnasium featuring one of the headliner presenters, and every hour there were five presentations going on simultaneously. In recent years the last session also featured an exhibition singles or doubles match—with commentary by Steve—often between top Minnesota high school players and/or U of M players and sometimes between top pro players. In 1991, for instance, David Wheaton played Rodney Harmon and in 1993 Jose Higueras played Tim Gullickson. As an added incentive to stay until after the exhibition match was played, there were closing remarks, special presentations; and drawings for clothing items, rackets, spots in tennis camps, and tennis merchandise donated by tennis suppliers. It was, all things considered, a gala kickoff to the spring high school season that sometimes

had the feel of a rock concert. It was also an annual tennis "family reunion," particularly for coaches during their noon lunch and meeting. All money raised from the clinic in recent years was distributed by the NWTA (now Northern Section) to junior development programs. When the clinic was held at Mound, for example, all profits went to the Westonka Tennis Association. Throughout the years the USTA, Prince, Head, Wilson, Penn, the USPTR, the USPTA, and the U.S. Racquet Stringers Association supported the clinic, provided presenters, and, of course, displayed their products.

Even when the NWTA began to sponsor the clinics in 1988, Steve still continued to recruit all the speakers, schedule the sessions, find new facilities to host the clinic, work with the MSHSL for approval, and coordinate with the Tennis Coaches Association. Wilkinson noted that "we produced a short video of the clinic in 1994, and in 1995 the Northern Tennis Association presented a description of the clinic at the annual USTA meeting as a model to other sections of what they could do to promote tennis." Unfortunately, the Clinic was discontinued, even though the last one (in 1997) was bigger and better than any previous one.

But Steve's Tennis and Life summer camps for juniors have continued to provide instruction for hundreds of budding young tennis stars, his camps for tennis teachers have helped countless area coaches with their own playing skills, his family camps have helped many develop parent-child relationships along with their tennis games, and his adult camps have provided solid instruction for players of all levels. Furthermore, many of his own players have expanded the ripple through successful professional, college, and high school tennis coaching: Paul Holbach, John Mattke, Tim Butorac, the late Kevin Ylinen, Jon Carlson (current GAC women's coach), Lee Kruger, Dan James (U.S. National Wheelchair coach), and Mark Ensrud, come to mind.

Of course the biggest influence Steve Wilkinson had was on those many young men he coached the past thirty-six years at GAC. On the Brown Courts and in the Swanson Tennis Center he has taught the virtues embodied in his "tennis and life" philosophy, a philosophy that he developed in this real-world laboratory of competitive college tennis. In addition to the inner game which Steve worked on with his players, he also emphasized the importance of being in good physical condition. And he prepared his netmen to be all-court players who knew how to play both singles and doubles.

While he has nothing but praise for high school coaches ("I have story after story of players coming down and describing an important mentoring role that their coaches played for them"), he finds the job of coaching a bit more difficult today. So one of the things he has done is to bring parents "into the loop," opening the lines of communication with them during the spring banquet and throughout the season. And instead of a "win at all costs" philosophy, Steve teaches his players "not to evaluate yourself on the basis of your position on the team" and to remember that "your success is someone else's failure." This sensible approach to competition may explain why so many top high school players come to GAC to play on one of Steve's three squads, knowing that they could play on the top six at most other MIAC schools but that they might never crack the top six at GAC.

Because of the many outstanding players he was privileged to coach, Steve was reluctant to single out any of them. However, he mentioned John Mattke as perhaps his best player because of his accomplishments in college and as a pro (he once defeated, among others, French Open champion and then No. 4 in the world, Andres Gomez). Another top former GAC player is recent graduate and Division 3 singles champion Eric Butorac, a doubles specialist on the pro circuit who is ranked No. 13 in doubles and will be playing in all the Grand Slam events in 2007. And Shaun Miller of Moorhead, who never even qualified for state tournament play, went on to win five national titles (two in team competition, two in doubles, and one in singles).

Steve's many coaching and teaching accomplishments in and of themselves are of mythic proportions, but he has also continued to compete at the highest levels of tennis. Throughout the years he has entered two or three national tournaments in the first two years of each age division, and few or none in the following three years. He has won enough titles to be ranked No. 1 at least once each in the 45s, 50s, 55s, and 60s and three times in the Men's Open Singles division (in 1972, '73, and '80). He's won

numerous Northern Section titles as well. In addition, he has qualified for a USTA Cup Team in each age category, playing on a team which won the World Championship for the Dubler Cup (45s) in Montevideo, Uruguay, in 1989. Most recently he won the 60s hard court singles and doubles (with John Powless) and the national indoor singles title in Seattle and was runner-up in the grass court tourney in 2001.

In addition, he has been involved in USTA affairs for years, renewing his friendship with Arthur Ashe. He first met Ashe when he and Darley played against him in doubles at the National Clay Court Tournament in 1965, but he also recalls an exhibition match he played against Ashe in 1966, when Arthur was in the army and Steve was the No. 1 seed at the Washington State Open, a Pacific Northwest Circuit Tournament. Ashe won 7-5. This and other encounters going back to 1965 enhanced their friendship and, with Ashe's influence, Steve would take a position on the Head Advisory Staff.

For these and other efforts on behalf of tennis, Steve was elected to the USTA/Northern Section Hall of Fame; and he was also awarded the NWTA President's Award and a Lifetime Achievement Award. In addition, he has won numerous regional and national coaching awards such as the 2006 USPTA College Coach of the Year.

Still coaching and running his Tennis and Life camps, Steve lives in St. Peter just a short walk from the GAC courts, with his wife Barbara, whom he credits for much of the success of Tennis and Life. Her behind-the-scenes work as the business manager of Tennis and Life puts her in charge of all registrations. In addition, she manages the pro shop and acts as head nurse when kids need comforting and a trip to the emergency room or the hospital.

Today Steve and Barb take delight in their three grandchildren and their extended family. Their two daughters, Stephanie Reddington and Debbie Sundal, both played high school tennis at St. Peter; and Debbie and her partner made it to the State Tournament. Both played junior varsity tennis in college, Stephanie at GAC and Debbie at Luther.

Jim Holden
Northfield (1997)

Like many other high school tennis coaches, Jim Holden (your author) took a road less traveled before landing a coaching job at Northfield High School. There was no high school and college apprenticeship for him, for neither Sherburn High School nor Augsburg College fielded tennis teams. Instead, his apprenticeship took place on the sanctified baseball grounds of Sherburn's Roman Catholic church. Here, right across the street from his house, he learned to throw, catch, and hit a ball with his younger brother Bob and his southside neighborhood chums. Then he added basketball to the mix and played both sports in high school, earning four letters in baseball and two in basketball.

After graduating from Sherburn High School in 1957, he enrolled at Augsburg, where he played baseball and basketball all four years. At first a pitcher and then a left-fielder, he played on two MIAC championship baseball teams (in 1959 and '61) and served as captain his senior year. He was never a starter in basketball but enjoyed the sport so much that he continued to play it until he was forty years old.

With a major in English, a minor in physical education, and a teaching certificate, he began teaching and coaching at Deep-

Jim Holden

haven Junior High School in Minnetonka. For four years he taught English at Deephaven and for two more years at the new Minnetonka East Junior High School when it opened in 1965. He took one year off (1965-66), to teach in Birmingham, England, then, in 1968, he accepted a job teaching English at Minneapolis Central High School. After just two years at Central (1968-70), Holden moved to Northfield, where he would teach high school English and begin his tennis-coaching career. While living in Northfield, he also completed his post-graduate work and earned an MA in English education from the U of M in 1972.

His first year in Northfield (1970-71) he was hired to direct the intramural sports program, but his principal asked him if he would be willing to coach tennis as well. Despite the fact that he had no previous tennis-coaching experience and only a few pickup tennis matches to cite on his resume, Holden accepted the job, with some trepidation. He said, "There were players on the team who had more tennis coaching experience than I had—from teaching summer recreation lessons—so I had to learn fast. I spent the winter before that 1971 season reading books such as Jack Barnaby's *Racket Work: The Key to Tennis* and practicing swinging my Jack Kramer Autograph racket in the living room."

That first year was a challenge, but it was one he relished; and by attending adult tennis camps, getting pointers from tennis-playing parents such as Tom Rossing (father of No. 1 player Erik), studying the game, and eventually playing in some tournaments, he became more confident in his coaching ability. For seventeen seasons (from 1971-87) he served as the head boys' coach and assisted his friend Wayne Kivell, the Northfield girls' coach, for one year (1985). And in 1990 he returned to the boys' program as an assistant coach for one more year. Though now retired from teaching and coaching, Holden still enjoys helping with the boys' and girls' programs in Northfield on occasion.

During his years at the helm of the Raiders, he coached five teams into the State Tournament, three other teams finished second in the region, and eight of his teams won Missota Conference championships. His 1975 team finished with a record of 22-1 and won the consolation title at State, his 1978 team won eighteen matches and lost just three and took third-place in the State Tournament, and the 1986 Northfield team finished fourth at State. Holden felt that his 1979 team may have been the best he coached, for they lost just one match during the regular season (to

Minnetonka) but were upset in the region tournament by Rochester Mayo 3-2. In addition, singles players Andy Ringlien, Steve Paulsen, and Paul Jenkins lost just one match total (Ringlien and Paulsen were undefeated and Jenkins lost only to Bill Sternard of Minnetonka) until that fateful loss to Mayo. And the sting of a 3-2 loss to Edina in the semis of the 1978 tournament still remains. Holden said, "Had we won that match we could very well have captured the state title." He concluded his coaching career with an overall dual meet record of 237 wins and 82 losses, a 74 percent winning record.

In addition to these team successes, he coached fifteen individual state tournament entrants (ten in doubles and five in singles). These included two third-place finishers in doubles (Tom Cieslukowski and Dan James in 1986 and Doug Cowles and Dan James in '87), one fourth-place singles finisher (Andy Ringlien in 1978) and several quarter-finalists such as Ringlien ('79) and Paulsen ('80) in singles and the doubles teams of Mark Welinski and Eric Jorgensen (1975), Pete Narum and Mark Peterson ('77), Narum and Paulsen ('78), Paulsen and Jenkins ('79), Steve Cieslukowski and Jon Stromseth ('81), and Tom Cieslukowski and Doug Cowles ('85), And in 1976 ninth grader Ringlien and senior Tim Ross captured the state doubles title. About the young men such as these whom he coached, Holden said, "I was blessed to coach so many wonderful young men (and a few young women) over the years, and it was also a great thrill to coach my son Chris for four years and my daughter Heather for one year." Many of his players also went on to play college tennis, including his only Division I player (Ringlien), who played four years at the U of WI. Others included Rossing at Augustana in Illinois, Stan Hunter at a small college in Florida, Welinski at the U of MN-Duluth, Ross at Augsburg, Peterson at Luther, Narum and Paulsen at St. Olaf, Al Updike at Carleton, Chris Holden at Macalester, Andrei Sivanich at Augsburg, Adam Buchwald at Whitman, Dan James at Gustavus, and Steve and Tom Cieslukowski and Cowles at St. Thomas.

With respect to his coaching philosophy, Holden believed that there were no short cuts to success: "You have to work hard and you have to give players an opportunity to hit a lot of balls in order to gain the confidence needed to come through when the pressure's on." As a result he often used station drills to keep players moving and also scheduled fifteen-minute private lessons with both his JV and varsity players every Saturday the team wasn't playing in a tournament. He also employed a no-cut policy and often inserted JV players into the varsity lineup when the Raiders played weaker teams. Said Holden, "Tennis is a lifetime sport, so I felt it was important to help all players develop their games, keeping in mind that varsity tennis is a 'gifted and talented' program for competitive tennis players." One of his former JV players, Carlton Lyons, expressed his gratitude to Holden for his philosophy of helping all players: "You gave me a chance to learn and improve my game of tennis. It was an honor to play and be taught under you."

Holden also felt it was important to be honest with players and to communicate with them. Another of his JV players, Paul Peterson, wrote these words in a thank you note: "You always treated me honestly and fairly throughout the seasons of tennis I played for Northfield. It is something few coaches have done."

To be sure, there were rules (and consequences if they were broken), as former No. 1 player and state doubles champion Ringlien noted in an article by *Northfield News* writer Bob Bradford: "It's not easy dealing with 17-18-year-old kids, but Jim manages to contain them. He sets certain rules that he wants followed." (July 3, 1986) One parent, in that same article, called his approach "principled firmness." Holden also emphasized that winning tennis matches wasn't everything. At the beginning-of-the-year organizational meetings he tried to put tennis into perspective by placing it fourth on a priority list of (1) family, (2) school, (3) faith-church-spirituality, and then (4) tennis.

During his years at Northfield, Holden belonged to the USTA, the MN State High School Coaches Association, and the MN State High School Tennis Coaches Association (MSHSTCA). As a member of the MSHSTCA he served as vice president in 1975-76, as president in 1976-77, and for two years as a member of the coaching ethics committee. As well, for many years he served as the Region/Section I rankings representative. And in Northfield he and girls' coach Kivell organized and ran summer tennis programs for children and adults from 1971-81, started a junior tennis league program in the late '70s, and continued to help organize the summer community recreation tennis programs from 1982-87. Over the years he has given private tennis lessons to many Northfield juniors and adults and still gives occasional lessons in the summer. For his coaching successes in Northfield he was inducted into the Northfield High School Athletic Hall of Fame in 1994.

In addition to this honor, Holden was twice elected as MN Boys' Tennis Coach of the Year (in 1979 and '87). But he regards his election into this hall of fame as his greatest honor. In an article in the *Northfield News* titled "Holden Inducted into Tennis Hall of Fame," he said about this award, "it's just a tremendous honor to be chosen by your peers... For an award like this, I'm joining the company of some of the great tennis coaches in Minnesota. Obviously, this award should also go to all the great kids and assistant coaches that I had in my program. I was just blessed to have wonderful kids" (April 18, 1997).

At the time of his induction, Holden was no longer teaching high school English. Instead, he had spent three years teaching in the education department at Gustavus (from 1991-94) and was then employed at St. Olaf, where he taught general education, English education, and first-year writing courses until his retirement in 2001. He still nurtures the active life—depicted so well in Michelangelo's sculpture of Lorenzo de Medici—by playing tennis one or two days a week, jogging, and flyfishing for trout. And he also continues to nurture Lorenzo's contemplative life by reading, teaching an occasional English class for senior citizens in Northfield, and writing things such as this book.

Lyle Steffenson
Hastings (2000)

Following the induction of Jim Holden in 1997, no coaches were admitted into the Hall of Fame until 2000, when three were chosen: John Hatch, Len McGuire, and Lyle Steffenson. For no particular reason except that I knew him best, let me begin these class of 2000 bioclips with that of Lyle Steffenson.

Though Lyle did not play competitive tennis in high school, he grew up in Brainerd where he came under the influence of tennis icon Bud Schmid, who taught him the

Lyle Steffenson

rudiments of the game in a physical education class. During his high school years he played a great deal of recreational tennis, but it wasn't until he took an intermediate tennis class at St. Cloud State that he got hooked on the game. After graduating with a social studies major in 1961, Lyle began his teaching career at Brooten, a small west central Minnesota community that did not have a high school tennis program. In 1965 he moved to Detroit Lakes, where for the first time he had an opportunity to coach tennis, albeit as a volunteer recruited by some of the players who, when they discovered that he played tennis, pleaded with him to help them. During this time he completed an MA degree in American history and then moved in the fall of 1967 to the historic river town of Hastings, named after a city and famous battle site in England—where William the Conqueror from Normandy made mincemeat of the Saxons and established his reign in 1066 CE. No doubt Lyle made mention of this fact in his history classes, but surely he would also have told his students about the great lumber floats down the St. Croix River in which this terrible cargo plunged into the mighty Mississippi near Hastings.

While he was regaling his students with the facts of

history, Lyle was also building a boys' tennis program in this picturesque river town. Here is how he described his first season (spring 1968): "The varsity tennis coach position became available—the only tennis position the school had at the time [there had been a makeshift program in Hastings since 1964]. I was encouraged by several friends to apply, even though I had not actually coached before. When asked to take the job, I told the athletic director that I would do it; but I insisted that they hire an assistant coach to work with the younger players to get experience to move up to varsity in the future." Thus was launched Lyle's twenty-nine-year coaching career.

He admits that it took a good deal of work to bring his Hastings teams up to a competitive level, but once that level was reached in 1975 his teams were very successful. That 1975 team, for example, led by Rick Kulla and Mike Humbert (who won the state consolation singles title that year), finished second in the St. Paul Suburban Conference and runner-up in the Region 3 team tournament. Lyle's teams would go on to claim thirteen St. Paul Suburban Conference championships (ten alone between 1986 and '96) and advance to the State Tournament six times during his tenure at the helm of the Raiders (in 1976, '87, '89, '90, '91, and '92). On his 1987 State Tournament team, Lyle was blessed to have four exceptional singles players whose combined record was 64 wins and 4 losses. These four were Rob Judge, Mark Horsch, Mitch Kranz, and Jim McNeary. Steffenson noted that neighboring coach Dick Hemberger from Park High School called them the "Untouchables." Judge and Horsch, who had successfully teamed in doubles to advance to the state doubles tournament in 1986, did so again in '87.

Most coaches find that one player usually emerges as the "top dog" on the roster, but Lyle experienced one season (1992) in which his top two players, Efren Maldanado and Brian Horsch, were virtually even in ability. So he decided that each would play number one singles every other match. This flipflopping arrangement drew the attention of the *St. Paul Pioneer Press* sports department, and they ran a story about this somewhat unorthodox plan, which saw Maldanado finish the season with just one loss and Horsch with only two.

When Steffenson put away his coaching whistle after the 1996 season, he had presided over a program that had produced many individual region singles and doubles state tournament entrants and very competitive teams (whose best results were two fourth place finishes in the 1991 and '92 State Tournaments). Cumulatively, his teams won 366 dual meets and lost only 105, a 78 percent winning record. And though the victories were always gratifying, Lyle said his biggest satisfaction "came from many players continuing on to play collegiate tennis. As best I know, at least fifteen went on to play college tennis in Minnesota and five other states." An amiable and friendly man, Lyle tried to live up to the description of a coach emblazoned on a plaque his wife gave him which he displayed on his desk: "A coach is a teacher who constantly strives to reach greater heights as a builder of lives... who advocates teamwork and proves every day that everyone wins in the game of fair play." As a coach whose teams competed against Lyle's Hastings Raiders, I saw evidence of this belief every time we played. Lyle's players were always well-behaved gentlemen on court, and he himself was the epitome of grace and sportsmanship, always treating his players, the opponents, and opposing coaches with respect.

Off court he also served with distinction as president of the MN Boys' Tennis Coaches Association during the 1978-79 school year, held the position of secretary-treasurer in that same organization for five years, and served two terms as a member of the Tennis Advisory Committee to the MSHSL, helping increase the team size to its present four singles and three doubles. It should be noted that Lyle was also active in the civic life of his community, serving as president of two Hastings' organizations—the Jaycees and the Sons of Norway. But it was for his long years of devoted service to high school tennis that Lyle was voted into the MN Tennis Coaches Hall of Fame. In addition, his peers voted him MN Tennis Coach of the Year for class AA in 1986; and during his career he was also voted Region 3AA coach of the year several times.

Today he lives in retirement in a townhouse on Fishtrap Lake near Nisswa, MN, close to his boyhood home of Brainerd. And though he thoroughly enjoyed a leisurely pace of life in retirement and the opportunity to spoil his nine grandchildren, he could not get tennis out of his blood. Shortly after moving north, a neighboring school (Pequot Lakes) recruited Lyle to begin a middle school girls' program there, a job he held for six years until re-retiring after the 2003 season. But now he has returned to coaching at the urging of his wife, Carol (perhaps she just wanted to get him out of the house). In addition, for the past several years he has also helped give tennis clinics in the Brainerd Resort area.

He has left a fine legacy and can rest in the knowledge that he has built boys' tennis at Hastings into a well-respected and highly competitive program.

John Hatch
Blake (2000)

The next coach to be voted into the Hall of Fame in 2000 is the first who guided a private school tennis team. From 1978-1994 (missing only the '82 season when he was on sabbatical leave) John Hatch presided over a program which felled the giant redwoods such as Edina in Class AA and the smaller birches in Class A, claiming two team titles in the big school class and five championships in the small school category during his tenure. This "little giant" is the Blake School of Hopkins, an independent private school with an enrollment of just 360 students in grades 10-12, a school perhaps best known for its strong academic college prep program. (For more on Hatch and his Blake teams, see Chapter Nine.)

The director of this very successful tennis program grew up in Detroit, MI, where he played spring baseball in high school and tennis in the summers. About his summer tennis experiences, Hatch said, "After taking some lessons from a pro for $5 an hour I played recreational tennis in the summers, once even competing in the 12-and-under doubles at Kalamazoo—I lost in the first round."

After high school, John spent his undergraduate years at Williams College in Massachusetts, graduating in 1956 with an English major. At Williams his outlet for competition continued to be baseball, which he played for four years. Captain of the team his senior year, he described himself as a Phil Rizzuto-type shortstop who was good enough to draw attention from Detroit Tigers scouts, primarily for his fielding prowess. Leaving his baseball

John Hatch

dreams behind after graduation, he took a teaching job at Hotchkiss, a prestigious boarding school in Massachusetts, then moved to Milwaukee, WI, in 1958 to take a position as an English teacher, admissions director, and baseball coach at Milwaukee Country Day School. It was in Milwaukee that he met his wife, Judith, and both agreed that they would like to live in the Twin Cities area.

After six years in Wisconsin, they moved to Minnesota in 1964 and John began his teaching and coaching career at Blake. During his first years there he taught English, earned a master's in education from Macalester, and coached baseball and ninth-grade soccer. But it wasn't until 1973 that he found his way over to the tennis courts, that year taking a position as ninth-grade coach. Then, when varsity coach Bill Fisher retired after the 1977 season, Hatch stepped in as head coach, continuing in that role (with the exception of that '82 season) until 1994. And in 1980 he assumed the role of head girls' coach, a position he would also hold until '94.

John would be the first to admit that, like his coaching colleagues at Edina, he often inherited talented players who had been taught by local teaching pros and had honed their games by playing both local and national tournaments during the summers. Still, helping these gifted and sometimes strong-willed players blend with less-talented individuals into a united team was not always an easy task. Nevertheless, by tournament time each year Hatch accomplished this goal, in part because he was a calming influence on his players but also because he knew how to help them deal with pressure. He said, "My job is to promote a team concept and have practice be useful and fun. I'm basically low key; most of the time I didn't say much. I saw too much overcoaching—too many guys going out on every changeover. Instead I would try to relieve pressure, deal much more with the head than the racket." 1988 State AA singles champion Chris Laitala, echoing this refrain, said of his former coach, "He had a calming influence and he also had a quiet intensity." But he knew how to prepare players in other ways as well. Two-time Class A singles champion Robert Keith praised Hatch as "a great coach who was very smart on drills and strategizing [sic] for matches."

Some tennis coaches were micro-managers, not so Hatch. For example, while some coaches slavishly adhered to a challenge method for determining their lineups, John used a very informal challenge ladder system and did not like to assign challenge matches during the season. He also said, "I'm a believer in allowing the kids to do what they do best." In addition, on the days before tournament competition, some coaches scheduled intense two-hour practices with fifteen minutes of calisthenics added before and ten minutes of running thrown in after practice. John, on the other hand, rarely conducted a hard practice the day before the State Tournament. "I wanted them rested," he said.

Hatch also placed a great deal of responsibility on the shoulders of his players and he believed in them. This belief in his players follows logically from his view that the best thing about coaching was establishing relationships with young people, relationships that found them practicing and competing together to accomplish common goals. He considered working with young people in the classroom and on the court to be "a real joy in my life." Over the years he established lasting friendships with his players, one of whom, Laitala, called Hatch "a great coach and a great supporter."

Beneath this calm exterior, however, was a fiercely competitive person who knew how to motivate players for top-level competition. So each year John scheduled as many dual meets and Saturday tournaments as he could with top Metro teams, took long road trips to play the best outstate teams and to help his players bond together (he recalls one such memorable trip to Hibbing, for instance), and wasn't above using a bit of reverse psychology to prepare his teams. Apropos this last point, Hatch said, "I never wanted to be undefeated going into the tournament." He reasoned that undefeated teams risked being complacent or overconfident, and so they were ripe for an upset. Sure enough, even his very best teams lost matches during the season (his 1981 Class A championship team was the only one to lose but a single dual match). And because many of his best players had become tournament tough during summer competition, he didn't need to do much to motivate them. "They were ahead of me; they knew the schedule as well as I did." Besides, they knew the top players in the state and had already played many of them in NWTA tournaments. As another advantage, true for many other Metro teams as well, John's teams had access to practice time at indoor clubs.

From his first day of coaching, when Louie McKee (1979 Class A singles champion) came to practice wearing a serape wrapped around his shoulders and John wondered what he was getting into, until his last day, he truly enjoyed coaching. Of course there were aspects of the job he didn't especially enjoy, like cutting players after tryouts or having to tell someone who had been on the 7-point team during the season that he wouldn't be on the 5-point Class A tournament team. And occasionally parents would complain, "Why aren't eleventh and twelfth graders playing?" But these were small irritations when juxtaposed against the pleasure he derived from coaching and the phenomenal success his teams experienced. Second all-time among boys' coaches whose teams won state titles (seven), John also coached fifteen conference championship teams and fourteen team region champions in sixteen seasons, and he mentored four singles champions (Robert Keith won two titles and McKee and Laitala won one each) and one doubles Class AA championship team (Stewart Barry and Fergus Weir). In addition, many of his other players excelled when they advanced to State. For example, in singles Scott Card finished second in 1981 in Class A; Laitala finished second in Class AA in 1990 and '91; and Keith took second in Class A in '92. And in doubles Chuck Ankeyney and Dave Meyers took third in Class A in '79, Scott Duncan and Tom Price second in Class AA in '83, Don Jackson and Scott Gage second in Class A in '87, and Jake Wert and Justin Wismer second in Class A in '94.

All told his boys' teams won 285 matches and lost just 49, a gaudy winning rate of 85 percent. Add to this his induction into the Hall of Fame, his election as MN Class A Boys' Coach of the Year in 1994, and his selection by the NWPTA as Section 1991 Coach of the Year and it adds up to an extraordinary coaching career.

After forty years of teaching English (thirty-two at Blake), John retired in 1996. He occasionally volunteers to help students at Creek Valley Elementary School in Edina with their writing. In addition, from time to time he and his wife relax at her parents' cabin on the Brule River in Wisconsin. He and Judith have three grown sons and they take delight in the pleasure of watching their seven grandchildren grow up.

Len "Mick" McGuire
Stillwater (2000)

The third of this year's nominees, Len "Mick" McGuire, is the only coach who claims membership in this and two other coaches halls of fame: high school skiing and the parent MSHSL Hall of Fame. He gained entry into the MSHSL Hall of Fame not only for his coaching but for his work with the League on behalf of tennis and ski coaches and for his longtime service as a high school and NCAA football official and basketball referee.

In addition to his productive tennis-coaching career, he had an even longer and more successful career as a ski coach. In sixteen years as the Alpine ski coach, his girls' teams compiled an unbelievable record of 132-2 and won five state championships; and his boys' teams won 170 meets and lost just 23. Their enviable record included four state titles and five runner-up finishes.

Like so many of Minnesota's top tennis players and coaches, this feisty and competitive man, diminutive in stature, grew up in the tennis hotbed of Rochester, graduating toward the end of WWII in 1944. He played tennis there, winning a doubles conference championship with

partner John Higgins his senior year. After graduation he attended pre-flight training for the military at Minot State U in North Dakota and, though its smallest member, he played on the football team. McGuire completed a two-year hitch in the Navy Air Corps, then enrolled at the U of M. When he completed his studies at the U (earning a BS in 1948 in education and an MA in history in 1949), he began teaching at University High School in Minneapolis, moving to Mason City, IA, after one year at U High.

He remained at Mason City for three years, then, more than 100 years after settlers came to "the city where Minnesota was born," Len "emigrated" to Stillwater from Iowa in 1953. It was in this picturesque town on the banks of the St. Croix River where he settled down for thirty-one years as a coach and teacher of social studies and history.

One of many pioneering Minnesota coaches who inaugurated tennis programs in their schools, Len started the boys' program at Stillwater in the spring of 1954 and led the Ponies for eight years before "retiring" to coach the combined boys' and girls' alpine ski team. But what wonderful years those were: a 61-10 dual meet record, five Suburban Conference championships, 1960 St.

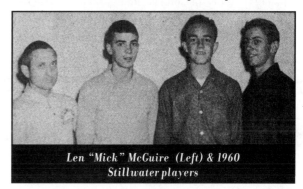

Len "Mick" McGuire (Left) & 1960 Stillwater players

John's Invitational champions, 1960 Pony-Polar Invitational champions, five District 14 titles, 1960 Region 4 champions, and 1960 state champions. A soft spot in his heart for tennis inspired him to return as an assistant coach from 1968-1979, working with his successor and longtime Stillwater coach Bill Herzog.

Former team members from his 1960 fall state championship team remember McGuire with fondness. Number one singles player Charlie Huss, who won the deciding third-place match that gave Stillwater the state title, recalls the sacrifices McGuire made to help a talented group of youngsters: "He discovered a group of kids in Bayport who played on the two courts there—there were no good courts in Stillwater at the time. We were all eighth graders and he came down in the summer to give us lessons." Jerry Wohlers, the No. 2 singles player on that 1960 team, said, "Len was instrumental in getting the program started; he found us at Bayport and came down every morning at 7:30 in the summer for two years and coached us." This was obviously a major commitment on his part, for McGuire had another full-time job in the summer, selling real estate.

Another member of that 1960 team, Tom Brown, remembers Len as an effective psychologist: "At the conference championships against North St. Paul, a very good team [coached at the time by Ed Sewell], we took Len's Cadillac convertible to the match. We drove up with the radio turned on to WDGY and my teammate Bob Olson strumming his guitar. When we got out of the car, we asked the North St. Paul guys where the food machines were? This scheme, which loosened us up, psyched them out and we wiped them out." Len's son Matt recalls a similar story from his time on his father's ski team: "He had a very purple ski jacket and warmups that had a wild floral pattern—ala 1969. We gave him tremendous grief for being so out of fashion, but he claimed it was all a ploy to 'psych out' the other teams. He said, 'They'll know Stillwater is on the hill.'" This example illustrated his self-deprecating sense of humor which also endeared him to his players and helped them relax before meets.

All this effort paid off with a well-earned team championship in 1960. The doubles team of Jerry Wohlers and Bob Olson (the guitarist), Region 4 champions, earned 6 points by virtue of their two wins in the doubles; and Charlie Huss earned 7 points for taking third place in singles. Wohlers recalls the unusual circumstances of Stillwater's 13-12 victory over Edina in these words: "We didn't know there were points for third place, so we flipped a coin for the trophy and Edina won the toss [the teams were then tied at 12-all]. When it was discovered that we had to play a third-place match, Charlie Huss came back the next day and won his match. Edina then brought the trophy back and we took it home."

These three Bayport boys, who lettered four years and helped the Ponies win the title as juniors, enjoyed playing for a man who truly loved coaching, a man who, as Wohlers said, "gave up a lot of his time to coach us." All three also recall that Len took them to tournaments in Rochester and other places around the state to help them sharpen their competitive skills. Further testimony to his commitment is the tennis court he built in his back yard for Stillwater kids to play on in the days when there were very few decent courts in town. According to 1960 player Tom Brown, though Len was not himself a skilled player, "he schooled us in groundstrokes and he knew how to get the most out of us." This schooling paid long-term dividends for Wohlers and Huss, both of whom went on to play college tennis—Wohlers at St. Cloud State and Huss at Hamline.

According to his wife, Barbara, "Mick was extraordinarily modest," but tennis coaches in Minnesota owe a great deal to him for his efforts on their behalf as president of the Boys' Tennis Coaches Association. For example, as president he presented and received approval for a proposal that allotted singles and doubles spots in the State Tournament on the basis of the number of teams competing in the region, a regulation that stayed in place from 1958-1972. And with chairman Ed Sewell and Reg Mead, he served on a committee that presented and received approval from the MSHSL for the current system which mandated both True Team and individual state tournament competition. These efforts alone justify his inclusion in the Hall of Fame.

But another important legacy he left for those who knew him well was his courageous battle against an opponent that he fought for thirty years and refused to give in to, muscular dystrophy (MD). His son Matt remembers his father's struggles only too well, but he speaks with admiration and respect for a man who "dealt with adversity, and taught me to do the same, by being active and athletic." An article by Stuart Groskreutz in the September 19, 2003, *Stillwater Gazette*, on the occasion of his death in 2003, noted that "McGuire worked out religiously which allowed him to retain a quality of life not always afforded those affected with muscular dystrophy."

One of the members of a Monday coffee and discussion group which McGuire belonged to, legendary Stillwater football coach George Thole, said of Len in the above article, "This was a tough little guy. He's probably the biggest little guy I've ever known in my life." His daughter-in-law, a former state champion skier on his coed teams, noted that he was one of the first people in Stillwater "to take on running as a form of exercise... at that time, running on the streets was unheard of" (September 19, 2003).

Ultimately, as for all of us, life is about giving things up; and though McGuire was forced to give things up earlier than most (for instance, he had to abandon his art hobby by age forty because his shoulder muscles had atrophied), he nevertheless made use of his remaining strength to do things such as throw a football underhanded to his son and to play golf. Charlie Huss saw him on a golf course once and Len said, "I'm playing both ways. I carry half left-handed and half right-handed clubs."

Rival coaches such as Ed Sewell, Tom Vining, and Hal Schroeder (who nominated him for the Hall of Fame) had great respect for Len; and though his tennis-coaching career was the shortest of current members of the Hall of Fame, it was nonetheless one that had a big impact on Minnesota tennis. Unfortunately, MD took McGuire at age 77. He is survived by his wife, son Matt, daughters Ann and Mary, and stepson Douglas Perrin.

Henry Dison
Lake City (2001)

The year 2001 saw two longtime coaches who were also outstanding tennis players earn their way into the Hall of Fame—Henry Dison and Oliver (Ollie) Guest. The first of these two, Henry Dison, was yet another of the many standout performers on outstanding Rochester High School teams of the early 1950s. Henry's tennis-playing career began modestly enough, for he and three of his friends traipsed down to the Soldier's Field outdoor courts to bat balls over the dilapidated nets (one was four feet high and another two feet high) during the summer after his ninth-grade year. Encouraged by his success that summer, he then tried out for the high school team in the spring of his sophomore year. This first taste of varsity tennis whetted his appetite for more, so the summer between his sophomore and junior years he "graduated" from the spartan Soldier's Field courts to the more elegant courts at the

Rochester Outdoor Tennis Club, where he came under the influence of teaching pro Hughes Davis, a former North Carolina Mens' Singles champion. Henry credits Davis for helping mold his game, and he especially took to heart Davis' advice: "Every time you hit a ball back, the other guy has to return it." One of the earliest memories of his days at the club is one that involves a job he took there in 1949. Given the task of cleaning the commode, Henry revealed his naivete, saying, "I didn't know what a commode was and had to ask three people before I found out what it was."

This humorous incident was to be one of the few glitches in Henry's road to success in high school, for he went on to win two state doubles titles (with partner Ron Trondson) and help his team capture team titles in 1950 and '51. During his high school career a meet consisted of six singles and three doubles matches, so Henry played both No. 4 singles and No. 2 doubles his junior year and No. 4 singles and No. 1 doubles his senior year. And while he was proud of the fact that he never lost a match at No. 4 singles and won many games in a row without losing a set at that position, he offered this modest disclaimer, "We didn't play teams from the Cities." (For more about Dison's exploits, see Chapters Six and Nine.)

Dison has many vivid memories of his high school years, but one in particular stands out. After winning the doubles title in 1950, he and his partner, Trondson, were privileged to serve as ball boys for matches being played at Rochester which featured touring pros Jack Kramer, Don Budge, Bobby Riggs, and Pancho Gonzalez. After one of the matches, Kramer went to the mike and said, "I hear there's [sic] a couple of hotshot doubles teams here and we'd [he and Budge] like to take them on." So Ron and Henry volunteered to challenge them. Here's Henry's account of this memorable challenge: "Before I served to Kramer in the ad court, Ron, who was an excellent volleyer, told me to serve to his backhand so he could poach. I served it there, Ron poached, and Kramer hit it behind his back for a winner. With a one-serve handicap they went on to beat us 6-0." It was, as Henry said, a humbling lesson.

After graduation in 1951 he attended the U of M for two years where, under coach Phil Brain, he played No. 5 singles and No. 2 doubles his first year and No. 4 singles and No. 2 doubles his second year. Henry recalls those years with some bemusement: "In those days we played more and didn't do many drills. Coach Brain would say, 'Here are the balls; go play and give me the results.'"

Adult life interrupted his college years, and in 1953 Henry took time off to attend to some family matters and get married. Then, lured by the prospect of reuniting with high school classmate Trondson, Henry enrolled at Mankato State Teachers College for his final two years. Playing No. 2 singles (behind Trondson) and No. 1 doubles, Henry's on-court success continued. He won the No. 2 singles title and he and Trondson won the No. 1 doubles conference title in both his junior and senior years; and Henry lost only two singles matches his junior year, both during a southern spring trip.

Graduating from Mankato in 1957 with a math major, Henry settled into his first teaching job at Hayfield. And since Hayfield did not then, and does not now, have a tennis program, Henry kept his tennis fires stoked by partnering with former Rochester teammates Dave Love and Roger Jackman to run the Rochester Outdoor Club for five years in the late 1950s and early '60s. In 1962 he moved to Lake City, a lovely Mississippi River town now perhaps best known as a mecca for sailors who come to catch the winds on Lake Pepin. Here he taught math and coached tennis for the remaining twenty-eight years of his career in education, assuming the head coaching job of both the boys and girls teams in 1981.

Lake City had never been a hotbed of tennis and it would not become a high profile team under Henry's direction, but he brought respectability to the program and raised it up from mediocrity. During his fifteen years as head coach his teams won three Hiawatha Valley League conference championships and he coached three singles players and ten doubles teams who advanced to the state boys and girls tournaments. The best of these performers was the girls' doubles team of Jodi Hinckley and Cindy Parrish, who finished fourth in the 1984 Class A tournament. Except for the presence of Class A powers Winona Cotter and Rochester Lourdes, who always stood in the way, his teams and players would have had more success.

Though he retired as head coach in 1995, Henry still serves as an assistant coach for the boys and girls programs,

even rushing home from his winter retreat in San Diego to hit the first balls in March with the boys' team.

When asked to describe his coaching philosophy, Dison replied, "I'm sort of an old-fashioned guy, somewhat of a disciplinarian. I believed that I was the coach and they were the players and that's the way it is." He would always meet with the players before the season to review the rules and go over situations. For example, Henry said, "I didn't like earrings and didn't allow players to wear them on court. It was sometimes funny to see them taking off their earrings as they walked to the courts."

In part this old-fashioned approach grew out of a belief that toughness was an important ingredient for success: "One of my theories was that you may not have the greatest talent but you shouldn't get outhustled." In addition, he wanted his players to believe that you "win by not losing"; therefore, you make your opponents hit one more ball (an echo from the voice of his first coach Hughes Davis). One story serves to illustrate just how tough Henry could be. His team was playing Austin Pacelli for the second time after an earlier rainout and it began raining again. Henry approached the coach from Pacelli and said, "Coach, I'm not coming back." So they finished the match in the rain and Henry told his players to "serve into the puddles." A man of few words during a match, Henry wanted his players to figure things out for themselves and believed that if players didn't hear from him during a match it was a good thing.

About the game he has played and loved for over fifty years he says, "I just think it's a great sport to continue on and you meet a lot of nice people. Besides, it's a great sport to keep you in condition. I always considered myself a person who loved to play and coach tennis and thought I worked pretty hard at it." Though the disciplinary part of coaching was difficult and losing tough matches was always disappointing, Henry loved the game and the competition. And he took great pleasure in watching young players develop their skills.

Still active in coaching, he lives in Lake City for most of the year but he and his wife, Janet, are snowbirds in February and March, traveling to San Diego to live near one of their two daughters. He and Janet also have one son and are the proud grandparents of five.

Oliver "Ollie" Guest
Robbinsdale and Robbinsdale Cooper (2001)

One of two coaches inducted into the Hall in 2001 and a coach connected to an earlier Minnesota coaching legend is Oliver "Ollie" Guest, a longtime stalwart in the Robbinsdale area who began his tennis coaching career as an assistant to Hall of Famer John Adams at Robbinsdale High School. John Mueller, former USTA/Northern Awards Committee Chair and Minnesota tennis historian, said of Guest, "When he started at Robbinsdale he knew almost nothing about tennis." But working with Adams (as an assistant coach from 1963-74) and playing the game helped him gain enough knowledge in order to take over as head coach when Adams retired.

So from 1975-88 Guest coached the Robbinsdale (1975-82) and Cooper High School (1983-88) boys' tennis teams. Of course his task of coaching tennis in Robbinsdale was as difficult as Hercules' task of cleaning the Augean stables, for he had to compete against strong Lake Conference teams, most notably Edina. So it is not for state championship trophies won that he was elected to the Hall of Fame, for there were none on his mantel. Instead, according to the person who nominated him, coach Lyle Steffenson of Hastings, "he was nominated for longevity of service and for doing the best he could in a difficult circumstance and for keeping the programs going in his schools." His son Jeff, the youngest of Guest's four children, added that "he [Ollie] had to make something out of nothing."

In addition, Jeff remembers his father's strong work ethic, which "exemplified what he wanted out of his players." And because he wanted to instill in his players a good work ethic and pride in sportsmanship, "he put in a lot of personal time which he wasn't paid for, working the players and drilling them hard. But," Jeff added, "he also made sure they hit the books—education was No. 1, athletics No. 2."

Despite having to compete against superior Lake Conference teams (Steffenson mentioned that on occasion Edina would send their JV squad to Robbinsdale and still win), Guest's players always competed hard; and in 1986 he coached a doubles team from Cooper into State. Senior John Andraschko and junior Craig Swanson took

second that year. In addition to his duties as boys' coach, Guest also piloted the girls' tennis teams at both schools for a number of years.

As a self-taught tennis player, Guest enjoyed a good deal of success (especially in doubles) and he truly loved the game. Playing with top-ranked senior player Jerry Pope, he earned a No. 1 55-and-over doubles ranking in 1987 (just ahead of Ken Boyum and John Bradley) and a No. 2 ranking in 1988, again with Pope. In addition, he participated in two 4.5 USTA Michelob national team championship tournaments, placing second in 1980 and third in 1981 on teams made up, according to Mueller, of teachers and players from the New Hope area.

Unfortunately, health problems cut short both his coaching and playing careers. Officially retired after spending two more years as an assistant coach at Robbinsdale Sandburg Junior High School, from 1988-90, Guest nevertheless continued to devote time to the game he loved. From 1990-94 he assisted Breck coach and longtime friend Chuck Anderson, and he was especially proud of his work with Breck's two-time state Class A doubles champions, Trace Fielding and Matt Drawz. Also, he continued to serve (until 2000) as Section 6AA manager for both the boys' and girls' tennis tournaments, a role he had held since 1985.

Both Mueller and Guest's mentor, Adams, spoke highly of him. Mueller remembered him as "a big, robust guy and a good friend for many years." Adams said of him, "He was a wonderful, competitive marine—a very nice man." And though he was, as Mueller said, "a robust guy," he couldn't beat his most fearsome adversary, cancer. According to his son Jeff, he contracted non-Hodgkins lymphoma, fought it successfully for a number of years until it came back, beat it again for a time, but then lost the battle in April of 2001. Guest was 70 years old.

He was survived by his wife and four children, two of whom became tennis players. While his two older daughters grew up in the days before girls' tennis and thus did not play in high school, Guest's son Jeff played for his father at Robbinsdale High School for one year before the school closed in 1982. He went on to play No. 1 singles his last two years at Robbinsdale Armstrong, then played mostly No. 1 doubles and singles for three years at the U of WI-River

Falls. Guest's oldest son Tim also played two years of tennis at Robbinsdale Armstrong, for coach Butch Derksen.

Growing up in Red Wing during the Depression and WWII years (he was born in 1931), Guest often had to work to support a large family for which his mother was the sole supporter. Nevertheless, he found time to play football and basketball, thus sparking a lifelong interest in playing sports and even in refereeing basketball.

When he graduated from Red Wing High School, he enrolled in what was then called Wisconsin State Teachers College at River Falls and eventually earned an education degree with a concentration in political science and economics. His education was interrupted by the Korean War, however, and he was on active duty as a marine from January 1951-May 1952. Then he returned to River Falls to complete his studies in 1956. Before coming to Robbinsdale, Guest taught at Rice Lake, WI, for one year (1956-57), worked in sales for a year, then taught in Plainview, MN, from 1958-61. In the fall of 1961 he accepted a teaching position at Robbinsdale Sandburg Junior High and taught ninth-grade social studies there until his retirement in 1990.

Guest will be remembered as a coach who, according to son Jeff, "taught his players more about life than tennis." And because he himself worked so long with underdogs, he is also remembered in a very tangible way, for there is a Section 6AA trophy named in his honor. Each year it goes to a male player from the Section—often not the most talented individual—who is a hard worker, a good sportsman, and a good student who participated in other activities. Said Jeff Guest, "This player represents the attitudes Dad tried to instill in his players." Not a bad legacy to leave the sport he loved so much.

Ted Greer
Edina (2002)

When the name Ted Greer is mentioned by the Minnesota tennis cognoscenti, the first reaction is usually, "Oh, yes. Wasn't he the Edina girls' tennis coach for many years?" Indeed he was the coach of the Hornets' incredibly successful teams in the late 1970s and early '80s; but less well known is his role as the boys' coach, for it was he and not John Matlon who started (in the spring of 1950) the

first boys' tennis program at what was then called Edina-Morningside High School. Greer would serve as the Hornets' boys' coach for seven years before turning the team over to Matlon in 1957.

During his first two years Greer's teams were nomads, practicing and playing matches on park board courts in Minneapolis. In his third year the school built five excellent courts, which helped lay the foundation for future success. Greer said of these early years, "There was no Lake Conference tennis organization. The only Lake Conference schools with tennis were Deephaven, Edina, St. Louis Park, and Robbinsdale. There was no Richfield or Minnetonka High School yet, and Hopkins, Wayzata, Mound, and Bloomington didn't play tennis."

And until his last year, when all Lake Conference schools finally fielded tennis teams, these were relatively lean years for Edina, years in which, he said, "no one even watched our matches except maybe a few parents." That final year (1956) Greer said Edina tied Roger Thompson's St. Louis Park squad for the conference championship. Minneapolis schools and Rochester were the powers in those days, but Greer said Blake and the old Deephaven High School were strong teams "because they had families that were serious about tennis—like Edina did eventually."

Greer left teaching in 1957 to take a job as an assistant principal at Edina High School, then for the next ten years he served as a junior high principal. After this twelve-year stint as an administrator, he went back to teaching math in 1969. And in 1974 he took another coaching job, as the first coach of the Hornets' girls' team, thus having the honor of inaugurating both tennis programs in Edina. With players like Anne Lemieux, Maura Bjerken, Stacy Husebo (1986 doubles champion Mike's sister), Michelle Houser, Carrie Odland (two-time singles champion Paul's sister), Jennifer Nelson, and Ginger Helgeson on his teams—first as Edina East then as Edina—Greer's teams won five team championships, the last coming in 1982. About these glory years, he said, "The last five years I coached we had outstanding experienced players and were state champions. The last three weren't even very exciting because we had no close matches."

He admits that he really didn't get very excited about tennis until he was about forty-five years old, though he had played some in high school at Blake (first doubles his senior year). Throughout his high school and college years hockey had been his passion. After graduating from Blake, he played varsity hockey for four years at the U of MI, serving as captain his senior year and playing center on the first line of the school's national championship team one year. But he was more than just a hockey player. An all-around sportsman, he even played football in high school and, living as he did on Wayzata Bay, it was inevitable that he would become a sailor as well. In fact, said Greer, "I became a fanatic sailboat racer and was a sailing instructor at the Minnetonka Yacht Club in the summers."

a tennis teaching pro for the Northwest Clubs. Said Greer about this new job, "During my twelve years at the Northwest Clubs I greatly improved my tennis teaching skills and my playing ability. Now tennis is my biggest interest." He began to play competitively as well, reaching his highest ranking in 1980 at No. 5 in the 55-and-over singles division. And today, retired and living in Gulf Shores, AL, for six months of the year, he still plays "three or four times a week with other old folks." In the summers he and his wife live across the bay from daughter Marnie in Brainerd, and in the fall, Marnie said, "I have gotten him to help me drill

Ted Greer (Left) and Les Szendrey

So when he came to Edina in the fall of 1949, he was also asked to coach the Hornets' first hockey team and ninth-grade football. He recalls the great satisfaction he experienced in starting up two sports programs (hockey and tennis), remembering especially those nomad days in tennis and the first four years of hockey when "all our games were outdoors on a rink the players helped maintain and a few parents stood in the snow banks to watch."

But eventually, in part because he had so much success as the Edina girls' coach, tennis won him over, and when he finished coaching the high school girls, he got hired as

the Brainerd girls' varsity team I coach." Once a coach, always a coach.

Marnie said about her dad's passion for tennis: "He'd probably play twice a day if his body would let him. He's left-handed but has worked extremely hard teaching himself to play right-handed so he could play either side if he was nursing a sore shoulder or elbow. He takes pride in switching hands to confuse his opponents or 'show off' serving with either hand." According to Greer's son Murray, a member of Edina's 1978 state championship team, his father's passion for the game is all the more remarkable considering he is eighty-five years old and has had artificial joint replacements in both knees. His mother has also had these replacements but still plays tennis several times a week.

Those who know Ted Greer speak of him with admiration and respect. Former two-time Edina state doubles champion Dave Mathews, who remembers that Greer hit with the JV players, said of him, "He was always so bubbly and enthusiastic, and he had a great positive attitude." One of his fiercest coaching competitors in girls' tennis, Cliff Caine of SPA, called Greer "a true sportsman who was so humane." Caine added, "He was so gracious and attentive to his kids." His son Murray no doubt shared this view of his father, for, as he recalled, "during the time my dad was in charge of the Edina junior high program (in the early 1970s), he encouraged me to start playing and was always more than willing to go hit with me." Murray recalls many exciting family tennis matches with his dad, his sister Marnie, his Mom, his dad's cousin John Rowe (a big Edina tennis fan), and other relatives and friends.

As for coach Greer himself, he enjoyed "getting kids to discover how much fun it is to strive to do one's best." His son also recalls his father's emphasis on enjoying the game, "not always with an emphasis on winning but on learning the game and enjoying it for life." Certainly there can be no better model for this creed, for Ted Greer continues to enjoy the game of tennis well into his eighth decade of life.

Bruce Getchell
White Bear Lake (2003)

The twentieth inductee into the Hall of Fame, and the only one in 2003, is Bruce Getchell, who had a great deal to do with shaping the landscape of boys' tennis in Minnesota in that formative early 1970s period. But for him and other visionaries such as Bud Schmid and Ed Sewell, it's possible that boys' and girls' tennis might be played in the same season or that matches would still consist of five points instead of seven.

More about this later, but what about this gentleman who spent his entire tennis coaching life in the northern St. Paul suburb of White Bear Lake (WBL)? Bruce grew up in

St. Paul, where he started playing tennis at age 14 with his cousin Carol. He recounts this experience in these words: "She was three years older and she wasn't a great player, but since I was just beginning she beat me. I guess this inspired me to practice and improve so I could beat her."

As a junior he went out for tennis at St. Paul Central and played doubles for two years, recalling that his best memory was of winning an individual Twin Cities championship doubles match against a good team from Minneapolis. After high school graduation in 1957 he continued his studies at the U of M for three years, then took time off to pursue other interests, including a lawn service business that he managed. In 1961 he transferred to Mankato State Teachers College, graduating with an all science major in 1963. And though he wanted to join the tennis team at Mankato, the athletic director told him he was ineligible for reasons he never fully understood—something about credits.

Fresh out of college, he took a teaching job in tiny Garden City, located close enough to Mankato so his wife, Janet, could complete her degree. After just one year at Garden City High School, Bruce worked for the Atomic Energy Commission as a peripatetic teacher, traveling around the state to present an assembly program called "This Atomic World." Moving in the summer of 1966 to the growing suburban community wrapped around the

Bruce Getchell

shores of lovely White Bear Lake, Bruce would settle there to teach biology and chemistry at WBL High School for the next thirty-one years, until his retirement after the fall semester in 1997.

He became involved in tennis even before the start of his teaching job in the 1966-67 school year, teaching that first summer and for many years thereafter in the WBL Recreation Department. Then, in the spring of 1967, Bruce began his coaching career as the boys' B-squad coach, remaining in that role until head coach Bill Kahl resigned in 1971. Jumping into the breach, Bruce took over the varsity coaching job in the spring of 1971 and held the reins until 1978 when he took a hiatus until '83. However, he continued coaching during those four years, but this time in a less stressful role at WBL Central Junior High School in order to coach his son Greg and Greg's friends.

When the call came from White Bear Mariner High School for a head tennis coach, Bruce answered it for the 1983 season, then returned to coach the WBL Polars again in '84 when the two high schools combined. Here he would remain until 1996 when he completed his very successful twenty-year career as boys' coach.

While Bruce was getting his feet wet in the boys' program in the early 1970s, he was also made aware of the need, in this pre-Title IX era, to provide equal tennis opportunities for girls. Bruce describes how he became involved: "In 1972 a group of girls approached me to start a girls' team, which we did in the fall that year." This "unofficial" team morphed into the first varsity girls' team in 1974, and Bruce would be their first and only head coach until 1997, a total of twenty-five years. And what a great run it was for his Polars. Overall they won 543 dual meets, the boys winning 257 and losing only 87 and the girls winning 286 and losing just 117. Within the North Suburban conference his boys' teams won seven titles, allowing zero points in conference play during the 1974 and '85 seasons. And his Polars won three region championships, taking second at State in the first two True Team tournaments (1973 and '74) and again in '85.

In addition, his 1972 team breezed through the season undefeated in dual meets; and over the years he coached many singles players and doubles teams that advanced to the State Tournament, including 1976 singles runner-up Paul Holbach and Getchell's son Greg and partner Gene Carlson (who finished fourth in the 1986 doubles tournament). Another of Getchell's top players was Tom Nelson, who went on to play at the U of M and serve as captain in 1977. Getchell calls Holbach "without a doubt the best player I coached. He was the first player to letter on varsity for four years and he advanced to State all four years. His record was 128-13. A lot of his skill was developed by hitting against a backboard in his early years." At Gustavus Holbach became a four-year All-American who won the 1980 NCAA 3 doubles championship with partner John Mattke.

Perhaps even more than the wins and losses, Bruce's integrity and commitment to tennis defined him as a coach and teacher. Future Hall of Fame coach Ken Peterson nominated Bruce, giving as part of his rationale for induction that Bruce was "always ethical and represented our profession with distinction." With respect to the latter point, Ken must surely have had in mind Bruce's exemplary service to the MN Boys' Tennis Coaches Association, a service that involved a one-year term as vice president in 1972-73 and two one-year terms as president (1974-76).

During that tumultuous period, a time in which the Vietnam War was coming to an inglorious end and a time in which many groups were fighting for equal rights—including girls who wanted to play tennis on a school team—Bruce used his considerable powers of persuasion to help convince the MSHSL to assign the girls' and boys' play to separate seasons and to increase the number of student varsity participants from seven players (5-point matches) to ten players (7-point matches). Apropos of this last change he helped lobby for, Bruce remembers that the North Suburban Conference was the first to use the 7-point matches during the season. All of his lobbying was done in a calm, low-key way, and always in a respectful manner. It was not in his nature to boast about these accomplishments or his success as a coach. In fact, when asked to provide information about his coaching record for the Hall of Fame nominating committee, he said, "Any success that I had should be attributed to the quality of the student athletes that I had the privilege to work with in White Bear Lake."

This is a man who, with the help of one or two

recreation student workers, took it upon himself to perform the upkeep of the school district's tennis courts. "It began by patching the cracks and ended up with my resurfacing all twenty-four of the courts at one time or another. This wasn't as good as a professional company's job would have been, but it kept the courts in decent playing condition and saved the district money," he said. Like so many successful Minnesota coaches, he did many other little things to keep his program going. For example, he bought an old stringer from coach Chuck Anderson and set it up in his basement. "I used to string rackets out of necessity so my players would have something the next day to play with."

These are just two of many examples to illustrate the quality of Getchell's character, and there are other testimonials from former players and coaching competitors as well. For instance, Holbach had this to say about Bruce: "Coach Getchell was a great coach and a great person and I have nothing but respect for him. I am sure I was difficult to work with. I was headstrong and cocky, but he handled me well and always demanded good behavior." Coach Bob Pivec of Coon Rapids spoke generally of the many fine coaches in the North Suburban Conference, including Bruce, in these words: "I really learned to appreciate their effort and realize how important we were for each other. We could not become competitive unless we played good competition. In the North Suburban area we had well-coached and competitive teams led by Ken Peterson at Anoka, Tom Vining at Roseville, Bruce Getchell at White Bear Lake, Chuck Anderson at Stillwater, and Mike Cartwright at Mounds View." Getchell returned the compliment, saying, "Overall it was great coaching in the St. Paul Suburban and North Suburban Conferences. The friendships I formed with other coaches such as Tom Vining, Ken Peterson, Bob Pivec, and Scott Swanson were special." Some of these friendships were cemented at the White Bear-Ramsey Tournament, one of the oldest in the state and the first to hold 7-point team competition.

In addition to providing guidance for his high school players, Getchell also devoted many hours to developing young players in the summer, serving as the coordinator of WBL recreation programs and the director of the annual Manitou Days Tennis Tournament—a tournament

that attracted many of the best Twin Cities players before the expansion of NWTA tournaments. Getchell noted that it was important to run a decent summer program in order to keep his varsity programs going. Said he, "We didn't have the USTA players some others had." So he started a program for beginners, expanded it for intermediate and advanced players, and encouraged kids to enter summer tournaments. The North Suburban Tournaments started by Peterson of Anoka and Pivec of Coon Rapids, priced cheaply at $2-3 and a can of balls, also provided an excellent opportunity for his players to hone their games. Getchell said, "They [these tournaments] guaranteed a consolation match or two and were completed in a day or two. And the parents didn't have to drive too far."

In addition, he was one of the first coaches to join Hall of Fame coach Bud Schmid at the Lake Hubert Tennis Camps (in 1974); and when Bud retired, Bruce and Todd Ruediseli directed the camps until Bruce retired in 2004.

Getchell spoke fondly of his coaching days: "The best thing about coaching tennis was getting to know the kids in a different setting than in the classroom. And 99 percent of the tennis players were great people and fun to work with." He also enjoyed seeing the excitement in players who qualified for State, some of whom, he said, "had never been out to eat at a restaurant before we had breakfast or lunch during a tournament." One time, Getchell recalled with a laugh, "I had to scramble to find matching shorts at a local sports store for a player who had forgotten his."

As for his coaching philosophy, he believed that tennis practices and matches should be fun but that it was also important to practice hard to win. To that end, he said, "We spent as much time in practice playing sets as we did doing drills." He felt it was more important to play points under game conditions than to drill one shot at a time. Getchell also thought "that trying to change grips and form during the short spring season resulted in hurting a player's game. So I told my players the time to change things and work on them was during the summer."

Like all Minnesota coaches, he had to find ways to get players ready during the often difficult spring weather. So his teams practiced serves and volleys as well as doubles positioning and strategy in the gym. In addition, he said, "We were able to scrimmage a few teams that had decent indoor courts like Brainerd, Tartan (with their Tartan surface), and Armstrong (a wood floor)."

A capable senior tennis player who played on a team that once qualified for Nationals at Palm Springs, CA, Getchell played until 2002 when, he said, "my knees and heart decided it was too much. After that I took up golf with little success but much enjoyment."

Getchell was justifiably proud of his contributions to WBL and Minnesota tennis, and of the fact that all three of his children (Greg, Anna, and Beth) played for him. Greg also had a very successful career at Gustavus and served for a time as a tennis pro at the Flagship Athletic Club. Bruce and his wife Janet lived in Vadnais Heights, not far from their children and five grandchildren, all of whom reside in the Twin Cities area. His only concession to our harsh winter weather was an annual two-week sojourn to warm-weather spots in Florida or Arizona. On December 7, 2006, Bruce passed away from cancer at the age of 67.

Cliff Caine
St. Paul Academy (2004)

An August 2004 article in *TennisLife Magazine* titled "News, Activities, and Happenings," spoke in glowing terms about this year's Hall of Fame inductees. "Three exceptional coaches were welcomed into the Minnesota State High School Tennis Coaches Hall of Fame on March 6 at White Bear Lake Racquet and Swim Club: Cliff Caine of St. Paul, Bill Ritchie of St. Cloud, and, posthumously, Dallas Hagen of Wells, MN." These three individuals were indeed exceptional coaches, and though two earned plaudits mainly as coaches of successful girls' teams (Caine and Hagen), they also coached boys' teams for many years. This year also signaled the beginning of a new era in state high school tennis, for it was the first year of the merged MN Boys' and Girls' Tennis Coaches Association. So it is perhaps appropriate that the 2004 biographies begin with those of Caine and Hagen, coaches who devoted their lives to working with both boys and girls.

Of all the coaches in the Hall of Fame, Cliff Caine had perhaps the most varied career, beginning at the college level and ending in high school tennis programs, and earlier involving many years of coaching private school teams

in the days before they were a part of the MSHSL. Although raised in the Dakotas, he moved to St. Paul his junior year and graduated from St. Paul Central High School in 1951. A man with a keen intellect and an appetite for learning, Cliff received his BA in history from Macalester in 1955, his JD from the U of M in 1958, and a PhD in American studies from the U of M in 1975. In addition, in 1976 he pursued further graduate study at Harvard U in education.

After graduating from Macalester, and after taking additional graduate studies, he returned to serve his alma mater as director of the student union and men's residence halls and, later, director of the Administrative Policies Study. From 1960-'71 he was also the Scots' men's tennis coach. It is probably not well known today, but during those years Caine's men's teams were the scourge of the MIAC, winning seven titles and finishing runner-up the other four years. Not quite Steve Wilkinsonesque, but had he stayed at Macalester his teams might have challenged the Gusties for supremacy in the conference. During his years at Macalester he also served as director of the MIAC Tennis Tournaments and as NAIA District Tennis chairman.

Leaving Macalester in 1970 to become assistant headmaster at St. Paul Academy (SPA), Cliff also took the reins

Cliff Caine

as head boys' tennis coach in the spring of 1972. During his first three years at SPA the private schools were not yet members of the MSHSL, so they held a separate Independent Schools State Tennis Tournament. (Note: See appendix G for information about these tournaments.) In those three years Caine's SPA teams won two state championships (1973 and '74), then in 1975 the independent schools joined the MSHSL. Despite the challenges of having to compete against bigger schools, Cliff's teams thrived under his leadership. For example, in 1976 they took third place in the one-class tournament, defeating big school powers Duluth East and Minneapolis Roosevelt by 4-1 scores and losing only to state runner-up Minnetonka in the semis 5-0. In addition, in 1979 they were runners-up in Class A to John Hatch's powerful Blake team; and they would advance to the state Class A tournament three more times during Cliff's tenure (1980, '81, '82). It is worth noting that his teams set the table for other successful SPA teams that would advance to the State Tournament seven more times between 1987 and 2003; and one of them, the '93 team, would claim the Class A championship. In addition, Caine was fortunate to coach many fine players who advanced to State, among them singles players Tom Braman, Todd Ward-who played Division 1 tennis at Miami of Ohio and is now a teaching pro, Matt Bellis, Mark Peterson-whom Caine coached until his senior year, and Darren Wolfson and the doubles teams of Fred Harris-Jeff Norton, Monty Flinsch-Chris Mulholland, Richard Kyle-Charlie Stringer, Ward Joyce-Wolfson, Matt Bellis-Matt Ravden (fourth in Class A in 1981), and Jon Libbey-Eric Dieperink. Caine keeps in touch with many of his former players and, in fact, Braman was for a time his doubles partner. Cliff said, "He and I were finalists one year in a St. Paul tournament when I was in my forties."

But it was as the SPA girls' coach that Caine cemented his high school coaching reputation. From 1974, the first year of girls' tennis competition in Minnesota, until 1984, his teams won seven state titles (the first two in the single-class tournament). During these years he also coached two state singles titlists: Lisa Martin (1979 and '80), and D'Arcy Kyle ('82). And though he was not then the coach, he was fortunate to have worked with four-time champion Kira Gregerson (1985-88) who had played No.

3 and 4 singles on his 1983 team and No. 1 singles on his '84 team. In addition, he coached five doubles teams to titles: Julie Brooks and Lucy Stringer in 1977, Beth Lilly and Elizabeth Mairs in '79, Beth Lilly and Becky Hart in '80, Carrie Stringer and Lindy Olson in '82, and Carrie Stringer and Cathy Paper in '83. These were remarkable players and remarkable teams, their reputation enhanced by the fact that they also played and defeated college teams such as those from Gustavus, the College of St. Catherine, Carleton, and Macalester in these early years. In fact, Cliff's 1974 team (still not a member of the MSHSL) compiled a 14-0 record against all comers and won the Independent Tourney, and his 1980 State championship team won all seventeen of its matches.

It is only fitting that Caine should be one of the honorees in this first year the Coaches Association was a combined organization, for he was one of the founders of the MN Girls' Tennis Coaches Association and its first president. His was one of the strongest voices in the quest to get girls' tennis started in the state. He was a member of the MN Boys' Tennis Coaches Association as well and he was a longtime member of the NWTA and the NWPTA (USPTA). In 1963 he served as director of tennis at Town and Country Club and, from 1964-73, at Somerset Country Club, both in St. Paul. And he and Bucky Olson were the original tennis professionals at the St. Paul Indoor Tennis Club.

For his contributions to high school tennis and tennis in Minnesota in general, he was voted 1976 MN High School Girls' Tennis Coach of the Year and 1980 Northwest Professional Tennis Association Coach of the Year. In 1976, '77, and '78 he was named one of the 100 Most Influential Persons in Minnesota Tennis by Bob Larson's *Tennis Midwest* magazine. Most recently, in 2007, he was elected into the Northern Section Hall of Fame, becoming only the fifth Minnesota high school coach to be so honored.

One of the best measures of a coach is how his or her players conduct themselves both on and off the court. On this measure Cliff Caine would get high marks. Current boys' and girls' tennis coach at Robbinsdale Armstrong High School and area tennis pro John Mueller said of Cliff, "His SPA teams were known for their sportsmanship. His players were always competitive yet respectful." As his Hall of Fame nominator, Mueller also commented about Caine's coaching prowess: "This man could flat out coach. SPA may have had some kids who came from the right background for success in tennis but they won titles because of Cliff." In addition, many of Cliff's players went on to have successful tennis-playing careers in college. For example, Tom Braman played No. 1 singles at Babson College in Boston, Kira Gregerson played for the U of WI, Lisa Martin played for the U of M, and D'Arcy Kyle played for Pomona College and St. Olaf.

In addition, his outside-of-tennis resume includes two books he wrote on the college admission process (*How to Get Into College* and *The College Entrance Predictor*), several articles about different educational matters such as liberal education and college admissions, and years of work as a consultant to schools and families. He speaks widely on educational matters and has appeared in the media throughout the country.

When Cliff left SPA in 1985, he was named Director of Student Services at the Breck School and served in this position until retiring in 1994. Since '94, as mentioned earlier, he has been an educational consultant.

Dallas Hagen
Wells-Easton
(Now United South Central–2004)

Though Dallas Hagen spent most of her coaching years as the head girls' coach at Wells-Easton High School (now United South Central), her story is included here because she also helped coach boys' tennis and because she gave so much to the sport during her career. And as the first female coach to be inducted into the merged Hall of Fame, she represents all the women who have worked so hard to find a place at the high school tennis table. Pioneer high school player Peg Brenden comes to mind, as does one of the first, if not the first, woman to direct a Minnesota boys' high school tennis team, Bloomington coach and Wimbledon doubles champion Jeanne Arth.

Dallas Hagen grew up near Heron Lake, MN, and then the family moved to Windom after her fifth grade year, where she graduated from high school in 1965. Though she did not play tennis in high school, she and her future husband Gary took up the game when they were students at Augsburg College because they wanted to play a sport together. Gary remembers going back to Windom in the summers "to play on cement courts built by the WPA during the Depression." Aside from tennis, Dallas played intramural sports at Augsburg during her years there (1965-1969). An aggressive and feisty competitor, "she broke several pairs of glasses during basketball games," Gary recalls. Unfortunately, she was born before the advent of girls' interscholastic athletics competition; but she knew it was imminent so she prepared herself—under the direction of MSHSL director Dorothy McIntyre—for a sport that was slated to be one of the first for girls, gymnastics.

Graduating with a teaching degree in physical education and health in 1969, she found a job at Mahtomedi, a job she landed, she believed, in part because they needed a gymnastics coach and because it was a sport she was prepared to coach. While there she started the high school gymnastics program in 1969 and also coached the girls' tennis team from 1974-77. Her early passion for gymnastics inspired her to co-found the MN Girls' Gymnastics Coaches Association—which she served as vice president for a year, to work as a gymnastics judge for thirteen years, and even to co-publish a gymnastics scorebook.

But her reputation as a tennis coach would be built in a most unlikely spot, Wells, a farming community of 2,400 located near the Iowa border in the southernmost part of the state. Here she would teach high school

Dallas Hagen

adaptive physical education, starting in 1986, and later elementary physical education. And even though she did not teach from 1978-1985, choosing instead to stay home to raise three daughters, she began coaching the girls' tennis team in 1978. At Wells she would preside over a girls' tennis program that for twenty-three years (from 1978-2000) would set the standard for other small-school coaches who saw that through hard work and sound coaching one could be successful even against some of the tennis giants. Her girls' teams won four Section 2 titles (1991, '96, '99, 2000) and six consecutive South Central Conference titles from 1995-2000, and she coached seventeen individuals in Girls' Class A singles and doubles State Tournaments. In addition, her teams won sixty-three straight regular-season matches from 1994-2000 and she compiled a coaching record of 223 wins and 93 losses during her years at Wells. Her best individual performers were two of her daughters and their partners, both taking third place in the Class A doubles tournament: Pepper Hagen and Angie Johnson in 1993 and Brooke Hagen and Johnson in '94.

While her contributions to girls' tennis are preeminent, it's important to mention her influence on boys' tennis and the sport in general as well. From 1979-86 Dallas served under head coach Jim Sand as an assistant boys' coach, directed adult tennis leagues in Wells, served as a clinician at Minnesota coaches sports clinics (in tennis and gymnastics), and started one of the first National Junior Tennis Leagues in Minnesota. As a result of her efforts, there are approximately 100 youth participating in this Junior Tennis League program in Wells today.

In addition, in her role as a member of the Wells Park Board, she helped develop summer youth programs in tennis and several other sports. Her husband tells about how adept she was at delegating the coaching to talented people who stayed with the program for years: "Continuity was a key element in her philosophy. She also had her three daughters run outreach programs in surrounding communities to increase the interest in towns which didn't have much of a tennis history."

Recognized by her coaching peers for her leadership qualities, Dallas was elected President of the MN Girls' Tennis Coaches Association for the 1996-97 school year.

She served on the MSHSL Advisory Board for Tennis and the MN Girls' Tennis Coaches Association Board from 1990-93 as well.

For her many efforts on behalf of tennis and sports in general, Dallas received a number of accolades. Twice voted Section 2A Girls' Tennis Coach of the Year (in 1991 and '96), she was also chosen as MN Class A Girls' Tennis Coach of the Year in 1991. Furthermore, Dallas was inducted into the Augsburg College Athletic Hall of Fame in 1999 for contributions to girls' sports. And in what must have been one of her proudest accomplishments, she and her family (husband Gary and daughters Pepper, Brooke, and Lindsay) were honored as USTA Northern Section Family of the Year in 1999.

A woman with great energy and a passion for life, Dallas served the greater community of Wells in many other ways as well. For instance, she served on the People's State Bank board of directors for three years, volunteered for the Special Olympics Track and Field Days program, and served as tournament director for a unique mixed doubles tournament for players with a "Wells connection." Sponsored by a Wells bank and organized by Dallas and her husband Gary, this tournament usually included 38-40 doubles teams divided into 7 or 8 flights. A round robin format was employed and no one was eliminated from the tournament.

Regrettably, Dallas died in the prime of her life on August 7, 2001, from an undetected congenital heart defect. Ironically, she died playing tennis with some of her good friends, including Hall of Fame coach Cheryl King. She was only fifty-four, getting ready to lead her girls' tennis team in the fall, to teach elementary physical education, and to continue to be a role model for young girls who, like Peg Brenden, just wanted a chance to play on a school sports team. One of those young women was her daughter Pepper, who today perpetuates Dallas' legacy by coaching girls' tennis at South St. Paul and serving in a leadership role in the merged coaches association.

Bill Ritchie
St. Cloud Tech (2004)
The other half of that dynamic duo (Jerry Sales being the

other) who guided the St. Cloud Tech Tigers to three state titles is Bill Ritchie, the last of the 2004 inductees and arguably one of the most successful boys' coaches in Minnesota tennis history. (For more about Ritchie and his St. Cloud Tech teams see Chapter Nine.)

Not a Minnesota native, Bill grew up in Menasha, a small town on the shores of Lake Winnebago in eastern Wisconsin. Though he couldn't hear the shouts of rabid fans on Sundays coming from Lambeau Field in nearby Green Bay just forty miles to the north, he must have been caught up in Packermania during these heady Vince Lombardi years. Nevertheless, it was not the siren song of football that lured Bill but rather the plaintive melodies of tennis rackets striking tennis balls. In Menasha he was to begin a tennis-playing and -coaching career that would last over forty years. At Menasha High School he played both No. 1 doubles and Nos. 4 or 5 singles for four years (in Wisconsin players were permitted to compete in both singles and doubles), graduating in 1961. Bill learned to play the game in a summer recreation program and recalls in particular two memorable experiences from his high school years. One was an upset of powerhouse rival Neenah in the conference finals and the other was a special memory that Bill recalls with some amusement. His dad came to watch a tournament match and, according to Bill, "he left before I finished. When I got home I asked him why he left and he said he thought he was bothering me and he thought I was losing. I won the match."

From Menasha he ventured south to attend Wisconsin State U at Whitewater to study and play tennis (mostly No. 4 singles and No. 1 doubles). Following graduation with a double major in physics and math, after the 1965 summer session, Bill joined the army in October 1965. Advancing through Officer Candidate School, Bill achieved the rank of second lieutenant and soon found himself in the jungles of Vietnam for a combat tour lasting from February 1967 to February 1968. Returning from Vietnam, he found himself stationed in St. Cloud, where he promptly enrolled at St. Cloud State Teachers College in order to become certified to teach.

In the fall of 1970 he took his first job, at St. Cloud Tech, and in the spring of 1971 he succeeded the legendary Mac Doane as just the third head coach at Tech, formerly St. Cloud High School. And what a career he had there—three state team championships (1976, '83, '85), nine runner-up finishes, five third place finishes, 464 wins and only 85 losses (an 84 percent winning rate), twenty-one Central Lakes Conference championships, and many individual singles and doubles state tournament qualifiers. All told, his was a most satisfying run of thirty-one years (1971-2001), a run that he enjoyed in large part because of "the enthusiasm and dedication of the high school tennis players at Tech."

In addition, Bill relished his partnership with Jerry Sales, finding in him a kindred spirit who valued hard work and discipline as keys to success. When asked what he liked best about coaching tennis, and what he did to prepare players for competition, Bill said, "I enjoyed coaching the mental toughness part of the game. I tried to make practices physically tough and then told the players the opponents have not worked as hard as you so don't let them beat you." His basic coaching philosophy, which of course included this emphasis on toughness and conditioning, was embodied in the motto "We win with class and we lose with class." One opposing coach who respected this attitude that Bill and Jerry instilled in their players was Tom Vining of Roseville, whose teams battled the Tech Tigers many times over the years. Vining said, "A perfectly suited pair emerged in the '70s at St. Cloud Tech, tall, soft-spoken Bill Ritchie and his assistant Jerry Sales. These guys were flat out superior coaches and Ritchie's low-keyed ego allowed Sales to deservedly share the spotlight. I always envied the players who were lucky enough to perform for these two." As mentioned in the profile on Sales in this chapter, if Jerry was Watson, Bill was Sherlock Holmes; and together they "solved many a puzzling opponent."

Over the years Ritchie considered it a privilege to coach so many fine young men. Of course there were the Helgeson brothers (see Chapter Ten for more on them), 1983 doubles champions Dave Nelson-Shawn Bresnahan and '84 champions Sean Potter-Todd Schlorf, Jeff and Jerry Schwanberg, Ken Dahlquist, Wade Bresnahan, Dan O'Shea, Adam Beduhn, Kevin Whipple, and Ajay Prakash, among others. Many of these players went on to tennis glory in college and some even challenged the sharks on the pro tour for a short time. One of these players, Brace

Helgeson, remembers Ritchie with fondness: "Bill Ritchie was a very understanding and effective coach by the time I became a junior and senior... He came to understand [as many who coached in this era of increased involvement on the part of tennis pros in high school programs came to understand] that he needed to allow for some flexibility to let us play outside of team practices in order to keep our games up. By my senior year he also did not make me play all of the matches as long as he knew I was getting a good match or practice in the Cities."

With so much talent available at Tech, Bill's most difficult job many years was choosing who would be in the starting lineup. For instance, in 1974 he and Jerry Sales allowed gifted eighth grader Brace Helgeson to join the varsity squad and, because they weren't sure where to play him, sent him to an indoor court in the Cities to challenge sophomore Jerry Schwanberg for the No. 3 singles spot. Brace won and thus for one year had the opportunity to play singles behind older brothers Grant and Kent. In trying to maintain a level of excellence in the program, Bill said, "we [he and Sales] counseled our returning players on what they needed to do before next season. And Jerry talked to the junior high players about what they also needed to do to play on the varsity next year."

When asked to name his best player, Bill, ever the diplomat, was reluctant to single out any of his players; but he said he has "many fond memories of his players and of the experiences they shared." One of the most memorable was of course Tech's first state team title in 1976, but he also recalls a tough 3-2 loss to Edina in the 1981 finals. In addition, there are the humorous moments, one of which found Bill thrashing around in a Twin Cities motel swimming pool when the players threw him in after someone posed the team (and Bill) for a poolside picture after Tech's 1976 state tournament victory. Bill also describes the following experience which was not so funny at the time: "On the way to a region championship match at Fergus Falls in 1978 we ran out of gas five miles from Fergus and were an hour late for the match." Luckily, coach Whitey Olson of Thief River Falls was a patient man and the match went off without a hitch, Tech in fact winning. (Where were cell phones when you needed them?)

A lifetime member of the MN Boys' Tennis Coaches

Association, Ritchie served this body as president for two years (1979-81) and was honored twice by his coaching peers as MN Boys' Tennis Coach of the Year (in 1975 and '85). Off the tennis court he served as an assistant football coach from 1970-1984, head boys' soccer coach for ten years, and for the past eight years—even since his retirement in 2001—he has served as an assistant girls' soccer coach at Tech. In addition, he has always been an active member of St. Peter's Catholic Church, today serving as an ordained deacon. He and his wife, Linda, raised two children, Scott and Maria, who played tennis at St. Cloud Apollo and St. Cloud Cathedral respectively.

John Eberhart
Pine City (2006)

You've seen the commercials on TV, the ones that try to persuade you that their batteries last forever. Of course, they're for Eveready and their pitch "man" is the Energizer Bunny which just keeps on going and going. Minnesota tennis's equivalent of the Energizer Bunny is Pine City's John Eberhart, the first of the 2006 inductees into the Hall of Fame (there were no inductees in 2005). Eberhart's boundless energy helped shape the direction of Minnesota high school tennis and played a major role in developing tennis in Pine City, a small town of about 3,000 citizens located north of the Twin Cities on the way to Duluth.

For example, since he began his career as the boys' coach in 1976, Eberhart helped create and organize the preseason coaches clinics, served for many years on the Tennis Coaches Advisory Committee to the MSHSL, helped establish the MN High School Boys' Tennis Coaches Hall of Fame, and served twice as president of the MN Boys' Tennis Coaches Association (in 1984-85 and 2002-04). In Pine City he started the Junior USTA Program in the early 1980s, organized summer leagues for adults, ran a local tournament—called the Koppens/Lees Open—for twenty-five years, and also served as the Pine City girls' basketball coach for eight years.

He is particularly pleased that he helped secure more tennis courts for his community. Eberhart said, "I worked with the superintendent to 'fix' the old courts and, when they realized they were beyond fixing, they gave us $320,000 for new ones. We now have eight in a row with metal bleachers and berms to sit on around the courts. A pretty nice setup for a small town." For his efforts, the courts were dedicated in his honor in 2004. John also said there are fourteen courts in town, "probably the most per capita in Minnesota."

In addition to his boundless energy, John had great competitive drive and a tremendous desire to learn and grow as a coach. He took pride in coaching teams that knew how to win (his boys' teams won fifteen conference titles and six section titles, for instance), and he spent a great deal of time learning how to play and coach tennis, a game he had not played as a youngster. These latter "energizer" efforts paid off in his becoming a successful USPTA professional.

And all this from a former Little Falls High School and Moorhead State College baseball player who, when asked to coach tennis at Pine City, didn't even own a tennis racket. So his wife, Merrilee, bought him a department store Chemold racket so he could at least look like a tennis coach for his first practice. He admits he knew virtually nothing about the game in 1976, but he had help from a number of knowledgeable people such as Matt Alexander, an executive at the 3M plant in Pine City, and capable assistant coaches such as Steve Eck, a local dentist. Another one of his excellent assistant coaches, Rick Engelstad, succeeded Eberhart as boys' coach in 2002.

John Eberhart

Eberhart liked his new job so well that he stayed to coach the boys until 2001 (twenty-six years), and he also coached the girls from 1981-2002 (twenty-two years). His Class A boys' teams never won a state title, but they finished third in 1981 and won the consolation title in '99. In addition, John coached thirty-eight individuals to State; and though none of them won championships, Tim Werner and Wayne Hagstrom finished second in 1981 in Class A doubles and third in 1980 and Zac O'Donnell and Jonah Ryberg-Sauter finished fourth in 1998. Eberhart says his best players were Hagstrom ("who had tremendous self-discipline and was a fierce competitor") and Tony Bacigalupi ("the most fundamentally sound player we ever had").

He is perhaps most proud of the Dragons' conference record of 120 wins and just 19 losses (with only four home losses in twenty-six years). Eberhart completed his career with a boys' team record of 291-110 and an even better girls' team record of 280-92. His girls' teams also won fifteen conference titles and made it to State twelve times.

For his coaching success and his tireless efforts on behalf of Minnesota high school tennis, Eberhart was voted Class A boys' coach of the year an unprecedented four times (1987, '91, '98, '99), and he was also recognized as Minnesota USPTA pro of the year twice. In addition, he was awarded the Frank Voigt Pro of the Year Award in 2002; and he was voted into the "first class" of the Pine City Athletic Hall of Fame.

Eberhart truly believed that a tennis team was like a family whose motto should be "We win together, we lose together, we eat together." He worked hard to develop every player, and that often showed up with crucial wins at Nos. 3 doubles and 4 singles. And while having fun was a top priority as well (John is a fun-loving guy), his practices were no-nonsense affairs that were, in his words, "super organized." In addition, he and his coaches really "tried to evaluate each opposing team and find weaknesses we might have in matching up with them and then working on these each day."

An optimistic guy who communicated positive energy to his players, Eberhart nonetheless expressed some frustrations with coaching high school tennis, frustrations which all coaches have expressed at one time or another. These include having to cut players (from a ten-person regular-season team to a seven-person team for tournament play) and "seeing tennis players not get the same recognition as the kids in basketball or football."

Now retired after teaching fifth grade his entire thirty-four years in Pine City and working for a time at a local bank in the financial planning department, he still plays tennis (and some golf) and works with the high school kids and the summer USTA program in Pine City. Eberhart says he wants to be remembered as one who "gave it 100 percent and cared for his kids." As someone who got to know John fairly well over the years, I was always impressed with his genuine concern for others and his belief that camaraderie among coaches was terribly important. He admitted as much when he said, "Without good coaches like Mike Premo, Tom Vining, John Hatch, and Dave Gunderson, we wouldn't have had to work so hard to be good. I'm glad I had the opportunity to coach against them."

John still makes his home in Pine City, though of late he and his wife have been spending the months of January-March in Virginia to be near their daughter Becky and her children. You see, Becky is married to former St. Cloud player and U of VA tennis coach Brian Boland. The Eberharts have two other daughters: Angie and Carrie. Becky and Angie both played high school tennis for their dad, and both made several trips to State as individuals or as members of the Pine City teams.

Mike Premo
Foley (2006)

One of my grandsons adores the cartoon character/toy "Bob the Builder." Somehow when I think of that fictional character I also think of a very real builder, the second of this year's Hall of Fame inductees, Mike Premo of Foley. Though he had already built a successful girls' tennis program at Foley since the school inaugurated it in 1978—stepping in after the first week of practice when the coach who had been hired to start the program resigned—it took Premo several years to lay the foundation for the boys' program which began in 1988.

For starters he agreed to take the post on a voluntary, unpaid basis. Secondly, it was difficult to schedule matches against the more established area teams and even more difficult to compete (and win) against them. For example, that first Foley team finished with an 0-9 record and lost seventeen matches over two years before earning a 6-1 win over Monticello in the second year, 1989. Third, though twenty-two players in grades 7-12 came out for

tennis that first year, none of them had much tennis experience. Finally, until six new tennis courts were built in 1991, Premo's boys' (and girls') teams practiced on three concrete courts that had been built in the '30s by the CCC and covered with asphalt in the early '80s.

Despite these humbling beginnings, within six years (1994) the Foley Falcons had advanced to the Class A State Tournament where they finished fourth. In addition, before he retired in 1999 after twelve years as the head boys' coach, the Falcons won three Rum River Conference titles and sent one singles player (Matt Emmerich in 1992) and three doubles teams to state (including Premo's sons Eric and Kris). Emmerich was Eric Premo's partner in '93, and Allen Smith and Ryan Zimmer were Kris Premo's partners the two years he made it to State, Zimmer and Premo taking fourth in the '97 doubles tournament. Premo is proud of his two sons, one of whom (Kris) is now the girls' coach at Mahtomedi and a USPTA pro at White Bear Racquet Club.

And though the foundation was at first a bit shaky, Premo's boys' finished with a fine record of 148 wins and 85 losses, one year (1991) also earning a MN State Academic Champion award. This is an admirable record, but on the boys' scene Mike is perhaps best known for his contributions as president of the MN Boys' Tennis Coaches Association during his 1992-93 tenure. He has also devoted a

Mike Premo

good deal of effort to promoting recent pre-season coaches clinics at the White Bear Lake Racquet Club, and he has advised the MSHSL on region alignments of teams for tournament competition. For his contributions to Minnesota high school tennis and for his team's successes he was voted MN Class A Boys' Coach of the Year in 1995.

It's fair to say that Premo had a more successful career as the girls' coach, for eight of his teams advanced to State (the 1998 team finishing second), nine won conference titles, and twenty-two of his singles players and doubles teams advanced to State in individual competition. His best singles player, Jessica Talberg, took third in the 1987 tournament, then went on to captain the Air Force Academy team.

Mike was twice voted MN Class A Girls' Tennis Coach of the Year (1993-94 and 1999-2000), and he finished his twenty-five-year girls' coaching career with an outstanding record of 362-147.

Premo grew up in Bemidji, where he played three sports: basketball until tenth grade, downhill skiing, and tennis. He made the varsity as a seventh grader in tennis and ended up playing No. 3 singles his senior year. After graduating in 1964, he enrolled at Bemidji State College, where he played just one year of tennis. Premo was in the army reserves for six years, and he took time off from college for one year of active duty in 1967; so he didn't graduate until December of 1969. After spending just one year at Mentor, MN, he took a job at Foley in the fall of 1970. His first coaching job was as a golf coach, so it was eight years before he became the girls' tennis coach.

A super nice guy with an amiable personality, Premo taught American history and government for thirty-two years at Foley and served as dean of students his last two years. Mike retired in 2003, then he and his wife built a home in the Tucson, AZ, area, where they now live. A USTA pro since 1987, Premo says he plays tennis five days a week and still does some racket stringing. In addition to his membership in this Hall of Fame, he is also a member of the Foley Athletic Hall of Fame.

Cheryl King
Anoka (2006)

Along with John Eberhart and Mike Premo, Cheryl King of Anoka joined the ranks of the newest Hall of Fame Coaches in 2006. Though she did not coach boys' tennis, she had a long and estimable career as both a player and girls' coach in Minnesota. As an adult player she was ranked as high as No. 3 in Women's 35-and-Over Doubles three times (twice with Cheryl Savage and once with Marge Champlin), and she has been involved with the NWTA since 1982—serving on the Board of Directors in 1995-96.

But it is for her coaching efforts that she was honored with this award. Hired to teach physical education and health at Jackson Junior High School in Anoka in 1970, King also started the girls' tennis program and coached there until 1976. Then she became the head varsity girls' coach at Anoka High School in the fall of 1976, succeeding the legendary Elie Peden. She held that post until 1992, when she moved to Champlin Park to take the head girls' job. She coached at Champlin Park until 1999 when she retired from teaching; but in 2001 she couldn't resist the siren call of tennis, so she signed up to serve as an assistant coach for the Park Cottage Grove girls' team, a position she still holds. In addition to her tennis duties, over the years

Cheryl King

King also coached gymnastics and track at Anoka.

During her long and successful career, King coached two girls' teams to the State Tournament, (in 1983 and '91), and seven of her Anoka Tornadoes' teams won conference titles. These good results are not surprising, for she was a hard-working, intelligent coach whose teams were always very well prepared. One of her coaching competitors, Tom Vining of Roseville Area, paid her the ultimate compliment, saying, "Cheryl King was a great coach—she had a way with her players. I felt we were always the underdog against her teams."

Honored as MN Class AA Girls' Coach of the Year in 1991, King also served the coaches association as president for one term and as a member of the Tennis Coaches Board for several years. In addition, she started the Maple Grove Tennis Association in 1994 and organized the junior team tennis program there that same year.

King grew up in Anoka, the child of a father who taught physical education and coached football and baseball. Stan Nelson passed his athletic genes on to Cheryl, who early on showed an aptitude for a variety of sports. For example, she swam, competing in AAU events for ten years; then, her tennis- and golf-playing mother got her started in those two sports. Both of her younger brothers also inherited what her dad called type PE blood (not type A or B); and one of them (Steve) played fourteen years in the NFL with the New England Patriots. Her other brother Dave is currently the Minnetonka football coach.

With such a family history, it was inevitable that Cheryl would become involved in athletics. So in high school she participated in GAA (Girls' Athletic Association) and girls' track. (Remember, these were the days before Title IX.) After graduating from Anoka High School in 1966, she enrolled at Augsburg College to major in physical education and coaching. At Augsburg she played three-forwards-three guards basketball until her senior year when they played regular five-on-five basketball. She graduated in 1970.

Re-introduced to tennis by her future husband Richard when both were Augsburg students, she continues to play USTA 4.5 league tennis and has competed in eight USTA national tournaments. She and her husband have two grown boys (both of whom played high school tennis

at Osseo), and they live in Prescott, WI. In addition to her membership in this Hall of Fame, she was inducted into the Augsburg Athletic Hall of Fame in 1990.

George Beske
Minneapolis South (2007)

The final Hall of Fame inductees are George Beske of Minneapolis South and Bob Pivec of Coon Rapids. We'll take them in alphabetical order and begin with Beske.

You could often pick out Beske in a tennis crowd because of his flamboyant attire, an orange Minneapolis South team shirt and zubas pants. No suit and tie for this self-described "Ghetto Tennis Coach," for he was truly a Minnesota tennis original. Moreover, his teams were extraordinarily successful in conference, section, and State play. In his eighteen years at South and six seasons at Minneapolis Central, he compiled a record of 360 wins and 217 losses. During his years at South he coached some of the best players in the state, including 2002 state singles champion D. J. Geatz, 2002 doubles titlists Mikey Kantar and Sion Wilkins, and others such as Tim Klein, Brandon Heath, Mike (fourth in the 1993 Class AA singles tournament) and Mark Chaly, Danny Kantar (who, with Mikey, finished fourth in the 2000 Class AA doubles tourney), Jesse Morgan (current South boys' coach), Casey Oppenheim, Jay Petrich, Taylor Hanson, and Bryan Baumann (a six-year letterwinner). As for his girls' teams, which he coached from 1978-2005, they won eleven city conference titles, finished as high as second at State (in 1996), and won 316 matches.

At South Beske was a tireless tennis promoter who also worked very hard to develop competitive teams. In addition, he always emphasized the importance of hard work. For example, one year he ordered shirts for his girls' team that said "Play hard or go home," a saying that became the team's mantra. He also said, "One huge deal I had was 'respect your opponent!' It is amazing what attitude can do for your game." In turn, he always respected his players and treated them fairly.

Since his retirement from teaching and his boys' coaching post in 2003 ('05 from girls' coaching), he has reflected about how much he enjoyed "coaching and working to develop discipline among the players and watching them have fun." He also enjoyed the interactions with students other than in the classroom (he taught math), and he has continued his relationships with many former players after they graduated.

For someone who began playing pick-up tennis for fun with his buddy Lee Raitz on the only court in his hometown, Beske has come a long way from Hector, a small community in southwest Minnesota which did not have a high school tennis team. He's coached one of the most successful city high school teams, helped develop the Urban Tennis Program in Minneapolis, and served the MN Boys' Tennis Coaches' Association as president from 1999-2001. For his success as a coach he was honored as the 2001 Class AA Coach of the Year.

Finally, Beske says his only regret was not trying out for the tennis team at Macalester, his alma mater. "I never had the guts to try out," he said, "and that story helped me to encourage my players on occasion." (For more about the South Tigers and Coach Beske, see Chapter Eight.")

Bob Pivec
Coon Rapids (2007)

"The best preparation for tomorrow is to do your best today." These words, which appear on a plaque at the Coon Rapids High School courts, represent for coach Bob Pivec his approach to life and to coaching tennis. During his thirty-two years at the helm of the Cardinals' boys' squad, he was careful not to look back or to look too far ahead, instead focusing on the present. To that end, Pivec believed that it was important "to make each season special for that year's players" and "to never have a team feel we were rebuilding or getting ready for the next season." In addition, said Pivec, "For the players making our team it would be their season and we expected each player to give his best each day in practice or when he played competitively."

Therefore, practices concentrated on improving skills and learning singles and doubles principles. Also, Pivec never took a day off from practice, taking some of the players to indoor clubs, working in the gym, or spending time in the "classroom" on bad weather days. In addition, he also used "classroom" days to "go over our expectations for playing out points and to talk about the

drills we would use so that when we got to the court players would know what they should do. We did not want to spend court time talking."

This meticulous attention to details and his "here and now" attitude helped his teams and players become successful. Under his guidance Coon Rapids won seven North Suburban Conference championships and seven section titles, finishing third at State in 1975 and second in '83. His career record was a sparkling 463 wins and 177 losses. And though none of his players won a state individual championship, Tom Olmscheid finished second twice—losing to two of the state's all-time great players, two-time champion Daryl Laddin in 1983 and ninth grade phenom David Wheaton in '84. In doubles Gerry Monus and Douglas Arntson took fifth in '76 and brothers Alfred and Sekou Bangoura finished second in '84. There were many others who made it to State during Pivec's years as the boys' coach, such as Elie Peden's son Dave, but he considered it "very special" to coach Olmscheid and Bill Ford, the latter the No. 1 player on Coon Rapids' first state tournament team in '75. He recalls that Olmscheid won thirty-two matches in a row before losing in the finals in '84.

Pivec grew up in Minneapolis, learning to play at courts located on the west side of Lake Harriet. He then played for three years at De LaSalle High School, holding down Nos. 3 singles and 1 doubles spots his senior year.

After graduating from high school in 1962 he attended the U of M, where he earned a freshman numeral in tennis, then transferred to Mankato State. He played just one year at Mankato, concentrating instead on completing his social studies major. Pivec finished his college studies at Mankato in 1967, then taught for two years in Milwaukee before coming to Coon Rapids in 1969.

Of his years at Coon Rapids, he said he is particularly proud of directing the first Cardinals' team in any sport that won a state trophy (third place in 1975). Perhaps most importantly, however, he will be remembered in Coon Rapids whenever players step on one of those fourteen courts next to the high school; for in October 2002 the coach who succeeded him, Scott Storrick, arranged to have the courts named after Pivec. These are the courts (now called the Bob Pivec Courts) where that plaque mentioned earlier resides. Pivec was also a member of the MN Boys' Tennis

Bob Pivec (Left) and George Beske

Coaches Association, serving the organization as treasurer for a number of years, and he was a member of the Tennis Coaches Advisory Committee as well.

Finally, Bob was yet another double-duty coach, serving as the girls' tennis mentor as well. In the twenty-nine years he coached them, the girls won fifteen conference championships, reached the section finals fourteen years in a row, and made eight state tournament appearances. And his doubles team of Renee Fournier and Joan Sundstrom won consecutive championships in 1975-76. Pivec also coached his three daughters, Katie, Sarah, and Amy; and two of them did well at State, Katie taking third in singles and Sarah third in doubles. All told, his boys' and girls' teams won 903 matches, an extraordinary record.

Still busy in retirement, Pivec plays tennis two to three days a week ("even on bad knees") and on Saturdays he teaches tennis for two hours at the Minnetonka Tennis Club. In addition, he teaches a women's tennis group at Coon Rapids. Ironically, one of his former players, Scott Swanson, is the pro manager there. In addition, he and his wife (who also plays tennis) travel a good deal, and he enjoys remodeling his house in Coon Rapids and doing garden and yard work.

Note: Ken Peterson of Anoka was inducted in 2008. For his profile, see Chapter Three.

They Also Served

Dedicated masochists, "fathers" (and "mothers") to many sons, persevering servants, tireless workers: all these phrases describe the best high school tennis coaches. But what characterizes them perhaps more than anything is the bond they share as members of an exclusive society of those who labor in the spring because they love the game of tennis. Unlike their players, most of whom only play high school tennis for two to four years and thus battle an opponent maybe only once each year, coaches compete against each other for many years. For example, for almost thirty years Bud Schmid of Brainerd and Reg Mead of Wadena competed against each other. And though some coaches don't get along, that was not the case with them. Their friendly rivalry helped forge a lifetime bond, a friendship that continued for over fifty years. Such relationships are forged through pre-match conversations—sometimes in the form of lively banter or kibitzing—and continue during the time the two coaches write their lineups in the opponent's scorebook and through to the end of the match. Sometimes they're even nurtured over a cup of coffee. Darwin Deim, during the one year he coached tennis at Northfield, tells the story about his first match. It was a typical blustery, cold spring day and the Raiders were playing at Rochester John Marshall. After the coaches wrote the lineups in their Wirtanen scorebooks and got the match started, veteran John Marshall coach Al Wold said, "Let's go out for a cup of coffee." They did, and when they returned the match was over.

In addition to these encounters during matches, coaches meet for seeding and conference meetings, interact at region and state tournaments, and often drive together to

> *"'Tis my vocation, Hal;*
> *'tis no sin for a man to labor*
> *in his vocation."*
> —Henry IV, Part 1

spring coaching clinics. Many also work together at summer tennis camps, and as a result the circles of friendship expand to include spouses and children. For instance, in the summer of 1980 my wife, Caroline, and I spent a week at the Lake Hubert Tennis Camp, in part because it gave us a free vacation (food and lodging provided in return for my services as a coach), but also because it gave our fourteen-year-old son Chris a chance to hit with top players like Myles and Roger Anderson. It also gave a jumpstart to the tennis career of our eleven-year-old daughter Heather, a heretofore reluctant tennis player. Perhaps most importantly for me as a coach, it was a wonderful opportunity to get to know Bud and Sue Schmid, Chuck and Ruth Anderson, Hal and Elaine Schroeder, and Bruce and Janet Getchell, among others. In fact, this still flourishing camp became a model for the tennis coaching fraternity and how it can be sustained.

This chapter, and the one on the Hall of Fame coaches, is meant to honor this close-knit fraternity, to inform readers of the accomplishments of these coaches, and to bring to light their stories. Here then are the stories of prominent Minnesota coaches who are not yet members of the Hall of Fame (and four USPTA coaches), some of whom are women, and all of whom were successful mentors of young tennis players. I have tried to say something about as many coaches as I could; however, there will be some whom I have not remembered or recognized. In addition, in some cases I simply could not find much information; so some profiles will be brief. To all those coaches and the many others who are not profiled here, I offer my sincerest apology. (See appendix E for a list of other longtime successful Minnesota coaches.)

Early Years (1929-50)

In these first years the power in Minnesota tennis resided in the Twin Cities. With the exception of Winona in 1947, Duluth Central in '49, and Rochester in '50, the unofficial (still not recognized by the MSHSL) team champions during those early years came from the Metro area. These were teams whose players had for the most part honed their skills on park board courts and/or at Nicollet Tennis Center.

Alas, we don't know much about the coaches from these years; but we do know that many of them were not tennis players themselves. Many were more or less chauffeurs who drove players to matches and sometimes even relied on their players to determine what positions in the lineup they should take. They were often just caretakers whose job it was to make sure that practices and matches went off without hitches. It's likely that many of them simply handed balls to the players during practice and said, "Here, Tom, take these balls and go play a match with Ralph on court four." In those days there were not many coaches who had played tennis and so the job was handed to someone who volunteered—and for very little or no pay as well.

One of the most successful of these first coaches was John Harp of St. Paul Central, coach of 1930, '31, and '35 state singles champions Robert Tudor, Roy Huber, and Myron Lieberman and of the 1935 and '36 unofficial team champions. The *Cehesian*, the Central yearbook, noted that Harp's 1929 team won the city title by beating Mechanic Arts, Humboldt, Johnson, and Cretin of St. Paul; U High and DeLaSalle of Minneapolis; Concordia College; and White Bear Lake. Harp's 1935 championship team lost only one point out of twenty in city competition (1935 *Cehesian*). He had perhaps the longest tenure of all these pioneer coaches, for in 1948 he moved to St. Paul Harding to coach the tennis team there. I do not know if Harp played tennis.

Ken Boyum's coach at Minneapolis West was Winworth Williams, who directed the Cowboys for many years in the 1930s and '40s. Unlike many of these early coaches, according to Boyum, "he could play a little tennis." Under his leadership West won team titles in 1940, '42, and '43; and he coached three state singles champions (Don Gunner in '40 and Boyum in 1942-43) and doubles winners Bill Ward/Bob Andrews in '31, Gunner/Fred Gulden in '40, Boyum/Wollin in 1942-43, and Ken Calhoun/Lenny Ferm in '45.

Other coaches from this early period included Washburn's Curtis Martin (see his profile in this chapter) and Fred Curtis; Central's Ed Weber, longtime coach of powerful Minneapolis Central teams and individual champions such as Christie Geanakoplos, Ed Von Sien, Wally Anderson, Dick Roberts, and Bill Kuross; North's Carl Larson and Marvin Skaurud; G. A. Ogden at Hibbing; Emil Anderson of Virginia; and Blake's Prescott Cleveland, who also coached at Minneapolis Roosevelt in the 1950s.

Middle Years (1950-73)

During this period, the last year of which was the year of the first True Team tournament, many coaches made their mark, including Hall of Famers Reg Mead, Bud Schmid, Hal Schroeder, John Adams, John Matlon, Jolly Carlson, Ed Sewell, and Len McGuire. This was a seminal period in Minnesota high school tennis history, for during this time many new schools were springing up in the Twin Cities and more and more outstate schools were adding tennis as an interscholastic sport. In addition, beginning in the late 1960s, the countrywide tennis boom was in full force. So there was a need for more tennis coaches, and many good men (and women) were stepping in to fill newly created vacancies. Many were tennis neophytes, to be sure, but great numbers of them, including most of the aforementioned Hall of Fame coaches, had played tennis and knew the game well.

The Later Years (1973-2003)

High school tennis flourished in Minnesota from 1973-2003, and many of the coaches who began their careers in the 1970s were still coaching at the turn of the century. And with more teams being added (and consequently more players), it is not surprising that the pool of potential coaches was increasing as well. So in the past thirty years many former Minnesota high school players have been filling tennis coaching slots.

Women Coaching Boys' Teams

It's important to note that many boys' team coaches have been women. I suppose it shouldn't be surprising that women have filled some of these boys' coaching vacancies, for girls have been competing on interscholastic teams since 1974 and attending tennis camps during the past thirty years. In addition, many players on high school girls' teams have been given a taste of coaching in the summer, for they were often hired to teach in recreation programs in their home towns.

So if you glance at the list of Minnesota boys' high school coaches today, you will see that many women are coaching boys' teams. This "crossover" coaching phenomenon is not unique to tennis; but my guess is that there are more women coaching boys in tennis than in any other sport. On the flip side, in part because there weren't many women with playing or coaching experience in the 1970s and '80s, most coaches of girls' teams then were men. That of course is changing, and now many girls' teams are coached by women.

In any case, it's worth acknowledging some of the women who have been successful boys' coaches; so I have included profiles of three of them (Jeanne Arth, Jane Kjos, and Katie Queenan). There are also profiles of two women who are Hall of Fame coaches (Dallas Hagen and Cheryl King) in Chapter Two.

In addition to these five women, here are some of the others who have coached state tournament teams. In Class AA, Carol King, who succeeded Cliff Caine at St. Paul Academy, coached the 1986 SPA state tournament team; and Naomi Hagestuen (who also served as president of the boys' tennis coaches association from 1999-2001), coached Apple Valley to three straight state tournament appearances (1991-93).

In Class A there have been even more women who coached boys' teams into the State Tournament. Perhaps the longest-serving of these coaches was Benson's Kjos, who coached four teams into the tournament; but the most successful was Breck's Queenan, who led the Mustangs to three Section 5A championships in four years and state titles in 1998 and 2001. Another woman who coached at Breck and also led them to the state championship (in 1997) was Dana Peterson, a former U of M varsity performer. And once again Carol King led SPA to State, but this time in Class A in '87. In 1992 Pat Sherman (a Winona State physical education professor who was for many years one of the top women players in the Northern Section) was the coach of the Section 1A champion Winona Cotter team. In '99 the Park Rapids Section 8A entry in the tournament was coached by Barb Thomason. Most recently, Mounds Park Academy coach Michelle Olson led her team to two state championships (in 2005 and '06).

Of course it hardly seems right to single out coaches of state tournament teams, so I'll cite two others I coached against (Sue Fischer and Denise Remak) and another one I know well. For starters, both Sue and Denise were good tennis players who commanded the respect of their players; and both were excellent coaches. Both began coaching in the late 1970s, Fischer at Lakeville and Remak at Apple Valley, and both continued in coaching after they gave up their boys' jobs. Remak, who played varsity tennis at Indiana U for four years, coached the Apple Valley boys for just two years (1979-80) but stayed on to coach the Eagles' girls' team until 1992. Fischer spent six years as the head boys' and girls' coach at Lakeville in the late 1970s and early '80s before moving to the U of WI-LaCrosse, where she headed up both the men's and women's tennis teams for eleven years. At Lakeville she inaugurated the boys' tennis program in the spring of 1978. (For more on Fischer, see Chapter Seven.)

On a more personal note, a coach who took over the Northfield boys' program for eight years in the 1990s was Tanya Thielman Will, a top high school player from Jamestown, ND, and a former No. 1 player at Concordia College in Moorhead.

Finally, when I checked the roster of boys' tennis coaches in 1978 (just four years after the first girls' tournament was held), there were six women listed as coaches of boys' teams: Marlene Bowen of Hermantown, Paula Douglas of Walnut Grove, Fischer of Lakeville, Deby Ostergren of Concordia Academy, Bonnie Strobbe of St. Paul Central, and Barbara Westman of Isle. Just twenty-seven years later, there were fifteen women listed as boys' coaches in the MSHSL Web site of coaches, including two expatriates from England, Apple Valley head coach Sue Furtney and her assistant Sue Hodgson. Furtney was an accomplished player in her home land (a county champion who played in the junior Wimbledon championships), and she was also a physical education teacher there and a tennis pro here. For the contributions she and Hodgson have made to youth tennis in the Metro area, both were awarded the prestigious Ward C. Burton Junior Development Award in 2002. The other thirteen women coaching boys' teams (in 2005) were Ali Barnett of Hopkins, Kathy Dumas of St. Paul Como Park, Mandy Larson of Minneapolis Edison, Thea Lowman of Cambridge-Isanti, Berit Merrill of Foley, Olson of Mounds Park Academy, Celine Pederson of St. Anthony Village, Tara Reichmann of Minnewaska Area, Rebecca Robertson of South St. Paul, Thomason of Park Rapids, Andrea Underhill of Holy Angels, Cammie Wadman-Day of Andover, and Kimi Wilson of Faribault.

As for the four USPTA coaches (Marv Hanenberger, Norm McDonald, Jerry Noyce, and Frank Voigt), I have included their profiles at the end of this chapter.

Following then are the profiles of selected coaches.

Gary Aasen
Edina

One of the most successful of the new breed of coach, the tennis teaching pro, is Edina's Gary Aasen. Since taking over from Steve Paulsen in 1994, Aasen has led the

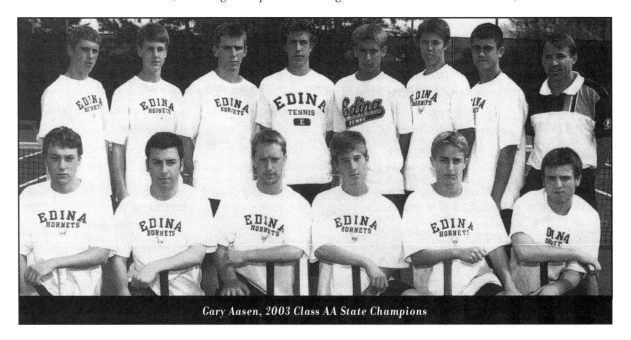

Gary Aasen, 2003 Class AA State Champions

Hornets to six state team titles (through 2006); and three of his singles players and four doubles teams have won individual championships. One of his teams—the 2002 squad—swept aside all opponents, winning the title and finishing with an unblemished 21-0 record. In addition, the Hornets have won eleven conference titles during his tenure and nine Section 6 team championships. For his efforts, his peers elected him Class AA Boys' Tennis Coach of the Year in 2000.

In the pressure cooker of Edina tennis, Aasen has been successful in part because he is a skilled player whose on-court experience helps him relate to Edina's top players. For example, he played four years of varsity tennis at Fridley under coach Dave Loo, receiving additional coaching from Lilydale pro Ric Yates. A 1982 high school graduate, he held down the No. 1 spot at Fridley for three years, advancing to State in singles his last three years where he made it to the quarters twice. He finished his high school career with a sparkling 82-19 won-loss record and led his team to State two years (1981-82). In junior play he was often a top-tenner and achieved a No. 6 ranking his last year in the 18s. Coach Gary Peterson of Minnetonka called him one of the toughest players in the state.

Aasen's tennis career continued in college, first for a year at the U of Nevada-Reno and then for three years at the U of M. A three-year letterwinner who alternated between Nos. 6-8 singles for the Gophers, he played on the 1986 Big Ten champions ranked No. 9 in the country. After graduating in 1986 and majoring in public health and psychology, he served as U of M coach Jerry Noyce's assistant for a year, then took a crack at playing in some satellite tournaments before, in his words, "slowly sliding into teaching full-time at the country clubs and winter clubs in Minneapolis." As an adult he has competed in age-group tournaments, earning No. 1 rankings in Men's 35-and-Over Singles (in 2001 and '02) and in Men's Open Doubles (with former U of M star and current Ohio State U women's coach Chuck Merzbacher in 1987). In addition, he's participated on a national championship 5.0 USTA team and has won three 30-and-Over Section championships (two in doubles with Randy Crowell in 1994-95) and one singles title in 1995.

As a high school coach he's a firm believer that "conducting yourself with integrity and professionalism is contagious to your team" and that it's important to be honest and open with your players. Team building is also essential to him, so he spends a great deal of time working with his young and inexperienced players and having them set performance goals. In addition, he credits his coach, Noyce, for showing him how a model tennis program works, one that is conducted with integrity.

Finally, Aasen counts winning the 100th state title for Edina High School as a highlight of his career, but he also takes pride in seeing individual players or doubles teams "do something exceptional during the two-day individual tournament" as well. (For more about Aasen, see Chapter Nine.)

Jeanne Arth
Bloomington Kennedy

One of most compelling stories in Minnesota high school tennis is that of Jeanne Arth, arguably the greatest female tennis player in the history of the state. This Wimbledon doubles champion (with partner Darlene Hard in 1959) and two-time U.S. doubles champion (in 1958 and '59, again with Hard), Arth was also a high school coach and

Jeanne Arth

teacher. But she was not just any coach, for ironically she coached a boys' tennis team in the days before girls could play competitively on high school teams. That team was Bloomington Kennedy, and she served as head coach from 1964-69. Of those years she said, "We had some good athletes, but no one played tennis in the summer and we barely had enough players for a team." Despite these drawbacks, one year her team finished 6-3 in the Lake Conference. One of her top players was future Anoka coach Ken Peterson.

A 1956 graduate of The College of St. Catherine in St. Paul, Arth taught physical education and social studies from 1956-76 at Holy Angels, Minneapolis South, and Kennedy, then served as a counselor from 1976-93 at Kennedy. She retired in 1993 after thirty-seven years as an educator and coach.

We honor her for inspiring many other women to become coaches of boys' teams, for she may have been the first woman to coach a boys' team in Minnesota; but it is her playing career we celebrate most. Remarkably, she never had a lesson as a child and never played tennis in the winter (at that time there were no indoor courts in St. Paul). Instead, after her mother bought her what Arth called "a dime-store racket," she started playing at age five at the St. Paul Tennis Club on Osceola Avenue. At first she and her older sister Shirley hit on the backboard there, thanks to club pro Louis Soukup, who gave them permission to do so; then they began substituting in with older women's foursomes when "they saw we could play." In addition, she noted, "They also gave us some pointers." And though her father played weekend tennis on public parks courts, neither he nor her mother were involved in her tennis. In fact, said Arth, "My mother never saw me play until my last two years of national junior girls' play."

Eventually she became so good that the St. Paul Central coach wanted Arth and her sister Shirley (who also became a top local adult player) to play on the boys' team. Unfortunately, the bureaucracy would not allow that, so instead she focused on tournament play during her four-month summer tennis seasons. During her high school years and her early twenties her results were astonishing for a woman living as she did in a state not noted for tennis: a No. 2 national junior doubles ranking with her sister and a

No. 4 national singles ranking in 1953, a No. 6 U.S. singles ranking and a No. 1 doubles ranking in '58, No.1 USLTA/ Northwestern Section junior singles and doubles rankings from 1947-53, a girls' 18 U.S. singles semifinalist in '53, and a national college tennis tournament singles finalist from 1954-56 and doubles champion from 1954-56.

In addition, she was the first state tennis player to compete overseas, at Wimbledon and as a member of the 1959 Wightman Cup team. She won her Wimbledon and U.S. doubles titles while teaching school (she did not regularly play the pro circuit), and after she won these tournaments she continued to compete in USLTA/Northwestern Section tournaments for many years. During these years, both as a junior and adult player, she dominated the local tennis scene, ranking No. 1 in Women's Singles from 1951-69 and in doubles from 1949-69. In addition, she won Sectional Women's Singles championships in 1949-52, 1955-56, and 1960-62 and doubles titles in 1948-52, 1955-56, and 1960-69.

Eventually she set aside her Maureen Connolly and Jack Kramer rackets, exchanging them for golf clubs. She hasn't done badly on the links either, for she's had seven holes-in-one thus far. A member of the NWTA Tennis Hall of Fame, the MN Tennis Hall of Fame, the MN Sports Hall of Fame, the St. Paul Central High School Hall of Fame, and the Wilson International Tennis Hall of Fame, Arth was also voted one of the Top 50 Minnesota Athletes of the twentieth century by *Sports Illustrated*.

Kurt Bartell
Duluth East, Duluth Marshall

Arguably the most successful of recent Duluth coaches, Bartell has led nine teams to State during his years as coach of the Duluth East Greyhounds and Duluth Marshall Hilltoppers. His 1991, '92, and '93 Class AA East teams and his 1995, '96, '97, 2000, '01, and '03 Class A Duluth Marshall teams advanced to State from Section 7A. Two of these latter teams finished second, the '96 and 2001 squads, and his No. 1 player (Peter Torgrimson) won the Class A singles championship in '02.

A native of Duluth, Bartell began his tennis career as a high school player at Duluth Central, where he played

No. 1 singles his senior year. Current Duluth East boys' coach and former Northfield No. 1 player Mark Welinski remembers Bartell as "a good player who spent a lot of time playing at the Longview Tennis Club in the summers."

After graduating from Central in 1982, he journeyed "south" to attend college at Gustavus, where he played (and lettered) for coach Steve Wilkinson's teams for four years. At Gustavus he played many varsity matches, but he was not in the top six singles or top three doubles for the conference tournament or NCAA nationals. Bartell remembers battling current Gustie women's coach Jon Carlson for the No. 6 spot his junior year.

A 1986 Gustavus graduate, Bartell credits Wilkinson "as a significant mentor in my development of coaching and teaching skills," for in addition to playing for Wilkinson, Bartell taught in the Tennis and Life program during the summers of 1983 and '84.

In addition to the aforementioned successful teams he led, Bartell coached numerous other state individual entrants, including 1992 Class AA third-place singles winner Erik Donley of Duluth East, '94 fourth-place Class A singles finisher George Grombacher of Duluth Marshall, and '97 third-place Class A doubles medalists Tom Valentini and Duane Johnson of Marshall. He is particularly pleased that nineteen of his players have gone on to play college tennis. Also a girls' coach for thirteen years (now retired from that post at Marshall), Bartell reflected on his successful career: "I never would have been able to foresee that I would enjoy being so involved in this life sport thirty years after becoming a player."

For his efforts as the coach of Duluth Marshall, Bartell was voted the 2005 Class A Boys' Tennis Coach of the Year by his peers.

Paul Bouchard
Greenway of Coleraine, Brooklyn Center

For a profile of Bouchard, coach of the surprising 1961 Greenway champions and the first tennis coach at the new Brooklyn Center High school, see Chapter Eight.

Merle Bryan
Simley

One of the best coaches in the south Metro area, Simley's Merle Bryan was another of those excellent athletes who took up tennis later in life and became not only a skilled player but a very successful tennis coach. Here's how he described that transformation: "I got started playing tennis at age thirty-five when my daughter's friend asked her to go out for middle school tennis. I went out and hit with her and had a great time; and soon the family was hooked." This initial introduction to the world of tennis led him to a job as the boys' coach (and later girls coach) at Simley and a summer avocation as an adult tournament player.

In his twelve years as the boys' coach (from 1979-90), his teams were always competitive, in part because Bryan prepared them well in practice. He taught them to be aggressive (just as he was when he played doubles) and tried to prepare them for competition by putting them in difficult, simulated match-play situations. For example, he said, "I had them play challenge matches—allowing only one serve, tiebreakers for challenge matches, and tiebreakers in which they used the other player's racket and were allowed only one serve."

Bryan loved coaching tennis for many reasons, but one in particular stood out. Said he, "One of the most unique and valuable things about tennis is that it is self-officiated. Players have to learn to call their own matches, and a high percentage of the time it works quite well."

Though his teams did not advance to the State Tournament, they lost 3-2 to powerhouse Austin in the 1982 region finals the year the Packers blitzed everyone at State, his Missota Conference teams won four conference championships, and he coached many fine players, such as Bill Brown and Joel Atkins. He also coached the Simley Spartans girls' teams for fifteen years (from 1980-94).

A 1960 graduate of Buffalo Lake High School, where he played basketball and ran track, Bryan went to Mankato State to get his degree in physical education. At Mankato State he continued to participate in track as a middle distance runner. After he graduated in 1964, he took a job at Hudson, WI, for two years, then moved to Simley where he taught and coached for thirty-three more years.

As a largely self-taught tennis player, Bryan

distinguished himself in doubles, earning No. 1 Northern Section rankings in the 35s, 45s, and 55s with partner John King, But he was also a capable singles player who earned one No. 1 ranking (in the 50s). Now living "down south—mostly in Arizona"—for five or six months in the winter, the "semi-retired" Bryan still keeps his hand in tennis. He works in the St. Paul Urban Tennis Program in the summer and helps as a volunteer coach at Simley and at Lake Havasu, AZ, in the winter. And he continues to play on USTA teams in Minnesota and Arizona.

Bryan takes pride in having coached his two daughters, both of whom played college tennis; and now he enjoys watching the next generation (his grandkids) play.

Tom Byrne
Owatonna

Amor vincit omnes! This Latin phrase meaning "love conquers all" could very well have been one used by tennis coach Tom Byrne to rally his troops to win games "at love," for he was a longtime Latin (and Spanish) teacher at Owatonna High School. Aside from the fact that he may have been the only Latin teacher who coached tennis in Minnesota, Byrne's tennis story is very much like that of so many in the early years of high school tennis in the state. He was a baseball player on high school, college, semipro, and army teams (in Hawaii in 1944-45); so, when hired in the fall of 1952, he wanted to coach that sport. However, there were no openings for baseball coaches, so the principal said, "Do you want to coach tennis or golf?" Byrne said he would try tennis, not knowing what he was getting into. This was the first year Owatonna fielded a team, and there was only one rundown court in town and often, Byrne said, "We had to use the two courts at nearby Pillsbury College for practice." In addition, only eight players came out for the team and Byrne was not paid that first year. And from his second to sixth years he received a salary of just $100 per annum. New practice facilities were added in 1958—when two courts were added at Dartts Park—and in '66, when four courts were finally built at the high school.

Though his teams never advanced to the State Tournament during his lengthy coaching career (1953-79), the Indians (now the Huskies) were usually competitive and won one Big Nine title. Led by Dan Halvorsen, Owatonna edged out Mankato East in 1969. Byrne called this win "my biggest thrill as a tennis coach." Halvorsen, arguably Owatonna's best tennis player, also took third in the state singles tournament that year after finishing fourth in '68 as a junior. One of Byrne's doubles teams also did well at State, the team of Jim Colton and John Wandus, fifth-place finishers in 1962. In addition, Pat O'Brien won the Big 9 tournament one year and Craig Halvorsen (Dan's younger brother) was a top player in the early '70s. Wayzata coach Roger Lipelt also played for Byrne. In his twenty-seven years at Owatonna, Byrne's teams won 135 matches and lost 74.

Born and raised in Dubuque, IA, Byrne played basketball and baseball at St. Columbkill High School (there was no tennis team). A shortstop and captain of the baseball team his senior year, Byrne described himself as "a fast runner." After he graduated from high school he played second base on semi-pro baseball teams in Dubuque, IA; Illinois; and Wisconsin and was once offered a pro contract. But Pearl Harbor intervened and altered that plan. Byrne served his country during WWII, then studied foreign languages in college. With an MA in Latin and a minor in Spanish, he taught both of those languages in high school

He retired from teaching in 1984 and was succeeded by Ron Phillips, who coached many strong teams—one of which (the 1987 squad) advanced to the State Tournament. When Phillips took over in 1980, Owatonna had an indoor tennis center with six courts and a total of twenty-six courts in the community—quite a contrast to that humble beginning in 1953, Byrne's first year of coaching. Now coached by former player Curt Matejcek, Owatonna tennis has flourished in part because players have access to winter court time and good coaching at the indoor tennis center under coaches such as Paul Jenkins—a former Northfield player, Tom Van Deinse, and Kevin Rust—who served for a short time between 2005 and 2006.

At eighty-five-years-young, Byrne continues to play doubles one day a week. This father of five daughters and grandfather of ten is proud of the fact that he taught tennis for almost thirty years and played a major role in the development of tennis in the town in which he has lived since 1952.

John Carlson
Litchfield

One of the most successful Class A tennis coaches, Carlson has led the Litchfield Dragons for twenty years. During this time the Dragons have advanced to State from Section 6A a remarkable thirteen times (eleven in a row through the 2007 season), winning the title in 1989. In addition, two of his doubles teams won championships (Tom Fenton/ Dave Huhner in 1989 and Alex Carlson/Chris Patton in 2000). Carlson is especially proud of his son Alex, whom he called "the best player that I coached in high school." He recalls that Alex and Patton won that 2000 final by a double bagel score, and he wonders if anyone has ever won by a 6-0, 6-0 score in the finals. (For more on Carlson and his two doubles titlists, see Chapter Six.)

For someone who did not grow up playing tennis (the six foot five Carlson was a football, basketball, and track star at Litchfield High School and a basketball player at St. Cloud State U), he has taken to tennis like a woodpecker to suet. Now a physical education teacher at Litchfield High School and Middle School, he learned the game when he worked at the Augusta Health and Racket Club in St. Cloud, initially assisting the pros. He then coached St. Cloud to a North Central Conference tennis title in 1986 before taking the job at Litchfield in the fall of '86. Carlson, whose coaching record is a sparkling 277-91 through the 2006 season, was honored by his peers as MN Class A Tennis Coach of the Year in '97.

One final interesting note is that another son (also named John), who played tennis, basketball, and football at Litchfield, was a starting end at Notre Dame and a finalist for the John Mackey Award for tight ends. He was also an academic All-American. John Carlson not only coached his son in tennis, but he also served as his coach in football. John, Jr., by the way, played on five of his father's state tournament teams (from 1999-2003).

Mike Cartwright
Mounds View

"The family that plays together stays together." This popular saying aptly describes the Mounds View tennis teams coached by Mike Cartwright. Mounds View tennis is truly a family affair in which siblings all want to be a part of the Mustangs' tennis "household." In 2005-06, for example, an incredible eleven out of twelve members of the rosters for the state tournament boys' and girls' teams were siblings of former or current players. Over the years there have been two Martin, two McCoy, three Olson, and three Torres boys; three Hickman girls; and a Vayghan boy and

John Carlson (Left) 1989 State Class A Champions

girl, to name a few. This could very well be a state record for a school's boys and girls programs.

The head of this family tennis program is Cartwright, himself a product of a tennis-playing family, who began hitting balls around on the court with his father, brother, sister, and grandfather as a junior high student. Thus inspired, he tried out for the tennis team at St. Anthony High School and played three years on the varsity, holding down a No. 1 doubles position his senior year. He also played football and basketball in high school. After graduation in 1978, he attended the U of M to major in physics. And while he did not play varsity tennis there, he participated in intramural sports—including tennis.

Then, after further study to receive his teacher certification at the U of M, Cartwright returned to St. Anthony to coach the boys' team at his alma mater. After five years there, he taught and coached boys' tennis for two years in Hawaii before accepting a job at Mounds View.

Luckily, he inherited a strong program which had been very successful under previous coaches Jon Staton and Richard Oxley. Under Staton Mounds View made three trips to State (1987, '88, and '89), finishing third in '87 and runnerup to Edina in '88. Oxley led the Mustangs to their first state title in 1990. And since Cartwright took over in the spring of '91 (taking the next year off to teach in Hawaii again), the Mounds View boys have advanced to State seven times (1998, '99, 2002, '03, '04, '05, and '06), winning Class AA championships in 2004 and '05. In addition, his girls' teams have done very well, advancing to State ten times and finishing second behind Edina in 2002 and '03.

From the beginning of the 2003 season until the semis of the State Tournament in 2006, the Mustangs' boys' teams won an extraordinary sixty-five matches in a row. Cartwright, who's not normally given to superstition, said of that semifinal loss to Rochester Mayo: "We were going for our sixty-sixth win on June 6, 2006, and we were ahead in all the doubles when the bubble came down at 98th Street and delayed play. Then we lost." Since True Team play began in 1973, this three-year streak is exceeded only by Edina's sixty-nine straight wins in the '60s (and by the Hornets' three championships from 1987-89).

In addition to their success at state, Cartwright's boys' teams have dominated the Twin City Suburban and now Suburban East Conferences, winning the last five in a row and a dozen all told. And many of his players have qualified for the individual tournament, one doubles team winning the 2005 title: Nick Crnkovich and Julian Tokarev. Of his other top players, Carl Wahlstrand and David Thawley took third in doubles in 1996, Walhstrand and Will Allen finished fourth in '97, Brody McCoy and Tokarev took third in '04, and Tom Ahlstrom and Andrew Tulloch lost in the doubles final to Mikey Kantar and Sion Wilkins of Minneapolis South in '02. And in '06 David Torres and Tyler Rice also finished as runners-up in the doubles tournament.

And while none of Mounds View's singles players have won a championship, that may soon change, given that sophomore Arya Vayghan finished fourth in the 2005 tournament and ultra-talented seventh grader Wyatt McCoy (son of White Bear Lake pro Brian McCoy) finished second in '06, only the third Minnesota high school player to take second at that age. The others were David Wheaton and D. J. Geatz.

Perhaps it's not surprising that Mounds View's teams and doubles pairs have done better than the singles players, for the family-team emphasis has been preeminent under Cartwright. After his team won the 2004 tournament, Cartwright, in an article by *Star Tribune* writer Jim Paulsen, said of his undefeated charges, "The challenge in high school tennis is to make a team out of an individual sport... The individual [tournament] is just play time" (June 10, 2004).

Under Cartwright the Mustangs' teams have become a family dynasty of over fifty boys and eighty girls; and with JV and B-squad coaches, everyone in the "family" plays competitively at some level. Cartwright's "no cut" policy has not seemed to hurt the Mustangs' prospects for success. Maybe instead it has helped foster that team-family spirit so evident at Mounds View.

Forrest Dahl
Minnehaha Academy
For information about Dahl, see Chapter Eight.

Merle Davey
Rochester

When Rochester began its ascendance as a tennis power in 1950, yet another of those unsung non-playing coaches, Merle Davey, was their leader. Described by 1950-51 doubles champion Henry Dison as "more a faculty advisor who drove us to matches and made the lineups out," Davey taught physics and also served as the head hockey coach for a time. During his lengthy tenure (he coached for many years in the 1940s and '50s), Rochester won five team championships and captured four singles titles (three by Dave Healey) and four doubles championships.

Dison praised him as "a super nice guy." And Healey, who got to know his coach very well—in part because he often babysat for his children—said Davey was "a very composed person who didn't say much." He credited Davey for "having a very calming effect on me."

"It's true," said Healey, "that he knew nothing about the mechanical side of tennis, but he was first-rate from the psychological side. For example, he could watch another player and figure out what you should do to beat him. He understood the needed mental aspects of how to get the best out of you to the fullest." Healey fondly recalls his freshman and sophomore years, when he and Davey traveled alone to the State Tournament. "He [Davey] would take me to the Varsity Café on University Avenue before a match at State. We always had BLT sandwiches and ice tea, then we chatted about my opponent and how I was going to play him."

Healey also remembers Davey as a strong-minded teacher who brooked no nonsense in his physics class, but as a tennis coach Davey recognized that his players knew the game better than he did so he often deferred to them. Said Healey, "He would toss out the balls and say, 'What do you want to work on today?' When we told him, he said, 'Go do it.'"

An Iron Ranger from Eveleth, Davey, now deceased, had more hockey in his blood than tennis; nevertheless, his name will be remembered as the coach of Rochester's first great tennis teams.

Ernie DeSantis
Minnetonka

One of the pioneer Lake Conference coaches, DeSantis coached some of Minnesota's top players during his nine years at the helm of the Skippers (1957-65). These included Dave Yorks, Brian Mahin, Tom Boice, Bill Crozier, Gary Peterson, Brian Stamp, and Dick Humleker. As high school players, none won state singles titles, but Peterson finished third in the 1959 tourney, Stamp second in '60, and Humleker fourth in '67 and '68. In doubles Crozier and Jim Bartsch finished third in '61, Crozier and Boyce took second in '62, and Mahin and Yorks came in second in '64. Finally, in '65, a DeSantis-coached pair won a state doubles title, as Mahin and Yorks upended the Daugherty brothers from Rochester.

Mahin recalls his years of playing for DeSantis with fondness. He said about their travels to meets that "we never took the same road twice with Ernie and he would say things such as 'Am I still in Kansas'?" Always looking for ways to motivate his charges, DeSantis invented mantras or acronyms such as RKYEOTBAFT. Mahin said that stood for "Relax, keep your eye on the ball and follow through." Mahin's teammate Yorks called DeSantis "a great philosopher-tennis coach who drove us around and told us about life."

Hired to teach English at 'Tonka, DeSantis had no tennis background. According to Peterson, after DeSantis signed his contract and was walking out the door, the superintendent told him he was the new tennis coach. DeSantis told his new boss that he knew nothing about tennis, but the superintendent replied, "Buy a book." DeSantis did and he became, as Peterson said, "a strategist and master of the mental game." Peterson also noted that "he was a philosopher who told you about life, often saying things like 'the measure of a man was the ability to adjust' [in tennis that meant adjusting to the wind, different styles of play, etc.]."

Though he quit coaching many years ago and has been dead for several years, he made a lasting impact on his players. Future Minnetonka boys' coach Gary Peterson said of DeSantis, "He was like a second father to me, especially after my dad died when I was in junior high school."

Geoff Docken
Hutchinson

With assistance from Brett Rasmussen, his only JV coach, Geoff Docken served as head coach of the Hutchinson Tigers from 1984-2004. Following in the footsteps of coaches Bernie Schepers (who inaugurated the Hutchinson tennis program in 1962), Jerry Carlson, and Bill Cauchy, Docken inherited a strong program that had seen teams advance to State in 1980-82 under Cauchy.

During Docken's tenure, "Hutch" continued its excellent tennis play, winning eight conference championships, making fifteen section final appearances, and winning seven Section 2 championships. In a fourteen-year period from 1986-99 the Tigers advanced to State seven times. At State the Tigers best finish was fourth in '88, and Docken also coached three singles qualifiers and eleven doubles teams for state competition. One of these doubles teams, coach Docken's son Jon and Dan Carlson, won the '90 Class AA title.

In addition to these two players, Docken coached other excellent performers such as Luke Wendlandt, Matt Jensen, the Remucal brothers (Jon and David), another son (Marc), and six-year letterwinner Sean McGraw. McGraw, son of Ron McGraw—a great tennis booster and founder of the Hutchinson Tennis Association—advanced to State twice in singles. Docken's son Jon also earned six varsity letters and, as with Carlson, made four State appearances. Overall Docken's teams won 199 dual meets and lost only 81 (a 71 percent winning record). And his teams also had a 114-31 record in the conference (an 80 percent winning mark). In 1989 he was voted MN Class AA Boys' Tennis Coach of the Year.

Another of a veritable legion of coaches who did not play tennis in high school or college, Docken instead played football and hockey at Grand Forks Central, ND, High School. He did not play sports in college (at the U of ND at Grand Forks), instead choosing to focus on his studies in industrial arts education. Docken then spent two years teaching at his hometown high school and came to Hutchinson in 1972 to teach industrial arts and to serve as an assistant coach under Bill Cauchy. (For more on Docken and his 1990 doubles champions, see Chapter Six.)

Loren Dunham
Fairmont

Truly a man of many parts, Fairmont's Loren Dunham was something of a vagabond in his early years who literally traveled with the railroad. His father's occupation as a telegraph operator for the Soo Line Railroad necessitated moving with the job, so Dunham was born in Thief River Falls, MN; began his schooling at Flaxton, ND; then attended high school in Belgrade, MN.

One part (or role) he played in high school was athlete, for he participated in four sports: football, basketball, baseball, and track. But he also played the part of worker, serving as a relief telegraph operator during the summers of his college years. "I earned my scholarship money from this job," and, he added, "since telegraph service has gone the way of the dodo bird, I may be the youngest living telegraph operator." Finally, he did not neglect his studies and so also played the part of scholar, a part he has continued to play well in his teaching career.

Like so many tennis coaches of his generation, Loren began his tennis career as a neophyte. He started playing tennis as a hobby, so when he took the boys' tennis coaching job at Fairmont in 1976, he knew very little about how to coach the sport. However, he said, "I always felt I understood kids and I went to the places where I could learn the game such as Steve Wilkinson's Tennis and Life camps and Nick Bollettieri's Tennis Academy" [which he attended on two occasions]. In addition, he accelerated his learning curve by reading tennis books and magazines, playing in some local tournaments, organizing and running these local tournaments, and attending tennis tournaments such as Wimbledon. He learned from fellow coaches as well by attending spring coaches clinics. Soon he became involved in the MN Boys' Tennis Coaches' Association and eventually served a term as president (1995-96).

All these efforts paid good dividends, for in his twenty-three years at the helm of the Fairmont boys' teams Dunham's Cardinals won 239 matches and lost just 136. And during a superb stretch in which Fairmont advanced to State in Class A three straight times (1990, '91, and '92), the Cardinals finished third each of those years. In addition, in '90 No. 1 player Joel Sagedahl finished fourth in the singles tournament and Dunham's No. 1 doubles team of Brad Hested and Cory Kallheim took second in doubles. Hested's and Kallheim's story is almost a Ripley's "Believe It or Not" tale, for they lost just three matches all year and all were to the same Blue Earth pair that beat them in the state final (Layne McCleary and Eric Lawatsch). Including team tournaments and post-season play, those three outstanding teams compiled records of 20-1 in '90, 20-2 in '91, and 20-4 in '92.

It's tempting for coaches to boast about their won-lost records, but Dunham did not. Rather, he tried to de-emphasize winning: "I tried never to ask, 'Are you winning?'" In fact, the one time he slipped up and asked one of his players if he was winning, the wise-beyond-his-years lad replied, "Not yet." In keeping with this civilized attitude, Dunham also said, "I never cut kids and we always gave B-squad players a chance to play."

When asked about favorite memories, he mentioned just one winning match, his first at Fairmont: "We were 0-5 and we beat Wells the same day my adopted son arrived. On the way home the engine in our van blew up and we were stranded in Blue Earth." Another highlight was the thrill of coaching his sons Jon and Mike, one of whom (Mike) played doubles in the state team tournament.

Dunham also coached the girls' tennis team for five years in the 1990s, leading them to State three times; but coaching in both tennis seasons got to be a bit much so he began to phase out of coaching. Thus, in '96 he dropped the girls' position, then retired from the boys' job in '98. And though retired from coaching, he continued to play the part of scholar. He taught upper level social studies and International Baccalaureate history classes; and he coached the Knowledge Bowl team since 1999, taking his new "team" to State each year. He also specialized in economics teaching, and in 2002, under his direction, Fairmont won its only national championship—an Economics Challenge title.

After earning a BA in history from Augsburg in 1967 and a master's in teaching from Oberlin in Ohio in '68, Dunham came right to Fairmont for his first (and what proved to be only) teaching job in the fall of '68. Almost forty years later he's ready to retire; but because he still loves "to be with kids," he plans to work with the Knowledge Bowl program as a volunteer and to run a fall invitational girls' tennis tournament named after him. Called the "Dunham Doubles Tournament," it features round robin flight play in which the four schools entered accumulate points based on games won in each match. Though aching knees keep him from competing, this tournament keeps him connected to the sport he has given so much of his life to.

Mike Geffre
Crookston

A tennis hot spot it's not, yet the northwest corner of Minnesota has produced some excellent tennis teams the past thirty years. For example, Thief River Falls, under Hall of Fame coach Whitey Olson, made it to State four times during the late 1970s; and Joe Joerger's Staples-Motley boys won two Class A titles (in '90, '91), both times defeating Metro power Orono in the finals. In addition, Wadena finished second twice (in '81, '82) and in '92 East Grand Forks also took second.

But perhaps the most remarkable tennis story from this remote corner of the state is that of the Crookston Pirates and their coach, Mike Geffre. Ten times in a span of fifteen years this Section 8 team made the 287-mile trip to the Twin Cities to play in the State Tournament (1988, '93, '94, '95, '96, '97, '98, 2000, '01, and '03). In 1995, '96, and '98 they finished third and in '94 they finished second behind powerhouse Blake. This is an even more remarkable story when one considers the relative isolation of this Red River Valley town of 8,500 people. And though there are indoor courts at Grand Forks, ND (forty-five minutes away), for the most part the Crookston lads have to hone their games during the summer. Furthermore, if they want to play tournaments, most of the time they have to travel to Moorhead (seventy miles away) or the Twin Cities to get good competition.

So what's the "X factor" here, the reason why Crookston has been so successful? Of course good players are needed, but in this case a good deal of the credit should go to coach Mike Geffre. Geffre admits that when he began coaching at Crookston in the spring of 1986, "There was a strong tradition of tennis here and I inherited dedicated kids." In fact, his first year the team was undefeated until it lost 4-1 in the section finals to St. Cloud Tech in the last year of one-class competition.

Nevertheless, there were a few obstacles to overcome, and one was that the tennis program had been in a revolving-door coaching cycle in which there were five different coaches in five years. In addition, that first year only ten players in grades 7-12 came out for tennis. Third, Geffre had little tennis background himself, having only played recreationally with friends in high school; so he had to learn fast. That he did, reading books, attending clinics, and, in his words, "learning the most from other coaches such as Whitey Olson and Terry Paukert (of East Grand Forks)."

Soon, however, he was at the head of the class of coaches in his section, taking the Pirates to State nearly every year and coaching many outstanding individuals and doubles teams, including two-time Class A doubles champions Troy Kleven and Jake Olson (1996-97). (For more on Kleven and Olson, see Chapter Six.) With a policy of not cutting players, Geffre said, "We get the competitive tennis player but we also get the social tennis player." He says his aim is to "keep it fun" and help his kids become better players and better persons. To focus on the latter goal, he encourages them to establish priorities: a spiritual life, family, and school coming before tennis. The results are impressive, for nearly every year the Pirates have been in the hunt for a section title and now Geffre has over forty kids coming out for tennis and both a junior high and JV coach.

He is proudest of the fact that "we've had some incredible wins as a team—the team is our No. 1 priority." He cites Chris Martin, the first Crookston tennis player to accumulate over 100 wins, as an example. Martin, who went on to play at St. Olaf College, "actually got us into State on a couple of occasions by beating top players such as Chris McDonald of East Grand Forks and George Grombacher of Duluth Marshall, players he then lost to in individual competition."

Another tennis coach who played other sports as a youngster, Geffre played baseball and basketball—his first love—and ran track at Mound-Westonka High School, graduating in 1976. From Mound he went to Bemidji State College to major in industrial arts education and to play basketball (for just one year). After graduating in December '82, he moved to the Twin Cities to do substitute teaching in the spring of '83, then took a teaching and basketball coaching job at Midway, ND, for one year. When he came to Crookston in the fall of '85, he was asked if he'd be interested in coaching tennis and he said yes.

So he coached the boys' team for twenty-one years, but he served as the girls' coach for eighteen years as well. He led the girls' teams to State seven times and coached 1997 doubles champions Liz Ames and Katie Hunt. In addition, he coached his daughter Amanda, Crookston's No. 1 singles player and a three-time section doubles champion. Geffre was also voted Class A Boys' Coach of the Year in 1993.

Geffre's a relatively young man who's still teaching industrial arts (now industrial tech) at Crookston, and he hopes to coach boys' tennis for a number of years more.

Tom Gillman
Red Wing

It certainly had not been 500 years, but for Red Wing it must have seemed almost that long since they had fielded competitive tennis teams. So when the Wingers, like the mythical bird the phoenix, rose up from its own ashes in the 1990s, it was a slow and sometimes painful process. Luckily for Red Wing, a young man from Edina came to this charming river town to oversee the Wingers' stunning resurrection.

His name was Tom Gillman, and when he took the coaching job in 1991, he inherited a program that had been struggling since the mid-70s. Coached by Jerry Childs in the early '70s, Red Wing fielded strong teams featuring players such as Scott Berg, Bob Behrens, Phil Duff, and the Fleming brothers (Stan and Bob). But from about '75 on, Red Wing tennis hit rock bottom. For example, I recall many matches in which the Northfield team I coached defeated the Wingers with lineups made up of several JV players and just a few varsity performers.

But under Gillman the Wingers soon became competitive and then became an elite team. This was Gillman's first high school coaching job, and he said about his opportunity, "It was a great way to start a career; we literally had to start from the ground up." Gillman's good friend Randy Anderson (an Austin high school standout and former women's coach at St. Bens, men's and women's coach at Carleton College, and boys' and girls' coach at New Prague High School) concurred with Gillman's assessment: "He was a grass roots coach who built the program from the ground up." At first, Gillman said, "There was such a fear factor when I came there—the kids didn't want to look dumb; they just wanted to know that someone would help them."

So, he observed, "I had to convince kids we could do it. At first we set short-term goals such as being competitive, staying in the match for more than forty minutes. By year three or four we started seeing results." These results were extraordinary, for in his eleven years at the helm (1991-2001), Gillman led the Wingers to State four times, including runner-up finishes in 1998 and 2000 (both times behind Edina). In addition, his teams won eight Missota Conference championships; and many of his individual players qualified for State from Section 1, including doubles runners-up Cam Goetz and C. J. Peterson in '99 and Goetz and Adam Witt in 2000. Paul Riedner and Jason Fregien also took fourth in doubles in '95 and Jesse Plote and Peterson finished third in '98, the year Gillman was voted MN Class AA Boys' Tennis Coach of the Year.

Not bad for a program that had been smoldering in ashes for so long, and Gillman has to be credited for helping the Wingers rise up. He started a summer tennis program in 1991 (one he still runs), sought out good athletes for his team, encouraged his lads to play summer tournaments, and essentially shepherded them as a herdsman tends his flock. Randy Anderson said, "The bottom line is that he cared about his players, some of whom were at-risk kids."

A 1980 graduate of Breck High School, Gillman played varsity tennis for the Mustangs for five years, holding down the No. 1 singles spot his senior year. His final year he and Mark Elert became the first Breck boys to qualify for State. From Breck he went to college at Stout State in Wisconsin, where he also played tennis (mostly at No. 2 singles with an occasional match at No. 1) on a strong team ranked No. 10 in the nation his senior year.

With a degree in hotel and restaurant management (he graduated in 1985), Gillman took a job with the Marriott Hotel chain in Charlotte, NC, for two years before getting his teaching certification at the U of WI-River Falls in physical education. While at River Falls he served as an assistant tennis coach for four years, then took a job as a substitute teacher at Red Wing in '91.

After leaving his post as Red Wing boys' coach in 2001, Gillman took the head men's and women's tennis coaching jobs at the U of WI-Eau Claire. He also resumed coaching the Red Wing girls' team in 2000 (a position he had held earlier) and has especially enjoyed coaching his daughters Lindsay (an '06 graduate) and Katie, a ninth grader who is the Wingers' current No. 1 player. Finally, he's pursuing graduate school studies while continuing to coach girls' tennis at Red Wing and men's tennis at Eau Claire.

Dave Gunderson
Virginia

A fixture in the tennis programs in this Iron Range town for over twenty years, Dave Gunderson has been instrumental in developing both the girls' and boys' tennis teams there. But it is his support for and efforts on behalf of the building of a new tennis center in Virginia (including an indoor facility with four courts) that he will also be remembered for. This facility will enhance the prospects for success of northern Minnesota youngsters for miles around and it will be a huge shot in the arm for community tennis in Virginia. Dave modestly credits others for doing the lion's share of work in bringing these courts to Virginia: Jim and Bob Prittinen, Eveleth coach Tom Prosen, Renee Galaski, and major contributor George Erickson—son of former coach Emil.

Gunderson, another coach who did not play high school tennis (though he played at Mesabi Community College), began coaching at Gilbert in 1984. He then came to Virginia in '85 where, with the exception of one year off to complete his master's, he has coached the girls' varsity program. And he presently coaches the boys' team as well, after previously coaching in that program for seventeen years off and on (as head coach from 1985-90 and 1995-98). Through the 2003 season his girls' and boys' teams have won 418 matches and lost just 122, so for his efforts he was voted the Class A Girls' Coach of the Year that year.

He says the greatest accomplishment of his career was coaching the 1989 girls' team that won the Class A tournament. But Gunderson has also coached some successful individual state performers such as Anne Lundberg and Julie Tomazin (runners-up in the '89 Class A doubles tournament and third place finishers in '90 and '91) and Tracy Erickson (second in the '90 Class A singles tournament). Gunderson said, "I credit much of the success of the Blue Devils to the dedicated people of the community. The school, businesses, parents, and volunteer coaches [such as dentist and some-time coach Jim Prittinen] enable the Virginia High School program to be successful."

Gunderson has also done yeoman service on behalf of the Coaches Association—he is in charge of the Class A state rankings and the Hall of Fame program.

Curtis Hatfield
Long Prairie/Grey Eagle

Coach of 2000 Class A singles champion Tony Larson, Curtis Hatfield has had a long run as the coach of the Long Prairie/Grey Eagle Thunder, heading up the boys' tennis program since 1978. In addition, he started up the girls' tennis program at nearby Swanville in '93 and coached there for twelve years; and he also assisted his wife (the Long Prairie girls' coach) for ten years in the late 1970s and early '80s. During his time as the assistant girls' coach at Long Prairie he helped coach Leslie Jacobson, a four-time state singles entrant whose only losses her sophomore and junior years were to four-time Class A singles champion Kira Gregerson of SPA. Jacobson was also at that time the only girls' high school player to make it to the semis in the singles tournament as a seventh grader.

Though none of Hatfield's boys' teams advanced to State, he coached several individual state entries, most notably Larson, who made five appearances, winning the title in 2000 after finishing third the year before. In addition, in 1989 the duo of Steve Rist and Bill Schleter finished second in the Class A doubles tournament, and

the next year Jay Monson and Brian Krousey took fourth in doubles. Schleter also made an appearance in singles in '87, becoming the first of Hatfield's players to make it to State.

Growing up in southwest Minnesota, Hatfield played four years of tennis at Mankato Wilson High School—mostly at third singles, then attended Mankato State U (MSU). With no tennis playing on his college agenda, he concentrated on earning a teaching degree with a math major, then continued on to earn a master's at MSU. In 1975 he accepted his first teaching job (at Lake Crystal), then came to Long Prairie in '77 where he still teaches math and computer science at the high school.

During his years as the boys' tennis coach, he also served as a section tournament director for four years and was privileged to coach his son and two daughters (one of whom made it to State twice, once in singles and once in doubles).

Dick Heunisch
Burnsville

Another pioneer who inaugurated his school's tennis program, Dick Heunisch began coaching at Burnsville High School in the spring of 1968 with a squad of seven players, just enough for a varsity team. Ruefully, he recalls that the school's best tennis player, NWTA Hall of Famer Wendell Ottum's oldest son, opted to play baseball.

Heunisch had been hired right out of college (in the fall of 1967) to teach social studies and to be an assistant hockey coach (he was a hockey standout at Hamline), but it was in tennis that he made his coaching reputation in Burnsville. That first spring he said there were no courts at the high school, so his lads practiced on the four new courts at Metcalf Junior High School.

Heunisch would lead the Braves from 1968-91, coaching two teams (1979, '89) and several singles players and doubles teams into the State Tournament. His best players were Rich Lacher and Doug Elsaas (who finished second in the doubles in '80), Stefan Kruger (a Swedish foreign exchange student who now runs a tennis club in Copenhagen, Denmark), his son Peter (a former No. 1 player at Mankato State U), and Jim Stahley (a small-college all-American at Swarthmore and probably Heunisch's best player). Elsaas played Division 1 tennis at Nebraska and is now a teaching pro in Minneapolis.

Heunisch played varsity tennis in high school for three years, holding down the No. 3 singles spot as a senior on the 1961 Bob Gustafson-led St. Paul Wilson team that finished third in the State that year. Playing with a TAD Davis racket his older brother bought him for babysitting his kids, Heunisch "tried to figure out how to play by watching '61 champion and future Hamline star Gustafson."

A jovial, good-natured guy, Heunisch said the best thing about high school tennis is that it's "kind of like organized play—a little bit of instruction, a bus to get kids to the matches, a place to play, and free balls." One of his players said he came out for tennis because "he just wanted to hit balls indoors for free in the first two weeks of the season."

Now retired, Heunisch often played tennis on the courts at the Burnsville Racket Club, engaged in some friendly doubles, often with his son, Peter, as his partner or opponent.

Jerry Hutchinson
Pipestone

Very likely the only Minnesota tennis coach who was a Golden Gloves boxing champion in high school (he was a bantamweight), Jerry Hutchinson of Pipestone brought the same toughness needed to survive in the ring to his tennis coaching. He was firm in enforcing discipline, even once suspending his star player, Jeff Stueven, for three matches for breaking team rules. Hutchinson's son Barry, while acknowledging that his father/coach could be pretty hard on his players at times, also said about him, "Kids really respected him and liked him. He was a real person, and many of his players still stay in touch with him." As for that incident with Stueven, Hutchinson said, "It never affected our relationship in the future."

So what do we know about the background of this old-school, tough-guy coach who retired in 2003 after twenty-one years at the helm of the Arrows boys' tennis team? Jerry grew up in Madison, SD, just forty-five miles from the place he would later call home for over thirty years,

Pipestone. There was no tennis in Madison, so, as mentioned earlier, he donned boxing gloves instead. A 1962 graduate of that high school, he joined the Navy for a four-year hitch before enrolling at Dakota State U in Madison. He graduated from Dakota State in '71 with an elementary education degree, then moved east to Pipestone, taking a job at Brown Elementary School, where he taught fifth- and sixth-grade classes.

During his first year in Pipestone he began playing tennis with a friend and some of his future players—including Dean Niehus—at a local park. At that time he had no thoughts about coaching tennis; in fact, in 1972 he coached junior high football and track. Then, in one of those accidents of fate, he traded his junior high track job for the head tennis job "with a guy who was hired to coach tennis." That "guy" was Don Helmstetter, ironically a future principal at the school which became the "bete noir" of Pipestone and all southern Minnesota tennis teams, Blue Earth. Said Hutchinson, "Tennis paid more so I gave him the difference he was going to get." He also noted that he knew very little about tennis and the first match he coached in the spring of 1974 was "the first I'd ever seen."

Despite this uncommon start to his tennis-coaching career, Hutchinson was able, according to his son Barry, "to get a lot of real good athletes to come out for tennis." These included Barry, with Kris Kluis a fourth-place finisher in the 1987 Class A tournament and a three-year No. 1 player for the Arrows; the aforementioned Niehus, who led Pipestone to the state tourney in '75; Stueven and John Chesier, runners-up in the '79 Class A doubles tournament; Stueven and Brad Sorenson, the '80 Class A doubles champions; and Sorenson, third place in Class A singles in '81. (For more on Sorenson and Stueven, see Chapter Six.)

In addition to the successes of these players (and others who made it to State but were not as successful), Hutchinson coached two state tournament teams, one in 1975 before two-class play was instituted, and one in Class A in 2003. Though his first fourteen teams never had a losing season, they could not get by powerhouse Blue Earth. For example, said Hutchinson, "Five times we were undefeated going into subsection play, but Blue Earth beat us every time. In 1981 we only lost two individual matches all year but Blue Earth beat us 3-2 in the finals of the region." He also noted that he coached thirteen Southwest Conference championship teams. And when he dropped the boys' coaching job for nine years (from 1988-96), Pipestone only had one winning season. For his successful 1981 season, he was voted MN State Boys' Tennis Coach of the Year.

All of this was in spite of the fact that the high school courts were so bad, according to Barry Hutchinson, "that we only played ten matches at home during my six years (1982-87); so we called ourselves the 'Road Warriors.'" However, Barry recalls all those road trips with great fondness: "He [Jerry] would drive the van and we talked about everything. You were close to your coach." This comment would no doubt please Jerry, for he considered himself "a player's coach" who, though also satisfied with his players' on-court achievements, was more proud of coaching a future doctor, architect, nuclear engineer, or priest.

Though he no longer engages in combat in the ring or on the court, he keeps active by doing some hunting and trapshooting near his Lake Madison, SD, home. In addition, though he retired in 2003 as the Pipestone boys' tennis coach, fourteen years as the girls' coach, and thirty-three years as an elementary teacher, he occasionally does some substitute teaching in the spring.

Joe Joerger
Staples/Motley

For a few brief but shining moments Staples-Motley and coach Joe Joerger were on top of the Minnesota Class A high school tennis world. During this six-year run his Cardinals advanced to State three times and won two team titles (in 1990 and '91), and to top it off, his son David captured the Class A singles championship and Mark Haglin and David Cizek won the doubles title in '92. In addition, Joerger's '87 Cardinals took fourth in the team tournament, David Joerger finished second in the '91 singles tournament and third in the '89 doubles tournament (with Greg Borstad), and Matt Peterson and Tim Goeden took second in the '91 doubles tourney.

And though these were the halcyon years for coach Joerger's teams, he also led Staples-Motley into the 1979

tournament and coached other state individual entrants such as his son Blaine, who earned a second-place doubles medal with teammate Mike Rollins in '95, and the 2001 fourth-place doubles team of Bob Anglin and Luke Grandlund.

Such coaching success was a bit surprising for a man who, by his own admission, was more in love with basketball. Joerger grew up in Henning, a west central Minnesota town that made a splash on the basketball scene in 1964 and '65. Joerger was a sub on those teams, and he continued to play basketball at Bemidji State College, albeit in an intramural setting. At Bemidji he majored in business and accounting and also picked up his coaching certification, with a goal of some day coaching basketball.

Joerger began his teaching career at Staples in 1970, first as an intern in a Bemidji State cadet teaching program; but he took over for his cooperating teacher after just six months and has taught his entire career at Staples. He also made good on that promise to coach basketball, serving as the boys' ninth-grade and B-squad coach for many years and as the girls' head coach for fourteen years. In addition, he donned his zebra shirt and refereed basketball for a number of years.

So while basketball continued to be a big part of his life, tennis gradually inveigled its way into his schedule. He recalls that Tom Wolhowe, a physical education teacher and the Staples' girls' tennis coach, "got me into the game." He added, "I started doing about everything wrong in the game. Whether it was the grip, stroking the ball, or getting into the right place, I was really a spectacle of what not to do. I could run down just about any ball hit my way but sure didn't know what to do with it next." But through the patient teaching of Wolhowe, and after spending "lots of time on ball machines, doing drop hits, and going to camps," Joerger said his game got better.

After agreeing to help Wolhowe teach summer recreation tennis, he began to learn how to coach. Because his children were moving through the elementary tennis program and because the boys' program had experienced a revolving-door coaching situation for years, Joerger agreed to take over the reins in 1976 (he had been serving as an assistant baseball coach in the spring). So he continued to learn by hooking up with people like Bruce

Boland of Brainerd [now the U of VA coach] and by "working the camp scene at St. Bens with Jerry [Sales] and the St. Cloud Tech crew. They always had 'Johnny Bread' as a treat for meals—one of those unpaid benefits." In addition, Joerger said, "I went to camps at Gustavus and took some lessons as well." He held on to the tennis job until 1993, dropped out of tennis coaching for a time, then served as head coach one more year, retiring from boys' coaching in '97.

He counts these years in tennis as some of the best in his career, speaking fondly of the many young men he coached, and remembering as well "the fine people you meet like Reg Mead and Sales who helped our kids a lot, too." Of course he also enjoyed coaching three of his sons in both tennis and basketball, and he's proud of the fact that all four of his boys and his one daughter played sports. Joerger said about his coaching, "I never really talked about wins and losses, believing that if you take care of the little things and concentrate, the big things will take care of themselves.

Joerger lives in nearby Henning (his hometown), but he is still teaching in Staples. A jack-of-all-trades, he teaches business and economics classes, operates a school bank, and does some online teaching. And he says he's going to get back into playing tennis, in a senior league in Alexandria. (For more on Joerger, see Chapter Ten.)

Jane Kjos
Benson

One of the most successful (and perhaps longest-serving) of all the women who have coached boys' teams in Minnesota is Benson's Jane Kjos. In her twenty years at the helm the Braves advanced to State four times (1992, '93, '95, 2000), and three of her players nearly won singles championships: Jon Koenigs finished runner-up to Blake's Robert Keith in '93, Ben Jacobson took third in '94, and foreign exchange student David Breyel lost to Grady Newman of Blake in the 2003 final.

One of her other thrills was coaching her son Andrew for five years. He and partner Jon Koenigs qualified for State in doubles in 1991 but lost in three sets in the first round. Another of her players who qualified for State in singles was Steve Wolf, a five-time All-conference player who played four years at St. Johns and later became a USPTA pro.

Kjos is justifiably proud of all her tennis "boys," many of whom have become coaches, including Wolf and Koenigs, a Gustavus grad who is now a teaching pro in Minneapolis. She has been recognized twice by her peers as Class A MN Boys' Tennis Coach of the Year (in 1996 and 2000), and her award in '96 was the first for a woman coaching boys in Minnesota. Kjos also served as president of the MN Boys' Tennis Coaches Association in 1996-97. No doubt her good relations with fellow male coaches earned her the votes needed to become president, for she said, "All the men coaches were nice to me. Some who stand out are John Eberhart, Gordy Kasal, George Beske, Dave Peterman, John Howard, John Carlson, Jolly Carlson (deceased), Joe Timmins, Hal Miller, to name a few."

Competing against strong area teams such as New London-Spicer and Litchfield, Kjos's teams nevertheless did well, winning two conference championships and four section titles. Now retired from coaching, she finished her career with 233 wins and 133 losses. She also coached the girls' team for several years and had the pleasure of seeing her daughter, Heidi, who played No. 1 singles for two years, make it to State in singles in 1987. She counts as one memorable moment the first time her boys' team qualified for State (in '92). Said Kjos, "I now know what it feels like to have a cooler of cold water thrown over my head. It was so surprising, but wonderful."

Though she did not have an opportunity to play tennis in her hometown of Hanley Falls, she began playing when she was married and living in Hutchinson. While there she took some tennis workshops at Carleton College in Northfield. These workshops were led by NWTA Hall of Fame member and legendary Carleton coach Pat Lamb. Kjos said of these experiences, "Pat Lamb was the most influential person and teacher I know. She is my mentor and idol, and I tried to pattern my coaching style after her." That style included "teaching skills, respect for the opponent, and most of all having fun." These workshops, and the support of her two tennis-playing children, inspired her to accept the boys' coaching job at Benson.

In fact, it was Heidi who encouraged her mother to apply for the job.

And while it was sometimes challenging to coach boys ("they always have to wrestle with each other"), she liked coaching them "because they are competitive, work hard in practice, deal with problems openly, and get over them quickly."

She is justly proud of her two children as well. Her son is the superintendent at the Trump International Golf Club in West Palm Beach, FL, and has a little boy; so Kjos is especially enjoying her new role as grandmother. Daughter Heidi is a major in the air force and a flight surgeon who recently spent four months in Iraq. Both continue to play recreational tennis.

Roger Lipelt
Wayzata

Dubbed "an awesome coach" by rival Lake Conference coach Rich Strohkirch of Eden Prairie, Roger Lipelt of Wayzata earned such praise by virtue of his mentoring of young athletes in four sports. After graduating from Hamline in 1965 with a political science/history major, he took a job as a social studies teacher and assistant basketball coach at West Concord, MN. Following a six-year stint at West Concord, he returned to his high school alma mater (Owatonna) to serve as an assistant coach in wrestling and football for one year. Then he moved west to Worthington, where he became the head coach in both football and tennis. During his five years at Worthington (1972-77), his tennis teams were often No. 2 in the region and he harbored visions of defeating Hal Schroeder's Blue Earth juggernaut. Alas, it was not to be, for those were Blue Earth's glory years.

In the fall of 1977 Lipelt moved north to take a job as the head football and assistant wrestling coach at Wayzata, and in '80 the boys' tennis job opened up. But when offered the position Lipelt told his athletic director, "I can't do wrestling and tennis both." The athletic director replied, "Pick one, then," so Lipelt chose tennis. This decision proved to be fortuitous, for under his direction the Trojans won two state Class AA championships (in '93 and '99) and finished second in '97, and David Hippee and Andy Calof claimed the '97 doubles title. In addition, Hippee finished second in the 2000 singles tournament and second in the '98 doubles tourney (with Trey Graft),

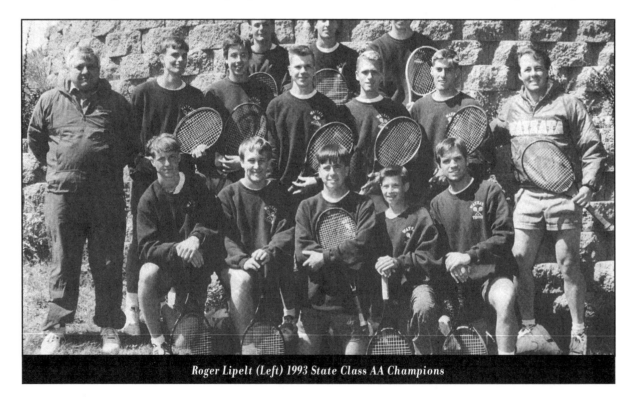

Roger Lipelt (Left) 1993 State Class AA Champions

Graft placed fourth in singles in '99, and several other Wayzata doubles teams acquitted themselves well at State. These included Lipelt's first top finishers, Matt Coyle and Hannus Gradischnig (fourth in '94), Coyle and Cory Ehlen (second in '95), Jon Annett and Mike Lidsky (third in '99), and Albin Hubscher and Amir Mirheyhder (second in 2001).

It is important to note that Wayzata earned its stripes during a decade in which the Lake Conference was loaded with talented teams and players, particularly from Edina and Bloomington Jefferson. Lipelt loved to compete against such teams, saying, "I always thought it was good to be in a region with Edina because it gave us a benchmark. If we could beat them, we knew we could win State." Sure enough, the Trojans' eventually reached this goal. Said Lipelt, "The highlight of those years was the first time we beat Edina in the region finals in 1993 (4-3) after we lost to them twice that year."

A modest man, Lipelt is quick to credit others for the success of his teams and players. "I was very lucky to get great assistant tennis coaches such as Bob Madson [who played at the U of M], Joe Nabedrick, and Dan Nabedrick [a former top Minnesota player from Robbinsdale Armstrong and a U of WI star]." In addition, he credits participation in the Stillwater Early Bird Tournament for helping his teams develop. He also jokingly referred to himself as more of a "shrink" than a tennis coach, something that anyone who has coached tennis can relate to.

After retiring from teaching in Wayzata in 1999 (the year he was voted Class AA Boys' Coach of the Year), Lipelt returned to coaching; so for three years he and USPTA pro Howard Johnson (one of David Wheaton's early mentors) directed the Providence Academy team. He also coached football there and taught social studies. As for his old tennis team, he's not worried about it because "it's in the capable hands of Jeff Prondzinski."

And though Lipelt downplays his tennis coaching abilities, he was no stranger to the game. He grew up in Owatonna and played No. 1 singles for coach Tom Byrne his sophomore and junior years; and though he did not play his senior year (1960), he continued to compete in the sport at Hamline, playing mostly doubles. As an adult he said he used to play with Hall of Fame coach Ollie Guest

and he continues to play doubles. Truly an all-around athlete, Lipelt participated in four sports in high school. In addition to tennis, he played guard in basketball and center and linebacker in football. Then in the summer he played baseball. At Hamline he also wrestled for one year and played four years of football, serving as captain his senior year.

Sometimes top athletes aren't able to translate their natural athletic abilities into coaching ability. Not so with Lipelt, for he has been a successful coach wherever he has taught and in whatever sport he has directed. Witness his two tennis titles and several Lake Conference and region football titles. For his success as a football coach he was elected to that sport's Hall of Fame. And after twenty-one years of teaching and coaching at Wayzata—and nearly forty years in the business, he's still going strong.

Dave Loo
Fridley

Dave Loo of Fridley, in the custom of Minnesota tennis coaches who took the job even though they had no tennis experience, symbolizes the tradition of committed, dedicated coaches who settled comfortably into their new roles and ably served the profession for many years. In Dave's case he coached the boys' team at Fridley for thirty years and the girls' team for twelve years (from 1988-99).

After serving as the JV boys' coach for several years, in 1978, the day before the season began, the athletic director introduced Dave to the varsity tennis team with these words: "Coach Loo will be the new head coach for at least this year and then we'll see what happens." Despite what Loo called sarcastically "that real vote of confidence," he seized his opportunity and became a student of the game. He said, "I learned as much as I could from the head coaches I coached against, and soon I began to attend workshops, tennis camps, and coaching meetings."

Like so many who had virtually no previous tennis experience and simply "fell into" coaching tennis, Dave was determined to succeed. And succeed he did, leading two of his teams into the State Tournament (1981, '82) and coaching several individual players into the tourney. For example, Todd Williams took third in singles in '82 and Tim Jachymonski and Jon Dean were a strong doubles team in '85. But Dave's best player was current Edina coach Gary Aasen, who twice advanced to the quarters in singles, where he lost to Alexander Ramsey's Steve Fosdick in '81 and "wunderkind" David Wheaton in '82.

Aasen has the utmost respect for his former coach, saying of him, "Fridley, not exactly being the hotbed of tennis, still had outstanding teams over the years. Somehow Dave seemed able to put together a few seasoned players with some inexperienced players and form a good team. Even without a previous tennis background, Dave Loo excelled in team building and personal motivation of his players."

His hard work produced several conference championships, including one in the Lake Conference in 1979, and an overall record of 261-158. Over the years he made many friendships with his players and considered it a privilege to have been a part of high school tennis during these past thirty years. But he was especially appreciative of the coaches that "came into his life," coaches such as George Beske of Minneapolis South, John Hatch of Blake, Randy Klassen of Elk River, Roger Lipelt of Wayzata, Bob Pivec of Coon Rapids, Ken Peterson of Anoka, and Tom Saterdalen of Bloomington Jefferson. He says there is "a link that ran through all of us and it was that we (1) took the game and competition seriously, (2) were devoted and dedicated to the game and our players, (3) respected the rules and taught the best ethics, (4) gave a good part of our educational careers for the promotion of high school tennis, and (5) coached life lessons to our players."

A 1967 graduate of Hibbing High School, Loo attended Hibbing Junior College for two years and then graduated from the U of M-Duluth (UMD) in '71 with a BA in language arts and a coaching certification. His athletic background included participation in track in high school and football at Hibbing Junior College. At UMD Loo played only recreational golf and tennis.

He came to Fridley in 1971 and taught English for twenty-eight years, then spent the last six years of his career as a high school counselor. In the coaching realm he also served as an assistant hockey coach for nine years and head coach for three years. And in addition to his BA, Dave also earned two master's degrees, one in counseling from St. Thomas and one in education from the U of M.

Curtis Martin
Minneapolis Washburn

One of the early pioneers who coached during the heyday of Twin Cities tennis, Curtis Martin led the Washburn Millers to four "unofficial" team state championships (1938, '44, '45, '47, and coached doubles champions Jim Hickey-Ed Struble ('38) and John Dunnigan-Jack Clements ('44). In addition, he coached Dunnigan ('44), Brad Pitney ('45), and Pudge Whitcomb ('47) to singles titles.

While it is difficult to track down records from this era, Washburn yearbooks show that Martin coached from at least 1938-47. His last state champion player, Whitcomb, said that though Martin didn't play tennis, he was "a terrific coach who would go the extra mile for this players." Noting that he was also an excellent tactician who knew how to help you win, Whitcomb recalls a city championship match he was playing on clay at Dunning Field with a St. Paul Humboldt player named Gerberding. "I'm down 4-1 in the first set," said Whitcomb, "and Martin, dressed in his usual suit and tie [which he also wore at practice], came over and said three words to me—'Get to net.' I then won that set 6-4 and took the second 6-2." After the match Martin told Whitcomb, "I've watched you play and when you go to the net you step into the ball and force your opponent."

A math teacher and later a principal, Martin was a very competitive guy who had what Whitcomb called "an analytical mind." He was, after all, a math teacher, so he was able to analyze his own players' games and assess the weaknesses of Washburn's opponents, according to Whitcomb. An active and healthy man, Martin could be seen walking around Lake Nokomis right up to the time he died at age ninety-one.

Greg Mathews
Litchfield

Also mentioned in the chapter about girls playing on boys' teams (he was the coach when Jody Nolen played on his boys' team in 1973), Greg Mathews coached some very strong Litchfield teams in the '70s, teams that unfortunately had to compete in the same region as the Lake Conference schools during the days of single-class play. In

'74, for example, his Litchfield team lost 3-2 in the region to state champion Minnetonka, which won all three of its matches at State by 5-0 scores.

Quite often during his eleven years as coach the Dragons were highly ranked, and he coached some top players such as Billy Nolen (Jody's brother), Steve Lundberg, Chuck Felling, and Steve Gabrielson.

A baseball player at Henry Sibley High School, Mathews took the tennis job at Litchfield because it was the only coaching vacancy in the fall of 1969. He decided to try it because he had played some recreational tennis in high school and could compete fairly well with a friend who was on the varsity team. Eventually Mathews also coached junior high football for five years, spent three years as an assistant wrestling coach, and served as the varsity softball coach for seventeen years.

Mathews said that he began running a summer recreation tennis program in 1973, partly, as he said, "to embellish the existing boys' program." During this time some parents of girls who had taken those summer lessons persuaded him to take the job as girls' coach, which he did in '79. So for eighteen years he coached girls' tennis, taking five teams to State and coaching one Class A singles champion (Allison Kramer) and two doubles champions (Tammy Ackerman-Sue Swanson in '86 and T. J. Satterlee-Amber Benson in '93). In addition, he had the pleasure of coaching his three daughters.

An innovator who may have been one of the first Minnesota coaches to recognize the potential of the two-handed backhand, Mathews taught nearly every kid in his summer program to use this stroke. Another of his innovations was an exchange program he inaugurated with coach George Beske and his Minneapolis South girls' tennis team. One year the Litchfield girls played a match at South and stayed overnight with their players and the next year South came to Litchfield. This was a program that continued for a number of years and Mathews called it "a terrific learning experience for his players" and "a country mouse-city mouse exchange" in which his girls (one of whom had never been to the Twin Cities before) and the urban girls had a chance to see how the other lived.

But getting back to boys' tennis, Mathews was a proponent of playing everyone on the team; consequently, he often took three or four vans (some driven by parents) to away matches. As a result, more kids got court time and, he said, "the whole mood of the team improved." His boys' teams won several West Central Conference championships during his eleven years.

One interesting footnote, according to Mathews, is that early on his conference employed a unique scoring system to prevent stacking lineups: two points for a first singles win, two for a first doubles win, and one point for all other matches.

Though no longer coaching, Mathews still teaches American and world history at the high school, thirty-nine years after arriving in Litchfield fresh out of Mankato State in the fall of 1968. At Mankato he did not play sports, but he was president of the weightlifting club and active in the student senate.

Joe Michel
Richfield

Another of the pioneer Lake Conference coaches is Richfield's Joe Michel, who often had to toil like an ironworker in a foundry to recruit enough players for his varsity team. In fact, he said that some years "we were fortunate even to have a junior varsity team." Because he did not have great numbers of players on his squads, he never had to cut even one player in his thirty years coaching the Spartans. These were challenging years for the Spartans, in part because they were competing against the best teams in the state, but also because they often had difficulty finding teams that were willing to play them. About this last point Michel said, "That was difficult at times because most teams wanted to play against teams that were better than they were for competitive purposes—we were often not good enough to be sought out for challenge purposes."

He also cited the usual challenges facing Minnesota tennis players and coaches: finding enough courts and court time for early season practice, dealing with the weather (and finding enough brooms to dry the courts), finishing a crowded end-of-season schedule that resulted from rainouts or other bad weather, transporting players to different sites for matches ("most schools did not have enough courts to play a whole team at once or at one site"), trying to decide who to seed for conference and region tournaments, and coping with challenges about players wearing (or not wearing) appropriate school uniforms during matches.

Despite these challenges, Michel truly enjoyed getting "to know another group of young men in a non-classroom environment [he was a science teacher] and challenging them to play the best they can and not get discouraged even when winning was not always possible." And though he never had the opportunity to coach year-round tennis players, he did coach one team that tied for the Lake Conference title with Edina and several players who made it to State in individual competition. His top players were Dale Chapman (who finished third in the 1963 singles tournament), Bill Stark (runner-up to Craig Jones of Edina in '72), and the '60 runner-up doubles team of Mac Lutz and Bruce Youngberg. He also mentioned two other good players he coached: Jay Marsh and Billy Kron. Michel is especially proud of the fact that six of his former players were or are coaching tennis in the area and two (Stark and John Roteman) are professional coaches.

He should be remembered as one of three coaches (John Matlon of Edina and Roger Thompson of St. Louis Park are the others) who helped get what he called "some clout with the MSHSL," in part because they organized the first tennis coaches association in the 1960s.

Though circulation problems prevent him from playing tennis today, he played the game most of his life, including for two years on his high school team in Monrovia, CA, and during his college years at Northwest Nazarene University in Nampa, ID. At Nazarene, though there was no intercollegiate program at the time, he and some friends started a club program so they could play tennis.

Michel retired in 1995 after thirty-seven years of teaching, including three years at U High in Minneapolis.

Hal Miller
Willmar

If you attend a Class A boys' or Class AA girls' state tennis tournament, you can't miss Hal Miller, for he seems to be ubiquitous. You'll see him behind the front desk patiently answering coaches' and players' questions, then you might see him out on the court arbitrating a dispute. And if you have attended the morning coaches/players' pre-match meetings, he'll be there. Also, you'll see him roaming the courts like a hawk looking for prey, only Miller's hawk eyes are scanning the courts, looking for problems or just making sure that everything is going smoothly (he calls this "preventative officiating"). He's there at the Burnsville or 98th Street Racquet Clubs at the first light of dawn and when the last ball has been struck each day.

Miller, a big guy with a big heart, has devoted almost forty years to the sport of tennis in Minnesota, both as a coach and as the face of the Class AA girls' and Class A boys' tournaments for eighteen years. While he is also proud of his years as head coach of both the Willmar boys' and girls' teams, he said about his job as tournament manager, "This is one of my greatest joys—to have seen how the MSHSL and the MN High School Coaches Association have worked together to make the tournament better." In addition, Miller said, "My involvement in the game has given me more than I can repay, so this is a way for me to repay some of my debt to tennis."

An Alexandria native and 1966 graduate, Miller played football and baseball in high school and football for one year at St. Cloud State. After earning his degree

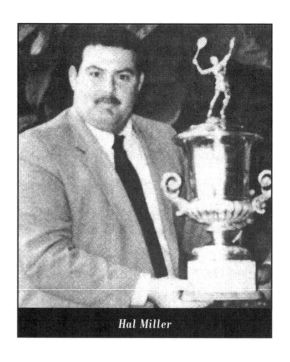

Hal Miller

in physical education and health, he signed a contract to teach and coach at Willmar in 1970. His main coaching responsibility that first year was as an assistant baseball coach, but when asked in '76 if he would like to coach tennis (a sport he had never played), Miller said sure. Thus was born his longtime affiliation with the game he came to love. He began coaching the girls' tennis team that fall, then took over the boys' team from longtime coach Gil Idso in '87 after serving as Idso's assistant for four years. He directed the Cardinals' boys' team for eighteen years.

As the coach of some very successful girls' teams for twenty-eight years, Miller led them to eight state tournament appearances, including a third-place finish in 1981. Twice his girls' teams were undefeated before losing to state powers Edina and Burnsville in the first round at State. And though his boys' teams could not get out of Section 8 (most often St. Cloud Tech cast a long shadow over all of its section competitors), he was privileged to coach outstanding singles player Matt Dawson (fourth place singles finisher in 1987) and two other state entrants (Miguel Busquets in singles in '92 and the '99 doubles team of Kyle Rice and Brian Benson). He is most proud of the fact that there were a number of teams such as Willmar, located as they were in outstate Minnesota, who competed well against teams from all over the state. Miller said, "Even though there were no indoor facilities in our area, there was some pretty good tennis played in our section. We just had to work harder in the summer."

He also counted it a privilege, as did so many coach-fathers, to have coached his two daughters (Jennifer and Patricia) and one son (James). And in addition to his yeoman service as the state tournament manager, Miller served two terms as president of the MN Girls' Tennis Coaches Association (one year as co-president with Cheryl King).

Now he's back home in Alexandria, semi-retired and living as Thoreau did ("in the woods") and working part-time as an adjunct professor at St. Cloud State U, where he supervises student teachers. In addition, he was persuaded to return to coaching and now serves as an assistant coach of both the boys' and girls' teams at Alexandria, enjoying all of the pleasures of coaching without the responsibilities of being in charge of the programs.

Tim Moynihan
Orono

Another successful west suburban area coach is Tim Moynihan from Orono, the coach of two-time Class A singles champion Tim George. Moynihan, who grew up in Edina, played basketball and football for the Hornets, graduating in 1970. In college, at the U of MN-Duluth, he continued to play football and also took up tennis, playing at the club level.

With a degree in elementary education and physical education in hand Moynihan settled in Orono in 1974, taking a job as a sixth-grade teacher at the middle school. Then, in '76, he signed on as the girls' tennis coach. He coached the girls for eighteen years, leading them to eight conference titles. The same year he began coaching girls' tennis, he assumed the post as boys' coach—in the spring of '77. Moynihan in fact inaugurated the boys' program (that first year as a club team), and he would coach boys' tennis until '95. All told he coached Orono high school tennis teams for twenty years.

During his nineteen years as the head boys' coach, the Bears advanced to State two times (in 1990 and '91), finishing runner-up both years to Staples-Motley. In addition, as mentioned earlier, he coached a singles champion (George) and several other players and doubles teams that advanced to State. One of them was foreign exchange student Mark Calander from Sweden, whom Moynihan credits for making the first breakthrough for Orono players (in '88). Thereafter, he said, "we had people in State each year." Another foreign exchange student, Erland Saaxegaard from Norway, finished second behind his teammate George in the '90 singles tournament.

And when Orono competed in the Suburban West Conference, Moynihan's teams won one conference championship, often finishing behind strong Hutchinson teams. Unfortunately, according to Moynihan, when Orono moved to the Tri-Metro Conference, "we could compete with teams like Blake and Breck but we didn't have enough depth in 7-point matches." Nonetheless, the Bears upended Breck "a couple of times" and "we were usually ranked in the top ten in the state in Class A and in the top fifteen in both classes combined," said Moynihan.

Moynihan believed in scheduling elite teams to challenge his players, so Orono always hosted what he called a Lake Minnetonka championship each year which featured four schools: Minnetonka, Wayzata, Mound, and Orono. In addition, he often brought in a northern school from Duluth and a southern school from Rochester for a weekend tournament; and Orono usually hosted the section tournaments as well.

A member of the MN Boys' Tennis Coaches' Association, Moynihan was nominated twice for Class A coach of the year. Though no longer coaching, he still teaches seventh-grade geography at Orono Middle School.

While he is justifiably proud of the accomplishments of his players, Moynihan said that his teams would not have been successful without "the support of many fine families, who often provided several siblings to Orono's teams." And in the broader picture of tennis in the community, Moynihan said, "I'm also proud of the fact that I started the Orono Tennis Association in 1983 and that it's still going."

Finally, young coaches could learn a thing or two about coaching from Moynihan, who felt that "the unwritten rules of tennis that govern a person's behavior are a great help to young people." He liked this aspect of the sport because tennis, like golf, is what he called "the last bastion of unofficiated competition." Accordingly, his motto was always "Let fair play be the way of the day."

Tom Osborn
Mound-Westonka

If dedication to the game of tennis is the first prerequisite for entry into a tennis Valhalla, Tom Osborn of Mound-Westonka would be a shoo in. For since 1981 his goal has been "to get as many young people involved in the great game of tennis that I possibly could." To that end he served as the high school girls' coach from 1981-91 and 1993-97 and the boys' coach from 1983-2006, organized and directed an elementary after-school winter tennis program in Mound for four years, organized and directed USTA-sanctioned tournaments in Mound for ten years, helped organize and direct Tennis and Life Coaching Clinics at Mound-Westonka High School

from 1982-90, directed Metro Alliance Conference tournaments for six years, served a two-year term on the MSHSL Tennis Coaches Advisory Board, and served for two years on the USTA Junior Advisory Council. Of this latter position he said, "I was an advocate for players who wanted to play tournaments but lacked money for private lessons."

The epitome of a player's coach, Osborn vowed early in his career that he would not cut players from his teams. This decision came when he experienced an epiphany after cutting the squad one year when he had fifty players and no assistant coach. He realized that if his goal was to get as many youngsters involved in tennis as he could, cutting players was not the way to accomplish that goal. Once the players came out for tennis, Osborn said he hoped they would "have fun playing the greatest sport on the planet" and that they would "make a commitment to tennis, play with passion, be dedicated, have integrity, and never give up."

And though his teams never made it to State (most often Blake stood in the way), Osborn's boys finished second in the section twice (1997 in Section 5A behind Blake and 2004 behind Waseca in Section 2A). In addition, they won four conference championships (1991, '92, '94, and '96) and several individuals made it to State during his tenure: Justin O'Keefe ('91) and Erik Martin (2001) in singles, and the doubles teams of O'Keefe-Aaron Searl in '92 and Brett Alness-Mitch Turner in '04. In his twenty-three years as the boys' coach the Whitehawks won 191 matches and lost 158. His girls' teams won three conference titles, and his sixteen-year record as the girls' coach was 122-119.

But more important than the wins and losses, said Osborn, has been the opportunity to meet "so many incredible people while playing or coaching tennis." One of these people was Arthur Ashe, a tremendous role model for youngsters who served as a clinician at one of the Tennis and Life Clinics held at Mound. Osborn also said, "Most of my friends are tennis players, and I continue to correspond with many of my former players and to play tennis with a few of them." In addition, his three daughters played tennis for Chaska and he considered that to be "a great family bonding experience."

And all this passion for tennis from a guy who didn't play the game at Minnetonka High School (Osborn was a 1966 graduate) but first learned how to play in a tennis physical education class at Mankato State College taught by the football coach, John Coatta. Osborn had good hand-eye coordination and seemed to do well at the game, so in '69 he took some additional lessons from pro Roger Boyer, then at Mankato. From 1970-72 he served in the navy, and for a time on a destroyer in Vietnam; but while stationed stateside, at Long Beach, CA, he found time to play tennis with a friend every day. After finishing up his military hitch, he came back to Mankato to complete his degree in elementary education and special education, graduating in '74.

Osborn landed his first job in Mound, as a fourth-grade teacher at Hilltop Elementary School, and he spent his entire career in this western Metro suburb. For fourteen of his thirty-two years at Mound he taught special education at the high school, then he returned to Hilltop for his last nine years. Though he retired in 2006, he still keeps busy: coaching the Mound-Westonka seventh- and eighth-grade girls' tennis team, doing volunteer work, and playing tennis four times a week.

He has many special memories from his years of coaching but one stands out. In 1995 he agreed to let his girls shave his head if they won the Maroon division of the Tri-Metro Conference. The Whitehawks won the title so the girls shaved his head after the last match of the year with non-conference foe Chaska, "in front of Mound High School with KARE 11 TV watching." Osborn added, "As it turned out, one of my players, Sarah Peterson, had her last chemo treatment for cancer that same night. Sarah had been an inspiration to the team, coming to most of the matches the last two years [when she was unable to play], even sitting in the car with her mom in inclement weather, wearing a red bandanna to cover her shaved head." As if that emotional drama wasn't enough, this final match with Chaska (won by Mound 4-3) took on added meaning because Osborn's daughter Christina played second doubles for the opposition.

Terry Paukert
East Grand Forks

One of the most prestigious Section awards is one that honors coaches who have "promoted the growth of tennis for juniors and served the junior tennis community in USTA Northern" (*2007 USTA Northern Yearbook*, "2006 Annual Awards"). On occasion this award is also given to a club, so, for example, in 2003 the Rochester Athletic Club was the recipient. However, since it was first established in 1963, it has seldom been awarded to high school coaches. Only Hal Miller, Hal Schroeder, Tom Kotsonas, Jim Prittinen, Kevin Rust, Susan Furtney, Sue Hodgson, and Fred King had won it until 2006 when another very deserving high school coach was so honored.

The winner that year was a coach who has made a huge impact on tennis, particularly in the northwest corner of Minnesota but also in the state, Terry Paukert of East Grand Forks. For twenty years he coached both the boys' and girls' teams there, leading the boys' teams to two Class A state tournament appearances, one in 1989 and one in '92 which produced a runner-up finish. In addition, he coached the '91 Class A doubles champions, J. P. McDonald and Brian Bakke, and the fourth-place doubles finishers in '92 (Tim Gee and Dan Harvey). And though he was not coaching the team in '97, he played a significant role in the development of third-place finisher Chris McDonald, brother of J. P. and a future Division 1 player at the U of WI.

After this stint at East Grand Forks, Paukert then served as an assistant coach at Grand Forks Central, ND, for eight years before returning to East Grand Forks to coach the boys the past three years. For his efforts at East Grand Forks he was honored by his coaching peers as 1992 MN Boys Class A Tennis Coach of the Year.

But Paukert has given of his time in so many other ways as well. For example, he has worked as a volunteer organizer of a summer tennis program for high school kids designed to help them develop skills needed to play high school tennis. Oh, yes, the drills are free of charge so no one is left out. Paukert also strings rackets and gives lessons to local players free of charge. He's a volunteer site director for the Grand Forks Classic Challenger I Junior Tournament as well and is a board member of the local

Community Tennis Association which built the Register Tennis Complex.

In addition, one can't help but be impressed with his generosity, because for most of his efforts on behalf of tennis he has not been paid. And as a coach who never cut a player, I am most impressed with his promotion of a no-cut policy that is gaining momentum among Minnesota high school coaches. According to the *Northern Section 2007 Yearbook*, as of December 31, 2006, 111 coaches had registered through the USTA as a No-Cut program—80 in Minnesota alone.

Steve Paulsen
Edina, Eastview

It must have seemed a bit overwhelming to twenty-five-year-old Steve Paulsen to be handed the daunting task of leading the Edina Hornets' boys' tennis team in the spring of 1988, but he was more than up to the job. For not only was he a teaching pro (then at the Northwest Club in Richfield), but he was a skilled player who could more than hold his own with his top players such as Mike Terwilliger, Scott Sanderson, and Marcelo Borrelli. He had also worked with some of the Edina players at his club, so he knew their abilities. In addition, he had served as the head coach for his alma mater (St. Olaf College) in 1986.

Even so, he could not have dreamed of a better place to coach than Edina, for he inherited an all-star lineup of Terwilliger (a junior) and seniors Mike Husebo, Jason Nasby, Charlie Eifrig, and Peter Erickson. The dream became reality when his first team won the 1988 tournament and, to add whipped cream to the coffee, Nasby and Eifrig won the doubles title. Under Paulsen's leadership, Edina would win two more titles during his six years there. Terwilliger praised Paulsen as a coach who "was consistent in enforcing team rules. There were a few times when he made decisions that involved people sitting out matches and we never felt like he was unfair or played favorites." Terwilliger also said of him, "I only remember him being positive, classy, and never cocky about our team or players—a really nice guy." Another of his players, 1993 singles champion Borrelli, said of Paulsen, "He was a good coach. He always seemed relaxed and he was a good

player—when he played he looked effortless." (For more on Paulsen's Edina teams, see Chapter Nine.)

Paulsen also coached the Eastview boys' team for five years (2000-04), leading them to three Lake Conference championships, but he has made more of a name for himself as the coach of the Edina girls' team—the juggernaut of Minnesota tennis. In his fifteen-year tenure the Edina girls have won eleven state championships (including ten in a row from 1997-2006) and 108 of 109 conference dual meets. Under his direction the Edina girls' team record is 320-9. In addition, he has coached many girls' state champions, including 1971 state doubles champion Ted Taney's daughter Whitney, an extraordinary talent who is arguably the best female high school player in the history of state tennis.

If the reader will forgive me for a bit of boasting here, I was fortunate enough to coach Steve in high school; for he grew up in Northfield and also played his college tennis there, graduating from St. Olaf in 1984 with a degree in math education. As a high school player he finished his career with 86 wins and just 18 losses, advancing to state individual competition three times (twice in doubles and once in singles). His senior year (1980) he lost a three-set match in the quarters to '81 champion Bob Bateman from

Steve Paulsen receiving the Sportsmanship Award

(where else?) Edina. With remarkable hand-eye coordination and great variety in his game, Steve was able to overcome his lack of foot speed to compete at the highest levels. For example, he was a two-time MIAC No. 1 singles champion and Division 3 All-American at St. Olaf, and for a few years he was one of the top male players in the Northern Section, ranking as high as No. 3 in Men's Open Singles in 1990 and No. 2 in Men's Doubles in 1991-92. For many years he also participated in the Pine Tree Apple Tennis Clinic at the White Bear Racquet Club, playing mixed doubles with a variety of different partners. And in '97 he was a key performer on a Men's 35-and-Over USTA team that won the Intersectional National championship. This was a team made up of Paulsen and several other former Minnesota tennis luminaries such as Greg Wicklund, Fred Budde, Chris Combs, and Glenn Britzius.

As a coach his low-key, even-tempered approach has a calming effect on his players; he's scrupulously honest and fair, and he always gives credit to a worthy opponent. He's still working as a teaching pro and coaching women's league teams and junior development groups. Also, he has presented at MN Tennis Coaches Association clinics and has been a clinician for the USTA at Fort Snelling Tennis and Learning Center. For all his efforts on behalf of high school tennis, in 2005 he was elected MN State High School Girls' Coach of the Year; and in 2007 he was named Girls' Coach of the Year by the National High School Coaches Association. Paulsen is a member of the St. Olaf College Athletic Hall of Fame as well.

Finally, he's married to a Northfield High School graduate, Jody James, sister of former Northfield High School and Gustavus standout Dan James, a White Bear Lake pro and the U.S. National Wheelchair coach and director. Steve and Jody have two daughters, one of whom plays tennis.

Dave Peterman
New London-Spicer

All across the state, often in off-the-beaten-path communities, the efforts of one individual helped put these places on the Minnesota tennis map. One such place is New London, a small west-central town of just over 1,000

inhabitants. For years New London had just one high school, but in 1963 it merged with neighboring Spicer (also with a population of just over 1,000) to become New London-Spicer High School.

That one individual who put the Wildcats' boys' tennis team on the map was Dave Peterman, a former high school basketball and football player at tiny Villard High School and basketball player at Bethel College. After graduating from Bethel in 1963 with a social studies major, Peterman took a job at Balaton, where he stayed for four years. Then, in '67, he came to New London to teach social studies and driver's education.

According to Peterman, there were no public tennis courts in town and no school team; so after he began to play some tennis in the mid-1970s on private courts at Green Lake near Spicer—with some high school players from Willmar—he got fired up about tennis. Soon he painted lines for three tennis courts on the elementary school playground and began giving lessons in the community education program in the summer of '75. He says he basically learned the game by playing, particularly with his pastor friend Ron Burke, a former college tennis player at Augsburg.

Next, he obtained a federal grant to build four courts (two at New London and two at Spicer), then took over as coach of the newly constituted boys' and girls' tennis teams in 1979. Peterman said he tried to get a head start for that first spring season of boys' tennis by taking prospective players to the former Willmar Community College courts to play twice a week in the spring of '78. Good results came immediately in '79, for his boys' team had a winning record; and by the mid-80s Peterman had built New London-Spicer into a Class A power that was the envy of many of its Section 6 opponents. Moreover, his teams gained respect from the Metro powerhouses as well. In fact, said Peterman, "We played Blake when Erik [Nelson—'87 Class A singles champion] was No. 1 and Andrew [Fernelius—'89 champion] was No. 2 and gave them good battles. As a result we were invited to Blake to play them during the season." He recalls that "we developed quite a good relationship with them and they also came to our place for an early-bird tournament." He also recalls that Blake always had a great feast for the New London team when we came there as well.

In the years Peterman has coached the boys' team (he "retired" in 1998 and then "unretired in 2003), the Wildcats advanced to State three times (1988, '95, '96), finishing third in '88 and fourth in '96. These were well-earned trips to State, for Peterman's lads always had tough competition, particularly from Litchfield, Staples-Motley, and St. Cloud Cathedral. According to Peterman, during the years that Nelson and Fernelius were on the team, "we never lost a West Central Conference match." During these years he also coached many top players who advanced to State, including the aforementioned Nelson and Fernelius. Others who fared well were the doubles teams of brothers Andrew and Jamy Fernelius (third in '87) and Jamy Fernelius and Jeff Gilson (runners-up in '88). (For more on Erik Nelson and Andrew Fernelius, see Chapter Five.)

Steve Wolf, a former Benson and New London high school player, remembers Peterman as "a very friendly man who always had a kind smile and a laugh to go with it."

Peterman also kept his hand in his first love, basketball, coaching that sport for fourteen years. In addition, he coached the girls' tennis team for twenty years, taking them to State five times. During his career he particularly relished the opportunity to coach his children, daughter Kristin and son Scott, who played six years on varsity and held the No. 1 spot his final three years.

Now retired from teaching social studies, Peterman continues to teach driver's education and coach boys' tennis; and he still finds time to play tennis at least once a week.

Edina in the section tournament and then winning its only state title. And though they finished second in 1976 and '77 in the State Tournament and were always competitive in the Lake Conference, their reign was relatively short.

The Skippers' mentor during these glory years was Gary Peterson, a former Minnetonka star player who returned to coach his alma mater. Peterson grew up playing on a tennis court outside his front door (in a communal neighborhood known as the Groveland Assembly Grounds) with his childhood friends Brian Stamp (1960 state singles runner-up) and Nancy Palm (the No. 1 junior girls' player in the Section). Palm's mother, Agnes "Ace" Palm, taught Peterson to play when he was in third grade, and he became one of the top junior boys in the Section, ranking as high as No. 2. A two-time third-place finisher in the state high school singles tournament (in 1958 and '59), Peterson was an all-around athlete who also played varsity football and basketball at 'Tonka.

It was his ability as a running back in football that helped him garner a scholarship at the U of IA; but he left after one year to join the army during the Berlin Crisis, at the height of the Cold War. After his tour of duty in Germany ended, he came back to complete his college career at St. Cloud State U. At St. Cloud he played No. 1 singles for just one year, winning the Northern Intercollegiate Conference singles title and leading the Huskies to a team championship.

After graduation he took a job at St. Louis Park, but he left after one year to move to Minnetonka. He taught health and physical education for thirty-two years at East Junior High and the high school and coached the high

Gary Peterson
Minnetonka

In our state lakes the muskie is the king fish, with the northern pike playing the role of prince regent. In tennis Edina is the undisputed king, and with such a long reign it's been difficult for other Section 6 teams to knock them out of the water. One team that managed to do so in the 1970s was Minnetonka, the prince regent which took the crown in 1974, beating

Gary Peterson (2nd Row, Center) 1974 State Champions

school tennis team from 1969-86. He also coached basketball, football, and cross country.

Peterson said of his experience as the tennis coach, "I had phenomenal players and I just had to get them to the court on time." While it's true that he had very talented players such as the three Wheaton brothers, Peterson was also an outstanding players' coach who never cut anyone from his squad and tried to find a spot for every player. During his tenure he coached three singles champions (Mark Wheaton in 1975 and '76 and David Wheaton in '84) and two doubles champions (the teams of Mark Wheaton-Roger Jenkins in '74 and Ben Ziegler-Dan Shannon in '79). But he coached many other skilled tennis players as well, including Bob Allen and Steve Nordbye ('71 doubles runners-up), Allyn Dart, Solomon Yohannes, Mark Burton, Bill Sternard, and Mark and Lee Kruger, to name a few.

Gary was a relaxed guy and his players loved playing for him; for example, Mark Wheaton said, "I was thrilled to have Gary as a coach." Mark and others also remembered some of Gary's funny sayings such as "Milk and cookies and be in bed by 10 tonight" or "No staying out with Betty Lou."

He thought it was also important to "give your best effort, be respectful of your opponents, and be proud of the school you play for." He credited assistant coach Tom Kotsonas (1958 state doubles runner-up and for years the Minnetonka girls' coach) for much of the success of his teams, and he took great pride in seeing his teams "come together and reach their full potential."

Ken Peterson
Anoka

While it might be an oxymoron, the term "servant leader" comes to mind when I think of Ken Peterson, the coach of the Anoka boys' tennis team. As the leader (coach) of the Tornadoes for thirty-three years (from 1972-2004), he led his team to twelve championships in the always tough North Suburban Conference, four region titles (with second, third, and fourth place finishes at State), and a record of 420 wins and 170 losses and only one losing season. In addition to these outstanding team records,

many of Ken's individual players qualified for State. And though none won titles, several did well. For example, two of his doubles teams finished fourth: Mike Fichtel and Jeff Scherrer in 1973 and Doug Marker and Bill Ervin in '81. Some of his other top players were Mike Borer, Paul Roback, Chris Janowiec, Mark Carlson, and Matt Jensen, all of whom, according to Peterson, "were top ten players in the state who led as captains and helped us win championships."

But when he is elected to the MN Tennis Coaches Hall of Fame, Peterson will perhaps be remembered most for service to his coaching colleagues and to the players they coached. As a young coach he made an early and favorable impression on his peers, so much so that in just his sixth year of coaching they chose him to serve as president of the MN Tennis Coaches Association for the 1977-78 school year. As president that year and in 1982-83 he worked hard on initiatives such as lengthening the boys' season, creating a consolation tournament, and helping persuade the MSHSL to institute the two-class tournament.

It is fair to say that Peterson has had a hand in most of the major changes in high school tennis over the past

Ken Peterson

thirty years. He, more than any other coach, was responsible for creating the Tennis Coaches Hall of Fame, for he wrote the original proposal and presented it to the membership for approval in 1987. In addition, for ten years he helped coordinate the statewide coaches ranking system and served for many years as the Section 4 rankings representative. Also, for several years he served on the Tennis Coaches Advisory Committee to the MSHSL and for five years on the Tennis Ethics Committee. He helped secure the present ethical lineup system as well, a system that requires coaches to hand in three possible lineups before tournament play begins. Perhaps it was inevitable that he would become an activist on behalf of Minnesota tennis players and coaches, for as a history teacher he was keenly aware of how important it is to help us remember our past.

A native Minnesotan, Peterson came to Anoka with a strong background in tennis. He played at Bloomington Kennedy, under coaches Joe White and Jeanne Arth, serving as captain his senior year (1966). At Kennedy he played No. 3 singles his sophomore and junior years and No. 1 singles as a senior. Then he walked on at the U of M, lettering his junior and senior years and earning a full scholarship those final two years. He remembers winning a key match against Michigan his senior year (1970) and also upsetting one of the top seeds at No. 6 singles in the Big Ten tournament that year. After college he joined the army, where he continued to play tennis, winning the Fort Lee Army Post Tournament in '71. He then served six years in the army reserves.

As a coach Ken stressed the following: (1) make tennis enjoyable and worthwhile for the players; (2) always demand good sportsmanship, integrity, and respect for the game; (3) set high expectations for hard work, effort, and commitment; and (4) never make winning the sole measurement of success. It's not surprising that he also emphasized "keeping your emotions in check in a match," for he was always calm and controlled while coaching.

In practice he worked on basic fundamentals and match-play tactics, encouraging his singles players to become more consistent and to work on placement and the doubles teams to keep their opponents off balance by "changing things up at least once a game if not more."

Despite the occasional run-in with an individual coach, a player "acting up" on the court, or a difficult parent, Ken enjoyed "the wonderful young men who played for me, the many quality coaches I competed against, and watching my program develop into one that was consistently competitive and respected."

And like so many coaches who were privileged to coach their children, Ken is proud of his son Mike, a former star player for neighboring Blaine who "always played with such class on the court." Mike and partner Allen Richels took third in doubles in 1991, and in his senior year Mike won the region singles and advanced to the quarters at State. Speaking of Blaine, it should be noted that Peterson also coached the very successful Bengals' girls' teams for fourteen years, teams which won 210 matches and lost just 70 under his direction. Three of his Blaine teams advanced to State, and he was blessed to coach the five talented Skogerboe sisters and his daughter Amy.

For his leadership of the Anoka boys' team and his service to the tennis coaches association, Ken was twice voted MN Boys' Tennis Coach of the Year (in 1981 and 2004). Peterson retired from teaching and coaching in '04 and resides in Coon Rapids with his wife Cami, and three young children. He played some competitive tennis after college (ranking as high as No. 10 in 35 singles and No. 4 in 35 doubles in '84, for example); and he continues to play some tennis in the winter, but he plays more golf in the summer.

Corey Prondzinski
Henry Sibley

Jeff Prondzinski
Wayzata

Growing up in a family of four boys, I have always been intrigued by sibling rivalries. Did Joe DiMaggio play harder when he and his Yankees tussled with younger brother Dom's Red Sox? Did Gaylord Perry put an extra bit of lather on his spitball when he pitched against brother Jim? Did Tim Gullickson's adrenaline amp up a notch when he saw brother Tom across the net? Does a Barry brother hoist up more three pointers when his brother is guarding him? And do our Minnesota tennis siblings compete a bit harder in practice (or in matches) when they hit against or coach against one another?

I expect that this is likely the case even in the coaching ranks—as the laws of nature and the reality of male testosterone dictate—for when brother coaches compete they want to win just a bit more than they normally do, if for no other reason than to give them bragging rights at family reunions.

Two of the brightest and best young high school boys' tennis coaches in the state happen to be brothers, Corey Prondzinski of Henry Sibley and Jeff Prondzinski of Wayzata. Over the years, and while coaching several different teams, they have locked horns eleven times. Thus far younger brother Jeff has the upper hand in the majority of these encounters. And yes, it's a competitive rivalry; but Jeff insists he has truly enjoyed competing against his brother and that when not playing each other's teams they are big supporters of one another. About their rivalry, he said, "We had a run of several wins in a row, but Sibley got us [Wayzata] this year [2007] 4-3." He also likes to tell the story of one of Corey's other wins, one that required the intercession of prayers on his behalf. It seems that Sister Margarita (their high school religion teacher) prayed for Corey's Austin Pacelli team when they were falling behind Jeff's Mankato Loyola team, and the Pacelli boys then rallied to win every match following Sister's divine intervention.

As mentioned earlier, older brother Corey currently coaches at Henry Sibley. Since taking the reins as the Warriors' boys' coach in 1998, Prondzinski has led his teams to the State Tournament six times (1999, 2000, '02, '04, and '06). In addition, he has coached several singles and doubles teams which have advanced from Section 3AA to State. The best of these performers advanced to the quarterfinals: the doubles team of Clay Sollenberger and Blair Madsen in 2000, Sollenberger in singles in '02, and Phil Haig and Stephen Grundhoefer in doubles in '04. Prondzinski is very excited about the possibilities for 2007 because he has a number of good players returning, including Anders and Chris Halvorsen, sons of former Owatonna and St. Olaf star Dan Halvorsen.

In addition, he will have what he calls his first legitimate top-ten player in seventh grader Matthew Schull, whose father played at the U of M.

A math teacher at the high school, Prondzinski has blended a philosophy of hard work and fun to develop competitive teams in a school that had not had much success since the late 1970s and early '80s, then under coach Elmer Vanderah. Said Prondzinski, "I believe in discipline and hard work; I'm demanding but I also make sure it's fun." One policy he employs is a "one-and-done" rule about drug use, a rule he says he's only had to invoke once. Another key to the success of the Warriors' teams, according to Prondzinski, is strong doubles play. "We've never had a top-ten kid, so we put a lot of emphasis on doubles. We [he and assistant Brian Schway, a former Sibley player] teach a very aggressive style, with lots of drilling, hitting balls to certain spots, and practice in knowing where to go on the court."

And while he is justly proud of the success his teams have had, he's quick to direct praise to his players: "I've had an incredible run of great kids."

Before coming to Henry Sibley, Prondzinski coached the boys' and girls' teams at his alma mater (Winona Cotter), leading both teams to State in 1994. During his time at Cotter (1993-94), he also worked as a USPTA pro. Following his gig at Cotter, and just before coming to Henry Sibley, he coached the boys' and girls' tennis teams (and served as an assistant girls' basketball coach) at Austin Pacelli from 1995-97.

When he was growing up in Winona he played baseball until he enrolled at Cotter in the seventh grade. Since the Ramblers did not field a baseball team, he tried out for the tennis team instead. And even though he'd had no formal tennis lessons (he learned the game by playing on a public court near his home), he became an accomplished player, lettering for six years. His last four years he played behind the very talented Derek Luebbe, the 1989 third-place Class A singles finisher. His senior year ('89) Cotter finished second in the team tournament behind Litchfield and Prondzinski lost to singles champion Drew Fernelius of New London-Spicer in the first round of the individual tourney. Though he was not a ranked NWTA junior player, Prondzinski improved his game by playing "lots of local tournaments in the area [Winona, Rochester, LaCrosse] almost every weekend."

After high school he stayed home to attend college at Winona State U. There he majored in math education but also continued to develop his tennis skills, playing No. 1 singles and doubles all four years. He was the conference singles champion his junior year and qualified for the national NAIA tournament his junior and senior years.

Reflecting on his seminal growing-up years in Winona, Prondzinski said, "I think a lot of my success comes from my parents, especially my dad, a hard-working, blue-collar guy. Even though he didn't play tennis, Dad often shoveled courts so we [he and Jeff] could go hit. Both our parents took us to tournaments as well."

Younger brother Jeff (he's three years behind Corey) also caught the coaching bug and he began his career while still a student at Mankato State U (MSU). Though he was a full-time student and a tennis player at the college, he drove to Winona to serve as an assistant coach (to Corey) in both boys' and girls' tennis in 1994. That year the girls finished as team runner-up (to Orono) at State and the brothers' younger sister Sally was the No. 1 singles player for the Ramblers. Then, with another intervention from a nun (Jeff's former elementary principal, Sister Mary Donald, who put in a good word for him), Jeff acquired the head boys' and girls' coaching positions at Mankato Loyola High School. During his years at Loyola he helped both teams achieve a measure of respectability, but he was most proud of resurrecting the girls' program. After completing his student teaching in Texas in the fall of his fifth year, he then took a full-time position at Loyola in mid-year, teaching and coaching there until 1997.

In the fall of 1997 Jeff also returned to his alma mater, Winona Cotter, to teach and coach the boys' tennis team. During his time at Cotter he led the Ramblers to four straight Class A appearances and its only state championship, in '99. In addition to this title, his teams finished second in '98 (behind Breck) and won consolation trophies in 2000 and '01. About these years Jeff said, "1999 was special because I had been the head tennis pro at the Winona Country Club and had worked with all the kids on the team."

During these years he also coached the girls' teams, but unfortunately they lost to powerhouse Rochester Lourdes each year. His top male players in these years were brothers John and Brian Thomas, who took second in Class A doubles in 2000; Brian Thomas, fourth-place finisher in the '01 singles tourney; Jared Novotny and Tony Rukavina, who also took second in doubles (in '01); and Novotny, fourth place in singles in '02.

In 2003 Jeff, like his brother before him, made the jump to the big school arena, taking the head boys' tennis job at Wayzata. His Trojans' have done very well in the highly competitive Classic Lake Conference, and one of his doubles teams took second at State his first year of coaching (Jon Reed and Jamie Rowland) and another (Ryan Gjoraas and Dan Mendelsohn) took fourth in 2005.

And like his brother, Jeff had no formal tennis instruction but learned to play on local public courts, playing challenge games against older players for court time. He noted that if you lost that challenge game you had to go back to the backboard to practice. Here on these courts and on the backboard he honed his two-handed forehand/backhand game—he claims he was forced into this ambidextrous game because his first wood racket was too heavy. Also like his brother he grew up as a baseball player first and, like Corey, once he got into tennis he played local tournaments in Rochester; LaCrosse, WI; and even Iowa.

No Johnny One-Note, he also played football and basketball in high school; but it was in tennis that he made his mark, lettering five years and moving up the ladder to No. 1 singles his senior year. His sophomore and junior years he played No. 2 behind Tony Baisley. During his years at Cotter his team took second in the 1989 Class A tourney (his freshman year) and they made it to the State Tournament his senior year as well ('92). As an individual he advanced to State in doubles his junior and senior years (first with Jon Schmid and then with Steve Knuesel), but they lost to the eventual champions in the second round both years. He counts as highlights of his years at Cotter the win to get to state over Blue Earth in '89 and the annual battles with Rochester Lourdes.

Even though he was juggling coaching and studying at the time, he was able to continue his tennis career at

MSU, playing No. 1 doubles all four years, Nos. 3 or 4 singles his first two years, and Nos. 1 or 2 singles his junior and senior years. His sophomore year the Mavericks were ranked in the top twenty in Division 2, and his senior year he was a finalist for MSU Male Athlete of the Year. Perhaps more importantly, he was an Academic All-American. Jeff graduated in 1996 with a major in social studies education with a history emphasis.

Now as a coach he said, "I try to make my players understand that tennis is a lifetime sport. But I also emphasize the team aspect of it and let them know it's a special privilege to play for your school or team." He really enjoys working with kids and seeing them improve, taking pleasure in seeing them "beat a kid they thought they couldn't beat." In addition, he said, "I'm big on doubles— I see parallels with basketball strategy. Doubles is more of a thinking man's game." Given the importance of backboard hitting in his life, it's not surprising that he's also a big proponent of the backboard as a learning tool.

Both Corey and Jeff live in the Twin Cities and both teach at their respective high schools. Perhaps we can look forward one day to a higher-stakes matchup between these two young coaches, say a team final at the State Tournament between Henry Sibley and Wayzata. A match such as this would really get their competitive juices flowing.

Katie (Mixon) Queenan
Breck

If you were a fan of girls' tennis in the late 1980s, you probably remember this Breck girl as a player and not as a coach. As Katie Mixon she cavorted on the courts for the Mustangs for six years 1985-90, beginning her career as a No. 3 doubles performer in seventh grade. From that lowly position she vaulted to No. 1 singles as an eighth grader and held down that spot in the Breck lineup throughout her high school career.

Advancing to State in singles her final three years, she lost twice to the eventual Class A singles champions. As a sophomore she lost to Kira Gregerson of SPA in the finals and her junior year she lost to five-time champion Gina Suh, also of SPA. Her senior year she lost in the quarters. On the summer junior circuit she also excelled, achieving

singles rankings of No. 1 in the 10-and-unders, No. 2 in the 12s, No. 5 in the 14s, and No. 6 in the 16s.

Mixon graduated from Breck in 1991, then enrolled at the U of VT. At Vermont she played No. 1 singles— and a variety of doubles positions—all four years. Mixon graduated in '95 with majors in political science and Asian studies.

She married in 1996, and in '98, as Katie Queenan, she took over the head boys' and girls' tennis coaching positions at her alma mater, Breck. During her five-year career as the boys' coach, she led the Mustangs to two state Class A team titles (in 1998 and 2001) and a runner-up finish in '00. In addition, she coached three state individual champions: '98 singles titlist Reven Stephens and doubles winners Jake Brenk and Brandon Fenn in '01 and Alex Clark and Fenn in '02. Her final year as the boys' coach was '02, but she continued as the Breck girls' coach until '04. During three of these years she worked on her master's degree in nutrition at the U of M, completing it in '03, and she also taught an evening course at the U.

While her girls' teams were often strong, none made an appearance at State; but several of Queenan's singles players and doubles teams advanced to the tournament. Overall, she said, "Coaching was fantastic because of the players—not the winning or losing. High school kids are great fun to work with; there is never a dull moment. More importantly, sports and teams can teach great life lessons." She also added, "As a coach I hope I was able to positively enhance the players' self-esteem and give them tools they could use the rest of their lives." She considered the exciting 2001 boys' State Tournament a highlight of her time at Breck.

Queenan's boys' coaching peers honored her by electing her MN Class A Coach of the Year in 2000. She moved to Chicago in 2005, where she works in commercial real estate and plays mother to two young children.

Mike Remington
Rosemount, Eagan

One of the young Turks when he began coaching at Rosemount High School in the spring of 1980, Mike Remington is now one of Minnesota tennis's elder statesmen who has coached for twenty-seven years. During his career he has coached several doubles teams into the State Tournament and, as the Rosemount girls' coach from 1979-90, he coached a top state competitor, Kris Gettler. Gettler finished third three years in a row during the reign of Edina and their three-time singles champion Ginger Helgeson.

He has also served a two-year term as president of the boys' tennis coaches association (1997-99), during which time he inaugurated an "Assistant Coach of the Year" award.

Mike is well known in his hometown of Richfield as well. A graduate of that high school, he played tennis for two years under coach Joe Michel, holding down the No. 3 singles position his junior year and then playing No. 1 singles as a senior. In addition, he taught in and directed a summer tennis program there for twelve years.

In 1979, fresh out of the U of M with a degree in math education, Remington took a teaching job at Rosemount High School. He then succeeded Barry Engrav as the boys' tennis coach in the spring of '80, and he remained at Rosemount until the new District 196 high school, Eagan, held its first classes for students in grades 9-12. The year was 1990, and Remington has been a fixture at Eagan ever since.

During his years in the Apple Valley-Rosemount district, Mike's teams have competed in two conferences (Rosemount in the Missota and Eagan in the Lake), but in all his years they have remained in Region/Section 1 for tournament play. And though he has not yet led a team to State (in 2006 his Eagan boys were undefeated until losing to Rochester Mayo in the Section 1 final), he has coached two Lake Conference championship squads. In addition, he has coached some excellent individual players over the years, including Kyle Freske, Eagan's No. 1 player for two years and a state entrant in doubles. Another good player he mentioned was Matt Kramer, also from Eagan.

One of the nicest guys in the coaching ranks, Mike has built solid tennis programs at Rosemount and Eagan. And while he has laid a good foundation for the coach who succeeds him at Eagan, he will also be remembered for his contributions to boys' tennis as president and as a longtime member of the tennis coaches association. He's still excited about coaching tennis because, he said, "I get a chance to work with great young kids and see how they develop and grow up."

Tom Saterdalen
Bloomington Jefferson

Some readers may be wondering, "Why is Tom Saterdalen included here? Wasn't he a hockey coach?" Indeed he was a hockey coach—and an extraordinarily successful one at that. In a thirty-eight-year career his teams won seven state titles (five at Jefferson and two in Wisconsin), thirteen Lake Conference championships, and fifteen section titles. In addition, seventy-two of his players went on to compete in Division 1 hockey and seven have played in the National Hockey League. And four times he was voted MN High School Hockey Coach of the Year.

But Saterdalen, who grew up in the tennis mecca of Rochester, knew how to wield a racket and to coach tennis as well. A three-sport athlete at Rochester John Marshall (JM), Saterdalen did not play high school tennis in the spring because he roamed the infield for his baseball team. However, he played pick-up tennis with his buddies and, because there was no baseball team at Rochester Community College (which he attended after graduation from JM in 1960), he decided to go out for tennis. During his two years there he held down the No. 6 singles spot, then played Nos. 3 and 1 his last two college years, at Bemidji State. His senior year at Bemidji he was captain of both the tennis and hockey teams, and he graduated in '64 with majors in social studies and physical education.

A bit of a nomad his first nine years of teaching and coaching, Saterdalen spent one year at Cloquet, one year at Bemidji State (as an assistant hockey coach), four years at Superior High School in Wisconsin—teaching physical education and coaching hockey—and three years at the U of M as an assistant hockey coach. Finally, he folded up his tent and moved to Bloomington Jefferson, where he taught and coached from 1973-2002. Though he had been a head boys' tennis coach (at Cloquet in '65), he admits that he didn't know much about coaching tennis when he stepped into the head job at Jefferson in 1980. It was also a challenge for him because, as he said, "I'm an emotional coach and that doesn't help in tennis because you have to

Tom Saterdalen (Left) 1994 State Class AA Champions

keep your emotions under control." And since he had only played an individual sport for a short time—in college, it took him a while to get used to coaching tennis. Eventually he adjusted, making the transition from coaching a team sport (hockey) to coaching the more individual-oriented sport of tennis.

His results during the twenty-three years he led the Jaguars speak for themselves: two state team championships (1994, '96), three section championships, eight Lake Conference championships, three state singles champions (Matt Peplinski in 1995 and '96 and Ryan Edlefsen in '97), two state doubles champions (Aaron Dvorak and Ben Bartels in '93 and Phil Woo and Rory Theis in '98), and an enviable overall won-loss record of 284-102. Most memorable about Jefferson's success is that it was often achieved against the best conference and section competition in the state, with Edina and Wayzata in particular standing in the way. Edina coach Gary Aasen praised Saterdalen, saying that "he always had his teams really prepared to play against us."

Reflecting on his career as a tennis coach, Saterdalen said that he particularly enjoyed hitting with his players: "Many times Jerry Pope [his assistant coach] and I would

stay out and hit with guys until 6:00. We would start practice at 2:30 and go officially until 4:00, but some guys wanted to stay and hit forever." In practice he also said he worked the players hard, believing that quality was more important than quantity. Sometimes, said Saterdalen, "when we had outstanding players, I would have them work out with us only forty-five minutes to an hour, then after conditioning send them in to work with the weaker players."

He also said he spent more of his time coaching the doubles teams, and he was quick to credit local teaching pros who worked with his top players and his longtime assistant coach, Pope. A USTA/Northern Section Hall of Fame member and an outstanding college player from Kentucky, Pope has been for almost forty years one of the top-ranked men's singles and doubles players in the Section, often dominating his age group for the past twenty-five of those years and even winning on the national scene. In part because of Pope's inspiration, Saterdalen began to play the summer circuit in the 1990s, partnering with his assistant coach and earning a ranking as high as No. 2 in the Men's 50-and-Over Doubles in '93. In addition, he and Pope captured 55 Sectional doubles titles in 1992 and '93.

Saterdalen of course counts Jefferson's two state championships as highlights of his tennis-coaching career. But the 1996 one was especially sweet because the Jaguars won it without No. 2 player Dvorak, who had broken his wrist during the section playoffs. In fact, said Saterdalen, "we still made it to State and beat Rochester Mayo 5-2 in the finals after we had only beaten them 4-3 with Aaron [Dvorak] in the lineup during the season."

Another story he recalls again involved Dvorak. Said Saterdalen, "In 1993 Aaron and Ben Bartels qualified for State as the runner-up team in Section 6. Jerry Pope and I played them in practice the day before the tournament and beat them 6-1, 6-3. We didn't think they'd get by the first round if they played like that, but they didn't lose a set at the State Tournament. They were state champs."

This one-time Class AA Tennis Coach of the Year (1994) is now semi-retired. I say semi-retired because he is still busy supervising student teachers for Mankato State U, working at his former hockey school, playing on USTA league teams (one of which, a super seniors team, went to nationals in both 2004 and '05), and doing some consulting work. In addition, he teaches a class for coaches designed to assist them in dealing with the pressures (such as from parents and unhappy players) and difficulties of coaching today. Called "Achieving Peak Performance," it's a college-credit class that also focuses on such things as structuring practices, conducting effective meetings with parents and athletes, and creating an environment to help students deal with both success and failure. It's not surprising that he has become a motivational speaker, for as a coach he was, according to 1997 state singles champion Ryan Edlefsen, "a good motivational guy." Two-time state singles champion Matt Peplinski also remembers Saterdalen as "one of the best coaches I ever had. He showed me how to take tennis and life to a better level." Added Peplinski, "Every time that we went out to play he would say, 'Just go out and have fun, win or lose.'"

Rich Strohkirch
Eden Prairie

Like the fictional character Forrest Gump, played by Tom Hanks in the film by the same name, Rich Strohkirch has been a participant in and a witness to so many important events the past forty years, though for Rich they've been in the smaller Minnesota tennis world. First, at St. Paul Wilson High School, he was a teammate of 1961 state singles champion Bob Gustafson; he played at Hamline with Gustafson and many other well-known Minnesota tennis players and coaches such as John Wirtanen and Jim Miller of Greenway of Coleraine, Roger Lipelt, Tom Hutton of Hopkins, and Charlie Huss of Stillwater; he started the boys' tennis program at Eden Prairie in 1968; he served as president of the MN State High School Tennis Coaches Association for two years (1993-95); he coached teams that successfully competed against powers such as Edina and Bloomington Jefferson and which even defeated Edina two years in a row; and he served for several years on the Tennis Coaches Advisory Board.

Strohkirch's tennis saga began on the public courts of St. Paul, when he first lettered for his St. Paul Wilson High School tennis team as a junior in 1960. He recalls that Gustafson played an important role in his life, first persuading him to try out for the Redmen tennis team and later convincing him to attend Hamline after his graduation in '61. Playing mostly doubles (often with his twin brother, Tom), Strohkirch lettered for two years. A good athlete, Strohkirch also played varsity hockey (he was a wing) and football at Wilson and at Hamline.

And though he described himself as "just an average high school tennis player," he improved greatly at Hamline under coaches Ben Lewis and Lowell Weber, moving up to the No. 4 singles spot on a strong team his senior year. During the three years he lettered in tennis, Hamline won the MIAC team championship each of those years and he had the privilege of once again playing with his brother (at No. 3 doubles). In order to complete his biology major and become certified to teach he stayed for a fifth year at Hamline. This gave him what he called "an awesome opportunity" to coach the tennis team when coach Weber was on leave.

Finally, in 1966 he was hired to teach biology and other subjects at the Eden Prairie Junior/Senior High School, and he continued to teach in Eden Prairie until his retirement in 1998. During his second year of teaching he was given the opportunity to inaugurate the boys' tennis program, and though he knew it would be hard slogging the first few years, he eagerly accepted the challenge. Sure enough, that first year was character building, for the Eagles won just one of ten matches. Strohkirch coached the team until 1975, took a hiatus for six years—when his wife joined the FBI— then returned as head coach in '81. All told he headed the boys' program for thirty years, retiring from coaching tennis after the 2003 season (the year his Nick Edlefsen won the Class AA singles title).

During those thirty years, Strohkirch's teams made four trips to the State Tournament (in 1987, '90, '91, and 2002), finishing second to Edina in 2002 and third in '91, a year in which they defeated Bloomington Jefferson 4-3 in the first round. These were years when the Eagles came out of Section 2, but they were also years when they more than held their own in the Lake Conference. I recall that my 1987 Northfield team lost 6-1 to an Eden Prairie squad that included three Class AA state champions: 1990 singles champion J. P. Demetriou and '87 doubles champions Steve Danielson and Paul Ezerski. Those were Strohkirch's first great players, but they were followed by many more, including future NCAA Division 3 All-American Ryan Haddorf from Gustavus (third-place in the AA '91 singles tournament), Chuck Schultz and Jeff Hahn ('96 doubles champions), and Edlefsen (2003 AA singles champion and two-time third-place singles finisher).

Like so many successful coaches, Strohkirch was quick to credit others for his players' accomplishments. He cited his faithful assistant Bruce Clark, who not only helped him establish systems for working with young people but "did so much for tennis in the Metro area." An accomplished senior player, Clark also helped Chuck Anderson coach the Edina girls' team for a few years and he and his wife Lois even babysat for Edlefsen. Sadly for the tennis community and all who knew him, Bruce passed away in 2006. Another coach who helped Strohkirch when he coached the Eagles' girls' team for ten years was Willmar's Hal Miller. "I learned so much about coaching from Hal—Willmar was the team to beat in our region," said Strohkirch. He also credits Bruce Clark's wife, Lois (for many years a JV and ninth-grade coach), for helping the girls' tennis program grow and succeed.

Still, Strohkirch was also successful because he worked hard, learned quickly, and dedicated himself to his players. About this last point he said, "They were my boys [and girls—he did not have children of his own], and I was there to help them any way I could. I wanted my kids to be competitive, so they always came to play hard and that's all I asked of them."

He was pleased when "my best players really responded to pressure and had an attitude of 'If I lose it's not because I didn't try.'" And because he believed in the power of positive reinforcement, Strohkirch made it a point to never put his players down and to "never focus on bad things." He had a rule that players needed to talk to him after the match and "before they left the site." As for his coaching philosophy, he said he spent more time on the mental aspect of tennis when he came back to coaching in 1981: "Skill with a racket is not the only thing it takes to win a match. It takes mental toughness and an ability to play calmly and without desperation."

After pounding the courts for so many years, including those ten years with girls' teams that advanced to State four times and produced back-to-back doubles winners in 1991-92 (Amy Hanson and Angie Henrikson), Strohkirch has put his rackets in storage. A leg injury forced him to give up the game, but he and his twin brother play golf and this satisfies his competitive urges for now. A one-time MN State High School Class AA Girls' Coach of the Year and two-time Boys' Coach of the Year (1991 and 2003), Strohkirch still resides in the community which became home to him when he left Hamline, Eden Prairie.

Laszlo "Les" Szendrey
Edina

Perhaps the most cosmopolitan of all Minnesota coaches, "Les" Szendrey was born in Hungary; played tennis as a university student in Germany, France, and North Africa; lived in Austria for two years and Italy for five while working at the American Consulate in those countries; and, as an American citizen, led seventeen student tours to Europe. He recalls etching his name on a bench while sitting with his tennis coaches on the banks of the Seine River in Paris and exploring exotic places such as Casablanca when he was a university student.

At one time the No. 6-ranked tennis player in Hungary, Les (the name given to him by American colleagues for who perhaps could not pronounce Laszlo) was an all-around athlete who played soccer and excelled in swimming as well. At the U of Budapest he played No. 1 singles on the tennis team all four years and also participated on the swimming team. As a swimmer he became one of the best at freestyle and breaststroke, ranking second in Hungary in the former event.

But we know him best as John Matlon's capable assistant coach and as the very successful head coach of some of the best Edina teams from 1978-87. (For more about Szendrey's coaching career, see Chapter Nine.) It wasn't easy to follow in the footsteps of John Matlon, but Szendrey handled the transition well. One of his best players, 1981 singles champion Bob Bateman, said of him, "Coach Szendrey followed a legend successfully. He integrated three new guys in his first year on the job [Batemen, two-time singles champion Brian Johnson, and Bob Bordewic]. He coached us to three team championships in my four years [1978-81]. He loved the game and he loved his players. I can't say enough about the man; he was a joy to be around." And while he could be tough when necessary (he suspended Bateman once for misbehavior and another time sent a player home and "told him not to come back until he apologized to the team"), he also believed it was important to have fun on the court. He took pride in developing "lesser-skilled players into competitive performers," and he taught his boys to be good sportsmen and gentlemen. Edina 1989 state singles champion Mike Terwilliger praised his former coach's attitude: "He was positive all the time, always happy and upbeat. He loved tennis, coaching it and watching it."

Another of Szendrey's "boys," two-time state singles champion Paul Odland, also remembers him as a friend: "He was even nice enough to have me over to his house from time to time for Hungarian goulash, a specialty of his wife's." Odland also spoke admiringly about his former coach's "understanding of how to get players focused on the task at hand and putting together the right players for doubles."

Szendrey, who was hired without a teaching degree in 1958 to teach German (he had received grants to study the teaching of German during two summers), also coached soccer at Edina. But he seemed destined to coach tennis; his father belonged to a country club in Budapest and little Les began hitting tennis balls when he was seven. Then he served as a ball boy for the "big boys," one of whom gave him a racket and also hit some balls with him. Finally, his dad bought him a racket and he and his three older brothers learned to play by hitting with each other. This training helped him garner a spot on the university tennis team after he graduated from high school in 1935.

After graduating from Budapest U in 1939, he earned a degree in international law from that university in 1943, then served as an interpreter in German and Italian with British and American forces until the end of WWII. He left home in 1940 when the Russian army occupied Hungary; and he came to the U.S. in '49.

Now over ninety years old, he lives in Edina with his wife, Hildegarde, also from Hungary, content in the knowledge that he made a difference in the lives of many Edina tennis players. He's had a good life here in the U.S., and he credits his skills in language (Hungarian, German, and Italian) for helping him succeed in the many different cultures and countries he's lived in.

Dick Thatcher
Rochester

Though he was known more in Minnesota coaching circles as a Rochester swimming coach, and though he only coached tennis for five years (1963-67), Dick Thatcher presided over one of the greatest tennis programs in state history. In those five years his Rockets won three team championships, and singles players from these teams took home five titles— Chuck Darley won three and Bob Gray and Rob Daugherty won one each. (Daugherty won another in 1968, under coach Terry Strawn.) And maybe Thatcher would have continued as the tennis coach, but in 1968 when the new Mayo High School opened, he moved to Mayo and quit his tennis job. He stayed on as swimming coach, resigning from that post in '83 after coaching many successful boys' teams.

He, too, did not have a tennis background when he took the job in 1963, but his competitive training as an elite swimmer helped in conditioning his tennis players. A '54 graduate of Austin High School, he swam there and was also a three-time all-American butterfly swimmer at the U of OK. He said, "I was a conditioner from my experience as a swimming participant and coach." One of his former tennis players, Bob Gray, said that "he [Thatcher] had some great leadership qualities as a coach." Gray also added that Thatcher was a coach who "was good at relational things, conditioning, and drills. He kept us in shape."

In addition, Gray recalls the time that Thatcher argued with MSHSL officials before the 1963 tournament to keep him (Gray) and Chuck Darley in opposite brackets. This dispute delayed the tournament for two hours, but Thatcher won his argument and Darley and Gray ended up meeting each other in the singles final. Oh, yes; their placement in opposite brackets also enabled the Rockets to win the team title.

Thatcher freely admits that Rochester's Mr. Tennis, Marv Hanenberger, was "my assistant" and that players such as Darley helped the younger kids and even suggested tennis drills he could use. He recalls being asked to put on a tennis clinic during the October MEA break for physical education teachers one year and turning to his players for help. "I talked to Darley and Dave Daugherty [Rob's brother and 1965 doubles runner-up] and they wrote a script for my forty-five-minute presentation," Thatcher said.

Describing his Rochester players as "dedicated and easy to coach," Thatcher noted that many of them were also members of his swimming team. He recalls his first salary being $300, acknowledging what all coaches know so well: "You coached because you enjoyed it, not for the money."

During his five-year tenure, Rochester lost just one dual meet (to Owatonna), so sometimes it was hard to find playing time for all his capable players. In 1963, he recalls, "We had no JV team and the first year we could only play three singles and one doubles in a meet; so sometimes I wouldn't play Chuck [Darley]. Bob [Gray], or Bob and Dave Daugherty." One humorous story Thatcher remembers had to do with the paltry meal money allowance schools were given for state tournament participation. "The night before the tournament we went to a fancy Minneapolis restaurant and blew all our meal money in one night, so we ate the rest of our meals with our own money. I also remember making the players dress in suits and ties."

Now retired from coaching and teaching business education, Thatcher still lives in Rochester and remains active in his business called Thatcher Pools and Spas, which sells swimming pools and spas. (For more on Thatcher and his Rochester teams, see Chapter Nine.)

Roger Thompson
St. Louis Park

Add the name Roger Thompson to the pantheon of eminent coaches in the early years of Lake Conference tennis, for he arrived in 1952 and stayed through the spring of '77. According to Thompson, St. Louis Park had fielded a team since '48 (under the direction of coach Del Daly), but there were only "two miserable courts on the school grounds and we had to use city park courts for practice and meets." So conditions were far from ideal until 1956, when a new high school with six tennis courts was constructed.

Thompson also recalls that there were only seven teams in the original Lake Conference at that time: Bloomington, Deephaven, Edina, Mound, Robbinsdale, St. Louis Park, and U High. Now there are sixteen in two conferences, the "Classic Lake" and "Lake."

During his twenty-five years as Park's coach (with one year off for a sabbatical), Thompson's teams were always competitive but, like most Lake teams, could rarely beat Edina. He will, however, be remembered as the coach of two state champions, singles titlist Carter DeLaittre (1970) and doubles players Bruce Edwards and Marty Lazniarz ('73). In addition, several Thompson-coached players advanced to State, including Dave Atlas and Jeff Carroll, who finished fourth in the '75 doubles tourney, and the unlucky Paul Krause. Krause, the upset winner over Bob Gray in the '64 tournament, was a tough competitor who played in the singles tournament for three years but did not advance to the semis in any of those years.

It is perhaps not well known, but Thompson inaugurated a Saturday invitational tournament (held at St. Louis

Park and Edina) that Park hosted for ten years before he asked Edina to carry it on. That tournament is the prestigious Edina Invitational. In addition, Thompson had what he called "the honor to be the first coach of girls' tennis at Park" (in 1974). His daughter, then a senior, played on the team. He also founded, with Roseville coach Tom Vining, the St. John's U summer tennis camp, and he was instrumental in helping draw up the first constitution of the incipient MN State High School Boys' Tennis Coaches Association.

Unlike many of his 1950s and '60s peers, Roger played tennis as a young man. An all-around athlete who liked most competitive sports, Thompson began playing tennis with neighborhood friends in northeast Minneapolis when he was twelve, then played No. 2 singles on the Edison High School team for two years. He graduated in 1943 and enlisted in the service, and after the war he attended the U of M. He completed his studies in '48 and taught math, science, and physical education in Tri-Mont, MN, from 1948-51. In the fall of '51 he moved to St. Louis Park to teach math and coach tennis. This gentle, soft-spoken man, described by one of his former math colleagues as "a peach of a man," died in 2006.

Milt Verant
Hibbing

Like the triumvirate of Marc Antony, Caesar Octavius, and Lepidus that ruled the Roman Empire after Julius Caesar's death, three teams ruled the world of Section 7 tennis from the beginning of True Team play in 1973 until 2003. Of these three northeastern Minnesota teams, Duluth East won eleven section titles and Virginia seven; but it is Hibbing (home of Bob Dylan, Kevin McHale, and generations of tough iron miners) which ruled this tennis triumvirate for the longest time. From 1974 until 2001 the Bluejackets won thirteen section titles.

At the head of this "scourge of the north" team for most of those years was Milt Verant, a local boy who came back to the Range and served as head coach of the Hibbing (now Hibbing-Chisholm) boys' teams for twenty-five years (1973-74 and 1977-99). Under his direction the Bluejackets won eleven of those thirteen section

championships, finished runner-up four other times, and sent many individuals on to state competition. When his last battle ended, Verant's teams had vanquished 402 foes and lost just 87 contests, an exceptional winning record of 82 percent.

Those who coach the so-called "outstate" schools cannot always measure their success by how well they perform in the State Tournament, for it was very difficult to upend the big dogs from the Metro area. A truer measure of their success is how they stack up against teams in their own section. Though Hibbing never finished higher than fourth in state team play, it often dominated the competition in its section.

Verant's individual competitors invariably exhibited a toughness and competitive spirit that characterized iron mining communities such as Hibbing. Many were excellent hockey players, so they knew how to play as a team and thus Hibbing players had more success in doubles. For example, four of these teams took third at State: Mike McDaniel and Mike Kasner in 1980, Jeff Lipovetz and Mike Vidmar in '84, Paul Wojciak and Marcus Karki in '90, and David Lindstrom and Scott Kolar in '95. In

Milt Verant

addition, Mark Kasner and Robbie Silas finished fourth in '83. Of Verant's singles players, he considered Laddie Gustin to be his best performer. With his "great overall game, good groundstrokes, and a tremendous serve-and-volley game," Gustin took fourth as a sophomore in '73. Vidmar played at Macalester and is now the manager at the Reed-Sweatt Tennis Center (formerly the Nicollet Tennis Center) and the Kasner brothers played at St. Thomas.

In addition to his duties as boys' tennis coach, Verant (who taught math and physical education at the high school and Lincoln Junior High) served as an assistant boys' swimming coach from 1968-81 and also directed the girls' tennis team for eight years (1978-86). And before coming to Hibbing in '68, he coached boys' tennis, gymnastics, and swimming and diving at North Junior High School in St. Cloud from 1966-68.

He says he was introduced to tennis by his older half-brother Vance Stanoff, a U of M physical education major who "helped me learn how to score and taught me a few basics." In high school Verant played tennis for coach Les Stark for two years before he had to work his junior and senior years to help pay for college. He then attended Hibbing Junior College for two years but did not play tennis there because they did not have a team. His last two years (1964-66) he attended Bemidji State College, where he played No. 6 singles on the tennis team.

As a coach Verant worked tirelessly to develop tennis in Hibbing and to help his players improve their competitive skills. For instance, from 1975-2000 he owned and operated a tennis pro shop called Range Tennis Supply, for four years in the late '80s he managed a sports and health club called the Mesaba Athletic Club, and for many years he was a tennis pro/manager in the summer at the Mesaba Country Club in Hibbing. During these summers at the country club he ran numerous USTA tournaments and team tennis programs, and he also instructed at the Lake Hubert Tennis Camps for a number of years. In addition, he served as president of the tennis coaches' association in 1983-84, as an ethics committee member, and as a member of the MSHSL Advisory Committee for Tennis. His coaching colleagues honored him as 1988 MN Class AA Boys' Tennis Coach of the Year for his coaching successes and for his contributions to the association.

All coaches could take a page from Verant's "book on how to coach," memorize it, and then use it in their own programs. For example, he believed in playing everyone: "We had as many as sixty-five boys out for tennis in the 1970s and '80s. Most of the Range teams did not have as many players so I would ask the other teams to play extra sets against our extra players. If one of our extras beat a varsity player from another team, he would earn points toward his letter." In addition, Verant prepared his players by varying practices and using different types of challenges each day. In order to accommodate all sixty-five players on Hibbing's four courts, he often scheduled practices in shifts, sometimes not finishing the last practice until 7:30 PM.

He also lined up competitive matches, often taking trips to the Twin Cities for Saturday tournaments. And he tried to expose the players to top-level tennis, so he took them to Minneapolis to watch the Gophers or pro tennis exhibitions. Finally, during the early season, he videotaped his players twice and critiqued their performance and spent a good deal of time talking about strategy and the mental part of the game.

Like a kid in a candy store, Verant recalls the pleasure he experienced in coaching his two sons, taking overnight trips with his team, eating in restaurants, meeting other teams and coaches, and soaking in the state tournament atmosphere at the 98th Street Racquet Club. Retired from teaching since 2000, Verant enjoys deer and bear hunting with a bow and arrow near his home on Swan Lake near the village of Pengilly.

Tom Vining
Roseville Area, Alexander Ramsey

While his boys' teams did not match the 641 wins earned by Hall of Fame coach Hal Schroeder of Blue Earth, Roseville's Tom Vining may hold a record unmatched in high school tennis history: 1,010 combined coaching victories. An article in *TennisLife* magazine titled "Roseville Coach Tom Vining Retires with More Than 1,000 Wins," said of this accomplishment, "With a won-loss record of 508-224 in boys' tennis and 502-172 in girls' tennis, Tom may be the only coach in Minnesota, and perhaps even in the country, to have won at least 500 matches with each gender" (November/December 2003). Vining retired in 2003 after thirty-five years as a high school English teacher at Brooklyn Center (one year), Alexander Ramsey, and Roseville.

During his years at Alexander Ramsey and Roseville, Vining's teams were always in contention in the highly competitive North Suburban Conference and in Section 3AA. And what seems most remarkable about his success is that without an established tennis program such as those at places like Edina, Vining was successful by beating the bushes for talent, often relying on "a network of teachers and graduates from my tennis program to alert me to any kids with potential." At one time, he said, "I knew of every kid in Roseville who was gifted at tennis by the time he or she was a fifth grader. I'd write their parents and encourage them to get their kids into more advanced lessons. Catching the kids early like that really helped perpetuate our success" (*TennisLife*, November/December 2003). In addition, he and coach Bob Pivec of Coon Rapids (his former college teammate at Mankato State College) organized weekly summer tournaments for northern suburban kids.

After being inspired by Steve Wilkinson's college coach Don Klotz, a clinician at the first Brainerd tennis clinic in 1973, Vining measured out two courts on the gym floor and established the Alexander Ramsey (later Roseville) "Indoor Tennis Club." Open every night from 6:30-10:00, it featured activities for players of all levels—and Vining was there every night and often on Saturday mornings. As a result, his teams did well that same year, with players whom he called "court rats, ... kids who had played some tennis but lacked the typical USTA tournament background you would find at the more elite schools" (*TennisLife*, November/December 2003). These extra efforts produced teams that advanced to State six times (in 1977, '88, '93, '94, '95, '96) and many individuals who qualified for state tournament competition. Of these individuals Vining calls current Moore Lake Club teaching pro Steve Fosdick the best player he coached. Fosdick finished fourth in the '81 tournament and, according to Vining, "was able to hit a swinging backhand overhead both accurately and hard." Another of his top players, Gregg

Cummings, took third in the '95 singles tournament. For his coaching success, Vining was honored as Class AA MN Boys' Tennis Coach of the Year in '95.

And though his boys' teams won six more matches than the girls' teams (508-502), Vining's girls' teams lost fewer matches (172 to the boys 224) and made it to State more often—thirteen times. They also finished runner-up to Bloomington Jefferson in 1995 and two of his singles players took third at State, Betsy Colby and Shari Lagen.

Like many other Minnesota tennis players, Vining credits a sibling for getting him started. Here's how he describes these early experiences with his brother Paul on neighborhood courts in West St. Paul:

We must have been quite a sight. He with his Bancroft racket on one side of the court and I with my Rawlings glove on the other. He'd hit tennis balls, I'd field them on a short hop, pivot, and fire them back so that he could hit each waist high on one bounce... he would remain in the center of the court while I would do the running. I was five years younger so it seemed right. But Paul always brought two rackets—an old Tad Davis was set against a net post. Sooner or later the temptation overwhelmed me and I traded my glove for the racket. My brother taught me how

Tom Vining

to hit tennis balls for two whole summers before we played one single point. Mechanics first, playing second."

With this training under his belt, Vining broke into the doubles lineup at Henry Sibley as a sophomore, then played No. 1 singles his senior year. In college at Mankato State, he played both singles and doubles and served as captain his senior year.

A coach who truly enjoyed "getting to know his players in a non-academic setting" and who enjoyed giving them a chance to see him as something other than "teacher," Vining was a players' mentor who realized that practices didn't have to be boot camps. In fact, he said he prepared his players by keeping practices "short (1.5 hours MAX), easy, and social."

So it was difficult for him when, because there were just seven courts available in Roseville, he had to cut players, particularly those good enough to play on other teams. Another difficult part of the job for Vining was "knowing what to say to a kid who has played his heart out and lost. Sometimes," he said, "I learned it's best not to say anything except 'good match' and give them a handshake." His philosophy was simple: (1) learn the game, (2) play hard, (3) have fun. And he believed you could achieve these goals without swearing at, ridiculing, or shaming players.

Finally, like so many in the profession, he enjoyed getting to know coaches from other schools, sharing what he called "a special bond" with them. That "bond" sometimes began to be forged during his early years of coaching when the U of M hosted a coaches' clinic the first Saturday in March. Said Vining, "It was a good place to bring your schedule book and pick up a half dozen match dates with coaches from other teams."

Still residing in Shoreview, the retired Vining said, "I've traveled, read, wrote, fished, hiked—done anything I've wanted." Well, most anything, for a severe case of tennis elbow and surgeries on both of his feet makes tennis painful for him today. He cited these maladies as one reason he retired from coaching.

Ted Warner
Blake

The hero of Edina's knuckle-cracking 23-22 team championship win over Rochester in 1968, Ted Warner is a successful Twin Cities tennis pro and, since 1995, the head boys' coach at Blake. Almost from birth it seemed that he could not escape his destiny as a tennis player and then coach. His first coach was his mother, Joan, for many years a top women's player in the Section who

Ted Warner (Right) 2002 Class A State Champions

excelled particularly in doubles. In 1961, for example, she and Muriel Cooper were ranked No. 1 in Women's Doubles and she and Cooper also won three national public parks doubles titles. Ted remembers his early tennis days with his mother in these words: "My mom started me at old Nicollet Park. She played at noon while I hit against a huge cement wall at the park, which also had basketball hoops. When my mom was done playing, she hit with me. I remember that my first racket was a reject from Bucky Zimmerman [1963-64 state doubles champion]." Eventually Warner played competitive doubles with his mother, and they earned an NWLTA ranking as high as No. 4 in mixed doubles (in 1971).

In addition to these home-cooked tennis sessions with his mother, Warner sampled tennis meals from other cooks and places. For example, like so many other young Twin Cities area players of his time, he was mentored by head tennis "chef" Norm McDonald. Said Warner, "Norm took an interest in me and asked me if I wanted to play with him. For some time after this he hit with me once a week on court 7 at Nicollet." As a result of this good mentoring, Warner became one of the top junior players in the Section, ranking No. 1 in 12-and-under singles in 1963 and No. 2 in Boys' 16 Singles in 1967 and No. 1 in doubles twice (in '67 with Peter Moose of Wayzata in Boys' 16s and in '69 with Marty Johnson of Brookings, South Dakota, in the Junior Men's 18s). He also played some national tournaments in places like Kalamazoo and St. Louis, often in doubles with Johnson.

And as a member of four exceptional Edina squads (even by their high standards), Warner played on teams which won sixty-nine straight matches and shared or won three state titles (1966-68). Also, in his senior year ('69), the Hornets finished runner-up behind Austin, losing by just one point. A varsity performer all four of those years, Warner played No. 1 singles his senior year and made it to State in singles his final two years. In '68 he won a memorable point, in what he called "the best match I'd played," a 6-1, 6-2 win over Dave Kubes of North St. Paul that gave Edina the team title and which earned him a consolation medal. Then he capped off his high school career with a runner-up finish (behind Tom Brennan) in the singles tournament in '69.

An all-around athlete who also played basketball (on yet another Edina team that won sixty-nine straight games) and baseball until his sophomore year, Warner described his tennis game: "I had a good head, my volleys were strong, and I had a good serve because I played baseball [he was a pitcher]. My groundstrokes were not as good." He remembers in particular his first-round match in the region tournament in 1968 in which he came from 5-2 down in the first set to beat Bill Babcock of Minneapolis Washburn, the No. 2-ranked player in the state that year, "by junking him."

Warner graduated from Edina in 1969 and walked on at the U of M, where he played No. 5 singles and No. 3 doubles for four years under coaches Joe Walsh and John Santrock. Then, after graduating from the U with a major in business in '73, another mentor stepped into his life, this time the legendary Frank Voigt. Though Warner had begun teaching at parks such as Powderhorn and Nicollet, and at the Minneapolis Tennis Club when he was just fourteen years old—after being hired by another of his mentors, Jack Roach—it was Voigt who helped him get a start on a tennis teaching career. Said Warner of this first full-time tennis teaching job, "I got hired in October 1973 by Voigt and Pudge [Miller, who with Voigt opened the Northstar Tennis Center in 1965] to work indoors at Northstar and at Woodhill in the summer." He served as the head pro at Northstar from 1973-87, then moved to the Crosstown Club in '87. In addition to these jobs and his position as the Blake coach, Warner spent twenty-two summers at Woodhill and continues to do some morning teaching at the former Northwest Clubs and in the summer program at Blake.

While he has truly enjoyed his work as a club teaching pro (he is a certified USPTA pro), he has also relished his years as the Blake boys' coach. "It [coaching] has been a good vehicle for helping kids learn about life and teaching them how to believe in themselves," Warner said. He added, "It gives you a chance to talk about things outside of tennis; too many coaches are just feeders or drillers." He enjoys being able to coach during a match as well, something coaches could not do when he played high school tennis.

At Blake he also coached the girls' team for several

years, taking them to State a number of times. His best player was Natalie Newman, two-time state Class A singles champion (in 2003 and '04) and sister of '03 boys' Class A champion Grady. Warner retired from this position after the '05 season, mainly so he could watch his daughter Emily play. The proud father saw Emily help Edina win yet another team championship in 2006 and also capture the doubles title (with Megan Gaard, 2000-01 Class AA singles champion Justin Gaard's sister).

His main day job today, however, is in real estate. He is the owner of a company called Warner Properties which manages eleven apartment buildings. As a spin-off of this work, he also runs Warner Properties and Communications, a firm that delivers satellite TV and internet service to apartments, condos, and health-care centers in the Twin Cities area.

Though he made a conscious decision after graduating from the U that he would focus on coaching tennis and not playing, he was called out of retirement to play on a USTA Over-50 team that won a national championship in 2002. This was a team made up of a Who's Who in Minnesota tennis: Warner, Dave Mathews, Carter DeLaittre, Tim Butorac, Tim Burke, and Dan Halvorsen. (For more on Warner and his Blake teams see Chapter Nine.)

Don Wojciechowski
Spring Lake Park

In many respects the tennis-coaching career of Spring Lake Park's Don Wojciechowski represents that of so many coaches from the late 1960s and early '70s. After all, he launched the school's first tennis program in 1968; he was an athlete but had not grown up with a tennis racket in his hand; he had played (and coached) other sports; he had to struggle like a desperate hiker stuck in quicksand to get his program going; and his teams had to battle much larger schools such as Anoka, Coon Rapids, and Mounds View in a very tough region. In addition, though his Panthers' teams won their fair share of matches, he emphasized playing tennis for the sheer joy of the experience.

Wojciechowski, who came to Spring Lake Park in 1963 after graduating from St. Cloud State with majors in math and physics, discovered that the school was starting a boys' tennis program in the spring of '68. He had taken two tennis classes in college and really enjoyed them, so he applied for the position. Since no one else had expressed an interest in the position, the athletic director gave him the job.

Realizing early on that he may have taken on a more difficult task than he imagined, Wojciechowski discovered that the school's six tennis courts were improperly surfaced and thus unavailable for matches. So that first year, in which the Panthers played only JV matches, he scheduled all games away. For the next year (the first of varsity competition) the courts were resurfaced; but, according to Wojciechowski, "they always had a crown on them." Despite these difficulties, and others like having to schedule early-season gym practices at odd hours such as 6:30 AM, Wojciechowski persevered and soon developed a very competitive boys' tennis program at Spring Lake Park.

Including that first year of JV tennis, he coached the Panthers for twenty-nine years. During this time his teams did well in first the Skyline Conference and then the North Suburban Conference, particularly in the late 1970s. In addition, Wojciechowski coached four doubles teams into the State Tournament; and his best player, Matt Hering, finished third in the 1996 singles tournament. He also coached two other players who advanced to State in singles (Mike Weller and Brad Olson).

Wojciechowski grew up in Little Falls where he played football, ran track, and competed in town team hockey during his high school years. After graduating in 1959, he moved on to St. Cloud State, where he played hockey for one year. Hockey remained a big part of his life, for he also started Spring Lake Park's interscholastic program in '69 and coached the team for five years. Though he gave up his varsity hockey job to focus on tennis (and his growing family), he continued to coach youth hockey teams and to referee games for several years.

Getting back to tennis, Wojciechowski said, "I enjoyed all my years of coaching—we had great kids. We didn't always win because we were one of the smallest schools in our conference, so I was more concerned with kids having fun." In addition to his coaching, he served the MN Boys' Tennis Coaches Association as president during the 1989-90 school year, and for ten years he assisted Ken Peterson as the rankings representative for Minnesota boys' tennis. Wojciechowski was a member of the MSHSCA for over twenty-five years as well.

Retired since 1997 after thirty-four years of teaching math and physics, Wojciechowski says, "I now do anything I want, when I want." Because of some problems with his achilles tendons, he no longer plays tennis; but he does walk the golf course on occasion.

Les Zellmann
St. James

A high energy guy with an almost thirty-year involvement in high school tennis, Les Zellmann coaches at St. James, a small south central Minnesota community of about 4,500 residents. The face of St. James tennis since 1979, Zellmann has been the Saints boys' coach for twenty-seven years and the girls' coach for twenty-two years. (For more about St. James tennis, see Chapter Eight.)

Zellmann, a basketball and baseball player in high school, graduated from Belle Plaine High School in 1973. He then went to Mankato State College, graduating in '77 with a degree in social studies education. Pursuing his dream of teaching social studies and coaching basketball, his first love, Zellmann took a job at Sioux Valley High School. In his two years there he served as head coach in both basketball and baseball, in fact starting the program in baseball. But then he moved to St. James in the fall of '79 to teach American government and psychology. In the middle of his first year at St. James he was assigned to coach tennis, with a promise that a baseball coaching job would open up soon. Luckily for St. James, and for Minnesota tennis, Zellmann liked the tennis job so much he had no desire to coach baseball.

So during his years at St. James, in addition to his high school tennis coaching duties, he has built a quality tennis tradition in the community, in part through his work as coordinator of the summer recreation tennis programs. In the broader picture of statewide tennis, he most recently served the sport as president of the merged MN High School Tennis Coaches' Association (2004-05). Earlier, as president of the MN Girls' Tennis Coaches

Association (2003-04), he was a key player in advocating for a merger of the boys' and girls' coaches associations— a reality since 2004. He said of this important action, "It started with some discussions I had with John Eberhart and Mike Premo [boys' coaches who also coached girls], and the concept was 'how can we make this happen?'"

He has been a dynamic leader for high school tennis in Minnesota, and he said about his involvement with the coaches association that "it [the association] is the life-blood for change and the promotion of high school tennis in Minnesota."

Though his boys' teams have not been as successful as his girls' teams (in part because there was a giant redwood to the east, Blue Earth, it could not cut down), they have always been competitive in the South Central Conference. Through the 2006 season his boys' teams have won 285 matches; and two of his singles players have advanced to State: Trevor Randall in 1995 and Andy Doll in 2006. He's also proud of his two children who played tennis for him, his son once holding down the No. 1 spot on the boys' team and his daughter a No. 1 doubles position on the girls' team.

His more successful girls' teams have reached the section finals the past five years and advanced to State in 1998, 2003, and '05. In addition, many of Zellmann's girls have earned trips to State as singles players or doubles teams. Going into the '06 season, his girls' teams have won 297 matches and lost just 127. For his successes in coaching, Zellmann has twice been selected as MN Class A Girls' Tennis Coach of the Year, in '99 and '05.

In addition to his job as a social studies teacher, Zellmann wears the athletic director's hat at St. James.

Professional Coaches

Finally, there are many professional teacher/coaches who devoted countless hours to helping develop young players in Minnesota. These include numerous former state high school stars who became teaching pros and/or high school coaches, players such as the following (listed in alphabetical order): Gary Aasen, Bob Amis, Randy Anderson, Paul Bates, Brian Biernat, Tom Boice, Mark Brandenburg, Glenn Britzius, Tim Burke, Tim Butorac, Dan and Jon Carlson, Chris Combs, Scott Danielson, Carter DeLaittre, Butch Derksen, John Desmond, Bernie Gunderson, Dan Halvorsen, Marv Hanenberger, Paul Holbach, Mike Husebo, Dan James, John King, Tom Kotsonas, Lee Kruger, Bill Kuross, Greg Lappin, Brian Mahin, Dave Mathews, John Mattke, Layne McCleary, Dave McGill, John Mueller, Paul Muesing, Dan Nabedrick, Scott Nesbit, Corey O'Brien, Bucky Olson, Wendell Ottum, Steve Paulsen, Dave Petersen, Ken Peterson, Corey Prondzinski, Jack Roach, Tim Ross, Dean Rudrud, Dan Shannon, Bob Speed, Bill Stark, Paul Steinhauser, Dave Stearns, Ted Taney, Jack Thommen, Paul Van Deinse, Mike Vidmar, Ted Warner, Jacob Wert, Bruce Westrum, Kevin Whipple, Marnie Wheaton, Greg Wicklund, Kevin Ylinen, Dave Yorks, and Bucky Zimmerman.

In addition to these coaches, there are numerous others (USPTA pros and non-pros alike, some not from Minnesota) who have been instrumental in developing players in the state. Again, this is, of course, a partial but impressive list and includes the following: Tunde Abe, Bill Babcock, Roger Boyer, Tom Boulay, Terry Bruestle, Randy Crowell, Connie Custodio, Hugh Curtler, Hughes Davis, Jack Dow, Jim Ebbitt, Steve Ehlers, Ernie Greene, Percy Hughes, Raman Jayapathy, Howard Johnson, Phil Johnson, Rajan Keswani, Fred King, Bob Madson, Dick Martinson, Brian McCoy, Norm McDonald, Marc Miller, Jerry Noyce, Nick Pappas, Dave Pettingill, Jim Prittinen, Ron Rieckenberg, Todd Ruediseli, Kevin Rust, Dick Schneider, John Shannon, Warren Swanson, Frank Voigt, Steve Wilkinson, Tom Wynne, Ric Yates, and Ron York. If I have missed some and/or misplaced some in these two categories, I apologize.

Of course there were also a number of high school coaches who were USPTA pros, among them Chuck Anderson of Elk River/Robbinsdale Cooper/Breck/Edina girls/Stillwater, Jeanne Arth of Bloomington Kennedy, Mark Muntifering of St. Cloud Apollo, Michelle Olson of Mounds Park Academy, Ken Peterson of Anoka, and Hall of Fame coaches Cliff Caine of SPA, John Eberhart of Pine City, Ted Greer of Edina, John Hatch of Blake, Mike Premo of Foley, Jerry Sales of St. Cloud Tech, and Bud Schmid of Brainerd.

Of all these pro coaches I've noted, four had an enormous impact on Minnesota tennis: Marv Hanenberger, Norm McDonald, Jerry Noyce, and Frank Voigt. There is a profile on Hanenberger in Chapter Nine and there is information about the other three scattered throughout this book, but I want to say just a bit more about McDonald, Noyce, and Voigt here.

Norm McDonald

A colorful character known as much for his story telling as for his playing, coaching, and generosity to junior players, McDonald was also the owner of the most famous tennis shop in the Twin Cities, Twin City Tennis Supply. From his basement store on 47ᵗʰ and Chicago Avenue, often sitting

Norm McDonald and wife, Carole

in a chair smoking a cigar with his dog Kramer by his side, McDonald (and later his son Kevin) sold tennis supplies, strung rackets, and dispensed advice. He was a fixture on the Minnesota tennis scene for over six decades, from the time he won a Minneapolis junior championship in 1932 until his death in 1996 at age eighty-one. For many years he was also a top adult player in the Section, even winning the 45 National Public Parks singles championship in 1961, a year in which he was the No. 1 Men's Singles and Doubles player in the NWLTA. When not in his shop, he was often playing on the courts at Nicollet Park, his home tennis base. Local Minneapolis teaching pro Greg Wicklund called him "a very quick and smart player" and remembers the time McDonald beat him when he (McDonald) was sixty-three and "I was a junior at Minneapolis Roosevelt High School."

Local pro Jack Roach recalls the times McDonald and Jeanne Arth drove to small towns in Minnesota to put on tennis exhibitions and how he brought touring pros Jack Kramer and Pancho Gonzalez to play at the Minneapolis

Armory. Roach called him "a great ambassador for tennis." Three-time singles champion Dave Healey remembers that McDonald "got me free rackets and a summer job at Woodhill Country Club working under Frank Voigt." Healey also said of McDonald, "everybody loved him."

But McDonald, the Twin Cities Wilson Sporting Goods representative for thirty-five years, did some coaching as well and was known for his great generosity to local tennis players. Wicklund also received free rackets from Norm and recalls that he supported the Minneapolis Roosevelt team by giving the players discounts on shoes, rackets, etc.

Called "Mr. Tennis in MN," McDonald won the second Ward C. Burton Junior Development Award in 1968 and is a member of the USTA/Northern Section Hall of Fame.

Jerry Noyce

The "maestro" of the U of M men's tennis team from 1974-88, Noyce has been an important figure on the Minnesota tennis scene since he came from Chicago as a heralded junior player to compete for the Gophers in 1963. He had a successful career as a player, and he served as the Gophers' captain his senior year. During his high

Jerry Noyce

school career at Evanston Township, his No. 1-ranked boys' team in the nation won four Illinois championships and he and partner Dave Power captured one state doubles championship. In his post-college years Noyce continued to play tennis competitively, winning many NWTA tournaments and earning top rankings. For instance, he was the No. 1 Men's Open Singles player in 1971, '74, and '75 and No. 1 in 35 singles in 1981 and '84. He was also the No. 1 Men's Open Doubles player in 1971, '72, and '74 (each year with Jack Roach as his partner); and he won four Section singles championships.

In the fall of 1973 he took over as the Gophers' men's coach, and under his direction the team experienced a renaissance, winning fourteen matches his first year and going on to win three Big Ten titles and the first (in '81) since 1933. In his fourteen years the Gophers had only three losing seasons and he also coached thirteen Big Ten singles champions and four doubles titlists. He is quick to credit the rise of Gopher tennis to the loyal Baseline Club founded by Bob Larson and Warren Jones, father of state singles champion Craig Jones. The club supported the program in so many ways, but much of the credit properly goes to Noyce, whose peers recognized him as NCAA Division I Coach of the Year in 1987.

During those years Jerry was perhaps as well known for his work as a tennis pro and supporter of high school and junior tennis. For about ten years he promoted coaches' clinics and helped start the STP junior development program, which, he said "raised the level of tennis in Minnesota." He credited pros such as Dave Mathews and Kevin Ylinen and the coordinator of the program for ten years, Paul Muesing, for making it work. Noyce took great pleasure in "watching the quality of play improve" and he considered it a privilege to coach so many home-grown stars at the U. Among them were Ted Taney, Carter DeLaittre, Bob Amis, Bill Stark, Dixon Dahlberg, Bob Van Hoef, Mark Brandenburg, the Helgeson brothers, Mark Wheaton, Mark Nammacher, Greg Wicklund, Dave Barnes, Bill Keenan, Tom Nelson, and Dave Morin.

As a coach of junior players, one of Noyce's goals was to prepare top youngsters for national competition, and he did that for so many Minnesotans, including future pros David Wheaton and Ann Henricksson.

For his remarkable resume he was honored by the USTA/Northern Section as 1982 Ward C. Burton Junior Development Award winner and '89 President's Award winner. His family was voted Tennis Family of the Year in '94 and he is also a member of the NWTA Hall of Fame. He has been the national president of the U of M Alumni Association as well and he was named to the President's Council on Sports Fitness by President George W. Bush in 2006.

In addition to his coaching jobs, Jerry is the former CEO of the Northwest Racquet, Swim, and Health Clubs and the former (now retired) CEO of Health Fitness Corporation in Bloomington. Noyce and fellow U of M graduate Jane Veker have been married for forty years and have two children (David and Jennifer).

Frank Voigt

Arguably the greatest pro coach in Minnesota history, Voigt had an enormous impact on players whom he coached, both in terms of the stroke mechanics they learned and the court behavior he insisted they demonstrate. Mark Wheaton, whose only pro lesson was from Voigt, said of the form Voigt taught, "It was always a classic continental forehand with no spin, low to high, no wrist." Bucky Zimmerman called him "a no-nonsense guy who taught you to do the best you can and be honest about what you do. He was a real inspiration to all the kids he came in contact with."

So many who either worked for Voigt or were taught by him praised him effusively. Dave Mathews called him a real people person and said of his teaching, "He had the ability to pick out the one thing that had the biggest impact on your game and then make a correction on it without overcoaching or totally dismantling your game." Jerry Noyce said, "Frank was one of the two or three greatest tennis teachers I've known." Dave Healey, who as a seventeen-year-old worked for Voigt in the summer, agreed with this assessment, calling Voigt "an unsurpassed tennis coach/teacher. He could take anyone and make that person a competent player in a short time. He had no peers, he was simply the best." Jack Roach added, "He told us how to teach and got us into the USPTA."

Healey also called Voigt "the most sage person I have

had the privilege to work with in my life. He taught me how to speak, how to carry myself, how to work with young people, and how to deal with wealthy people."

Described as a "transplanted Easterner" in the 1981 *NWTA Yearbook* (he was from Newport Beach, RI), Voigt became the professional at Woodhill Country Club in Wayzata in 1942 and remained there until he retired thirty-eight years later (in 1980). In addition to his teaching, he influenced many fine teacher/coaches such as Ken Boyum, Dave Healey, John Brennan, Dave Stearns, Dave Mathews, and Ted Warner; and he figured in several "firsts" in Minnesota tennis. For example, he was the first full-time professional coach to take up residence in the state; he and the late Budge Miller opened the first permanent indoor club here (North Star) on March 10, 1965; and he was a founder of the MN Northwest Professional Tennis Coaches Association.

And for many years Voigt managed a major junior tournament at Woodhill (eventually the Sectional Tournament) and generously donated discarded rackets (which he renovated) to inner city and Park Board youngsters. In addition, he helped develop the Junior Tennis Champions program.

The NWTA showed its gratitude to Voigt by electing him to its Hall of Fame, by naming its Pro of the Year award after him, and by giving him the Ward C. Burton Junior Development Award in 1973.

Finally, Voigt could walk the talk, for he was himself an exceptional player who competed on the pro circuit from 1939-41 against some of the greatest American players of all time such as Bill Tilden, Don Budge, Frank Parker, and Pancho Segura. As a high schooler he led his team to three state championships, then, after graduation, he began teaching tennis at an Eastern club in the summer and at Palm Beach, FL, in the winter. During these years (the late '30s) he taught future Presidents Jack Kennedy and George Bush the elder, and, according to Healey, used to regale the young teachers at Woodhill with stories about Budge (who became a great friend of Voigt's) and his days of teaching the likes of Fred Astaire, the Kennedys, and other celebrities during his time in Florida. Voigt died in 1988.

Multiple Singles Champions

As a young English teacher at Minnetonka East Junior High School in the early 1960s, I taught *Julius Caesar* to novice Shakespeare scholars, ninth graders who were mostly unimpressed with the high-sounding oratory of Brutus and Marc Antony and the iambic pentameter rhymes that characterized this classic historical drama. But I hoped that they would learn something about the character of this "noblest Roman of them all," Julius Caesar, and the awesome power he held in first century BCE Rome. He reigned over the Roman Empire for five years, and his name was known and feared in all the surrounding world. So perhaps it's not a stretch to call our Minnesota tennis champions who won at least two singles titles the Caesars of their day. They didn't conquer Gaul, but they conquered the known Minnesota tennis world and reigned supreme for two or three years and were much admired. For example, my frequent doubles playing partner Dick Kleber (brother of 1954 singles runner-up Ron Kleber), tells how he was in awe of Minnesota's first multiple champion, Ken Boyum, envying Ken's drop shot and wishing he could play like Boyum.

> *"Why, man, he doth bestride the narrow world like a Colossus."*
> —Julius Caesar

Another Caesar of the Minnesota tennis world was Chuck Darley, three-time singles winner from Rochester (1962-64) and arguably the greatest high school champion our state has produced. Brian Mahin, a '65 doubles champion from Minnetonka, speaks in almost reverent tones about his first encounter with Darley in a summer junior tournament. According to Mahin, "I played the best match of my life and he beat me 6-0, 6-0."

This latter-day Caesar (Darley) came to Rochester, saw, and conquered every opponent during his three years of competition, losing only seven sets, all to teammate Bob Gray, the '65 champion. But we begin with the first of our multiple champions, our first Caesar, Boyum.

Ken Boyum
Minneapolis West (1942-43)

Ken Boyum was one of the many Park Board boys (from the 1930s, '40s, and '50s) who learned to play on the public parks of Minneapolis and St. Paul. His was a learning path different from that of most young tennis players today, who often receive professional coaching at early ages, unlimited court time at one of our indoor tennis clubs, rides to summer tournaments, and lots of support from doting and sometimes overbearing parents. Ken received no coaching, but instead learned to play tennis by hiking down to the Bryant Square courts and watching players like Don Gunner (the 1940 Minnesota boys' singles and doubles champion and '41 National Public Parks champion), skilled women's players like Muriel Magnuson, and top men's players such as the legendary Norm McDonald. From the time he started playing at age eleven, Ken honed his game by imitating the strokes displayed by these players. He noted, "All of them had the same game, and you didn't play at the net at that time."

Ken Boyum

Growing up during the Depression, Ken and most of his tennis playing buddies did not have enough money to buy tennis balls (one can cost 75 cents in 1937), so he helped put up nets and served as a ball boy for Mort Roan at the Parade Stadium clay courts during the summer. Occasionally players whom he served as a ball boy would hit with him, but his biggest reward for working at Parade was an occasional "gift" of nine to twelve used tennis balls. This gift gave him instant cachet with the older and more experienced neighborhood tennis-playing crowd: "I was king of the walk when I brought tennis balls with fuzz on them. They let me hit with them until their partners came."

Entering Minneapolis West High School with a polished game, Ken soon made his name known by sweeping aside all competitors to reach the finals of the State Tournament in 1941, where he lost to little Joe Armstrong, Jr. (called "the two-handed swatter" in a June 4, 1941, article in the *Minneapolis Morning Tribune*), 6-2, 5-7, 6-4. This match in his sophomore year was the last Boyum would lose in high school, for he would go on to claim state titles in both singles and doubles in 1942 and '43, becoming the only Minnesota player to twice claim titles in both events. (By 1950 players could enter only the singles or doubles competition, a rule that is still in place). In 1942 Ken led his West Cowboys to the team title as well, helping them earn the maximum possible points (13) by defeating teammate Kess O'Bryan in the singles final 6-2, 6-3 and by teaming with Harold Wollin to win the doubles 6-4, 6-3. He had advanced to the singles final with an easy win in the semis over Ted Taylor of Minneapolis Southwest but in two very difficult prior matches (1-6, 6-1, 6-3 over St. Paul Johnson's Bucky Olson—future St. Thomas coach and well-known St. Paul tennis pro—in the first round) and 6-4, 3-6, 6-3 over Minneapolis South's Norman Rice in the quarters.

The year 1943 proved to be, in the words of one of America's most original language manglers, Yogi Berra, "déjà vu all over again" for Ken and his West teammates. Once again they claimed the team title by scoring the maximum number of points (13), and once again Ken defeated a teammate, this time Bob Herman, to claim his second singles crown and then paired with Wollin to repeat as doubles champions. His task was made more difficult because that year's tournament was held at the U of M courts on June 8th, meaning that Ken had to play all his singles and doubles matches in one day. However, unlike in 1942, his road to the finals was a leisurely walk in the park; for he won all four of his matches in straight sets, including his 6-3, 6-3 win in the finals over Herman.

When I spoke with Boyum, I was struck by how modest and unassuming he seemed; but his friend Pudge Whitcomb (1947 State singles champion) talked about Ken's intense, competitive nature: "He hated to lose." Whitcomb tells about the time Boyum challenged him to a set in which he (Boyum) would only use his weakest stroke, the forehand. "He beat me 6-4," relates Whitcomb. Pudge also had this to say about his good friend Ken's game: "In terms of quickness of foot and balance, it was so hard to force him. His backhand was his best shot—he could hit it down the line, lob, or change the angle." Boyum was one of those players I would characterize as "rabbits," players who seemed to make difficult-to-get shots look easy because their first three steps were so quick. Whitcomb said Boyum had "a tremendous quickness at the start and an ability to maintain his balance almost against the laws of physics when he stopped." Another Minnesota player who admired him, 1963-64 doubles champion Bucky Zimmerman, called Boyum "the Ken Rosewall of our era."

Boyum remembers his high school sports career (which included playing on the West High varsity basketball team) with great fondness, recalling in particular how much more coverage the high school and U of M sports scene received in the days before the arrival of pro sports in the Twin Cities: "I was even on the front page of the [Minneapolis Morning] Tribune once." As for any recollection of particular matches, Ken cites the three-setter he lost to Armstrong his sophomore year and one with John Dunnigan of Minneapolis Washburn (the 1944 singles champion) his senior year, a match in which he had to fight through cramps in his arms in order to prevail. Ken also spoke highly of his coach/history teacher Winworth Williams, who had been coaching tennis at West since the

early 1930s. "After he retired, we took him out for lunch once a month for many years." But one of Boyum's best memories is that of driving in style in 1942 to a match (there was no van or bus travel to meets in those days), he in his dad's 1941 Pontiac and his teammate, Bob Herman, in a new Packard, the Cadillac of its day.

A member of the "Greatest Generation," Boyum was drafted into the army after he graduated from West in 1943. Because he wore glasses he was put in the medical corps. According to his obituary in the November 11, 2005, Star Tribune, "He landed on a beach in Normandy the day after D-Day in 1944 and followed the army as it fought its way to Germany" (Trudi Hahn).

After his stint in the service, Ken attended the U of M where he played No. 1 singles for Coach Phil Brain for three years, losing in the finals to Andy Paton of Michigan in 1948 and in his senior year to Northwestern's Grant Golden, a member of the U.S. Davis Cup team. In addition, he served as captain of the Gophers tennis team all three years (1947-49).

After he graduated from the U, he worked for the Veteran's Administration in the Twin Cities until the summer of 1953, then took that summer off to play in major U.S. amateur tournaments. He returned to the Metro area to take "a position with Hennepin County District Court, providing social services related to court services" (Star Tribune, November 11, 2005). In 1955 he was married, and in 1962 he earned his second master's degree at the U of M (this one in hospital administration—the first had been in social work) and he moved to Michigan to work with Blue Cross Blue Shield.

He brought his family back to Minnesota after just one year in Michigan, for he was appointed administrator of the Sister Kenny Rehabilitation Institute. In 1971 he resigned from that post to become administrator of the Minneapolis Children's Health Center, then under construction. After just one year there he resigned to become a freelance medical administration consultant, a position he held until his retirement. In addition, he served four years as a supervisor in the Hennepin County Probation Office and for five years he helped develop a domestic relations section for the county.

As for his adult tennis life, for two summers (1949-50)

he assisted Frank Voigt as a tennis pro at Woodhill Country Club. And during his post-college years he earned a reputation as one of the greatest amateur male tennis players in Minnesota history, holding down the No. 1 Section ranking in Men's Open Singles for eleven years and earning numerous top singles rankings in every other age category from Junior Veteran's to the 65s. In addition, he held a No. 1 ranking in doubles with many different partners. For example, in 1967 (when he was fifty-one years old), he and Bill Kuross were the top-ranked Men's Open Doubles team. Also, in his later years he won Sectional doubles titles in the 50-and-over division with Kuross and Bill Bradley and in the 65-and-over division with local teaching pro Dick Martinson.

Boyum was elected to the NWTA Tennis Hall of Fame in 1981. And in '97 he was elected to the U of M M-Club Hall of Fame, one of only two tennis players to be so inducted (the other is Jerry Noyce). Perhaps more than anything else he will be remembered as a great sportsman, gentleman, and family man. In the aforementioned obituary, his wife, Claire, said of him, "The competition is what drove him, but he was a nice player, never mean, in a sport that gets personal when your opponent is right in front of you" (November 11, 2005). The NWTA recognized his good sportsmanship by presenting him with the Al Teeter Sportsmanship Award in 1977.

Boyum died of cancer at age eighty on November 2, 2006.

Dave Healey
Rochester (1953-55)

After Ken Boyum it would be almost a decade before we would have another multiple singles champion, namely Dave Healey of Rochester, one of only two Minnesotans (both from Rochester) to win three titles. When Dave first made a name for himself in tennis, winning the first of his championships in 1953, the city of Rochester had already produced a number of outstanding players (beginning with Charles Britzius and Walter Hargesheimer, the No. 1 doubles champions in the first State Tournament in 1929) and would dominate Minnesota high school tennis for almost twenty more years. (See Chapter Nine for more

about Rochester tennis.) During these years (1953-74) this hotbed of tennis would produce five singles champions—three of whom would be multiple winners—four singles runners-up (including Bob Gray twice), three championship doubles teams, six runner-up doubles teams, and seven team titles. And prior to 1953, Rochester produced one singles champion, three singles runners-up (one with the wonderfully eponymous name of Johnny Lobb), three championship doubles teams, two runner-up doubles teams, and two team champions.

There must have been something in the Rochester water that could produce a Dave Healey and so many other accomplished tennis players. In Dave's case it may have been a bit of serendipity, for until the age of thirteen he had been an all-star midget baseball player who excelled at three different positions: shortstop, second base, and catcher. Then came that fateful summer when he was thirteen, as Dave tells the story: "I wanted to play American Legion baseball during the summer, not midget baseball. Finding out that I had to be fourteen to play American Legion, I was most discouraged. A friend, Roger Jackman [1955 state doubles champion], asked me if I wanted to play tennis instead. I joined him at the Rochester Tennis Club and by the end of the summer became the Club junior champion, beating Roger in the finals. Thus, my tennis career started and I never went back to baseball."

Of course it helped Dave (and the other Rochester players) that they had access to tennis instruction in the summers at a tennis club—a luxury most Minnesota tennis players did not have, but they also had Marv "Hanny" Hanenberger to help them out. (See Chapter Nine for more about Hanenburger.) Hanny approached Dave and offered to hit with him, volunteering to provide free instruction—good news for Dave since he had no money for lessons. A tough taskmaster, Hanny took Dave under his wing and quickly realized that playing the backcourt would not suit Dave's game. So, honoring Dave's athletic ability, Marv decided that an aggressive serve and volley style would be best for Healey.

Healey remembers Marv as a coach who was "verbally skilled at explaining the mechanics of each part of the game" and who "coached to the talent he saw and didn't attempt to clone himself." Most importantly, however, Hanny gave his time to help boys such as Dave, even helping him shovel off the cement courts at Soldiers Field on winter days when it was warm enough to play tennis. While these and other hitting sessions were not always amicable (Hanny would sometimes infuriate Dave by telling him over and over that he wasn't hitting a particular shot correctly), Dave learned to play all kinds of players—including "pushers"—because Hanny was a master at hitting slice, spin, backspin, sidespin, and overspin.

Though Hanny convinced Dave to quit playing football so he could practice tennis in the fall, he continued to play basketball, starting at guard as a ninth grader and playing through his senior year and one year at the U of M. He must have had some regrets about giving up football though, for every day during the fall the football team would walk past the tennis courts where Dave was practicing tennis and some of the players directed snide epithets at him. Nevertheless, giving up football gave him extra court time which no doubt helped him achieve his goal of becoming a state tennis champion.

So after losing in the semifinals his freshman year to eventual champion Charles "Chuck" Edwards of Minneapolis Washburn, he won the first of his titles, avenging that 1952 loss by defeating Edwards in the '53 final 6-2-6-3. Rochester coach Merle Davey, in a *Rochester Post-Bulletin* article titled "Rockets Take State Title in Tennis Meet," said Healey was outstanding and "showed everything that a champion possibly can in lifting the singles title from Edwards' shoulders" (June 3, 1953). Just a sophomore, Healey blasted his way through the draw in what could

Dave Healey

be called a blitzkreig, giving up just nine games in four straight-set wins. And three of these wins came against formidable opponents, two of whom later finished second in state singles (Ron Kleber of St. Cloud and Chauncey Riggs of Duluth Central) and another who had already won a singles title (Edwards).

In 1954 Healey, a junior, won his second title by outlasting Kleber 6-3, 4-6, 6-4. Except for this challenge from Kleber, his other matches were relatively uneventful two-set wins, including one in the semis over freshman Mark Anderson of St. James, whose two previous wins helped the Saints win the state team title. The match with Kleber was Healey's most challenging during his three-year championship run, for it was his only three-setter.

He capped his brilliant career with a straight set win (7-5, 6-3) over Riggs in 1955—leading the Rockets to their second team title during his four-year career. A June 8, 1955, article in the *Rochester Post-Bulletin* said of the final between Riggs and Healey, "Riggs, a heavy-set senior, displayed a large quantity of spirit and determination in the finals. After being extended to the upmost in the semis [an 11-9, 6-2 win over St. James' Mark Anderson], he [Riggs] led Healey 4 to 2 in the first set. The Rochester boy, playing under loads of tension as he tried to become the first player to ever win three straight singles titles, came back strong to take the set 7-5." With the exception of one other 7-5 set, against Mickey Edwards of Minneapolis Washburn in the quarters (in a match he won 7-5, 6-1), Healey cruised through his other two matches.

Healey accomplished his three-peat without losing a match in those three years, using his excellent serve and quick feet to help him become the first three-time Minnesota singles champion.

And though the pressure to succeed accelerated with each victory during his senior year and he admitted to being so nervous during his final match in 1955 that he could hardly swing his racket, these competitive experiences laid the foundation for his success at the U of M. There he was awarded the first full-ride, non-revenue sport scholarship (the Henry L. Williams Scholarship) and played No. 1 singles for three years (freshman couldn't play then) under the tutelage of legendary coach Chet Murphy, a master strategist and author of books such as *Tennis for the Player.* Healey also served as captain for two years (1958-59).

His experiences in tennis altered and eventually helped direct his life, as he noted:

> Tennis taught me how to compete within the rules and not be satisfied with being second. Tennis taught me integrity—being on one side of a tennis court all by yourself with the intent of beating your opponent within a set of rules that you have to administer fairly and honestly without an umpire. Tennis provided me with an education which launched my career in business [mostly as an executive recruiter]. I built two businesses by hard work, honesty, and drive to succeed. Tennis was also a launching pad for me to become involved with the USTA.

For a young boy growing up in Rochester who rode his bike by the Taystee Bread Factory to the Rochester Tennis Club every day in the summer, Dave could not have imagined the places he would see and the people he would meet because of his involvement in tennis. For example, when a younger Marty Riessen (later a top pro player) came to Rochester in the summer of 1955 to play in a tournament, Dave played and defeated him. Also, in high school he had the privilege of playing other Minnesota legends such as Ken Boyum, Bill Kuross, Wendell Ottum, and Norm McDonald. And in summer tournaments he played the No. 1-ranked junior player, Gerry Moss from Florida, and Art Andrews from Iowa (a Don Klotz protégé ranked in the top ten in the country). At the U of M Healey lost in three sets to Barry McKay of the U of MI, the No. 1 male tennis player in

the U.S. at the time, in 1959. He remembers playing with his first Jack Kramer racquet, then later meeting Kramer and becoming friends with him. In addition, when he was on the USTA board he often played customer tennis with the likes of Jimmy Connors and John McEnroe.

And perhaps there was something about playing tennis in those early years at the Rochester Tennis Club, which Dave fondly referred to as "a lovely green oasis with clay tennis courts," that gave him the confidence to volunteer for USTA work. In any case, he soon moved up the ladder in the Northwestern section, serving first on the Board of Directors, then becoming Vice-president, President, and Section Delegate. This groundwork set the stage for positions with the USTA where he chaired three committees and eventually served as a vice president on the Board of Directors.

Among the honors Dave treasures most are these: being named by Governor Orville Freeman as a Minnesota Sports Champion of the last 100 years and being elected to the USTA Northern Section Hall of Fame. After a distinguished career, first at Honeywell and then as a recruiter of business executives, Healey is now retired, spending winters in Naples, FL, and summers at his cabin in Wisconsin.

Charles "Chuck" Darley
Rochester (1962-64)

Nine years would pass before another multiple singles champion would emerge, and he would be the great Charles "Chuck" Darley, also from Rochester. Darley grew up in Iowa City, IA, and he remembers his early tennis days of "playing with my dad on the U of IA courts and at Fayetteville, AR, where my mom's grandparents lived." He recalls "the wonder of hitting the ball over the net three or four times and the ritual of sharing an orange drink with his dad at the Fayetteville Dairy" after their hitting sessions. Once he began to show promise as a player, he took lessons from celebrated U of IA men's tennis coach, Don Klotz, who also transported his pupils to tournaments in the summer. One of these tournaments was the Rochester Invitational run by Marv Hanenberger. Chuck remembers playing there for the first time when he was ten years old and returning each summer for several years thereafter until his family moved to Rochester before his sophomore year in high school.

The rest, as they say, is history, for Darley's dominance of the Minnesota high school tennis scene began that first year in Rochester. Using his incredibly skilled

Charles "Chuck" Darley

volley technique (Darley was called the best amateur volleyer in the U.S. at that time by Jack Kramer, according to Hanenberger) and his quickness and good footwork, Chuck defeated southpaw teammate Bob Gray in the 1962 final 6-0, 6-1. Though Gray must have been crestfallen to win just one game against his teammate, he had good company; for Darley did not lose a set and surrendered just nine more games against his other three opponents.

Given the fact that he was ranked No. 10 in the national 15-and-under category, it was not all that surprising that Darley was able to capture his first title at such a young age.

In 1963 Chuck repeated as champion, once again defeating teammate Bob Gray in the finals, but this time in a much more difficult match, a hard-fought three-setter that he won 6-1, 2-6, 8-6. Though the Rockets' No. 1 ace, now a junior, had a more difficult tournament this year, he still won all his matches leading up to the final in straight sets.

Leading the Rochester John Marshall Rockets to their third straight team title and eighth overall, Darley capped his illustrious career by securing his third singles title, defeating four-time state tournament entry Dennis Chez of Hibbing 6-3, 6-0 in the 1964 finals. His most difficult match, however, came in the semis—a hard-fought 6-3, 7-5 win over Edina's Chip Otness, a match the Rockets needed to secure the team title. This third title run demonstrated once again Darley's dominance, for he swept through the draw with only one really competitive match, giving up just sixteen games in four matches.

Amazingly, Darley did not lose a match in three years of high school competition, despite the fact that he played very little tennis in the winter (he played basketball all three years, once on a team that lost to Luverne in the state finals). In fact, he only lost seven sets in that time, all to teammate Bob Gray, who reminisced about his teammate's prowess: "Darley gave himself the chance to be the best he could be. He didn't waste his time playing small tournaments. When he came in tenth grade, that summer he had beaten national champion Bill Harris. I saw that match. Chuck won the first set 7-5, lost the second 1-6, then won the third 13-11." Gray said that Darley even held double match point against Stan Smith at Kalamazoo in the boys' 17s before losing.

Considered the greatest high school tennis player in Minnesota history by many who played against him or hit with him (among them Healey, Gray, John Brennan, Dave Yorks, Brian Mahin) or saw him play (coaches John Matlon, Chuck Anderson, and Tom Vining), Darley established a reputation and a standard of play that future players tried unsuccessfully to emulate. For example, Scott Nesbit from Edina, who paired with Bill Arnold to win the 1975 state doubles title, told about how during practice Coach Matlon always used Darley as an exemplar. "If you hit what looked like the best volley you'd ever hit, Matlon would say, 'Oh, but it was nothing compared to Darley's volleys." Yorks, a 1965 doubles champion from Minnetonka, said of Chuck, "He was just playing a different game than the rest of us." And his partner Mahin, recalling that 6-0, 6-0 thrashing administered to him by Darley (see earlier reference), also spoke about Darley's humanity: "He wasn't in your face. He was so much better and he could have acted like a jerk but he didn't." Coach Tom Vining of Roseville called him "the best state champion in my memory." And in an article by Rich Melin in the *Rochester Post-Bulletin* (June 8, 1964), his coach, Dick Thatcher, said of the 145-pound Darley: "He was by far the best player. He was not only a good tennis player, but he had a lot of finesse and he was very cool." Added Thatcher, "It'll be a long time before another like Darley comes along." One could argue that David Wheaton was the greatest Minnesota player, by virtue of his success as a pro player, but he and Darley were different players from different eras, so we'll never resolve this issue.

Future state champion Rob Daugherty, also from Rochester, called Darley his hero. He recalls how he was "so nervous in his presence." Daugherty added, "I saw him play in tournaments and I tried to imitate him, move like him, play tennis like him." Later Daugherty, who had just won his second state high school singles title, played an exhibition match with Darley, then a senior at the U of CA-Berkeley, the No. 20 player in the U.S., and a recent quarterfinalist in the NCAA tournament. It was June 1968 and 300 spectators packed the Rochester Athletic Club to watch this battle of state champions. Daugherty said of the encounter, "It could easily have been love and love. Chuck was a gracious champion and gave me a few games." In fact, because a point system was used for the first two sets, Darley gave Daugherty a few points and two games, the score being 21-12, 21-13, 6-2.

As with so many of the former players I spoke to, Darley commented about the value of the team aspect of tennis and how, in his case at least, tennis became a refuge for him, a place where he could overcome his "social shyness." Memories of his years at Rochester include practicing with teammates such as Gray on the white cement courts at the high school (the present John Marshall High School), and laughing at jokes Coach Thatcher told in the car on the way to meets. He also recalls learning how to drive in Marv Hanenberger's Corvair, feasting on sumptuous meals at the Hubbell House Restaurant—courtesy of Marv—and learning how to slide as if on clay while practicing in the rain.

Chuck also recalls one time that the usually genial Coach Thatcher was not pleased: "In an early match on a cold day at Owatonna my senior year, Bob [Gray] and I finished early; so we sat in Coach's car, which we dubbed the 'Purple Bitch,' listened to music—I remember one song called 'You Can't Sit Down'—and ran the battery down." Another episode in a car occurred during the summer when Gray and Darley drove to Duluth for the Arrowhead Tournament in the Gray family Buick. It had a bad battery, so they had to jump start it many times or park on a hill so they could get it going. A State Tournament memory during Chuck's sophomore year involved a player named Dave Rosenberg from St. Paul Central. When Chuck arrived to play, he saw Rosenberg practicing his serve by trying to hit a trophy he had won in a previous tournament.

When asked who were the best players he competed against in high school, Darley named Andy Goddard of Edina, Dave Nash of Blake (for years a top adult player in the Northern Section and once the No. 1-ranked mens' 55 player in the U.S. and a member of the U.S. International Club team), and especially his teammate Bob Gray. Of Bob, Chuck said, "He was a scrapper, a lefty who had good groundstrokes."

After completing his spectacular high school career, Chuck enrolled at U CA-Berkeley where he played No. 1 singles for three years, competing at the highest level of collegiate tennis and twice earning all-American recognition. During his college years he played against the likes of Stan Smith and Bob Lutz from the U of Southern CA and he played "professionally" (remember, this was before the Open era of pro tennis) during two summers, achieving a U.S. Men's Singles ranking of No. 20 and, with partner Armistead Neely, a doubles ranking of No. 5 the summer between his junior and senior years, and the No. 1 ranking in Northern California singles. This was pretty heady stuff for a lad from a state not noted for tennis, and it would be several years before another Minnesota boy would crack this elite group. Howard Schoenfield, a transplanted Rochester native and another pupil of Marv Hanenberger, then living in California, would be ranked No. 1 in Boys' 18 Singles in 1975. Still later, in 1987, David Wheaton (another Minnesota native but then a Florida resident), would be ranked No. 1 in the 18s—ahead of such famous future stars as Pete Sampras, Andre Agassi, Jim Courier, and Michael Chang.

On the tournament circuit Chuck and his doubles partners, first future World top-ten player and future U.S. Davis Cup coach Tom Gorman and then Neely, played four future World No. 1 teams: Roy Emerson and Fred Stolle at the National Doubles Championship at Longwood Cricket Club, John Newcombe and Tony Roche in the Northern California Championships, Marty Riessen and Clark Graebner, and the aforementioned Stan Smith and Bob Lutz. In singles Darley played Arthur Ashe twice (once at the National Clay Court Junior Championships in Chicago and another time at the Pan American Games tryouts held at the Minikahda Country Club in Minneapolis). Chuck described Ashe as "a terrific guy, such a mentor to young players and a super sportsman."

Because of his lofty U.S. ranking, Darley was privileged to gain entry into the main draw of the U.S. Open (then held at Forest Hills, NY) on two occasions, losing in 1967 on the grandstand court to then No. 1 in the World John Newcombe 6-3, 6-1, 6-1. As an amateur Chuck earned nothing from these appearances, but his expenses were covered by the Northwestern Tennis Association for tournaments such as the Eastern Grass Courts and Southern Clay Courts the summer after his sophomore year in college. An interesting side note is that Chuck played his college tennis for Coach Chet Murphy, the very same gentleman who coached Dave Healey at the U of M.

When Darley retired his college sneakers, he gave the Satellite Tour a try for six months, traveling around the country in a motor home with his wife and two-year-old son in an attempt to earn a ranking. Attending graduate school after his four years at Berkeley, he earned a PhD in cognitive psychology but decided that tennis was his first love so he taught the game at several Northern California private courts from 1975-84. Returning to his roots in Iowa, Chuck accepted the job as head women's coach at the U of IA, serving in that role from 1984-87. For some time thereafter he continued teaching tennis while also working in both the athletic department and student services offices (career development) at the U of IA. Today he teaches for the Great River Tennis Association in the Iowa City area, and he says he thoroughly enjoys working with both promising young junior players and adults of all abilities.

Rob Daugherty
Rochester Mayo (1967-68)

In 1966, after four straight years in which Rochester players captured singles titles, Edina's Robb Jones claimed the state championship. However, the parade of Rochester champions continued in 1967 when Robert "Rob" Daugherty, an imposing six-foot-five-inch player with a booming serve, took the first of his two titles. The making of this fourth state multiple singles champion also

Rob Daugherty

began at the Rochester Tennis Club. Daugherty recalls "dragging a racket behind me when I was five or six years old, returning from backboard hitting at the Club." Like so many young Rochester tennis players in the 1950s and '60s, Rob spent his summer days at the Club, taking a sack lunch with him for nourishment. It was here that he became immersed in the culture of tennis, working at the tennis shop with older brothers Tom (who ran the shop) and Dave and learning to play the game. It was here where he won his first tennis trophy, a runner-up award in the 1959 15-and-under club doubles tournament when he was just nine years old. And it was the court time he logged here that gave him the confidence to begin playing summer tournaments at age nine. Rob remembers his mother (who didn't even know how to keep score) driving him to tournaments, quietly watching his matches, then driving him home. Another fond memory is playing with his dad and winning a Rochester Club father and son doubles championship, beating Mark Brandenburg and his father in the 1970 finals. It was his good fortune to be raised in a tennis-playing family, but what motivated him most was the fact that he really had a passion for the game.

Success came quickly for Rob; he was ranked No. 2 in the Northwestern Section in Boys' 14 Singles, he held the No. 1 spot in Junior Men's Singles in 1967, and he and teammate Bob Brandenburg were ranked No. 1 in doubles one time as well. He was also ranked No. 39 in the nation in the 16-and-unders in '66, and he burst onto the high school scene by finishing second in state doubles competition (with his older brother Dave) as a ninth grader.

His sophomore year (1966) he earned a runner-up finish in singles, losing to Robb Jones of Edina in what was something of an upset and in a match moved to an indoor club (North Star) for the first time in tournament history. Daugherty, with a 19-0 record, had defeated Jones twice before they met in the state finals. Ranked No. 1 in the state and a favorite to win the singles title, Daugherty felt he was ready to win it all. He admitted, to *Rochester Post-Bulletin* writer Joe Long in a June 8, 1966, article, that "the pressure is on"; but he also felt that "last year's exposure to state competition should be a big help this weekend."

Despite these good signs, he lost 7-5, 6-2. Nevertheless, coach Thatcher praised him for the year he had. In a June 13, 1966, article in the *Post-Bulletin*, Thatcher said, "You have to give Daugherty a lot of credit. He had the pressure on him all the way being ranked No. 1... And Jones played much better Saturday than he did in their two meetings during the regular season." Daugherty finished the season with a 23-1 record.

The next year, as a junior, Daugherty avenged his 1966 loss to Jones by defeating him in the final match 6-4, 7-5. After a first round bye, Daugherty began play by knocking off the dangerous Reid Pederson of Coon Rapids (the 1966 doubles champion) 6-2, 6-4. Then things got even stickier, for it took him three sets to win his next two matches against two of the top-ranked players in the state. Daugherty needed every bit of his competitive fire to win these matches, for he lost the first sets in each of them. In the quarters he nipped future Minnetonka coach

Dave Stearns of St. Cloud 2-6, 9-7, 7-5; and in the semis he defeated Dick Humleker of Minnetonka 4-6, 7-5, 6-2. Had a point or two in either of these matches gone to his opponents, Daugherty would not have won that year.

After another first-round bye in the 1968 tournament, Daugherty opened play with a second-round 6-2, 6-1 win over Anoka's Greg Lappin (who ironically became the director of the Rochester Athletic Club in 1993), then upended his next two opponents in straight sets. His finals opponent was No. 2-ranked Tom Brennan of Minneapolis West (Daugherty was No. 1). Though this was also a straight-set win (6-3, 6-1), Daugherty called Brennnan his toughest opponent. There were no dramatic come-from-behind escapes in this year's tournament, and his win gave him a perfect two-year record of 51-0 and a four-year career record of 81-4.

A June 10, 1968, article in the *Minneapolis Tribune* called Daugherty "the Mayo Mauler" who had a "cannon-ball serve as accurate as it was fast." No radar guns were on site to record the speed of his serves, but it's clear that Daugherty was at the time the Andy Roddick of Minnesota tennis, a player who could dominate opponents with his big weapon: the serve. One of his opponents, former Edina star and current Blake coach Ted Warner, tried without success to fend off that cannonball serve on a lacquered gym surface in North St. Paul. Said Warner, "I played him [Daugherty] indoors once on a high school gym floor and he killed me with his great serve which in normal conditions was tough enough." Warner called him "the best guy I played."

But he was more than a big server for, according to his sometime unofficial coach, Marv Hanenberger, he also "hit groundstrokes very hard and at six foot five inches he could cover the court easily." By the way, Daugherty praised Hanenberger, saying that he "had a huge impact on me and everybody around who played tennis in Rochester before me and up to Mark Brandenburg. He hit for hours with us and took us to restaurants." Daugherty was a good athlete as well, playing center for the Mayo basketball team and earning all-Conference honors in 1968.

Unfortunately, Rob's exploits were not enough to earn multiple team titles for his Rochester Mayo team (in 1967 divided into two schools, John Marshall and Mayo), for his four-year career coincided with the arrival on the

Minnesota scene of the next and greatest tennis dynasty, Edina. In 1965, the year he and his brother took second place in the doubles competition, (a new high school in 1966) Rochester John Marshall won the title with 19 points; but his last three years the Mayo Spartans finished tied for third in '66, third in '67, and second in '68. Each of those years Edina either tied for or won the team title outright.

Most of the players I spoke with chose not to focus on the championships they won but instead focused on the camaraderie and fun they had going on trips, practicing with friends, or sharing good times. Rob was no exception, saying, "The championships were OK, but it was more fun being part of a team." When asked about memorable high school experiences, Daugherty mentioned three. First, he enjoyed playing doubles in the State Tournament with older brother Dave. "I was six foot five and he was six foot eight and we intimidated other players." Secondly, he remembers a scrimmage match in 1967 with a good team from Onalaska, WI. Little did Rob know that he would play one of the Gullickson twins that day (who, by the way, he called his toughest opponent in high school). Third, he cites his fortunate "escape" in a semifinal match in 1967 with Dick Humleker of Minnetonka, noting "I was down match point, he served to my backhand, and I hit a return and he missed it."

During his high school years he had three coaches (Dick Thatcher at John Marshall in 1965, Bill Fessler at Mayo in '66–67, and Terry Strawn at Mayo in '68), but, speaking in an article by Rochester writer Bob Brown, he credited his first coach for "getting me off on the right foot" (*Rochester Post-Bulletin*, June 10, 1968). That first coach was his father, Dr. G. W. Daugherty. "When I was about six or seven years old, he got me started," Daugherty explained. "We play together often, but I passed him up about three years ago." A humble young man who doesn't "gloat over his achievements," Daugherty stores his many trophies "in the attic of the family home" (June 10, 1968).

Another important figure in Daugherty's tennis development was U of M tennis coach Joe Walsh, who invited Rob (and Robb Jones of Edina) to live with his family in California the summer between Rob's junior and

senior years. Walsh was on sabbatical leave, and he generously took time to hit with Daugherty and Jones and to get them into tournaments. Said Daugherty about Walsh, "He believed in us and yet there was never a mention of wanting us to come to his school to play. He and his wife, Margie, were incredibly generous people."

Tennis fans in Rochester must have been very proud when they learned that Daugherty decided to "walk on" at Stanford to play for Dick Gould, now retired as perhaps the most celebrated and successful NCAA tennis coach in U.S. history. As a freshman in the fall of 1968, Rob recalls playing on a team that included nine nationally ranked players. Daugherty was, as he said, "on the bottom of the heap," and the next year Gould recruited Roscoe Tanner and Sandy Mayer. So he gave up college tennis after two years to concentrate on a humanities major for pre-med students. After completing his medical studies at the U of M, he worked for two years as a general practitioner in Homer, AK, then spent two years in family practice in Spokane, WA. Rob today serves the Eugene, OR, community in a family practice clinic with seventy doctors. As for tennis, he still plays, enjoying time on court with his two daughters and "playing with hotshot high school kids looking for competition."

Mark Brandenburg
Rochester Mayo (1973-74)

Though Rochester's tennis dynasty was now on the wane, the city produced yet one more multiple singles champion, Mark Brandenburg. Mark dominated Region I opponents from the moment he first donned a Mayo warmup suit as a freshman in 1971. Playing No. 1 singles all four years, he lost only three matches in his exceptional high school career, one each in his first three years and all in state tournament competition. And after claiming his first title as a junior, he fought off all challengers his senior year, compiling a perfect 22-0 record in 1974 to claim that elusive second title. (On a side note, Mark's tennis career began the same year mine began as a coach at Northfield; so it was a privilege to share, if only vicariously during the few times I saw him play, in his success. He was a marvelous athlete, quick of foot and so balanced; but even more importantly, he was a gracious sportsman who treated all his opponents with respect.)

Brandenburg first strolled onto a tennis court at the age of seven. Two years later he was ready to give up tennis, but he overcame what seemed at the time a devastating 6-0, 6-0 drubbing in a tournament match ("I cried and told my parents I was never going to play again") and began playing serious tennis at age ten. At age fourteen he began traveling around the summer tennis circuit with Marv Hanenberger and it didn't take him long to establish his reputation, for his success in summer tournaments soon earned him a No. 1 ranking in the 12-and-under bracket in 1968. And though he continued to play other sports (even football through junior high school), Mark maintained his dominance of the summer circuit all through high school, holding the No. 1 position in his age group every year he played enough tournaments to qualify for a ranking. So he was No. 1 in singles four times (once in each age bracket from the 12s to the 18s) and No. 1 in doubles three times (in the 14s

Mark Brandenburg

with Rob Davies and Bruce Mannes—both from Aberdeen, SD—and in the 18s with Grant Helgeson).

Following in the shoes of Rochester's two other multiple champions, Dave Healey and Rob Daugherty, Mark also played basketball. In fact, he was a star point guard on a team that finished fourth in the State Tournament in 1974.

Perhaps more than any other player before him, Brandenburg's ride to his championships was a bumpy one characterized by moments of high drama. His junior year (1973), for instance, in the first official True Team State Tennis Tournament, Mark was playing senior Craig Jones of Edina in the semifinal match. The match was tied

2-2 and Mark had an opportunity to help Mayo advance to the finals and have a chance to win its first team title in any sport. (The other Rochester tennis titles were achieved before the advent of the True Team format.) Here's how Mark described that fateful match: "I had a match point in the second set when I started to develop cramps after hitting a backhand groundstroke and coming to the net. Craig hit a sitter on my forehand side, but I couldn't switch my grip so I hit it wide." Mark tried unsuccessfully to complete the match after a couple more games in the third set, so his coach, Bob Riege, said, "That's it, we're stopping it." And thus Mark's dream of leading Mayo to a state team championship ended ingloriously, for after reluctantly defaulting he was taken by ambulance to a hospital.

Despite this devastating loss and injury, Brandenburg came back on Friday to win two matches and then defeated two very tough opponents on Saturday (Grant Helgeson of St. Cloud Tech and his Thursday nemesis Jones, the 1972 singles champion) to claim the first of his two titles. His 6-4, 9-7 win over Jones in the final, one of the most hotly-contested two-set matches in state tennis history, was something of an upset because Jones was undefeated. Coach John Matlon of Edina, quoted in the June 8, 1973, *Minneapolis Tribune*, had been so confident that he said, "He [Jones] shouldn't have any trouble defending his title."

Along the way Brandenburg also had to contend with three other top-rated players, Tom Nelson of White Bear Lake, Billy Nolen of Litchfield, and Helgeson of St. Cloud Tech. Helgeson presented the biggest challenge, and it took Brandenburg three tough sets to defeat his Tech opponent in the semis (6-3, 1-6, 6-4).

In his senior year, 1974, Mark did not have to carry a burden for his team (Austin had upset Mayo in the Region 1 finals), but once again he had to dig deep just to get out of a very difficult match with Allyn Dart of team champion Minnetonka in the first round of the State Tournament. Dart, a formidable opponent, was ranked No. 2 in the NWLTA Section in Boys' 18s (behind Brandenburg) and so it was probably not fair that Mark had to play him in the first round. (Remember that pairings were drawn in advance and that winners from one region played the runners-up from another region and Dart had lost to Claude Peterson of Hopkins Lindbergh in the Region 6 final.) This was also the first year that the famous James Van Alen 9-point tiebreaker was employed, so of course Mark's match with Dart reached that dreaded simultaneous match point in the third set. Dart had won the first set in a tiebreaker and Mark had won the second 6-3. Brandenburg recounts the point this way: "I remember hitting an approach shot and coming to the net, then he hit a passing shot wide. I dropped my racket and came up in a manner not befitting a winner because I was a little disappointed in my play."

As a bystander stationed several courts away, I remember the confused looks on the faces of my fellow spectators, for in truth, by the demeanor of both players (and because from our vantage point we could not tell whether Dart's shot was in or out), we had no clue who had won the match. It was not until we saw the score posted that we realized Brandenburg had moved on to the next round.

And move on he did, motivated in spite of or because of this match, to defeat three other worthy opponents: seniors Paul Holbach of White Bear Lake in the quarters, Mark Hempel of Edina East in the semis, and Claude Peterson of Hopkins Lindbergh in the finals. Two of these matches would also go to three sets, the semi with Hempel (6-1, 4-6, 6-3) and the final with Peterson (6-7, 6-1, 6-0). In the Peterson match the drama of the tiebreaker was played out again, this time though in the first set (which Brandenburg lost), but Mark would earn decisive wins in the second and third sets. Perhaps the regular season had been too easy for Brandenburg—after all, he had not lost a single set until the State Tournament, but his mettle was sorely tested during these two grueling days.

With two state titles in hand, he could look back with pride on one of the great careers in Minnesota tennis history, a career forged by hard work, persistence, and exceptional athletic gifts. In addition to these accomplishments he, like many of the champions, spoke of the joy he experienced in being on a team. Getting in the van and going on long trips was especially enjoyable. He said, "For me the tennis was fun but being with the guys was the best part."

And as with so many of Marv's pupils, Mark was quick to credit Marv Hanenberger: "He was really generous with his time [often hitting with Mark for two hours on Sunday nights during basketball seasons] and helped out however he could. He really took an interest in me, and he was passionate about tennis." Hanenberger praised Mark for his "well-rounded game, good strokes, and good anticipation."

Always gracious in victory or defeat, Mark spoke well of his high school opponents, but he had special praise for Bob Amis, the 1971 champion from Edina. He said, "Bob was a relentless serve and volleyer who kept a lot of pressure on. He was a very solid player who played a very disciplined game, and he was very tough mentally." In an article in the *Minneapolis Tribune*, Mayo coach Bob Riege also praised Amis before also extolling Mark: "I think Amis was possibly the best I've seen in years. He was a natural, but Mark's all-around game is better. He doesn't have that powerhouse serve but he has great quickness and agility" (June 8, 1974). Ironically, Amis and Brandenburg became teammates at the U of M.

Other contemporaries shared Riege's opinion of Brandenburg. Future U of M teammate Grant Helgeson thought Mark was the best player he competed against in high school, and Paul Holbach of White Bear Lake said, "I would say Mark Brandenburg was the best. We all felt he was a god; he had perfect form and complete composure, and he was a great athlete." In addition, he was always a fair and considerate competitor. Northfield's No. 1 player in 1973 and '74, Stan Hunter, considered playing Mark the highlight of his career, saying, "He was a nice guy and I had nothing to lose. I remember not knowing whether to call his serves in or out because they were the fastest I'd seen up that point and I couldn't tell."

After leaving Rochester, Brandenburg had a very successful college tennis career, playing four years for coach Jerry Noyce at the U of M. He and Amis played No. 1 doubles, qualifying for the NCAA Tournament in Mark's sophomore year by virtue of a second-place finish in the Big Ten tournament. They would lose their first round match, but Mark had another crack at nationals his senior year in singles. This time he would lose, also in the first round, to Larry Gottfried; but he was thrilled to play next to John McEnroe the year he (McEnroe) won the NCAA singles title (1978). He was also a member of a very successful team his freshman year—the Gophers finished second in the Big Ten and were ranked No. 21 in the nation. In his four years he played No. 4 as a freshman, No. 2 as a sophomore, and No. 1 his junior and senior years, earning All-Big Ten honors for three years. During these four years he also played some NWLTA summer tournaments, twice earning No. 3 rankings in Men's Singles and in 1978 earning the No. 1 ranking (with former U of M player Bob VanHoef) in Men's Doubles. In addition, he served as captain his senior year (1978) and won two other coveted honors: the Louis Ratner Memorial Award in 1976 (for outstanding contributions to the team) and the Most Valuable Player Award in 1977 and '78.

As with many top-notch Division I college players who wonder how they might do at the top level of competition in their sport, Mark decided to give the pro circuit in Europe and the U.S. a try after graduation, playing sporadically for two years. In 1979 he earned a world ranking of 640 ("the same ranking as Rod Laver," he quipped) and defeated several higher-ranked players, including an Australian Davis Cup player. When he had satisfied this urge, Mark taught tennis at clubs in Chicago for six years, where he had the pleasure of hitting with pro women players such as Andrea Jaeger and Barbara Potter—whom he worked with as a traveling coach. In 1987 Brandenburg came back to Minneapolis, earned an MA in counseling psychology at St. Thomas, and, in 1997, began training to become a personal life and business coach. Mark is today a contented family man whose work as a certified sports counselor reflects his desire to help people (especially youngsters) become happy and well-adjusted individuals. He still plays a little recreational tennis and an occasional tournament such as the Pine Tree Mixed Doubles Tournament at White Bear Lake.

Mark Wheaton
Minnetonka (1975-76)

In 49 BCE Julius Caesar crossed the Rubicon, a river separating Gaul and Italy, conquered Italy and Spain, and, for his efforts, was named dictator of Rome. Our next tennis Caesar came, saw, and conquered the Minnesota high school tennis world in 1975, a year after the previous crown-bearer, Mark Brandenburg, graduated. His Rubicon was a difficult river to cross, for on the other side were formidable opponents such as Mark Nammacher from Minneapolis West, a player who had defeated him three times in this, his junior season. More about this encounter later, but let's travel back in time to discover how this newest Caesar got started in tennis.

As with all his siblings (older sister, Marnie, and younger brothers, John and David), Mark was encouraged by his parents (especially his mother, Mary Jane) to participate in an individual sport and then was taught tennis by his grandfather, John Hessey, on the community courts near his parents' home in Deephaven, just up from the beach on Lake Minnetonka. (See Chapter Ten for more about the Wheaton siblings' introduction to the game of tennis.) His grandfather taught him the fundamentals of the game, beginning when Mark was seven years old. Hessey's oft-repeated phrases were, "Hit it where they ain't" and "Let the other guy make the mistakes." This last admonition Mark applied unfailingly in his early tournament days in the 12-and-under division as he kept the ball coming back with the monotony of a metronome. In his first sanctioned tournament in the summer of 1967—he was only nine and playing in the boys' 12 division—he experienced both the lows and highs of tennis in one weekend at the Northwest Sectional played at Lafayette Country Club. While he lost to the No. 1 seed in the first round 6-0, 6-0, he was serendipitously paired with his first-round nemesis (Tom Clayton of Sioux Falls) in doubles and they won the title.

An all-around athlete, Wheaton participated in hockey and swimming as well as tennis throughout his formative years. Living close by Lake Minnetonka, it's not surprising that he took to these other sports like a duck takes to water, for in summer he could swim in the lake and in winter he could skate on its icy surface. Mark was in fact very successful in both sports, once holding an A.A.U. state record in the breaststroke in the 10-and-under age group, but hockey and tennis were his great passions. One of his main goals as a youngster was to win a state hockey title, and he had great memories of playing against such future stars as Neil Broten (former Gopher, North Star, and 1980 Olympic Miracle on Ice hero) and Rob McClanahan (also a former Gopher and 1980 Olympian), but when it wasn't as much fun any more he gave up hockey to focus completely on tennis. This turn of events was a real bonus for his tennis game. Now he could play with pros such as Dave Mathews, Dave Stearns, Connie Custodio, and Kevin Ylinen, giving him an opportunity to improve his game against older, stronger, and craftier players who played with different styles. Coach Chuck Anderson of Robbinsdale Cooper even let him practice with his team on occasion while he was still a ninth grader attending Fourth Baptist Christian Day School in Minneapolis.

Mark Wheaton

One of the best predictors of success at the state tournament level is a player's performance in summer tournaments, so it's not surprising that Mark ultimately won two state titles. In the 12-and-unders, for example, he finished No. 1 two times in singles and No. 1 in doubles three times (with Jim Norton of Wayzata, Bill Nolen of Litchfield, and Kent Helgeson of St. Cloud). In the 14s he was ranked No. 2 one year and No. 1 the second year in singles and No. 1 in doubles twice, both times with Helgeson. He closed his spectacular junior career with rankings of Nos. 3 and 2 in 16-and-under singles and No. 1 in 18 singles. One of his main goals was to qualify to play the Boys' National Junior Championship Tournament, which he did each year from age eleven in the 12-and-unders in Chattanooga, TN, through his final year of the 18-and-

unders in Kalamazoo, MI.

All of Wheaton's summer play was backstage preparation for the mainstage on which he would play for three years, the State High School Tournament. Mark attended the aforementioned Baptist school from his fifth-to-ninth grade years and so did not play high school tennis until he transferred to Minnetonka for his sophomore year. Soon he became part of an historic event, Minnetonka's first and only state tennis championship in just the second year of True Team competition. The year was 1974 and Mark quickly asserted himself by securing the No. 3 singles position in the lineup behind two stalwart senior players, Allyn Dart and exchange student Solomon Yohannes from Ethiopia. Mark recalls that his Skippers lost only one singles point the entire year during their undefeated 24-0 season—Dart lost a No. 1 singles match to state singles runner-up Claude Peterson of Hopkins Lindbergh. In a match to decide who would advance to the State Tournament, Minnetonka beat Lake Conference power Edina 3-2 in the Region finals, losing only the two doubles points. The Skippers capped this magical season in dominating fashion, rolling to the state title by blitzing Hibbing, Austin, and White Bear Lake by 5-0 scores. Following the championship match, No. 2 doubles player Mark Burton quipped that Wheaton and his singles compatriots Dart and Yohannes "didn't even need our doubles teams to win a match the entire year."

While the team championship was great fun for Mark, he had begun to establish his reputation in the individual competition as well, winning the state doubles title with Roger Jenkins. This reputation would be enhanced the next year, for he would capture the first of his two singles titles in 1975. Here's where Mark Nammacher comes back into the story. Nammacher, whom Mark considered the best player he competed against in high school, was "well-schooled at all points of the game. His lefty serve was almost impossible to return, he was lightning quick, he had an exquisite volley, and he had pinpoint accuracy. Though his groundstrokes were flat and aggressive, he didn't make errors. He also had a strong mental game and he was always prepared." Mark went on to say that Nammacher had been taught by Frank Voigt (who Mark said was "the only guy who gave me a lesson other than my grandpa"), so he used a classic continental forehand and hit low to high with no spin or wrist movement. And while Mark had beaten Nammacher on several occasions between the time he was eleven and sixteen years old, the gap had rapidly closed. Nammacher, a year older, hadn't had much trouble beating Wheaton in the 18-and-unders and into the 1975 high school season. In fact, Mark had lost to Nammacher three times this season, and by decisive scores of 6-1, 6-1; 6-1, 6-2; and 6-2, 6-2, the last match in the Region finals.

Now a senior, Nammacher, had been groomed to win the title this year, and he had a phenomenal regular-season record of 33-0. In the State Tournament he easily defeated junior Paul Holbach of White Bear Lake in the quarters, the player he felt was his only serious threat to the title. Meanwhile, Wheaton had won his first two matches in straight sets, setting up this memorable semifinal match on Saturday morning at the U of M courts. Here's how Mark described it: "I honestly felt I could beat him, but it would take something special, a different game plan just for him. He was an aggressive player and he was on top of his game, so I wrote out a game plan a week before the State Tourney, literally a 'Plan A' and a 'Plan B' and took it on court with me." This was a tactic, by the way, that Mark encouraged younger brother David to employ when he played in the State Tournament from 1982-84 and throughout his pro career. Simply titled "How I am going to beat Mark Nammacher," it was a game plan designed to get Mark to the net before Nammacher could. Here's how Wheaton remembers the end of this memorable match:

> I got help from the No. 6 player from the U of M, Danny More, my main sparring partner the week prior to State who also gave me a few tips of his own. I was really relaxed and confident, which was unexpected considering the thrashings he had given me already that season. We were playing on the first court near the bleachers, and I

won the first set 6-3, which really stunned him. Nammacher won the second 6-3 and the third set was really a close battle. At break point for me at 5-all, he hit his most dependable lefty first serve out wide to my backhand [in the ad court]; I lunged for it and returned it down the line. My return didn't have much on it and he was closing quickly to knife a backhand volley crosscourt. I sprinted across court determined to at least get my racket on his volley. In full stretch I not only got to the ball but took a big swipe at it. I never saw the shot because I went head first into the bleachers where some fans caught me, patted me on the back, and yelled, "Great shot, Mark!" As the ball passed him down the line (I was later told), I heard Nammacher yell out in despair, "Oh, no!" I jumped out of the bleachers and went to change sides knowing that I needed to serve out the match so I had to keep my composure. For the first time he seemed rattled. I felt very calm as I stuck to my game plan, winning the game at 15 and the match 7-5 in the third.

Speaking of the crowd, Mark was quoted in a June 8, 1975, *Minneapolis Tribune* article as saying, "Yeah, I kinda like it when there are more fans and it's an important match... I think I play better when there's some pressure." His assessment was confirmed by Coach Gary Peterson, who said in this same article, "Wheaton is a pressure player, a money player."

Nammacher was shocked, of course, for this was a huge upset, and now Mark had to guard against overconfidence for his finals match against another Frank Voigt pupil, senior Greg Swendseen of Edina East, a player Wheaton had beaten twice during the season. He did not let down or lose his focus and defeated Swendseen 6-4, 6-0 for his first state singles title.

The next season brought with it high expectations for Mark; he was, after all, the defending state champion and the No. 1 ranked 18-and-under singles player in the Northwestern Section, so he was a marked man. Despite this pressure, or maybe because of it, he handled the role of favorite very well during this 1976 season, defeating one of his chief competitors, No. 2 ranked Holbach (now a senior), at the Edina Metro Tournament and coming into the State Tournament with an undefeated record of 34-0. But once again he would have a difficult time crossing his Rubicon, overcoming an injury in the first round and a loss in the team tournament finals. (Minnetonka had advanced through the minefield of Region 6 competitors for the second time in the past three years).

Wheaton's first No. 1 singles match in the team tournament, however, was against senior Dave Peden of Coon Rapids, and he remembers racing along the back fence of the court to return Dave's overhead with a lob and then smashing into a bench behind the court. As a result, he cut his leg open, with blood streaming down on the court. Mark said, "I thought when I hit the bench it [his tournament] was all over." But after continuing to play, urged on by Coach Peterson, Wheaton limped through to victory. After the match he received assistance from the on-site U of M trainer and didn't worry about the injury until the dressing kept coming off due to sweat. During the next team match, against St. Paul Academy, Coach Peterson told him to tear off the bandage and to forget about his injury. Mark did as his coach told him, he won his match, and Minnetonka advanced to the team finals.

His second obstacle, this in the individual tournament, was underrated senior John Mattke, a great athlete whose tennis career blossomed at Gustavus and later as a player on the pro tour. Mark struggled against Mattke in his first-round match (7-5, 4-6, 6-3) to get to the quarters. Wheaton said that Mattke's athletic serve and volley game was the toughest he had faced all year.

His third impediment was a very disappointing three-set loss to St. Cloud Tech senior Kent Helgeson in the team finals, a match in which Mark held a 6-2, 5-1 lead and a match which gave Tech a 3-2 win and its first team championship. In addition, it was blistering hot—90 degrees—and the team and individual finals were held on the same day. A lesser mortal might have wilted, literally from the heat and figuratively from such a demoralizing loss, but Mark came back an hour later in the semifinals of the individual tournament to beat his friend, senior Jeff Steiner of Chaska 7-5, 6-2.

He then had two hours to freshen up before his final match with Holbach, the second-ranked player in the state behind Wheaton and the possessor of a big western forehand. So while Holbach was engaged in a titanic three-set battle with Helgeson for a place in the finals, Mark took a cool shower, ate, rested, and prayed with his pastor just before the match. The result was a well-deserved 6-4, 7-6 win. "Because of fatigue and the heat," he recalls, "I put everything into the tiebreaker, realizing a third set would be up for grabs." Thus, he became just the sixth Minnesota high school player to win multiple singles championships. Oh, yes, his other match in the singles draw was a surprisingly easy 6-0, 6-2 quarterfinal win against junior Greg Wicklund of Minneapolis Roosevelt, a future U of M player and prominent local teaching pro.

It should be noted that Wheaton was the first multiple champion since Ken Boyum to also claim a doubles title, which he won as a sophomore. Recalling that year, Mark recounts a sophomoric incident that took place before the final match against Brian Weinreis and Steve Quello of Hopkins Eisenhower: "We went to Bridgeman's Restaurant one-half hour before the match to have a sandwich but before we left one of the guys said, 'We'll pay for it if you'll eat a lollapalooza,' a mammoth ice cream dessert with several toppings. I ate it with ten minutes to spare but I felt sick as the match began, knowing I couldn't run or bend for fear I'd throw up. I had to sit in a chair right after the warmup, and I told Roger, 'You're gonna have to hold us up in this first set.' We got through the first set 6-4 and by the second set things had settled down a bit."

As a high school player Mark also earned an honor normally given only to pro sports athletes, having his picture on the back of a family-size WHEATIES breakfast cereal box. He had been chosen by the President's Council on Fitness and the WHEATIES Fitness Federation to encourage a healthy and fit lifestyle. His father, Bruce, had always eaten WHEATIES. And because of Mark's last name, his teammates had dubbed him "Wheaties" a year before the picture appeared on the cereal box. That year, 1975, his picture appeared on five million boxes nationwide. A fifteen-minute film, called "Portrait of a Champion," featuring Mark's training routine, was also made available to non-profit organizations.

Mark Wheaton had a magical high school career, and though he considered the singles titles as very special, he particularly remembers how much fun he had during the year Minnetonka won the team championship—1974. "I always wanted to be a part of a team sport *and* an individual sport. High school tennis had both aspects. Enjoying the season with my teammates and being a part of the winning team at state was a great memory for me." Mark was also generous in his praise of Coach Gary Peterson, saying, "He made tennis so much fun. He knew the technical things but practice wasn't drudgery for us. It was always enjoyable to come to practice. He always had a smile on his face and had many witty sayings."

Mark also expressed thankfulness to God and his family. "My parents and grandfather got me started in tennis, and I am thankful for their support and dedication. God truly blessed me through their guidance on and off court as well as in the contributions of others along the way. The victories and defeats on the court prepared me for many lessons in life God wanted me to learn. No one can accomplish anything significant in life without the help of others."

Several of Mark's contemporaries, including Kent Helgeson, Paul Holbach, and Greg Wicklund, considered him one of the best they played. He took his polished game to the U of M, where he competed for Jerry Noyce for four years. He played No. 1 doubles with former rival Mark Brandenburg one year and played various positions in the singles lineup. An injury to his lower back during the Big Ten tourney his junior year caused him to redshirt his senior year. He came back from the injury in 1981 and won the No. 3 Big Ten doubles title with Mike Hoeger, helping the Gophers win their first Big Ten team title since 1933.

Mark loved the way the human body worked, and as a result he thought he would become a surgeon some day. So as an undergraduate he majored in physiology with the idea of going into the field of sports medicine. He took the MCAT (Medical College Admissions Test) and then applied to the U of M Medical School but was turned down on the first go-round. He took the MCAT again while attending Moody Bible Institute in Chicago the year after graduating from the U, then applied to several medical schools and was wait-listed at George Washington U (GWU) in Washington, DC. While awaiting their verdict,

Mark took bold action, writing a blind letter to then Surgeon-General C. Everett Koop to see if he (Koop) could put a good word in for him for admittance to the GWU Medical School. Mark had briefly met Koop after a lecture Koop had given in Minneapolis earlier in the year and thought that, even though Koop certainly wouldn't remember him, he would be out only a postage stamp if he got no response. Surprisingly, Koop called him and told him he'd see what he could do for him. Shortly thereafter, Mark was admitted to GWU Medical School, which he felt was due in large part to Koop. He then kept a personal pledge to meet with Dr. Koop during each year in medical school at the Office of the Surgeon General on Capitol Hill.

After completing his medical degree at GWU, Wheaton finished his internship at Loma Linda U Center in Southern California, then took a break from his medical training to travel with and coach younger brother David on the pro tennis tour in 1988-89. He returned to Southern California to complete his physical medicine and rehabilitation (physiatry) residency training in 1989-92 and a sports medicine fellowship at the Southern California Orthopedic Institute in '94. Deciding that he wanted to return to Minnesota to be closer to his family, especially his grandparents who were approaching 100 years of age, Mark came back to his Deephaven roots to live and practice medicine in the same area where he grew up and learned to play tennis. Since '96, as a board-certified physiatrist, he has been diagnosing and treating professional athletes like his brother David, weekend warriors, and those with chronic pain conditions. Wheaton is trained in the specialized natural injection technique called prolotherapy which has been used successfully for many years as an alternative to drugs, cortisone, shots, and surgery, in the treatment of a wide range of back, neck, and joint conditions.

Brian Johnson
Edina East (1978-79)

Though Edina/Edina East had already won or shared eight team titles since its first in 1959 and captured seven doubles titles, only four singles players from the school had won titles and none of them were multiple singles champions during those twenty years. That would change in the years 1978-79, for the Hornets' No. 1 player, Brian Johnson, stung all competitors in state competition these two years and became the first of four Edina multiple champions.

Of all the multiple champions, he might be the one who got the most out of his ability. It wouldn't be fair to call him an "overachiever," for anyone who could win two state titles was no slouch; but he was not as naturally gifted as some of his contemporaries such as Dave Morin, Louie McKee, Brace Helgeson, or Andy Ringlien. Perhaps he could be compared to Michael Chang, a gritty pro of the 1980s and '90s who kept the ball coming back and made his opponents earn every single point. Well-known tennis guru Vic Braden, who said, "Give your opponent one more chance to pass gas," would have been admired Johnson; for he employed these good ground-stroke skills to earn four state tournament appearances in individual competition (three in singles and one in doubles) and also led Edina East to two team titles (in 1978-79).

As a ninth grader (he had just moved to Edina from Michigan), he and teammate Bruce Irwin took fourth in the doubles, and as a sophomore he lost to Brace Helgeson in the second round of the singles tournament. His big breakthrough came in his junior season, for that year (1978) he led Edina East to the team title and swept through five matches (winning each in straight sets) to take home the top prize in singles. In the process he eliminated his nemesis, '77 champion and top-ranked Kevin Smith of Hopkins Lindbergh in the quarters. Smith, a senior, had beaten him in the Region 6 tournament two years in a row, this year dealing Johnson a heartbreaking three-set loss. In a June 10, 1978, article

Brian Johnson

by Bruce Brothers in the *Minneapolis Tribune*, Johnson said, "I almost had him in our last match (in region semifinal play). I had three match points... I was ahead 6-2, 5-2 and then lost 7-5 in the third set. I was just waiting for him again." Johnson's victory over Smith was as much of a stunner as Smith's victory over No. 1 Greg Wicklund in the semis the year before. Smith admitted he was tired after a grueling 7-6, 2-6, 7-6 win over third-ranked Brace Helgeson (a senior) of St. Cloud Tech the previous round: "I was really tired. But he played well. I was missing a lot of shots, and he was keeping the ball in play" (June 10, 1978).

After dispatching Smith 7-6, 6-2, Johnson took care of Northfield junior Ringlien in the semis on Saturday (6-4, 6-3) and then beat Mounds View senior Steve Brandt in the finals (7-5, 6-2). This was a well-earned triumph for Johnson, in part because he had to win five matches to secure the title, four of which were against exceptional players. In one of those quirks of state tournament scheduling (where there is no seeding), he also had to overcome No. 5-ranked Louie McKee of Blake in the first round (7-6, 6-2).

Johnson's first singles championship was a surprise for a number of reasons: he barely qualified as the third entry from his region (after Smith and Dan Shannon of Minnetonka), he was ranked just No. 6 in the final coaches' ranking, he defeated three players ranked ahead of him (No. 1 Smith, No. 4 Ringlien, and McKee), he lost to Ringlien in team play two days earlier, and he had to win three matches on a sweltering 90-degree day with winds gusting at up to 40 mph. In a curious bit of scheduling, the MSHSL scheduled the semis of individual play on Saturday morning, the team finals (which Edina East won over

Minneapolis Roosevelt) at noon, and the individual finals at 3 PM. So Johnson had to defeat Ringlien in the morning, Roosevelt's Dave Schultz at noon in the final team match (a match he won 6-0, 6-1), and finally Brandt.

Unlike in 1978 when he was not expected to win, Johnson's 1979 singles championship was one the Las Vegas oddsmakers could have predicted. Ranked No. 1 by the coaches all year in Class AA, he wore the mantle of champion very well, leading his team to overwhelming 5-0 wins in each of its state matches and another title for Edina East. With only a 16-draw now that there was a two-class tournament, Johnson breezed through his first three individual tourney matches against seniors Dan Paulson of Austin (coach Keith Paulson's son), Wayne Rice of Willmar, and Dave Schulze of Minneapolis Roosevelt in straight sets.

But then he had to fend off a determined Dave Morin from White Bear Mariner in the finals. The third-ranked Morin, a senior who had beaten second-ranked Ringlien in the quarters, was a talented player who later had a fine tennis career at the U of M; so Johnson struggled mightily the last two sets to overcome Morin 6-1, 5-7, 7-6. Johnson admitted as much, in a June 2, 1979, article in the *Minneapolis Tribune*: "I played the first set well. After that I was just hanging in there and waiting for a break." In the third-set tiebreaker, the article continued, "Morin double-faulted twice and Johnson picked up three more points in rallies to Morin's one. Johnson saved his title on a shot by Morin down the middle that sailed past the base line." Johnson said, "That's the second tie-breaker I've been in this year. I usually do pretty well in them 'cause I play the percentages. I just keep constant pressure on the guy and make sure I don't make stupid mistakes" (June 2, 1979). Maybe this is how Johnson should be remembered, not as a crazed riverboat gambler who goes for broke in hopes of winning the jackpot but as a steady poker player who wins with safe bets.

Though he achieved good results in junior tournament play during his four years in Minnesota (once ranked co-No. 1 with Ringlien in the 18-and-under singles and No. 1 in doubles with Brian Lew of Edina one year in the 16s, for example), he did not do as well at the next level of tennis, in part because players with big serve and volley games were able to overpower him.

Johnson enrolled at the U of IA after graduation but played just one year of tennis there, perhaps because, as one of his high school competitors, Ringlien of Northfield, said, "He was a hard worker but did not possess abundant physical athletic talent. Maybe he just reached the highest level he could go." At the same time, Ringlien praised Johnson for having "good passing shots and an ability to close on the net and put away his volleys." One of Brian's high school teammates echoed Ringlien's comments about Johnson's steadiness and how he used his good two-handed backhand and "waited more for others to make mistakes." So though he may not have done as well at the next level of tennis as some of the other multiple champions, Johnson was still one of our great state champions.

Darryl Laddin
Hopkins Lindbergh/Hopkins (1982-83)

Both of this multiple champion's two titles had as much to do with his talent as it had to do with his rivalry with the young upstart David Wheaton, a rivalry that even produced a well-publicized altercation between their two fathers at the 1983 State Tournament. Like Chuck Darley and Brian Johnson before him, Laddin was another of our transplant champions. His family moved to Hopkins in 1980 from Highland Park, IL, where, according to an article by Charley McKenna in the May 12, 1983, *Minneapolis Star and Tribune*, Laddin had been "the second-ranked 14-and-under player in the Chicago area and among the top 60 in the nation." Making an immediate impact his first year in Hopkins, Laddin quickly helped his team become competitive and advanced all the way to the '81 singles final, where the sophomore lost to senior Bob Bateman of Edina 7-6, 6-2. He followed this auspicious debut up with two dominating seasons.

As a junior he posted a 24-0 record and won all four of his matches at State in straight sets, surrendering a total of just eleven games. In his toughest match, the final against seventh-grade phenom Wheaton, he gave up only five games in his 6-2, 6-3 win. Like the young piano recitalist who breathes easier after the last piece has been played, so did Laddin express relief when the last ball was struck. "I'm glad it's over," he said after beating Wheaton. "All season I felt the pressure of being rated No. 1," the unbeaten left-hander confessed in an article in the *Minneapolis Star and Tribune*. "I was supposed to win, and anything less wouldn't be good enough. It was the same in the championship match with Wheaton. He's young and the crowd sentiment was all for him. He's a good player, smart, and I might have been psyched out by all the media attention on him" (June 17, 1982).

And though his 1983 title was even more dominating (Laddin gave up only six games in four matches), his senior season was in some respects a more difficult one. For one thing, though he finished with more wins (twentynine), he did lose a match during the year, to the talented eighth grader Wheaton at the Metro tournament 6-2, 7-5. (Unfortunately for Minnesota tennis fans, an expected final between Wheaton and Laddin did not materialize because an injured Wheaton lost to Tom Olmscheid of Coon Rapids in the semis of the State Tournament.) Secondly, like Wheaton, Laddin had a hard time finding good competition during the season to stay sharp. However, he had prepped for the season during the summer

Darryl Laddin

of 1982 by playing the local circuit and four national tournaments. He reached a No. 64 national ranking in the 18s that year and also won the NWTA 18-and-under Sectional singles title.

In two other summers Casey Merickel of St. Cloud (who no longer lived in or and played high school tennis in Minnesota) challenged him as they jockeyed for the No. 1 ranking in NWTA play; but except for Wheaton no one challenged him in his 1983 high school matches. In the previously mentioned article by McKenna, Hopkins coach Tom Hutton is quoted as saying, "Darryl is a step above

high school players." Laddin admitted to being bored in some matches. The article noted, "in some ways they [these matches] hurt his game—a bad shot he hits for a winner against high school players would be slammed back down his throat by top level competition." And in many other states the high school competition is stronger, so why did Laddin stay in Minnesota for his senior year? He said, "I had thought about not playing high school tennis this year. But I figured if I was not going to play, I should come up with something better to do. And what else am I going to do? So why not play?" (*Minneapolis Star and Tribune*, May 12, 1983).

So he began to challenge himself, to play against himself, as it were. He told McKenna, "That's the only way to do it because there are a lot of guys you play who are not really that good" (May 12, 1983). To that end he set goals such as winning every point in the match (once he only gave up five points) or winning every game. During the season Laddin accomplished the latter goal five times and no opponent (except for Wheaton) won more than six games against him (May 12, 1983).

A good team player who practiced with his mates four times a week, Laddin was also given leave during the season to hit with pros to upgrade his game. In that same article by McKenna, it was noted that "Laddin usually plays against local pros six days a week... With Laddin's superior talent in mind, Hutton allows him to skip practice to play with local pros [particularly Jerry Noyce and Kevin Ylinen] and college players." But Hutton also commented that having Laddin in practice has helped his Nos. 2 and 3 players, Bill Marker and Scott Slick. "He has been accepted by the rest of the team and isn't above anybody," Hutton said. "He didn't ask for any special treatment" (*Minneapolis Star and Tribune*, May 12,

1983).

Having Laddin on the team gave Hutton, coaching the first combined Hopkins Lindbergh-Eisenhower team, the luxury of having, for the first time, a formidable team and a No. 1 player that everyone else tried to avoid. Though the Flyers did not make it to State, they won the Lake North with a 6-0 record, compiled an 11-0 dual meet record, and even beat Edina 4-3. Though Laddin said, "I'd like to win it [the team title] for the school" (May 12, 1983), St. Louis Park represented Region 6 in the state team tournament and St. Cloud Tech won the 1983 title.

After he knocked off Wheaton in the region finals, Laddin roared through the competition at State, beating junior Matt Boos of Apple Valley and highly regarded sophomore Mark Peterson of St. Paul Highland Park the first day. An article by Ralph Thornton in the *Minneapolis Star and Tribune* described Laddin's "quickness and leaping style at the net." And Laddin said of his own game, "I guess I'm an inch or so taller, my serve is harder, my volley better and I'm quicker (than last year)" (June 11, 1983).

Then in the Saturday matches he dispatched junior Jon Carlson, future Gustavus star and later the Gusties womens' coach (6-1, 6-0) in the semis; and in the finals he rolled over Coon Rapids senior Tom Olmscheid, the upset winner over Wheaton, by a similar 6-1, 6-0 score. Perhaps Olmscheid had run out of gas, for it had taken him two tough, three-set matches, including the emotional semifinal win over Wheaton, and 77 games (compared to Laddin's 41 games) to reach the final. Nevertheless, Laddin was clearly the better player who capped his two phenomenal seasons with excellent play in the championship match. "I'm as strong as he is as far as being able to hit the ball," Laddin told sports writer Howard Sinker, comparing himself to the huskier Olmscheid, a junior. "But I was able to get to his shots and move him around. At the beginning I made some nice passing shots and since I started out well, I think I just carried on." Though the score didn't reflect it, Olmscheid said he wasn't disappointed in his effort—and he hadn't given up. "I've never played anyone before that's as good as him," he said. "I didn't expect to get beat this bad but I didn't get my (first) serves in and he didn't miss a shot" (*Minneapolis Star and Tribune*, June 12, 1983).

Following graduation, Laddin took his two-handed backhand and steady game to courts around the country, particularly in California where he participated in the Junior Davis Cup trials "as one of the thirty best young male players in the country." After losing just two matches in three years of state competition, Laddin looked forward to improving his tennis in the summer. "I've got to work on my serve-and-volley game," he told Sinker. "At the national level kids hit harder and serve and volley a lot and you can't really beat them from the baseline" (June 12, 1983). After this exciting summer he enrolled at Harvard to continue his education and to play tennis.

Laddin had a fine career at Harvard, even returning home for an encore in the spring of 1984 to take part in the Republic Airlines Showcase Tourney hosted by the U of M and his former junior pro coach, Jerry Noyce. It was a triumphant return, for he claimed the No. 6 singles title.

Paul Odland
Edina (1985, 1987)

A tennis player who relaxed between matches at the State Tournament by angling for bass, Paul Odland reeled in two state singles titles during four seasons as Edina's No. 1 player. The only multiple singles champion from Minnesota who did not win his titles in back-to-back years, Odland loved to escape to Indian Head Lake for a few hours of bass fishing on occasion. He called this spot "a place I could go and totally unplug for a few hours." During his senior year, for example, he and sophomore teammate Mike Terwilliger "used to head there together and catch a few 'hogs' [big bass] between matches or just after practice."

But when he wasn't employing his fishing skills on his favorite lake, he was using his considerable tennis skills to out-angle his opponents on the tennis court. Except for a short time during his freshman year on the Edina team when Cort Larson played No. 1 singles, Odland held the top spot in the lineup for four years. This was a remarkable feat, given that he played with incredibly talented players such as Terwilliger (the 1989 singles champion); Chris Michaelson; and state doubles champions Mike Husebo,

Guy Carteng, Jason Nasby, and Charlie Eifrig. This was a team that advanced to State all four of those years, winning the title in Odland's senior year and finishing third his first three years. Practice matches for Odland, especially against Terwilliger, certainly made him a much better player, and often he had to defeat a teammate to advance in individual region and state competition as well. Terwilliger remembers these practice times, praising Odland as one of the two best players he competed against: "I was lucky to be able to play against Paul [Odland] in practice for two years. I thought he was great because his ground-strokes were so heavy and deep. He was tough to get to the net against."

This fisherman-tennis player got his start in tennis on the public parks with his father, Lynn (who took up the game and became an accomplished player in his own right). After his oldest sister Amy showed an interest in the game, Paul's parents got involved (his father hitting balls with Amy and his mother taking Amy to tournaments and practices); and soon he, Amy, and sister Carrie were out hitting balls during the summer. Paul said, "I was only eight or nine at the time, but soon I played my first 10-and-under tournament." Incidentally, both of his sisters became key players for the Edina teams which dominated Minnesota girls' tennis in the late 1970s and '80s, Carrie also claiming a doubles title in 1983. After this introduction to the game, Odland began to take group lessons at the Northwest Clubs. His first coach was Bill Keenan, a former high school and U of M player. Later on he received help form another local pro, Steve Benson, who also traveled to some national tournaments with the Odland family.

Once he began logging more time on the court, Odland became a very successful junior player. His first high NWTA ranking was a No. 1 in his final year in 12-and-under doubles with Ryan Skanse, a year the pair won the Sectional doubles title; and he earned two No. 1 singles rankings, one in the 14s and one in the 16s. In addition, he and Skanse won a second Sectional doubles championship in the 14s. He also played national tournaments in the summer, reaching a ranking of No. 122 in boys' 18 singles one year. Competing with the bigger fish on bigger waters, in addition to the good competition he

experienced in the NWTA, prepared him well for fishing on the smaller waters here in Minnesota. So he made it to State his freshman year, losing to senior Tom Trondson of Mounds View in the first round.

Then, as a sophomore, he surprised the Minnesota tennis world (and probably himself) by sweeping four matches to claim the 1985 singles title. Along the way he

Paul Odland

upset two older pre-tournament favorites, senior Mark Peterson of St. Paul Highland Park and junior Jason Hall of Minnehaha Academy, the player who would knock Odland out in the 1986 semis and go on to claim the singles title. It took three sets to dispose of Peterson (2-6, 6-4, 6-4), but Odland dispatched Hall in straight sets. Tom Briere, in an article in the June 9, 1985, *Minneapolis Star and Tribune*, said of the final match, "Edina sophomore Paul Odland used superior shotmaking in a match of baseline styles to dispose of Minnehaha Academy junior Jason Hall 6-1, 6-3."

The Peterson match illustrated Odland's penchant for coming from behind to win. In fact, Edina coach Les Szendrey called Odland "Mr. Comeback." Summing up, a July 1985 article in *Tennis Midwest* titled "Odland Wins Minnesota Singles Title," noted this about his play in the final match: "Odland, who was an underdog throughout the tournament, said patience paid off for him. His pre-match strategy was to keep the ball in play and allow Hall to make errors." Despite the 90 degree heat, Odland "never appeared tired in his victorious match" (July 1985).

While he was Mr. Comeback on Saturday, Odland was Mr. Ho-Hum on Friday, easily dispatching two opponents in straight sets. Since this was a 24-player draw and three players advanced from each region, it was possible to meet a teammate in an early-round match, so Odland played (and defeated) Edina's Chris Michaelson in the first round.

In 1986, even though Odland led his team to the State Tournament and he advanced in singles (though as runner-up from Region 6, having lost to freshman teammate Terwilliger in the finals), he must have been a bit disappointed in the outcome of both endeavors. His Edina team lost to the Cinderella boys from Minnehaha Academy 4-1 and had to settle for third place, and Odland lost to Hall in the semis and to St. Cloud Tech's Todd Schlorf in the third-place match. One consolation is that his 7-5, 6-3 two and one-half-hour match with Hall was one for the ages, a memorable match in which Hall was knocked down but not out (see Chapter Five for more on Hall). There were two other factors that conspired against him in this year's tournament: (1) he had to play three matches the first day because he lost in the region finals and (2) he was, by his own admission, a bit tired of tennis. "I felt a little burnt out until the match this noon," he told John Gilbert in an article in the *Minneapolis Star and Tribune.* "There wasn't much we could have done against Minnehaha yesterday because they played so well. I felt better today, but it's hard to say if I'm at the top of my game. I played almost every day all year, all through the winter, and once the high school season starts we play all the time" (June 7, 1986). Adding insult to injury, Odland broke strings on two rackets in the match with Hall and finished with a borrowed racket.

But just as some days and some years are better for fishing, so some are better for tennis. Odland stormed back his senior year to lead his team to its thirteenth team title (first since 1981) and to take his second singles title, thus becoming the ninth Minnesota player to do so. In the first 7-point team tournament Edina lost only one point in three matches and Odland won each of his matches easily.

After dispatching his first two opponents on Friday in straight sets, a rejuvenated Odland told *Minneapolis Star and Tribune* writer Ralph Thornton, "I'm going for it. I've changed my game, improved my volley, so I feel more well-rounded than last year." Ever the realist, he also said, "But you never know what can happen" (June 6, 1987). What happened is that he had to reach into his bag of tricks to defeat stubborn senior Matt Dawson of Willmar 6-2, 5-7, 7-5 in Saturday's semis, then he finished the day with a splendid 6-3, 7-5 win over Minnehaha Academy senior Ryan Skanse (who would go on to earn all-American status for three years at Gustavus). He had genuinely earned these two titles against a slew of top players, including 1986 champion Jason Hall, who said of Odland, "One of my top three opponents because he had a huge forehand."

Maybe it was his "gone fishing" approach that helped Odland again this year, for after Friday's matches, according to a *Minneapolis Star and Tribune* article by Ralph Thornton titled "Edina's Odland Relaxes, Wins Singles Title," he and Terwilliger once again "went fishing on a little private lake for three and one-half hours to relax" (June 7, 1987). Odland said, "We caught eight nice bass. Between matches today (Saturday) I went home, lay down and listened to some music." The article went on to say, "So Odland didn't get excited when Skanse had three set points in the first set and let him off the hook. After that, Odland's lobs and passing shots were too devastating for his opponent." Naturally, Skanse was disappointed that he let the fish get off the hook, so to speak, but Odland noted, "It's hard to say who let up and who came on strong. I got my timing on better in the second set, but I never felt it was in the bag" (June 7, 1987). It was a hot day (90 degrees) and Odland had played a total of 53 games and two long matches, but he survived and put an exclamation mark on his terrific four-year career at Edina.

About these high school tennis years he said, "My fondest memories of those times were of the sense of accomplishment that they provided." And while he has no desire to live in the past, he noted that "winning two titles did give me a sense of confidence that I have carried on ever since." He also said that being a part of a team created a new sense of purpose for him.

When he left Edina he enrolled at Notre Dame, a school better known for football than for tennis. While he appreciated the good education he received there, he also played a huge role in revitalizing the Irish tennis program. Odland played up and down the lineup during four years there (from No. 2 to No. 6 singles—and some doubles) and served as captain for coach Bob Bayliss his senior year. Assisting in recruiting "some great new talent that helped the team move from a decent regional team to a national contender" was what he considered his greatest contribution to the program. His senior year the Irish made the NCAA tournament, and the next year they finished second to Stanford.

No longer a tennis fanatic, he still plays from time to time and also runs and plays golf to stay fit. After working in sales in the San Francisco area following graduation from Notre Dame in 1991 with a bachelor's degree in business, Odland went back to school to get an MBA from the U of CA-Berkeley and now works in the real estate investment business. He is president and CEO of a company called Concierge Asset Management and lives in the Bay area.

Tim George
Orono (1990-91)

The careers of the next two multiple champions overlapped in many ways: they were the same age, both led their teams to state tournaments, both were top-ranked juniors, both played high school hockey, both were excellent groundstrokers, both played for west suburban schools, and both won two state singles championships. These two players were Tim George of Orono and Scott Sanderson of Edina. We begin with George because he won his first title earlier than Sanderson, as a sophomore, giving him an excellent chance to become only the third three-time champion (after Dave Healey and Chuck Darley).

Though there were these similarities between the

two, there were also significant differences. First of all, George was the champion in Class A and the first two-time winner in the small-school class; so it's fair to say that the competition at the state level for him was not quite as stiff. This comment is in no way meant to demean his accomplishments, for there were many strong players in Class A, including Staples-Motley's David Joerger—who upended George in 1992 to prevent him from achieving his three-peat dream—and Blake players such as two-time

Tim George

singles champion Robert Keith. Moreover, George played summer tournaments and more than held his own against top Class AA players. A late starter who didn't begin playing tennis until he was in eighth grade, he rose up the ladder from NWTA rankings of No. 22 his first year in 16 singles, to No. 10 the next year, and to No. 2 his first year in 18 singles (behind Erik Donley of Duluth East). That last year he also received Sectional endorsements to play in several national tournaments.

Sanderson, on the other hand, had been playing summer tournaments since he was nine years old, and he earned high rankings in every age group except the 18s. And though George did not have the good fortune to hit with as many skilled teammates as Sanderson did, in his sophomore year his teammate Erlend Saxegaard was a good match for him. Sanderson, in his senior year, had the luxury of being able to bang heads in practice with future singles champion Marcelo Borrelli, 1992 doubles champions Scott Riley and Tom Danford, and even coach Steve Paulsen (himself a top high school and college player).

But back to George. He claimed his first title in 1990, beating his teammate Saxegaard (a ninth-grade exchange student from Norway) in the final. The two good friends had battled all year in practice and had split matches against each other, George winning the subsection final and Saxegaard the section final. George, serving lefthanded but hitting with his right hand (perhaps because of his ambidexterity, given his hockey skills), dispatched Saxegaard 6-3, 6-4 in the state final. "It was hard, closing out on somebody I know as well as that," said George in a June 10, 1990, article in the *Star Tribune* by Nolan Zavoral. On his way to this matchup with his teammate, George won two matches, his first opponent providing the stiffest resistance. That player was junior Tony Baisley of Winona Cotter, and it took George three sets to put him away (6-3, 3-6, 6-3). He had less trouble in the semis against junior J. P. McDonald of East Grand Forks.

A pressure-packed year for George, 1991 saw him play three matches with the player who would help define his career, the aforementioned David Joerger. In these clashes of the titans, Joerger (the top-ranked player all year in Class A) won the first battle at the Pine City Invitational and George took the second in the state team final match won by Staples-Motley 4-1. And though this latter match was a tough three-setter which George won 6-4, 4-6, 6-0, the individual singles final (expected to be a classic matchup between the No. 1- and 2-ranked players) was not close, perhaps in part because summer surgery made it difficult for Joerger to run. In a June 9, 1991, article by Judd Zulgad in the *Star Tribune*, George said he was a bit surprised by the ease of his 6-1, 6-2 win because "there was [sic] a lot more people that picked Joerger to win." According to Zulgad, "The match featured Joerger's booming serve against George's finesse." George said of the match, "I just think that I figured out his weaknesses and I was able to exploit them... I kept a good balance of

lobs and good passing shots." After holding up his medal and finally being able to exhale, George talked about the pressure of defending his title but added that he thinks the stress will not be as great next season (June 9, 1991).

En route to his final match with Joerger, George dispatched his three other opponents in straight sets, including 1990 doubles champion Eric Lawatsch of Blue Earth in the semis (7-5, 6-2).

Though George traded his tennis racket for a hockey stick during the winter of his senior season, leading the Orono Spartans to the first Tier 2 hockey tournament, he didn't completely neglect tennis, sneaking in a few practices during the hockey season. His tennis coach, Tim Moynihan, speaking to *Star Tribune* writer Brian Wicker (April 23, 1992), said, "What he's done to improve has been largely out of season. It's not uncommon for him to play three or four hours a day, every day... He wants to be a nationally ranked player, and he will be. People who know him know he's not afraid to stick his nose in there and work hard." Calling him a player with a killer instinct, Moynihan also said of George, "He really goes after his opponents" (April 23, 1992).

So when the tennis season began in the spring of 1992, it took George a few weeks to become accustomed to the courts again after skating on ice for such a long season. But once he got his strokes back, he rolled through section play and headed to Eden Prairie High School—site of this year's State Tournament—primed for a run at his third title. An article in the *Star Tribune* (titled "Joerger Hopes to Avenge Big Loss to George in '91") described George's attempt to win his third title. First, coach Moynihan said of his star player, "Really, in the last week he's started to play the best he can." Said the still slightly rusty George, "I'm used to playing in the team tournament [Orono's team didn't make State this year]. (In the first match) I was nervous because I hadn't played in a while, but I played pretty well" (June 6, 1992).

So the stage was set for the last battle between George and Joerger, but because the MSHSL does not seed players at State, it would be in the semis instead of the finals. Both swept their first two matches easily, and thus this matchup would essentially be for the championship. Sophomore Robert Keith of Blake, a future two-time

Class A champion and three-time victim of George this year, said of the impending match between the two top players, "Joerger's knee is fine now and George is such a tough baseline player. Both are so tough and they won't let up a bit" (June 6, 1992).

Unfortunately for George, his old antagonist Joerger denied him the coveted three-peat, knocking him out in a veritable street brawl 7-5, 1-6, 7-6 (8-6) and then upending Keith in the finals to take home the 1992 singles title. *Star Tribune* writer Judd Zulgad said of the match, "George had opportunities to win, but [he] failed to capitalize. In the first set he was ahead 5-2 and serving when Joerger rallied, and in the third set George was serving for the match at 5-4, but [he] could not finish off Joerger." Generous in defeat even though a crucial call went against him in the tiebreaker, George credited Joerger: "I don't know if that is the best I've seen him (play), but he did play well. It was a good match" (June 7, 1992).

George's coach, Moynihan, called him "a truly enjoyable player to watch. He never gave up on a point and he had a very unusual playing style." Moynihan explained that "George served lefthanded (but could also serve right-handed) and hit overheads with either his right or left hand. And he could also hit a two-hand drop shot and topspin lob effectively." According to Moynihan, George learned some of these shots from Mark Calander, a Swedish foreign exchange student who finished third in Class AA singles in 1988 while playing for Orono. But above all, said Moynihan, he remembers that George "had an all-court game and a two-hand backhand he could do anything with."

It's also worth noting that George played the game fairly and with respect for his opponents, as evidenced by the 1992 Boys Junior Sportsmanship Award given him by the NWTA Northern Section.

It must have been heartbreaking for George to come so close and yet be so far from his goal, but he expressed genuine satisfaction in his accomplishments and said he was looking forward to continuing his tennis career the next year. Unlike two other Minnesota champions who also played hockey and chose that sport over tennis in college, Mike Terwilliger and Scott Sanderson, George chose tennis after receiving a partial scholarship to Bowling Green U. He stayed at Bowling Green for two years, then transferred to the U of M, where he tried out for but did not make the tennis squad.

Scott Sanderson
Edina (1991-92)

While George worked his racket magic against his Class A challengers on a slightly smaller stage (his senior year the matches were played at Eden Prairie High School), Sanderson performed on the larger Class AA stage at 98th Street Racquet Club. And while George won his two titles as a sophomore and junior, Sanderson won his back-to-back titles his junior and senior years. In addition, though George's accomplishments were perhaps less predictable, Sanderson seemed a lock to win at least one title. From the age of nine he had been competing in and winning junior tournaments in the summer. For instance, he was No. 1 his second year in the 10s, and in the 12s he was ranked No. 3 his first year and No. 1 the second year (a year in which he also won the Sectional singles championship). In the 14s he was ranked No. 3 and No. 2, taking his second Sectional singles championship his first year in the 14s. And in the 16s he was ranked No. 2 his first year in singles (behind Chris Laitala) and took the Sectional doubles championship (with Erik Donley); he followed this up his second year in the 16s with his fourth Sectional championship (again in singles) and a No. 1 ranking.

He did not play enough local tournaments to be ranked in his first year of the 18s, focusing instead on national tournaments, and his second year in the 18s he did not play NWTA tournaments because he was prepping for a college hockey career. In addition, he received NWTA endorsements to play national tournaments nearly every year of his junior career, earning a top 30 ranking in the 14s one year. Sanderson remembers finishing fourth that year in the National Hard Courts in San Antonio and recalls how that success helped him "realize I could compete on the national scene."

At Edina he joined the high school team as a sophomore (1990) and assumed the top spot in the lineup, following in the departed Mike Terwilliger's footsteps. Not only did he lead his team to a third-place finish at State that year, but he also advanced through Section 6 competition, beating Andy Ray of Hopkins in the final to claim a spot in the 16-draw singles competition. With unexpected victories over Eden Prairie's J. P. Demetriou (the eventual '90 singles champion) and Mounds View's Derek Howe during the season, Sanderson was ranked No. 4 in the last coaches' poll and had established himself as a force to be reckoned with.

Though drawing the very tough fourth-ranked Blake Bears in the first round of team play, the Hornets triumphed 4-3, in part because Sanderson (dubbed "their giant-killer" by *Star Tribune* writer Nolan Zavoral) whipped 1988 champion Chris Laitala 6-2, 6-0. Zavoral also said, "One of Sanderson's most effective shots was a backhand that moved Laitala around the court. Even Sanderson seemed surprised by his domination of the former state champion. 'I thought it'd be a really tough match, and that if I won, it'd go to three sets,' he said. 'I've only beaten him once in something like ten times. He still doesn't look fully recovered (from an arm injury) to me'" (June 7, 1990). Despite

Scott Sanderson

the giant-killer's efforts, Edina fell to the eventual team champion, No. 1-ranked Mounds View, in the semis and had to settle for third place. In singles Demetriou got his revenge, ending Sanderson's splendid sophomore season by eking out a monumental "3-hour, 40-minute quarter-final grind" (*Star Tribune*, Nolan Zavoral, June 9, 1990).

Sanderson's junior season (1991) was personally satisfying but disappointing from a team standpoint, for Hopkins beat Edina in the section semifinals and kept them out of the team tournament for the first time since 1983. Individually Sanderson again advanced to State as Section 6 champion and proceeded to win four matches against very talented players to secure his first Class AA singles title. His wins came at the expense of three former

or future champions and one future Gustavus star player. The first day he disposed of two future champions, ninth grader Scott Bowlby of Minneapolis Washburn (6-1, 6-0) and sophomore Marcelo Borrelli—then playing for Hill-Murray—in a tough three-setter in which he dropped the first set (4-6, 6-3, 6-1). In the semis he took out future Gustie Ryan Haddorf of Eden Prairie (a senior) 6-1, 6-1, then he had to get past senior and 1988 champion Chris Laitala of Blake again, a player who had shone like the North Star in the Minnesota sky for four years but whom Sanderson had beaten earlier in the year.

According to *Star Tribune* writer Judd Zulgad, Sanderson was frustrated early on in the first set with Laitala and looked up at the heavens and cried out, "Somebody help me" (June 9, 1991). That somebody turned out to be coach Steve Paulsen, who advised him when he was behind 5-2 in the first set "to slice the ball a lot more." This tactic kept the ball low and brought Laitala up to the net, and Sanderson closed out the set by winning five straight games. Said Sanderson, "I got down and I was playing tentative... I have to guard against getting mad at myself" (June 9, 1991).

Nevertheless, Sanderson fell behind in the second set as well 4-1. Once again he came storming back to tie the set at 4-all, but Laitala took a 5-4 lead, Sanderson went up 6-5, then Laitala evened the set at 6-6. The tiebreaker went to Sanderson 7-3, so with this 7-5, 7-6 win he had his first title. In that same article by Zulgad, coach Paulsen said of Scott's play, "He played very, very well. Variety was the key to his game. We came into the match thinking Scott [Sanderson] could come up (to the net) but Chris [Laitala] took the net away. This match could have gone either way." For his part Laitala credited Sanderson ("He played tough when he was down") but expressed disappointment that "I didn't go for it when I had the lead" (June 9, 1991).

Expected to win again in 1992, Sanderson did not disappoint, even though, according to an April 23, 1992, article in the *Star Tribune* by Brian Wicker, he took time in the winter to skate with "Team Minnesota, a high school all-star squad that had recently won a national hockey tournament in Chicago." As noted in the previous sketch about Tim George, Sanderson was an all-around athlete who wasn't consumed by tennis. "Ever since I was little, I've played a lot of sports," Sanderson told Wicker. "I don't want to concentrate on just one. I'd get tired of it." He recalls that he played baseball, football, soccer, hockey, and tennis until "at age twelve or thirteen I realized that I needed to concentrate on tennis in the summer" (April 23, 1992). So he established a schedule of playing just tennis and hockey, dividing the year into six-month segments. Though he eventually had to concentrate more on these two sports, he refused to bow to the pressure from some in the local tennis world to focus just on that sport, a rare concession in an age of increasing specialization in sports.

In addition, it never took him long to get his tennis legs back and his coach, Paulsen, wasn't worried: "I don't think it affected him that much." Paulsen also noted, in the aforementioned article by Wicker, "Scott is a very hard worker and a perfectionist. He's not happy unless he's in there and doing things well" (April 23, 1992). Another factor in the No. 1-ranked Sanderson's favor that season was that he gained the No. 3-ranked player in the state as a teammate and sparring partner, junior Borrelli, a transfer from Hill-Murray. And, as mentioned in the profile on Tim George, he also had senior teammate Tom Danford to contend with in practice. Coach Paulsen, in a *Star Tribune* article by Brian Wicker, said, "Scott hasn't lost a set all year and only one last year, to Marcelo (4-6, 6-3, 6-1 in the state quarterfinals). Tom's only lost three times. Marcelo has just lost to Scott" (June 3, 1992).

Although Sanderson's attempt to go undefeated for two high school seasons was thwarted by second-ranked Erik Donley of Duluth East in the team quarterfinals, this blip on the radar screen did not stop Edina from sweeping the field to claim the team championship in 1992 and it only fueled Sanderson's desire to do better in the

singles competition. Easily winning his first two matches in straight sets on Friday—against junior Brian Horsch of Hastings and senior Chris Hirsch of St. Cloud Apollo—Sanderson then hammered Donley 6-1, 6-1 in a fifty-two-minute semifinal match (after losing 16 games in that three-set loss to Donley on Wednesday). And in the finals he steamrolled over teammate Borrelli 6-0, 6-2. Including his two team matches on Thursday, Sanderson was so dominant that he gave up only eleven games in his final six matches. And in one of the most dominant performances in the Minnesota singles tournament, Sanderson gave up only seven games in those four matches. Borrelli told *Star Tribune* writer Brian Wicker, "He (Sanderson) just doesn't miss. I made a lot of errors, but he doesn't make any" (June 7, 1992).

In the foregoing *Star Tribune* article titled "Edina's Sanderson Dominates to Repeat As Singles Champion," Wicker also said, "The beauty of Sanderson's game is that it doesn't fit neatly into a category. He can play the heavy-topspin, baseline style of Borrelli; he's just as suited to serve-and-volley, as Donley prefers. Those two are generally regarded as the second- and third-best high school players in the state. Sanderson showed them how wide the gap is between them and No. 1." Against Donley Sanderson said, "I tried to attack more and come up to the net more. I think I had him guessing the whole time." And after settling for a baseline match against Borrelli in the section finals (a match Sanderson won, but in three sets), he changed strategy in this match, using an assortment of drives, chips, and volleys. "I didn't want to stay out there all day," Sanderson said. "Marcelo loves pace. He thrives on it. That's his game" (June 7, 1992). For Sanderson, this ability to change his game was possible because he had no glaring weaknesses. He described his own strengths as "consistency, strategy, variety, and a strong backhand."

Borrelli praised Sanderson, calling him "the best player I played against because he was in great condition [he was a great athlete], he was very steady, and he knew how to play each player differently."

So Sanderson closed his sterling career with two straight singles titles (with just two losses) and a major role on a team that took third place once and a championship this year. He'll be remembered in part as someone who was not consumed by the sport in his growing up years (remember, he played competitive hockey his junior year on legendary Edina coach Willard Ikola's final team, for instance), but he worked very hard to become a champion. At age eight or nine his mother, whom he called "a great athlete with a pretty competitive spirit," introduced him to tennis. According to Scott, "She hit balls with me and taught me some strategy and techniques she picked up by watching kids play." She played no favorites, also helping Scott's sisters Kristin, who played college tennis at Duke, and Kari, a 1989 state doubles champion.

Soon thereafter he enrolled in the STP junior development program, but his tennis skills blossomed during the fourth quarters of his seventh-, eighth-, and ninth-grade years when he attended Rick Macci's Grenelefe Tennis Academy in Florida. One of his training partners at the Academy was tennis prodigy and future pro Jennifer Capriati, and Sanderson remembers having many spirited hitting sessions with her.

Most important to him during these formative years were the friendships he made through sports. "Many of my current friends are teammates or acquaintances from sporting teams and events," he noted. But he counts his second tennis title as his most memorable event. "It was bittersweet as I knew it meant the end of competitive tennis because I was going to play hockey at Wisconsin," Sanderson said. In addition, he felt that high school tennis taught him about life and relationships and "how to focus and bear down when I needed to. I feel it's helped me personally and professionally in this regard." He also credited his Edina high school coach for helping him develop as a player and a person. "I think of how fortunate I was to have Steve Paulsen as my coach," Sanderson said. "He had a calming effect on me and he was such a great strategist who knew how to approach different players. He was a great player as well and he understood the game. And he had a great temperament and knack for knowing when to coach and when to observe," he continued.

Alas, Sanderson's tennis followers and fans were not able to watch him play tennis in college (even though he wasn't that far from home) because he chose to play Division 1 hockey at the U of WI. He did give tennis a brief try as a freshman, but the allure of playing college hockey in front of 8-15,000 screaming fans and in the hockey-mad atmosphere at Wisconsin was too tempting. Playing center for the Badgers for four years, he helped his team advance to the quarterfinals of the national tournament three times. As he was working toward a pre-med course of study and because hockey trips made it difficult to schedule his needed labs, it took him five years to graduate with his psychology major.

After a short stint with Andersen Consulting after graduation, Sanderson enrolled in the U of M Medical School in 1998. He completed his studies there and is now an ophthalmologist at Ophthalmologist P.A. in Edina. Sanderson has truly returned full circle, for he now makes his home in Edina.

Robert Keith
Blake (1993-94)

From the time that Blake won the first of its twelve state team titles in 1979, the school has produced seven state singles champions, but only Robert Keith won more than one title. And all but one of these seven titles, the one claimed by ninth grader Chris Laitala in 1988 when Coach John Hatch elected to enter his team in Class AA competition, was won in Class A competition. So Keith, a winner in his junior and senior seasons (1993-94), became the twelfth multiple singles winner in Minnesota and second (and thus far last) from Class A.

Growing up in a loving and close-knit family, Keith and his younger sister Laura (1994 Class A girls' singles champion) benefited from some quality family time on the tennis courts. Keith's father, who had also played tennis at Blake, began tossing balls to them from the time they were tiny tots. But soon he began taking lessons from pros such as Brian Biernat, Marc Miller, Dan Shannon, and Mike Ach and playing local and national tournaments—in the 14s.

He joined the Blake varsity team as an eighth grader. The next year he played a key role on the 1991 AA championship team, then assumed the mantle of No. 1 singles player in '92 and led the Bears to two more championships, these in Class A. And though he did not participate in state individual competition during that magical year of '91, he won all three of his No. 3 singles matches in the team tournament, including a pivotal one against St. Cloud Tech in the finals that helped Blake win 4-3. After losing to Tech during the year, Coach Hatch knew that, because of the strength of Tech's doubles, his team needed to win all four singles in order to take the match; so he moved doubles specialist Fergus Weir into the pivotal No. 4 singles spot. As noted in an article in the June 7, 1991, *Star Tribune*, "The match went according to Hatch's expectations—with Blake winning all four singles matches, while Tech swept the three doubles matches."

Weir had not played singles all year, and yet he rallied from a set down to secure the third point against Tech's Dave Holly. Keith said of this coaching move, "It was an extremely smart strategic move by Coach Hatch to move Fergus from doubles into the singles lineup. We kept Fergus a secret, playing him in doubles" (June 7, 1991).

Meanwhile, Keith, playing on a court adjacent to Weir, knew that he also had to win (Chris Laitala and Stewart Barry had won their matches and the doubles teams were losing). But he, too, lost the first set and wasn't altogether confident. "I saw Fergus [Weir] lost the first set... but I had faith in him," Keith told Wicker in that June 7 article. "I'm not sure if he had faith in me." However, once Weir won his match, Keith "disposed of Tech's Lou Thomas quickly" (June 7, 1991) and Blake had its championship. Even though Keith would go on to win two singles titles, serve as captain of his team for three years, and lead Blake to two more Class A team championships, his experience of playing (and winning) in this pressure-packed Class AA big school championship match was one of his best memories of high school tennis. He loved the team camaraderie of high school tennis and said, "It's much

Robert Keith

more exciting and frankly more difficult to play the team matches because your teammates depend on you. You're winning or losing for the team, not just for yourself."

If he needed incentive his junior year, Keith had only to recall his runner-up finish in the 1992 individual tournament when, as a sophomore, he lost to David Joerger of Staples-Motley 6-3, 6-2. He had lost three times during the season to Orono's two-time champion Tim George and then received what he thought would be a huge break when Joerger tripped up George in the semis. An article by Judd Zulgad noted Keith's delight in his good fortune: "I was excited when I saw I didn't have to play George. But David played a great match. It surprised me because I expected him to have a letdown after the first [semifinal] match" (*Star Tribune*, June 7, 1992). And Joerger admitted that after his tough match with George he had to guard against a letdown: "It was very emotional beating George. It was a long match, and while I'm in good shape physically, it took a lot out of me emotionally" (June 7, 1992).

Call it overconfidence, the breezy optimism of youth, or just plain being outplayed in the 1992 finals, there were none of these things in evidence in Keith's 1993 performance at State. He won his two Thursday matches in straight sets, then defeated junior Ben Jacobson from Benson (the eventual third-place winner) in the semis 6-4, 6-3 and Jacobson's senior teammate, Jon Koenings, in the finals (7-5, 6-2).

Reflecting on the previous year's loss to Joerger, Keith said a lack of mental toughness kept him from winning. "I've been trying to work on that, and I didn't allow myself to be angry or anything and give away any free points," he told *Star Tribune* writer Heath Smith (June 12, 1993). The first set was highly competitive, with both players holding serve until the final game, when Keith broke Koenings to take the set 7-5. "I think when I broke him at the end of the first set, that was big," said Keith. "He let down a little bit after that. Then I immediately broke him to start out the second set, so I think that was the turning point." Koenings, a six-year stalwart for coach Jane Kjos's team, said, "It was a mental letdown, and he really picked up his game... His swing got going and there was not much I could really do" (June 12, 1993). Final score: Keith 7-5, 6-2.

So Keith took home his first championship medal, satisfied with his individual play but disappointed that he was unable to lead his top-seeded Bears to what would have been their third straight team title (they finished third after being upset 3-2 in the semis by eventual champion SPA).

Using this upset loss to SPA in the 1993 team semis as inspiration, Blake, led by senior Keith, destroyed all comers in '94 to take its third title in the last four years. Unfortunately for them, SPA lost in the semis to Crookston, so Blake wasn't able to exact revenge against them; however, they swept all three matches by 5-0 scores, losing only one set in the process. It took just forty-two minutes for Blake to win in the finals, as all three singles players won their matches against Crookston without losing a set; and in what might be a team tournament record for one player, No. 2 singles player Ben Wismer did not lose a game in all three of his matches. But the impetus for such a dominating performance came in large part from Keith, who told *Star Tribune* writer Rachel Blount, "When we came out here, to get the guys motivated, I told them to look in the [tournament] program. SPA's picture was where ours could have been. Losing to them was a blow" (June 9, 1994).

This dominating team play fueled Keith in the singles competition, for he breezed through four matches on the way to his second singles championship. Getting through a straight-set first-round match on Thursday with SPA senior Travis Meldahl gave him some redemption for last year's team loss to SPA, then he defeated sophomore Monti Ossenfort of Luverne in the quarters. On Friday he defeated ninth grader George Grombacher of Duluth Marshall in the semis. That set up yet another encounter with the unfortunate Rob Warn of Minnehaha Academy,

a sophomore and eventual state singles champion (1996) who had already lost to Keith five times this season. Said Keith, in a June 11, 1994, article by Roman Augustoviz, "I had played [Warn] twelve times in high school matches but the thirteenth was kind of big. He had always given me trouble. He's a good player and I tried to think of this as the first time I was playing him" (*Star Tribune*).

There would be no unlucky thirteenth, for Keith handled Warn in straight sets 6-1, 6-3. Warn, whose only losses this year were to Keith (two of which were in three sets), gave credit (in the aforementioned article by Augustoviz) to his senior opponent: "I felt good about getting another shot at him, but he played real tough even when I was up on him. I tried to out-consistent him and he was more consistent. I tried to hit to his backhand but he kept everything deep." Warn's chance to get back in the match came at 3-4 in the second set, but after climbing back to deuce from 15-40 down on his serve he "double-faulted twice to lose the game." At match point "Keith hit a forehand winner deep into the right corner," then celebrated by blasting a ball almost to the top of the roof of the 98th Street Racquet Club building next to his court. Understandably relieved, Keith, who had played with a target on his back all year as the No. 1 player in Class A, said, "It (winning the title) was harder the senior year. Rob Warn always played me well, so I was pretty ecstatic to win" (*Star Tribune*, June 11, 1994).

Though he became a varsity high school player in eighth grade, Keith was not a highly ranked junior player until he entered the 18-and-under division. His early rankings were decent enough (No. 12 once in the 12s and once in the 14s, and No. 11 one year in the 16s; but his rankings in the 18s demonstrated the progress he made: No. 5 his first year, No. 4 his second year, and a No. 153 national ranking in 1993. After winning his second state title, he said, "Since tenth grade I've made a lot of strides. It was all too much for me as a sophomore ... Now I'm stronger, bigger and faster, but the key is mental focus" (*Star Tribune*, June 11, 1994). The boy tennis player had in fact become a man, a man who would take his mature game to Yale in the fall of 1994.

Coach Hatch (whom Keith called "a great coach and a fantastic person on and off the court") also noted how much Keith had improved over the years. But he also said of him, "Robert was a real worker and a tenacious competitor, a no-nonsense guy." Furthermore, Hatch praised Keith's mental game, which he said "was at least as good or better than his physical play." Adding praise was Ted Warner (Keith's "pro" and later the Blake coach), who said of Keith, "He was a very, very smart kid, a great competitor, and a very hard worker. What also made him successful was that he learned to not overswing with his arm." A quiet young man, Keith instead let his racket do the talking for him on court.

At Yale he played just one year before deciding that "there were other things I wanted to do." After completing his studies in economics at Yale in 1998, Keith worked for three years for Morgan Stanley in New York, then journeyed west to Stanford where he earned his MBA. With his second degree in hand (2003) he worked for a time as a venture capitalist in Palo Alto, CA, and then started his own investment firm. Today he lives in the San Francisco Bay area.

Matt Peplinski
Bloomington Jefferson (1995-96)

Minnesota's next multiple singles champion played for Coach Tom Saterdalen during the golden age of Bloomington Jefferson tennis, a period in which the boys' team won two state championships and three individual titles and the girls, led by Anh Nguyen's Class AA state record five straight singles titles, won three team championships and three doubles titles. For the boys' team this scintillating run began in 1991, when the team advanced to State from Section 6. Then, in '93, ninth grader Aaron Dvorak and senior Ben Bartels won the state doubles title. Next came team championships in '94 and '96 and two singles titles won by the subject of this sketch, Matt Peplinski. (After Peplinski graduated in 1996, Ryan Edlefsen claimed the singles crown in '97 and Phil Woo and Rory Theis won the doubles in '98; so this Jefferson run extended almost through the entire decade of the '90s.)

But this portrait is of Peplinski, a tennis prodigy who began "painting the lines" on the Nokomis Lakes Park tennis courts in Minneapolis at the age of three with his

hitting partner and future teammate Dvorak. Soon thereafter he moved to Bloomington and started to play more competitively. "We (Peplinski and Dvorak) both took more lessons, played more tourneys, and became better players," Peplinski said. Once he began competing in local and national summer tournaments, Peplinski became one of the top junior players of his era, earning high rankings in every age grouping. For instance, he was No. 2 in boys' 10 singles one year, No. 3 both years in 12 singles (and No. 1 in doubles with Justin Wismer his second year), and No. 2 his second year of 14 singles (and Section singles champion). But when he reached the 16s he really hit his stride, ranking second in singles and doubles (he and partner Trace Fielding won the Sectionals that year) his

Matt Peplinski

first year and No. 1 in both singles and doubles his second year in the 16s. In addition, this latter year he won the Section singles and doubles championships (with teammate Phil Woo) and earned a No. 44 national ranking in singles, even reaching the round of 16 at Kalamazoo that year, where he lost to future pro Alex Kim.

He continued this outstanding play in the 18s, taking both the singles and doubles (with Gregg Cummings)

Section titles his first year and earning a No. 1 ranking in both singles and doubles. Then, in his final year as a junior player, he was ranked No. 3 in the 18-and-under singles. And though he did not achieve another national ranking as high as No. 44, he was ranked in the top 135 both years in the 18s and he was chosen to participate in the Intersectional Team Championships as a member of the Northern Section team each year he played in the 16s and 18s.

His would be a storied career even if he had never played high school tennis, but Peplinski made his mark as a high school player as well, helping his team win those two state championships and claiming back-to-back Class AA singles crowns in 1995-96. First cracking the Jaguars' lineup as a No. 3 doubles player when he was in seventh grade, he helped Jefferson reach the State Team Tournament for the first time. Then, after a period of learning on the job as the new kid on the block, Peplinski made a big splash his sophomore year, leading his team to its first AA team title and advancing to the state singles tournament, where he lost in the semis to Winona foreign exchange student Rafael Gonzales and in the third-place match to Hopkins' Shai Ingber, the player who had also beaten him in the Section 6 finals. In the team competition, though he lost in the semifinal match to 1994 singles champion Todd Bowlby of Minneapolis Washburn, Jefferson took the match 4-3. He won both of his other team matchups with No. 1 singles players, including one in the Jaguars' title-clinching final against Blaine.

In 1995, though Jefferson did not defend its '94 team title (Edina beat them in the section final), Peplinski celebrated the first of his two undefeated seasons by capturing the coveted singles title. His first two opponents made Peplinski work, the second making him play three sets. Nevertheless, he overcame them, beating junior Casey McLain of Prior Lake in the first round 7-6, 6-4 and sophomore Matt Lipinski (brother of future two-time singles runner-up Brian) in the quarters 6-2, 3-6, 6-3. In the semis he easily defeated senior Greg Cummings of Roseville Area 6-1, 6-1 and then dominated senior Shawn Simmons of Burnsville in the finals 6-1, 6-2.

The next year was a spectacular one for Peplinski and his talented teammates, the most brilliant of all during this dominant stretch of Jefferson tennis. With a nearly unbeatable singles lineup of senior Peplinski at No. 1, senior Aaron Dvorak at No. 2, sophomore rising star Phil Woo at No. 3, and sophomore Ryan Edlefsen (1997 singles champion) at No. 4, Jefferson finished the season with an unblemished record of 23-0. In addition, Peplinski won his second singles title and the team of Woo and Edlefsen took second in the doubles competition. So it was nearly a sweep for the Jaguars in 1996, but winning the team championship did not come without some high drama. It seems that a "friend" of Dvorak's pulled a most untimely stunt on him before the section semifinal match with Eden Prairie. According to an article in the *Star Tribune* by Roman Augustoviz, [the "friend"] "pulled a chair away as a practical joke as Dvorak, one of the state's top singles players, was about to sit down. Dvorak tried to brace his fall with his right hand, the same hand he uses to grip his racquet. And snap—a broken knuckle on his little finger" (June 4, 1996). Dvorak was the 1993 doubles champion and a mainstay for the Jaguars since his seventh-grade year, but after this unfortunate fall his season was over. So coach Saterdalen moved Woo and Edlefsen up to Nos. 2 and 3 singles respectively and brought eighth grader Rory Theis ('98 doubles champion) up from doubles to No. 4 singles. Despite this setback, a confident Peplinski said, "Our No. 1 doubles team [seniors Nate Hultgren and Brett Dahlof] is playing at its peak right now, so losing [Dvorak] won't affect us. It just means everyone will have to play that much harder. We still have a good chance to win" (June 4, 1996). His confidence was well placed, for, after advancing through section play, the Jaguars bounced Stillwater Area 6-1, St. Cloud Tech 5-2, and Rochester Mayo with the horses that had driven them to the front of the race all year, their singles players. Even without Dvorak, the 1-2-3 punch of Peplinski, Woo, Edlefsen (each with undefeated season records) set the pace in the Jaguars' 5-2 win over Mayo in the finals.

After leading his mates to the team title, Peplinski capped a tiring and triumphant week by leaving no doubt about who was the No. 1 player in the state in 1996. Described by *Star Tribune* writer Nolan Zavoral as a player with "a steaming serve and stoic demeanor" ("Peplinski Ends Perfect Season with AA Title, June 8, 1996), Peplinski knocked off Edina senior Derek Brandt in the finals 6-2, 6-2, the third time he had beaten his Section 6 foe during the season. The article also noted that "Peplinski finished his senior season with a 27-0 record, and was 52-0 over the past two years. His last high school defeat was in the '94 State Tournament, where he finished fourth" (June 8, 1996). Perhaps it was only fitting that he hit a service winner on match point, for he had relied on his big serve all year.

In addition, maybe he wanted to end the match quickly, for he admitted to being tired. " I went to graduation last night and then to an all-night party at the school," Peplinski told Zavoral. "The principal came up and said he wanted me home by midnight. That was fine with me. I was really tired [after his two singles matches that day, two on Thursday, and three matches on Tuesday and Wednesday]." Peplinski's father Steve also acknowledged that Matt was weary: "He wouldn't get up. Then again, he's always hard to get up" (*Star Tribune*, June 8, 1996). Though he "woke up" in the final against Brandt, he showed evidence of his fatigue in the semifinal match with Spring Lake Park's Matt Hering, who pressed Peplinski and forced him into only his second three-set match of the year, a match he won 6-2, 3-6, 6-3. The day before he had little trouble with senior Chris Canniff of Hastings or with rising star Kevin Whipple of St. Cloud Tech, a ninth grader, defeating both in straight sets.

With two well-deserved state titles in hand, Peplinski set off with teammate Dvorak to the U of M to continue his schooling and tennis. However, he was redshirted his freshman year and decided to drop out of school to go to work. In the end he had to settle for some wonderful memories of playing for a coach whom he admired a great deal (Saterdalen) and socializing with good friends "I still hang out with." After teaching tennis in Atlanta for a time, he now lives in the Twin Cities area.

Coach Saterdalen of course remembers the six foot three Peplinski's overpowering tennis game, but he credits Matt's parents for their support which helped him achieve his goals. "One thing that made Matt so good was the tremendous support he got from his parents. They weren't pushy," said Saterdalen. And of course Peplinski will be remembered by Minnesota tennis fans as a tremendously gifted player. Greg Wicklund, one of his junior coaches,

said about him: "He was very talented. He had great hands and he had all the shots."

Justin Gaard
Edina (2000-01)

En garde! A phrase that literally translates from the French into "On guard!" is an expression we have heard in movies about pirates, mythical figures such as Robin Hood, and French adventurers such as the Three Musketeers. The *American Heritage Dictionary* says it is "used to warn a

Justin Gaard

fencer to assume the first position preparatory to a match" (1969, 433). Remember those swashbuckling films such as *Robin Hood*, with Errol Flynn wearing a jaunty hat and green tights and sporting a cocky grin, initiating a fight with a confident cry of *En garde*? Somehow, if you will excuse the lame homophone ("garde" and "Gaard"), I can picture Edina's Justin Gaard raising his racket and saying something like that, maybe a tamer "Let's go" or "Bring it on."

In any case, this last of Minnesota's multiple

champions (2000-01), like the movie swashbucklers, did not back down from a fight. And perhaps like few of the other multiple champions, he took more nicks and cuts along the way; but he always came back fighting. Early in his tennis career, for example, he lost many a racket battle with his peers, and yet he became a two-time champion. About his early career he said, "The first couple years the good players just killed me. The first time I played D. J. Geatz [2002 champion] when I was twelve, I lost 6-2, 6-0. David Hippee [of Wayzata], who had a good lefty serve, beat me 0-0 the first time I played him."

Always talented and an all-around athlete who played on the Edina varsity basketball team for three years, Gaard, said, "I was never a twelve-month-a-year tennis player. I didn't start playing tennis until March and I had a lot of other interests, including choir."

In fact, Gaard admitted that he didn't even like tennis until he saw four of America's young swashbucklers play exhibition matches at Target Center in 1991. These now legendary tennis stars were Andre Agassi, Pete Sampras, Jim Courier, and Minnesota's own David Wheaton; and their on-court skirmishing so inspired him that he began taking lessons again (his first group lessons at age four or five had not panned out). These lessons, when he was eight or nine, were first with Steve Molen from Gustavus and then with David Wheaton's brother John who "got me focused." He said, "I was spoiled because I worked with a number of other outstanding local teaching pros," including Greg Wicklund (who hit with him during his fifth- and sixth-hour study hall periods and before practice). Gaard called Wicklund "the best coach around here for strategy," but he also hit with former U of M and Chicago Bulls basketball star Trent Tucker on Sundays, eventually beating him when he was sixteen.

Gaard played his first tournament at age nine, then began playing in what he called "the whole circuit" the summer he turned eleven. Perhaps because he did not play all year, or maybe because (as he admitted), "my biggest challenge was getting over memories that these guys [the top players] used to kill me," he did not rise to the top until the summer of his second year in the 16s. Though he had secured some early national rankings (No. 224 in the 14s and No. 225 his first year in the 16s) and was No. 4 in his last year of the 14s in local Northern Section rankings

and No. 5 his first year in the 16s; it wasn't until his second year in the 16s that he established himself as a player to contend with. That year he won the 16 Sectional singles and doubles titles (with Trey Graft of Wayzata), played in the Zone Team Championships, and was ranked No. 1 locally and No. 132 nationally. The next year, his first in the 18s, he was again ranked No. 1 in the Northern Section and finished the year at No. 232 in the nation. Finally, focusing mostly on national tournaments his last year in the 18s, Gaard earned his best national ranking (No. 111) and won the 18 Sectional singles title.

And though he could not completely erase the memories of painful losses to his toughest competitors such as Hippee ("Dave had beaten me nine or ten times in a row") and Geatz ("I only beat him four or five times out of twenty"), Justin plugged away until he began to overcome these and other foes who had played more tennis than he had.

Breaking into the Edina lineup in 1997 as an eighth grader at second singles, Gaard was forced to move down to fourth singles in '98 when Cesar Vargas—state singles champion that year—and Geatz transferred to the school. This potent lineup produced a state title for Edina. The next year, though his No. 1-ranked team was upset 4-3 by Wayzata in the Section 6 final, Gaard made it to State and sent notice to future opponents to be "on guard" by taking third place in singles. His summer doubles partner, Trey Graft, had taken out pre-tournament favorite and top-ranked Geatz—now playing for Minneapolis Southwest, so Gaard felt confident going into the semis: "Any time the top dog goes out, you have to like your chances," he told *Star Tribune* writer Michael Rand in a June 4, 1999, article. Hoping to play his friend Graft in the finals (he had beaten him in the section finals), Gaard did not get his wish. Instead he fell to eventual champion Eric Butorac of Rochester John Marshall in the semis 6-4, 6-2 and had to settle for a third-place match with Graft, which he won.

Brandishing his graphite Head Agassi racket like a swashbuckler of old waving his sword, Gaard finally banished all those memories of losses past by claiming the 2000 singles title in his junior season. In addition, he led the Hornets to yet another team championship (their eighteenth), with 7-0 wins over Fergus Falls and Minneapolis South and a 6-1 triumph over Red Wing in the finals. And though he had beaten consensus No. 1 David Hippee in the section finals 6-4, 6-4, he was not necessarily the favorite to win the singles title. Given that Hippee was in the draw and that two other top players advanced to the semis with Gaard (Winona sophomore Brian Lipinski and Chaska foreign exchange student David Allahverdizade from Germany), this was a year when no clear-cut favorite could be identified. According to an article by *Star Tribune* writer Jim Paulsen, "Allahverdizade is undefeated (26-0), big (six foot three) and possesses perhaps the most intimidating arsenal of the four. His first serve booms, his second kicks high and he comes in behind his powerful forehand with skill and precision" (June 9, 2000). Lipinski was a formidable opponent with smooth strokes, impeccable footwork, and great foot speed, and Hippee has a "polished serve-and-volley game" (June 9, 2000).

Playing, by his own admission, his best tennis of the year, Gaard overcame the odds and rolled to the title, beating Lipinski in the semis 6-3, 2-6, 6-0 and his old nemesis Hippee in the finals 7-6 (10-8), 6-1.

Unlike most of the top players, Gaard did not play tennis year-round but instead took four months off to play basketball. In an article by *Star Tribune* writer Jim Paulsen, Gaard Expressed no regrets about this decision, saying, "I know if I played tennis all year long, I'd get sick of it. I play tennis eight months of the year, and I know that by the end of the summer I'm ready to take a break. So I'm notorious for starting slow, but it's not where you start, it's where you finish" (June 10, 2000).

So although he began slowly against Hippee, falling behind 3-0, Gaard won the next three games, lost the next two, and won three of the next four to send the first set to a tiebreaker. The article by Paulsen described the tiebreaker thus: "And what a pivotal and entertaining tiebreaker it was. Gaard and Hippee traded winners before Hippee won three points in a row to go up 6-3... Again Gaard rallied, winning the next three points and eventually winning the tiebreaker 10-8 and the set 7-6." Hippee had struggled in a two-hour, three-set semifinal match with Allahverdizade and he was tired, so Coach Gary Aasen told Gaard to "wear David [Hippee] out more by going over and under him. I told him to hit the ball more at David's feet, to make him bend down more. And Justin hit some great top-spin lobs. He made David work" (*Star Tribune*, June

10, 2000). The strategy worked, and after Gaard served a love game to wrap up the second set 6-1, he had his first title. Though both of his matches this final day of the tournament made some Edina hearts stop, his two matches the first day were danger free, straight-set wins.

Employing the same strategy in 2001 (dropping tennis for a time to focus on other pursuits), Gaard once again won the state singles championship, becoming the fourth Edina lad to accomplish this difficult feat and the fourteenth in state boys' tennis history. But the tournament season was a bit more challenging than he might have liked, for not only did he have to deal with normal graduation activities that go with being a senior, he had to perform on a stage other than that of tennis. According to an article by Jim Paulsen in the *Star Tribune*, what really concerned Gaard on the day of section individual tennis competition was his singing: "He sings with the Edina choir... And for the first time, [Justin Gaard], who sings with a resonating bass that belies his five foot ten, 160-pound stature, will perform with a small a capella group" (June 5, 2001). Not to worry; he cruised through his two section singles matches and "then he performed flawlessly with the choir" (June 5, 2001).

And though he was nervous about his singing, he was accustomed to pressure in other venues, most notably basketball and tennis, noted Paulsen. "He's a point guard on the basketball team, a position that requires decisiveness and leadership skills, and it shows through in his demeanor on the court. Gaard doesn't so much play an opponent as stalk him, with an aggressive all-around style that can produce a blistering baseline winner on one point and place a decisive volley on the next." In short, he is the very model of the swashbuckling fencer, whose *En garde!* means "Look out; I'm coming!" He admits to being very aggressive and intense in basketball, but he told Paulsen, in tennis "I'm not quite that intense, but I don't just sit back and hit, either" (June 5, 2001).

He would need all of his poise and aggressiveness to win this year, for his other old nemesis, junior D. J. Geatz, stood in his path in the quarterfinals of the singles competition. Geatz had beaten Gaard three times this season, most recently in the team semifinals which Minneapolis South (Geatz's new team) won on the way to its first title, so Gaard knew he'd have to contend with what

Jim Paulsen, in an article titled "A Change in Tactics: Gaard Beats Geatz in Class AA Singles," called "various displays of the disruptive on-court behavior that have become something of a dubious trademark [of Geatz's]" (*Star Tribune*, June 8, 2001). Gaard, who had been routed by Geatz in the team match the day before, said, "I tried to play his game and hit from the baseline. He killed me." So despite the fact that Geatz once screamed at Gaard and another time took a strategic bathroom break, Gaard was not distracted. He said, "He's been around college teams and has hit with college guys for so long that it gives him an edge. But it doesn't faze me. I've seen it before" (June 8, 2001). So instead of hanging on the baseline, Gaard chose the more aggressive style of serving and coming to the net at every opportunity. Doing so produced a 6-2 first-set victory, but he had to rally from 5-2 down in the second set to force a tiebreaker which he won 7-2 to make the score 6-2, 7-6.

Though he easily disposed of two other opponents, Gaard had difficulty overcoming the talented Lipinski, a junior, in the finals. In an article in the *Star Tribune*, writer Jim Paulsen said Gaard had to be patient because "After losing a close first set 7-5, Lipinski played virtually mistake-free tennis in winning the first five games of the second" (June 9, 2001). And though Gaard plugged away to make it 5-3, Lipinski closed out the set and took a 2-0 lead in the third. Hoping to "see a few chinks in [Lipinski's] armor," Gaard remained confident and "rallied to tie the set at 3-3 by breaking Lipinski's serve—and perhaps his heart—in a spectacular sixth game that went to deuce six times." Gaard sensed a letdown, so, according to Paulsen, he "went on the offensive. Gaard attacked Lipinski's second serve the rest of the match, coming to the net at every opportunity and winning three of the last four games with relative ease." After the match (a 7-5, 3-6, 6-4 Gaard victory), Lipinski credited his opponent by saying, "What can I say? [Gaard] never gives up. He's a great player" (June 9, 2001).

USPTA pro Greg Wicklund, who had worked with Gaard, wasn't surprised by his success. Said Wicklund, "He was a great athlete with good volleys and a good all-around game. But most importantly, he had a world-class backhand."

Admitting that defending his title had been difficult, Gaard savored even more this win; for he had outlasted two extremely tough and talented opponents on the way and had fought back in the final match, one in which a lesser player might have given up. His season officially over, Gaard looked forward to some rest and a resumption of his tennis career in college the next year. Looking back on his high school and junior tennis career, he cited a number of memorable events and highlights:

- His 24-0 record at fourth singles as a freshman.
- Edina beating Bloomington Jefferson to get to State and then winning the state title his freshman year.
- As a junior, winning another team title and upsetting Wayzata on their court.
- Fun conversations on bus rides.
- Team dinners provided by the parents, who gave his team a lot of support.
- Friendships with guys on the team.
- Losing to future pros Robby Ginepri (6-3, 6-4 in a national Tournament) and Andy Roddick in the third round at Kalamazoo (6-2, 6-2) in his second year of the 16s.

Gaard took a tennis scholarship to the U of IA and played one year there, compiling an 11-10 record at No. 1 doubles and a 12-10 record at No. 5 singles. After a year at Iowa he transferred to Normandale Community College for a semester, then enrolled at the U of M to play tennis and major in journalism. While studying at the U, he obtained a job as what he called a "gofer" at KFAN radio station, covering games, interviewing players after games, and helping produce the 9-12 morning "P. A. and Dubay Show" and Dan Barreiro's "Sunday Sermons Show." He's also finishing a journalism program in night school at St. Thomas and, though no longer competing at the U, he still keeps his hand in tennis helping coach the Blake girls' team and the Benilde-St. Margaret's boys' team.

Justin Gaard was a deserving champion, but he will also be remembered for his refreshing approach to sports and life in this increasing age of specialization. He was a young man who refused to become "just a tennis player."

One-time Singles Champions

1920s

This is a chapter about those who seized their opportunities or, as Shakespeare said, "took the current when it came." Some benefited from good fortune, but most were deserving champions who earned their medals. Their story began in the last decade of the 1920s.

It was 1929. The bubble had not yet burst; but ominous storm clouds foretold the end of a decade, variously dubbed "the Roaring 20s" or "the Jazz Age," of both incredible decadence and progress. There were parties in the mansions of newly minted millionaires, illegal drinking in speakeasies, a chicken in every pot, and two cars in every garage. It was also the beginning of the nation's love affair with celebrities such as movie stars Charlie Chaplin and Mary Pickford, aviator Charles Lindbergh, and sports figures Red Grange, Bobby Jones, Babe Ruth, and tennis legend Bill Tilden.

"We must take the current when it serves,
Or lose our ventures."
—Julius Caesar

But before it came crashing to an end in the Black Monday stock market demise of 1929, the Minnesota State High School League (MSHSL) launched a modest experiment in June, a state tennis tournament sanctioned by the League. The USLTA Northwestern Section had sponsored an Interscholastic Tournament for high school players since 1903, but it was not sanctioned by the MSHSL and was thus not considered an official high school competition. Held in conjunction with the second annual State Golf Tournament June 25-26, this first official high school tennis competition (and subsequent tournaments until 1949), permitted contestants to play both singles and doubles. An individual tournament in which member schools were allowed to enter two singles players and one doubles team, it was held on the thirty courts at the U of M tennis grounds on Washington Avenue.

In this first year, eight of the singles entrants also played doubles—one player from the Rochester pair that won the doubles title (Charles Britzius) finishing second in the singles, for instance. All matches leading up to the finals were two out of three sets, but both the singles and doubles finals were three out of five sets. It's not certain how individuals qualified for the tournament because there were very few inter-school matches and not many of the 437 member schools offered tennis as a competitive sport, but only one singles player and one doubles team emerged from the competition between the twelve Minneapolis and St. Paul schools fielding teams in Region 5. Some schools from other regions very likely entered players because they had no competition in their region, and not all regions sent players to this first tournament which has now been a Minnesota spring event for over three-quarters of a century. (See appendix C for the draw sheet from the tournament, with ten singles players and six doubles teams entered.)

In these early years from 1929 to 1949, every singles champion except two came from a Minneapolis or St. Paul school; and they all most likely grew up playing on public park courts in the Twin Cities. Unfortunately, there is not much information about the earliest champions, so I have not included biographical sketches of all of them. But when I was able to interview those still living or gain information about them from other sources, I have tried to bring them to life through short profiles. In every case I have included scores of their final matches and names of their opponents (and scores and names of other opponents if those matches were significant), all of which were gleaned from MSHSL bulletins. (In some cases only the last names were listed and in a few instances no scores were given.)

1929—Walter Monson
Minneapolis South

Claiming the gold medal this first year (a silver medal was awarded to the runner-up) was Walter Monson of Minneapolis South, an 8-6, 4-6, 7-5, 6-4 winner over Charles Britzius of Rochester. (For more about Britzius, see Chapter Six.) Monson's victory was well earned, for it took him 46 games to dispatch Britzius and another 26 games to defeat J. Halverson of Proctor in the semis (6-1, 3-6, 6-4).

1930s

This was the decade of the great worldwide Depression which contributed to the rise of fascism in Italy, Spain, and, of course, Germany. And in Russia the Stalinist killing machine was at work even before Hitler created his concentration camps. Here in the U.S. Prohibition ended in 1933 but life was bitterly hard for nearly everyone. John Steinbeck's *The Grapes of Wrath* captured the plight of poor migrant workers who left Oklahoma for what they discovered was not the promised land—California. Milk cost 14 cents a quart and bread 9 cents a loaf, but many could not afford to buy them.

Despite the privations of the time, people found hope in FDR's upbeat "fireside chats," in jobs created by the WPA, and by attending escapist films. And people gathered around their radios to listen to baseball games; the music of the Benny Goodman and Glenn Miller Big Bands; and popular programs such as "The Lone Ranger, The Green Hornet," and "Jack Armstrong, the All-American Boy." Comedy radio shows featuring Jack Benny, George Burns and Gracie Allen, and "Amos and Andy" were also popular. But in perhaps the greatest irony of the time, though most had little disposable income, Americans flocked to the movies. Sometimes considered Hollywood's golden age, this was the era of the Marx Brothers, Charlie Chaplin, Clark Gable, Greta Garbo, Shirley Temple, and many others. The Social Security system was introduced in 1935, Monopoly was the most popular board game, children studied from *Dick and Jane* readers, and Jesse Owens destroyed Hitler's notion of a master Aryan race by winning four gold medals at the 1936 Berlin Olympics. And the 1939 World's Fair in New York, a symbol of progress, marked a renewal after the Depression.

In sports the Yankees still ruled baseball (winning four World Series titles) and for much of the decade tennis was dominated by the likes of Fred Perry of England and Americans Ellsworth Vines, Don Budge, Helen Jacobs, and Alice Marble.

1930—Robert Tudor
St. Paul Central

In the first full year of the Depression, the State Tournament stage in Minnesota was dominated by twin brothers from St. Paul Central, seniors Robert and Dick Tudor. Both had honed their games by practicing and playing against each other for years; in fact, Robert had defeated Dick in the Interscholastic Tournament a week before the State competition in an epic five-set match. Dick did not make it to the state tournament singles final, though he and Robert claimed this second official doubles title. But Robert added the second major singles title in two weeks to his resume (including the Interscholastic), defeating teammate Roy Huber (the 1931 champion) in the finals 3-6, 6-3, 6-0, 6-1.

His match with Huber was Tudor's only test, for he sliced through the first three rounds like a knife through butter on a hot day, defeating each opponent in straight sets—one of whom was future state champion Paul Wilcox of Mountain Lake, an eighth grader.

1931—Roy Huber
St. Paul Central

From a draw of 24 singles players, the winner who emerged this year was senior Roy Huber of St. Paul Central (the 1930 runner-up), who defeated an opponent from Rochester with the wonderfully eponymous name of Johnny Lobb. One wonders if he used the lob in trying to ward off Huber, who defeated him in what the *MSHSL Bulletin* described as "a wearying contest of five sets: 6-4, 4-6, 6-3, 4-6, 6-1."

An article in the *Minneapolis Tribune* said of Huber's win, "The triumph of the St. Paul youth was the reward after he had played almost five hours of tennis during the closing rounds of the tournament Friday... the final singles match was not concluded until 7:45 PM" (June 13, 1931). Prior to this compelling final, Huber defeated Hansen (no school listed) and Venske (or Venzke) of Alexandria, then upended St. Paul Humboldt's Grover Fletcher (the 1932 champion) in another difficult match 6-4, 8-6. Lobb had knocked off ninth-grade prodigy and 1934 state singles champion Wilcox in the semis. In addition to his singles triumph, Huber also finished second in the doubles (with Albin Anderson).

The June 13 *Minneapolis Tribune* article also noted that "a calculating style of play with accurate placements helped Huber use his energy more wisely than his foe and despite his length of service Friday he was in as good shape as Lobb at the finish." Capricious late spring weather, more typical of March and April, bedeviled this third tournament: "Harassed by rainfall, the state high school tennis tournament at the U of M developed into a two-day affair Thursday when matches were forced into the confines of the fieldhouse and play was continued on Friday" (June 13, 1931).

Huber continued his tennis career at the U of M, winning a Big 10 doubles championship in 1935 with Bill Schommer and playing on two team champions (1932-33), the last Gopher team titlists until Jerry Noyce's 1981 squad.

1932—Grover Fletcher
St. Paul Humboldt

In 1932 there was a full draw of 32 singles players for the first time, and the trophy once again stayed on the east side of the Mississippi River. After prevailing over Rochester senior Marv Hanenberger in a marathon 9-7, 6-4 semifinal match, Grover Fletcher of St. Paul Humboldt defeated Mountain Lake's Paul Wilcox in a one-sided final 6-0, 6-0, 6-2.

In the first two rounds Fletcher easily dispatched Fred Pierce (no schools listed this year) and Gordon Sangsland. His next match was a donnybrook with eighth-grade prodigy Myron Lieberman of St. Paul Central, a future singles champion (1935) and two-time Interscholastic singles titlist. Fletcher, a senior, outslugged Lieberman 12-10 in one of the longest sets ever played in the singles tournament, then coasted to a 6-3 second-set win. In five matches Fletcher had played 104 games, earning a well-deserved title and a good night's sleep.

1933—Carl Hovland
Minneapolis Central

Perhaps because it was nearly a 32-draw in singles and a 16-draw in doubles, and because the finalists would have to play five singles matches and possibly three doubles matches if entered in both events, the MSHSL decreed that finals would not be three-out-of-five-set matches this year. So the 1933 singles winner, senior Carl Hovland, who also won the doubles title, only had to win two out of three sets in the championship match. Hovland, called by a *Minneapolis Tribune* staff writer "a well-built youth from Minneapolis Central" (June 7, 1933), defeated another Minneapolis player, Jack McKecknie from West, 6-1, 2-6, 6-2. McKecknie advanced to the finals with an upset win over favorite Paul Wilcox, the 1932 singles runner-up who was considered by many to be the best junior player in the NWLTA Section at the time.

After a first-round bye, Hovland defeated Winfield Thundstedt of Willmar and Hershman of Minneapolis North (no scores given). His semifinal match was another three-set tussle, this one a 6-2, 3-6, 6-4 win over Wallace Nosek of Proctor, brother of 1938 champion Henry.

1934—Paul Wilcox
Mountain Lake

After three previous tries, Wilcox (now a senior) finally broke through in the 1934 tournament, the first to be held over three days and the first in which team points were kept. Son of the principal at Mountain Lake, Wilcox had not only competed well at the State Tournament for three years but had also finished runner-up in the 1933 Interscholastic Tourney to Marvin Doherty of Fargo, ND. An article in the *Minneapolis Tribune* said of Wilcox's state tournament triumph, "Persistence won its reward Wednesday at the U of M. Paul Wilcox, in his third and last tournament, won the state high school tennis championship, an objective of himself [sic] and his brother Bob for several years, by defeating Arzy Kunz of Minneapolis Central 6-4, 9-7" (June 6, 1934). This win was even more noteworthy because it broke the string of five straight titles won by Twin Cities players and would be the first of only two singles championships won by outstate players until 1950 (the other by Henry Nosek of Proctor in 1938).

His was a well-deserved title, for he had to win five matches, three of which went the distance. Wilcox's first-round match did not foreshadow his troubles, for that was an easy 6-2, 6-1 win over Donald King of St. Paul Humboldt. But in two of the next three matches he had to pick himself off the mat after first-set losses (4-6, 6-2, 6-3 over Howard Taylor of Minneapolis Central and 4-6, 6-2, 6-4 over Lester Druck of St. Paul Central). And in a spirited semifinal, he outlasted Wallace Nosek 6-4, 1-6, 6-4. All told Wilcox played an astounding 123 games (19 more than 1933 champion Fletcher), a state record for a Minnesota singles or doubles champion.

Paul Wilcox

Wilcox was yet another local Minnesota lad who went on to play tennis for his home-state univerity team after graduating from high school.

1935—Myron Lieberman
St. Paul Central

Metro area dominance of Minnesota high school tennis was restored in 1935 when Myron (Mike) Lieberman of St. Paul Central, a junior, claimed the title by defeating Stan Brain of Minneapolis Roosevelt (son of U of M coach Phil Brain) 6-4, 6-4 at the U courts. Though this would be Lieberman's only state singles title, he would later make a name for himself by winning both the 1936 and '37 Interscholastic singles and doubles titles. His doubles partner was Central teammate Jack Marsh.

An article in the June 6, 1935, *St. Paul Pioneer Press*, titled "Central Player Downs Brain in Two 6-4 Sets," said of Lieberman's win, "Dropping the first two games in rapid succession to his Roosevelt rival, Lieberman settled down to take the next five straight games in the initial set and clinched the issue a short time later after Brain had run the score to 4-5. In the second set Brain took 3-1 and 4-2 leads before "the southpaw [Lieberman] returned to his cunning playing for the lines and corners, and successfully out-maneuvered the Roosevelt star and took the next four games." The article credited Lieberman's "subtle chop stroke and a smashing drive with his fairly consistent services" (June 6, 1935) for helping subdue Brain.

Lieberman's consistent play enabled him to subdue his previous two opponents with ease, Bill Deitrich of Minnepolis Washburn in the quarters and Albert Johnson of Hibbing in the semis.

After high school Lieberman also enrolled at the U of M and played tennis there.

1936—Richard McGee
University High School

For the next two years Twin Cities players captured the singles titles again, continuing the dominance of city tennis players. In 1936 senior Richard McGee of U High

defeated Brain (giving him two runner-up finishes) 6-3, 6-4 in the final after upsetting defending champion Lieberman in the semis 6-2, 5-7, 6-4. Except for that three-setter with Lieberman, McGee sailed through the draw like a catamaran racing across a lake on a windy day. His first three victims fell in straight sets: Ken Sather of Minneapolis Roosevelt, Dick Detchens of Minneapolis West, and Marv Hanenberger's brother, Duane, of Rochester.

Hall of Fame coach Cliff Caine, a sometimes doubles partner of McGee's, said of him, "He became the No. 1 player in western Pennsylvania. In some ways, even though he was much older at the time, he was the best player I ever played with."

1937—Jack Marsh
St. Paul Central

In 1937 Lieberman's former teammate from St. Paul Central, Jack Marsh (who had an all-around game, according to 1939 champion Christie Geanakoplos), vanquished unheralded Henry Nosek from the Northern hamlet of Proctor 6-1, 3-6, 6-3. And even though he, like the previous three champions, had to win five matches in order to claim the title, none but the final with Nosek provided a challenge for him. His first four victims all fell in two-set matches: Jack Roebke of Fairmont; Laurence Johnson of Hibbing; Clarence Higbie of Rochester; and Ed Von Sien of Minneapolis Central, 1937 doubles champion, in the semis.

And though St. Paul Central did not win the team title, Marsh's singles championship was the fourth for the school in the first nine years of state competition.

1938—Wallace Nosek
Proctor

By now a well-known quantity, Proctor senior Wallace Nosek, described by Minneapolis Central's Geanakoplos as "a hard hitter with firm groundstrokes," defeated all comers in the 1938 32-draw tournament. In a hotly contested final (6-4, 3-6, 7-5), Nosek took out Geanakoplos, a '37 doubles champion and the '39 singles champion.

Wallace Nosek

Nosek's victory would be the last by an outstate player in singles until Don Ranthum of Rochester in 1950 broke the ironclad grip on the trophy held by Twin Cities competitors.

As in 1937, when Marsh stormed through the draw, Nosek did the same, defeating his first four opponents in straight sets. These were, in order, Monroe Isenberg of Minneapolis North, Leonart Karkon of St. Paul Johnson, '39 doubles champion Wallace "Wally" Anderson of Minneapolis Central, and John Adams of Minneapolis West.

Nosek, too, went to the U of M to play tennis after graduation from high school.

1939—Christie Geanakoplos
Minneapolis Central

Geanakoplos (also spelled Geankoplis) brought the singles trophy back to Minneapolis in 1939, and he won the doubles with partner Wally Anderson as well, becoming the first Minnesota high school player to win three state individual championships. His hard-fought 8-6, 1-6, 6-2 win over Joe Armstrong Jr. of St. Paul Central also helped secure the unofficial team title for a very strong Central team coached by Ed Weber. Utilizing his excellent foot

speed and a bigger serve-and-volley game, Geanakoplos finally outlasted the tenacious young Armstrong, who was just a sophomore. His wins in singles and doubles helped Central take its second state championship in three years, the other coming in 1937.

Geanakoplos's road to the final was not entirely smooth, for he had to overcome a huge bump in the semis, the talented Don Gunner of Minneapolis West, a junior who would win the singles the next year. Nevertheless, he outdueled Gunner 9-7, 6-4. Earlier, he easily handled Richard Anderson of St. Paul Marshall and Laurence Johnson of Hibbing.

Arguably the most successful prep tennis player of the 1930s, Geanakoplos's 1939 state singles title, a runner-up finish in singles in '38, and two doubles titles would be enough to cement his reputation; but he was also very successful in summer junior play, in college, and as an adult player. As a junior player he won six Public Parks singles titles from 1936-39 and the '39 Interscholastic doubles championship. And after graduating from Central he would play three years at the U of M (serving as captain his junior and senior years of 1942-43 and playing No. 1 singles both those years). He also won five Mens' Open Singles titles from 1944-1954 in places such as Philadelphia; Edmonton, Canada; and Louisville, Kentucky. All told he won eighteen major singles and doubles championships in twenty years of competition at very high levels of tennis.

Born and raised in Minneapolis, Geanakoplos first learned the game on public park courts, particularly on the hallowed Nicollet Field courts at 40th and Nicollet which gave birth to so many of Minnesota's early tennis champions. He remembers being taught by his older brother Deno and defeating him after about two years even though Deno was four years older. Mineapolis Central played its matches at Nicollet so Christie also learned the game by watching players such as Ed Olson and Ed Von Sien (whom he would win a doubles title with in 1937). There was no coaching or instruction in those days; therefore, one needed to be self-reliant. So in addition to watching older players in action, Christie bought illustrated flip books featuring demonstrations and instructions written by top players such as Bill Tilden and Don Budge. "You flipped the pages so you could see motion. It was better than a

VCR because you could stop any time. That was the best instruction I ever had and I showed it to my high school team," said Geanakoplos.

In keeping with this theme of self-reliance, Christie and his doubles partner, Anderson, established their own racket stringing company in order to earn money to buy tennis rackets and equipment ("In high school they didn't give us any uniforms or tennis shoes"). Commenting about this business enterprise, Christie said, "I bought a tennis vice for $6, told my friends, printed cards, and called it 'Gopher Tennis Company.'" In the summer between their junior and senior years, he and Anderson rode the trolley downtown for twenty cents, set up shop in Donaldson's and Dayton's Department Stores, and strung two or three rackets a day for fifty cents apiece.

Geanakoplos has fond memories of these spartan, late-Depression, WWII years of high school and college tennis—"punching" the ball on the hardwood gym floor before the weather permitted outdoor play; playing in the junior boys' tournament on the grass courts at the Burton Estates in Minnetonka; competing against two-handed terror Joe Armstrong Jr. on the clay at the Parade Grounds for the 1939 state championship; helping his Central team claim two state championships, three city conference crowns, and thirty-straight dual meet wins; hitting with his favorite Don Budge Autograph or Maxply rackets; wearing discarded and of course oversized basketball uniforms at the Big Ten Tournament; and wearing out tennis shoes "about every three weeks in college."

But perhaps more important than all the tennis success he had was his prowess in the classroom. At the U Geanakoplos was named the top Gopher athlete-scholar of the year in 1943. A *Minneapolis Tribune* writer said, "A brilliant classroom average of 2.5 points out of a possible three was credited with making Christie Geanakopolis [sic] the first Minnesota tennis player in history to win the conference medal [at MN]. He is the second 'minor sport' athlete in 29 years to win the conference medal" (May 14, 1943). An oddity in his story is that he had earned enough credits to graduate after the winter quarter in his senior year, so he had to obtain a special Big Ten ruling in order to play on the tennis team in the spring of '43.

After earning his BS degree in chemical engineering in 1943, Geanakoplos attended graduate school at the U of Pennsylvania in Philadelphia and, because he worked for Atlantic Richfield Corporation on a project to make aviation gasoline, he was deferred from service in WWII. He completed his PhD at the U of PA in '49 and taught chemical engineering at Ohio State U for thirty-three years before moving back to Minneapolis where he continued to teach chemical engineering at the U of M almost until the time of his death in 2005. He also wrote two chemical engineering texts titled *Transport Processes and Unit Operations* and *Mass Transport Phenomena*.

1940s

Even though the Depression was winding down, according to a *Wikipedia* Web site featuring historical information from the 1940s, there were still over eight million unemployed Americans and the minimum wage was just 43 cents an hour at the beginning of this decade. Aside from the war, which took up the first half of the decade, there were scientific breakthroughs such as the first computer (called ENIAC) and the first commercial TV stations—thirteen of them in 1947. You could buy frozen dinners covered in aluminum foil and you could keep food in Tupperware dishes. Rhythm and blues music was popular, and African American musicians such as Dizzy Gillispie, Billie Holliday, Louis Armstrong, and Ella Fitzgerald appealed to all audiences. And children were regaled by the newest Disney animated films such as *Fantasia*, *Dumbo*, and *Bambi*.

According to the *Bud Collins' Tennis Encyclopedia*, in 1940 tennis was on hold all over Europe because of WWII—for example, the French and Wimbledon championships were not contested from 1940-45, the Italian Open from 1936-49, and the Australian Open from 1941-45 (appendix B, "Records," 586-618). However, since the North American continent was not a battlefield, the U.S. Open was played during the war, albeit with notable absences of tennis players serving overseas. In this shortened decade of international competition, Frank Parker, Pancho Gonzalez, and Jack Kramer were the dominant male players and Pauline Betz, Margaret Osborne Dupont, and Louise Brough were three women players of note.

1940—Don Gunner
Minneapolis West

Here in Minnesota, on June 3-4, 1940, at the U of M courts, the duo of Don Gunner and Fred Gulden from Minneapolis West took the prizes in singles and doubles at the eleventh annual State Tournament. Together they won the doubles and Gunner routed his partner in the singles final 6-0, 6-1. En route to his singles triumph over Gulden, Gunner won two easy matches, but he was fortunate to escape from his first-round match. After winning a marathon first set 10-8, Gunner lost another agonizingly protracted battle in the second set 9-7, then finally took control in the third set, winning 6-1 over his tenacious opponent, Roger McGee of U High (brother of 1936 champion Richard). And his semifinal match was also a test for him, but he overcame Hibbing's John Caliguiri 7-5, 4-6, 6-2.

Gunner was a worthy champion who excelled on the national level as well, winning the National Public Parks Tournament in 1941 and reaching the finals of the Northwest Interscholastic Tournament that year as well. Eventual two-time champion Ken Boyum remembers trying to pick up some tips from Gunner when he (Boyum) saw Gunner play at the Bryant Square courts.

After high school Gunner entered the service and, after WWII, enrolled at the U of M to play tennis, earning his first letter in 1946.

NOTE: while John Mueller's history of Minnesota high school champions lists Gunner as the 1940 winner, the MSHSL yearbook for that year lists his teammate Fred Gulden as the singles champion.

1941—Joe Armstrong Jr.
St. Paul Central

1941 marked the coming-of-age party for Joe Armstrong Jr. For three years this "little giant," called in various newspaper stories "the two-handed swatter, the two-handed clubber," or "the peewee backhander from St. Paul Central," had befuddled most opponents but never won a state championship. He had, however, won Interscholastic singles titles in 1939 and '40 and reached the finals in '41. As a sophomore he lost at State to Geanakoplos, who said of Armstrong, "He sat back and was accurate as Hades; he could hit a dime." When he played and defeated Armstrong for the state championship in '39, Geanakoplos struggled because, as he said, Armstrong hit "fantastic drop shots in my left-hand [backhand] corner." But he eventually turned aside Armstrong's challenge "by hitting deep and down-the-line."

Armstrong, a redhead, was the son of Joe Armstrong Sr., a top player who had won the Interscholastic Tournament in 1908 and '09. Using his patented two-handed stroke on both sides, Armstrong Jr. defeated six opponents in the two-day tournament, vanquishing sophomore Ken Boyum in the final 6-2, 5-7, 6-4. It was the only singles match Boyum lost in his high school career. With forty players in the draw, Armstrong needed to defeat five opponents to reach the finals. But he was not fazed, defeating each one decisively. In the first round his victim was Pemberton (no first name given) of Rochester, who fell 6-2, 6-2. Then, in succession, he took care of Kufus of Hutchinson 6-1, 6-0; Schul of Cloquet 6-0, 6-1; Fuller of Mineapolis South 6-1, 6-1; and, in the semis, Bucky Olson of St. Paul Johnson 6-2, 6-3. So after beating Boyum in the finals, Armstrong had logged 103 games on the U of M courts—not quite the 123 played by Paul Wilcox in 1934 but very impressive nonetheless. In winning six matches, Armstrong became the only Minnesota state champion to do so. No other champion required more than five matches to take home a title.

1942-43—Ken Boyum
Minneapolis West

The next four years were lean years for everyone in the U.S. as the war raged on across Europe and the Far East, and though it would cause a three-year cancellation of the Northwest Section's Interscholastic Tournaments, it did not prevent the MSHSL from holding state tennis competitions. To be sure, money was tight and schedules had to be reduced drastically; for example, in 1943 Minneapolis Southwest played only four scrimmages and no official matches before the State Tournament. In some years the state meet was just a one-day event, and there were also fewer participants (only eighteen in singles and nine in doubles in '43, for instance). Nonetheless, the quality of play was still very high, in part because of the play of two-time champion Ken Boyum of Minneapolis West in 1942 and '43. (See Chapter Four for his profile.)

1944–John Dunnigan
Minneapolis Washburn

In 1944 John Dunnigan of Minneapolis Washburn won the singles title by defeating Clyde Dedahl of Cloquet in the finals of this abbreviated one-day tournament. An article in the June 7, 1944, *Minneapolis Morning Tribune* spoke of Dunnigan's "classy network that paced his Washburn teammates to the team championship" and that no doubt helped him and teammate Jack Clements win the doubles title as well. Dunnigan was, according to '43 champion Boyum, "a very good athlete who had good strokes. He was so relaxed." Clearly outdistancing the field, Dunnigan romped through the draw without losing a set and dropping only nine games in four matches. His scores were 6-0, 6-0 over Jack Bernstein of Minneapolis West; 6-1, 6-2 over Jim Ellertson of Deephaven; 6-1, 6-2 over L. Youngdahl of Minneapolis Roosevelt; and 6-2, 6-1 over Bedahl.

Dunnigan enrolled at the U of M in 1944, but he was soon drafted and spent two years in the army. When he completed his term in the service, he returned to the U and asked coach Brain if he could try out for the team. According to his son Dave (who also played high school tennis in Minneapolis), Brain said, "If you think you're capable of being on the team, you need to beat this guy" [Ken Boyum]. He did beat Boyum—the only time he did so—and thus made the team, playing No. 2 behind Boyum and with another important Minnesota tennis figure, future highly ranked senior player and NWTA Hall of Fame member Bernie Gunderson.

His son Dave described him as an "incredibly modest person" who simply did not talk about his tennis accomplishments, choosing instead to let his racket do the talking on court. He continued as a strong player almost to the time he died. For example, with partner Dick Flom he was ranked No. 1 in the 45 doubles in 1972 and with Dave he was highly ranked for many years in Father/Son Doubles, reaching the top spot in 1979. He and his son played men's doubles tournaments together for thirty years, the last one in 2001 when he (John) was 75 years old. Dunnigan died in 2004.

1945–Brad Pitney
Minneapolis Washburn

For the first time since 1940, the tournament in 1945 consisted of a full 32-draw in singles and a 16-draw in doubles. Emerging as champion was Brad Pitney of Washburn, a 4-6, 6-1, 6-2 winner over Jack Thommen of Minneapolis Southwest, a big server who would go on to win the doubles title (with Edmund Gould) in '46.

Pitney earned his title against a strong field, defeating three future champions and five opponents. In the first round he upended the '45 doubles champion, Kent Calhoun, 6-4. 6-2. Next was a very difficult match with Kermit Johnson of Minneapolis Roosevelt, but Pitney prevailed 6-8, 6-0, 6-2. Then came future singles champion Esser Shragowitz of Minneapolis North, and this, too, was a three-setter Pitney won after dropping the first set (2-6, 6-4, 6-2). In the semis he won in straight sets over Jack Lee of Deephaven (6-2, 6-4), but once again he had to rally from a set down in the finals, pulling off another Houdini act to defeat Thommen. With 115 games under his belt, Pitney ranks second behind Paul Wilcox in most games played by a Minnesota singles champion in the State Tournament.

And once again, as it did in so many of these early years, the U of M snagged its high school singles champion; so Pitney too played his college tennis there. According to Thommen, Pitney left the state after graduating from the U of M and eventually became a wealthy Texas oilman.

1946–Esser Shragowitz
Minneapolis North

Claiming the singles title in 1946 was Esser Shragowitz, one of four tennis-playing brothers from Minneapolis North. Defeated by pre-meet favorite Thommen in a regular season meet, Shragowitz turned the tables on Thommen (a senior) by ousting him in the semifinals 6-3, 6-4. An article by Jim Byrne in the *Minneapolis Morning Tribune* titled "Shragowitz Family Shows 'Net' Profit," said this about Shragowitz's upset of Thommen, "Esser [Shragowitz] turned the tables on the likable Thommen, who has earned 12 letters at Southwest. After beating Thommen, Esser's prep tennis season was a success as far as he was concerned. He topped it off by beating sophomore Edmund Gould of Southwest [Thommen's teammate] in the finals for the State title." (June 3, 1946). The score was a decisive 6-0, 6-2.

This was a huge win for Shragowitz, in part because it was secured by beating five players from a strong field of 40 contestants, but also because, including summer tournament play, it was only his second junior title up to that time. He would go on to win the Interscholastic singles title (again over Thommen) that year and the 1948 Interscholastic doubles championship with partner Al Goldstein, but the 1946 state title would be the brightest feather in his cap.

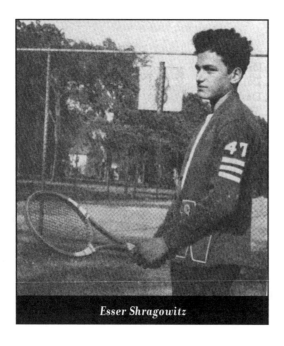

Esser Shragowitz

Along the way he easily defeated Jack Lloyd of St. Paul Marshall in the first round, but Bob Bergfalk of Minneapolis Washburn gave him a scare in the second round before falling 5-7, 6-2, 6-3. From then on it was smooth sailing, for he dispatched both Bob MacKinnon of St. Paul Johnson, Thommen, and Gould in straight sets.

1947–Rollin "Pudge" Whitcomb
Minneapolis Washburn

As an experiment, part of the new Summer Program of the MSHSL, the 1947 State Tournament was held as a one-day event on August 18. There were only thirteen singles players entered, and the champion was Rollin "Pudge" Whitcomb of Minneapolis Washburn. Whitcomb defeated all four of his opponents in straight sets, first knocking out William Gerberding of St. Paul Humboldt and then Herman Muus of Fergus Falls. His semifinal victim was Tsatsos (no first name given) of Winona; and in the final he took out Bert Willamson of St. Paul Marshall 6-1, 6-1.

Rollin Whitcomb

A baseball player until he was 14, Whitcomb was a late convert to tennis whose first experience of the game was a 6-3 loss to a girl-friend. Determined to improve his game, he went to Corrie's Sporting Goods store on Nicollet Avenue and bought an instructional book by Helen Hull Jacobs (a bit ironic because it was a book by a female player) which he studied carefully. He then played his girlfriend again and beat her 6-3, and thus became serious about the game. He credits baseball for some of his success ("a great game to take up tennis"), but he also recalls learning about volleying by watching Don Budge volley against Bobby Riggs in a 1946 match he saw them play in Minneapolis. Of the event, he said, "I had never seen anybody volley before."

One of his favorite memories from high school was

the sound of opening a tennis ball can, for he had but one can to use his first year of playing: "My dad bought me three balls and they were tiny at the end of the year." And despite the fact that he had no formal tennis instruction, he won 19-straight matches his senior year, capturing the city, region, and state titles. In addition, Whitcomb captained a Millers' team which won its second Twin Cities team title in a row and which won 20-straight dual meets his junior and senior years.

Whitcomb also recalls winning the Twin City singles championship at Dunning Field with a come-from-behind win over the aforementioned Gerberding. Though he doesn't have many vivid memories of his state tournament matches, he recalls one of the now-discredited remedies (recommended by coaches) used to prevent cramping and fatigue while playing: "They gave us salt pills [tablets] and told us not to drink water." He remembers clearly how much he loved match point "if I had it"; and he spoke highly of the value of high school sports, saying, "A competitive sport is the only way at an early age you can learn how to deal with problems of adulthood. Sports provide a laboratory for training and transfer."

After graduation from Washburn Pudge attended the U of M and played tennis for coach Phil Brain for two years. He served as an officer in the navy during the Korean War and from 1955 (when he graduated from the U law school) until 1992 he practiced law in Minneapolis. As an adult player he was fortunate to win some NWTA doubles titles when he partnered with Ken Boyum and was ranked as high as No. 5 in Men's Singles in 1961.

1948—Edmund "Chiefie" Gould
Minneapolis Southwest

In a scheduling anomaly, two State Tournaments were held during the 1948-49 school year, one in August (the '48 tournament), and one June 6-7, 1949. The '48 tourney was a one-day summer event (August 18) that featured a small draw of just 14 singles players. Edmund Gould of Minneapolis Southwest, the '46 doubles champion with teammate Jack Thommen (who called Gould "Chiefie"), claimed the singles title with a 6-3, 6-4, 4-6, 6-4 win over Dean Constantine of U High. Except for this match

with Constantine, Gould had little trouble, though he won an 8-6 set over Dresser (no first name given) of Winona in the first round. He closed that match out 6-3, then defeated Jacobson of Cloquet and John Nutting of Duluth Central in the semis in straight sets. Nutting would go on to win the '49 doubles title. The year before, according to Thommen, the unlucky Gould missed the streetcar and was thus defaulted from the tournament. Another peculiarity of this tournament was the return of the three-out-of-five-set format in the finals, a format that would finally be abandoned the next year. Gould, who had lost to Shragowitz in the finals his sophomore year, also won the doubles this year. These two state titles gave him three in his high school career, a distinction matched by only two previous champions: Geanakoplos (three titles) and Boyum (four).

(For more on Gould see Chapter Six.)

1949—Al Goldstein
Minneapolis North

Returning to a two-out-of-three-set format and to a spring schedule, the 1949 State Tournament produced a champion from Minneapolis North, Al Goldstein, a come-from-behind, three-set winner over Don Korn of Minneapolis Roosevelt (2-6, 6-1, 6-2). To reach the finals Goldstein defeated L. Nelson of St. Paul Murray, Araskog (no first name given) of Fergus Falls, and 1950 champion Don Ranthum of Rochester in the semis—all in straight sets.

Al Goldstein

As an aside, the MSHSL presented the first team championship trophy this year to Duluth Central, but the League did not officially recognize team champions until 1950.

1950s

The '50s began with the Korean War and extreme anti-Communist feelings which resulted in the notorious Army-McCarthy Hearings in 1954. Eisenhower became President in '52 and the decade was one of relative peace and calm after the Korean War ended. Queen Elizabeth ascended to the throne in '53, construction on the Interstate Highway System began in '56, the AFL and CIO merged, the Salk polio vaccine was perfected in '56, and science fiction became popular in both books and films. Disneyland opened; blue jeans became popular; drive-in movies were the rage; kids played with Silly Putty, Matchbox cars, Yahtzee, and Barbie dolls; teenagers swooned at Elvis Presley concerts; rock and roll was introduced to our culture; and Dick Clark's "American Bandstand" debuted. Alaska and Hawai became the 49th and 50th states in '59 and emerging anti-establishment voices arose in writers such as Jack Kerouac, Allen Ginsberg, Lawrence Ferlinghetti, and in books such as *Catcher in the Rye*.

Still, all was not as calm as it may have seemed. There was trouble in the South as Jim Crow laws were being tested: Rosa Parks refused to give up her bus seat in 1955, the '54 Brown versus the Board of Education Supreme Court ruling crippled the "separate but equal" school doctrine, and the schools in Little Rock were integrated in '57. And people were so worried about the "Red Menace" of Communism that they were building bomb shelters in their basements. The Cold War was in full swing.

International tennis saw the emergence of the first African American champion, Althea Gibson; the successes of American men such as Tony Trabert and Vic Seixas and the Aussies Lew Hoad, Ken Rosewall, and Frank Sedgman; and several Grand Slam victories by American women Maureen "Little Mo" Connolly, Doris Hart, and Shirley Frey.

For the first time in Minnesota (1950) players had to qualify for the State Tournament through region play, and for the first time an official team champion was crowned—though teams still earned points in individual competition and not in head-to-head matches between teams. In addition, players could no longer compete in both singles and doubles, so there would never again be a dual state champion in a single year. There were also no more Interscholastic Tournaments, so the State Tournament was now the marquee competition preceding summer junior tennis circuit play. The '50s witnessed the ascendance of southern Minnesota tennis power Rochester, a team that would win five team, four singles, and four doubles titles in this decade alone. And though Minneapolis Central in '57 and Minneapolis Marshall in '58 won team titles, these would be the last championships the previously dominant Twin Cities schools would win until Minneapolis South broke through in 2001. Just over the Minneapolis border were the new suburban tennis powers such as Edina, which would win its first title in '59.

1950—Don Ranthum
Rochester

Emerging as the singles titlist from a 16-draw in the 1950 tournament was junior Don Ranthum of Rochester, a 6-1, 6-1 victor over sophomore Vincent Bugliosi of Hibbing. Ranthum began his tournament run with an easy win over Norm Wigg of Duluth Central but ran into trouble in his quarterfinal match with Don Hufford of Minneapolis Southwest. "After winning the first set, 6-3, Don broke a string in his racket and lost the second set 6-3. After the set, a new racket was used and Ranthum won, 6-0, to take the match," noted an article in the *Rochester Post Bulletin* ("Rocket Net Team Pacing Field in State Tourney," June 6, 1950). Then in the semis Ranthum easily dispatched Charles Welman of Fairmont.

Future Hall of Fame coach Henry Dison, Ranthum's teammate, said of him, "He had fantastic concentration and that made him the player he was. He was very steady and good on the tough points." Marv Hanenberger remembers that Ranthum "had a well-rounded game and was a very steady competitor who made few errors." Very likely the only Minnesota tennis champion to become a professional bricklayer, Ranthum earned 20 of the 44 points the Rockets garnered in winning this first official state team title. Not much is known of Ranthum's whereabouts after high school, but Dison said he is deceased.

NOTE: In order to determine this first official team

champion, the MSHSL instituted the following system, assigning points in this manner: in round one, two points for a singles win and three for a doubles win; in round two, four points for singles and six for doubles; in round three, six points for singles and nine for doubles; and in round four, eight points for singles and twelve for doubles. This system remained in place for just two years, for in 1952 the League began using a two-points-for-singles/three-for-doubles scoring system that would more or less remain in place until the advent of True Team play in 1973.

1951–Vincent Bugliosi
Hibbing

Perhaps the most famous of all Minnesota champions—for something other than tennis, that is—Bugliosi would exact a measure of revenge against Rochester by defeating the Rockets' No. 1 player, Bob Reid, in the 1951 championship match 6-2, 6-0. Before beating Reid so soundly, Bugliosi disposed of three other opponents with equal ease: Richard Trumanhauser of Fairmont, Russell Holman of Deephaven, and '50 champion Ranthum (also of Rochester) in the semis. All told, he gave up just seven games in four matches.

Reid, a retired IBM employee, remembers well this second player from northeastern Minnesota (the first being Henry Nosek of Proctor) to win a state singles title. In a May 13, 2001, article in the *Duluth News Tribune* by Mark Stodghill, Reid is quoted as saying, "The first year [1950] he really did not look like a very good tennis player. It looked like he could hardly see over the net." Perhaps Reid had forgotten that Bugliosi had finished runner-up to his teammate Ranthum the previous year. In any case, he changed his view the next year. Said Reid, "It was a whole new Vince, and I'll tell you he was good. He'd stand at the baseline and return every ball you hit. He wore you down." And, he added, "He was a little on the cocky side, but anybody who is any good is—that's not degrading him" (May 13, 2001).

After Bugliosi won his championship, as a junior, he transferred to Hollywood High School in California because his parents wanted him to develop his tennis game further.

The son of Italian immigrants, Bugliosi recalled his hardscrabble early childhood growing up during the Depression as the son of a grocer. He especially remembered how hard he and his parents worked, saying, "You had to earn everything you got. There were no such things as credit cards. All the kids worked and gave the money to our parents. It was the normal thing to do. You earned your keep" (*Duluth News Tribune*, May 13, 2001). According to this same article, Bugliosi "delivered newspapers, mowed lawns, picked up garbage and painted lights on Howard Street." And "he hit tennis balls at every opportunity." He considered it a huge challenge to become a good tennis player, but he developed his game by hitting against a wall at the Memorial Building. "I used to hit a tennis ball hour after hour. I got very steady," he said (May 13, 2001). In fact, two-time state doubles champion and Hall of Fame member Henry Dison of Rochester called Bugliosi "a steady Freddy."

After his graduation from high school in 1952, Bugliosi had a conversation that summer with former Miami star and tennis legend, Pancho Segura. Bugliosi had received a partial scholarship to play tennis at the U of Miami and Segura convinced him to take it. However, at Miami he soon realized that only a few great players made money playing tennis in that era, and he didn't want to be a tennis bum; so "he buckled down on his studies and graduated from Miami with a bachelor's degree in business administration in 1956" (May 13, 2001).

Bugliosi then attended UCLA, where he received his law degree in 1964. He soon became one of the most celebrated trial lawyers in the country, according to a December 2, 2005 Web site article titled "Best Selling Author to Speak at Conference." The article notes that he won 105 out of 106 felony jury trials and never lost a murder case as a prosecutor for the Los Angeles County District Attorney's office." Described by famous trial lawyer F. Lee Bailey as "the quintessential prosecutor," he was also called in the article "a lawyer who has captivated courtrooms and audiences nationwide with his dynamic and tenacious approach in meticulously surrounding a criminal case with a web of facts from which there is no escape." Veteran criminal defense attorney Harry Weiss called Bugliosi the best trial lawyer of the past thirty years;

and another famous defense attorney, Gerry Spence, called Bugliosi "a giant in the legal profession" (Web site, December 2, 2005).

But he is best known for his prosecution of the 1969 Charles Manson "family" following the Sharon Tate/LaBianca murders and the book he wrote about the trial, called *Helter Skelter*, the top-selling crime book ever published by W. W. Norton. He was a young lawyer at the time and he said "he worked seven days a week, 100 hours a week" on the case (*Duluth News Tribune*, May 13, 2001).

Bugliosi, who parlayed his talents into writing, has received numerous awards for his best-selling true-crime books. These include *'Til Death Us Do Part*, an Edgar Allan Poe Award winner, and *Outrage: The Five Reasons Why O. J. Simpson Got Away With Murder*, which was No. 1 on the New York Times bestseller list. In addition, he wrote *None Dare Call It Treason* and most recently penned a book about the Supreme Court ruling regarding the Florida balloting irregularities in the 2000 election (*The Betrayal of America*). Still active in the legal profession—he is a partner in the Steinberg and Bugliosi firm—he continues to be in demand as a public speaker as well.

1952—Charles Edwards
Minneapolis Washburn

In the third year of the Korean War another player from Minneapolis, junior Charles Edwards of Washburn, captured the singles title. Though he garnered all eight points for his team in the new format of two points for each singles win and three for each doubles win, it was not enough to enable his team to wrest the team championship from Minneapolis Southwest. His opponent in the singles final was Jack Fithian of Minneapolis North, whom he conquered 6-3, 6-2. Before this match Edwards foiled Richard Trumanhauser of Fairmont 6-3, 6-0, then came from behind to upend Warren Olson of Lakeville (6-8, 6-2, 6-1). In the semis he vanquished freshman Dave Healey of Rochester 6-1, 7-5.

Edwards continued his fine play as a senior, but he gave up his crown in the 1953 tournament to young Healey, a rising star on the high school scene who would win three straight singles titles. Healey described Edwards

as "a very cerebral player." 1953 doubles champion Jack Roach said of Edwards, "He was a big strong guy who hit the ball hard and was very steady. A nice guy who went on to play at Harvard."

1953-55—Dave Healey
Rochester

For an account of Healey's 1953-55 championships, see Chapter Four.

1956—Charles Hawke
Minneapolis Central

Though Rochester continued its dominance of team play in 1956, Healey had graduated, opening things up for junior Charles Hawke of Minneapolis Central, who defeated senior Mark Anderson of St. James in an exhausting three-set final 5-7, 6-4, 9-7. Anderson had won two crucial singles matches in the 1954 state singles draw, earning four points for the '54 Dark Horse team champions from St. James. This loss to Hawke was especially painful for Anderson because he came so close to winning. He recalled, "I had match point against him and I hit a shot to his backhand corner and came in, but he threw up this beautiful lob to win the point." Anderson said of Hawke, "He wasn't a big guy; he was small and slight but in good shape. I was a little intimidated by him because he was a city guy." Another of Hawke's contemporaries, 1958 doubles champion John Desmond, called Hawke "Boomboom" because "he was a big hitter, a lefty who was all power and no touch."

Hawke wasn't tested in the tournament until the semis (he defeated Richard Ostram of Rochester in the first round and Minnesota governor Levander's son Harold Jr. in the semis) when he met up with Karl Honigman of Duluth East, who had participated in the doubles in 1954 and '55 with John Hatten. After dropping the first set 6-1, Hawke turned the tables and won the match 1-6, 7-5, 6-2.

After graduation Hawke went to the U of M but didn't play tennis there.

1957–Willie Hernandez
Hopkins

Once again a defending champion was dethroned, for in 1957 Hawke fell to Hopkins' Willie Hernandez, an exchange student from the Philippines, 6-2, 6-4, in the finals. Before knocking off Hawke, Hernandez double bageled his first two opponents: Albert Everson of Olivia and Harold Levander Jr. of South St. Paul. And in the semis he blitzed Gene Hovden of Fairmont 6-0, 6-2; so in four matches he gave up a total of just eight games. Not only was he the first foreign exchange student to win a state singles title (there would be just two more: Jakob Victorin and Cesar Vargas), but Hernandez was the first singles champion from a suburban school.

Willie Hernandez

Future state doubles champion John Desmond said this about Hernandez: "He was a short guy and was fast. He grew up on clay and had great groundstrokes; he hit hard but didn't make mistakes." 1960 singles champion Frank Kleckner also remembers Hernandez as having a clay court game. "He had a fine game and he was very smooth with big sweeping strokes. He really was a classy player," said Kleckner.

According to John Mueller, Minnesota's tennis historian, Hernandez once played in the Minikahda Tournament and also played for the Philippine Davis Cup Team. That's all we know of him, for he left the U.S. shortly after his high school year was completed.

1958–Bob Luck
St. Paul Monroe

The 1958 singles draw included Lake Conference notables such as future Minnetonka coach Gary Peterson, his teammate Bryan Stamp ('60 singles runner-up), and Robbinsdale standouts John Adams and Ken Franko; but it was a "lucky" lad from inner city St. Paul who took home the singles trophy. Bob Luck of Monroe dominated the competition all year, going undefeated in 32 matches and becoming the first champion from the capital city since little Joe Armstrong Jr. in '41. In the final match he dispatched Dave Poehler (a future high school coach and top NWTA player) from Hastings 6-1, 6-2. But it would take a bit of luck for the aptly named champion to get through to the finals. Said he, "There's no way in the world I thought I'd ever win a State Tournament. I should have lost to Gary Peterson [of Minnetonka] in the semis. The only way I won was to charge on every point—in those days most guys stayed back." Eventually he overcame Peterson 6-3, 2-6, 6-3.

Luck's longtime friend and that year's doubles champion, John Desmond, would have agreed with Luck's strategy: "He [Luck] liked to get to the net. He was a serve and volley guy who had a good volley. But he was also real consistent." Luck's other two matches were not close, straight-set triumphs over Thomas Olson of Detroit Lakes and Bill Zell of Mankato.

No country club player was he; in fact, Luck (the son of a streetcar and bus driver) grew up hitting tennis balls against the family's garage for hours and hours. In addition to practicing "100 hours on the wall for every one hour played," Luck also recalled that "I never had a tennis lesson, but my father used to take us to play at the St. Paul Central courts. We didn't have a lot of money, so I had to use rackets that my dad bought from the Salvation Army for a quarter." And though Luck honed his tennis game by hitting on that garage wall, he also enhanced his athletic skills by playing hockey and running cross country in the fall to stay in shape. "I was primarily a hockey player," Luck said. "My dad used to flood the rinks near Adams Elementary School and I played from 8 in the morning until 8 at night."

A four-year letterwinner in tennis who played No. 1 his last three years at Monroe, Luck reminisced about his junior-and senior-year tournament experiences. He recalls playing Governor Harold Levander's son (also named Harold) those two years in the region tournament. "I met Hap [his nickname] at Hamline for the region playdowns my junior year. He was a big guy (six foot three) and I was six feet and he blew me off the court. My senior year I'd gotten better and we met again in the regions and I was able to beat him." Luck added, "My closest match was with Tom Hutton (future Hamline basketball and tennis player and Hopkins basketball and tennis coach) to get into the State Tournament."

Of course he considers the highlight of his tennis career winning the state singles title, the only one for St. Paul Monroe. "The match was on Court 1 and my parents were in the stands," he recalls. His only regret is that Monroe was unable to win the team title as well. Teammates John Heuer and Dick Saser won the consolation title in doubles, and if he (Luck) had received two points for his first-round bye (which had been standard procedure in previous years), Monroe would have edged out Minneapolis Marshall 13-12. Instead, Marshall earned 12 points (to Monroe's 11) by virtue of the doubles title Desmond and Don Cooper won.

Offered a full ride to play tennis at the U of M by coach Chet Murphy (who had seen Luck play at State), Luck couldn't resist this gift, though he had also been offered a partial hockey scholarship at Rensselaer Polytechnic Institute. After sitting out his freshman year (frosh couldn't compete in those years), Luck played mostly No. 5 or 6 singles during his sophomore year at the U. A credit snafu—he had too many lower division credits and not a high enough grade point average for upper division courses—forced him to drop out of school his junior year, then he was drafted during the Vietnam War. He went to Army Medical School and served as a medic in Norfolk, VA. While serving there, he renewed acquaintances with another game he had played in high school, golf, a game he still plays today.

Married right after his discharge from the service in 1965, Luck embarked on a rigorous schedule in order to complete his college studies: taking college classes at River Falls State College during the day, working at Sperry-Rand from 3:30-11 PM, driving home to Como Park, then getting up at 6 AM to start up again. And though he wasn't playing college tennis, he tells a story about how tennis helped him get through college. "I had a class at River Falls, and the teacher (also the tennis coach) said, 'If you can beat me, you don't have to do a 3 PM lab class.' I beat him 6-0 so I didn't have to take the lab."

Luck completed his studies in 1967 (with degrees in business and math), and from then until his retirement in 2001 he worked as a computer programmer at Lockheed-Martin. Ironically, Luck has been a close friend of one of the high school competitors who helped deprive Monroe of that team championship, John Desmond. For a time he and Desmond played tournaments together, with rankings as high as No. 7 in Men's Doubles and No. 5 in the 35-and-Over division, but a severe case of tennis elbow cut short Luck's adult tournament career. After age 50, however, he took up the game again, but only for non-competitive play.

Luck has two boys (both of whom played high school tennis and hockey), and he has lived in Burnsville since 1968.

1959—Keith Butterfield
Edina

The final year of this decade was a coming-of-age party for Edina, a school which would become a dominant power in both boys' and girls' tennis in Minnesota. (See Chapter Nine for more on the Hornets.) By virtue of a second place finish in doubles and a singles championship, Edina earned 19 points to runner-up Faribault's 14.

The singles title went to Edina's No. 1 player, Keith Butterfield, who defeated Harold Dirksen of Rochester 11-9, 0-6, 6-1 in a final match in which the players had one competitive set and two very lopsided sets (the 20 games played in the first set were the most ever played in a set in a singles final). And it was just seven games shy of the number of games Butterfield played in his first two rounds. Those scores were 6-1, 6-0 (over Rolf Kolden of Bemidji) and 6-2, 6-0 (over Jerry Roth of Mankato). Then he defeated Tom Chamberlin of Duluth East in the quarters 6-0, 6-4; and in the semis he had a tussle with 1961 champion Bob Gustafson, a sophomore from St.

Paul Wilson. After dropping the first set 6-1, Butterfield recovered to win the next two sets by scores of 7-5, 6-3. All told, Butterfield was on court for 104 games.

1960s

An extraordinarily traumatic decade, the '60s was defined in this country by anti-establishment protests on college campuses (especially against the Vietnam War), racial violence in our cities, Civil Rights marches in the South, and assassinations (first John F. Kennedy in 1963, Malcolm X in '65, then Martin Luther King Jr. and Robert Kennedy in '68). Bob Dylan intoned "The Times They Are a Changin'" and indeed they were. The Civil Rights Act of 1964 banned discrimination in education, housing, and employment; women, through the efforts of people such as Bette Friedan and Gloria Steinem, were striving to obtain equal rights; and the Space Race with the Soviets was moving at warp speed. Marshall McLuhan coined the term "global village," pot smoking was in vogue, and many women lauded the "pill" as a development that gave them control over their bodies. Hippie was a new word in our lexicon and "women's lib" was a rallying cry. Also, the Berlin Wall was erected and we had two flareups with Cuba: the Bay of Pigs fiasco and the Cuban Missile Crisis.

In the entertainment world folksingers such as Joan Baez; Peter, Paul, and Mary; Dylan; and Pete Seeger were popular. And the Lads from Liverpool, the Beatles, became the dominant group of the decade. There were six James Bond movies, Woodstock became a symbol of the age, we were fascinated by pop artists such as Andy Warhol, and African American writers such as James Baldwin, Maya Angelou, and Gwendolyn Brooks educated us with their stories and poems.

This was also a watershed time for tennis in the open era of professionalism that began in 1968. On the international tennis scene Harry Hopman's boys from "down under" (Rod Laver, Roy Emerson, Neale Fraser, Fred Stolle, Tony Roche, Ken Rosewall, John Newcombe) were the kings of the court, while their female counterparts—the queens—were the up-and-coming Billie Jean (King) Moffitt and the nearly invincible Aussie, Margaret (Court) Smith.

In Minnesota two tennis powers ran roughshod over the competition, Rochester in the first half of the decade and Edina in the last half—Rochester taking home four team championships and finishing second another year and Edina winning two titles and finishing second four other times. In addition, Rochester players won six singles titles and Edina took one.

1960–Frank Kleckner
Minneapolis Roosevelt

Once more the MSHSL experimented with a fall tournament, holding the 1960 competition in October 1959. This year's singles champion was junior Frank Kleckner of Minneapolis Roosevelt, a 6-3, 6-2 winner over Bryan Stamp of Minnetonka. Undefeated in city conference play, Kleckner had lost only one match during the year, by an almost identical score, to the aforementioned Stamp in the finals of the region (6-3, 6-1). After losing to the tall and rangy Stamp in that regional final, Kleckner changed strategy when they met at State (thanks to some advice another player gave him), choosing to hit right at him

Frank Kleckner

instead of moving him from side to side.

The word "uneventful" describes Kleckner's first- and second-round matches, for these were straight-set wins over Richard Olson of Cloquet and Andrew Hanson of St. Peter. But in the semis Donyeyszyn (or Danylyszyn) of Minneapolis Central made Kleckner earn his trip to the finals, succumbing after a long struggle 6-4, 8-10, 6-1. About his state tournament experience Kleckner recalls that there wasn't much of a crowd at the meet and that it was "nasty weather." He also said, "I was really excited to win."

Unable to repeat in 1961, Kleckner was upended 6-2, 6-3 in the semis by the eventual champion, Bob Gustafson of St. Paul Wilson. Then, during the second set in his third-place match with his good friend Andy Goddard of Edina—a match Kleckner was winning handily—Goddard injured himself and his coach asked Kleckner if the match could be completed the next day. The good-hearted Kleckner agreed, but unfortunately for him, he, too, sustained an injury that evening, tearing the skin on both of his hands as a result of an accident on a trampoline. Said Kleckner, "I couldn't even hold a racket in my hand, so I had to forfeit the third-place match to Goddard."

Kleckner was always one of the top junior players in the Northwestern Section and was ranked No. 4 in singles his final year in junior play and No. 1 in doubles (ironically with Goddard, the player whom he forfeited to in the 1961 State Tournament). He had a blue blood tennis pedigree—his father (also named Frank) was a top player who finished second in the 1933 State doubles tournament. Unfortunately, because his father died unexpectedly when he was just 14 years old, Frank Jr. had to work to help support his family. According to his friend John Mueller, even though Kleckner continued to play tennis, his father's death and subsequent need to work took a lot out of him: "No question it affected his high school and college results." Kleckner said that he "worked construction during the day, changed clothes in the car, then played tennis at Nicollet until dark."

Kleckner remembers the trauma surrounding his father's death in July of 1958 as if it were yesterday. He had qualified for the national junior tournament at Kalamazoo, and the night before his father died he recalls playing guitar with Ricky Nelson, the famous son of Ozzie and Harriet Nelson. "The next day I won my first-round match but then got a call to come home," said he. "I flew home—it was my first time on a plane—and when I arrived Norm McDonald put his arm around me and told me my

dad died. Dad was only 43."

An all-around athlete who also played baseball and football in high school, Kleckner recalls that he donned his football gear after the 1960 fall tennis tournament and ran for a 68-yard touchdown on his first carry as a halfback in his first game, against Edison.

Like so many of the great Minnesota high school players of the 1940s, '50s, and '60s, Kleckner learned to play on the famed Nicollet Tennis Center courts. And except for the pointers he received from mentors such as McDonald, "Doc" Roberts, and Wendell Ottum, he never had any coaching. He also credits Bill Kuross for helping him learn how to compete. Kuross told him, "If you get into tennis, once you start to get tired, you dig in and that's when you play your best." In part because of this advice, Kleckner became a tenacious competitor who could run down anything and who did not like to lose.

His competitive fire continued to burn after high school, for he played two years at the U of M (he was No. 1 as a freshman and No. 2 or 3 as a sophomore). A *Minnesota Daily* article called Kleckner "a human dynamo" (May 7, 1963). Then he took up racketball after college, winning many tournaments and once even beating a national champion in a match in San Diego.

Though he began as a pre-med student at the U, he ended up going into the business world. Kleckner owned his own construction company and is proud of the fact that he built 200-300 homes in the Apple Valley/Burnsville area. Now semi-retired, he has gotten back into the home building and real estate business. He has one daughter, Mandee, and a son named Luke who played tennis for Apple Valley High School and Luther College. Unfortunately, Kleckner has had some serious health problems over the years. While in San Diego to play in the aforementioned racketball tournament he contracted a virus and almost died from a resulting heart difficulty. Kleckner was just 27 at the time, and this problem eventually made it necessary for him to get a heart transplant in 1998. Amazingly, he remembers playing in a father-son tournament (with Luke as his partner) the fall after he had his transplant and actually winning a round.

In the winter of 2005 he also contracted a serious staph infection which nearly claimed his life, but he credits his son's love and devotion for helping him survive. "My dad (Frank Kleckner Sr.) and I were very close and so are Luke and I. He's my reason for living," said Kleckner. One has to believe that he's also alive today because of that competitive will to win which carried him through during his high school tennis days.

Harking back to his days as a high school and junior player, Kleckner remembers winning a father-son tournament two weeks before his father died, meeting at Norm McDonald's tennis shop on 45th and Chicago Avenue for "Dave's popcorn and root beer floats," never losing a match in city play, and winning many local summer tournaments and qualifying for three national tournaments. Finally, he remembers the generosity of those who helped him, particularly Norm McDonald who provided him with rackets throughout his high school and junior career.

1961—Bob Gustafson
St. Paul Wilson

"If at first you don't succeed, try, try, again" could very well have been the motto of 1961 champion Bob Gustafson of St. Paul Wilson. One of the very best Minnesota junior players of his time—he was ranked No. 1 in his final year of what was then called Junior Singles, Gustafson finally broke through after three tries—he had finished fourth at State his sophomore year and fifth his junior year. But this was Gustafson's year, for, according to a June 7, 1961, article in the *St. Paul Pioneer Press*, "he didn't lose a set in district, regional, or state tournament playdowns, and no opponent won more than three games in any set."

After dispatching defending champion Frank Kleckner in the semis 6-2, 6-3, he overwhelmed Dave Rosenberg of St. Paul Central in the finals 6-0, 6-3 and took home the first place medal. His other results in the tournament were two-set wins over Art Johnson of Robbinsdale in the first round and Oliver Larson of Faribault in the second round.

Then Minneapolis West coach and Minikahda pro Bill Kuross, in an article in the *Minneapolis Morning Tribune* by Jim Byrne, predicted Gustafson's success in the tournament because, he said, "Gustafson has been playing some of the older tennis players around the Twin Cities all spring... I've played him myself and so has Norm McDonald" (May 29, 1961). While Gustafson rolled over all four of his opponents, he knew the match with 1960 champion Kleckner was the big one. Said he, "I feel my victory over Frank Kleckner of Roosevelt in the semifinals did the most to put me over" (May 29, 1961).

After graduation Gustafson attended Hamline where he continued to excel on the tennis courts and help the Pipers win MIAC titles.

NOTE: The Rosenberg brothers of St. Paul Central were top players for years in NWLTA play and both did well in state competition. For example, Dave was No. 2 in Junior Singles in 1961 behind Gustafson and Al was No. 2 in Boys' Singles. At State Dave finished second in '61 and fourth in '62 and Al finished third in '62 and fifth in '63.

1962-64—Chuck Darley
Rochester

Like a comet blazing across the sky, Iowa import Chuck Darley, perhaps the most dominant high school tennis player in state history, arrived on the Minnesota scene in 1962. And for three years (1962-64) this Rochester Rocket took home the singles prize. (See Chapter Four for a full account of the Darley years.) It is worth mentioning that many top players chose to play doubles these years in order to avoid an inevitable loss to Darley. For example, Andy Goddard of Edina, the 1961 singles third-place finisher and '59 doubles champion, played doubles again in '62 and won another title with partner Bill Jevne. Other elite players such as Charles (Bucky) Zimmerman and John Brennan of Minneapolis West opted for doubles in 1963 and '64. The result was two doubles titles for them. There were also many hard-luck stories of singles players who chose to compete during those years but could not break through, in part because of Darley. One was Dennis Chez of Hibbing, who made four trips to Minneapolis and came up empty each time, though he would finish runner-up to Darley in '64 after bouncing Paul Krause of St. Louis Park (an upset first-round winner over Darley's teammate Bob Gray) in the semifinals.

1965–Bob Gray
Rochester

But of all the players most negatively affected by Darley's move to Minnesota, none had reason to curse his fate more than Darley's teammate Gray. If it hadn't been for Darley it's possible that Gray could have won multiple state championships. Instead he had to settle for one which he claimed his senior year (1965), the year after Darley graduated.

Not born with a silver tennis spoon in his mouth—his father was in the trucking produce business and his mother, like most married women of her generation, was a homemaker—Gray was fortunate to live next door to a private tennis court. His neighbors, George and Jean Waters, had inherited a dilapidated tennis court that needed a good deal of refurbishing. Once they restored the court with a clay surface similar to the one then in use at Woodhill Country Club, the Waters gave Bob ready access to it. George Waters, a Rochester businessman who often took time to hit with Bob, was his first mentor and the person "most responsible for getting me started in tennis." Waters also took him to the Rochester Outdoor Tennis Club for the first time, a place which became his home away from home in the summer. Gray recalls that "my world for ten years was three things: going to Woolworth's for 5-cent candy, going to various local parks to play football, and going over to the tennis club." He recalls that junior memberships at the club were $12 and that sometimes the Mayo Clinic, which owned the club, paid membership fees for kids who couldn't afford them. And often they hired a summer pro for the members.

Another person who had a huge impact on the development of Gray's tennis game was Marv Hanenberger, his

Bob Gray

second great mentor who saw promise in him and began to work with Gray when he was 13 years old. Bob said of Marv, "He would pick up his guys and, if you were having trouble with your shots, say a backhand, he'd hit 1,000 balls with you until the shot got better." In addition, Bob remarked, "When you were Marv's boy, he'd take you out to eat at the Hubbell House in nearby Mantorville and that was a treat. $3.95-$4.25 for filet mignon and your choice of potato, garlic bread, soup, salad, shrimp cocktail, and a deluxe sundae." And while Hanenberger played a key role in his development, Gray also became a top player through hard work and dedication. Three-time singles champion Dave Healey praised Gray as "a self-made player."

Though he had good reason to be jealous of his teammate Darley, after all, he lost eleven matches to him in high school, Gray was nevertheless magnanimous in his praise for someone he recognized as "one of the best players in the nation" [Darley was at one time ranked No. 10 in his age group in the U.S.]. Bob also said of Darley, "I'm glad Chuck came to Rochester. He was a great friend and he made me a better player, and that meant more to me in the long run." He has no regrets and values his ongoing lifetime friendship with Darley.

For three years Gray lost to Darley in the Big Nine and district tournaments; and in each of those years he qualified for the State Tournament by virtue of a runner-up finish to Darley in the Region I tournament. Of his state tournament appearances, Gray says he remembers them all vividly. Even though he lost decisively to Darley in the 1962 state final, he considered it quite an accomplishment to make it that far as a ninth grader. The next year Bob played maybe his best match against his Rochester teammate in the state finals, losing a hard-fought three set match 8-6 in the third. Perhaps his biggest disappointment, in what John Mueller called "the greatest upset in Minnesota high school tennis," was a first-round loss to Paul Krause of St. Louis Park his junior year, his only high school loss to a player not named Darley. Generous in praise of a most worthy opponent, Bob said of Krause and that match, "Paul played an excellent match and really deserved it. He was always a challenge and you had to play your best to beat him; he was a tenacious player."

Gray redeemed himself the next year by beating Krause 6-4, 6-4 in the quarters, after he had blitzed next year's champion, Robb Jones of Edina in the first round 6-0, 6-0. Krause was a senior and Jones just a sophomore. In the semis he easily disposed of Hibbing's Merle Kerr 6-0, 6-1, then defeated John Brennan (a senior and two-time doubles champion from Minneapolis West) 6-3, 6-1 in the championship match. Gray, a lefty, considered this 1965 win his best achievement because there was "so much pressure my senior year." After all, he had been ranked No. 1 all season and came into the tournament undefeated.

Bob's three-year "friendly rivalry" with Darley, which on a smaller scale has a parallel in the great Aussie rivalries of players such as Laver and Rosewall, was built on a foundation of mutual love and respect similar to that of Harry Hopman's boys in the late 1950s to early '70s. There is probably no other teammate rivalry in Minnesota to compare to it, and Bob speaks glowingly of those days. Darley's great volley technique and solid groundstroke game pitted against Gray's concentration, consistency, and percentage tennis game made for some classic matchups. Here is how Bob described their playing styles: "Chuck's great volley was what took him as far as it did, but his anticipation was also great. He came in after every serve and my undercut backhand hurt me against him because it would float just a bit and he was able to exploit that. I was quick and consistent and hit a flat forehand. Those times I played well against him I was able to chip and come in on short balls—I had a good net game and my serve was pretty strong. I didn't double fault much and kept my groundstrokes in. If someone beat me, they had to earn it."

Gray spoke wistfully of his blissful growing-up years in which "we played one sport in the fall, one in winter,

and one in spring, and we played tennis for camaraderie, enjoyment, and memories." He also said, "There were no outside expectations except those you put on yourself or what the team members put on themselves and there was absolutely no parent interference." For example, his mother never saw him play and his dad maybe saw three matches. "To my parents, tennis was like horseshoes—'nice but it didn't amount to much; it was just a game.'"

And summers were idyllic in this tennis Eden of Rochester. He hit with Marv Hanenberger, practiced at the Outdoor Club, and traveled all over the Upper Midwest to play tournaments. "We couldn't stay in the Holiday Inn so we'd stay with families and I'd make wonderful friendships with people in Sioux Falls, Duluth, Minneapolis. Some parent drove us there and picked us up, and you took $5 with you—enough for miniature golf and the go-kart track for four days. In addition to his fond memories of playing in the State Tournament, Bob also recalled the not-so-pleasant smell of a seed factory near the U of M courts. "I ran a mile to warm up and I remember that smell. It was so nauseous that it will never leave me," he said.

His one regret is that he did not play more national tournaments, for after defeating a player ranked No. 23 in the U.S. at a National Junior Chamber of Commerce tournament in East Lansing MI, one year, Bob wondered "if I could have made the top 20." But there was no one at the Rochester Club at the time who had the perspective on national tournaments to be able to help him and no one to sponsor him or chauffeur him, so he had less experience on the national stage than did Darley, who played in the Missouri Valley Section and in many national tournaments. Gray did, however, play at Kalamazoo five times and in the national Junior Chamber of Commerce (JC) tournaments for three years (tournaments financed by the NWLTA and the JCs, respectively), and he recalls with pride his victory (over Jerry Krause when he was only 13) in the 15-and-under JC Tournament at Nicollet Park, a victory that earned him his first trip to nationals. On the local scene he was most often ranked No. 1 in NWLTA junior tennis singles divisions and was also ranked as high as No. 2 in doubles one year with John Brennan.

Most of the players on his Rochester team were good

students so they had a significant influence on his decision to pursue further education. Therefore, after graduation Bob accepted a full scholarship to play tennis at Indiana U. Ironically, in one of those twists of fate that life brings us, shortly thereafter he received a call from U of M Assistant Athletic Director Glen Reed offering him the first full-ride tennis scholarship from the U. He wonders how his life might have been different if he had gone to the U of M. Nevertheless, he played two full years at Indiana, competing very well at No. 4 singles his sophomore year. Unfortunately, he was forced to quit the team after both his parents died in December of his junior year. He was just 21 at the time.

For two and a half years after graduating with a degree in elementary education, he taught fifth grade in an Indianapolis inner city school, then, answering the siren call of home, he came back to Rochester to teach. For thirty years Gray taught fifth or sixth grade at Gage Elementary School. During this time he also coached the Mayo boys' tennis team (from 1975-1982),

Robb Jones

describing himself as a "relationship coach." And while he occasionally hit with his high school players, he spent more time on the racketball courts, earning a ranking as high as No. 3 in Minnesota in the Over-45 division.

Now retired, he still lives in Rochester, where he often holds court at the "Bob Gray Booth" at the Rochester Athletic Club. He continues to keep in touch with both of his mentors, George Waters and Marv Hanenberger; in fact, Bob helped inaugurate an award named for Marv at the Rochester Outdoor Club. Called the Marv Hanenberger Trophy, it is given each year to the most deserving junior player in Rochester and focuses on sportsmanship and work ethic.

1966—Robb Jones
Edina

In a mild upset, a young man from Edina, junior Robb Jones, slashed his way through the jungle of a very tough draw to win the 1966 singles title. Along the way he blitzed Tim Kuzma of Ely in the first round; defeated John Mueller of Robbinsdale in the second round; and dispatched Dan Bomgren of St. Paul Johnson in the quarters. In the semis he took out Dave Stearns of St. Cloud Tech (future Minnetonka coach and local tennis pro) 6-3, 6-3. Then in the finals he upended tourney favorite, previously undefeated six-foot-four-inch sophomore Rob Daugherty from Rochester Mayo 7-5, 6-2. It took him five matches to claim his title, but none went to three sets and all told he gave up just 16 games. Truly he was a deserving champion.

Jones, no relation to 1972 champion Craig, had excelled on the junior scene for years, reaching the No. 1 spot once in singles (in the 14s) and the No. 2 spot his final year in the Junior Men's Singles. In addition, he was an excellent doubles player who was ranked No. 1 twice, in the 14s with John Ahern of Minnetonka and in the 16s with Bruce Laidlaw of Edina.

1967-68—Rob Daugherty
Rochester Mayo

In the 1967 tournament Daugherty turned the tables and defeated Jones (whom he had already beaten twice during the year) in the final 6-4, 7-5. This was another outstanding singles draw of 26 players (5 from Region 5 alone) that included Dick Humleker of Minnetonka, a fourth-place finisher this year and in 1966; Dan Halvorsen of Owatonna (a three-time singles contestant who took third in 1969); and rising star Tom Brennan, a sophomore from Minneapolis West who finished third by beating Humleker. Brennan, brother of former doubles champion John, defeated 1966 champion Robb Jones during the year and later claimed a singles title (in 1969).

Form would hold in 1968, for the No. 1-ranked Daugherty won again, this time defeating No. 2-ranked Brennan 6-3, 6-1. (For more about Daugherty, see Chapter Four.)

1969—Tom Brennan
Minneapolis West

In 1969 senior Tom Brennan of Minneapolis West finally achieved his dream, winning the singles title with a well-deserved 6-4, 6-4 victory over senior Ted Warner of Edina (future local tennis pro and current Blake coach) in the finals. In the semis he defeated Halvorsen of Owatonna, who had bested 1970 champion Carter DeLaittre of St. Louis Park in the quarters in an exhausting 6-8, 6-4, 7-5 three-setter. Clearly the dominant player in the field, Brennan did not lose a set in four matches and gave up games grudgingly. In fact, he surrendered just 16 games, an average of four per match. After a first-round bye, Brennan trounced Tim Hanson of Moorhead 6-0, 6-1, then defeated Steve Hunter of Sibley 6-3, 6-3 before taking out Halvorsen—a senior—by a 6-1, 6-0 score.

Without question one of the most dominant players of the late '60s, Brennan was a top-ranked junior on the local and even national scene in addition to being a nearly unbeatable high school opponent for three years. In his previous two years, for example, he lost just two matches, both to his nemesis Daugherty in the State Tournament. Playing No. 1 singles for Minneapolis West for three years, Brennan won the Region 5 singles title each of those years (beating city conference rival Bill Babcock of Minneapolis Washburn in the final each of those years). He remembers "getting killed" by big-server Rob Daugherty in the '68 final held indoors at the Southdale Tennis Center—rain had stopped play at the U of M courts—but he's justly proud of never losing a set during his run to the title his senior year. At six feet one inches tall, he was able to leverage that big serve of his into a dependable weapon, but he also said of his tennis, "I had a big power game."

Tom Brennan

Brennan recalls his summer tournament tennis career with fondness as well. He was, after all, ranked No. 1 in junior singles play three times and twice in doubles (once with Bob Brandenburg of Rochester and the other time with Babcock), and his No. 40 national ranking in the 18s was pretty heady stuff for a lad from snow country. That year Tom reached the semis at Kalamazoo where he faced the three-years-younger Jimmy Connors. Connors whipped him 6-3, 6-2 and Brennan was devastated, saying, "I thought he'd ruined my career."

Hungry for some tougher competition to challenge him, Brennan also played in Men's Open Singles tournaments his last two summers as a junior player, often beating some of the top adult players in the Section such as Minnesota tennis legends Ken Boyum and Jack Roach and earning a No. 13 ranking in 1968. And just a year out of high school ('70) he and brother John's doubles partner Bucky Zimmerman even won the National Public Parks doubles championship held at the Nicollet courts in Minneapolis, beating the aforementioned Boyum and Roach in the finals.

Possessed of a photographic memory, Brennan is a reservoir of great tennis stories. For instance, he remembers the summer of 1964, when tennis hustler Bobby Riggs came to work at the Minneapolis Tennis Club for eight weeks. Tom was just 14, but he recalls witnessing one of Riggs' favorite tricks, tying a rope to a chair and fastening it to his leg, then hobbling around the court to beat a disbelieving opponent. His best memory of that summer, however, is of learning more about tennis by watching Riggs play and later talking to him about tennis. Later he ran into Riggs at the Forum in Los Angeles at an Elton John AIDS Foundation tennis benefit attended by such tennis luminaries as Martina Navratilova, John McEnroe, Tracy Austin, and Pete Sampras.

A terrific athlete who played three sports in high school (he was a football quarterback and a left wing on the hockey team), Brennan did not play tennis in college, even though he had a tennis scholarship at the U of M. A free spirit who perhaps embodied the mood of the tumultuous '60s, Brennan spent his summer after graduation teaching tennis at the Cold Springs Harbor Tennis Club on Long Island, NY. Then, though he had qualified at a grass court tournament to play in the U.S. Open at a grass court tournament (scheduled to play next to Margaret Court by the way), he partied at Woodstock instead.

When he came home to enroll at the U, he learned that he was about to become a father; so that ended his college tennis aspirations and his wandering ways. With a family to support, he was compelled to go to work after finishing just one year of college. So for twenty years he was employed (in California) as a divisional sales manager for Advance Machine Company, a firm which manufactured maintenance floor equipment. He quit the corporate world in 1994, but during his years in business he continued to play tournament tennis, always ranking in the top five in the 35s, 40s, 45s, and 50s in the ultra-competitive tennis hotbed of southern California. During these years he often competed against the likes of touring pros Alex Olmeda and Pancho Segura.

Since leaving the corporate world, he has enjoyed the more laid-back life of a tennis teaching pro, working at the Ritz Carlton Club in Laguna Niguel, CA. (For more about Tom and his brothers, see Chapters Six and Ten.)

1970s

This decade began inauspiciously with the so-called "massacre" at Kent State in 1970 and deeply divided feelings about the Vietnam War. But it was also the decade of the VCR, floppy discs, smiley faces, pet rocks, streaking, Nerf Balls, the Rubik's Cube, and discos. It was a time of blockbuster movies such as *The Godfather*, *Star Wars*, *Jaws*, *American Graffiti*, *The Deer Hunter*, and seminal TV shows such as "Saturday Night Live" and "Sesame Street." There

were momentous events such as the Watergate scandal in '72, President Nixon's resignation in '74, and the fall of Vietnam in '75. Margaret Thatcher became Prime Minister of England, Nixon went to China, and Palestinians murdered Israeli athletes at the Munich Olympics.

On the national and international tennis scene, however, things were never better. The sport was attracting millions of new players and fans who watched on TV as Jimmy Connors battled Bjorn Borg and a young John McEnroe, and Chris Evert struggled against Billie Jean King and rising star Martina Navratilova.

Perhaps it is worth mentioning here that the decade of the '70s, one which saw tremendous growth in the game of tennis, also saw the rise of indoor clubs in Minnesota. There was the indoor club at the Roller Rink in St. Louis Park and one at Richfield in the early '60s. But for the most part there had only been public or school courts and outdoor tennis clubs such as St. Paul, Somerset, Town and Country, Minneapolis, Duluth, Nicollet, Rochester, Hibbing, Morgan Park, Macalester, and North Oaks, and country clubs such as Wayzata, White Bear Yacht Club, Woodhill, Minikahda, Edina, Interlachen, and Lafayette. That all changed when Harvey Ratner and Marv Wolfenson began building a string of indoor clubs (called the Northwest Clubs) in the '70s. (For more on Ratner and Wolfenson, see appendix G.)

1970—Carter DeLaittre Jr.
St. Louis Park

On the tennis courts in Minnesota teams from Edina/Edina East would win six titles and a young man with the very French name of Carter DeLaittre would capture the first singles title of the '70s, defeating sophomore Bob Amis of Edina in a three-set final 3-6, 6-4, 6-2. DeLaittre, a senior, had lost to Owatonna's Dan Halvorsen in '69, but this year he emerged from the scrum to claim the first and only singles title for a player from St. Louis Park. His victory indeed had the feel of a rugby scrum, for he earned it by pulling out four three-set matches; in three of the matches he lost the first set.

Truly the "comeback kid" in this year's draw, he avenged a loss to Martin Bornemann of Bloomington

Lincoln (a foreign exchange student from Germany), defeating him in the quarters 0-6, 6-2, 6-0, and he then took out Graham Gie of Aurora-Hoyt Lakes in the semis— also in three sets (6-1, 2-6, 6-1). Bornemann had beaten DeLaittre 7-5, 6-3 in their Region 5 match and, after getting clobbered in the first set of their state tournament match, DeLaittre changed tactics, coming to the net and overpowering Bornemann in the final two sets. In addition to these three very difficult matches, his first two opponents gave DeLaittre all he wanted. In the first round he defeated Winona's Ron Koehler 7-5, 6-1 and in the second round he had to come back after once again losing the first set, finally overcoming Colin Ham of St. Paul Murray 4-6, 6-0, 6-2. One could argue that he was a cat with nine lives who had used up at least three of them in come-from behind wins against Ham, Bornemann, and Amis. Furthermore, he had labored on court through a total of 112 games, only 11 fewer than the record set by Paul Wilcox in 1934. In addition, DeLaittre had qualified from region play as the fifth and last contestant, so that made his win all the more remarkable.

Carter DeLaittre Jr.

As a junior player he worked his way up the rankings ladder, twice reaching a high of No. 2 in both singles and doubles, once in the 16s and once in the 18s. His doubles partners were Rip Rapson of Minneapolis and Dale Stockdale of Edina. 1971 champion Bob Amis called DeLaittre the best player he competed against in his sophomore year. He said of DeLaittre's game, "He had a huge serve, a lot of power. And he had big fluid groundstrokes with a lot of topspin. He had a loose arm like a big thick rope with no joints." Carter's coach, Roger Thompson, lauded him for an excellent senior season in which he won 25 matches and lost but the one to Bornemann. Thompson also spoke of his aggressive serve and volley style.

It is worth noting that his father, Carter Sr., was a good player as well, so one could argue that Carter the younger inherited some of his tennis ability. Carter the elder was a top-ten senior player, and in two years (1970

and '78), he and his talented son were the No.-1 ranked father-and-son team in the Section.

After graduation DeLaittre enrolled at the U of M where he played tennis for four years with many of Minnesota's other top former high school players such as Bob Van Hoef, Tim Burke, Greg Lappin, Dave Mathews, and Dave Stearns. He had a very successful career there, moving up the ladder from No. 4 singles his first year to No. 2 singles his sophomore year, then to No. 1 singles his junior and senior years. And all four years he played No. 1 doubles. A two-time Gopher captain (1973-74), DeLaittre also won the coveted Phil Brain Memorial Award for Most Valuable Player twice (1973 and '74 again) and was All-Big Ten those same two seasons, his junior and senior years.

When he completed his degree, majoring in anthropology, he flew to London in 1975, where he met Gopher teammate Bob Van Hoef for some tennis-playing adventures in England and Belgium. Then, in '76 he joined Bill Babcock and Bob Amis for more tournament play in Europe and South Africa, finally returning to the U.S. to take a tennis teaching job at Lafayette Country Club in the fall of '76. Carter worked there until 1980, coaching a number of top junior players, including '81 singles champion Bob Bateman, who said of DeLaittre, "He was fantastic to work with and helped me a lot my first year of tennis." During these years he also found time to play summer tournaments, and in '78 he was ranked No. 1 in Men's Open Singles.

After completing his coaching stint, he enrolled in Hamline Law School, graduating in 1984. Today he works for the firm of Henson and Efron, specializing in real estate law. Tennis is back on his schedule as well, and in 2002 he and his teammates won the national 4.5 USTA League tournament.

1971–Bob Amis
Edina

After finishing second in the previous two State Tournaments, Edina reclaimed the team title it had last won in 1968, thanks in large measure to its No. 1 player, 1971 singles champion Bob Amis. One of the hardest-working champions in Minnesota tennis history (in part due to coach John Matlon's emphasis on rigorous conditioning), Amis also relied on superstitions to give him that extra edge. An article by Roxie Aho in the May 23, 1971, *Minneapolis Tribune* said of Amis, "First he makes sure his lucky rabbit's foot is in the handle of his tennis racket. He picks up his lucky rubbing stone. He pins his Snoopy pin to the front of his tennis shirt. Then he puts on his sunshine yellow tennis hat." And though it was this yellow hat that became his signature adornment, he also used his good luck charms to help him slow things down and regain his composure. Coach Matlon added, "Bob is smart, too. He doesn't show these things off, although the hat certainly is noticeable... Practically everybody has his little quirks, and they're valuable when things go badly. Watch a mature boy like Bob. He'll turn his back and fiddle with his luck pieces or he'll go back against the fence to slow things down and regain his composure" (May 23, 1971).

Bob Amis

Perhaps it was the hard work, perhaps it was the superstitions, but it was certainly Amis's talent that enabled him to win the 1971 title over three-time state singles contestant Bob Van Hoef of St. Paul Harding, who would be ranked No. 1 in the 18-and-under age group in NWLTA play that summer.

Born in Memphis, TN, Amis played "very casual" tennis until he was 12 or so, though he remembers his second tournament well. "I was 8 playing in a 14-and-under tourney. My mother dropped me off with my $3 entry fee and racket in wooden press. When my Mom picked me up two hours later, I was beaming on the street corner and I told her, 'I got bombed 6-0, 6-0—but I had a good time.'"

When he moved to Edina at the age of 11, he became more serious about tennis even though he continued to play basketball through his tenth-grade year. That first summer and for two more summers his mother, herself a tennis player, sent him to the Bob Speed Tennis Camp where he met future teammates Chris Barden, Craig Jones, Ted Taney, and Dixon Dahlberg. This experience inspired him to become a serious tournament player as well, and during his junior career he gradually moved up in the rankings, in part because he often "played up" a division while also competing in his own age brackets. For example, the only time he was ranked No. 1 in singles (in the 16s) he was also ranked No. 6 in the 18s. But he was a successful doubles player as well, earning several top rankings with teammates Chris Barden and Ted Taney, including a No. 1 ranking with Barden in the 16s.

At Edina he made the varsity as a ninth grader, earned the No. 1 singles spot as a sophomore in 1970, and, after finishing second to DeLaittre in the '70 tournament, broke through his junior year-'71, in part because of his superb conditioning. On the day of the singles tournament it was a hot 85 degrees, but Amis wasn't fazed by the heat. In a June 13, 1971, article in the *Minneapolis Tribune*, he is quoted as saying, "The heat doesn't bother us because Mr. Matlon gets us into such good physical condition. I do a little more work on my own." That "little more work" included skipping rope "for twenty minutes without a miss" and extra running in addition to the six-minute mile runs demanded by Matlon. Teammate Craig Jones (the '72 champion) remembers Amis's unfailing energy and work ethic: "At the beginning of the season the team ran a mile as Matlon called quarter mile splits. During the 1971 spring, Bob and I would go back to the courts [after practice] and play until dark, usually another one and a half to two hours. Then Amis would want to run again. I would keep up with him for one-half to three-fourths of a mile run and then yell at him that he was nuts."

Jones called Amis the best player he competed against in high school, saying, "His intensity was beyond anyone.

He had great concentration which was years beyond competitive players at that time." Jones and Amis had one of the great teammate competitions, not unlike that between Bob Gray and Chuck Darley; and just as Gray never beat Darley, so Jones never defeated Amis, even though they had many epic battles in various high school tournaments.

In the 1971 tournament, Van Hoef, ranked No. 7 by the Coaches Association, had beaten second-ranked Kevin Ylinen of Robbinsdale Armstrong in the first round (4-6, 6-3, 6-4) and top-ranked Dave Petersen of Hopkins Lindbergh in one of the most competitive of all state tournament matches 5-7, 14-12, 6-2 in the quarterfinals. That 14-12 second set against Petersen, his tough first-round match with Ylinen, and then a hard-fought 6-2, 3-6, 6-2 semifinal win over future state champion Craig Jones of Edina (just a sophomore) drained Van Hoef. Amis, on the other hand, encountered very little resistance in his first four matches, winning each of them in straight sets. His first two victims were Mark Thies of Aurora-Hoyt Lakes and Jeff McFadden of Stillwater. Then in the quarters he bounced senior Chuck Puleston of Robbinsdale Cooper before defeating Bemidji's Gary Conda in the semis.

So the final was anticlimactic, as Amis dispatched the weary Van Hoef in straight sets 6-4, 6-0. In a June 13, 1971, article in the *St. Paul Pioneer Press* by Jim Wells, Amis is quoted as saying, "It didn't seem like he (Van Hoef) was really on today. When he is, he's really tough. He aims for the white (court border) and not the green (court surface)." So in these five matches Amis gave up just thirteen games, an average of less than three per match.

Amis, who had played in just three local tournaments the summer before his junior year (winning them all), put most of his energies into national tournament play instead, honing his game against top U.S. junior players. So his senior year must have been bittersweet, for though he was not able to defend his title, he helped Edina win another team championship and gained some satisfaction in seeing his junior teammate Jones win the singles title by beating the player who had upset him in the semifinals, Bill Stark of Richfield. For the first time Amis had been ranked No. 1 (by the Tennis Coaches Association), and he came into the tournament undefeated. After that

disappointing loss to Stark (who had only beaten him one other time in high school), Amis recovered his composure and defeated future two-time champion Mark Brandenburg of Rochester Mayo for third place.

While it's true that he came so close to becoming a two-time or even three-time champion, his two state tournament defeats in no way tarnish his image. For his was one of the most successful careers in Minnesota boys' tennis history; after all, he won one singles title and finished second one year and third another and he played on teams which won two state titles and came agonizingly close to winning two others. One might argue compellingly that he played on four of the greatest high school teams in state history, teams that also featured 1972 singles champion Jones and doubles titlists Chris Barden (a two-time champion), Ted Taney, and Dixon Dahlberg, among others. (See Chapter Nine for more on these Edina teams.)

After graduation he took his tennis game to the Division 1 college level, playing for a year and a half at Southern Methodist U., then transferring to the U of M the winter of his sophomore year to play for coach Jerry Noyce. In his two years there he played No. 1 singles and No. 2 doubles—with Dave Barnes—his junior year and No. 1 singles and doubles (with old high school rival Mark Brandenburg) his senior year, participating in the NCAA Tournament both years and twice earning All-Big Ten honors.

Though his was a short career at the U of M, he earned many other honors as well: Most Valuable Player in 1975 and '76, the Louis Ratner Memorial Award for Outstanding Contributions to Golden Gopher Tennis in '75, and co-captain of the team in '76 (with Stark).

During his college years Amis also played summer satellite tournaments to try to pick up ATP points, then joined Bill Babcock and Carter DeLaittre to play in Europe in September 1976. Following that brief European adventure Amis and DeLaittre played what Amis called the "Sugar Circuit" in South Africa for two months and then returned to Europe. Amis spent the next two years playing for three different clubs in Germany, and small money tournaments in France, Spain, and Italy. Of all the good things that happened to him in Europe, two stand out, as Amis explains: "I met my wife in Luxembourg and I learned German because I had to teach tennis at the club." It was truly a memorable experience for him, and even though he didn't get rich ("I made enough money to keep going"), he had the priceless opportunity to explore Europe, play the game he loved, and learn the nuances of playing on slow, red clay. "It's the greatest surface of them all. The game was meant to be played on clay," he said. In addition, he met many touring pros such as Tim and Tom Gullickson, Victor Amaya, and Vitas Gerulaitis, whom he described as a "friendly, charismatic guy who was a lot of fun."

In addition to these young adult tennis memories, he has fond recollections of his years as a junior and high school player as well. Like so many players of his generation, he recalls that his "parents were supportive but they let us be kids." So he and his Edina pals always entered the Rochester Invitational Tournament in June and the Duluth Tournament over the fourth of July. About the Duluth tournament he noted, "It was so cool. We went up on the train a couple of times and billeted in homes." And when they went to Rochester they stayed at the Galaxy Motel. A bit nostalgically, Amis added, "Of course you couldn't do that any more." And like many of the pre-indoor court champions, he has distinct memories of the U of M tennis courts, describing "the smell of the grain elevators, the three rows of courts, the green tennis shack, a long backboard wall, and dusty old canvas windscreens." And, he added, "It was always sunny and hot."

Like breathing and eating, tennis became an essential in his young life, for even when he wasn't playing, he served as a ball boy at Nicollet Tennis Center, all the while learning by watching the top Upper Midwest players of the day such as Noyce, Steve Wilkinson, Jack Roach, and Wendell Ottum. He also remembers state tournament day lunches at Bridgeman's (under the watchful eye of coach Matlon), 5 AM Saturday practices at Northstar Tennis Club, donut sale fundraisers, and most of all the friendships he made on the Edina tennis team. In addition, tennis gave Bob a self-identity boost: "It was nice to have something to call my own through my adolescent years. At times it was a refuge from adolescence."

When his tennis ramblings abroad were over, he and his wife moved to a 20-acre farm in Scott County, where they grew organic vegetables in the summer for a few years

while he taught tennis in the winter, mainly at the Northwest Club. Then, in the mid-1980s, he worked for his father in an equipment leasing business. After his father retired, Bob ran the business for twelve years, selling it in 2000. His life then took a 180 degree turn, toward teaching. So he is now a middle grades teacher at City of Lakes Waldorf School in Minneapolis.

1972–Craig Jones
Edina

For Craig Jones of Edina, 1972 was a magical year, for not only did his Edina team win another championship, but he emerged from the singles competition with a crown on his head. His win was not a complete surprise, for he had announced his arrival on the tennis scene the previous year when, as a sophomore, he took third place, losing to runner-up Van Hoef in a three-set match. But he would be the first to admit that the gods were on his side in '72. His teammate and nemesis Bob Amis had been upended in the semis by senior Bill Stark of Richfield; and as a junior who was ranked behind Amis and even his teammate Chris Barden in the early season MN Coaches Association rankings, he was certainly not favored to win. Nonetheless, his victory was no fluke, for he defeated future champion Brandenburg (a sophomore) in the semis 8-6, 6-3 and champion-killer Stark, with whom he had split two matches during the year, in a superb final 3-6, 8-6, 7-5. His route to the semis was not difficult, however, for he defeated his first three opponents in straight sets: Steve Benson of Bloomington Jefferson; Laddie Gustin of Hibbing; and Joe Elling of Alexander Ramsey.

In his senior year, 1973, he came into the tournament ranked No. 1 by the coaches (just ahead of Mark Brandenburg). And though he would defeat Brandenburg in that epic team No. 1 singles match Brandenburg described so eloquently in his profile, thus securing the first True Team title for Edina East, he, like so many champions, was not able to defend his title. Instead, Brandenburg dethroned him in a stirring 6-4, 9-7 final.

Jones began playing tennis in the rarefied competitive air of Edina where, he says, "I remember seeing Chris Barden [future teammate] play tennis and finding out he was a ranked player in the three-state area. I thought I could beat him with a couple months' practice, so I immediately went to Walgreen's and had my dad buy me a racket for $1.99. I spent the summer banging the ball against the backboard to learn." Soon Jones was entering NWLTA summer tournaments, where he enjoyed success and earned rankings as high as No. 2 in 14-and-under singles and No. 6 in the 16s.

When he shook the dust off his Edina tennis shoes, Craig enrolled at the U of WI on a full tennis scholarship. During his four years he played a variety of singles spots for the Badgers, but he enjoyed his greatest success in doubles, twice finishing runner-up in the Big Ten at the No. 2 position. Returning to Minnesota in 1977 after earning a BA in economics and communications, he completed work for an MBA at the U of M and then spent twenty years working on Wall Street for Lehman Brothers and Alex Brown. Now he runs a senior housing finance group for Red Capital (owned by National City Bank) and makes his home in Columbus, OH. Though he took a long break from tennis, he has recently rediscovered his love for tennis competition and has taken up the game again.

1973-74—Mark Brandenburg
Rochester Mayo and

1975-76—Mark Wheaton
Minnetonka

Except for Kevin Smith's breakthrough in 1977, the remainder of this decade would be ruled by two-time champions Brandenburg (1973-74), Mark Wheaton (1975-76), and Brian Johnson (1978-79). (See Chapter Four for in-depth profiles of these players.)

There were of course many other outstanding players during this decade who, though they did not win singles titles, made good showings at State. These included Dave Petersen and Claude Peterson (both of Hopkins), Mark Nammacher of Minneapolis West (ranked No. 1 by the coaches in 1975), Van Hoef of St. Paul Harding, Stark of Richfield, John Mattke of Centennial, Greg Swendseen of Edina, Paul Holbach of White Bear Lake, Scott Jacobson of Blue Earth, Steve Brandt of Mounds View, Greg Wicklund

of Minneapolis Roosevelt, the three Helgeson brothers of St. Cloud Tech (Grant, Kent, and Brace), Dave Morin of White Bear Mariner, and Andy Ringlien of Northfield. Two won doubles titles (Dave Petersen and Ringlien); and some, like Van Hoef, Stark, Claude Peterson, Swendseen, Holbach, Jacobson, Brandt, and Morin took consolation in finishing second. And all were highly ranked juniors, often No. 1 or 2 in their age groups in the NWLTA; but such are the vagaries of life and there can be only one winner. Their losses, however, do not diminish their high school careers, for all went on to successful college and even pro careers (Mattke especially but also Wicklund and the Helgesons, to a lesser extent).

Holbach, who claimed never to have had a private lesson until college, was always a top four junior who played No. 1 for four years, never losing a Suburban Conference match in that time. He went on to play at Gustavus with Mattke, whom he called the best player he ever competed against in college. Both of them also became tennis pros and coaches, Mattke in the Twin Cities and Holbach for the Desert Princess Country Club in Cathedral City, CA. Most of the others also spent some time as coaches or pros and Wicklund especially, who starred at the U of M and became a top local player as an adult, has had a long and successful career as a pro with the Northwest Clubs, in particular working with talented junior players. (For more on Wicklund, see appendix G.)

Perhaps one other player worth noting from this period is Park High School's Bruce Nadeau, who, despite suffering from cystic fibrosis, in 1974 earned All-Suburban Conference honors for the second year in a row. His story represents that of so many players who never played in the State Tournament but who loved the game and gave it their all nonetheless—in Bruce's case even in the face of enormous physical obstacles.

These are just a few of the hard-luck players, and I apologize to any I've left out, but we move on to the year 1977, since Chapter Four chronicles the triumphs of the 1973-76 champions Brandenburg and Wheaton.

1977—Kevin Smith
Hopkins Lindbergh

Taking the top prize in the 1977 tournament was a Johnny-come-lately from Hopkins Lindbergh, five-foot-six-inch, 115-pound Kevin Smith. Smith, a new arrival in Minnesota, came from Tampa, FL, where, according to an article in the *Minneapolis Tribune* by Bruce Brothers, he was "rated 17th in the state in Boys' 16-and-Under singles at the age of 15" (April 24, 1977). A year earlier, in the 14-and-unders, he had been ranked 33rd in the nation and 7th in the tennis hotbed of Florida. When he came to Minnesota, Smith was soon knocking down opponents of all ages like a tornado destroying a village: "Lindbergh junior Kevin Smith has been having such an easy time against high school opponents that he's been playing some members of the University of Minnesota tennis team—and beating them." Among those players were Grant Helgeson, Jeff Steiner, and Judd Larson, former St. Louis Park No. 1 singles player. Brothers said of the diminutive Smith, "He hits the ball harder than anyone else in high school" (April 24, 1977).

In addition, according to his coach, Pat Anderson, "He's just so consistent. He hits the ball so well he doesn't have to be that strong. And he can put it anywhere" (April 24, 1977). This article by Brothers also mentioned that Smith rarely rushed the net but that he didn't need to because his groundstrokes were so solid.

Coach Anderson also noted, in the article by Brothers, that he was a very hard worker who stuck around after practice to work "against anyone who is good who is available." The article also mentioned his positive attitude and his high expectations: "I want to win the state high school championship and be in the top 20 in the country, I guess... I think I can do it" (April 24, 1977). He did indeed do it, knocking off pre-tournament favorite, undefeated and No. 1-ranked Greg Wicklund of Minneapolis Roosevelt (a senior), 6-3, 6-4 in the semis and then taking out No. 2 Scott Jacobson of Blue Earth (a junior) in the finals 7-6. 6-1. Talking to himself from the start of his match with Jacobson, Smith jumped out to an early 3-0 lead in the first set but let Jacobson back in the match. In an article by Gary Olson in the *St. Paul Sunday Pioneer Press*, Smith described what happened in the match when

it got to 6-all: "Things started to go my way in the first-set tie-breaker when I got a couple of returns in. A lot of lefthanders (Jacobson is a lefty) have a really weird spin on their serves but Scott's wasn't too bad... In the second set I didn't make nearly as many errors as in the first and I think Scott may have been a little tired" (June 12, 1977). Jacobson was playing his third match of the day and Smith beat him with lobs and "maddeningly accurate [passing] shots that just seemed to nick the line" (June 12, 1977) when Jacobson rushed the net.

On the first day of competition, after receiving a first-round bye, Smith had defeated seniors Steve Lundberg of Litchfield and Ben Streitz of Waseca in straight sets. (Wicklund, by the way, then defeated senior Pat Luebstorf of St. Paul Monroe to claim third place and finish the season with a stunning 41-1 record.)

After this successful tournament experience, Smith continued to work on his game in an effort to prepare for his senior season and his goal of becoming only the seventh Minnesota high school player to win multiple singles championships. In a March 28, 1978, article in the *Minneapolis Star* by Chan Keith, Smith was quoted as saying, "As a rule I work out two hours a day, five or six days a week. I've been on the schedule for quite awhile." In addition, he spent the summer of 1977 playing tournaments. "He won every local tournament he entered, then won the Northwest Sectional, which in turn qualified him for several national events." On the national circuit he "finished in the top 12 in the National Clay Court Championships...won his first two rounds in the nationals at Kalamazoo before losing to the tournament's third seed... Smith also became the youngest player to compete in the Intersectional team championship held in Edmond, OK" (March 28, 1978).

At the end of the summer he was ranked No. 1 in the 16s in the NWTA and No. 17 nationally. During the off-season he continued his blue-collar schedule and added private lessons with Minnetonka pro Dave Yorks.

And while he improved his game a great deal over the summer and had another outstanding high school season his senior year—1978 (he was ranked No. 1 all year by the coaches and came into the tournament as a prohibitive favorite), Smith was surprised by Edina's Brian Johnson, ranked No. 6, in the quarters 7-6, 6-2. Johnson then defeated Northfielder Andy Ringlien in the semis and Mounds View's Steve Brandt in the finals. This would be the first of Johnson's two singles titles, and Smith would become yet another champion who could not defend his title this decade in the competitive cauldron of Minnesota high school tennis.

1978-79—Brian Johnson
Edina East

So the decade came to a close with the implementation of the first two-class tournament in both team and individual competition and a second title for Johnson, as well as a medal hanging around his neck that read "1979 Class AA Singles Champion." Hereafter this narrative will continue with a focus on the AA champions (and the combined class champions in the years in which two-class competition was aborted, 1983-86), with a separate section devoted to the Class A singles champions from 1979-82 and then from 1987-2003. That section follows the profile of the 2003 Class AA champion, Nick Edlefsen of Eden Prairie. (For more on Johnson's two titles, see Chapter Four.)

1980s

A time of extraordinary economic prosperity in the U.S., this period became known as the "Me decade." "Greed is good" was a mantra, and conspicuous consumption, Reaganomics, and insider trading also became buzz words of the day. On the international scene the Berlin Wall came down and students were massacred in Tiananmen Square in Beijing. Gorbachev unwittingly planted the seeds for the dissolution of the Russian empire and the end of the Cold War with his calls for "glasnost" and "perestroika." There were also horrible environmental disasters such as Chernobyl; the poison gas leak in Bhopal, India; and the Exxon-Valdez oil spill in Alaska. AIDS, our modern Black Plague, was identified and pictures of emaciated and starving Ethiopian children roused the world to action (Live-Aid and Ethiopian Famine Relief).

Indira Gandhi and John Lennon were assassinated, the Space Shuttle Challenger exploded, and the Pan Am flight was destroyed over Scotland. Prince Charles and Diana were married and Ronald Reagan and Margaret Thatcher dominated the political stage.

On the entertainment front, *Gandhi*, *Amadeus*, and *Platoon* were the Academy Award-winning films; games such as Pictionary and Trivial Pursuit were popular; and youngsters played with Cabbage Patch Kids dolls.

"Magic" and Bird, Joe Montana, Michael Jordan—these were four of the top sports figures of the day. And tennis players John McEnroe, Ivan Lendl, Jimmy Connors, Pete Sampras, Andre Agassi, Monica Seles, Steffi Graf, and Martina Navratilova dominated their sport in the '80s.

Here in Minnesota there was a four-year return to a single-class tournament from 1983-86; and in '87 the two-class tournament system, begun in '79, resumed. So from '87 on there would be two singles champions each year.

1980—Chris Combs
Edina West

He was ranked No. 1 all year, and Edina West senior Chris Combs did not disappoint, beating frequent hitting

Chris Combs

partner and good friend Bob Bateman of Edina in the 1980 final. A June 1980 *Tennis Midwest* article noted that "with a noisy crowd of 400 spectators watching the final match, the lanky 6-foot 4-inch Combs dominated his favorite hitting partner 6-2, 6-2 with his strong serve and volley game." Bateman had given Combs his only loss of the year in the Region 6AA final a week before (7-6, 7-6), but the junior was no match for Combs this day, perhaps in part because he was favoring a sore ankle. Throughout the year the two had pushed each other, as Combs confided: "Bob [Bateman] and I live real close, so we play a lot of tennis after our regular school practices" (June 1980).

Combs had beaten Bateman twice before during the regular season, but he certainly wasn't overconfident going into the finals, according to an article in the *St. Paul Pioneer Press* by Gregg Wong. "The fact that Bob beat me was always there, Combs said, "but I told myself to pretend this was the first time we had ever played. And once I started hitting the ball, I had completely forgotten about that loss [in the region final]" (June 1, 1980).

The article by Wong noted that Combs broke his five foot eight opponent twice in the first set, then broke Bateman in the first game of the second set to keep his momentum going and again "at 4-2 with a crisp cross-court backhand passing shot." After finishing off his close friend, Combs said, "It was one of my best matches all year... This is the best graduation present I could ever give myself" (June 1, 1980).

Bateman praised his rival and friend, calling him the best player he competed against in high school: "Though I practiced against him a lot, I couldn't beat him when it really mattered. He was tough. Big serve, tall, agile. Good guy. Good player" (June 1, 1980).

In his other matches Combs defeated each of his opponents in straight sets, first brushing aside Virginia's Ben Deutsch, then taking out Austin senior Dan Paulson in the quarters. In the semis he disposed of sophomore Todd Ward of St. Thomas Academy.

Combs had lived a gypsy life before moving to Edina in 1979, having experienced tougher competition in California, Georgia, and Illinois. In a May 31, 1980, article in the *Minneapolis Tribune* by Howard Sinker, Combs is quoted as saying, "Tennis here isn't as good as in other places... This area is lagging behind, although it's beginning to catch up." Playing just two summers of junior tournaments here, Combs earned Nos. 3 and 4 rankings in 18-and-under singles and a No. 2 (with Dave Schultz) and No. 3 (with Bob Bateman) in doubles.

He finished his senior year with a 30-1 record, then took his tennis game to the U of M, where he played just one fall (1980) before taking a tennis teaching job with Steve Ehlers at the Minneapolis Tennis Club. Then he worked at Somerset Country Club and Arden Hills before taking a position at the newly opened White Bear Racquet Club. He's been a tennis teaching pro there since that opening year ('88). Combs has five sons, the oldest a varsity tennis player at WBL who earned all-conference honors in 2007.

1981—Bob Bateman
Edina East

Though he was pressed by eventual two-time champion Darryl Laddin of Hopkins Lindbergh, senior Bob Bateman took home the trophy in 1981 with nary a blemish on his record. He was ranked No. 1 from the get-go and maintained this position all the way through to the final, where he defeated sophomore Laddin 7-6, 6-2. His other three opponents all succumbed to Bateman without much of a struggle. In the first round he upended senior Mark Johnson of Hutchinson (a future boys' and girls' tennis coach at Northfield); defeated Rochester Mayo's Riley Horan in the quarters; then bounced the unlucky Ward of St. Thomas Academy. It was the second year in a row that Ward, now a senior, had lost in the semis, and in both years he finished third.

A feisty competitor, Bateman didn't start playing tennis seriously until he was older than most junior players. As he put it, "We played just about all sports as kids. Boredom with Little League baseball and the fact that Edina had a great tradition of tennis led me to try tennis as my summer sport when I was 12. It didn't hurt that tennis was booming then." His next-door neighbor, Mark Brosius, an Edina player at the time, allowed Bob to tag along to the courts, where he (Bob) spent hours "hitting against Edina East's big green backboard that summer." He also played with Brosius and his friends when they needed a doubles fill-in or wanted an occasional singles match. Brosius also introduced Bob to an older gentleman named Per Palm, a legendary figure in Edina tennis who played matches with Bob and many budding young Edina players. (For more about Palm, see Chapter Nine.)

While hanging out at the high school courts, Bateman learned that some of the Edina guys actually traveled around the state to play tournaments in the summer. So in the summer of 1975 his mother bought him a pair of shorts, he borrowed his sister Tracy's racket so he'd have a spare, and his mother drove him down to Austin to play in the 12-and-under tournament. Amazingly, he advanced all the way to the finals, then later that summer lost a competitive match (in the quarterfinals) to a top player, Steve Rost from Sioux Falls, in a tournament in Northfield. These experiences whetted his appetite

Bob Bateman

of indoor clubs. And he was quick to credit local tennis pros for his success. For example, he remembers struggling in national and regional matches outside the NWLTA section, in part because, he said, "I was trying too hard." Former state champ Bob Amis, then a pro at Northwest, told Bob that if he just played his game and hit the shots he could and didn't try to play better than he was capable of, he would rarely if ever lose in the upper Midwest and even outside the Section, too. After getting that sage advice, Bateman soon did well in a tournament in Madison, WI, and thereafter rarely lost a match in the Northwestern Section. Focusing primarily on singles, Bateman was the No. 1 NWTA player four times (once each in the 14s and 16s and twice in the 18s) and also won the Sectional 18-and-under singles title one year. In addition, he won matches outside the Section on the national level, achieving a ranking of

for more tennis, so, determined as a bulldog to improve his game, Bateman soon began taking lessons at the Midwest Club in Edina that winter. His first group lessons were with Connie Custodio and John Desmond, whom he described as "great guys who tolerated my attitude and made tennis fun."

Bateman may have been one of the first Minnesota high school tennis stars who owed a great deal to junior tennis programs established in the relatively new phenomenon

No. 58 in the 18s his last year as a junior player.

There were many others who helped build the foundation of his game: Jack Roach, Greg Lappin, Steve Wilkinson, Ric Yates, and Ron York and John Mattke (two "fantastic guys" who served as sparring partners for him during high school seasons). Ron, a pro at 98th Street at the time, and John played weekly matches with Bob his senior year. About these teaching pros, Bateman said, "Both were far better players than I was and it was extremely helpful to have them to play against every week." Bob also credits Jerry Noyce, for he arranged these hitting sessions and "a couple of group lessons each week my senior year." In truth, by his own admission, he was mentored by what he called "a veritable Who's Who of Minnesota coaching."

Back on the high school courts, Bateman was nearly unbeatable during his four-year career. Playing first doubles as a freshman with Tom Szarzinski, he won most of his matches; and playing No. 2 singles his sophomore year behind Brian Johnson, he lost only one match, that to John Wheaton in Region 6 individual play. His junior year, playing No. 1 singles, he lost just three matches (all to Combs), and his senior year he was undefeated. Despite all of his on-court successes, his best memories are those of teammates and team competition. "For me high school tennis was all about the team competition. I'm proud of my individual results, but I don't have any special memories about my individual play. I remember the great guys who played on our teams those four years from 1978-81." One, said Bateman, was classmate Bob Bordewick, "with whom I played and practiced from probably age 13 on. Without him as a friend, teammate, and practice partner, I can't imagine getting all I did out of tennis." Bateman saw high school tennis as a continuation of junior circuit play in which he enjoyed friendly rivalries with the likes of Dave Schulze, Combs, Ward, Mark Covin, Dan White, and others.

As a performer he was, in the words of his coach, Les Szendrey, "a superior shot-maker" who "has the ability to move the ball anywhere on the court... He can make shots other players couldn't think of" (*Tennis Midwest*, May 1981). Never a power hitter, he was instead an intelligent and skillful player. But like some teenage players, Bateman had his demons. He himself admitted that he was no angel on court, and he credits Coach Szendrey for helping him to avoid crossing the line. "To his credit Coach Szendrey suspended me for poor behavior my freshman year and would not allow me to play unless I agreed not to blow my top on the court. He said that once I agreed to return to the team, my next offense would be my last. I didn't appreciate the suspension at the time, but I think it helped me be a little more civil on the court."

After his career at Edina ended, Bateman enrolled at the U of Colorado and played four years of varsity tennis from 1981-85. Playing No. 1 doubles all four years and a variety of singles positions, he was runner-up in the Big 8 conference at No. 2 singles his junior year. He graduated in '85 with an economics major, then took nine years off from tennis to work in business before returning to the game. Now he works as a teaching pro at the Harvest House Club in Boulder, CO.

1982-83—Darryl Laddin
Hopkins Lindbergh

1982 and '83 were the Laddin years (see Chapter Four), but there were other stalwarts on the scene as well. 1983 runner-up Tom Olmscheid of Coon Rapids, '83 fourth place finisher Jon Carlson of Hutchinson (future Gustavus Adolphus women's tennis coach), and of course '82 runner-up David Wheaton, come to mind. Olmscheid and Carlson would not win a state singles title, but Wheaton did, breaking through in '84.

1984—David Wheaton
Minnetonka

A precocious talent who had been groomed by his tennis-playing family to be a champion, David Wheaton became the first seventh grader in Minnesota history to compete in a state tournament singles final (D. J. Geatz would be the only other, in '97), losing to Laddin in 1982. Then, after finishing third in 1983, he won his one state singles title in '84 as a ninth grader and moved on to national prominence during his final three years of high school in Florida. Except for aching knee problems, Wheaton might well have won the title as an eighth grader, for he had beaten Laddin during the season. Nevertheless, he finished third in '83 and came through in '84, becoming the youngest Minnesotan ever to win a state singles title. The only other ninth graders to win singles titles were Chris Laitala from Blake, who accomplished this feat in '88, and Ross Greenstein of Blake, the Class A champion in '97.

David grew up as the youngest of four children in Deephaven-Cottagewood, where his mother, a teaching pro at Minnetonka Country Club, began tossing tennis balls to him when he was four. Also a hockey player, Wheaton developed a strong backhand from an early age and he recalls how his grandfather, John Hessey, even tried to make him into a left-handed player. A self-described "rink rat in the winter and court rat in the summer," Wheaton recalls hitting against a screen in his driveway and later honing his game on public courts, particularly on a court right in his Cottagewood neighborhood a block away where he hit with his older siblings Marnie, Mark, and John. He also credits Jerry Noyce for helping him, beginning when he was about 10 years old, when they would play before

every high school player in the Upper Midwest. But he had to be given permission to play on the team by Coach Gary Peterson and he had to integrate into a squad of mostly junior and senior boys. This proved not to be a problem, thanks in part to Peterson, a cooperative group of guys, and co-No. 1 player Mark Kruger, who made David feel at ease right away. He loved being part of a team, and he also excelled in individual competition, losing to the much older and undefeated Laddin in the state finals 6-2, 6-3. Although he did not win the title, tennis fans hailed the arrival of a new prodigy, this Mozart with a racket. Howard

David Wheaton

school regularly. "We played for yoghurt cones. He let me win some and taught me the daily discipline of the game." Always a thoughtful, self-analytical person, David said of his early years in tennis, "I had a really good environment to become a tennis player because of the three C's: court time, coaching, and competition."

With such a firm foundation, laid through tournament playing and coaching from his family and many others, David was ready to play high school tennis. Coming into his seventh-grade year with a national ranking of No. 5 in the 12-and-unders, he was already better than nearly

Sinker, in an article about the tournament, commented, "David Wheaton, a boy among older boys, captured the fancy of the audience during the state tennis tournament Saturday afternoon at the 98th Street Racquet Club" (*Minneapolis Star and Tribune*, June 13, 1982).

Though his eighth-grade season was surely a disappointment for him in some respects, for he had beaten Laddin during the season at the Metro Tournament, he nevertheless finished third in the state singles tournament that year, losing to junior Tom Olmscheid of Coon Rapids in the semis and then beating junior Jon Carlson of Hutchinson. A knee injury he sustained before the tournament while skipping rope for conditioning, as well as extreme heat, took a great deal out of him. "It was hot out there," said a flushed-faced Wheaton, who had to play 49 games and three matches to reach the Saturday semis. "The temperature was way over 100 degrees. I'm going home and jump in the lake [he lived on Lake Minnetonka], then go to bed early," he told *Minneapolis Star and Tribune* writer Ralph Thornton. (June 11, 1983).

That summer David traveled with brother Mark to play tournaments on the national circuit. When his ninth-grade season rolled around, Wheaton, who had given up hockey to concentrate on tennis, was primed to win the state title that had eluded him the two previous years. Undefeated during the regular season, he rolled through the 24-draw, winning all but one of his three matches leading up to the final in decisive straight sets. His first victim was junior Jeff Demeray of Rochester Mayo (future Mayo tennis coach). The only glitch was a 7-5 loss to junior Mark Peterson of St. Paul Highland Park in the first set of his next match on Friday. After dispatching Peterson 6-0, 6-0 in the last two sets, he then took out senior Matt Boos of Apple Valley in the semis and senior Olmscheid 6-3, 6-0 in the final on Saturday. A metronome with perfect pitch on all his strokes, Wheaton dominated his older but less-experienced opponents. In an article in the June 10, 1984, *Minneapolis Star and Tribune* by Tom Briere, U of M tennis coach Noyce said about his pupil David's game, "The freshman just turned 15, but he plays with the experience of a 25-year-old." The match was over in less than an hour, for, according to an article in *Tennis Midwest* magazine, "After a rocky start in the first set, Wheaton settled down to play his game of backboard tennis, returning everything the bigger and stronger Olmscheid could hit" ("Wheaton Stops Olmscheid," July 1984).

Wheaton said of the match, "I played real well. It would have to rate with my best ever. In the second set, I never felt better—serving, passing shots, whatever" (*Minneapolis Star and Tribune*, June 10, 1984). As a spectator at that match, I personally remember how impressed I was by this youngster's concentration and focus. On the changeovers, for example, he pulled out notes he had written to remind him of strategies to use against Olmscheid.

He was indeed our tennis Mozart, so rumors about his departure for a more competitive tennis environment began to surface when he was still playing in the 12-and-unders, a division he dominated for four years (he was No. 1 four straight times). And after he won his third Sectional singles title, this one in the 14s (he eventually won a total of eight Sectional singles titles, every one he competed in through his second year of 16-and-under competition), it was apparent that he was already thinking of a pro tennis career. However, his intentions were to return to Minnetonka for his sophomore year, even though it was becoming more difficult for him to find good local competition.

An event in mid-January 1985 would soon change his life. Nick Bollettieri came to Minneapolis to do a clinic for local youth and David's mother asked him if he wanted to attend the clinic. David eagerly agreed, and at the clinic he had a chance to hit some balls under the watchful gaze of Bollettieri. Here's how Wheaton describes that serendipitous meeting: "Nick saw something in me and offered to have me come to his tennis academy for a month to see how I liked it." His mother then asked David if he wanted to be a big fish in a small pond or a small fish in a big pond. David replied, "I want to be a big fish in a big pond."

Thus, according to David, "We left in mid-January 1985 and Nick put me in a room with Aaron Krickstein." Wheaton improved his tennis immediately, Bollettieri gave him a full scholarship, his parents rented out their house and took a nearby condo in Florida, and David enrolled in a private Episcopal school, St. Stephen's. Though he never played in another high school match, his afternoon sessions with Bollettieri and his practice battles with Agassi, Courier, and other top juniors such as Chris Garner and Martin Blackman, prepared him for top-level junior competition. As a result, he became only the second Minnesota teenager (along with Howard Schoenfeld of Rochester) to achieve a No. 1 national ranking in the juniors, which he achieved in his last year in the 18s. So in 1987 he could boast that he was ahead of Pete Sampras, Agassi, Courier, and Michael Chang; for that year he won both the U.S. Open (over Andrey Cherkasov of Russia) and U.S. Clay Court junior tournaments to secure that No. 1 ranking.

No slouch in the classroom either, David graduated as valedictorian of his class at St. Stephen's; so despite the lure of increasingly big prize money that enticed his compatriots at Bollettieri and Nick's own encouragement for him to turn pro, David opted for college after graduation. Though he had a strong allegiance to Jerry Noyce, he chose Stanford over the U of M, in part because he had a chance to play on a top-level team with the likes of Patrick McEnroe, Jeff Tarango (his doubles partner), and Blackman. Under the tutelage of legendary coach Dick Gould, who "forced me to become a serve-and-volley player, urging me always to 'get to the net'," Wheaton helped the Cardinal win the 1988 national championship. That year he also won the Block S award as most outstanding freshman athlete at Stanford. Oh yes, he earned all-American status as well. On the court he reached the final of his first college tournament, the All-American Tournament at UCLA, but in December of '87 he put his hand through a dorm window while roller-blading. He cut two tendons and partially tore a nerve in his left wrist. As a result, he had reparative surgery and couldn't hit his patented two-handed backhand for weeks. When he returned to action, he started at No. 3 singles and finally moved up to No. 1 for the NCAA Tournament.

After this heady athletic and academic experience, the lure of the pro tour was too great; so on the 4th of July in 1988 he embarked on a career that would take him all over the world in quest of the Holy Grail of tennis stardom. While one might fairly argue that Chuck Darley was the greatest male Minnesota high school player, I don't think there's any question about who was the greatest male professional player from the state. David Wheaton earned that honorific by virtue of his remarkable record in thirteen years on the pro tour: five times ranked in the top ten in the U.S. (his highest ranking was No. 5 behind Courier, Sampras, Agassi, and Chang in '91), U.S. Davis Cup team member in '93, semifinalist at Wimbledon in '91 (losing to Boris Becker), U.S. Open and Australian Open quarterfinalist in '90, U.S. Open and Australian Open doubles finalist in 1990 and '91 respectively (in '90 he and partner Paul Annacone lost to Piet Aldrich and Dannie Visser and in '91 he and Patrick McEnroe lost to Scott Davis and David Pate). In addition, he won

three ATP Tour singles titles (Grand Slam Cup, Kiawah Island, and Newport) and three ATP doubles titles; and he earned a world No. 12 ranking in '91, his best year. By the way, that Grand Slam Cup win in Munich earned him two million dollars. All told he won over 5 million dollars and held career victories over Agassi, Jimmy Connors, Stefan Edberg, Ivan Lendl, Courier, Chang, and Michael Stich, among others. Not bad for a kid from the frozen northland.

Though there are now other things in his life, David has continued to play competitive professional tennis after leaving the tour in 2001. He has played World Team Tennis with the Delaware Smash and many special events. In addition, in '04 he and partner T. J. Middleton won the 35-and-over doubles title at Wimbledon, his first Wimbledon title. And beginning while he was still on the tournament circuit he also began giving motivational speeches to Christian, corporate, and athletic organizations; led an e-mail Bible study group for pro players on the ATP and WTA tours; appeared in various television and print ads/articles; received numerous corporate endorsements from the likes of Northwest Airlines, Nike, Wilson, and Head; and even did commentary during the '91 Wimbledon final won by Stich over Becker.

Returning to his hometown, David lives once again on Lake Minnetonka, not far from his siblings and parents, and he is involved in a host of enterprises, some of which are related to tennis. For example, you can read his column in the *Star Tribune* four times a year when he writes preview reports for the four Grand Slam tournaments. In addition, he has a radio talk show program on KKMS called "Beyond Sports-The David Wheaton Show" and he occasionally serves as an emcee for exhibition tennis events in the Twin Cities, most recently serving in that capacity when the Davis Cup boys (Andy Roddick, Mardy Fish, and the Bryan brothers) came to the Excel Energy Center in December of 2004.

He is also a member of the USTA Board of Directors, participates in numerous charitable fundraising events, and supports inner city tennis programs in Minneapolis by doing occasional events for them. He's a bright guy whose interests include sailing and wilderness sports, current events, politics, and history; and he recently completed a book titled *University of Destruction—Your Game Plan for Spiritual Victory on Campus*. In addition, he continues to do some coaching, even serving as the interim U of M men's coach in 2005. Most recently, he signed on as the touring tennis professional at the Wayzata Country Club. For all his contributions to Minnesota tennis, he was inducted into the Northern Section Tennis Hall of Fame in 2005.

Although he has gained a good deal of fame from his tennis experiences, he remains grounded in Midwestern values and in his faith and he is quick to credit his family, some investors in his career, and people like Jerry Noyce (who gave him free court time and invested his time in him) for his success. And despite the fact that he spent years on the dog-eat-dog pro tour, he relishes his years as a team player, saying, "Being in a ruggedly individual sport like tennis, it was a pleasure to be on a team. I always enjoyed Davis Cup and Stanford because they were team sports. It adds a dimension to tennis that's not normally there, that is, the team aspect. It helps you in so many ways—it's for a greater good, mental control, courage under pressure, discipline. Your match is one cog in a wheel, and you learn to accept authority from a coach."

1985—Paul Odland
Edina

In the void now left by Wheaton's departure, the field was wide open in 1985, and the player who came out of the pack was another young and talented performer, sophomore Paul Odland of Edina. (Once again, see Chapter Four for more about Odland, a two-time winner.)

1986—Jason Hall
Minnehaha Academy

The runner-up in 1985 as a junior, Jason Hall of Minnehaha Academy defeated Odland (now a junior) in the semis, then beat Odland's ninth-grade teammate Mike Terwilliger in a grueling three-set final to claim the '86 title. Terwilliger, who would finally win the title as a senior in '89, upset Odland in the region finals; so while Terwilliger and Hall—winners of their regions—played only twice the first day, Odland had to play three matches

on Friday just to get to the semis (the tournament was a 32-draw with 24 players, so the 8 region winners had first-round byes). This was a magical year for Hall and his Minnehaha teammates, for they stormed through the team competition to claim the first-ever team championship in any sport for the school, and he capped it off with the top individual medal.

Losing only one match during the year, Minneha-

Jason Hall

ha's ace—the only Minnesota tennis player recruited by Jerry Noyce that year—beat Odland twice in the tournament (once in the team semifinal match) and knocked off Edina's No. 1 and 2 players back to back in the individual semis and finals. John Gilbert, in a June 8, 1986, *Minneapolis Star and Tribune* article, described these two matches thus, "Hall completed a spectacular week at the 98th Street Racquet Club by beating Odland 7-5, 6-3 in the morning semifinals, then overtaking Terwilliger 4-6, 6-4, 7-5 in the title match." Remarkably, the two-set match with Odland in the semis took two and one-half hours, so Hall only had a one-half hour break before the finals. In the match with Odland, the first set ended after the other singles semifinal (a 6-3, 6-4 Terwilliger victory over Todd Schlorf of St. Cloud Tech) and both doubles semis were completed, so both Hall and Odland played on in a state of near exhaustion. Gilbert picks the match up at 2-2 in the second set: "He [Hall] came back to win that game, but he had to pick himself up off the asphalt—literally—to win the match. Up 5-3 in games and leading 15-love, Hall tried to chase a perfectly lobbed shot by Odland past his baseline. As he looked up at the ball, he crashed heavily into the outer fence and tumbled to the court, stunned, the wind knocked out of him. But he came back to finish off Odland, who broke strings on two rackets and had to borrow another to finish" (June 8, 1986). With no time for a meal, Hall gulped down some gatorade and snacked on a banana before taking the court for the final match.

Against Terwilliger, Hall lost the first three games in the first set, rallied to win the next four, but lost the next three and the set. After losing the set, Hall told Gilbert, "It was almost good that I lost that set. The last time I beat Terwilliger, I lost the first set and came back to beat him." In the Odland match Hall had come to the net often, but this strategy didn't work well against the canny young Terwilliger, who, according to Gilbert again, "foiled those moves with precise shots just inside either sideline for consistent winners." And when Terwilliger came to the net, Hall couldn't pass him. So after he fell behind 3-1 in the second set, Hall resolved "to play patiently at the baseline" (June 8, 1986). This tactic garnered him four straight games and some much-needed momentum; he then closed out the set 6-4. Leading 5-2 in the last set and seemingly in command, he saw the youngster claw his way back to 5-all; but even though he had some trouble serving and was battling leg cramps, Hall summoned enough energy to win two more games and the match. Terwilliger later praised Hall as the toughest player he faced all year. Before overcoming the terrible two from Edina, Hall won straight-set matches the first day: over senior Tim Turnquist of White Bear Lake and junior Eric Bracht of Stillwater.

Though he didn't start playing tennis until he was 12, Hall had excellent coaching from the likes of Ron York, Randy Crowell, Scott Danielson, Mark Wheaton, and Paul Muesing. By age 16 he began to make his mark in NWTA tournaments, achieving a No. 2 ranking in boys 16 singles in 1985 and a No. 1 ranking in boys 18s, a ranking which he held for two years (1986-87). In addition, he and high school teammate Ryan Skanse won the Sectional 16-and-under doubles championship one year. However, he counts winning the state team championship and the singles title as highlights of his high school career, especially because this was the last year of the combined one-class tournament and also because Edina was a big favorite. With some amusement he recalls his parents saying that high school tennis was good for him because it kept him out of trouble after school. On a more serious note, Hall said, "Personally, high school tennis gave me a lot of confidence. Overall, I think of my junior and senior high school years as being the best of my life."

Hall went on to play four years at the U of M (two years for Noyce and two for Dave Geatz), mostly at Nos. 4-6 singles and 2-3 doubles. His best U memory is winning the 1989 team tournament during a year in which players such as Todd Martin of Northwestern and Mal Washington of Michigan were competing. And as a sophomore he won the Jerry Noyce-Nike Most Improved Player Award ('88).

Jason lives in Prior Lake, the town where he grew up, and works for a firm called Innovative Marketing Solutions. Oh, yes; he still finds time to play tennis a couple times a week. In fact, his USTA league teams have won two national titles, one in the 5.0 division and another in the 5.5 division.

1987—Odland
Edina

After finishing fourth in 1986, Paul Odland came back as a senior to win his second title in '87 and help Edina claim the team title they last won in '81 (then as Edina East). (Again, see Chapter Four for Odland's story.)

Chris Laitala

1988–Chris Laitala
Blake

In 1988 another tennis prodigy, Chris Laitala, surfaced to win the state singles title. Only the second ninth grader (after David Wheaton) to win the championship, he played for Blake, normally a Class A school. Blake could have chosen to play in the small-school tournament, but coach John Hatch opted to give his players a chance to compete against the larger Class AA schools. This decision proved to be a good one for the team (which advanced to the State Tournament) and for Laitala.

Like Wheaton, Laitala's potential had been evident for some time. Bob Larson, in his "Ad In" column in the May 1988 issue of *Tennis Midwest* magazine, said of Laitala, "Chris has the best potential among Minnesota boys for a professional career." Local pro Howard Johnson, a former Pepperdine player and local USPTA pro who once worked with Vic Braden, said, "Chris is very close in ability to David [Wheaton] at 15" (May 1988).

Unlike Wheaton, Laitala stayed in Minnesota to complete his high school career. But even though he was always one of the top players his last three years, finishing second his junior and senior years, for example, his

championship this year would be his only one. After losing a tough match to Mounds View's Dean Hlushko in a first-round team match on Wednesday, he came back on Friday to beat seniors Steve LeGuen of White Bear Lake in the first round and Dan James of Northfield in the quarters of the individual tournament. Then in the Saturday semis he polished off foreign exchange student Mark Calander of Orono and Robbinsdale Armstrong junior Dan Nabedrick in the finals 6-4, 6-3.

Nabedrick, by the way, took third in the 1989 singles tournament and went on to play at the U of WI (rotating between Nos. 5 and 6 singles and Nos. 1 and 2 doubles). He then played some professional tennis tournaments and is today the director of tennis at the Golden Valley Golf and Country Club and owner/director of Twin City Tennis Camps, Inc. In addition, he served as an assistant boys' tennis coach (under Hall of Fame coach Roger Lipelt) at Wayzata for several years.

It is perhaps no coincidence that Laitala's name should be linked with David Wheaton's, for he began taking lessons at age 11 on the very same courts in Cottagewood where David got his start and from David's coach, Howard Johnson. And in his first out-of-state tournament, the 12-and-unders at the Orange Bowl in Florida, he traveled with Wheaton and his two brothers. He had begun playing with his parents when he was 9 or 10, and he remembers well his first tournament at the Edina Country Club. "I got to the finals in the 10-and-unders and this spurred me on."

From this first successful experience at age 10, Chris's precocious talent helped him carve out an incredibly successful junior career on both the local and national tennis stages. In his rookie year of competition (1984) he was ranked No. 2 in the NWTA in the 10-and-unders. Moving up to the 12-and-unders the next year, he was ranked No. 4; from then until he graduated from high school he was the No. 1 ranked boys' player every year in which he competed in NWTA tournaments.

On the national stage he was the most successful male Minnesota junior of his era, ranking No. 15 his second year in the 14-and-unders and No. 8 in the 16-and-unders in 1989. That year he finished 8th at Kalamazoo, losing to future touring pro Vince Spadea in the quarters, a player whom he eventually trained with. But his most outstanding feat as a junior was winning a doubles silver medal in the Olympic Festival in '90.

After completing his brilliant high school and junior career, Laitala played four years of Division I tennis at Harvard on a team that was always ranked in the top twenty in the country and as high as number ten his freshman year. Playing between Nos. 4-6 singles with the likes of Tom Blake (current pro James Blake's brother), Chris thoroughly enjoyed his college tennis experience. After completing his studies at Harvard he worked for a banking firm in Baltimore for two years, earned an MBA from Howard U, worked for a venture capital firm, then did leveraged buyout work for two years. He continues to play tennis once a month or so and today works for a medical sales firm in Greenwich, CT.

Although he won just one state singles title, he expressed no regrets: "I didn't measure my success by how many tournaments I won or lost; I loved the game and the competition." Laitala also spoke about how much he enjoyed the team camaraderie of high school tennis and the adrenalin rush of state tournament competition. "I loved being able to play in front of a larger crowd." Of course he valued winning the singles title as a freshman, but he considers being a part of the AA team champions his senior year a highlight of his career. Also, in his sophomore year (1989) he lost only one match, to champion Mike Terwilliger in the state singles quarterfinals (6-4, 6-4), and led Blake to a second-place team finish. Chris then lost in the finals his junior and senior years to J. P. Demetriou of Eden Prairie in '90 (2-6, 7-5, 6-2) and Scott Sanderson of Edina in '91 (7-5, 7-6).

Greg Wicklund, one of the local pros who helped shape Laitala's game, said of him, "He was a great baseliner who had a terrific two-handed backhand and a solid return of serve. He was a very smart player with lots of national experience." Two-time Class AA singles champion Scott Sanderson said of Laitala, "Chris had great groundstrokes and a great mind for the game." And another of his coaches, Dave Mathews, who served as Laitala's traveling coach to national tournaments, praised Chris as "a very intense player and hard worker."

In addition, he was a resourceful player. Chris recalls an experience during the early spring of his senior season that exemplified his resourcefulness. Even though his left arm became increasingly sore, he continued to hit his two-handed backhand until he realized that his arm was broken. This didn't seem to be a problem for Laitala, for he just switched to a one-handed backhand for two weeks until he could return to his patented two-hander.

All things considered, even though he won only one singles title, he will be remembered as one of Minnesota's most successful high school players at the local and national level. In addition, he was a consummate sportsman, earning the 1991 NWTA Junior Sportsmanship Award.

1989—Mike Terwilliger
Edina

1989 was finally Mike Terwilliger's year. After bursting on the scene as a freshman in '86 (finishing second to Jason Hall in the singles tournament), Edina's Terwilliger won the state title that had eluded him for three years. One of the best athletes to capture the singles crown, he played several sports as a youngster but excelled in both tennis and hockey. The son of former state senator and current chairman of the Metropolitan Sports Facilities Commission, Roy Terwilliger, Mike rolled through the singles draw in '89, first blitzing senior John Dawson of Duluth East 6-0, 6-2, then beating '88 champion Chris Laitala (still only a sophomore) in the quarters 6-4, 6-4. Then he defeated senior Tommy Tauchnitz of Austin 6-2, 6-0 and Mounds View senior Brian Benkstein in the finals 6-1, 6-1. This victory capped a glorious season for him, a season in which he won every match and also led Edina to the team title. In addition, a measure of his dominance in the state singles tournament was the fact that he gave up just 14 games in four matches.

Terwilliger's tennis career began innocently enough with some recreational hitting with his family and neighborhood friends such as Charlie Eifrig (1988 doubles champion) when he was 9 years old. At age 12 he played some summer tournaments for fun and did so well that he became more serious about tennis. Mike said, "The next summer, when I was 13, I hit with Brace Helgeson and started doing STP in the fall and winter and taking lessons." After working with Brace for a year or so,

Mike Terwilliger

Terwilliger then hit "quite a bit for the next few years with Randy Crowell, a great guy." Periodically, he took lessons from other pros such as Howard Johnson, Ron York, and Brian Biernat; but mainly he hit with Randy. These lessons and hitting sessions, combined with his raw athletic talent, helped him carve out a very successful junior career in the NWTA Section. Beginning in 1984, when he was ranked No. 2 behind Dan Nabedrick in the 12-and-under singles, Mike was ranked No. 3 in the 14s, No. 2 in the 14s, and No. 1 in the 16s for two years. In addition, for many years he played national tournaments in the summer and in '85 earned a ranking of No. 49 in boys 14s.

Never one to boast about individual accomplishments, Terwilliger considered being a part of three championship teams to be his most memorable tennis accomplishment in high school. "I liked being a part of our team—my main goal each year was to help our team win State." He also talked of all the fun times he had with his teammates off the court; for example, playing basketball games and being "as concerned about winning a game of 'cutthroat' or 'horse' as with a challenge match against each other." He enjoyed hanging out with his teammates for breakfasts

at Perkins or team meals at Davanni's; and he especially delighted in playing golf with coach Steve Paulsen his senior year. One time, on a team trip to his family's cabin near Brainerd, he and Steve got up at 5:30 and played 18 holes of golf at Breezy Point before 8:00 AM.

Unlike most of our Minnesota champions, Mike did not continue in competitive tennis after high school, instead opting to play Division I hockey at St. Lawrence U in Canton, NY. A defenseman, he helped his nationally ranked St. Lawrence team reach the quarterfinals his junior year. After graduating with an English major, he indulged his passion for golf by working for the Burnett Senior Classic Golf Tournament (now the 3M Professional Championships) as a paid volunteer coordinator, then attended the U of M in 1998-99 to become a certified elementary teacher. For the past seven years he has been teaching first grade in Eden Prairie and helping coach the high school hockey team. He lives in Eden Prairie with his wife Cara (daughter of *Tennis Midwest* magazine's Bob Larson and herself a top player at Edina) and their young son.

Mike is remembered by former competitors such as Chris Laitala as "a great athlete who, when he was focused on tennis, was an excellent player." Both Laitala and 1986 champion Jason Hall spoke of Terwilliger's great two-handed backhand, Hall calling it "unbelievable." Laitala also noted that Terwilliger nearly beat Michael Chang one year, losing twice to him in three sets, once at Kalamazoo. His teammate Odland considered Terwilliger the best player he competed against in high school. "While he was two years younger than me, he was a natural. His two-handed backhand was as good as I had ever seen in the juniors," Odland remarked. "Outside of David Wheaton, he was the best tennis player in Minnesota at the time. He could have been a college player on a top-20 NCAA Division 1 team," he added.

Perhaps in the end he will be remembered more for being a part of three state championship teams, but he should also be remembered as a great champion who competed against some of the best tennis players in any era of Minnesota high school tennis, state champions such as Odland, Hall, Laitala, Roger Anderson of Blue Earth, J. P. Demetriou, and other top competitors such as Nabedrick and Ryan Skanse of Minnehaha Academy. His first high school coach, Les Szendrey, also remembers him "as a gentleman and an exemplary person as a player who commanded respect from everyone." All things considered, he has quite a legacy to leave to his grandchildren.

1990s

An extraordinary time both at home and abroad, this last decade of the 20th century featured cataclysmic political and historical world events such as the collapse of the Soviet Union in 1991, Operation Desert Storm (the Gulf War) in that same year, the end of the Cold War in '92, the Balkan War in the former Yugoslavia, and genocide in Rwanda beginning in '94. Here in the U.S. the World Trade Center was bombed in '93 (a prelude to the horror of 9/11/01); Waco, Texas, became infamous as the site of another tragic cult massacre; O. J. Simpson was tried and found innocent of murder in '94; there was the Oklahoma City bombing in '95; and in late '99 alarmists feared the

Y2K bug would wreak havoc all over the globe.

For the most part, however, this was, like the '80s, a decade of prosperity in the U.S.—and most young people knew only one president, Bill Clinton. Even those who were technology-phobic couldn't escape the explosion in communications represented by the growth of the Internet, DVDs, CD players, and cable TV. Some of the Academy Award-winning films of the decade were *Dances with Wolves*, *The Silence of the Lambs*, *Schindler's List*, *Titanic*, and *Forrest Gump*.

In sports, women in the U.S. had opportunities to earn a living by playing professional basketball (in the WNBA) and by boxing, and the decade featured some remarkable tennis talents, especially among the men. In a "class" that came of age roughly at the beginning of the '90s, future champions emerged such as Pete Sampras (the Grand Slam record-holder with thirteen singles titles), Andre Agassi (eight Grand Slams, including one each of the four majors), Jim Courier (four Grand Slams), Michael Chang (a French Open champion), Todd Martin, and our own David Wheaton, among others. Among the women we had two talented Americans who would flame out for different reasons, Jennifer Capriati (eventual winner of three Grand Slams) for her indiscretions and the transplanted Monica Seles (nine Grand Slams) because a crazed Steffi Graf fan stabbed her in the back. Speaking of Agassi's future wife, Steffi Graf, she was still at the top of her game, tromping all comers on the way to her twenty-two Grand Slam singles titles; and the star of the late '90s was the Swiss Miss, Martina Hingis, winner of five Grand Slams in just three years.

1990—J. P. Demetriou
Eden Prairie

Here in Minnesota, in Class AA, there would be two players claiming two singles titles (Edina's Scott Sanderson in 1991-92 and Bloomington Jefferson's Matt Peplinski in 1995-96), and the others all came from Metro area schools except '99 winner Eric Butorac from Rochester John Marshall. The inaugural winner in 1990 would be Eden Prairie's J. P. Demetriou, who upset '88 champion Chris Laitala in the finals 2-6, 7-5, 6-2. Laitala, now a

J. P. Demetriou

junior, admitted that he may have been overconfident, as he told *Star Tribune* writer Nolan Zavoral: "I won the first set and was up in the second and began thinking of what I'd do when I won" (June 10, 1990). The article by Zavoral continued by saying that Laitala "swept through the first championship set by breaking his opponent twice. In the second set Laitala led 5-3 but Demetriou drew even as he saved three match points. There was no panic in Demetriou's play. He concentrated on keeping the ball in play with soft shots to win the second and third sets."

Demetriou said, "All I could think about was getting back even." Zavoral then noted that "in the deciding set, Demetriou kept getting stronger. On the other hand, Laitala seemed to be weakening from his semifinal grind [a two-hour 2-6, 7-6, 6-2 win over Mounds View's Derek Howe]. Buying time after a point, he would circle behind the baseline, catching his breath and summoning his strength" (June 10, 1990).

"I could see him getting tired," Demetriou said. "He wasn't running as much." Laitala admitted he was tired in the third set, and he showed it by double faulting match point. The victory was especially sweet for Demetriou because Laitala had eliminated him in the first round in 1989 (June 10, 1990).

In addition to this tough match against Laitala, the road to the finals for Demetriou was full of huge boulders: future champion Scott Sanderson in the quarters (whom he overcame in a 4-6, 7-5, 6-4 dogfight); the up-and-coming sophomore star from Duluth East, Erik Donley, in the semis 6-2, 7-5); and, of course, Laitala. His only easy match was a 6-1, 6-0 win over senior Josh Roering of Mounds View in the first round.

Demetriou finished his triumphant season with a record of 32-2 and, according to the aforementioned article by Zavoral, "his only losses were to Edina's Scott Sanderson. Demetriou won 11 of 12 three-set matches, dropping his only three-setter in a regular-season defeat to Sanderson" (June 10, 1990).

After years as a successful junior player in the then Northwestern section, Demetriou finally cracked the code to win a state title in his final season of high school competition. Beginning in 1983, when he was ranked No. 6 in Boys 12 Singles, he was always one of the top juniors in the Upper Midwest. In '84, for example, he was No. 3 in Boys 12 Singles and No. 1 in doubles (with Andy Ray); and in '89 he secured the No. 1 ranking in his last year of junior competition, the 18-and-unders.

Edina's Sanderson called him "a great all-around player with a great mind for the game." And his coach, Rich Strohkirch, said of Demetriou, "He was a steady player who played long points and very seldom made mistakes." His mother also weighed in with an opinion, saying of her son, "He's so loose and quiet that he might seem lackadaisical. But he's not" (June 10, 1990).

After graduation he went to Ball State and played tennis for four years. He lives in the Twin Cities today.

1991-92—Scott Sanderson
Edina

In what was another mild upset in 1991, Edina junior Scott Sanderson deprived Chris Laitala (in his final year of competition) of a second title, beating him 7-5, 7-6 to take home the first of his two singles medals. He repeated in '92, that time defeating teammate Marcelo Borrelli in the finals. (See Chapter Four for details about Sanderson's two titles.)

1993–Marcelo Borrelli
Edina

As the global village expanded even into small towns in Minnesota, foreign-born players began to turn up on the rosters of schools all over the state as early as the 1950s. Some were foreign exchange students such as Willie Hernandez from the Philippines (the '57 champion from Hopkins) and Jakob Victorin from Sweden (the '81 Class A champion from Morton), but others were foreign-born players who moved to the U.S. when their parents emigrated. One such player was '93 champion Borrelli, whose parents, natives of the Dominican Republic, brought him and his family to Minnesota in the summer of '89. For two years Marcelo dominated the junior summer circuit in the Section (ranking No. 1 in the 16s in '91 and No. 1 in the 18s in '92) and excelled in high school play for three years (reaching the quarterfinals in '91, finishing second in '92, and of course winning the AA title this year).

Borrelli spent his first two years at Hill Murray, then transferred to Edina for his last two years. As a sophomore at Hill Murray he soon became acquainted on the court with future teammate Sanderson, losing to him in three sets in the quarterfinals of the 1991 tournament. The next year he lost to Sanderson twice, once in a close two-set match in the region finals and again in the finals of the State. That match would not be close, Sanderson winning 6-0, 6-2. Despite this lopsided score and Sanderson's domination of him, his teammate praised Borrelli, calling him one of his toughest opponents because "he had an incredible topspin forehand he hit with an extreme Western grip. He hit the ball with a lot of pace, and when he was on he was difficult to beat."

With Sanderson gone the next year, Borrelli finally won the singles title, defeating senior Mike Ghaly of Minneapolis South in the semis and future champion Todd Bowlby, a junior from Minneapolis Washburn, in the finals by a score of 6-2, 6-2. After absorbing a season-opening 7-5, 6-1 loss to Bowlby, Borrelli was looking for redemption in his rematch with the Minneapolis Washburn star. Said he after the match, in an article by Jeffrey Shelman, "Of course I wanted to make up for the state title [loss to teammate Sanderson in 1992], but getting back at Bowlby was great, too. I hoped Bowlby would get to the finals so

no one could doubt I could beat him" (*Star Tribune*, June 12, 1993). In this same *Star Tribune* article, Borrelli said about his matchup with Bowlby, "If I was going to lose, I would go down swinging... I knew I could rally with him all day." In their earlier match Bowlby had forced Borrelli to come to the net, but using his big forehand and backhand this time, Marcelo didn't have to come up to the net. Giving credit to Borrelli, runner-up Bowlby said, "He wanted it more. He played the big points better than I did" (June 12, 1993).

Borrelli's dominance of the field was complete, for he gave up only eleven games in four matches, an average of not quite three per match. The match with Bowlby was the closest, and his first two were routs over seniors Chris Anderson of Brainerd-Motley-Pillager and Kim Pederson of Buffalo.

Borrelli's journey to the top of the tennis ladder in Minnesota was that of a nomad. Born in the Dominican Republic, he first began playing on clay courts there at age 6; then at age 12 he began playing three times a week at a tennis academy in Buenos Aires during his family's residence in Argentina. Still, he didn't become really serious about tennis until he moved to Minnesota the summer before his freshman year and when his family joined the White Bear Racquet Club. There he took lessons from former Gustavus player Rajan Keswani and often hit with some of the top players from Mounds View's 1990 State championship team such as Derek Howe and Josh Roering. After two years with Rajan, Marcelo then worked with '80 champion Chris Combs and another White Bear Lake pro named Mike Olson, and his senior year he worked with Brian McCoy. All four coaches were instrumental in making him a champion, but Borrelli is especially grateful to McCoy for taking him to the top level.

Recruited by several top schools, Marcelo accepted a tennis scholarship to the U of NM, then the 18th-ranked team in the nation. Unfortunately for him they had, in his words, "some REAL good players from all over the world that were semipros," so he did not make the top six traveling team. In a bit of serendipity, his parents then moved to Texas; so, in order to be closer to his family, he transferred to Texas Tech to play for the 33rd-ranked team. For two years he played great tennis, and even considered going to Europe to play the clay court circuit; but after receiving the MVP award his junior year, he put his rackets in mothballs. He said, "There is a very big difference between a great college player and a top tennis pro." At Texas Tech he had played some doubles and mostly Nos. 4-6 singles, compiling the best winning percentage on the team his MVP year (1995).

Instead, he focused on getting "a real education and pursuing a professional corporate job." Since graduation he has been working as a financial consultant (stock broker), first for Morgan Stanley and now as a second vice president for Smith Barney-Citigroup, in Florida.

Like so many players, he counts the friendships he made in tennis—and getting out of school to play in the State Tournament—as favorite memories of his high school years. As for playing highlights, he cites winning the 1992 team championship and the '93 singles title and getting to play his teammate Scott Sanderson his junior year in the finals of the region and State. The No. 1-ranked high school player going into his senior year, he lost his only match, to Bowlby, in that first meet of the year. Ultimately, Borrelli got his revenge, soundly defeating Bowlby in the state finals: "I still have the tennis ball that I used on the last point that day with the date and score."

1994—Todd Bowlby
Minneapolis Washburn

Speaking next of Bowlby, he was a determined player who came through his senior year, 1994, to claim the singles title that had eluded him the year before. In doing so he became the first Minneapolis city player to win the championship in twenty-five years, the last being Tom Brennan of Minneapolis West in 1969. In addition, the stylish lefty, along with teammate and No. 2 player Bobby Hansen, led Washburn to two third-place team finishes in 1993 and '94. A dominant player both on the junior scene for years (he was, for example, ranked No. 1 in Boys 14 Singles in '89 and boys 18s in '93 and No. 2 in boys 16s in '91 and in boys 18s in '92) and in high school, Bowlby wore the uniform of the Minneapolis Washburn Millers. As Washburn's No. 1 player, he advanced to the State Tournament in singles all four of his high school years, losing to '91

champion Sanderson in the first round his freshmen year, to '92 runner-up Borrelli in the second round his sophomore year, and to champion Borrelli in the finals his junior year.

Todd Bowlby

But he would not be denied his senior year, triumphing despite a good deal of adversity that would have felled a lesser mortal. Rachel Blount, in a June 11, 1994, article in the *Star Tribune*, first talked about Bowlby's draining two-hour and fifty-minute semifinal match with Hopkins senior Shai Ingber which he won 6-1, 5-7, 7-6. "He maintained his focus through a rain delay that caused the match to be suspended and moved from the 98th Street Racquet Club to the Burnsville Racquet Club." And in the finals he needed every ounce of his boundless energy to defeat Rafael Gonzales, a previously undefeated foreign exchange student from Mexico playing for Coach J. Paul Richards at Winona. Willing himself on through what

Blount described as "a number of surges and lapses," Bowlby won the match in an anticlimactic fashion after Gonzales cramped up in both legs and was unable to complete the match. The final score was 6-4, 4-6, 2-0 (default) and after the match Bowlby proudly wore the champion's blue medal around his neck. Though Gonzalez had to get through rising star and future two-time champion Matt Peplinski from Bloomington Jefferson in his semifinal match, he nevertheless won in straight sets and had more than the thirty-minute break between matches that Bowlby had.

The final match was a classic baseline slugfest, with both players pounding groundstrokes at each other and waiting for the other to make a mistake. Both were broken several times, but in the end it was Bowlby who weathered the storms. In the article by Blount, Washburn coach Dean Rudrud said of his player, "The delays and the length of the first match didn't bother [Bowlby]. He's so well-conditioned he could go all day... Once he set this goal [winning the state title], he was ready to fight to the finish." Speaking after the match of needing his heart and desire, Bowlby also said, "This shows how important mental toughness is. I got an opportunity and I took advantage of it. My business is taken care of" (June 11, 1994). During a season in which he was ranked No. 1 by the state tennis coaches, Bowlby lived up to his reputation. He won all four of his matches at State, including two straight-setters on the first day: over junior Tom Fleming of White Bear Lake Area and senior Brian Cardinal of Henry Sibley. This state title, and a summer of tournament play which earned him a national ranking of No. 147, gave him a nice boost in confidence for his tennis future, a four-year career at Gustavus Adolphus College.

At Gustavus Bowlby played No. 1 singles for four years on teams that finished as high as fourth in the NCAA Division 3 Tournament, and as an individual he was exceptional. For example, he won the ITA Midwest Regional singles all four years, and three years in doubles (with three different partners: Paul Jeffries, Adam Beduhn, and Ryan Dussault); the MIAC No. 1 singles title every year (1995-98); and the No. 1 and 2 MIAC doubles twice each (with two partners: Jeffries and Dussault). A four-year NCAA all-American (1995-98), Bowlby was the singles

runner-up at Nationals his sophomore year and a quarterfinalist his senior year. In addition, he was voted ITA Rookie of the Year in '95 and Midwest Regional Senior Player of the Year in '98.

Matt Peplinski, next year's singles champion, called Bowlby "the best player I played against. His mental and physical game was so hard to beat. He's the only one I haven't beaten." And his college coach, Steve Wilkinson, said of him, "Todd was a dedicated work horse, a steady baseliner who never gave up."

Today Bowlby continues in tennis as a part-time teacher at the Eden Prairie Lifetime Fitness Club.

1995-96—Matt Peplinski
Bloomington Jefferson

After a sophomore year in which he finished fourth in the state singles competition, Matt Peplinski was ready to take his place at the head of the class in 1995. Not only did he win the title this year, but he would join the ranks of multiple champions by claiming a second singles championship as a senior in 96. (See Chapter Four for the profile on Peplinski.)

1997—Ryan Edlefsen
Bloomington Jefferson

One of Peplinski's teammates, Ryan Edlefsen, who as a ninth grader was an important member of the Jefferson team which won its first-ever AA team title in 1994, emerged from Peplinski's shadow to take the singles crown in 1997. He and teammate Phil Woo had finished second in the doubles competition in '96, so this singles victory, though not unexpected because Edlefsen had been ranked No. 1 all year by the coaches, rounded out his successful junior season. These were glorious years for Edlefsen and his Jefferson team, for they clawed their way out of the ultra-competitive cauldron of Region 6 to win two State AA team titles in addition to the three singles titles he and Peplinsli won.

Edlefsen advanced through the draw to the singles final where he found seventh-grade phenom D. J. Geatz of Minneapolis South waiting for him. Geatz was only the second Minnesota player to reach the finals as a seventh grader, the other of course being David Wheaton in 1982. Both, however, would lose, Wheaton to Darryl Laddin and Geatz to Edlefsen, who dispatched his youthful adversary in straight sets 6-0, 6-1.

Carrying the burden of No. 1 didn't make things easy, but Edlefsen handled it well, overcoming a stiff challenge from sophomore Eric Butorac of Rochester John Marshall in the first round, then dispatching his next two opponents in straight sets. Against Butorac, he had to come back after losing the first set 6-3. In the quarters he easily handled junior Neil Kolatkar of Maple Grove, then upended another rising star in the semis, sophomore Ajay Prakash of St. Cloud Tech.

His coach, Tom Saterdalen, in an article titled "Edlefsen Shows Why He's No. 1," is quoted as saying, "There was a lot of pressure on Ryan and he did a good job of withstanding it... Everyone thought he should win it. That's what makes it so much harder. D. J. had

Ryan Edlefsen

nothing to lose" (*Star Tribune*, June 7, 1997). *Star Tribune* writer Joy Spencer added, "Most of the pressure Edlefsen faces is self-imposed; his game speaks for itself. His serve is a killer. His backhand causes crowds to gasp. He is good. Very good. He also was playing a 13-year-old" (June 7, 1997).

And though Edlefsen experienced some temporary anxiety after winning the first set ("When I got up 6-0, I got nervous. I started losing points"), he kept his focus. Edlefsen also told Spencer, "You're expected to beat this kid... I stayed aggressive. He played better than I expected. He was really returning balls. I had to put more on my second serve" (June 7, 1997). Geatz won the second game of the

second set and had many chances to win the fourth game, but Edlefsen's big game was too much for the kid. Still a bit nervous on his first match point, an overhead that Edlefsen almost put in the parking lot, he then ended the match with an authoritative ace. About his missed overhead, Edlefsen said, "I wanted to nail it away, but I didn't want to hit him." In less than an hour Edlefsen had taken care of business against Geatz, exclaiming after the match, "I'm still surprised but relieved" (June 7, 1997).

In some respects this match was anticlimactic, for, as Edlefsen noted in the June 7 *Star Tribune* article, "My toughest match was in the first round against Rochester John Marshall's Eric Butorac. He was up in the first set and there were a lot of people cheering for him." Edlefsen nevertheless prevailed 3-6, 6-2, 7-5.

Unfortunately for Edlefsen, he was unable to defend his singles title his senior year (1998), for a foreign exchange student from Mexico, Cesar Vargas of Edina, thwarted his efforts. And though he finished as the runner-up, this loss had to have been painful for a number of reasons. First, Edlefsen was bidding to win the fourth AA singles title in a row by a Bloomington Jefferson player. Secondly, Edlefsen was undefeated during the regular season and had not lost a set all year. Thirdly, if Vargas had not shown up at Edina High School, Edlefsen would surely have become Minnesota's fourteenth multiple singles champion. In addition, he had beaten Vargas twice in the past month, including their match in the Section 6 final, and three times during the year. Finally, he injured his chronically weak achilles tendon (which had from time to time bothered him since a childhood bicycle accident) in a difficult semifinal match with St. Cloud

Tech's Kevin Whipple and so was not at full strength for the final against Vargas.

A key member of Bloomington Jefferson's teams, Edlefsen had been appearing at State since he was an eighth grader when he played No. 4 singles. As a ninth grader he again played No. 4 singles and as a sophomore in 1996 he anchored the first doubles spot and he and Phil Woo teamed up in doubles to take second in the individual State Tournament. Then as a junior he took over the No. 1 singles spot after Peplinski graduated.

Claiming that he really wasn't very athletic as a youngster, Edlefsen said he got started in tennis because his dad "wanted to get me into a sport I could play in high school." Soon he began to take private lessons, especially from former Minnetonka player and Twin Cities teaching pro Glenn Britzius, who was his main coach early in his career. Then, like nearly all the modern-era state champions, Edlefsen rose up from the ranks of junior tennis, beginning with rankings of Nos. 12 and 3 in the 12-and-unders. In 1994 he earned the No. 2 ranking in boys 14s, and in '96 he reached the top of the peak in boys 16s, then concluded his junior tennis career with a No. 2 ranking in boys 18s in '97.

In addition, he began competing in national tournaments when he was very young, often participating on boys' intersectional and zone teams for the NWTA. His rankings were respectable—always in the 100s—and his best was No. 128 in the 16s. So his high caliber performances in state tournament competition were not surprising.

After leaving Jefferson as one of the best players on some of the top high school teams of the 1990s, the six-foot-three-inch Edlefsen took his considerable tennis skills to Pepperdine U in California to play Division 1 tennis on a top-ten college team. In a most unusual twist, however, Edlefsen entered Pepperdine not with a tennis scholarship but with an academic scholarship for his prowess in math (he had earned a rare perfect score on the math SAT test). He stayed two years, playing mostly No. 6 singles and Nos. 2 and 3 doubles, then decided he wanted to transfer, in part because he had broken a vertebra in his back his last year and was actually bedridden for six months. So he transferred to a top-thirty college, Northwestern, in the Big Ten, where

he could play higher up in the lineup. Here he played No. 3 singles his junior year and Nos. 1 and 2 singles his senior year and No. 1 doubles.

Following his graduation from Northwestern, Edlefsen took his math major into the business world, but not before playing a few futures pro tournaments during the summer after graduation. Today he lives in downtown Chicago and works for Northwestern Mutual. His busy life does not keep him off the tennis courts, for he continues to play once a week or so at a local country club.

1998—Cesar Vargas
Edina

They could have played the Mexican national anthem following the conclusion of the Class AA singles tournament in 1998, for a lad from south of the border, now wearing a green and white Edina uniform, fought through the draw to claim the one and only AA title won by a non-Minnesotan since True Team competition began in '73. (Willie Hernandez of the Philippines won a title in '57 when there was only one class and Sweden's Jakob Victorin won a Class A title in '81.)

Seeking to learn English, play tennis, and gain experience in order to obtain a tennis scholarship, Vargas applied for an exchange program that only took students

Cesar Vargas & host parents
Barbara & Mark Carlson

from Mexico and placed them in Minnesota. So in an incredible bit of serendipity, Vargas ended up in the tennis hotbed of Edina, much to the dismay of other potential suitors. Of course some tennis coaches wondered if he was recruited, but Vargas maintains that this was not the case at all, claiming, "I just happened to take advantage of an opportunity I had."

A relatively late-blooming star, Vargas was first introduced to tennis by his father; but initially he was not fond of the game, preferring the more popular international sport of soccer. And though he never had a coach in Mexico, eventually at about age 10 he took an interest in tennis and by age 14 was playing some national tournaments. When asked about his ranking, he said, "Right before I moved to Minnesota I was No. 9 in the national 17-and-under division."

So he left Mexico, calling the opportunity to attend school in Minnesota and play tennis "an incredible experience." He added, "It was an amazing year and my host family (Mark and Barbara Carlson) was wonderful." He said of them, "Nothing would have been possible without the effort they put in." He also benefitted from participation in the STP junior program, often hitting with pros Paul Muesing and Greg Wicklund. Wicklund called his star pupil "a real smooth player with a big first serve and exceptional backhand. He was a great baseliner, a relaxed player." More importantly, Wicklund said, "He was a fun, happy-go-lucky guy."

Thus it was *hola* to Senor Vargas, a most hearty welcome to this young man who not only won the singles title but helped the Edina Hornets win yet another team title. Edina's *buena suerte* (good luck) was *muy mal* (very bad) for the other AA teams in the tournament and also for singles players such as 1997 champion Ryan Edlefsen. To get to the finals Vargas won two easy matches and one barnburner before reaching the finals. In the first two rounds he upended seniors Andy Musser of Mankato West and Nils Ahlgrimm of Cambridge-Isanti. Waiting for him in the semis was the up-and-coming eighth-grade prodigy from Winona, Brian Lipinski. Vargas would need all of his senior guile to overcome Lipinski, for the lad from Winona went the distance with him. Final score: Vargas 6-4, 3-6, 6-3. And in the finals he

had to play the match of his life to upset the previously undefeated Edlefsen.

After losing in the section finals to Edlefsen, Vargas learned his lesson. With a strategy of pinning his tall and rangy opponent back on the baseline, Vargas negated Edlefsen's big serve-and-volley game. An article by Jim Paulsen in the June 6, 1998, *Star Tribune* spoke of Vargas's new tactic: "Coming to the net less than he had planned, Vargas kept his opponent pinned at the baseline with deep groundstrokes and an extremely effective topspin lob. He also countered Edlefsen's vaunted first serve with strong backhand returns."

So after squeaking out the first set in a tie-breaker, Vargas held on for a 6-4 second set win. His victory was, of course, a huge disappointment for Edlefsen, but he was gracious in defeat and credited Vargas for keeping "me back with some deep balls so I wasn't able to get in and volley like I usually do." Edlefsen also said, "This wasn't my best day. I played a lot better in the section finals. But he played well today. You have to give him a lot of credit" (June 6, 1998).

Often when a player can tough out the first set, he gains momentum and confidence, and such was the case for Vargas. Jim Paulsen noted that "the pivotal stretch for Vargas came midway through the first set. With the score tied 2-2 and both players having held serve, Vargas rallied to win three games in a row after trailing by two points in each game. Suddenly Edlefsen found himself on the verge of losing a set for the first time all season" (*Star Tribune*, June 6, 1998).

Paulsen continued, "The defending champion fought back to tie the set at 5-5, then 6-6, but Vargas took advantage of numerous unforced errors to win the tiebreaker 7-3." Once he took the first set, Vargas relaxed and played confidently; and Edlefsen "appeared to lose his focus early in the second set." This lapse allowed Vargas to storm out to a 4-1 lead and eventually a 6-4 second-set win. Perhaps Edlefsen was stunned because he was not used to playing from behind, but make no mistake, Vargas was a deserving *campeon* (champion) who saved his "best for last." Coach Cary Aasen said of his star player's performance, "That was the best I've seen him play for an entire match. He had stretches like that against Ross Greenstein [1997 Class A champion from Blake but now of Hopkins] in the sections, but not for the entire match like today" (June 6, 1998).

Aasen also said, in the same article by Paulsen, "We talked about him [Vargas] countering Edlefsen's serve-and-volley, and he did. Cesar didn't attack as much as he could have, but he didn't need to." As a result, even though things didn't always go his way, Vargas held on for a well-deserved 7-5, 6-4 win. Aasen praised him for keeping his head in the match "even with all the foot faults and close calls that went against him. He kept his poise and didn't flinch" (June 6, 1998).

What a thrill it was for this young man from Mexico. "One year ago, Cesar Vargas was playing tennis in his hometown of Mazatlan, Mexico, a long way from the hard courts of Minneapolis' western suburbs," said Paulsen in a June 4, 1998, *Star Tribune* article. Having played mostly for individual honors in Mexico, Vargas was ecstatic after leading his Hornets to the team title. "This is incredible," he said. "I've never been a part of a team in tennis before. Back home, we only play as individuals in tournaments and things. This is different and a lot of fun" (June 4, 1998).

Regarding his singular individual accomplishment, Vargas said, "I never thought this would happen when I got here last summer. This is awesome. I had no idea I could do this well" (*Star Tribune*, June 6, 1998). While he surprised himself, his coach was less taken aback by his accomplishments. "He's really played well the past three weeks," Aasen said. "He's got great hands, moves the ball around and is playing with a lot of confidence" (*Star Tribune*, June 4, 1998).

Not knowing about the ins and outs of obtaining a college tennis scholarship, and realizing that most schools had already filled their rosters, Vargas finally secured a scholarship to play at the U of TX-Pan American after graduating from Edina. Though he achieved his goal of going "somewhere I could play," he was not happy there and left after two years, spending a year back home in Mexico before enrolling at the U of NE. Unlike his experience in Texas, he had a happy two years at Nebraska, playing No. 2 singles his senior year until he got hurt and then playing mostly No. 5. Needing a fifth year to complete degrees in international business and marketing, Vargas stayed on at Nebraska and also served as a volunteer assistant coach.

Vargas now works at a private tennis club in Raleigh, NC. Life in the U.S. has been good to him, but I imagine he isn't afraid to fly the Mexican flag in front of his home on occasion.

1999–Eric Butorac
Rochester John Marshall

If you've ever had to compete with your best friend for a job, for the last spot on a sports team, or maybe for the affection of the same woman, you have some idea what must have been going through the minds of Rochester John Marshall's Eric Butorac and St. Cloud Tech's Kevin Whipple just before they stepped on the court to compete against each other in the 1999 Class AA singles final. Good friends since their early days of combat in summer junior tournaments, they had played each other many times over the years, but never had their friendship been tested with so much at stake. So on this day both had to set aside their friendship, and the result was a somewhat surprising 6-1, 6-2 victory for Butorac.

Eric Butorac

Butorac's win was surprising for two reasons. First, some tennis observers thought that ninth grader D. J. Geatz of Minneapolis Southwest would win the title. In the team competition the day before he had defeated top players Whipple and Wayzata's David Hippee, and Hippee told *Star Tribune* writer Jim Paulsen that he liked Geatz's chances. "He's a great player," Hippee said. "I think he's going to win it all" (June 3, 1999).

But predictions don't always come true, and Butorac didn't have to worry about Geatz, who was upset in the first round by Wayzata's No. 2 singles player, junior Trey Graft. Secondly, though they had not played during the regular season, Whipple seemed to "have Butorac's number" in their recent encounters. "I haven't beaten him in about two years," Butorac told Paulsen in a June 5, 1999, *Star Tribune* article. "It's been at least five times." Nevertheless, both were pointing toward their date in the finals, Whipple driving down to Rochester before the tournament to play "a couple of three-out-of-five-set matches," said Butorac. In addition, Butorac drove to St. Cloud on a weekend two weeks before the tournament to practice with Whipple. The two mates then warmed up together the morning before their semifinal matches; and after their hitting session Butorac told Whipple, "Here's our chance."

Considering themselves outsiders, they relished the opportunity to bump off the big city boys. And, as he recalled their youthful dreaming, in the June 5 article by Paulsen, Butorac said, "We must have talked about it [meeting in the state finals] 100 times." Even in summer tournaments, according to Butorac, "we'd look at the draw to see if we played each other" (*Star Tribune*, June 5, 1999). Both made sure their dream would come true by winning their semifinal matches, Whipple ending the Cinderella run of Graft 6-2, 6-3 and Butorac disposing of Edina sophomore Justin Gaard 6-4, 6-2 after surviving a first-round scare from Fridley senior Steve Solberg (4-6, 6-2, 6-2) and winning a routine quarterfinal match over senior Mike Marshall of Duluth East (6-0, 6-1).

Their dream had indeed come true and though Butorac said it made things awkward, once they began the match the awkwardness ended and he played nearly a perfect match. The above article in the *Star Tribune* noted Butorac's dominance in these words, "The rangy lefthander was in control from the outset, keeping the usually ultra-conservative Whipple guessing with an array of blistering serves, well-placed approach shots and soft volleys." Butorac, a senior who completed a magical undefeated season with this win, said of the match, "He likes to go back and forth across the baseline, so I wanted to keep him from getting into a rhythm, get him moving front to back." In addition, Butorac observed, "Everything was working, and with me, I play better when I'm in the lead. And that was probably the best I've ever played" (June 5, 1999). Retired Hall of Fame coach Jerry Sales of St. Cloud Tech, of course cheering for Whipple, agreed with Butorac, "I have never seen a more flawlessly-played match in high school championship play."

For Whipple, also a senior who was making yet another appearance at State after winning the Section 8 singles title (which he had won five straight times), this was only his second loss of the year. Sitting quietly by himself after the match, Whipple said, "He was clearly better. We've always played close before, but today he never gave me a chance." Though disappointed in the loss, Whipple could take pride in his second-place finish and in two previous third-place wins against some excellent Minnesota players. Moreover, he was not jealous of his good friend's accomplishment: "I'm glad he won. I'd rather lose to him than anyone else" (*Star Tribune*, June 5, 1999).

For Butorac the dream was reality and he became, surprisingly given the talent that has come out of this southeast Minnesota tennis hotbed, the first singles champion from Rochester since Mark Brandenburg in 1974.

After each spent a year playing Division 1 tennis following high school graduation (Butorac at Ball State and Whipple at New Mexico State), the two friends continued their tennis relationship by enrolling at Gustavus. Both played No. 1 or 2 on teams that finished fourth once and third twice in the national Division 3 tournament (with Butorac more often occupying that coveted No. 1 spot) and both earned all-American Division 3 honors. Butorac ended his career in 2003 with three national ITA doubles championships (with Whipple as his partner), one singles finalist place in 2001, and a clean sweep in 2003 of the national NCAA Division 3 singles and doubles championships. Whipple also reached the singles final to once again face his high school friend. Only this time Whipple defaulted, wanting to conserve his energy for the doubles final, thus giving Butorac his bittersweet singles championship. Butorac and Whipple also won two No. 1 MIAC doubles championships and Butorac took home two conference singles titles: one at No. 1 and one at No. 2.

Butorac's coach, Steve Wilkinson, called him "the best doubles player in Gustavus history." Wilkinson also said Butorac was "very receptive to coaching and appreciative of what he he learned while at Gustavus." It should be noted that one year Butorac also won the highly prized Arthur Ashe award for sportsmanship given to an MIAC tennis player as well.

Though he didn't start swatting tennis balls in his crib, it wasn't long before Butorac had a tennis racket in his hand, thanks to his tennis pro father. Tim Butorac, a high school standout at Robbinsdale Cooper High School and like his son a collegiate all-American at Gustavus, is a tennis pro at Rochester and he often brought Eric with him when he went off to work. Eric recalls that his dad got him started in tennis when he was five years old, commenting that "it was a good way to bond with my father. My favorite thing as a kid was to go to the Club and hang out, playing tennis and ping pong."

Even though he later worked with other teaching pros in Rochester, he credits his dad for giving him a passion for the game. And while his dad was the one who got him started, Eric liked it that "he [his dad] let me take an interest for myself—he never pushed me to come out and play." Eric continued, "We had something in common and both of us had a passion for tennis."

So his dad laid the foundation, but Eric had to build the structure, and build it he did, eventually securing a No. 1 singles ranking in his last year of the 16s and finally holding up the singles championship medal he won at State in 1999. After some early success in summer NWTA play (one year he was ranked No. 3 in the 10-and-unders), it took him awhile to reach that No. 1 spot in the 16s. For example, in the 12s one year he was No. 2—but just in the Challenger Level singles division—and No. 4 in the Open Doubles division, No. 10 in Open Singles in the 14s, the year Whipple was No. 1, and No. 12 his first year in the 16s. The year he was ranked No. 1 in singles ('97) he also won the Sectional championship, finished No. 1 in doubles, and had a No. 193 national ranking. In the 18s Butorac climbed up to a low-100s national ranking.

Meanwhile, back at John Marshall High School he had moved into the varsity lineup as a seventh grader, playing No. 1 doubles. As an eighth grader he jumped up to No. 1 singles, a spot he occupied for an almost-unprecedented five years. Then, for four straight years he graced the 98th Street courts at tournament time, losing in a first-round doubles match as a ninth grader to the eventual champions, Chuck Schultz and Jeff Hahn of Eden Prairie. Playing singles as a sophomore, he again lost in the first round, this time to that year's champion, Ryan Edlefsen of Bloomington Jefferson. As a junior he won a round before getting dumped by his buddy Whipple in the quarters.

Finally, his big breakthrough came in his last crack at a singles title, and his good fortune has continued on apace. After his extraordinarily successful career at Gustavus, he decided to pursue the vagabond life of a tennis pro. About his pro career he said, "It was a dream growing up and it just fell into my lap. I kept overachieving and it got better." Get better it did, particularly in doubles for Butorac and his partners, Chris Drake (son of Bill Drake, a standout Gophers player from the 1970s) and Jamie Murray of Scotland (brother of World top-tenner Andy Murray). He's played doubles at Wimbledon with both partners and as of July 2007 he and Murray are the thirteenth-ranked doubles team in the world. They have won two ATP titles and lost in the finals of a Los Angeles ATP event to the Bryan brothers.

A January 4, 2006, article in the *Star Tribune* by Michael Rand gave some insights into the often bizarre and difficult life players like Butorac have to endure in the minor leagues of pro tennis. "He [Butorac] has been asked by a doubles partner to smuggle him across an international border in the trunk of his car (and politely declined); he has flown across the ocean to sleep on the floor and lose in the first round; and about 100 times he has eaten spaghetti with ketchup to load carbs and save money, sometimes combining the ketchup with mayonnaise to make a sauce that he says tastes 'surprisingly good.'"

Through all of these adventures and successes, however, the lefthander with the big serve- and-volley game has remained grounded in solid Midwestern values. He comes home on occasion to watch local high school tennis matches and to keep in contact with friends like Whipple (who has also stayed in tennis, but as a teaching pro at the Flagship Club—now Lifetime Fitness). He also gives credit to his two most important mentors—his dad and Steve Wilkinson, and even finds time to play some father-son doubles tournaments. He and his dad have bonded well enough on court to win two national grasscourt father/son titles (in 2003 and '05), and in '04 they were also honored with the first USTA/Northern Section Hall of Fame Achievement Award.

Looking back on his high school career, Butorac recalls what it was like to negotiate the difficult transition to varsity tennis at an early age and he credits "the senior guys on my team for taking me under their wing when I was a seventh grader." He counts the friendships he made with teammates and the opportunity to influence younger players when he was a senior (thus giving back what others once gave him) as two of his fondest memories of high school tennis.

2000s

The new millennium brought with it a host of terrors, imagined or real: the Y2K bug, global warming, weapons of mass destruction, and, worst of all, 9/11. September 11, 2001, our modern "date with infamy," showed us how vulnerable we are in this age of the global village. Following 9/11, the U.S. drove the Taliban out of Afghanistan and invaded Iraq, eventually capturing Saddam Hussein. These conflicts also gave us new names and words to learn as the airwaves and newspapers intoned stories about Osama Bin Laden, Al Qaeda, Islamic fundamentalism, jihad, the Taliban, Shiites, and Sunnis. And we lost another space ship, this one the Columbia.

Here in the U.S. George W. Bush was declared president in 2000, after the "hanging chads" controversy in Florida was resolved by the Supreme Court. In the "no child left behind" era of accountability, voices also clamored for choices in education such as vouchers and charter schools.

And we entered a new age of technology in which people began to publish their own private newsletters ("blogs") on-line, TiVo shows on television, carry ipods around, listen to radio shows streamed on-line, look up information on Google or on-line encyclopedias (such as Wikipedia), and download music on YouTube. In addition, hybrid cars, the Segway scooter, wind power, living green, buying locally—these sustainability and environmentally friendly words have all become a part of our early 21st century lexicon.

On the men's tennis front the great American champions Sampras and Agassi retired (with a record fourteen Grand Slam singles titles for Sampras and eight for Agassi) and a new king emerged, the Swiss assassin, Roger Federer. Others will challenge him (the American Andy Roddick, the Russian Marat Safin, the Aussie Lleyton Hewitt, and the dynamic Spaniard Rafael Nadal, for example), but none can knock him off his No. 1 perch. On the women's side the Williams sisters dominated early in the decade, but they were challenged by the Belgians Justine Henin and Kim Clijsters, the young Russian Maria Sharapova, and Frenchwoman Amelie Mauresmo.

2000-01—Justin Gaard
Edina

Here in Minnesota the decade began with the Justin Gaard years, so for his story see Chapter Four.

2002—D. J. Geatz
Minneapolis South

Since he first entered the race for a singles title as a seventh grader in 1997, a young stallion who nearly won the prize in his first sprint, D. J. Geatz had not managed to win, place, or show. To be sure, he sometimes lost to talented players (Ryan Edlefsen in that '97 final and two-time champion Justin Gaard of Edina in the 2001 quarters, for example), but in '99 he didn't even place (losing to Wayzata's Trey Graft in the first round), and in 2000 he was ineligible and so did not even "show" up in the tournament. For someone so gifted, one must wonder why it took him until his senior year to cross the finish line first.

When the game comes easily to a player, sometimes it's difficult to focus, so that's probably one reason why he didn't always do well at State. In addition, he expressed frustration with the MSHSL policy of not seeding players: "It makes no sense that they don't seed the teams or players," he noted in a June 4, 2002, article by Jim Paulsen in the *Star Tribune*. As a result, he sometimes became rattled when he had to play a tough player such as Gaard early in the draw. On another occasion (in 1998) a difficult section draw kept him from making it to State, for Cesar Vargas and Ryan Edlefsen stood in his way. And his mother, Pam, offered the view that he was often just too hard on himself, remarking, "He's been such an intense competitor since he was a baby." For D. J. there have always been the high expectations others had for him as well. "Ever since I made the finals in seventh grade, people have been surprised when I didn't win. It's been a lot of pressure," he remarked. "It's bugged me that I haven't won the state championship," he admitted. "It's about the only tournament I haven't won" (June 4, 2002).

But this year he had the focus and the will he may have lacked in the past, a focus that came in part because of the untimely death of one of his best friends, Blake Rogers of Edina. According to *Star Tribune* writer Paulsen, "Geatz's world was rocked late on Feb. 26 when he heard Rogers had been shot and killed in his own bedroom by an acquaintance." Though Rogers was not a tennis player, he loved the way D. J. played the game. So, the day before the funeral, his friend's mother came up to D. J. and noted, "how much he [Blake] was looking forward to seeing me finally win state." Said Geatz, "That's when I decided this season was for him... I really want to win it for Blake" (June 4, 2002).

His friend's death seemed to be a catalyst for D. J. His Minneapolis South coach, George Beske, took notice of his newfound maturity: "D. J. has always practiced hard. I've never coached a more talented player. The difference this year has been his focus. I see utter concentration on his face" (*Star Tribune*, June 4, 2002). So after racing through the regular season without a loss—and dropping only one

D. J. Geatz

set, to Blake's Chi Pham at the Edina Invitational—Geatz came in to the tournament as the overwhelming favorite.

But wait, there was yet another impediment in his path, this time an injury he sustained practicing in the rain the Monday before the tournament began. He slipped and sprained a ligament in his right knee, keeping him out of the team lineup for South's first-round team match with Mounds View on Tuesday. Understandably upset, Geatz said, in another article by Paulsen, "I iced it all night, hoping it was just bruised, but it was really painful this morning. I wanted to play but the trainer said no... I just can't believe this happened. It doesn't seem fair" (*Star Tribune*, June 5, 2002). His inability to compete in the team tournament cost the South Tigers a chance to win a second consecutive title, but it brought him some much-needed time to recover for the individual competition to be held on Thursday and Friday.

Though at times hobbling around the court, he easily won his first two matches on Thursday (over Irondale senior Alex Vu in the first round and Henry Sibley senior Clay Sollenberger); but on Friday things got tougher. Future high school champion, junior Nick Edlefsen of Eden Prairie, extended Geatz to three sets in the semis, but D. J. survived 5-7, 6-1, 6-4. Then he faced his future U of M teammate Brian Lipinski of Winona in the finals. Once again Geatz lost the first set (7-5), but in the last two sets, seemingly oblivious to the discomfort in his knee, he dominated Lipinski 6-1, 6-1. This hard-earned triumph gave him the title he had for so long sought and, according to an article by Paulsen titled "Elusive Title Is His, Geatz Wins Singles; Fulfills Expectations," the win "also silenced those who questioned his resolve" (*Star Tribune*, June 8, 2002). Expressing relief, Geatz said, "Man, this feels great. This is the biggest load off my back. I wanted to win this one for so long." As he iced his knee after the match, he also said, "My knee was really stiff, but I had to give it a try. I didn't feel it that much once the match [with Lipinski] started" (June 8, 2002).

This loss was another disappointment for Lipinski, a high school star for five years who, because he lived in Winona and often played competitively in southeast Minnesota, was not as well known as some of the top state players. Lipinski had appeared in five state singles tournaments and Geatz in four, Geatz finishing second as a seventh grader and Lipinski finishing third as a sophomore and runner-up in 2001 as a junior. For Geatz this singles championship validated his sometimes luckless and often disappointing career, for the injured warrior fought through his pain to a well-deserved victory.

While Lipinski was cutting his tennis teeth by playing mostly in southeast Minnesota in the summers and in fewer tournaments, Geatz for the most part eschewed local junior competition in favor of national tournament play. However, he did play in USTA/Northern Sectional singles tournaments for six straight years, winning all six, probably a state record. His first was in the 10-and-unders, then he won two in the 12s, two in the 14s, and one in the 16s. During these years of playing in the Section, he lost only two matches, one to Justin Gaard and the other to Nick Edlefsen. In addition, he and Mike Solum won two Sectional doubles championships, he and his father, U of M coach Dave, won the Father and Son Sectional title another year, and he was ranked No. 3 in Men's Singles in 2001, though still just a high school student.

And while Geatz played few NWTA tournaments, he was distinguishing himself on the national scene. In 1995, not quite 11 years old, he earned a ranking of No. 161 in boys 14s; and the next year he moved up to No. 134 in the 14s. Then, in his last year in the 14s, he was once ranked No. 9 and finished with his highest year-end ranking, No. 17. In the 16s he earned national rankings of Nos. 103, 77, and 28. Geatz concluded his extraordinarily successful junior career ranked No. 97 in the 18s.

Jim Paulsen, in that June 4, 2002, article, noted that in some respects Geatz seemed a most unlikely candidate to be a successful tennis player: "At first glance, Geatz doesn't look like your typical tennis star. Tall and narrow-shouldered, he walks with a bounce on the balls of his feet. A two-inch-long pillow of curly reddish-brown hair makes him appear almost gangly." But once he stepped on the court he used his "powerful right arm, an instrument that can rip forehand winners from anywhere on the court" (*Star Tribune*, June 4, 2002) to demolish his opponents. In addition, he had a strong return of serve and his game has been honed by long hours on the court. Paulsen also said of Geatz that he was " a 'backboard' when waiting for an opponent to make a mistake," but now "he has become stronger and added that to his accuracy, honed by hitting thousands of groundstrokes" (June 4, 2002).

And though there have been (and will be more) high school players who participate for more than one team in their careers—thanks to a policy of open enrollment in Minnesota—it's not likely anyone will challenge the nomadic Geatz for changing schools and helping those schools succeed at the state tennis level. For example, in 1997 as a seventh grader at Minneapolis Southwest he finished second in the singles tournament, then transferred as an eighth grader to Edina and helped the Hornets win yet another team title in '98. Back to Southwest for his ninth-grade year in '99 he led the Indians to a runner-up finish in the team tournament; but the next year, still at Southwest, he was ineligible to play tennis. He then finished his stellar high school career at Minneapolis South, as a junior leading the Tigers to their first and only team tennis title in 2001 and advancing to the quarterfinals in singles competition where he lost to champion Justin Gaard. And of course his senior year he led South back to the tournament and won the singles title.

Now he has taken his game to the Division 1 level, playing for his home state team and his father at the U of M after a short stint at the U of NE. At Nebraska he played just one year, but it was a good one; for he held down the No. 1 singles spot in the lineup, won the most matches for a freshman in school history, and earned a runner-up award for Regional Player of the Year. At Minnesota, playing mostly No. 1 singles, he distinguished himself in 2006 by earning All-Big Ten honors and entry into the NCAA Division 1 national tournament.

He says his best memories from high school were individual victories as a member of his teams, one in particular being the deciding match he won against Phil Woo from Bloomington Jefferson to give Edina a 4-3 win and the section title in 1998. However, he said a later experience was even more memorable: "My best moment was beating Justin Gaard and our team [Minneapolis South] beating Edina in the State Tournament." He also spoke highly of his coaches (John Pratt of Southwest, Gary Aasen of Edina, and George Beske of South), calling them "great guys and great coaches." Further, he said of them, "Each of them had distinct qualities that made them good coaches."

Coach Beske lavished praise on D. J. for playing injured and still winning his 2002 title even after losing the first sets in his semifinal and final matches: "This guy knew how to dig down deep." Beske also defended D. J. after the local press came down on him following a controversial loss to Justin Gaard (his only loss in two years at South) in the 2001 singles tournament. "It was especially gratifying to see an injured Geatz win [in 2002] after enduring uncalled for bad press during the '01 season... Even if D. J. was not perfect, there is no reason for sports writers to criticize high school athletes publicly."

An incredibly talented and competitive performer with outstanding groundstrokes, Geatz was a colorful personality who will be remembered as one of the best players in state high school history. Two-time champion Gaard of Edina called him "a great competitor who had an aura about him since he was 10. You had to play really well to beat him; he rarely lost matches here [in Minnesota]. I only beat him four or five times out of about twenty."

2003—Nick Edlefsen
Eden Prairie

Though he had not advanced past the semifinals in his two previous state tournament appearances, Eden Prairie's Nick Edlefsen nonetheless approached the 2003 Class AA singles tourney with the confidence of a lion chasing a crippled baby zebra. No false bravado here; Edlefsen came into the tournament with a 29-0 record having not lost a set. In addition, he was the top-ranked 18-and-under singles player during summer 2002 NWTA play, winning the Sectional title over his soon-to-be state finalist opponent Charlie Seltzer of Edina 6-2, 7-5. He also came from a family with an excellent pedigree (older brother Ryan won the '97 AA singles championship).

A supremely gifted player possessing a monster serve as his weapon of choice, there were nevertheless reasons

for others to doubt his confidence. As *Star Tribune* writer Jim Paulsen reported in a June 3, 2003, article, "For four years the Eden Prairie senior has been something of an enigma on the boys' high school tennis scene. Always among the most talented players in the state, Edlefsen's worst enemy often has been himself." Not disputing Paulsen's assessment, Edlefsen said, in a matter-of-fact tone, "I was better than most of the other players, but I would take it too seriously and make mistakes" (June 3, 2003). One might argue, however, that in the past two years his opponents had something to do with his semifinal lapses, for in 2001 he lost to runner-up Brian Lipinski of Winona and in 2002 to eventual champion D. J. Geatz of Minneapolis South.

But this was a new year and both Geatz and Lipinski were gone, so Edlefsen believed it was his time. Therefore, in a statement that created the biggest buzz during the week before the tournament, Edlefsen said, "I'll win it. I've been getting my game ready to play satellite tournaments in northern California during the summer. I'm really confident that I'm more than ready for the State Tournament" (June 3, 2003).

Edlefsen's coach, Rich Strohkirch, agreed with his star player's bold prediction because "he's become quite a mature young man. Now, if it gets serious, he'll play long and deliberate points, setting up the win, instead of just going out and practicing to hit winners" (June 3, 2003). The only concern Strohkirch had was that Edlefsen hadn't faced enough tough competition during the year; so he enlisted the help of volunteer assistant coach Tim Smith, a former St. Olaf College player. According to a June 7, 2003, article by Paulsen, Smith made him work in practice but deflected any praise by saying, "Nick deserves all the credit because he did what it took. I was just around to help him work up a sweat" (*Star Tribune*).

Backing up his bold talk with a "big serve and blistering groundstrokes" (June 7, 2003), the six-foot-two-inch Edlefsen roared through the first three rounds without dropping a set and with the loss of just six games. First off he dispatched Cretin-Derham Hall junior Aaron Zenner; and in the quarters he took out Mounds View junior Brody McCoy; then he clobbered Apple Valley Eastview's ninth grader Derek Peterson 6-1, 6-0 in the semis. These wins set up the rematch with Seltzer, a player whom he had met several times, including in the third-place match last year, a match Edlefsen had won 6-2, 6-4.

According to Paulsen, "Seltzer started strong, winning two of the first three games. But Edlefsen found his groove in the fourth game and seized control of the match," wearing down "the tenacious Seltzer." So, in Paulsen's words, "what at first appeared to be cockiness now looks like nothing more than self-confidence." Wanting to prove he wasn't just blowing smoke, Edlefsen said about the match with Seltzer, "I didn't feel really nervous at all—just a little before this match because I know Charlie is a good player—because I knew that I would win if I played like I can." Taking stock of his own play, Edlefsen said, "My serve was amazing today. Seltzer hit some good shots, but I think he made a few more mistakes than I did. I think I played pretty darn good" (*Star Tribune*, June 7, 2003). Like quarterback Joe Namath, who guaranteed a victory for his New York Jets' team in the 1969 Super Bowl, Edlefsen backed up his talk with his racket and his prediction also came true. The result was a decisive 6-3, 6-3 win for Edlefsen. (For more about Seltzer, see Chapter Six.)

Edlefsen finished his illustrious high school career with two third-place medals in singles, this 2003 singles championship, and a medal for his role in helping Eden Prairie earn a second-place team finish in '02. And, in addition to a No. 1 ranking his final year in the 18s, he also held the No. 1 ranking his first year in the 18s. These two years, his best in junior tennis, he won the Sectional title (over Seltzer in 2002 and Lipinski in '01) and he held national rankings of Nos. 152 and 112 as well. While he did not burn up the courts in his first years of junior competition, he did get an early start in tennis, hitting balls when he was 8 or 9. And though he often played three or four times a week, he said, "I didn't take it [tennis] seriously until I was 14 or 15." Of course he played with his older brother, and he named Dave Petersen and Glenn Britzius as the coaches who worked most with him.

After achieving modest success in the 12-and-unders (he was ranked alphabetically for three years in Challenger 1 level play), Edlefsen began to make his mark in the 14s, ranking No. 7 his first year and No. 4 the second year. In the 16s he was once ranked No. 2 (behind Seltzer), and finally he perched at the top of the ladder both years he played in the 18s.

His high school tennis career (like that of Geatz's) was something of a nomadic one, for he started out on his brother's team, Bloomington Jefferson, as a seventh grader. That year he played No. 4 singles, but his parents moved and so he played No. 1 singles as an eighth grader at Chaska the next year. Finally, he switched to Eden Prairie to complete his career. Although he played No. 1 singles for for five years, it must have been difficult for him to live up to the expectations set by his older brother; and even though he (Ryan) still gave him a hard time, Nick didn't waver. According to that June 3, 2003, *Star Tribune* article by Paulsen, "He [Ryan] told me I'd better win it," said Nick. He professed not to be worried, saying, in all seriousness, "The only way I can see me losing is if I don't wake up in time" (June 3, 2003). You see, he had literally almost missed his Section 2 finals match when he overslept and missed the bus. Here's how he described this almost disastrous experience to me: "We had a banquet the night before and I woke up late—at 7:15. Coach Strohkirch called me and told me I had to drive down to St. Peter, so I jumped out of bed, threw my clothes on, and got there just a bit late for my match."

This time he had no problem getting to the courts on time, and despite the huge expectations put on him, he earned the top prize, becoming with his sibling Ryan just the third brother combination to win state singles titles (the others being Mark and David Wheaton and Gregg and Roger Anderson in Class A).

Edlefsen's outstanding play in high school and on the junior circuit won him a tennis scholarship to the U of Santa Barbara in California, but he spent just one year there. Leaving because "my teammates didn't care about tennis as much as I did" and because "it wasn't a serious tennis program," Edlefsen decided to transfer after just one year in sunny California. So he obtained a release from Santa Barbara, enabling him to play right away at the U of M. In 2005 he played anywhere from Nos. 2-4 singles, and in 2006 he played mostly No. 3 singles. Both years he played a variety of doubles spots. He also shared the Most Improved Player Award in 2005 with Brian Lipinski. In the summer of 2006 he played some futures satellite tournaments to see how he matched up with other young pro hopefuls, and he completed his tennis career at the U in 2007.

Singles Champions
Class A

In 1979, with the required 10 percent or more of small schools now fielding teams (fifty-one), Minnesota tennis entered the era of multiple-class competition that began with two-class boys' basketball in 1971. Now more teams and individuals had a chance to compete for state laurels; now small schools had a chance to compete on a level playing field; and now there would be two team, singles, and doubles champions instead of just one. Critics of multiple-class tournaments are quick to dismiss small-school competition as second-rate and inferior to the play in the large-school class. And while it is for the most part true that the strongest teams and best players come from the Class AA teams which simply have strength in numbers, one cannot overlook the "Hoosiers Factor." Just as that small town of Milan, Indiana, felled the big elms and won a state basketball title in 1954, so have some teams and youngsters felled the tennis giant redwoods in Minnesota tennis.

For example, since 1973, when True Team play was inaugurated, both Blue Earth in '77 and Blake in '84 and '91 have won titles against the big schools. And since the beginning of individual competition in 1929, there have been a number of singles players and doubles teams from small schools who have gone toe to toe with their big-school rivals and snatched titles from them. For example, small-school doubles champions have included Dave Anderson and Gerald Kintzi of St. James in 1954, John Wirtanen and Jim Miller of Greenway of Coleraine in '61, Doug Luebbe and Tom VanDeinse of Winona Cotter in '77, Greg and Jeff Carlson of Madison in '78, and Myles and Roger Anderson of Blue Earth in '85.

In singles some of these giant-slayers have been Paul Wilcox of Mountain Lake in 1934, Henry Nosek of Proctor in '38, Jason Hall of Minnehaha Academy in '86, and Chris Laitala of Blake in '88. But the focus in this chapter is on singles winners from Class A, victors who hoisted the trophy after beating their peers from small schools, so here's a look at these champions from the years of Class A competition (1979-82 and 1987-2003).

1979–Louie McKee
Blake

The honor of claiming the first Class A singles title went to Blake's Louie McKee, a gifted player who could very well have competed for the AA crown if he had been in that draw this year (1979). In 1978 he had been ranked No. 5 by the coaches, one spot ahead of the eventual AA champion, Brian Johnson of Edina, and behind big-school players like Kevin Smith of Hopkins Lindbergh ('77 champion), Brace Helgeson of St. Cloud Tech, and Andy Ringlien of Northfield. Moreover, he had been one of the top-ranked juniors for years, ranking No. 1 his second year in boys 14s and No. 1 in doubles twice, with Brian Lew in the 14s and with Brace Helgeson in the 18s. A strapping young man with a big game, McKee held down the No. 1 singles spot at Blake for two years. A two-time singles participant in the State Tournament, as a junior in '78 McKee lost to

Louie McKee

champion Brian Johnson of Edina East in the first round of the singles competition.

Entering the 1979 tournament as the top-ranked singles player in Class A, he rolled through the draw without losing a set in his four matches, all against senior opponents. His first victim was Jeff Carlson of Madison, then came Tim Staley of Rochester Lourdes, who took the most

games from McKee but nonetheless fell 6-3, 6-4. In the semis McKee defeated Dave Baukol of Mahtomedi, and for the fourth time this year he had to play his No. 2 singles teammate Tom Ferris. This time the stakes were higher, however, for the winner would be a state champion.

Though McKee had beaten Ferris in the conference, subregion, and region finals, he respected his teammate's strong baseline game. An article in the June 2, 1979, *Minneapolis Tribune* titled "Edina East, Blake Tennis Players Win," noted that the two obviously had a good deal of knowledge about each other's play but that McKee executed his game plan better. Said McKee of his 6-1, 6-2 win, "When he's (Ferris) playing well, his strokes from the baseline are great. He can play better than he did today." McKee, with powerful serves and aggressive net play, dominated the match. About his strategy, McKee was quoted as saying, "I knew I had to serve well and get to the net." Although McKee hoped he and Ferris would meet in the finals, saying "We're good buddies and we said it'd be nice to play each other in the finals" (June 2, 1979), this was of course a bittersweet victory.

Earlier in the tournament McKee and Ferris led Blake to its first state team title, and both went on to play college tennis, Ferris at Carleton and McKee at the U of M, where he helped the Gophers win the 1981 Big Ten title.

Current Blake coach Ted Warner said of McKee, "He was a very talented player who had a flamboyant game. He was a big hitter who was also very athletic."

1980–Gregg Anderson
Blue Earth

In this second year of Class A play, another player who more than held his own against AA competitors, Gregg Anderson of Blue Earth, took the title. A senior who finished the season with a 46-0 record, Anderson won his first three matches in straight sets before giving up a set for the first time all year in the final against senior Raoul Madrid of Marshall-University High. The No. 1-ranked Class A player all year, Anderson opened the tournament with a win over pre-season No. 2 player Greg Weitzel of St. Cloud Cathedral—a senior, then dispatched LeSueur junior Jack Elvestrom in the quarters. In the semis he

Gregg Anderson

bumped senior Andy Odegaard of Roseau and Anderson earned his title with a hard-fought 6-2, 6-7, 6-0 win over Madrid in the finals. *Minneapolis Tribune* writer Roman Augustoviz said of the match, "Anderson won 6-0 in the third set, giving him 91 straight wins (counting doubles matches) over the past two years. He lost his opening match last season" (June 1, 1980). After the match, and after that unexpected loss of a set, Anderson kidded coach Hal Schroeder: "I was just trying to give you some more gray hairs" (June 1, 1980).

So in four extraordinarily successful years at Blue Earth, Gregg helped his team take home two state titles (1977, '80) in addition to winning a doubles title in '79 and a singles championship this year. Coach Schroeder did everything he could to give Anderson and his talented teammates high caliber opponents, arranging tournament competitions all over the state on weekends for example; but more often his players weren't challenged, particularly in conference play. Nevertheless, Gregg kept his focus even during easy matches, commenting that "my senior year I never lost a game in the conference matches (all were 6-0, 6-0) at No. 1 singles."

When asked to reflect on his high school days and to comment about highlights of his tennis career, Anderson mentioned several, some of which involved matches in which he played with his brothers. First, he recalled winning the state championship in 1977 when Blue Earth became the smallest school to win a True Team title and playing with his oldest brother Chris who held the No. 2 doubles spot in the lineup. Second, he mentioned upsetting John Wheaton of Minnetonka 6-1, 6-4, at No. 2 singles, to clinch Blue Earth's 3-2 win over the Skippers in the finals when he was just a ninth grader. Next, Gregg spoke of this, his senior season: "Winning the team title again in 1980 with my brother Myles on the team and winning the Class A singles title were also high points." And he counts a summer tournament victory over '80 Class AA champion Chris Combs of Edina West as a fitting climax to his junior career.

He also recalls humorous moments such as "going to tournaments and having the amount of lunch money decided by your won-loss record that day." Finally, he said the best thing about high school tennis was "the opportunity to compete on a best-shall-play basis."

In addition to his extraordinary success as a high school tennis player, Gregg was a highly ranked junior player from the time he began playing in the 12-and-unders, often competing in doubles with his brother Chris. Their best ranking was No. 5, but Gregg also earned a No. 1 doubles ranking his second year in the 16s with Duke Paluch from South Dakota and a No. 2 ranking with Nick Gustilo of St. Louis Park his last year in the 18s. That final year he also achieved a singles ranking of No. 3, the second time he had done so (the other time was in his second year of 16s). (For more about the life and tennis career of Anderson, see Chapters Six and Ten.)

1981–Jakob Victorin
Morton

"The Swedes are coming! The Swedes are coming!" On the international scene and even in the Unites States Swedes were making themselves known in the tennis world in the late 1970s and into the '80s. At home they were developing a training system that produced future No. 1 singles players Mats Wilander and Stefan Edberg, U.S. college champions such as Mikael Pernfors, and doubles champions such as Edberg and his partner Anders Jarryd, and the team of Wilander and Joakim Nystrom. All of this success would not of course have been possible if a sensational talent named Bjorn Borg had not sprung up from Swedish soil to inspire his countrymen. At 17 he won the French Open (a championship he would win five more times), and at 20 he won the first of five-straight Wimbledon titles. In 1981 he won the last of his French Open titles and lost to John McEnroe in both the Wimbledon and U.S. Open finals.

Here in Minnesota one of Borg's countrymen, a young lad named Jakob Victorin (or Viktorin) became just the second foreign exchange student to win a state high school singles title, knocking off future Class A champion Scott Card of Blake in the finals 6-1, 6-1. Arguably the second best player in Minnesota this year—after Class AA titlist Bob Batemen, his frequent hitting partner—Victorin landed in the most unlikely place, a small town of 600 souls located 90 miles west of Minneapolis, Morton. An article in the June 6, 1981, *Minneapolis Tribune*, titled "Swedish Exchange Youth Is Morton Tennis Hope," described his odyssey: "Viktorin lives in Eskilstuna, Sweden, a city of 100,000, 60 miles west of Stockholm. He knew when he applied to the foreign exchange program that

Jakob Victorin

he would have no control over where in America he would be assigned. So he was curious to find out exactly where this place called Morton, MN, was. 'I found out,' Victorin said, 'in a very big atlas.'" The article continued, "Viktorin was Sweden's 15th-ranked junior tennis player." Said Victorin, "But I'm not going to be a tennis pro anyway... So I could take that chance. I wanted to see America and learn English" (June 6, 1981).

Because he needed stiffer competition to make him tournament tough, Victorin came to Minneapolis to play on weekends, often staying at newfound friend Bob

Bateman's home. Bateman said of this experience, "My sister, Tracy, was off at college so we had an extra room in the house. It was no problem. We probably could have fed him dog food and he wouldn't have complained. He's too nice" (June 6, 1981).

Meanwhile, back in Morton, Jakob had displaced former No. 1 player Nathan Hjulberg (ironically also a Swede, though of the Minnesota variety), but Hjulberg had no complaints. He echoed Bateman's comments about Victorin's pleasant personality and added, "I'm really thankful he came... he amazes me with some of the shots he makes" (*Minneapolis Tribune*, June 6, 1981). Hjulberg no doubt benefitted from hitting with Victorin, for he also advanced to the State Tournament in singles. Adding her praise to the mix, Morton coach Bonnie Scheitell said of her five-foot-eight-inch player, "He hits the ball like a rocket" (June 6, 1981).

Before the State Tournament began, Victorin had modestly exclaimed, in a June 7, 1981, *Minneapolis Tribune* article, "It would be more fun for the people of Morton [than for me]. It seems they are so excited about it. So I would like to win it for them." And win it he did, in grand style. The first day he easily disposed of LeSueur senior Jack Elvestrom and Minnehaha Academy's Chris Lund (a junior). In the semis he defeated Pipestone junior Brad Sorenson before meeting up with Card, a junior, in the finals. "His 6-1, 6-1 victory took less time than it took Bateman and Laddin [Class AA finalists] to play their first set." (June 7, 1981). Perhaps Card was a bit fatigued after his come-from-behind 4-6, 6-4, 6-1 semifinal win over Wadena's sophomore ace Chris Grabrian; however, this should not diminish Victorin's dominance. He won all four of his matches in straight sets and lost only 11 games in the tournament.

With one more year of high school to complete in Sweden, Victorin thought about attending Minnesota's Swedish-heritage college, Gustavus, to play tennis; but he opted instead to return to his native land.

1982–Scott Card
Blake

In a year in which his achievements were overshadowed by the drama of the Class AA final between seventh-grade phenom David Wheaton and Darryl Laddin, senior Scott Card of Blake quietly moved through the 1982 Class A draw without losing a set until he faced teammate Scott Duncan, a junior, in the finals. Ranked No. 1 all season in his class, Card bounced out ninth grader Steve Muller from Rochester Lourdes in the first round. He followed this up with a win over senior Matt Bellis of SPA, then defeated a tough opponent in the semis, junior Chris Grabrian of Wadena, 7-5, 6-1. In the finals against his teammate and summer doubles partner Duncan, Card rallied from a 6-4 first-set loss by employing his plan of serving hard and volleying to claim the final two sets 6-1, 6-2. Ironically, though Card had beaten Duncan every time he had played him during his career, he came into the tournament as the second-place finisher from Region 5 by virtue of his first-ever loss to Duncan in the region finals.

Scott Card

In this last year of Class A competition until it resumed again in 1987, Card had also led his Blake squad to the team title, adding another laurel to his crown.

Though he did not show up in the NWTA junior rankings until his second year in the 16s (at No. 7 in singles), Card began playing the summer circuit when he was 11. A late-bloomer, Card cited the fact that he "often went to our lake home in summers and so I didn't play the full circuit" as a reason why he wasn't ranked until the 16s. His top ranking was No. 4 in singles and No. 3 in doubles (with Duncan), both in the 18s. While his parents played recreationally and he often hit with them, he credits Jerry Noyce for getting him started when he was 10 years old. Jerry, and to a lesser extent two other pros at Interlachen Country Club, Bill Babcock and Ted Taney, laid the foundation for his game in the summers of 1974-75. As a national tournament player Card also had a run to the fourth round of the Fiesta Bowl Tournament during the winter of his junior year, and one can only speculate about "what might have been" if Jakob Victorin had not shown up in Minnesota in 1981. Very likely Card would have added his name to the multiple champions roster.

After graduating from Blake he attended the U of IN for a year but did not play tennis there. Lured back to Minnesota by his first coach, Noyce, Card walked on at the U of M and played "20-some Big-Ten matches in two years on a team that lost in the finals to Michigan one year, 1985." Though he then dropped out of college for a year, he came back and completed his BA in finance and economics, with additional studies in Spanish language, in '87. An outdoorsman whose early years at his parents' lake place whetted his appetite for nature, Card satisfied this appetite by working early in his adult life as a fishing guide in Alaska, as an Orvis salesman in Minneapolis, and as a game fishing lodge manager on the banks of the Rio Orinoco in Venezuela for two years, where his college Spanish studies came in handy. Then he began selling commercial real estate, and since 1992 he has sold residential real estate in the Metro area.

Card still plays tennis once or twice a week and hopes

to get back into tournament competition when his three children are older. And he still indulges his passion for the outdoors, flyfishing on Minnesota and Wisconsin trout streams and offering free guiding trips for various charity contributors.

1987—Erik Nelson

New London-Spicer

Class A competition resumed again in 1987 after a four-year break during which the small schools were thrown back into the fray against big schools. And this year the singles winner came from the first hyphenated, combined school to produce an individual tennis champion, New London-Spicer (population just over 2,000). That winner was Erik Nelson, an all-around athlete who lettered in four sports for the Wildcats: football, basketball, cross country, and tennis. Nelson, New London-Spicer's No. 1 player for four years, had gotten a taste of state tournament competition as a junior, advancing to the one-class tournament in '86 and winning a round before losing to Duluth East foreign exchange student Jose Colmenares in the round of 16.

Erik Nelson

So back in Class A as a senior he battled through the draw against three talented sophomores to win his title. With just an eight-player draw he only needed to win three matches, but all were close. In the opening match he rallied after losing the first set to defeat Blue Earth's Troy Thompson 4-6, 6-1, 6-3. His semifinal match against Chris Essler of Sauk Center was a straight-set win, but it was a close 6-3, 7-5. Then, as *Star Tribune* writer Ralph Thornton said, Nelson "survived a first-set scare from Wade Martin and took a 3-6, 6-0, 6-4 victory from the Breck player for the individual championship" (June 7, 1987).

Had he chosen to focus specifically on tennis, it's likely Nelson could have become one of the top junior players in the state. Given his focus on other sports, it's a credit to his athletic ability that he was able to earn NWTA singles rankings as high as Nos. 10 and 14 in his final two years in the 18-and-under competition. Nelson, who told Thornton that "he took up tennis at the age of four when his father traded some land for a tennis court to be built beside their home in Spicer," nevertheless didn't get serious about the game until later. He also said, "When I started beating the No. 1 singles player in our high school I got interested in the sport" (June 7, 1987). A six-year letter winner, Nelson began as the Wildcats' No. 3 singles player as a seventh grader and took over the No. 1 spot as a freshman. His accomplishment paved the way for some successful teams from New London/Spicer and for another singles champion, Drew Fernelius, who would emerge in 1989.

Nelson's high school coach, Dave Peterman, said of him, "He was one of the hardest-working players I coached. He never sloughed off in practice. His strengths were a devastating forehand and a good serve—a very strong kid."

After completing his storied high school athletic career, Nelson enrolled at Gustavus for more tennis. Playing mostly No. 6 singles, he won MIAC singles titles in 1989 and '91 at that position. Today he lives in St. Louis and works as a pilot.

1988—Roger Anderson

Blue Earth

Between the triumphs of two west-central players in 1987 and '89 (Nelson and Fernelius), the singles title in '88 went to the last and arguably most celebrated of the four Anderson brothers from Blue Earth (then Blue Earth/Frost/Winnebago and now Blue Earth Area High School), Roger. Ranked No. 1 all year in Class A and a prohibitive favorite to win the title, Anderson came through the junior-dominated draw to win his third individual championship (his two others were in doubles) and also lead his Bucs' squad to its final team championship under Coach Hal Schroeder. The owner of an 80-straight singles match winning streak coming into the tournament, Anderson first defeated junior Scot Skogerboe of East Grand Forks and Breck's ever-dangerous Wade Martin, also a junior, in the semis before meeting Fernelius, another junior, in the finals (after playing and defeating him in the team semis in a hard-fought three-set match).

Anderson said of his worthy finals opponent, "I loved to play against him because I matched up well against him and had a lot of success against him even though he was a tremendous player who had excellent results throughout his career." This time the match did not go three sets, Anderson prevailing 6-4, 6-3. Aware that everyone expected him to win, Roger noted in a *Star Tribune* article by Wayne Washington: "There was more pressure on me than there was on him [Fernelius]. I was expected to win" (June 12, 1988).

Once again with just an 8-player draw, Anderson had to win only three matches; but his encounter with Martin in the semis was not without some drama, in part because a large crowd from Breck cheered Martin's every successful shot. Nevertheless, Anderson took care of business, remarking, in another article by Washington, that "I've played here every year since I was a seventh grader... It's something I'm used to" (*Star Tribune*, June 10, 1988).

Perhaps more than any Minnesotan who ever played competitive tennis here in the northland, Anderson was at home in the State Tournament. From the time he was seven years old, when he watched his brothers play on the U of Minnesota's 4th Street courts, he had been around the pressure cooker of state-level competitive tennis. He

recalls watching his brother Gregg play in the 1980 Class A singles final at 98th Street:

> I remember walking around the site trying to find the best place to watch the match and soaking in the atmosphere. By this time I was ten, had some success in summer tournaments and was doing what all ten-year-olds do, dreaming of following in my older brother's footsteps and doing great things. My strongest memory is of looking up at the people two deep lining the up-sloped sidewalk overlooking the first tier of courts. Seeing so many friends of the family, people from the tennis community, and fans involved was like being in a candy story.

And his was also a very familiar name on the summer junior tennis tournament circuit. Beginning in the days when there were 10-and-under rankings, Roger's name appeared as one of the top players. For example, his first year in that division he was ranked No. 2 behind David Wheaton in singles, the second year he was No. 3 (right behind Michael Chang—yes, that's the Michael Chang, who lived in Minnesota during his early tennis years) and Chris Boily, then in his final year in the 10s he was co-No. 1 with Sean McGraw. In the 12s he was No. 3 (behind Boily and Wheaton) and No. 1 his second year—a year he also won the Sectional singles title; and in the 14s he was Nos. 3 and 2. Then in the 16s he was Nos. 10 and 3, and he completed his outstanding junior career with rankings of Nos. 3 and 2 in the 18s. In addition, Roger won two Sectional singles titles, one in the 12s and one in the 14s. This youngest in the Anderson clan was also endorsed for national tournament play many times and achieved modest success playing outside of the friendly courts of Minnesota, once earning a No. 121 ranking. And while he was a student-athlete at the U of M, he and his teammate Dean Hlushko, former Mounds View star, won the Men's Open Sectional doubles title in 1991.

Like his brothers before him, he lived with an aunt in Blue Earth so he could play tennis there, usually commuting to his parents' home in New Hope on weekends. And like his brothers he was an exceptional doubles player (see Chapter Six for more about his doubles prowess); but as his rankings attest, he was also a terrific singles player. Possessed of a booming forehand and an instinctive knack for knowing how to hit the best shot in nearly every circumstance, Anderson was described by his coach (Schroeder) as "a very versatile player who didn't get uptight about anything." In addition, Schroeder said, "He had a lot of ability and he put it to use."

He went on to play at the U of M for coach Dave Geatz, helping the Gophers win Big Ten titles in 1992 and '93 and serving as co-captain his senior year ('93). In addition, he won two coveted Gopher awards: "Unsung Player of the Year" in '89 and the "Team Spirit Award" in '93. (For even more on this last of the Anderson clan, see Chapter Ten.)

1989—Drew Fernelius
New London-Spicer

With the Anderson era finally over at Blue Earth, the 1989 singles tournament featured seven seniors and a sophomore (J. P. McDonald of East Grand Forks) vying for the title won last year by Roger Anderson. Out of this pack emerged Drew Fernelius, the lad from New London/Spicer mentioned earlier. After making an appearance at State as a sophomore with his brother Jamy in doubles ('87), he came back the next year in singles and advanced to the finals, where he fell to Anderson. So this was his year to shine, and shine he did, taking out three seniors: Winona Cotter's Corey Prondzinski (now the boys' coach at Henry Sibley) in the first round and Breck's J. P. Gallagher in the semis. Then, according to *Star Tribune* writer Bob Schranck, he had to beat back a major challenge in the finals from perennial top player Wade Martin of Breck (who went on to Michigan State to play college tennis). Not satisfied with his play, even though he was mostly ahead in the match, Fernelius "berated himself repeatedly, and loudly, during his play yesterday when he made what he considered foolish mistakes. He was at match point in the second set, when Martin came from behind to win in a tiebreaker. Two double faults in the third set didn't help Fernelius' disposition. Martin was trailing 2-5, then used his strong serve to battle back to 4-5" (June 11, 1989). About his worthy opponent, Fernelius told Schranck, "Wade made some awesome shots. You know he's going to

hit that way, so you have to keep the ball in play and wait for your chance." Composing himself, Fernelius closed out the match, winning 6-2, 6-7, 6-4.

Known as much for his feats on the football field and the basketball court as for his skills on the tennis court, Fernelius moved on to St. Thomas College where he continued his tennis career. Like his former teammate Erik Nelson, he had not focused exclusively on tennis in high school. Nevertheless, he worked on his game in the summers and enjoyed a good deal of success in tournament play, first cracking the top ten in the 14s at No. 5 singles and No. 4 in doubles (with Lindsey Nelson). In the 16s he was ranked No. 24 his first year and No. 10 his second year, and he capped his NWTA summer play with rankings of Nos. 13 in singles and doubles (with Jeff Gibson) his first year in the 18s and another No. 5 ranking in singles his final year of competition.

And like his teammate and fellow state champion Nelson, Fernelius was a six-year letterwinner for the Wildcats. He played third singles as a seventh grader and backed up Nelson at No. 2 singles until his junior year, when he finally took over at No. 1. Coach Dave Peterman, noting Fernelius's competitiveness, said, "I've never seen a kid who wanted to win at anything as much as Drew." As for his tennis-playing skills, Peterman said, "He was a finesse player, a smart player who could work the ball until he saw a weakness. He hardly ever made mistakes and often berated himself for unforced errors." In addition, said his coach, "He would run around his forehand to hit his tremendous two-handed backhand."

Now living in the Twin Cities, he works in the real estate business.

1990-91—Tim George
Orono

The years 1990 and '91 brought the Orono Bears into the spotlight, for they finished second both years in team competition and produced the next multiple singles champion, a player with the two-first-names moniker of Tim George. (For the story about George, see Chapter Four.)

1992–David Joerger
Staples-Motley

If you start driving from Moorhead, MN, on U.S. Highway 10 and head east, you will pass through the towns of Staples (population 2,973) and then Motley (population 495) before the highway turns south toward the state's more populated centers such as St. Cloud and the Twin Cities. Just seven miles apart, these two towns today share one high school combining their two names.

Known perhaps more for its championship wrestling teams, Staples-Motley also worked some tennis magic, under head coach-magician Joe Joerger, in the early 1990s. With a strong cast of performers, including coach Joerger's sons Blaine and David, the Cardinals not only pulled rabbits out of the hat, taking home Class A team championships in 1990 and '91, but star player David Joerger also employed some magical strokes to win a singles championship in '92. (For more on the Joergers, see Chapter Ten.)

David Joerger

Frustrated after losing in the finals as a junior to Orono's Tim George, Joerger was determined to make amends this year. Though he would not use it as an excuse, Joerger was not full strength in 1991. *Star Tribune* staff writer Judd Zulgad noted Joerger's condition on the eve of his rematch in the '92 semis with George (also a senior): "Unlike last year, Joerger will be healthy heading into today's match. Last spring, Joerger was playing on a bad right knee (which he had initially injured playing football when he was in 7th grade) that required him to wear a brace. Surgery took care of that problem and Joerger is now able to play at full speed" (June 6, 1992). His father and coach, Joe, also said, "He can get to the ball so much quicker and his lateral and vertical movement are much better" (June 6, 1992).

And in that same article by Zulgad, David remarked about his own play this year: "I can get around better now. Last year I had to end points quickly if I wanted to win." That's what he tried to do against George in 1991; but because his mobility was impaired George beat him handily 6-1, 6-2. This time Joerger played with the confidence that a healthy body granted him, and he was relaxed. Said he before his last high school matchup with his long-time foe George, "There is no pressure on me. He won last year and won big" (June 6, 1992).

So in the match of the tournament, Joerger hung on and upended George 7-5, 1-6, 7-6 (8-6). (For more on this match and the 1991 final between George and Joerger see the profile of George in Chapter Four.)

After the match Joerger told Zulgad, "I'm not big on revenge but losing last year hurt a lot. It's fun to play him because he's such a good athlete. This victory is something that means a lot. He's going to play Division 1 tennis (at Bowling Green) and beating him tells me where my game is at" (*Star Tribune*, June 7, 1992). Elated as he was to beat George, Joerger nevertheless kept his eye on the real prize, a Class A State title, telling his father, "One more to go Dad, one more to go" (June 7, 1992).

And keep his head he did, defeating sophomore Robert Keith of Blake in the finals 6-3, 6-2, thus beating in the same year two Class A multiple singles champions (George in 1990-91 and Keith in 1993-94). Joerger had to be at his best in these two matches against exceptional players, but his first two matches on Friday did not tax him. In the first round he defeated senior Matt Meyer of Fairmont, then needed only one set to take out senior Daniel Lopez of Chisago Lakes, who retired after dropping the first set to Joerger.

One of a select band of tennis champions who competed at the varsity level for six years, Joerger as a seventh grader made an appearance at State as a first doubles player on a team which lost to Blue Earth Area 4-1 in the first round of the 1987 tournament. As an eighth grader he and partner Greg Borstad advanced to State in doubles, losing in the first round to the '88 third-place winners Paul Schroeder and Layne McCleary of Blue Earth Area. In '89 he and Borstad returned and took third in doubles; then, as a sophomore, he and Borstad (now a senior) teamed up for one final crack at the doubles title. Unfortunately for them, they lost to a team from Fairmont in the first round, Brad Hestad and Cory Kallheim, a team that went on to finish second.

With Borstad gone in 1991, Joerger advanced to the State Tournament in singles, where he lost to George in the finals. But then came his breakthrough in '92. The oldest of three tennis-playing siblings, David was a superb athlete who excelled in basketball as well as tennis in high school. Though not particularly tall (he was five foot ten), Joerger had a good kick serve and controlled it well. His dad said, "Like a good pitcher who used a change of pace on his pitches, David also mixed up his serve well." And though he did not have the big weapon that some champions possessed, Joerger nonetheless excelled on the tennis court because he used his head. His father said playing David was like competing in poker against an opponent who never tipped his hand. Coach Joerger also said, "David had very good racket control and excellent touch."

In addition to his distinguished six-year high school career, he enjoyed success during the summers in which he competed in junior tournaments as well. His best singles rankings were in the 10-and-unders (he was No. 6 his first year and No. 3 his second year), but he was also ranked No. 3 in the 14s once and Nos. 7 and 4 in the 16s. Also, he was No. 1 in doubles (with Edina's Tom Danford) his second year in the 16s.

But the most noteworthy accomplishments of his junior tennis career perhaps had more to do with his character than his tennis skills. In 1990 he was named the NWTA Sportsmanship Award winner and in '91 he was chosen as the USTA Central Region William Talbert Junior Sportsmanship Award winner. This last award also gave him an opportunity to attend the International Tennis Hall of Fame ceremony in Newport, RI, that summer.

After high school Joerger attended Chapman University in California, a Division 2 school, to play tennis. But the temptation of his first love (basketball) was too great, so he left the sunny climate of California after two years, returning to the the northland to attend school and play basketball at Concordia College in Moorhead. Following that year, a year in which he also played tennis, he sat out a year in order to compete in Division 2 basketball at Moorhead State U. In just one year as the point guard at Moorhead he became the all-time assist leader and one of the school's top three-point shooters.

Though his tennis is temporarily on hold, he is still very much involved in sports. In fact, he was a part-time player and assistant coach for an International Basketball League team in Bismarck, ND, for two years and then a head coach his third year. The following two years he coached his Bismarck Wizards team, now in the new CBA, to a championship. After one more year at Bismarck he coached the Sioux Falls team to a championship, and after two years there he returned to Bismarck to coach. And in 2007 he achieved his career goal to coach in the NBA, when he was named an assistant coach of the Memphis Grizzlies.

1993-94—Robert Keith
Blake

With both Joerger and George gone, the next two years were dominated by Blake's Robert Keith, who became just the 12th player (and only the second from Class A) to win multiple singles championships. (For an account of Keith's 1993-94 accomplishments, see Chapter Four.) For the next five years Class A singles champions would come from three private schools, Breck, Minnehaha Academy, and Blake, a run that would finally be broken in 2000 by Long Prairie/Grey Eagle's Tony Larson.

1995–Trace Fielding
Breck

First up in 1995 is sophomore Trace Fielding from Breck. Perhaps known up to this point in his high school career more for his excellent doubles play (he and Matt Drawz won the Class A doubles titles in 1993 and '94), Fielding was, according to Breck Athletic director John Thiel, "a tall, lanky kid with a tremendous wingspan." Both Thiel and Fielding's '95 singles opponent in the state finals, Rob Warn, also commented about his big serve and his volley skills. At six feet two inches tall, he used this big serve as a weapon to win a lot of free points.

Fielding had an outstanding junior career in singles. For example, in 1988 he was the top-ranked 10-and-under singles player in the NWTA (ahead of future two-time Class AA champion Matt Peplinski). Then in the 12s he was No. 2 his first year (behind Bloomington's Aaron Dvorak and once again ahead of Peplinski) and No. 1 his second year. He slipped a bit in the 14s to Nos. 9 and 4, but in the 16s he rebounded to place No. 7 his first year and No. 2 his second year (behind Peplinski). And in his first year in the 18s he finished No. 7, a year he won the Sectional championship. He capped his junior singles career with a No. 2 ranking (again behind Peplinski) his final year in the 18s.

Trace Fielding

That final year he was also the highest-ranking Minnesotan in the national 18-and-under bracket, ranking seven places ahead of Peplinski at No. 113, so here was another small-school champion who could very well have competed for a title in Class AA.

In addition, until he began to focus more on singles, he won those two state doubles championships and he was always ranked near the top in doubles in summer tournament play. He was No. 2 his first year in the 12s (with Dvorak as his partner) when he was just 10 and No. 1 with Dvorak the next year, No. 2 with Peplinski his first year

in the 16s and co-No. 4 his second year (when players were first ranked individually in doubles). And though he did not play a great deal of doubles every summer, he nonetheless won Sectional titles in the 12s and 14s (with Dvorak) and in the 16s with Peplinski one year. (For more about his doubles successes at State, see Chapter Six.)

Back on the high school courts in 1995, Fielding first took care of senior Chris Martin from Crookston (a future St. Olaf player). Next he bounced juniors Justin Jeffrey of Orono and Toby Erdman of Lac Qui Parle Valley-Madison, surrendering just two games total in both matches. Then, for the fourth time this year, Fielding found himself across the net from Minnehaha's Rob Warn, also a junior. A rematch of the Section 4A final, which Fielding won, this final produced the same result. Fielding won 6-1, 6-4 and took home his fourth state tournament gold medal (two in doubles and another for his part in the team championship Breck won this year). Unfortunately for Breck, this would be Fielding's final year of high school competition in Minnesota. He left after this, his sophomore year (though he would return in the summer to play junior tennis), to enroll at a tennis academy in the Lone Star State of Texas, where he honed his game in preparation for a college tennis career at Texas A and M. After playing four years there he gave the pro tour a try, enjoying some success in smaller satellite tourneys, especially in doubles.

Had he chosen to stay in Minnesota to finish his high school career, he could very likely have become just the third three-time singles winner in state history (after Dave Healey and Chuck Darley of Rochester). And if he had done so, he might have become the most decorated player of all time, for with two doubles titles and a team championship medal, he would have had at least six gold medals to pin on his letter jacket. But all of this is pure speculation. What remains is that he was an awfully good high school player for the time he played here.

Moreover, he was, according to Thiel, "a wonderful kid, very courteous and understanding." Thiel also said that Fielding was a perfect gentleman on the court, even though he easily defeated most of his opponents: "Kids never felt they didn't belong on the court with him." One final observation from Thiel supports this "nice guy" image. "He could have won three singles titles, but Trace felt that his teammate [Matt Drawz] should have a chance to win a doubles title, so he took him on as a partner. That act was so unselfish that he will forever have my respect, not only as a tennis player but as a human being," said Thiel. In addition to his performance on the tennis courts, Fielding was also an all-around athlete who played soccer in the fall and basketball in the winter.

1996—Rob Warn
Minnehaha Academy

For three years Minnehaha Academy's Rob Warn had been knocking on the door in the Class A singles tournament, twice finishing as runner-up—in 1994 to Robert Keith and in '95 to Fielding. This year, 1996, would be different, for Warn stroked his way through the draw to win four matches and a well-deserved state title. First he trounced ninth grader Lucas Elliott of Benson 6-0, 6-0, then blitzed junior Adam Rowekamp of Winona Cotter 6-1, 6-1. And in the semis he overcame future singles champion Reven Stephens of Breck, a sophomore, in a spirited and very competitive match (7-6, 6-4), to set up a final contest with senior Justin Wismer of Blake, the '95 doubles champion. After toughing out a 6-2, 4-6, 6-4 battle with Wismer, according to *Star Tribune* writer Nolan Zavoral, Warn smiled and said, "It feels so great. I'm finally done with it. I've got a title in the bag" (June 8, 1996).

All of Warn's hard work finally paid off, and he said, "I've been practicing and practicing for a match like this—the third set of the State Tournament with the title on the line." Now, like his Class AA counterpart Matt Peplinski, the AA champion, he could relax and look forward to something other than tennis. "We've got graduation and all-night parties coming up," Warn said. "What's not to like?" But for the moment he could look back on this day

with fondness: "It was the end of the school year and all my friends were there" (June 8, 1996).

Like the beautiful giant white trillium flowers which bloom late in the spring here in the Upper Midwest, so did Warn's tennis career bloom later than that of most state champions. Warn admits that he didn't play his first tournament until he was 14, and his best early ranking was just a No. 4 in the Challenger Level 16-and-under singles. His final year in the 16s he came into full bloom, however, with a co-No. 3 ranking (with Aaron Dvorak). Said Warn about his junior playing days, "I played all the summer national junior grand slam events my second year of 16s and both years of 18s." His reward for this dedication was a No. 133 national ranking and a solid NWTA ranking of No. 3 (behind Peplinski and Fielding) his last year in the 18-and-under division.

Though he had first played some tennis with a good friend when he was 10 or so, his entrée into competitive tennis came as a result of summer lessons taken in the Urban Tennis Program in Minneapolis. Then, according to Warn, "I got hooked up with the Northwest Clubs and Greg Wicklund was my coaching mentor for four or five years." Warn gives a great deal of the credit for his success to Wicklund: "Without him taking me under his wing I wouldn't have gotten anywhere in tennis. He made it fun." Wicklund in turn praised him as "a hard-worker and a lefty who was very quick."

With continued confidence in his game Warn enrolled at Notre Dame, where he became a member of some very successful Irish tennis teams from 1996-2000. And though he played just "a handful of matches at No. 6 singles and some tournament matches," he enjoyed playing against and practicing with so many top Division 1 players.

Describing his tennis game, Warn said, "My forehand was a weapon but I didn't have an overpowering serve." Bob Bayliss, his college coach, called Warn a counterpuncher.

He left Notre Dame with an accounting degree and now lives in Minneapolis where he works for DeLoitte and Touche in the audit practices department. Lamenting that his busy work life keeps him away from tennis, Warn contemplates a return to the game he once played so well.

1997–Ross Greenstein
Blake

After some family bonding in 1996, when they teamed up to take second in the Class A doubles tournament, cousins Ross Greenstein and Blake Baratz of Blake opted to play singles in '97. The result was a singles championship for ninth grader Greenstein and a fourth-place finish for Baratz, a junior. Both were also key members of the '96 state championship Blake team and this year's runner-up squad.

Now it was their turn to show the way for their teammates, Greenstein as the No. 1 singles player for the Bears and Baratz as No. 2. And they did not disappoint, advancing out of Section 4A as the two singles entrants (Greenstein beat Baratz 6-3, 4-6, 6-1) and both winning their first two matches at State. (Greenstein opened with a straight-set victory over senior Adam McNicol of Martin County West.) However, both had won difficult matches in the quarters, Baratz topping St. Peter sophomore Troy Brovold 6-4, 6-3 and Greenstein edging Duluth Marshall senior George Grombacher 6-4, 7-6. These victories set up the potential for a family feud in the finals, but it was not to be. While Greenstein advanced with a win over senior Chris McDonald of East Grand Forks in the semis, Baratz lost a heartbreaker (4-6, 7-5, 7-6) to future singles champion Reven Stephens, a junior from Breck and this year's other finalist. Baratz then lost to McDonald and had to settle for a fourth-place finish.

Greenstein, on the other hand, gained family bragging rights by upending McDonald, then turning the tables on Stephens in the finals. No doubt smarting from his 6-1, 6-7, 6-2 loss to Stephens in the team finals, a loss that gave Breck an important point in its 4-3 win over Blake, Greenstein was eager for revenge. And get revenge he did, taking the opening and third sets with ease after

dropping the middle one. Final score: Greenstein 6-3, 4-6, 6-1.

One of only three players to claim a singles title as a ninth grader, Greenstein first appeared in the Blake lineup as a seventh grader. Though he was just a youngster, Greenstein was already a mature tennis player, having logged hundreds of hours on the court and having been a top-ranked junior player for years. For instance, in 1991 he was No. 1 in NWTA 10-and-under singles and participated in the Boys' 12 Zone Team Championships. In his first year in the 12s he was ranked No. 4 (behind Charlie Schultz of Edina, his older teammate Baratz, and Ryan Edlefsen of Bloomington) and No. 2 in doubles with another Blake teammate, Drew Zamansky. Again he was a member of the Zone Team for the NWTA. Still in the 12s in '93, he was ranked alphabetically and participated in both Zone Team play and the National Challenge Cup.

Then, in his first year in the 14s, he was ranked No. 5 (behind Baratz who was No. 4) in singles. The next year he was No. 2 in the 14s (behind St. Cloud Tech's Kevin Whipple) and was ranked No. 75 nationally (the highest ranking of any Minnesota boy in all divisions). By the way, that second year in the 14s he lost a close match to Andy Roddick.

His first year in the NWTA 16s he was No. 6, with a No. 186 national ranking. In 1997 he moved up to the 18s, where he ranked No. 7 in the Northern Section and No. 86 nationally. Then, though he had a No. 93 national ranking, he did not play enough in the Section to be ranked locally. However, he won the 18 Sectional championships in 1998 and '99 and earned terrific national rankings (Nos. 62 and 26). Once again, these were the highest national rankings of any Minnesota male player.

After winning the Class A singles title, Greenstein won a major summer NWTA tournament in Sioux Falls,

Ross Greenstein

SD, an 18-and-under competition which he won at age 15 after beating Class AA champion Ryan Edlefsen of Eden Prairie in the finals. In addition, that summer he won a gold medal in mixed doubles and a bronze medal in singles at the Junior Maccabiah Games in Tel Aviv, Israel.

That fall he transferred to Hopkins High School but did not make it to State in 1998, losing in the section tournament to Class AA champion Cesar Vargas. He then decided to set his tennis sights a bit higher, in part because he wanted to compete in the Easter Bowl tournament his junior year but could not have done so if he had played high school tennis. So he moved to the San Diego, CA, area the second semester of his junior year to compete in tournaments there. Then he returned to Hopkins but graduated early his senior year.

For the most part Greenstein's success was achieved without any coaching until he moved to California, though he credits U of M coach Dave Geatz for letting him play with some of his players in the summer. A good athlete who also played varsity basketball at Blake his ninth-grade year, Greenstein described himself as a serve and volley player. "I came to the net all the time, chipping and charging and basically living at the net. It wasn't until I moved to California that I developed an all-court game," he said.

After high school he moved to the sunshine state to play tennis at the U of FL. No doubt that No. 26 national ranking had something to do with the scholarship the Gators' coaches offered him. He played just two years there, mostly at Nos. 5-7 singles and No. 3 doubles. Greenstein enjoyed being a part of a top-ten team, and he said that he clinched a number of matches for his team; but after having toe surgery and enduring other nagging injuries he decided to end his tennis career after his sophomore year.

With a business degree in hand, he moved back to San Diego to establish a program (called Scholarships for Athletes) designed to help highly ranked athletes find the best college setting for them and to get scholarships. He also teaches tennis a few times a week.

1998—Winfield Reven Stephens
Breck

Since Staples-Motley's David Joerger claimed the singles title in 1992, every champion until 2000 would come from private Metro schools. Three were from Blake (Robert Keith, who won two; Ross Greenstein; and Drew Zamansky), one was from Minnehaha Academy (Robert Warn), and two were from Breck. Trace Fielding was the first champion from Breck ('95) and in '98 the second Breck player, Winfield Stephens (called by his middle name Reven), came to the fore. After losing to Greenstein in a three-set final in '97, the road was clear for Stephens this year. Having already led his top-ranked Breck Mustangs to the team championship, its third in the past four years, Stephens was battle-tested for the singles tournament. He opened individual play with two easy wins on Thursday, giving up only one game in those matches. First he double-bageled senior Jason Kuehn of Crookston and then demolished junior Chris Kindler of Mounds Park Academy. In the semis he defeated sophomore Mike Solum from the Academy of Holy Angels 6-2, 6-2. Waiting for Stephens in the final was his good friend and national doubles tournament partner, senior Blake Baratz of Blake, last year's fourth-place singles finisher.

Unfortunately for Baratz, Stephens showed no mercy to him, defeating Baratz 6-1, 6-1 in just forty-five minutes. Said Baratz of Stephens's play (in a June 6, 1998, article in the *Star Tribune* by Kristen Davis), "He was outstanding. There was nothing I could do. If anyone's going to [beat me], I'd want it to be him." Just two weeks earlier Baratz had lost to Stephens in a pair of white-knuckle tiebreakers, so the ease of Stephens' win was somewhat surprising. His coach, Katie Queenan, told Davis that "this is the best I've seen [Stephens] play all season. He really peaked at this tournament. He was so focused and really wanted this and it showed in his play. He just played phenomenal." Blake coach Ted Warner, though sorry to see his player (Baratz) take such a licking, couldn't help but admire Stephens' play. "I told him [Baratz] he should have been on the sidelines with me. He could have enjoyed it more," said Warner, who added, "For me, it's just fun when you get someone to win who plays so well." As for Baratz himself, he remarked, "I felt hopeless. I could have played my best and still lost" (June 6, 1998).

In that same June 6 article, Davis said of Stephens' play, his "powerful serve was his best friend Friday. Baratz made 15 errors trying to return the rocket." Stephens, called by his coach "an all-court player with good hands who could bang against the baseliners and do everything," agreed that he had just played the best match of his life. And while Reven always competed hard on the court, even against his friends, he said that after the match he and Baratz "made plans to 'hang out' Friday night" (June 6, 1998).

So it had been a glorious tournament and career for Stephens. He won the biggest individual prize in high school tennis and helped Breck defeat three foes to claim the team title. In addition, he finished second in the singles in 1997, third in singles in '96, and third in doubles in '95 (with partner Ryan Burnett). And he was a key member of two other Breck championship teams in 1995 and '97.

Queenan, his coach for that special senior season, said of her star player, "He was a great guy who had a great attitude; and he didn't take himself (or tennis) too seriously." She added, "He really enjoyed himself on the court." With the natural talent he possessed, he stomped on most of his Class A opponents, losing just one match this year, that to 1997 AA champion Ryan Edlefsen.

His talent was apparent as a youngster, for he began taking lessons at age four and first appeared in the NWTA rankings at No. 6 in singles and No. 3 in doubles as a 12-and-under player in 1992. That year he was also a member of the Boys' 12 Zone Team. Then, in '94, he was the third-ranked 14-year-old singles player and earned his first national ranking (No. 150). And though he won the NWTA Sectional singles championships both years he played the 16s, he did not play enough tournaments to be ranked locally. However, he earned national rankings of Nos. 168 his first year in the 16s and 136 in his second year. In his first year in the 18s he was No. 4 in singles locally and No. 147 nationally. His final year in the juniors he did not have an NWTA ranking but he achieved his highest national rankings (Nos. 111 in singles and 23 in doubles, with Baratz).

Off to the U of KY with a partial tennis scholarship, Stephens played three years for the Wildcats. His freshman year he played No. 3 doubles on a team ranked No. 12 in the nation, his sophomore year he played Nos. 2 doubles and 6 singles, and his junior year he played Nos. 6 singles and 1 doubles. Then he returned to Minnesota—as many who have gone to supposedly greener pastures have done—where he played No. 2 doubles and No. 6 singles for coach Dave Geatz's top-35 team his senior year. That year (2002) he also won the "Team Spirit Award."

After graduating from the U of M with a degree in community recreation, Stephens worked at the Baseline Tennis Center on the U campus as an assistant teaching pro for a time and is now the co-director of the Center. He also continues to play some competitive tennis. In 2003, for example, he achieved a No. 3 ranking in Men's Open Singles in the Northern Section. He also serves as an assistant coach at St. Catherine's College.

1999—Drew Zamansky
Blake

In this the final year of competition in the 20th century, another big fish from Blake, that small independent school tennis power, won the 1999 singles title. For nearly the entire decade of the '90s, Class A tennis had been dominated by Metro area private school teams and players, with Blake, SPA, and Breck winning seven of the ten team titles

Drew Zamansky

and players from those teams (and one from Orono) taking home eleven of the twenty singles and doubles championships. In singles these schools produced eight of the ten titlists. And in most cases these eight champions were the lunker trout controlling the biggest pool in the stream, feasting on the small fish which dared to venture into their territory.

So this year was no exception as the singles champion once again came from Blake. And though he may not have been the biggest "trout" coming into the tournament (that honor went to undefeated and top-ranked Mike Solum of Holy Angels, a junior), senior Drew Zamansky was right up there at the top of the food chain (No. 2). After devouring his first two opponents easily (juniors Matt Reich of Park Rapids Area and Tim Slama of Blue Earth Area), Zamansky swallowed up Eveleth-Gilbert's Kyle Hawley, also a junior, in the semis and then ate up the favored Solum in the finals 6-4, 6-4.

Though this was Zamansky's first appearance in the singles draw, he had played an important role in the success of Blake's teams for five years, first playing as an eighth grader on the 1995 team which lost to Breck in the finals. Then, as a ninth grader, he made it to State in doubles with partner Benji Hartman, losing in the first round to Breck's Jon Simmons and Tom Pohlad, and helped the Bears win the team title. As a sophomore he and his partner, Chris Laurey, finished second in doubles, and as a junior in '98 he entered the singles competition but did not make it to State.

As a summer junior player Zamansky first made his name known with a modest No 23 ranking in the 12-and-unders as just a nine-year-old in 1990. Then, playing in both the 10s and 12s in '91, he was No. 2 in the 10s (behind Ross Greenstein) and No. 10 in the 12s. In addition, he and Ryan Edlefsen were third in the 12-and-under doubles. In '92 he ranked No. 7 in the 12 singles and No. 2 in doubles (with Greenstein) and qualified to play in the USTA Boys' 12 Zone Championships. His last year in the 12s he was ranked alphabetically, and in his first year in the 14s he was the No. 1-ranked doubles player but just the No. 6-ranked Challenger 1 singles player. In '95 he was back in the championship rankings (No. 6 in the 14s) and earned a No. 169 national ranking. Then in the 16s he was

ranked locally at Nos. 11 and 8 (and No. 4 in doubles) his last year of the 16s. That last year in the 16s he was also ranked No. 227 in national singles play. He was not ranked in the 18s.

So for someone who wasn't always in the upper echelon of local junior players, this accomplishment (winning a state title) was a bit of a surprise to some in the Minnesota tennis community. However, he was the No. 1 fish at Blake his senior year, so he had the best competition.

His coach, Ted Warner, called him "probably the smartest player I ever had—he could read other players' footwork." Since he was only about five feet six inches tall, he had to rely on his brain; but, according to Warner, "he was also a feisty player who had all the shots." Warner began coaching him when Zamansky was 10 years old and tried to find "a label for his game." That label became his service return, but Zamansky also had "great hands and a great half-volley," Warner noted. He also volleyed well and had a knack for anticipating court position.

He left Blake to attend George Washington U where he played Division 1 tennis for two years, mostly at Nos. 4-6 singles and a variety of doubles positions. Tendonitis cut his career short, and after graduating from George Washington he earned a law degree at Denver U. Today he works for his father's law firm in Minneapolis, Zamansky Professional Association.

2000—Tony Larson
Long Prairie/Grey Eagle/Swanville

Like the surprise ending in an O. Henry short story, the 2000 Class A singles tournament produced an unexpected winner, sophomore Tony Larson from the west-central paired school of Long Prairie/Grey Eagle/Swanville. Though he first earned a spot in the singles draw as an eighth grader and finished third in last year's tournament as a ninth grader, he was not given much of a chance to win, particularly since pre-tourney favorite Mike Solum of Holy Angels stood in his path in the semis. Now a senior, Solum (who finished second in '99), easily advanced to the semis, as did Larson. On the other side of the draw junior Jarrett Cascino of Rochester Lourdes and talented ninth grader Grady Newman of Blake squared off.

In the biggest upset of the tournament, Larson bumped off Solum 6-3, 6-3, then beat Cascino in the finals 6-3, 6-4. Solum had defeated Larson in last year's tournament in straight sets and, according to *Star Tribune* writer Michael Rand, "seemed to have the edge entering the rematch. But Solum ... had problems with his serve, enabling Larson to get the breaks he needed" (June 10, 2000). And though he acknowledged that he was the underdog against Solum, Larson said, "I played my best tennis today." A disconsolate but magnanimous Solum said, "I needed to serve better to win, and I didn't. He had the best day of his life and I give it all to him" (June 10, 2000).

While Solum was easily winning his third-place match, he kept peeking over to catch glimpses of the championship match on an adjoining court. Here, according to the above *Star Tribune* article, "he saw more of the same play he had witnessed earlier. Larson constantly pounded deep ground strokes and hit hard, accurate serves in the early stages against Cas-

Tony Larson

cino." But a match that started out to be a rout got closer when "Larson tightened a little while serving for the title and started making the errors he had been forcing earlier. Cascino climbed within 5-4, but Larson was still up a break. After regaining his composure, he took the final game and the championship" (June 10, 2000).

Larson had broken Cascino at 4-3 in the first set, and, after taking that set 6-3, raced to a 5-0 lead in the second. According to this same article (titled "Class A Underdog Wins Title in Singles"), after Cascino broke him twice in the second set, Larson said, "I got pretty nervous when he broke me a couple of times. I just had to forget about it and start playing like I was when everything wasn't on the line" (June 10, 2000).

It was a splendid tournament for Larson, for not only did he upset Solum and upend Cascino in the finals, but

he won all four of his matches in straight sets. He was, as tennis pundits like to say, "in the zone." In the first and second rounds he upended sophomore John Kuntz of East Grand Forks and eighth-grade phenom Chi Pham of Blake.

The next year (2001), with a reputation to uphold and a title to defend, Larson advanced to the State Tournament for the fourth year in a row. Unfortunately, however, he did not make it to the semis, losing in the quarters to the eventual fourth-place finisher, senior Brian Thomas of Winona Cotter, 1-6, 7-5, 6-4 in a huge upset. Perhaps he was a bit over-confident, but the truth is that these years featured some of the toughest singles draws in the history of Class A play. Had he been able to win his quarterfinal match, he would have needed to beat Peter Torgrimson of Duluth Marshall and then he would have faced the eventual champion, senior Cascino, his victim the previous year.

Entering the 2002 tournament, Larson, now a senior, was confident he could repeat his sophomore performance. He was, after all, undefeated coming in and he was now as experienced as a trial lawyer arguing his 500th case; for this was his fifth appearance at State. But the tennis gods and the competition (or his lack of it) were not kind to him again this year. In the first round he had to play future champion Grady Newman of Blake—a junior—barely escaping in a three-set, three-hour match (7-5, 4-6, 7-5) that drained him so much he suffered leg cramps after the match. Nevertheless, he survived the first day and moved into the semis with a 6-1, 6-1 win over Minnehaha Academy junior Scott Bean. Next up for Larson was Winona Cotter's Jared Novotny, a senior whom he dispatched 6-4, 6-3. Waiting for Larson in the finals was Duluth Marshall's Peter Torgrimson, who also had to survive a grueling three-set semifinal match (against Chi Pham of Blake) that took a great deal out of him. Even so,

Torgrimson got the better of Larson to win the title in a close two-set match 7-6, 6-4. Despite having to endure that grueling first round match and despite re-injuring his back in the match with Torgrimson (Larson first hurt his back during the basketball season), Larson did not use these events as excuses. In fact, he said, "My losses in high school were the best thing that happened to me."

Taking nothing away from Torgrimson, Larson's coach, Curt Hatfield, noted that his player didn't have enough tough competition in his section during the year. Hatfield told *Star Tribune* writer Jim Paulsen, in a June 7, 2002, article that "he came out of a really tough section that year [2000]. He had played in some matches that tested him by the time he got to the State Tournament. He hasn't had that in the past two years. I don't think he's had a close match all year." Paulsen supported Hatfield's view: "competitive tennis in Minnesota revolves around the metropolitan area, and Larson and Lipinski [Winona's Brian—Class AA] rarely get the chance during the high school season to test themselves against the best in the Twin Cities." He called them "mystery men; talented players who toil in the relative obscurity of their outstate schools" (June 7, 2002). While Paulsen's assessment might not be altogether fair (both Larson and Lipinski made five appearances at State, after all), the truth is that they perhaps could have done better if they had competed against more Metro-area players. In a June 8, 2002, *Star Tribune* article, Paulsen noted that "the silky smooth Larson did win one title, but Lipinski finished his career without taking home a first-place medal."

Much has been made of the lack of competition for Larson during the high school season, but the truth is that he honed his game by playing summer tournaments (often against his Metro-area peers) and more than held his own. His credentials speak volumes about his prowess: No. 2 in singles and a Section doubles champion (with Zach Smith of Rochester) his second year in the 14s, rankings of Nos. 5 and 3 in the 16s and No. 4 in the only year he was ranked in the 18s. And if anyone ever doubted his ability, he laid those doubts to rest by securing the No. 1 ranking in Men's Open Singles in 2005, while still a student in college.

For Larson, an excellent athlete who also played basketball in high school, it was inevitable that he should turn to tennis as his sport of choice after his parents moved to a house with a court in the back yard. In addition, he started playing in the summer recreation program run by his coach, Hatfield. A precocious talent, he moved to the varsity as a seventh grader, where he played No. 3 singles. The next year he moved up to No. 1 singles, a position he would hold for five years, advancing to the first of his five straight State Tournament singles appearances.

After finishing his illustrious high school career, Larson played tennis at Westmont College in Santa Barbara, CA, for two years before returning to Minnesota to attend school and to play tennis. At Westmont, an NAIA school, Larson played No. 1 singles his sophomore year, often competing against Division 1 players who, he said, "gave me tough competition and made me a much better player."

He completed a physical education degree at St. Cloud State U with a goal of coaching a college tennis team or working at a racket club. Of course he played tennis at St. Cloud as well, holding down the No. 1 singles spot his junior and senior years and compiling a record of 48 wins and just 3 losses. His senior year he was ranked No. 43 in Division 2 and his Huskies reached the second round of NCAA team play.

Since completing his college eligibility, Larson has been challenging the big "boys" of Minnesota tennis, in 2005 earning that aforementioned No. 1 Men's Open Singles ranking and defeating D. J. Geatz to win the Men's Open Sectional championship in 2006.

His coach, Hatfield, described him as not only a great tennis player but a great kid. Said Hatfield, "He was always polite and respectful of his coaches and teachers. And he always had a lot of fun with the other players on the team. He especially took some of the younger players under his wing and spent a lot of time with them improving their tennis games. He has also come back to see how his old team has been doing and to hit with the current players."

2001–Jarett Cascino
Rochester Lourdes

In a decade that began with an outstate player (Larson) taking the top prize in Class A, that trend continued for two more years. Following Larson's triumph in 2000, a lad from Rochester Lourdes who had distinguished himself in doubles took the 2001 title, becoming the first player from Lourdes to win a singles championship. After appearing at State in doubles as a ninth grader and a sophomore (with partner Phillip Johnson), he took home gold medals in doubles both years. (For more about these doubles wins, see Chapter Six.)

As a junior he got a whiff of the roses in singles when he finished second to Larson, so in 2001 he was determined to take home a bouquet. And take it home he did, thanks in part to Brian Thomas, the other outstate entrant from his section, who upset Larson. In his first match Cascino knocked off senior Johann Liljengren of St. Peter, a formidable opponent who finished second in the 1999 doubles tournament. Then he beat senior Pete Spreitzer of Duluth Marshall, setting up a semifinal encounter with the very dangerous Grady Newman, a sophomore from Blake. Defeating Newman in straight sets, he advanced to the finals for the second year in a row, where he met Duluth Marshall's Torgrimson, who had beaten Cascino in a dual meet a month ago. In a highly competitive, entertaining match, Cascino triumphed 6-4, 4-6, 6-3 to earn a championship in his last year of high school competition.

Unlike Tony Larson, Cascino had no difficulty finding good hitting partners or tough opponents in southeast Minnesota, including his doubles partner Johnson. In addition, there were strong area teams in the section such as Winona Cotter in Class A and Rochester Mayo in Class AA. He also became tournament-hardened by playing junior tennis in the summer, earning NWTA singles rankings as high as No. 2 in the 12s and No. 3 one year in the 14s and also his first year in the 16s. Cascino also played national tournaments, and in the 14s he was once ranked No. 225. At Lourdes he played No. 2 until his junior year (behind Johnson), then took over the No. 1 spot for two years.

Recruited by the U of WI-Green Bay, Cascino went off to Packerland to play his college tennis. After four good years there (Cascino captained the team his senior year), he went on to play some pro tournaments in Europe, often traveling with Eric Butorac, and he has done some tennis coaching as well, some of it in Rochester. After graduation from Green Bay, he attended graduate school at his alma mater and also helped coach the men's tennis team.

2002—Peter Torgrimson
Duluth Marshall

After a fifty-one-year drought, a northeastern Minnesota school finally produced another singles champion, Peter Torgrimson of Duluth Marshall—the former Duluth Cathedral but now a school for students of all religions with just

Peter Torgrimson

500 students in grades 5-12. (That 1951 champion, by the way, was the famous Los Angeles trial lawyer and prosecutor of Charles Manson, Hibbing's Vincent Bugliosi, whose accomplishments are described earlier in this chapter.) Torgrimson, the 2002 champion, had been planting the seeds for four years, first making an appearance in the singles draw as a ninth grader. And though the seeds were slow-growing (he did not survive the first day of competition his first two years at State, losing to Mike Solum of Holy Angels both times), he demonstrated last year that he might have what it takes to sprout up by taking second, beating top-ranked players Chi Pham of Blake and Brian Thomas of Winona Cotter before losing 6-4, 4-6, 6-3 to Jarett Cascino in the finals.

Easily advancing through the first two rounds with wins over seniors Robert Moore of Park Rapids Area and Sam Conway of Waseca, Torgrimson ran into a buzz saw in the 2002 semis in the person of sophomore Pham of Blake. The *MSHSL 2002 MN Boys' State Tournament*

Program noted that "Torgrimson claimed the first set 6-2, but Pham roared back to win the second 6-2. In the third, Pham pushed Torgrimson to the tie-breaker, but Torgrimson was able to win 7-6 (8-6)."

A relieved Torgrimson did not let down his guard, however, for his next opponent was 2000 champion Tony Larson, now a senior. An article by Ben Noble in the June 8, 2002, *Star Tribune* said about the early stage of this final match: "The first game set the tone for the rest of the match; Torgrimson and Larson brought the game to deuce five times." Trading games until 6-6, Larson then "built a 5-0 lead in the first-set tiebreaker and was on the verge of winning the first set. But Torgrimson rallied, reeling off seven points in a row to win the set 7-6 (7-5)." Said Torgrimson of his remarkable comeback, "When I get down like that, my brain just shuts off and I play my game" (June 8, 2002).

Apparently now in the driver's seat, Torgrimson, with the second set tied at 1-1, began to cramp up, perhaps because of his strenuous match with Pham in the semis. He said, "I guess I wasn't in as good of shape as I thought I was" (*Star Tribune*, June 8, 2002). Nevertheless, he "toughed it out, winning his serve and breaking Larson's to take a 3-1 lead." But Larson refused to fold, breaking Torgrimson and serving at 4-5. Then, according to the June 8 *Star Tribune* article, "That was when Torgrimson showed why coach Kurt Bartell calls him the definition of mental toughness. Still hobbled by cramps, he was able to break serve and win the match."

So in the first singles final featuring two performers from north of the Metro area, Torgrimson prevailed 7-6, 6-4. This win was a fitting reward for a young man who led his team to two team appearances at State (one of which resulted in a runner-up finish in 2001) and who played No. 1 singles for four years.

Duluth Marshall's athletic director, David Homstad, called Torgrimson "a tremendously hard-working, talented kid."

Torgrimson's win was remarkable for several reasons. First, players from the northern part of the state don't often get enough outdoor court time in the spring to be competitive. Secondly, though they can get good coaching at the Longwood Tennis Club, often the lack of

tough opposition puts them at a disadvantage. And thirdly, at least in Torgrimson's case, he was not one of Minnesota's top-ranked junior players. To be sure, he did earn some decent rankings (No. 6 one year in the 16s and No. 11 in his final year in the 18s, for example), but in two of his last four years he wasn't even ranked.

After graduation, Torgrimson headed off to the U of OR to play tennis, but he did not play there so he transferred to the U of M and earned his first varsity letter in 2005.

2003—Grady Newman
Blake

Another singles player from Blake in the finals, another Blake team championship, another feather in the hat for this storied program. In a year in which he led the Bears to their twelfth State team title (a record ten in Class A), Grady Newman became the sixth Blake player and seventh all told to win a singles title (Robert Keith won two). Finally, after five straight advances to State in singles, Newman came through. As a neophyte in 1999, eighth grader Newman lost in the first round to that year's runner-up, Mike Solum of Holy Angels. Then, in three of the next four years he advanced to the second day of play, finishing fourth in 2000 (as a ninth grader) and third in '01. And in '02 he experienced the bad luck of the draw, meeting up with and losing to '00 champion Tony Larson in the first round.

So in 2003, in relatively easy straight-set matches, Newman defeated junior Adam Altepeter of East Grand Forks, ninth grader Max Busch of Duluth Marshall in the quarters, and senior Scott Bean of Minnehaha Academy in the semis. On deck waiting for Newman was the pride of Gilhorn, Germany, foreign exchange student David Breyel. Playing for coach Jane Kjos's Benson team, Breyel came into the tournament with a spotless 27-0 record. In what *Star Tribune* writer Jim Paulsen called "the showcase match of the first day," Breyel had defeated Newman's teammate, junior Chi Pham, one of the pre-tournament favorites, in a two-hour quarterfinal 6-4, 7-6 (10-8). Said Paulsen, "Pham led at some point during both sets, but eventually Breyel's soft hands and deft backhand proved too much" (June 6, 2003).

Newman was also one of the pre-tournament favorites, and he knew he was in for a tussle after he saw Breyel defeat Pham and SPA's Sam Salyer in the semis (in a come-from-behind 4-6, 6-1, 7-6 match). Said Newman of his finals opponent, in a June 7, 2003, article by Paulsen, "He's from Germany. He's a clay-court player. You can't really hit it by him" (*Star Tribune*). Knowing that Breyel would get everything back, Newman's "game plan was to stay on serve and maintain rallies long enough to use his powerful forehand to force the issue" (June 7, 2003). His calculated plan worked, and he earned a 6-4, 6-4 win to claim the title. Breyel admitted to being tired (the earlier three-set semi and the long quarterfinal match with Pham had drained him), but there's no denying that Newman deserved his medal.

Newman, who went off to study at Williams College in Massachusetts in the fall, had a glorious career at Blake, winning this singles title and also helping his team win three championships in four years. In addition, he had been a stalwart on the junior scene since 1993, first appearing as one of the top 10 players in the 10-and-unders. His best ranking was No. 1 in his last year in the 12s, a year he also claimed the Sectional singles title. Thereafter he earned Section rankings as high as No. 5 in the 14s (also achieving his highest national ranking—No 119) and Nos. 2 and 4 in the 16s. So in a sense it was a bit surprising that it took him so long to win a title. But there were many strong players in Class A during his years at Blake, including his teammate Pham. Often they competed against each other in section play; and theirs was one of the greatest inter-team rivalries in state tennis history, for in four years they met each other in subsection and section play. And each time both advanced to State, this year with Pham having won the section final over Newman.

But it was Newman who claimed the prize, finally achieving the goal he had long ago set for himself. And though he was justifiably proud of his singular accomplishment, he also took pride in seeing the progress made by younger members of his team. In addition, he was pleased to see his close friend David Baker get elected as co-captain of the team.

Reflecting on his strengths as a player, Newman said, "I had a good serve and forehand, and I showed a lot of intensity on the court. I had the ability to get my adrenalin going when it was needed and to pull out some tough matches." He credited two individuals for helping develop his game: his favorite pro coach, former Gustavus star Marc Miller, and his sometime hitting partner, Aaron Dvorak (1993 State doubles champion). The result of his effort and their help was this state championship and four years atop the ladder at Blake (a position he occasionally relinquished to Pham this season).

Newman graduated in 2007 from Williams with an economics major and today works in his father's business (Newman Capital Group) in Minneapolis.

Double Your Pleasure
The Doubles Champions

Those who play doubles, for all sorts of reasons including advancing age, can't understand why doubles has often been considered the neglected stepsister of singles in high school, college, and professional tennis competition. Though "its the most popular grass-roots form of the sport, not only in the United States, but worldwide," according to an August 2004 article by Richard Eaton in *TennisLife* magazine, its popularity has especially waned among the pros. Sure, there are some top women pros who play doubles, but none of the top ten men were ranked in doubles and only one of the top fifty male singles players, No. 33-ranked Max Mirnyi, was ranked in the top five in doubles in 2005. To some extent this lack of interest in doubles is a result of the increase in prize money for singles (close to a million dollars in 2005 for the singles champions in Grand Slam events) and much more modest prize money for doubles. But singles also gets the attention of the press and the fans; Arthur Ashe Stadium simply wouldn't fill up for a match between the Bryan brothers and the team of Jonas Bjorkman/Leander Paes like it would for a singles match between top-ranked male or female players. Let's face it, singles is the glamour game, the heavyweight boxing match to the doubles light-weight match. People still prefer the brutal *mano a mano* spectacle of a singles bout, the sight of two heavyweight punchers such as Rafael Nadal and Roger Federer trying to knock each other out with hard-hitting serves and punishing groundstrokes. This despite the fact that doubles is a more tactical game often featuring incredible angle shots; soft, touch volleys; ever-changing formations and tactics; and spectacular retrieves off overhead

"We were as twinn'd lambs that did frisk in the sun And bleat the one at the other"
—The Winter's Tale

smashes. And it no longer generates the buzz it did in the days when John McEnroe and "anyone else" (but usually Peter Fleming) were entertaining fans all over the world. Paraphrasing the words of the late Rodney Dangerfield, a popular film comedian, doubles "don't get no respect."

And while doubles still remains a staple in both college and high school competition, it does not have the cachet that singles does at either level. In college competition, only three of the nine matches are doubles, and often just one point out of seven can be earned in doubles (by virtue of winning two out of the three matches). Even if all three points count when nine points are scored, these are just 8-game pro-sets instead of full two-out-of-three-set matches. In college this change was made to shorten the matches.

At the high school level in Minnesota it's a bit better, for in most dual meets three of the seven points (or two out of five) are scored in doubles and all are full two-of-three-set matches. But when it comes to individual competition leading to the State Tournament, there's no doubt about which competition takes center stage: it's singles in a walkover. Not many of the top players aspire to be state doubles champions; in fact, many simply refuse to play doubles even though they know they have no chance to win a singles title. They would rather reach the quarters in the singles draw than take home a state championship medal in doubles. A win in doubles is seen as a consolation prize. It's like kissing your sister—not quite the real thing.

Let me focus for a bit on the positive aspects of doubles competition, then highlight the stories of those who chose to play doubles and became state champions. For starters, doubles can be a steppingstone for future stars, a chance for soon-to-be singles champions such as Christie Geanakoplos, Mark Wheaton, Gregg Anderson (all sophomores at the time), and ninth grader Roger Anderson to showcase their developing skills. It also provides a chance for other top players, often with no opportunities to advance to State from tough sections, to extend their seasons and perhaps gain some recognition. In addition, it's often an excellent opportunity, especially for outstate coaches, to pair up their top singles players in hopes of making runs for a title. In addition, some players, perhaps lacking the mobility needed to excel in singles, nonetheless have superb doubles skills that make them ideal partners. And isn't that what doubles is all about: cooperation and teamwork? Oh, sure, the doubles tournament can be just as much about the law of the jungle as singles is, but in doubles you have a friend to help you tame the tigers on the other side of the net.

Finally, as touring pro Ai Sugiyama noted, in an August 2003 article in *TennisLife* magazine by Richard Eaton, doubles is fun: "It [doubles] should be fun. People talk [between points] and smile. You talk to your partner, which is something that can't happen in singles. I enjoy it because it's a chance to share court time with friends."

So this is a chapter about successful partnerships that have earned championships for doubles teams since 1929, those "twinn'd lambs that did frisk in the sun" (or now indoors) on our state tournament courts.

Note: In some of the early years the MSHSL yearbooks do not list first names of the players and in some cases they list just the name of the school for the doubles teams.

1920s

1929—Charles Britzius & Walter Hargesheimer
Rochester

In the state's first MSHSL-sanctioned doubles tournament in 1929 just six doubles teams competed for the first-place prize, and all but two tandems participated in the singles draw as well: Cool and Watson of Minneapolis West, and Spurbeck and Brophy of Proctor. Both lost in the first round, but for Charles Britzius, a member of the winning team from Rochester (Walter Hargesheimer was his partner), the two-day tournament provided a daunting physical and mental challenge, as it would do for many top players entered in both singles and doubles until the MSHSL decreed in 1950 that players could participate in only one event. Britzius took second in the singles, winning two matches and losing a marathon four-setter in the finals; and coupled with two wins in the doubles he played 133 games, thirteen sets, and five matches in two days.

In the doubles final, Britzius and Hargesheimer took the gold medal, defeating C. Roslen and R. Campbell of White Bear Lake 6-3, 6-3, 6-4. As in singles in the early days of the State Tournament, the doubles final was a three-out-of-five-set match. The lads from Rochester only had to win one other match to get to the finals, that being a 6-3, 6-4 triumph over the Wilcox boys of Mountain Lake, Bob and his seventh-grade brother Paul (the 1934 singles champion).

Of the two champions, Britzius is the one we know the most about, for he became a Big 10 champion playing for the U of M Gophers, winning the No. 1 singles title in 1933 (his senior year) and the No. 1 doubles championship in '32 (with John Scherer). He also served as captain of the Gophers' tennis team in 1932 and '33 and led his team to Big Ten titles both those years. In addition, he was a 1933 and '34 National Public Parks men's doubles champion.

And he was for many years a top-ranked player in the then NWLTA Section as well. For example, in 1972 he was No. 4 in Men's 55 Singles, in '69 No. 1 in Senior Men's Doubles (with former U of M teammate Paul Scherer)

and in '77 No. 2 in Men's 60 Doubles (with partner Art Weiner) behind Lach Reed and Norm McDonald. A better doubles player than singles player, according to 1932 doubles runner-up Marv Hanenberger, Britzius earned rankings with many different partners, including Hall of Fame coach John Matlon of Edina. For his many contributions to Minnesota tennis and his outstanding accomplishments as a player, Britzius was elected into the Northern Section Hall of Fame.

A Lake Minnetonka area resident, he lived to be 92 and, according to an article titled "Section Mourns Loss of 5 Tennis Role Models," in *TennisLife* magazine, "He became a role model and mentor for many Section players, including sons Dale and Glenn who were college players" (April 2004). He earned bachelor's and master's degrees in civil engineering from the U of M and for many years owned a company called Twin City Testing and Engineering Laboratory that specialized in concrete and structural-steel inspections. But, according to his obituary in the *Star Tribune*, it also did metallurgy and soil testing, so Britzius "tested everything from vegetable oil to the soil under Southdale Shopping Center" (Trudi Hahn, January 15, 2004). During WWII his company "studied everything from Navy rope to rivets to gun-mount bearings" and "took samples to determine soil density for military bases at such sites as Grand Forks and Minot" (January 15, 2004).

Because soil testing became such a huge part of his business, Britzius organized a separate company in the 1950s called Soil Exploration Co. In 1985 he sold Twin City Testing, and Soil Exploration was closed, but Britzius remained with Twin City Testing until '94. A civic-minded individual, Britzius served on many professional boards and was mayor of Deephaven from 1964-68.

As for Hargesheimer, Britzius's partner in this 1929 final, he was a solid player with good strokes who joined Britzius to play tennis at the U of M.

1930s

1930—Robert & Richard Tudor
St. Paul Central

If you believe in horoscope readings, 1930 was a good year for the sign of Gemini, for it was twin brothers Robert and Richard Tudor of St. Paul Central who earned the hardware that year. Robert won the singles, then teamed with Richard to claim the doubles championship with a decisive 6-3, 6-0, 6-3 win over Robert Carlson and O. Venzke of Alexandria. Robert thus became the first Minnesota player to hold both the singles and doubles titles in the same year.

The Tudors needed to win only two other matches to advance to the finals, easily handling Matzke and Jeroniums of Duluth Central in their first match and Putnam and Aanes of Red Wing in the semis. The victory of the brothers Tudor was all the more remarkable because the tournament was just a one-day event, so Robert had to play six matches that day, including two three-of-five-set finals.

Theirs was also a noteworthy win because they were the only twin brothers to claim a doubles title. (The luckless McGregor twins of Duluth East finished as runners-up twice, in 1976 and '77.) (For more about Robert Tudor's singles win, see Chapter Five.)

Robert & Richard Tudor

1931—Bill Ward & Bob Andrews
Minneapolis West

In 1931 a pair from Minneapolis West, Bill Ward and Bob Andrews, won the doubles title, defeating singles champion Roy Huber and his partner Albin Anderson of St. Paul Central in a tough four-set match 6-2, 0-6, 6-3, 6-4.

Earlier on the final day Ward and Andrews defeated a team from Eveleth, then broke a good sweat in their next two matches. First they knocked off a team from Glenwood 6-2, 2-6, 6-1; then in the semis they took out the Wilcox brothers of Mountain Lake, Paul and Robert, 6-4, 6-3. It should be noted that more and more schools were now sending players to the tournament; so, for example, there were 12 doubles teams in the draw, up from 8 in 1930 and 6 the first year (1929).

1932—Gordon Sangsland & Peter Kehne
St. Paul Mechanic Arts

With a perfect draw of 32 in singles and 16 in doubles, the 1932 tournament marked a significant milestone in Minnesota tennis. Now a player or team that won a title truly earned it, for an individual had to win five matches in singles and a team had to win four in doubles. Emerging from this first 16-draw as doubles champions were Gordon Sangsland and Peter Kehne of St. Paul Mechanic Arts, winners of an epic 5-set final match over Marv Hanenberger and Fred Hargesheimer of Rochester 6-8, 6-3, 6-2, 1-6, 6-4. By the way, the doubles final was moved from the Northrop Field courts indoors to the U of M Field House at 2-all in the second set and finished there.

Hanenberger, the future "Mr. Tennis" of Rochester who served as both coach and player for his team, recalls his tournament play in these words: "I also was beaten in the semis in five sets. In those days all semis and finals were three-out-of-five-set matches. The tournament was held in two days, and I played around 125 games each day. I had the worst cramps ever in my tennis life."

In the first-round Sangsland and Kehne defeated a pair from Eveleth, received a free pass into the semis, with a default over a team from St. Paul Humboldt, then defeated a team from St. Paul Central.

1933—Carl Hovland & Howard Taylor
Minneapolis Central

As millions of Americans continued to tighten their belts in the midst of the Great Depression, the MSHSL did some belt tightening of its own, reducing all 1933 matches to the current best two-out-of-three sets. And though there were as yet no tie-breakers to shorten sets, there would be no more grueling five-set matches. In this first year with the new format, Carl Hovland became the second dual winner, taking home the singles title and winning the doubles with partner Howard Taylor. In the final match, held on the U of M Washington Avenue courts on Wednesday, June 6, the Minneapolis Central duo defeated Frank Kleckner (father of 1960 singles champion Frank Kleckner Jr.) and Jack McKecknie of Minneapolis West 7-5, 8-6.

The unfortunate McKechnie finished second in both the singles and doubles, and in both cases Hovland was on the other side of the net.

To reach the finals, Hovland and Taylor first upended Flickson and Ferris of Minneapolis Washburn and then Allen and Fuhrman of St. Paul Central. In the semis they defeated Thundstedt and Duncan of Willmar.

(For more about Hovland, see Chapter Five.)

1934—Arzy Kunz & Rodney Loft
Minneapolis Central

1934 was a good year for Arzy Kunz and his Minneapolis Central teammates; they won the first "still unrecognized" team championship; Kunz finished second to Paul Wilcox of Mountain Lake in singles and, with Rodney Loft, he won the doubles. In this first year that the tournament was extended to a three-day format, Kunz and Loft defeated Harry Johnson and Walter Nosek from the small northern town of Proctor in the finals 6-3, 6-3.

The Central pair drove through the field on cruise control, taking all four of their matches in straight sets. First, they thrashed Andrews and Rhodes of U High; then they defeated Fletcher and King of St. Paul Humboldt in the quarters. And in the semis they took care of 1935 singles champion Myron Lieberman and his partner Feinberg from St. Paul Central.

1935—Neil Kidwell & Lenny Johnson
Minneapolis Central

While St. Paul Central, which had won three of the four singles and doubles titles in 1930-31, returned to prominence in 1935 by claiming the second unofficial team title and the singles crown (Myron Lieberman), a team from Minneapolis Central captured the doubles title. Neil Kidwell and Lenny Johnson beat Stan Brain (son of U of M tennis coach Phil Brain) and Ken Sather of Minneapolis Roosevelt 6-4, 6-2 in the finals. They had advanced to the finals with straight-set wins over Lieberman and his partner Jack Marsh in the semis and over McGuigan and Stolpe of St. Paul Johnson in the quarters.

This was Central's third straight doubles title, and an article in the June 6, 1935, *St. Paul Pioneer Press* described the final match in these words: "Johnson and the vociferous Kidwell released a well-coordinated attack, punctuated with mutual pep talks, to clearly establish their rights to the doubles title." The article went on to say the Central pair handcuffed their opponents "with a stellar game at the net" (June 6, 1935).

1936—Neil Kidwell & Rodney Loft
Minneapolis Central

In one of those curious personal oddities of sport, in 1936 Neil Kidwell and Rodney Loft of Minneapolis Central became (simultaneously) the first Minnesota two-time doubles champions, each having paired with different partners in winning their first title (Loft with Arzy Kunz in '34 and Kidwell with Lenny Johnson in '35). And once again Stan Brain and Ken Sather of Minneapolis Roosevelt were the victims, losing 6-2, 6-4. Brain was surely the first and maybe the unluckiest always-a-bridesmaid-never-a-bride competitor in state tennis history, for he not only finished second in doubles in 1935 and '36, but he was also the runner-up in singles both those years. He could, I suppose, take comfort in knowing that his runner-up finishes helped Roosevelt tie for the team title in '36 with 7 points.

Except for the final match with Brain and Sather, Kidwell and Loft encountered little resistance, defeating their first two opponents (duos from St. Paul Johnson and

St. Paul Humboldt) in straight sets. No score was given for their semifinal win over Minneapolis Central.

1937–Ed Von Sien & Christie Geanakoplos
Minneapolis Central

This year marked the arrival on the scene of a player who would become the first three-time state champion, sophomore Christie Geanakoplos of Minneapolis Central. He and senior Ed Von Sien won the doubles, helping Central earn its second team title. The Central pair advanced to the semis with a straight-set win over Haugen and Tvedt of St. Paul Mechanic Arts; waltzed over a pair from Minneapolis Roosevelt, R. Brain (brother of Stan Brain) and Skrivseth in the semis; then outlasted Duane Hanenberger (Marv's brother) and Clarence Higbie of Rochester 6-1, 5-7, 6-4 in the finals.

Ed Von Sien (Right) & Christie Geanakoplos

Geanakoplos said of his partner, Von Sien, "He was extremely accurate and made few errors. He didn't go up to the net at all, but if you left a corner open he would hit it." Von Sien, like his partner, went on to play college tennis at the U of M, serving as captain of the Gophers in 1940 and '41. He is also a member of the USTA/Northern Section Hall of Fame.

Remarkably, this was the fifth year in a row that a team from Central claimed the doubles crown, a record that still stands today. In addition, except for Loft and Kidwell, who won two titles, eight different players shared in this glory. (For a profile on Geanakoplos, see Chapter Five.)

1938–Jim Hickey & Ed Struble
Minneapolis Washburn

In 1938 a team from Minneapolis Washburn ended Central's unprecedented five-year run. With Jim Hickey and Ed Struble claiming the title this year, Washburn also won the team title. Their opponents in the final match were sophomore Don Gunner (who would go on to win both the singles and doubles titles in 1940) and John Adams of Minneapolis West. The score was 6-3, 6-4.

And though their first match over Richard Thielen and Bob Dahl of Mankato was a breeze, their next two encounters tested their mettle. In both the quarters and semis they had to go three sets to win: 7-5, 5-7, 6-4 over Gangelhoff and Nelson of Minneapolis Central and 10-8, 4-6, 6-0 over Johnson and Caliguiri of Hibbing.

1939–Christie Geanakoplos & Wally Anderson
Minneapolis Central

After dispatching little Joe Armstrong Jr. in the 1939 singles tournament, Christie Geanakoplos and new partner Wally Anderson brought glory back to Minneapolis Central, capturing the school's sixth doubles title in seven years and helping it win the team championship. The final was a hard-fought three-setter against Bill McKerney and Tom Daniel of Minneapolis West (4-6, 6-3, 6-3), a match won by the well-paired team of the five-foot-nine-inch Geanakoplos and Anderson. Geanakoplos described Anderson as "a six-foot-three-inch power player who would crowd the net. Though slightly erratic, he hit very hard and put points away. We complemented each other well because I was fast and consistent." Both were seniors and would go on to play together at the U of M.

Theirs was an easy route to the finals, for they only needed to win two matches and these they took in straight sets, the first over John Culligan and L. Johnson of Hibbing and the second over Bob Dahl and Richard Thielen of Mankato in the semis.

1940s

It is not an exaggeration to say that the early years of high school tennis in Minnesota were thoroughly dominated by Minneapolis and St. Paul schools. Until 1950, when Rochester won the first of its nine championships, city schools won all but two of the first sixteen unofficial team championships. In addition, Metro players dominated singles and doubles play, winning all ten singles championships in the decade of the '40s and nine of the ten doubles championships. Only a doubles team from Duluth Central was able to break the stranglehold that Minneapolis and St. Paul players had on state tennis, and then only in 1949, the last year of the decade.

1940—Don Gunner & Fred Gulden
Minneapolis West

As the pre-tournament singles favorite in 1940, Don Gunner from Minneapolis West had a target on his back all year. However, this "Gunner" dodged all bullets and hit two bullseyes in this first year of the new decade. Gunner outshot teammate Fred Gulden in the singles final, then teamed with Gulden to vanquish outstaters Larry Johnson and John Caliguiri of Hibbing in the finals 6-0, 6-1. Their exploits also earned a team title for West.

No score is given for their first-round win over Krawetz and Mark of St. Paul Central but they won their final three matches in a commanding fashion, giving up a total of just two games. Gunner and Gulden blitzed through the Zalk brothers of Duluth Central; Fuller and Houdek of Minneapolis South in the semis; and Caliguiri and Johnson. Because we don't have a score from that first match, we may have to put an asterisk beside their names, but no doubles champions in Minnesota history gave up only two games in winning a title. (For more on Gunner's singles triumph, see Chapter Five.)

1941—Joe Armstrong Jr. & Harry Moreland
St. Paul Central

In 1941 it was St. Paul Central, led by little Joe Armstrong Jr., which took home the prizes in both the team and individual competition. Armstrong (son of Joe Armstrong Sr., a former Interscholastic champion and top adult player from St. Paul) had earlier bested future champion Ken Boyum of Minneapolis West in the singles final, then teamed with Harry Moreland in doubles to hand sophomore Boyum just his second loss of the year. Boyum and his partner Bud Weigant won the first set 6-0, but Armstrong and Moreland stormed back to win the next two sets, and the match, 6-4, 6-1.

For Armstrong (a senior) the tournament had been something of an endurance test, for he had to win six matches to claim the singles title and he and Moreland had to come back from first-set losses in three of their four doubles matches. In the first round they rallied to defeat a Minneapolis Central pair 3-6, 6-3, 6-2 and the next round was almost a carbon copy of their first match, a 3-6, 6-3, 6-4 win over a team from Minneapolis Washburn. Their semifinal win over a Hibbing team in the semis was a breather (6-2, 6-1) before their three-set triumph over Boyum and Weigant in the finals. All told, Armstrong played ten matches and an astonishing 194 games in the tournament, a state record which will never be equaled because players can now only play singles or doubles and tie breakers are used. (For more on Armstrong, see Chapter Five.)

1942-43—Ken Boyum & Harold Wollin
Minneapolis West

Continuing the domination of city schools, Minneapolis West, with its No. 1 cowboy Ken Boyum leading the way, won team and individual honors the next two years. In fact, Boyum so mastered the competition that he won both the singles and doubles titles in 1942 and '43, the only player ever to do so. His sidekick in both years was Harold Wollin, and together they hogtied the team of Earl Rice and Harold Wexler from Minneapolis South in the '42 finals (6-4, 6-3).

Earlier, after receiving a first round bye, Boyum and Wollin trounced Feldman and Hastings (no school listed), then took out Olson and Molander of St. Paul Johnson in the semis.

And even though there were some very strong players in the 1943 draw ('44 singles champion John Dunnigan of Minneapolis Washburn and '46 doubles champion Jack Thommen of Minneapolis Southwest, for example), Boyum and Wallin corralled all three of their opponents in straight sets. First they double-bageled Silverstein and Culp of Minneaplis North; then they took out Thommen (just a freshman) and Hastings of Southwest; and in the finals they bucked off Dunnigan and his partner, Burgeson, 6-3, 6-2. One oddity of their run through the draw is that all of their opponents were familiar faces from Minneapolis schools.

West's team championship was also its third in four years, and with 13 points it won nearly as many individual points as it was possible for a team to earn.

(For more on Boyum, see Chapter Four.)

1944—Jack Clements & John Dunnigan
Minneapolis Washburn

Once again one team, this time Minneapolis Washburn, took home the first-place hardware in the individual competition in 1944. Senior John Dunnigan won the singles, and he teamed with Jack Clements to take the doubles title, beating Frank Bruce and LeRoy Nyhus of Minneapolis Central 6-3, 6-1 in the finals.

This was clearly Dunnigan's year, for he stormed through the singles and doubles fields without losing a set. Before thumping Bruce and Nyhus in the doubles final, he and Clements did not give up a game to Sheldon and Goldstein of St. Paul Marshall. Next they took out Clyde Bedahl and Tom Benson of Cloquet; then in the semis they defeated Jim Larsen and Jim Rush of Minneapolis West.

On a side note, because of transportation problems resulting from belt-tightening during WWII, Washburn played just a few matches, and those only with schools in their neighborhood: Roosevelt, Central, West, and Southwest. Matches in those days were played at public parks

such as Kenwood, Folwell, Pershing, Hiawatha, and Lynnhurst—Washburn's "home" court.

(For more on Dunnigan, see Chapter Five.)

1945—Ken Calhoun & Lenny Ferm
Minneapolis West

In 1945, though Washburn once again won the team title and the singles championship (Brad Pitney), the combo of Ken Calhoun and Lenny Ferm of Minneapolis West came out of the pack to claim the doubles title. They defeated Bill Kuross and Bob Haiker of Minneapolis Central 6-3, 6—0.

Ken Calhoun (Left) & Lenny Ferm

Calhoun and Ferm opened the tournament with a straight-set win over Phil Meziasky and Munroe Tapper of Minneapolis North, then upended Jack Thommen and Edmund Gould of Minneapolis Southwest. Their semifinal match was a tough 6-4, 3-6, 6-4 win over Dwight Hall and Kermit Johnson of Minneapolis Washburn. As in the 1944 tournament, their four wins were earned solely against players from the city of Minneapolis.

1946—Jack Thommen & Edmund "Chiefie" Gould
Minneapolis Southwest

The first two post-war years featured two aforementioned players who became important figures in the Minnesota tennis world, Jack Thommen and Bill Kuross. Thommen, the 1946 doubles champion and 1945 singles runner-up, was one of the top junior players in the Upper Midwest and later a central figure in the development of inner city tennis programs for youth in the Twin Cities. (See Chapter Eight.)

Much like other youngsters of his era, Thommen got his start in tennis when his parents bought him two Wilson Jack Kramer rackets and told him to go play. And, like past champions such as Ken Boyum, he spent many hours watching the big boys play at public parks near his home. An all-around athlete who also played basketball and ran track and cross country for legendary Southwest coach Al Halley, Thommen remembers a lesson his father taught him about controlling one's emotions in competition. "After a loss in a junior match in 1940, I was so upset I threw one of my rackets in Minnehaha Creek. My dad gave me a dressing down and locked my other racket up until April."

After he learned this lesson, in one of those serendipitous events some are privileged to be a part of, Jack received lessons from the great tennis pro and tennis hustler Bobby Riggs. Thommen's junior doubles partner Scott Donaldson's father flew Riggs in for lessons with his son and Thommen tagged along four times. In addition, Thommen took lessons in the summer from a pro at Minikahda three days a week and later from Paul Scherer, a former U of M tennis standout.

All of this training finally paid off in 1946 when he and Edmund Gould became the first players from Southwest to win a state tennis title. Known for his booming serve and hard groundstrokes, Thommen was the pre-tournament singles favorite entering state competition. He had defeated eventual champion Esser Shragowitz from Minneapolis North during the season, but Shragowitz upended him in the semis 6-3, 6-4, opening the door for Gould, who took second. But the strong play of Gould and Thommen in both singles and doubles helped Southwest take home the team title as well.

Gould and Thommen were deserving champions, for they swept through the draw without losing a set. With a first-round default from Porter and Fredrickson of Stillwater, they advanced to the semis with a victory over Bjerken and Peterson of Minneapolis Roosevelt. Their semifinal match was an easy win over Nelson and Morris of Albert Lea; then in the finals they defeated the 1947 champions, Kuross and Dick Roberts of Minneapolis Central 6-2, 6-2.

Though he did not win a singles title, Thommen was a formidable player who defeated many top juniors both in Minnesota and on the national scene. For example, in high school and college he defeated Kuross every time he played him, though Kuross would give him a drubbing when they were adults after Kuross returned from playing in the navy in the late 1950s. The self-effacing Thommen, who played tennis (1) in the service from 1946-48, (2) for Gustavus, and (3) for the U of M, recalls that he wasn't even the best player at Southwest. "A classmate of mine named Jim Holker, the most natural athlete I ever met, beat me every time I played him, including one day when he was dressed in street clothes. He humiliated me in front of my U of M teammates 6-2, 6-2. At the time he was playing baseball for Coach Dick Siebert."

As a junior in high school Thommen advanced as far as the third round in a national tournament in 1946 and at Gustavus he won the '49 singles title over Bucky Olson of St. Thomas. An article in the *Minnesota Daily* by Doug Pearson, titled "Minnesota's Comeback Kid," described Thommen's penchant for losing first sets and then recovering to win matches: "His sizzling backhand smashes and cannonball serves have worn down countless opponents into ultimate three-set defeats... The only 12-letterman ever to graduate from Southwest, versatile Thommen won four letters in tennis, three each in track and cross country, and two in basketball" (May 7, 1951). A member of the Gustavus Athletic Hall of Fame (for tennis), Jack was also given the USTA/Northern Section President's Award in 1975 for his contributions to the development of inner city junior tennis and the Section's Community Service Award in '80. And for his lifetime service to tennis in Minnesota and his playing skills (as an adult player he was often ranked), Thommen was inducted into the Northern Section Hall of Fame in 2007.

1947—Bill Kuross & Dick Roberts
Minneapolis Central

The second of these post WWII state doubles titlists highlighted here, 1947 champion Bill Kuross also began his tennis career on the public courts of Minneapolis, first at Powderhorn Park (where, he said, "Norm McDonald gave us balls") and then on the clay courts at the Minneapolis Tennis Club, site of the annual Interscholastic Tournament in June. Kuross said that all his neighborhood friends, including Dick Roberts, Frank Bruce, Bill South, Bob and D. J. Olson, and the legendary Norm McDonald, played at Powderhorn during and after the war. During the war, Kuross recalls, "We had paper routes, so we'd pedal our routes in the morning, then play tennis until our afternoon routes, deliver our papers, come back, then play until dark. The big thing during the war was getting tennis balls—they were all reconditioned balls which we played with until they were rubber." But for Kuross the "highlight was to go down and play in the MN Clay Court Tournament at the Minneapolis Tennis Club." Eventually, in 1949, the tennis house at the Parade Grounds was moved to Nicollet, and the courts there became a magnet for all aspiring young Minnesota tennis players. Kuross remembers playing matches there against the likes of Thommen and Gould, whom he called the best public high school players he competed against ("These guys were too steady"); top private school players like Harry Adams and Henry Norton from Blake (the latter Kuross called the best junior player in the state); and later against adult players such as Ken Boyum, Howie Atwater, Ed Von Sien, and McDonald. Kuross was also an all-around athlete who played football and hockey in high school and college.

So in 1947, instead of "three strikes and you're out," the third time at the State Tournament was a charm for Kuross and his two-time partner Dick Roberts, who came

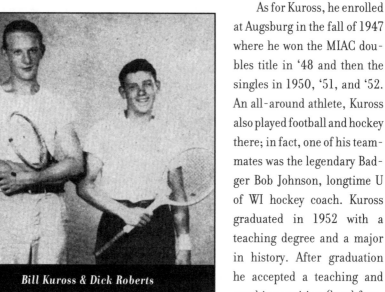

Bill Kuross & Dick Roberts

through with a 6-0, 7-5 victory over the outstate team of Dwayne Lidke and Welchlin of Fairmont in the finals. The Central lads needed only two wins to advance to the finals, taking both in straight sets. First they knocked out Don Mulligan and Bill May of St. Paul Central; then they manhandled Arndt and Modisette of Detroit Lakes in the semis 6-0, 6-1.

We don't know as much about Roberts, but Kuross called him "a real fine tennis player who joined the navy after high school. He was also a great football player, an elusive and fast halfback."

As for Kuross, he enrolled at Augsburg in the fall of 1947 where he won the MIAC doubles title in '48 and then the singles in 1950, '51, and '52. An all-around athlete, Kuross also played football and hockey there; in fact, one of his teammates was the legendary Badger Bob Johnson, longtime U of WI hockey coach. Kuross graduated in 1952 with a teaching degree and a major in history. After graduation he accepted a teaching and coaching position (head football) at Slayton, but he stayed for just one year before taking a job at Ramsey Junior High in '53. Drafted into the navy, he would serve from 1954-56; and it was during these years that his tennis career blossomed. These must have been heady times for a young man from the frozen north country, for during these two years he earned All-Navy in tennis and crossed paths (and rackets) with some of the great American tennis players of the '50s.

For example, he played in the 1956 U.S. Open, beating John Leach from Southern California in the first round, then losing to one of the great characters in U.S. tennis history, the talented but goofy Art "Tappy" Larsen 6-4, 7-5, 17-15 in the third round (Larsen then lost to Ken Rosewall in the next round). In addition, he earned two silver balls for runner-up finishes in national 45 senior tournaments, one in 1955 in Pittsburgh and one, much later, in a match in Philadelphia when he and his partner Charlie Oliver lost to Bobby Riggs (the same Bobby Riggs who had given lessons to Jack Thommen) and Riggs' partner Dick Sorlien.

And in 1956, in the week between tournaments featuring the top four players from each of the service branches, Kuross played in the national Public Parks Tournament, losing to his friend Ken Boyum in the quarters and finishing second in the doubles to a nationally ranked team which included a top ten U.S. player named Gene Bassett.

In addition, Kuross had the privilege of practicing with the great Vic Seixas, at the time ranked third in the U.S. and fourth in the world. Here is how he describes this serendipitous connection: "I practiced with Vic Seixas at the Marion Cricket Club in Philadelphia—on grass... He wanted me to practice with him because I could get off early before dark." One time, when he and Seixas were relaxing and watching some older men enjoying a game on the clay courts at the Cynwyd Club in Philadelphia, Seixas said, "I wish I could enjoy tennis again." No doubt Seixas was feeling the pressure of playing top-level competitive tennis. Shortly thereafter he took up the game of squash and introduced it to Kuross, who became an accomplished player himself, winning the state squash championship ten years in a row during the 1960s.

Returning to Minneapolis after his stint in the navy, Kuross took a job in the fall of 1957 as a jack-of-all-trades teacher at Washburn (economics, business law and government, American history, health, and physical education), where he also served as the head football coach for three years. After nine years he left teaching for a job with a company called Advance Machine, and in '86 he bought Savoie Supply Company.

For his exploits on the courts, his service to the NWTA, and for his efforts on behalf of tennis in Minnesota (he also coached boys' tennis at Minneapolis West for two years and girls' tennis at Washburn for one year and served as the summer head teaching pro at Minikahda from 1957-66), Kuross was given the Northern Section President's Award in '73. In addition, he is a member of the Northern Section Hall of Fame, elected in '79.

While at Minikahda, he organized and directed the

enormously successful Minikahda Invitational Tournament which featured six touring male pro players (even Andre Agassi one year) and two top local players who earned spots in the draw by winning a feed-in tournament. Kuross directed the tournament for many years, worked with new director Dick Martinson for a time, then continued to assist for many years thereafter. Three-time state singles champion Chuck Darley said of Kuross' efforts to bring top players to Minnesota, "He ran a terrific tournament."

And while Kuross called Ken Boyum and Wendell Ottum the two best players of his era, he certainly ranks near the top of male Section players of his time. His former nemesis, Jack Thommen, would agree, for he recalls playing Kuross after he (Kuross) returned from the navy: "I played the best tennis of my life and he beat me 1 and 1." And though he did not play Section tournaments until he was 35 (in 1966) because he was considered a professional, once he began competing he excelled. For instance, he was ranked No. 1 in Junior Veterans Singles in 1970 and No. 1 in 45-and-over singles in '77. And he and Ottum were ranked No. 2 in 35-and-over doubles on at least three occasions. Well-known local teaching pro John Mueller also praised Kuross, saying, "His hand-eye coordination was incredible and he had great strokes."

1948—Edmund "Chiefie" Gould & William Moses
Minneapolis Southwest

The decade of the 1940s would end with teams from Minneapolis Southwest and Duluth Central capturing titles. Thommen's teammate from 1946, senior Edmund "Chiefie" Gould, teamed with William Moses to defeat James Lillo and James Stenerson of Moorhead in the '48 final 6-0, 6-3, 6-1. Gould and Moses had breezed into the finals on the strength of straight-set wins over Emme and Welchlin of Fairmont and Gronum and Furuseth of Thief River Falls.

Gould also won the singles title in this second (and last) fall tournament, leading Southwest to its second unofficial team championship in three years. As mentioned in the chapter titled "One-Time Singles Champions," this was also the last year for three-out-of-five-set matches. (For more on Gould, see Chapter Five.)

1949—John Nutting & Bruce Dikson
Duluth Central

In 1949 the MSHSL began to legitimize team competition by awarding a team trophy, this first one to Duluth Central, whose nine points was one more than Minneapolis North. This title was won on the strength of three doubles wins (each now worth three points) by the championship duo of John Nutting and Bruce Dikson. As in 1947, a team from Fairmont finished second. One member of that Fairmont team was the unlucky Dwayne Lidke (paired with Welchlin), who lost in the '47 final and was paired this year with Donald Jaqua. The score was a decisive 6-3, 6-1.

In their other matches Nutting and Dikson came from behind to defeat Wendell Ottum (later one of the greatest adult players in Minnesota history) and Ralph Price of Minneapolis Roosevelt 5-7, 6-0, 6-1 and Lester Fiegel and Bob Reid of Rochester in the semis.

This win by Nutting and Dikson was the first doubles title for a northern Minnesota pair and the first non-Metro doubles championship since Rochester's Britzius and Hargesheimer won the inaugural state title. Moreover, in the twenty-one years of state high school competition since that 1929 tournament, only two other singles players not from Minneapolis or St. Paul took home a first-place trophy, those being 1934 champion Paul Wilcox of Mountain Lake and 1938 champion Henry Nosek of Proctor.

1950s

While the 1950s marked the coming-out party for powerhouse teams and players from Rochester, a Cinderella team from St. James claimed a team and doubles title; and two future influential figures on the state tennis scene, Jack Roach and John Desmond, burst onto the tennis stage.

1950-51—Ron Trondson & Henry Dison
Rochester

In the history of doubles competition in Minnesota, multiple titles by the same pair are almost as rare as snow in Los Angeles. Often one of the partners graduates or chooses to play singles the next year, one player transfers to another school, or the duo loses before reaching the finals. Despite these obvious roadblocks, the team of Ron Trondson and Henry Dison became just the second tandem to win two doubles titles (the first being Ken Boyum and Harold Wollin of Minneapolis West). They were a formidable pair whom Marv Hanenberger called "by far the best Rochester doubles team. They played well together and knew what moves to make at the net."

As juniors in 1950 they opened the State Tournament with a bye, then beat John Dunlap and Chuck Van Lenen of Mankato. In the finals they defeated a team from Minneapolis Central, Dick Pearson and Bill Hardie, thus completing an undefeated season. Dison, who became a successful some-time tennis pro at Rochester and full-time teacher and coach at Lake City, recalls the final match his junior year: "These guys [Pearson and Hardie] stayed on the baseline and lobbed us and won the first set 8-6, so we decided to bring them to the net. We then beat them 2 and 1."

(Left to right) Donald Ranthum, Henry Dison, Ron Trandson, and Robert Reid

As seniors in 1951 they struggled against Larry Covin and Jack Fithian of Minneapolis North before winning an epic three-set final (6-8, 6-4, 6-3), helping Rochester win its second team crown in a row. Their other two matches were not so taxing. First they took care of Ed Rice and Brad Hanson of Mankato; then they rolled over Tom Lindblad and Dick Hanson of St. Paul Johnson in the semis.

So in two years of doubles play together—during the season and in tournaments—this dynamic duo lost just one match (to a Faribault Shattuck pair in 1951).

Trondson, the father of successful top state junior players named Tom, John, and Ann, followed Dison to Lake City where he taught for three years before becoming a State Farm agent in the Metro area. Trondson is deceased, but Dison continues his active life in tennis. (For more on Dison, see Chapter Two.)

1952–Tom LaMott & Greg Heimark
Minneapolis Southwest
In 1952 the doubles title went to the tandem of Tom LaMott and Greg Heimark of Minneapolis Southwest, whose three victories gave the Indians all the points they needed (9) to win the team championship over Minneapolis Washburn. In the finals they overcame the same Brad Hanson and Ed

Rice of Mankato who had lost to Dison and Trondson in '51—with a score of 7-5, 6-1.

The lads from Southwest struggled in their first match, a 6-3, 5-7, 7-5 win over Ronald Gover and Dennis Robertson of South St. Paul, but they cruised into the finals with a 6-2, 6-2 semifinal triumph over Robert Schoonover and George Tsatsoes (or Tsatsos) of Winona.

1953–Jack Roach & Mike Dunn
Minneapolis Central
The 1953 final showcased the talent of a young man from Minneapolis Central who has been a fixture on the state tennis landscape for over fifty years, Jack Roach. A future member of the Northern Section Tennis Hall of Fame, Roach grew up on the same Powderhorn Park courts that had nurtured earlier standouts such as Kuross, Norm McDonald, and Howard Atwater (all of whom also became members of the Hall of Fame). Roach remembers watching a Powderhorn Park team led by McDonald play Sunday matches at Powderhorn against competitors from cities such as Duluth, Rochester, and St. Cloud. "Kids would ride their bikes to come and watch them play," said Roach. "After the matches the players gave us balls and at the end of the season they gave us rackets. We used these old balls and rackets, and eventually I entered my first

Greg Heimark (Left) and Tom LaMott

Mike Dunn (Left) and Jack Roach

tournament at Nicollet Tennis Center—the Aquatennial. This was my earliest and most thrilling memory because I was able to win my first trophy in the first tournament I ever played in," Roach stated. At the time Jack was 14 and he took second place.

Soon, as he became a more accomplished player, he began to hang around the place to be if you were a tennis player, the twelve courts at Nicollet Tennis Center. He rode his bike down to Nicollet from his home near 34th and Chicago, took his lunch, and stayed all day, playing with the ten or twelve kids who also showed up there and/or with the older men who, in Jack's words, "beat up on us but helped us learn." He credits McDonald, who often played with him and gave him the Wilson Tony Trabert rackets he always used, and a dentist named Doc Roberts, as major influences on his growth as a tennis player. Of Roberts he said, "He took juniors and helped them by playing against them and by giving them balls and rackets." Sometimes Roach would also hit on the wall at Nicollet for hours, waiting for someone to come by and offer to play with him.

Then, in what would be unthinkable today, he hitchhiked to Rochester to play in summer tournaments. Once he even rode to Sioux Falls with Ottum, Bernie Gunderson, and Pudge Whitcomb to play in a 16-and-under event. Roach said that he began playing tournaments in part because his high school coach, Whitey Thoreson (known more as the Central basketball coach), encouraged his players to play in the summer. And, said Roach, "He also made every kid join the Nicollet Tennis Center. He got us a deal there and I think it cost us about $10 or $15."

All this effort eventually earned Roach a No. 2 ranking in boys' 18 singles and a state doubles title in 1953. Jack explained that he decided to play doubles again that year (he and partner Jerry Rudquist, well-known artist and art teacher at Macalester, had lost in the district finals in '52), in part because he had lost to '52 champion Charlie Edwards of Washburn during the year. "He beat me as a junior and senior in conference play—my only losses at No. 1 singles." This prudent decision resulted in a well-earned doubles title for Roach and his new partner Mike Dunn.

Well earned indeed, for what started as a picnic in the park on a sunny day for seniors Roach and Dunn (a first-round bye and a 6-2, 6-2 win over Truman Porter and Bog Shapiro of St. Paul Central) soon became an outing plagued by storms—in the form of two worthy opponents. In the semis the Central boys had to rally from a set down to overcome brothers Robert and John Hatten of Duluth East (5-7, 6-4, 6-2), then in the finals they again had to go three sets against formidable opponents from Rochester, Roger Jackman—a doubles champion in 1955—and Larry Parker, defeating them 6-2, 4-6, 6-0.

After graduation from high school he enrolled at Macalester, then a Division 2 school which gave athletic scholarships, where he had an outstanding career. He played No. 1 singles for three years, winning one MIAC singles title (as a junior) and finishing second two other times. Roach's partner from Central, Mike Dunn, competed at St. Thomas, and Roach remembers defeating him in college. About Dunn, Roach said, "He was an accomplished, ranked player and we played a number of tournaments together in the summer."

When Roach graduated from Macalester, he coached high school tennis at three schools: Minneapolis Edison for four years, Kellogg for nine years, and Aitkin for one season. At Kellogg he taught social studies and physical education and also coached basketball. About his job at Edison he said, "We didn't have many good players, so we took spring break to schedule two matches a day. We took our lunches along and played twelve matches in six days. My first year we won only one match, the next year we won six, and the third year (1962) we won ten and took the City championship. We did this every year and that's how we got better."

Roach was then offered tennis teaching jobs: first at Southdale as an indoor pro and at the Wayzata Country Club in the summer. And when Harvey Ratner opened the Northwest Clubs, Roach was the first head pro hired. He was in charge of all the clubs but spent a good deal of time at the first one which was located at 494 and Penn Avenue, Richfield.

For twenty years he worked for the Northwest clubs, then for four years he served as the women's coach at the U of M before returning to his work as a teaching pro. In addition, in the summer he often served as the head pro at the Minikahda Country Club. One year he helped supervise the Pan-Am Games trials at Minikahda—Arthur Ashe played there when he was the No. 1 player in the world. Now the head pro at the Interlachen Country Club in the summer, he still teaches a bit in the winter at the 98th Street and Normandale Clubs.

Because he was a teaching pro, Roach, like Kuross, could not compete in Section tournaments until this ban was lifted. But when he began playing, he was very successful, earning No. 1 rankings in the Pro Division in 1968, Junior Veterans Singles in '71, and the 35s in '73. He also held two No. 5 rankings in Men's Open Singles when he was well over 30 years old (1968, '70) and several No. 1 rankings in doubles in the Open Mens' division with his partner Jerry Noyce in the early '70s. (For more on Roach, see Chapter Eight.)

1954—Dave Anderson & Gerald Kintzi
St. James

In 1954 a Minnesota "Hoosiers" story unfolded at the state tennis tournament, for that year a doubles team from the small town of St. James, seniors Dave Anderson and Gerald Kintzi, captured the doubles title. And with help from Dave's brother Mark, the Saints also won a team championship over heavily favored Rochester. A profile of this team and players appears in the chapter called "Dark Horse Teams," but it is certainly appropriate to say a few words here about the doubles championship won by Kintzi and Anderson.

Kintzi had played No. 1 singles from ninth to eleventh grade; but because he injured his knee in basketball his senior year he played No. 1 doubles during the season, then teamed with Anderson for tournament play, figuring this was their best chance to do well at State. After waltzing through district and Region 2 competitors, the pair swept all three state matches in straight sets. In the first round they beat Merle and Bob Speed of Brainerd, then defeated Karl Honigman and John Hatten of Duluth East in the semis. Their final match was tighter, but it was still a straight-set win over Bob Bates and Daryl Hagman of Minneapolis Patrick Henry (6-4, 6-4).

1955—Roger Jackman & Roger Riege
Rochester

Still smarting from the previous year's losses in both the team and doubles competition, Rochester restored order in the Minnesota tennis house in 1955 by taking home all three titles. Dave Healey won his third straight singles title, the team claimed its fourth title in six years, and the doubles pair of seniors Roger Jackman and Roger Riege won three matches to earn the doubles medals.

In the finals they dispatched the team of Stan Palmer and Bob Adolphson of St. Peter, 6-0, 6-2; but they were sorely tested in their first two matches. For example, in round one they defeated Don Hendrickson (a future top-ranked NWLTA adult player) and Ray Radasorich of Minneapolis Roosevelt 6-3, 7-5. Next up was the team of Karl Honigman and John Hatten of Duluth East, semifinal losers in 1954, and they made life uncomfortable for Jackman and Riege before falling 3-6, 6-3, 6-0.

Former Rochester doubles champion Henry Dison praised the 1955 champs, saying, "Jackman was a good athlete who was quick. He also had good concentration; he was a non-quitter. And all of Riege's strokes were good."

Riege's brother Bob became the coach at Rochester Mayo in the early 1970s, and Jackman went on to play college tennis at the U of M.

1956—Chuck Baker & Dave Love
Rochester

Though Rochester did not win the singles in 1956, it still won the team title, edging Minneapolis Central and Duluth by one point. This title was earned solely by the doubles team of Chuck Baker and Dave Love, for their three victories brought Rochester the 9th point needed to stave off the two runner-ups teams. They easily overcame Alan Hoag and Larry Enger of Minneapolis Washburn 6-3, 6-1 in the finals.

But as in the previous year, the winning pair survived a more difficult semifinal match, having to overcome a first-set loss. After losing this first set, however, Baker and Love demolished Charles DeWett and Ralph Olson of St. Paul Central, surrendering not even one more game and winning 4-6, 6-0, 6-0. In a sense this was a double bagel, the same score of their first round match against Bill Goetzman and Jerome Brust of Olivia; but that was a two-set 6-0, 6-0 score.

Love was a senior, but Baker—a junior—came back in 1957 with a different partner (Dick Ostrom) to take second in the doubles tourney.

1957—Dan Olson & Don Larson
Minneapolis Central

Not only did a Minneapolis Central team dethrone Rochester in 1957, but a duo from Central also upended '56 champion Chuck Baker and his Rochester partner Dick Ostrom to win the doubles title. Dan Olson and Don Larson took that match in a close three setter, 6-4, 3-6, 6-4.

After an easy straight-set win over Jerome Brust and Boyd Goetzman of Olivia in the first round, the Central pair had a tussle against Dick Faser and John Heur of St. Paul Monroe in the semis, winning 8-6, 6-4.

We don't know much about the Central pair, though Olson went on to play tennis at the U of M with three-time singles champion Dave Healey. In 1961 he served as captain of the Gophers' Big Ten squad.

1958—John Desmond & Don Cooper
Minneapolis Marshall

"Local Lads Win State." That could very well have been a sports news headline in 1958, for this year a Minneapolis Marshall team, John Desmond and Don Cooper (whose school was located just six blocks from the site of the State Tournament at the U of M courts), won the doubles and the team championship for their school. We know more about Desmond, for he became one of the most popular and successful Metro-area teaching pros and adult tournament players, but in fact Cooper was the No. 1 player for Marshall that year. Desmond, who had played baseball in the spring, didn't start playing tennis until his ninth-grade year, and then only because the tennis coach (George Patten) coaxed him into coming out. Patten told him, "You're not going to make the baseball team, so why don't you come out for tennis?" Though he had no

previous experience in tennis, Desmond made the varsity his freshman year, playing No. 2 doubles, then moved up to No. 1 doubles as a sophomore and No. 2 singles as a junior and senior. Desmond also ran cross country in the fall and played basketball in the winter, which he credits for keeping him in shape for tennis.

He has wonderful memories of his senior year, including playing with a $10 racket in Bermuda shorts and basketball shoes and helping his team embarrass mighty Edina 4-1. He also recalls (1) playing an early season match while wearing gloves, (2) taking their own nets to matches on the two courts at Tower Hill or the three at Prospect Park, and (3) playing with only one racket. About the latter experience, Desmond said, "Every guy had only one racket. If you broke a string, you had to play with it." Desmond commented that one of his teammates, Bruce Maxwell, played all four years with the same racket and same strings.

He also recalls this advice given to the team by his then coach Patten: "Keep the ball in play and run like hell." (Sounds like the advice given by a more famous Patton during WWII.) In this modern day of organized coaching, with some top players even flying off before the State Tournament to tune up their games with pros in South Carolina or Florida, it would be impossible for players to compete and win without a coach. But that's what Desmond and Cooper did. When the last ball was struck in their fourth and final win, a 6-0, 3-6, 6-3 win over Tom Kotsonas (a future Minnetonka assistant boys' and head girls' coach) and Ron Miller of Minneapolis Central, their coach, Joe Arnold, was nowhere to be seen. Desmond recalls that "Coach Arnold, also the Marshall football coach, never came to practice or even to the State Tournament. We were on our own."

Perhaps Desmond and Cooper could have used some coaching help in their three-set final, but not so in their first three rather uneventful straight-set wins. First they dispatched John Fitzpatrick and Ben Pulkralek of Brainerd; then in the quarters they took out Bill Hickock and Dick Haight of South St. Paul. Their semifinal match against Leroy Lidstrom and Harold Dirksen of Rochester was a bit more of a challenge for them, but the Marshall duo still triumphed 6-2, 7-5.

Despite the lack of coaching, he and Cooper were unbeaten in 20 matches that spring, including all 4 matches at State, matches that earned them—and their team—the 12 points needed to stave off second place St. Paul Monroe (11 points) for the team title.

Other "prominent" Minnesotans in the draw in 1958 were Harold Levander Jr. of South St. Paul (Governor Levander's son), Gary Peterson of Minnetonka (third-place singles finisher and future coach of the Wheatons), and Bryan Stamp of Minnetonka ('59 singles runner-up).

After graduation Desmond began to devote more time to tennis, playing eight hours a day at Nicollet Park and the University courts that summer and fall. Desmond said, "I watched people play and felt I could do it." He enrolled at the U of M to play first for coach Chet Murphy (his freshman year) and then for Don Lewis. During his three years as a Gopher netman, Desmond made a steady climb up the ladder until, in his senior year (1962), he played No. 1 singles and doubles. His sophomore year (remember, freshman were not eligible to play yet) he held down the No 5 singles position and No. 3 doubles (with Bob Luck), and in his junior year he moved up to No. 2 singles and No. 1 doubles. His senior year he captained the team and gave a good account of himself in the Big Ten singles tournament, losing to Marty Riessen of Northwestern in the semis. Riessen, a future touring pro, went on that year to finish second in the NCAA tournament.

Desmond spent a fifth year at the U, coaching the freshman tennis team and finishing up his physical education major and social studies minor. But the military changed his plans, and he was drafted in 1963 and served two years in the army. He recounts that he was on the flower detail for the Kennedy funeral and that he spent seventeen months in Germany, where he played tennis and won the All-Europe doubles championship.

After he left the service he attended graduate school at the U of M, majoring in physical education and educational psychology. During that time he also coached the freshman tennis team. After graduating with his MA in 1967, Desmond taught history and coached in Indiana for a year, then took a position as the head men's tennis coach and physical education teacher at the U of WI for

four years. He taught tennis at a YMCA in Eau Claire for a year and a half, then came back to Minneapolis in '74 to work at the Northwest Tennis Club in St. Louis Park.

Now semi-retired from his day job, Desmond had a very successful career as a USPTA pro coach and teacher in the Metro area until 2002. For example, he coached and taught at the St. Louis Park, Normandale, and 98th Street Racquet Clubs (this last his main haunt). But he had the privilege of being the first pro at the Highway 100 Club and he and Ted Warner also opened the Crosstown Club. He remembers especially the good times he had working in the STP program (mostly doing group work/drills) with "my best buddy, Kevin Ylinen." During the days he most often worked with women players.

In addition, he found time to play summer tournaments, and in these endeavors he did very well, particularly in doubles. For example, he and Gopher teammate Dan Olson were ranked No. 1 in Men's Doubles in 1961, he was No. 2 (with Jerry Noyce) in '66, and he and Jack Roach were Section doubles champions in '80 in the Men's 35-and-Over division. And he earned some top rankings in singles as well, No. 1 in Men's 35 Singles and No. 4 in Men's Open Singles in '79, for example.

Despite the usual aches and pains associated with advancing age, Desmond still finds time to do some coaching, particularly for his daughter Amy, a women's coach at Benilde-St. Margaret's. Desmond has two daughters (Amy and Elaine), but the only other tennis player in the family was Amy.

As for his partner Cooper, Desmond said, "He was tall (six foot four) and had a big serve. He was also good at the net and he covered a lot of the court." Desmond says he has lost track of him; however, he noted that Cooper played college tennis at Carleton.

1959—Jeff Fisher & Mike Parmelee
Faribault

In one of those "Where did this come from?" moments, a junior duo from Faribault (Jeff Fisher and Mike Parmelee) came from nowhere to claim the 1959 doubles title. And they did it with relative ease, taking all four matches in straight sets. Their first round match was a cakewalk, a 6-0, 6-0 win over William Marinac and Luke Davich of Hibbing; and in the quarters they had to work a bit harder but nevertheless won 6-4, 6-3 over Ken Klaffky and Bill Naegele (the outdoor sign mogul) of Minnetonka. In the semis they dispatched Mike Birch and Tom Griffiths of Minneapolis Washburn. This unheralded team then knocked off future doubles champions, Andy Goddard and Franz Jevne of Edina, in the finals 6-2, 8-6, helping Faribault (a town not noted for its tennis) earn a second place finish behind the rising tennis power of Edina.

It is one of those surprising moments in sport when a David (in this case Faribault) can slay a Goliath (Edina). Neither Fisher nor Parmelee had any sort of coaching and neither played much in the summer. Parmelee, in fact, worked at the Faribault Canning Company in the summer and admitted that "I wasn't a tennis bum." He basically learned to play tennis by watching others play and by hitting on a warehouse wall in the summers. He said, "I had to hit it [the ball] hard to get it back into the street." Parmelee and Fisher received no coaching as junior players, and their high school coach, Jim Warren, was primarily a football coach. Warren, however, sometimes gave him balls to hit with after he (Warren) saw Parmelee wearing the balls out on the wall. In addition, except for playing one national Jaycee tournament when he was 15, Parmelee did not play summer tournaments. And for years he played with cheap rackets, many of which he broke. Finally, said Parmelee, "I got a Jack Kramer Autograph from Norm McDonald which I restrung with gut a couple of times. I still have it, even though it's pretty warped." What also helped his tennis game was playing ping pong during lunch breaks at school and playing other sports—football and basketball.

Together he and Fisher won the region twice, losing as seniors in the second round at State in 1960 to '59 finals foes Goddard and Jevne. Parmelee noted that their success together was built on good court coverage ("We were pretty agile") and being able to put points away quickly. "Fisher," he said, "was a lefty who didn't have a lot of form but was fairly effective." About his own game he commented that he had several different serves he used to good effect: "a slice, a reverse slice (twist), and a flat serve." He remembers hitting a winning overhead smash

on match point in the final against Goddard and Jevne.

The No. 1 player for four years and the first Faribault player to letter in tennis for six years, Parmelee secured a partial athletic scholarship to Mankato State College and played tennis all four years there. After earning a BA in business administration and a BS in commercial teaching, Parmelee journeyed north to the frozen tundra, Alaska. He taught for twelve years in Nome and also got into the business of buying old houses and fixing them up. Then he returned to Faribault where he worked as a substitute teacher and assistant tennis coach for ten years. After living in Florida for the next twelve years, he settled in Rio Verde, AZ.

Fisher, the No. 2 player in 1959-60, did not play college tennis but instead moved to Canada and became an artist.

1960s

1960—Andy Goddard & Franz Jevne
Edina

Denied a first-place medal in 1959, the Edina team of Goddard (a sophomore) and Jevne (a senior) rebounded to claim the doubles title in '60, defeating Mac Lutz and Bruce Youngberg of Richfield 6-1, 6-1 in the finals. It was also sweet revenge for the Hornet duo, for they took out last year's champions (Fisher and Parmelee) in the second round by a decisive 6-3, 6-1 score.

And in one of the longest and most hotly contested doubles matches in state history, the team of Jerry Wohlers and Bob Olson of Stillwater (the eventual third-place finishers) beat Robert Perfette and Mike Vidmar of Hibbing 18-16, 7-5 in the second round. I mention this match for two other reasons: (1) without this win Stillwater would not have won the team title and (2) Vidmar is the father of Mike Vidmar the younger, a top player for Hibbing and Macalester College in the 1980s and now a tennis pro at the Reed-Sweatt (formerly Nicollet) Tennis Center.

But back to Goddard and Jevne. They also won two other matches on their march to the title, over brothers Dave and Don Jokela of New York Mills in the first round and the aforementioned Wohlers and Olson in the semis.

In Goddard's final two years he finished third in the 1961 singles tournament and won another doubles title in '62, with Jevne's brother Bill.

1961—John Wirtanen & Jim Miller
Greenway of Coleraine

1961 was the year of the Iron Rangers, for the unheralded team of junior John Wirtanen and senior Jim Miller of Greenway of Coleraine stunned the Minnesota tennis world by winning the doubles title and, by earning 12 points, also capturing the team title for their school. Theirs was just the second doubles title won by a northern Minnesota school—John Nutting and Bruce Dikson from Duluth Central won in 1949.

Tennis coaches will recognize Wirtanen, for it was the green scorebook bearing his name that nearly all state coaches used for almost forty years. Wirtanen sadly died of cancer at age 22. (For more about Wirtanen and Miller and their doubles triumph, see Chapter Eight.)

For now it's enough to say that he and Miller won three matches and dug out of a hole to prevail in a three-set final over Ronald Jarvis and Dennis LeBarron of Austin 4-6, 6-2, 6-3. Prior to this match they received a bye in the first round, came from behind to defeat Charles Berry and Len Bjeldanes of Minneapolis Roosevelt in the second round (3-6, 8-6, 7-5), then won a straight-set semifinal match against Gilbert Rozman and Jules Beck of Minneapolis North.

1962—Andy Goddard & Bill Jevne
Edina

In 1962 senior Andy Goddard of Edina became just the fifth player in state high school tennis history to pair up with a different partner and win a doubles title. As a sophomore in '60 he won the title with Franz Jevne; this year he hooked up with another Jevne, Franz's brother Bill, to defeat future Minnesota teaching pro Tom Boice and his partner Bill Crozier of Minnetonka 6-0, 6-3 in the finals. Never challenged in their four matches, these Hornets stung all challengers and left them for dead. First they swarmed all over Tom Mattson and Tom Reitman of Elk River 6-0, 6-1; then in the quarters they gave up just one more game in defeating Tom Wheeler and Dave Honigman of Duluth East 6-2, 6-0. And Gary Fleming and Brad Offerdahl of St. James fared no better, falling 6-1, 6-0 to this buzz-saw duo. Shades of 1940, when doubles champs Don Gunner and Fred Gulden gave up just two games in their three matches. This Edina team gave up just seven games in four matches.

Like the Biblical Daniel, who interpreted the handwriting on the wall for King Belshazzar, Goddard saw the obvious and decided to play doubles rather than face certain defeat at the hands of the great Chuck Darley of Rochester, who this year won the first of his three singles titles. Though he was no match for Darley, Goddard was a top player who had finished third in the singles tournament in 1961, but he knew his chances were better in doubles and he was right. He had also been ranked No. 1 in Junior Doubles with '60 singles champion Frank Kleckner the summer before, so that gave him an additional reason to "go doubles." In addition, he had been a top singles player, ranking No. 3 in NWLTA Junior Singles in '61.

By the way, '61 champion Wirtanen and his new partner Jack Stebe lost in the quarters to Boice and Crozier 6-3, 8-6.

1963-64—John Brennan & Charles "Bucky" Zimmerman
Minneapolis West

Though Rochester, with top singles players Darley and Bob Gray and doubles teams such as John Lillie and Bob Bergstedt, dominated team competition in 1963-64, it was a city pair from Minneapolis West (John Brennan and Charles "Bucky" Zimmerman) that took home the doubles crown both years, becoming only the third doubles pair to win two titles together.

In 1963 they defeated the above-mentioned Rochester pair (Lillie and Bergstedt) 6-3, 8-6 to capture the title. Theirs was not an easy ride that year, but the Cowboys' duo nonetheless won all four tournament matches in straight sets. It took them 59 games to get to the semis, their first match (against Jack Nist and Chris Hagen of Anoka) going 7-5, 12-10; and in their quarterfinal matchup with Derald Johnson and Dick Lahti of Hibbing they prevailed 9-7, 6-3. Finally, in the semis they caught their breath and easily outclassed Fairmont's Al Hansen and Sam Larson 6-0, 6-2.

In 1964 they vanquished the team that would take the crown in '65, juniors Dave Yorks and Brian Mahin of Minnetonka. This was a three-setter which Brennan and Zimmerman won 6-0, 5-7, 6-1. On the way to this final match, Brennan and Zimmerman defeated Bill Sederberg and Tom Young of Mankato Wilson; then they drubbed a team from North St. Paul in the quarters (Richard Swanson and Steve Anderson). Their semifinal opponents, Duluth East's Tom Wheeler and Dave Honigman (fifth-place finishers last year), gave the West pair a tussle but fell 7-5, 8-6. This second-straight title meant that Brennan and Zimmerman finished their time together with an unblemished record.

In a tournament anomaly that occurred only once before and would happen only one more time, the same team, singles player, and doubles partners swept every state title this year and in 1963. In 1942-43, Minneapolis West won the team title, Ken Boyum the singles, and Boyum and Wollin took the doubles. This was the only time all six titles were claimed by one team in consecutive years. In 1967-68 Edina won the team championships, Rochester's Rob Daugherty took the singles title, and Edina's Dave Mathews and Jim Mitchell claimed both doubles crowns. So these two years (1963-64) Rochester won the team titles, Chuck Darley the singles, and Brennan and Zimmerman the doubles. An article in the June 7, 1964, *Minneapolis Tribune* said about this 1964 déjà vu competition, "They might just as well have told the competitors in the 36th annual High School

tennis tournament to go home after Friday's first and second round action... when finals were completed it was an exact duplicate of last year as far as the individual and team champions were concerned." This second doubles championship was the eighth for West and twenty-second for Minneapolis teams.

The senior member of that duo, Zimmerman, who credits tennis for "creating the bedrock for me as a person," began playing the game at age 10. "My first lesson was at the Minikahda Club with Bucky Olson [a singles semifinalist in the 1942 singles tournament and a former MIAC standout at St. Thomas College], then Frank Voigt worked with me once or twice a week until I was

John Brennan (Left) and Charles "Bucky" Zimmerman

17." According to Zimmerman, "Voigt was a real inspiration to all the kids he came in contact with" and thanks in part to him, Bucky did well both in summer tournaments (which he called "cutthroat competition") and in high school tennis play. For example, he recalls being ranked No. 3 in singles his last summer in NWLTA play and No. 1 in doubles three times, once with Al Rosenberg of St. Paul Central, once with Dennis Chez of Hibbing, and once with his teammate Brennan.

And under the guidance of coach Bill Kuross while in his sophomore year in high school, he swept through all comers in the City League. The No. 1 player for West for three years, he became a better competitor because he had an excellent sparring partner, No. 2 player Brennan, on his own team. In fact, they practiced four times a week together from the age of 11 or 12 and often played practice matches. Zimmerman recalled, "John Brennan and I always had a battle royal, but we were always good friends."

Of his two state tournament doubles titles, Zimmerman remembers two things especially well: how dominant he and Brennan were and what a big deal his small city school made of their triumphs. Personally, he said, "It was the start of something where I got some recognition."

A good athlete who played junior football, participated on the swimming team for one year, and was a fast sprinter, Zimmerman nonetheless had to overcome one obstacle: he was slight of stature and short (five foot five or so). But what he lacked in size and power he made up for in speed and consistency on the tennis court. A lefthander, he was extremely fast ("I could run things down"), had a good serve and overhead, and played an all-court game. His teammate Brennan added, "Zim had a wicked slice backhand."

Like so many other players, Zimmerman valued high school tennis because, for the first time, "It made me understand the importance of team play and being recognized as part of a team, even when cheering for our fourth or fifth singles players." For him it also provided opportunities to "bring something back to the school" and taught lessons about growing up.

After graduating from West he enrolled at the U of M, where he played tennis and earned his degree in history and political science. His sophomore year he played No. 1 doubles with Jerry Noyce, then teamed with Chez at No. 1 doubles his last two years. As seniors they took third in the Big 10, qualified for the NCAA tournament, and had the privilege of playing great NCAA champions and future pro tennis stars Stan Smith and Bob Lutz in the first round. Zimmerman also played No. 2 singles his final two years and is perhaps most proud of the fact that he served as captain for two years. He also recalls that he and Brennan played each other once in college, with Zimmerman winning. And though the U was at the time the largest campus in the U.S., Zimmerman felt at home in the company of his tennis teammates who helped "make the U small."

After graduating from the U, he tackled the pro circuit for a year, even playing in the U.S. Open in 1968 and earlier that year losing to Arthur Ashe at the National Clay Court Tournament in what he called "a pretty good match." But perhaps his most notable tennis achievements took place during the three years he participated in Mens' 35 Singles tournaments at the Maccabiah Games held in Israel, Venezuela, and Uruguay. In three different games he won two gold medals, one each in singles and doubles, one silver, and one bronze.

Zimmerman also earned a law degree from his alma mater and in 1982 he started his own firm (Zimmerman Reed), a firm that specialized in class action suits. He recently married former WCCO TV anchor Pat Miles and they live in Arizona.

His partner, Brennan, the son of a novelist and one of the top senior men's players in the Section named Dan, was the first of three brothers who excelled for the West Cowboys. Tom finished third in the 1967 singles tournament, second in '68, and first in '69; and John also finished runner-up to Bob Gray his senior year, in '65. Youngest brother Mike was also a top player for West. (For more on the Brennan boys, see Chapter Ten.)

John Brennan, at six foot one a good deal bigger than Zimmerman, won these two titles as a sophomore and junior with what his partner described as "a very natural, fluid game. He also had an excellent forehand and backhand and a good overhead." He was, in addition, a very good athlete who played quarterback for the West football team which finished 7-1-1 his senior year, the best school record in many years.

Zimmerman called him "a gentle soul and a really nice guy." Brennan returned the compliment, saying of his joined-at-the-hip partner, "We spent a lot of time together in the summer and my fondest memory was growing up together on the tennis court."

And though he also played basketball in high school, it was tennis that gave Brennan recognition. He said, "I still have my medals from high school. It [tennis] gave me an identity in my high school and in the city." In addition, he added, our doubles championship "really brought attention to our high school." His senior year he lost only to champion Bob Gray in the 1965 singles final and that was his only loss in three years of varsity competition.

When he completed this remarkable career at West, he headed off to college at Northwestern U to play tennis. He played mostly No. 4 singles and No. 1 and 2 doubles for coach Claire Riessen (Marty's father), and his senior year he won the Big Ten playbacks at No. 4 singles.

After graduating in 1969 with a history major, Brennan was drafted and spent three years in the U.S. Air Force. When he got out of the service, he enrolled at the U of Chicago Law School, graduating in '76. For fifteen years he practiced in Chicago and was for a time a Cook County Public Defender in the felony courts before heading back to school to get his MA in journalism. He's lived in Washington, D. C., since 1991, working as a TV reporter and assignment editor and now a media consultant. Before that he also worked as an administration cabinet member during the Clinton presidency. Brennan says he still plays a good deal of tennis.

1965—Dave Yorks & Brian Mahin
Minnetonka

As more and more suburban ring schools began to develop tennis programs, the balance of power shifted from the Metro area to the west, first to Edina (which won its initial title in 1959) and in '65 farther out on Highway 7. That year a team from Minnetonka claimed the first tennis championship for the school, a doubles title won by Dave Yorks and Brian Mahin. During the season Dave and Brian alternated at No. 1 and 2 singles, but they also played doubles and were undefeated in nine matches.

However, their road to the title was not necessarily a smooth one. Yorks remembers that they won handily against Benson's Dennis Peterson and Gary Foster in the first round, struggled to a 7-5, 9-7 quarterfinal win over Steve Anderson and Al Hansen of North St. Paul, then ousted Wayzata's No. 1 and 2 guys (Rob Meads and Charles Gudger) in the semifinals 7-5, 6-2. The ease of this straight-set victory surprised Yorks because "We went to Wayzata and played them before the tourney for a warmup and just got killed."

In the finals they met future two-time singles champion Rob Daugherty and his brother Dave from Rochester, who had earlier knocked off Dave Stearns and Dave Woodward of St. Cloud Tech. Yorks said of this match, "We dropped the first set 7-5, won the second 6-2, then broke at 5-all in the third set. I served for the match and Brian, who was so fast, hit three winners." So after coming close in 1964 (they lost to Brennan and Zimmerman in a three-set final), Yorks and Mahin saw all that hard work that began on neighborhood courts in Minnetonka finally pay off.

Both spoke of those early years with great affection. Mahin played on what he and others later called the "Wheaton Memorial Courts" in Cottagewood, and his mother signed him up for East Tonka community lessons when he was 12. But it was a night out with his father that really turned him on to tennis, Mahin recalled: "One night when I was 12 or 13 my dad took me to see Pancho Gonzalez, Jack Kramer, Frank Parker, and Pancho Segura play at the Minneapolis Armory and I was really impressed."

Yorks grew up on the Groveland Assembly Grounds, playing with the likes of Bryan Stamp, Tom Boice, Gary Peterson, and Nancy Countryman. Here's how he recalls these early years: "I also learned by watching these players and they took me with them for tournaments. Sometimes I went with them to Nicollet Tennis Center, but more often I hitchhiked with 50 cents in my pocket and played all day. I don't ever remember waiting for a ride and I have no negative memory of a bad person picking me up during those four or five years before I learned to drive."

Brian Mahin (Left) & Dave Yorks

Yorks and Mahin began playing together in seventh grade, but Yorks said, "I had to talk Brian [Mahin] into playing tennis instead of baseball because I felt he could earn a letter in ninth grade." Both truly enjoyed tennis and thrived on the competition, though Mahin wishes that he had played more tournament tennis. He was never a highly ranked player and Yorks' best showings were No. 9 rankings in the 16-and-under singles and doubles (with his high school teammate Gordon Stamp).

For Mahin high school tennis and junior tennis in the summer called to mind so many pleasurable experiences. For example, he remembers that "we used to play some of our home matches at Bill Naegele's two private courts and the one court at John Gabbert's." Naegele of course became the owner of the Minnesota Wild hockey team and president of the billboard company that bore his name and Gabbert was the founder of the well-known Edina furniture store, so these matches gave Mahin and some of his teammates a glimpse into a world very different from their own. And in what was a kind of initiation rite many young tennis players also experienced, Mahin recalls "riding in back of a station wagon and sitting on top of rackets and luggage on my way to tournaments in Sioux Falls—with the big guys in front."

Mahin joined the navy right out of high school, serving for four years (with a hitch in Vietnam); then he became a USPTA pro and taught tennis in a number of clubs in Indiana, Wisconsin, and Minnesota. In 1981 he got involved in local tennis association work, serving in a variety of roles on the NWTA executive committee until '96 and one year as president. Gradually weaning himself out of the tennis world, in the late '80s he purchased his father's business, one that involved installing movable wall systems.

Yorks went on to play tennis for three years at the U of M with some of his former high school antagonists such as Bucky Zimmerman, Paul Krause, and Denny Chez. After graduation, like Mahin, Yorks chose to put his tennis efforts into coaching and serving the greater Minnesota tennis community.

So he served for many years as a local pro and NWTA official, as president of the USTA/Northern Section in 1989-90, as a Sectional delegate to the USTA in 1991-92,

and as vice president of the Section for five years. In addition, he served on many national and local USTA committees, was president of the Northwest Professional Tennis Association from 1975-79, and for many years served as director of the Minnetonka Racquet Club and Wayzata Country Club. He also served for a time as head umpire for the U of M men's tennis matches and as a director of the American Family Mortgage USTA Women's Tournament held at Fort Snelling.

For his lifetime service to tennis he has been honored many times: as 1978 NWPTA Pro of the Year, as the 1994 USTA/Northern Section President's Award recipient, and as a 2001 USTA/Northern Section "Special Award" recipient. But his highest honor is his membership in the NWTA Northern Section Hall of Fame.

1966—Greg & Reid Pederson
Coon Rapids

One of the most difficult things to overcome in life is sibling rivalry, a normal consequence of adolescent selfishness and the natural inclination to gain the attention of our parents in order to show them that we're better than our brothers or sisters. How hard it must then be for two brothers to put aside their petty jealousies and differences to play tennis together. Oh, sure, the current No. 1 doubles team in the world, the Bryan brothers, demonstrate that it can be done. But in Minnesota high school tennis such brotherly love has only produced five state championship doubles teams, the first being the Tudor twins of St. Paul Central in 1930.

Thirty-six years later the second brother duo captured a doubles crown. Senior Greg and junior Reid Pederson of Coon Rapids took the 1966 title by defeating Jerry Burnham and Dwight Dahlen of North St. Paul in one of the most dramatic and exhausting finals ever (5-7, 10-8, 12-10). This 52-game final doubles match is a state record that will never be surpassed now that tiebreakers are played at 6-all in all sets.

By the time they had hoisted their medals wearily in the air, the Pedersons must have been hoping to take a nap, for their other three opponents had also made them expend a great deal of energy. In fact, they had to overcome a first-set loss in round one, finally prevailing 5-7, 6-3, 6-1 over Richard Taylor and John Weddle of Richfield. Their quarterfinal opponents, Dan Wolesky and Randy Klemmer of Owatonna, also did not give up without a good fight (7-5, 6-3). And while they won their semifinal match in straight sets against Mike Vogel and Volker Henning of White Bear Lake, 6-4, 6-1, the first set was competitive. Their total of 118 games played was a record for doubles champions.

According to their sophomore- and junior-year coach, Chuck Wennerlund, the Pedersons came from Rochester with an established tennis reputation. Coon Rapids High School had just opened in 1963 with only a sophomore class, and Greg Pederson was a member of that first class. Both boys were good athletes who also played basketball; Greg, who was a couple inches taller than Reid, played forward and Reid played guard.

In tennis the year they won State, Greg, "a more natural tennis player," according to Wennerlund, held down the No. 1 singles spot in the lineup while Reid played No. 2 singles. Wennerlund added, "Both were very smart, good competitors. And while Greg had more natural ability, Reid was good at strategy." More importantly, said Wennerlund, "They were both intelligent, quality people."

And both had some success in junior tournament play as well, Reid achieving rankings of No. 16 in the 16s and No. 18 in the 18s in singles and Greg earning a No. 8 ranking in 16-and-under doubles with Greg Reed of Coon Rapids. Reid went on to play tennis at St. Cloud State Teacher's College.

1967-68—Dave Mathews & Jim Mitchell
Edina

Remember the story about the 1963-64 years, when one team, one singles player, and the same doubles pair swept the competition. Well, it happened again in both 1967 and '68. Edina won both team championships, Rochester's Rob Daugherty took the singles, and the team of Dave Mathews and Jim Mitchell of Edina captured the doubles titles, in so doing becoming only the fourth duo (after Boyum-Wollin, Trondson-Dison, and

Brennan-Zimmerman) to win two in a row. After being upset in the quarters in '66 by the runner-up team from North St. Paul (Burnham and Dahlen) in a tough 12-10, 9-7 match, Mathews and Mitchell stormed through the draw in '67 and knocked off Jim Colwell and Dale Britzius of Minnetonka in the finals, 6-4, 6-4. These two 6-4 sets and a 7-5 set in their semifinal match were the only ones in which opponents won more than two games a set against Mathews and Mitchell. In round one they defeated Chuck Peterson and Jim Frederickson of Mankato, then took care of Bruce Filsin and Tim Kuzma of Ely in round two. Mathews and Mitchell struggled but won their opening set (7-5) in the semis against Dave Woodward and Larry Nelson of St. Cloud before closing out the match with a 6-2 second-set win.

Then for an encore they won the 1968 title with a flair, beating Tim Burke (future Twin Cities pro) and Bob Brandenburg of Rochester Mayo by a score nearly identical to that of the '67 final (6-4, 6-3) and giving up just 6 games in their three matches leading up to the match with the Mayo lads. These were, following an opening round bye, a 6-3, 6-1 win over Tim Johnson and Charles Berquist of Stillwater; a 6-0, 6-1 blitzing of Bob Thorson and Harlan Brooker of Bemidji; and an almost identical 6-0, 6-1 romp over Jim Henry and Ron Koehler of Winona. All told they surrendered just 13 games in 4 matches, an average of just over 3 games per match.

One could have predicted a championship for these Edina lads, for both had been successful junior

Dave Mathews (Left) & Jim Mitchell

tournament players. Mathews was once ranked No. 5 in Junior Men's Singles and No. 2 in doubles (with Mitchell). And Mitchell was ranked nearly every year, reaching the No. 2 spot in singles in both the 14s and 16s and the No. 1 ranking in the 16-and-under doubles with Rochester's Bob Brandenburg.

Mathews, who played college tennis at the U of M and became a successful local teaching pro, cherishes these two doubles titles and the experience of playing on a team: "I liked the camaraderie, the team aspect, getting to know the group and having an identity." He didn't start playing tennis until the summer before his eighth grade year, and then only when a classmate gave him a racket and told him he had to learn to play tennis. Soon he was hitting at the Wooddale Public Courts on 50th and Browndale in Edina and taking park and recreation lessons from Rob Granger and Dave Warner (Ted's brother). He made the tennis team his freshman year, becoming with his pal Mitchell the only ninth graders in the school to earn varsity letters that year. Therefore, when they weren't teaming in doubles for tournament play, he and Mitchell alternated at Nos. 2 and 3 singles.

Mathews gave up hockey after his sophomore year in order to play tennis and work at the Southdale club in the days when indoor tennis was just getting a start in Minnesota. In the off-season he also had the opportunity to play with great women players such as Jeanne Arth and Betty Swanson; and like so many top juniors of his era, he took lessons at the Northstar Club from Frank Voigt and also hit with Jerry Noyce from time to time.

Heading south after graduation from Edina, Mathews enrolled at North Texas State to play tennis. However, he stayed there just one year, playing No. 6 singles and Nos. 1 or 2 doubles and helping his team win the Missouri Valley Conference title. After his year in Texas he transferred to the U of M to play two more years for Coach Joe Walsh. Mathews sat out a year, then as a junior he played No. 1 doubles with Dave Stearns. As a senior he teamed with Bob Van Hoef to reach the semis of the Big Ten tournament at No. 1 doubles (losing to a pair from Michigan). In singles he played No. 3 his junior year (1971) and No. 2 his senior year, a year in which Mathews won the playbacks at his position. His senior year he also served as co-captain with his former doubles partner Stearns.

Before he graduated from the U, he began his tennis coaching career by working with Jack Roach at the Richfield club. When he graduated in 1972, he became the first "'out-of-college' teaching pro for Marv [Wolfenson] and Harv [Ratner] to handle lessons at Richfield." Then, Mathews said, "for seventeen years I went to new clubs (Northwest, 98th Street, Burnsville) to get programs going." For his work as a teaching pro he was voted Northwest Tennis Association Pro of the Year in '82, and for his lifetime service to the NWTA, he was elected to the Northern Section Hall of Fame in 2007.

After he completed his teaching career, he became a manufacturer's rep for Dunlop—a position he held for seven years—and then switched to Head as a rep for four and one-half states. Once voted the Dunlop Representative of the Year, he also earned a Rookie of the Year Award for Head and today serves as district sales manager for that company. And though he has not played a great deal of competitive tennis as an adult, he did team up in 1986 with Tim Burke and they won the 35 doubles Sectional championship.

From those early days as a shy freshman riding on the team bus to Rochester, tennis has been Mathews' passion and his life. In fact, he even played the pro circuit in the Northeastern U.S. his junior year with partner Greg Lappin and once hit with Arthur Ashe at Minikahda in Ashe's warmup for the Pan-Am Games. And today, he said, "I'm playing senior tennis with all the guys who played in colleges."

Regarding his teammate Mitchell, Mathews said, "He was a very explosive power player with a big serve and overhead and he volleyed well." Mathews called him "a very positive and upbeat guy who was extremely bright." Also, Mathews said, "We had a lot of fun playing together and he never got down on his partner."

Mitchell did not continue his tennis in college, but he went out for hockey as a walk-on player at Harvard. From Harvard he went to Duke U Medical School to become an ophthalmologist. Today he is a neuro-optical eye surgeon in Minneapolis and lives in Edina. His high school teammate Mathews added about him, "He is so bright that he tested out of his freshman year at Harvard and graduated early with honors. He is also truly a class person."

1969—Steve Runtsch & Greg Knutson
Austin

In the final year of the tumultuous '60s, a doubles team from Austin swept through the draw and, in the process, won a state team title for coach Keith Paulson's Packers (see Chapter Two for more on their victory). Senior Steve Runtsch and junior Greg Knutson had played singles all year, so it was a bit of a surprise that they did so well. But excel they did, beating a team (Steve Yoss and Tony Bianco) from their region in the finals, 4-6, 6-3, 6-4. Steve Yoss and Tony Bianco of Rochester Mayo.

Leading up to the final, after they dispatched Harlon Booker and Bob Thorson of Bemidji handily in the first round, the boys from Austin ran into some alligators in the swamp in their quarterfinal and semifinal matches. In the quarters they almost saw their dreams of a title die out after they were trounced in the first set 6-1, but they persevered and came back to win 1-6, 6-3, 6-2 over Bruce Meese and Brian Saksa of Robbinsdale Cooper. And their semifinal match was a grinder that they took 9-7, 6-3 over Tom Driscoll and Jerry Hanek of Moorhead.

Greg Knutson (Left) Coach Keith Paulson & Steve Runtsch

1970s

Like the giant Kodiac brown bear sitting on top of the food chain in his native Alaska, so the new super power teams and individuals from the Lake Conference sat atop the tennis food chain in Minnesota during this decade. Teams from the conference feasted on their competitors and won eight of ten state team titles, and individuals gobbled up eight singles titles and seven doubles titles. Of the doubles titles, Edina took three, Minnetonka two, and St. Louis Park and Hopkins one each.

1970—Dave Petersen & Pete Maeder
Hopkins

Hopkins claimed its first doubles championship, in 1970, with the team of junior Dave Petersen and senior Pete Maeder overcoming a strong pair from team champion Robbinsdale Cooper in the finals (Kevin Ylinen and Tim Butorac) by a score of 6-3, 6-4. Giving little comfort to their opponents and less hope to their opponents' fans, Petersen and Maeder methodically dismantled four doubles teams without losing a set. In the first round they trounced Dick Skaden and Doug Rome of Blue Earth; then in the quarters they took out Chuck Dillon and Steve Moore of Waseca. Their semifinal match with Edina's Ted Taney and Scott Benjamin was competitive, but Petersen and Maeder triumphed 6-4, 6-4.

This year's doubles featured an outstanding draw which showcased several players who would become college standouts and one junior (Taney) who would win a doubles title in 1971. In a quirk of fate, three of the four finalists went on to play for coach Steve Wilkinson at Gustavus: Petersen, Ylinen, and Butorac. Petersen, after spending a year at Edison Junior College in Florida, became a three-time all-American at Gustavus who won the 1973 NAIA doubles championship (with Butorac) and the '75 NAIA singles championship his senior year. His sophomore year he also finished second in the singles tournament. Butorac was a three-year all-American as well and, again with Petersen, finished second in the

Pete Maeder (Left) & Dave Petersen

NAIA doubles tournament in '74. In addition, he and his son Eric (1999 Class AA singles champion) were national father-son grass court champions in 2002 and '04. Ylinen played two years at Gustavus, winning the MIAC singles and doubles titles his senior year (1975) and also earning all-American status that year.

After completing their careers at Gustavus, the three became successful teaching pros in the area. Ylinen, who died unexpectedly at the age of 39, was one of the founders of the Northwest STP junior program; and Butorac has been a teaching pro for many years in Rochester.

But back to 1970 state champions Petersen and Maeder. Their victory was no fluke, for the summer before they were the top-ranked doubles team in the Section and Petersen was ranked No. 2 in singles behind nationally ranked Howard Schoenfield of Rochester, one of Minnesota's greatest male junior players. Petersen was a big lefthander who was a magician with the racket. Taney, who later played doubles with Petersen in mens' tournaments, said of his game, "He was a very good doubles player who was excellent at the net. I've never seen a ball that had so much movement, a ball that danced. He could get anybody tangled into the nets at the side of the courts." In addition, according to Taney, "He had an unusual style to his game—a lot of slices, and he never hit a normal ball. He also had a very good twist serve that was very hard to return."

Taney described Maeder as "a steady player who did everything well." As a junior player he appeared only once in the singles rankings, at No. 12 in the Junior Men's 18s in 1970.

His senior year Petersen was ranked No. 1 all year in the state coaches rankings, but he lost in a grueling three-set match in the 1971 singles tournament to fifth-ranked Bob Van Hoef of St. Paul Harding in the quarters 5-7, 14-12, 6-2.

After graduating from Gustavus, Petersen also competed in and dominated the Men's Open Singles field in the Section for several years in the middle-to-late '70s, ranking No. 1 for three of those years (1975-77) and second behind Carter DeLaittre one year and his coach Steve Wilkinson another year. In addition, Petersen won one Sectional singles championship each in the 35s and 45s. Today he still plays a bit of tennis and occasionally gives lessons to selected young players, but he travels a great deal and is, according to Taney "a salesman, a bit of an entrepreneur."

1971—Ted Taney & Chris Barden
Edina

If 1971 had been a Chinese New Year, we might have called it the "Year of the Horse," for one thoroughbred (the undefeated Edina team) so dominated the competition that it doubled up on the team score (32-16 over second-place Robbinsdale Cooper) and won both the singles (Bob Amis) and doubles crowns (Ted Taney and Chris Barden).

After tripping up St. Paul Murray's Paul Steinhauser (a future Twin Cities area club pro) and Jim Merrill in the semis, Taney and Barden defeated another Lake Conference pair, Bob Allen and Steve Nordbye of Minnetonka, 6-3, 6-1, in the finals. And like Petersen and Maeder, the Edina duo took no prisoners, winning all four of their matches in straight sets. Their first victims were Kevin Coughlin and Tom Nelson of White Bear Lake, then in the quarters they dashed the hopes of Sandy Ruttger (of the Ruttger's Resort clan) and Dave Shanks of Brainerd.

Jim Wells, writing in the *St. Paul Pioneer Press*, said of the Taney-Barden win, "Perhaps the most excited on the Edina team was Taney, a senior. The Hornets' doubles team last year, on which he played, finished third in the State Tournament. 'This had to be it... all there was for me in high school competition,' Taney beamed. His partner, Barden, is a junior." In their first year of playing together, they lost nary a set. Taney said, "I guess we just complement each other in our game" (June 13, 1971).

Perhaps because a harried mother wanted to get Taney (and her son) out of her hair, he got his start in tennis. Ted was about 10 when his friend's mother "gave me and him a tennis racket and balls and said, 'You guys should go and play.'" Then, just as the lion cub learns to hunt by watching its mother, so Taney learned the game by watching older players such as Jack Roach and Jerry Noyce. His future coach, John Matlon, also saw him hit and encouraged him to play tournaments. As a tournament player he was most successful in doubles, achieving a ranking as high as No. 2 in Boys' 18s (with Bob Amis) in 1971; but he also earned a No. 10 singles ranking that year.

Cracking the deep Hornets' lineup as a ninth grader, Taney played second doubles that year, then played mostly No. 1 doubles his last three years (with Scott Benjamin his sophomore and junior years and with Barden as a senior). In 1971 he and Barden resembled almost unhittable baseball pitchers, hurling straight-set wins in every one of their matches, including four in the State Tournament. Taney, recalling how satisfying these team and individual titles were, in part because he and his teammates had worked so hard, said, "The harder we worked, the better we would get. We didn't take anything for granted." Like his coach he was also a wrestler in high school (and wrestlers know the importance of hard work), so perhaps that's one reason he had such great respect for Coach Matlon. He is proud of having been a part of a winning team and tradition at Edina, and the camaraderie he shared with his teammates endures today.

Taney continued his tennis career after high school, playing for Coach Jerry Noyce at the U of M (mostly at No. 4 singles and No. 3 doubles with Bill Stark). In addition, he captained the Gophers his senior year (1975). After graduation he worked as an assistant pro at Interlachen and the Northwest Clubs for four years and is now a senior vice president and financial advisor for Smith-Barney, a

firm he has been employed with for the past twenty-nine years. He hasn't played a great deal of competitive tennis in the Northern Section, but he was ranked No. 9 in Men's Open Singles one year and No. 5 in Men's Open Doubles in 1973 (with his college teammate Stark).

Taney and his wife, Jane, the ultimate tennis mom and a player herself, have three daughters, the youngest of whom inherited Ted's tennis genes. Whitney Taney has carved out the most remarkable high school career in Minnesota girls' tennis history. (For more on Whitney, see Chapter Seven.) Of their other two girls, middle daughter Ashley did not play tennis but oldest daughter Lauren played in high school at Benilde-St. Margaret's.

1972—Chris Barden & Dixon Dahlberg
Edina

In an even more dominant performance in 1972, Edina once again swept all three titles, annihilating all comers in the team competition with a 20-point margin (32 to St. Cloud Tech's 12). And once again Barden, described by '75 doubles champion Scott Nesbit as "a bit of a free spirit," won the doubles, this time pairing with Dixon Dahlberg and defeating Grant Helgeson and Jeff Schwanberg from St. Cloud Tech in an epic two-hour and fifteen-minute final match 6-3, 3-6, 10-8.

In the leadup to the finals, Barden and Dahlberg had little trouble with three opponents, defeating Scott Bjella and Virgil Malbraaton of Bemidji, Mark Thies and Gerry Gray of Aurora-Hoyt Lakes, and Moorhead's Grandon Kjesbo and Rick Sullivan in straight sets.

Their win was not unexpected, for Barden and Dahlberg were the No. 1-ranked 18-and-under doubles team in 1971 NWLTA Section play, and they were also top-ten singles players (Barden had been No. 4 in both the 16s and 18s and Dahlberg No. 8 in the 16s and 18s and No. 3 in 18 singles his last year of junior competition). Barden was also No. 1 in doubles in the 16s (with Bob Amis), the same year that Dahlberg was No. 2 (with Rob Tesar of St. Paul).

Barden's 1971 partner, Ted Taney, described him as "a consistent player who had a pretty good forehand. He didn't miss a lot and he was a positive player on the court."

After high school he enrolled at the U of M, where he tried out for tennis but did not make the team. Barden holds a law degree from Harvard and a doctorate in psychology from the U and today lives and works in Salt Lake City.

Dahlberg, according to former teammate Taney, was "a lefty with a good serve that gave him a real advantage." Taney also called him "a good doubles player who was very consistent and hit a topspin backhand." After graduation Dahlberg also attended the U of M and played tennis, mostly Nos. 5 or 6 singles.

When he left the U he worked in the bakery business for about ten years, Taney noted, and today he is in the real estate business in Edina. For a time he played competitive tennis as an adult, and in 1979 he and Tom Boice earned the No. 1 Men's Doubles ranking in the Section.

1973—Marty Lazniarz & Bruce Edwards
St. Louis Park

In the first year of True Team competition, a team from Edina (now Edina East) took home a third straight title, but both the singles and doubles went to outsiders, the singles to Rochester Mayo's Mark Brandenburg and the doubles to the tandem of seniors Marty Lazniarz and Bruce Edwards of St. Louis Park.

Bruce Edwards (Left) & Marty Lazniarz

In another hotly contested final, Lazniarz and Edwards triumphed 6-8, 6-4, 6-1 over Randy Oldenburg and Randy Quint of Blue Earth. This was on the heels of two previous tough matches the St. Louis Park team won,

coming from behind to defeat Greg Gohlke and Bob Marshall of Edina East 8-10, 6-1, 6-4 in the quarters and struggling a bit to overcome Brian Parr and Tom Griffith of Duluth East in the semis 7-5, 6-3. Their only easy match was a 6-1, 6-4 first-round win over Jeff Hagen and Ben Underwood of Fergus Falls.

Longtime St. Louis Park coach Roger Thompson said about his charges, "Bruce Edwards and Marty Lazniarz, the 'Dynamic Duo,' went undefeated in doubles during the spring of '73. A record of 25-0 brought them the state doubles championship. During their final match against Blue Earth Marty suffered a foot injury but he refused to quit. I told him to forfeit, but he limped on, with Bruce, and they won."

Neither had been highly ranked players (Edwards did not appear in the rankings and Lazniarz appeared only once, at No. 18 in the 18-and-under singles), so their triumph was yet another unknown underdog win.

1974—Mark Wheaton & Roger Jenkins
Minnetonka

Except for Mark Brandenburg's second-straight singles title, the 1974 tournament belonged to Minnetonka, a team led by Allyn Dart, foreign exchange student Solomon Yohannes, Roger Jenkins, Mark Burton, and sophomore standout Mark Wheaton. The Skippers won the True Team title, Yohannes took the consolation singles medal, and Wheaton and Jenkins won the doubles, defeating Brian Weinreis and Steve Quello from Lake Conference rival Hopkins Eisenhower in the finals. The score was 6-4, 7-6.

For Wheaton and Jenkins there was only one glitch along the road to the finals, a comeback win against Blue Earth's Mark Schroeder (coach Hal Schroeder's son) and his partner, Mike Weise. They lost the first set 6-1 but dominated the next two to win 1-6, 6-1, 6-3. This was in the quarters; in the first round the lads from Minnetonka beat Steve Krahn and Jeff Mash of White Bear Mariner in straight sets. Then in the semis they dispatched another Lake Conference team, Mike Lilly and Kelly Frost of Robbinsdale Armstrong.

Jenkins, a senior and thus the elder statesman of the team, was never a ranked junior player; however, he was an important member of Minnetonka's championship team, playing first doubles with Glen Wertheim. Wheaton described him as "a streaky player who could run off a string of winning shots, both on the return and during a rally, with his good forehand. He always seemed to play up to the occasion." In addition, Wheaton said, "we meshed well on the court not only due to our complementary styles and opposite personalities (I was serious and he was more of a fun-loving guy), but because he could win some quick points in the deuce court while I worked the opponents in the ad court until they made an error or went for a low percentage shot." This combination of Wheaton's height and reach and Jenkins' physical strength and power pressured opponents and enabled them to sweep through region and state competition.

Wheaton of course followed up this doubles win by taking home singles medals the next two years. (For more on Wheaton, see Chapters Four and Ten.)

1975—Bill Arnold & Scott Nesbit
Edina East

Though Wheaton took the singles title in 1975, Edina East won the team title and the doubles. Junior Bill Arnold and senior Scott Nesbit defeated the team of Larry Stolte and Greg Dubois of Park of Cottage Grove 6-2, 6-0 in the finals, after knocking out Doug Arntson and Jeff Welter of Coon Rapids in the first round and surviving two difficult

Bill Arnold (Left) & Scott Nesbit

matches in the semis and quarters. In the semis they topped Dave Atlas and Jeff Carroll of St. Louis Park 6-2, 4-6, 6-1; in the quarters they scraped out a 7-6, 6-7, 6-2 win over seniors Mark Welinski and Eric Jorgensen of Northfield.

As the coach of Welinski and Jorgensen, my first-ever doubles entry in the State Tournament, I took the loss pretty hard, especially since we had a chance to upset an Edina team. However, over time I have forgiven Arnold and Nesbit for this indiscretion; in fact, since Nesbit now lives not far from me and coaches at St. Olaf, we have become good friends.

Both Arnold and Nesbit were stalwarts on Edina teams for three years, beginning in 1973 when they anchored the No. 2 doubles spot for the undefeated East team which won the first True Team Minnesota championship. As a junior Nesbit played mostly No. 1 doubles and Arnold stayed at No. 2 doubles. In their championship season Nesbit alternated between Nos. 1 and 2 singles (with Greg Swendseen) and Arnold played No. 1 doubles (with Don Howard) in team competition, but these former partners joined up again for doubles play in the individual tournament.

The two had come up through the Edina system, though Nesbit began playing at age nine in California. His parents played, and they "signed me up for lessons at the Newport Beach Tennis and Yacht Club." Nesbit was placed in the intermediate group and remembers beating the pro's son. Until age 14 he also played baseball, ice hockey, and "a ton of street hockey," but after that he became serious about tennis. He earned a spot on an outstanding JV team—one of only three ninth graders to do so, then began playing tournaments the summer of his tenth-grade year. Tennis soon became an obsession with him, as he recalls, "I was a maniac. I played all the time, even on Christmas day."

Though neither he nor Arnold were imposing figures on the court (Nesbit in fact was and still is slight of frame), they were both very consistent and accurate in their placement. Their success certainly confirmed the truth that one need not be a Charles Atlas in order to win at tennis. Scott tells a story that so aptly illustrates this point. "My sophomore year Bill Arnold and I were playing doubles at Anoka against two guys who were six foot seven and 220 pounds and really sculpted. I weighed 89 pounds at the time and Bill was about the same. Together we didn't weigh as much as one of them, but we beat them 6-0, 6-0. I hardly know if they won a point, and I knew then I was in the right sport. Tennis is like that and that's one of the reasons I like it." Another indication of their consistency could be seen in the second set of the doubles final in 1975, for Arnold and Nesbit made only three unforced errors.

He also has fond memories of summer junior play, especially of matchups he had with top players such as Mike Brennan of Minneapolis West ("a very stylish player"), Brennan's teammate Mark Nammacher ("a lefty with a lot of experience—great quickness with good technique"), and Allyn Dart of Minnetonka ("another tough lefty, a big guy who had the talent but was inconsistent").

After high school Nesbit enrolled at the U of WI-Eau Claire, where he earned a degree in history education with a coaching minor and played varsity tennis for an NAIA team which advanced to the Nationals three of the four years he played. Scott played Nos. 1 and 2 singles for the Bluegolds his first three years and No. 1 singles as a senior and No. 1 doubles his last three years. His senior year he finished second at No. 1 singles in the conference tournament and he and his partner won the No. 1 doubles title. As a team Eau Claire was ranked as high as No. 11 his senior year, and Nesbit also earned academic all-American honors in 1979.

Though Nesbit was a successful singles player in college and as an adult (he was once ranked as high as No. 2 in the men's 35s), he excelled in high school as a doubles player. In addition, as an adult he won the 35-and-over Section doubles title in 1992 (with former Austin Pacelli star Fred Budde) and was ranked as high as No. 4 in Men's Doubles (with high school teammate Greg Swendseen). A clever performer with a wonderful feel for the ball, Nesbit also earned two 18-and-under No. 1 Section doubles rankings (with Swendseen). Perhaps he liked doubles so much because it reminded him of chess: "You can put so much variety in it and you have to mix it up." But he was also a skilled high school singles player whose highest summer ranking was No. 4 his final year in the 18s.

Nesbit's partner, Arnold, received a great deal of encouragement and help with his tennis from two former U of M players—his stepfather and Bob Van Hoef. As a youngster he worked at the Edina Country Club "stringing rackets and saving to buy a metal racket." At the Club he also had opportunities to hit with the likes of Craig Jones, Ted Taney, and Butch Derksen.

In what must have been a bittersweet moment for Arnold, he capped a successful 1975 spring season by winning the state doubles title. His heart heavy with sadness, for his stepfather had died in March and did not get to share in his joy, he nonetheless persevered, "trying to win it for my dad." He also recalls that "I had a partner (Scott) I could completely trust to be a perfect sportsman and fierce competitor." For his part Nesbit enjoyed playing with Arnold as well and said of Arnold's game, "He had a great kick serve that people had trouble returning."

Though he played first singles his senior year, Arnold remembers that the season had an unhappy ending because of what he called "a combination of stupidity and youth." It seems that he reached the finals of an arm wrestling competition (held in front of the entire student body), lost badly, and in the process injured his shoulder. As a result he developed severe tendonitis and missed the last three weeks of the season. He did not play tennis in college, but he graduated from the U of M and since then has been doing standup comedy and magic shows.

In addition to their success in tennis, Nesbit and Arnold have made names for themselves as adults, but on very different stages. With his partners Michael Pearce-Donley and Bob Stromberg, Arnold helped create one of the most successful local stage shows in recent years, "Triple Espresso," a show that has been performed before adoring audiences in Minnesota, all over the U.S., and in Europe. In fact, it was even translated into Danish for an eleven-week run in a Copenhagen theater. Nesbit, on the other hand, has stayed with tennis and today serves as the men's and women's tennis coach and a physical education teacher at St. Olaf College.

1976–Andy Ringlien & Tim Ross
Northfield

In what was considered a significant upset, a team from Northfield stopped the six-year run of Lake Conference doubles champions by claiming the 1976 title over a strong field of 24 entrants. An article by Jim Wells in the *St. Paul Pioneer Press* said of their win, "The biggest surprise of the tournament, however, was in doubles competition where Northfield's Andy Ringlien and Tim Ross beat the favored Edina East team of Bruce Ervin and Brian Johnson in the semifinals and then Don and Doug McGregor of Duluth East for the title... Ringlien, a 15-year-old freshman, and Ross, a senior, came into the tournament unseeded and unsung" (June 6, 1976).

Andy Ringlien (Left) & Tim Ross

Their victory was even more remarkable considering that they had finished second in Region 1 competition (behind 1977 champions Tom Van Deinse and Doug Luebbe of Winona Cotter) and that they had to win five matches because they did not receive a first round bye. So on the first day of competition they played three matches, winning each in straight sets: over Jim Scipioni and Gary Flaim of Virginia, Al Damerow and Rick Balamut of Columbia Heights, and Irv Neumann and Tom Groff of North St. Paul.

But the semis and finals would not be so easy, for both those Saturday matches were nail-biting three-setters in which the Raiders' duo lost the opening set. In all five tournament matches, Ross and Ringlien used an aggressive, attacking style featuring crisp volleys and booming overheads hit with new metal rackets (a Head Professional

and a Head Master) to overcome their opponents. This was especially true in their upset over Johnson and Ervin of Edina East.

Ringlien, from his perspective as an adult, made an astute observation about these new metal rackets and how they transformed the game of tennis: "Playing with wooden rackets required consistency, placement, foot speed." But, he said, "The new rackets started to allow power with enough control so bigger players could trump consistent smaller players who relied on control." As a result, with his six-foot-three-inch wingspan and big serve and volley game, he (and the six foot one Ross) could hit winners from everywhere on the court.

Though their 2-6, 6-3, 6-1 win over the Edina pair was huge, the final match against the McGregor twins, though a bit anticlimactic, was closer (4-6, 6-4, 6-4). Ringlien recalls that the McGregors "were so identical that people in the crowd accused them of not rotating serves in the third set." Another interesting footnote to this story is that Ross and Ringlien stayed up until two AM the night before the finals, eating pizza and chatting.

This doubles pair took very different roads on the way to the title, still Northfield's only tennis championship in either boys' or girls' tennis. Both were all-around athletes, but Ross did not begin playing competitive tennis until his junior year. He and another refugee from the baseball program, Mark Halvorson, joined the team that year and helped Northfield advance to the State Tournament for the first time as a team, where they lost only one match on the way to the 1975 consolation championship. In fact, Ross played very few tournaments in high school and was content to hone his big serve and volley game in high school competition and in sparring matches with his teammates.

Ringlien, on the other hand, began playing with his older brother, Jeff, at age 6 or 7. They tagged along when their parents played, then accompanied their father Warren on "some nights when he played with the Northfield Tennis Club." These adult members, whom he called "my first coaches," allowed him to hit with them and later, according to Andy, "convinced my parents to enter me in my first tournaments at about age 9." He remembers playing with his mother's wooden girls' racket and losing to an older ranked player 6-0, 6-0 in his first junior tournament, but this would be a rare loss, for Ringlien went on to carve out a very successful junior and high school career for himself. Twice ranked No. 1 in NWTA singles (once in the 16s and once in the 18s), he was also ranked No. 1 in doubles two times (once in the 12s with Jeff Carlson of Madison and once in the 18s with Duke Paluch of Rapid City, SD), and two other times he was ranked No. 2 in singles. During the summers, traveling with Mike Quinnell of Lakeville, he also played on the national circuit. And his senior year in high school the coaches ranked him No. 2 behind 1978-79 singles champion Brian Johnson.

Though Ringlien advanced to State in singles his last three years, he would come up short, finishing fourth his junior year and losing in the quarters to runner-up Dave Morin of White Bear Mariner his senior year. He finished his high school career with an eye-popping 133-17 record and earned the first of only three Division 1 tennis scholarships for players from Northfield (in 2005 Christina Keesey earned the only one for girls' tennis and that same year her brother Matt earned one as well).

Also a terrific all-around athlete, Ringlien held the school record for interceptions (sixteen) as a defensive back in football and was a high-scoring forward in hockey for three years. In tennis he had a smooth, all-around game honed at tennis camps such as Ramey in Northfield and Tennis and Life at Gustavus, and he had a big serve and volley. *St. Paul Pioneer Press Dispatch* writer Jim Wells said of his game, "He's smooth with a capital 'S,' moves gracefully, seemingly without effort. His serve carries a whistle with it. He can play with power, keep the tempo swift or slow it down... But Ringlien's greatest asset is his mental toughness" (June 10, 1978). His opponents all respected his game, and some, including Jeff Carlson of Madison, considered him their toughest opponent in high school.

At the U of WI Ringlien played four years on the varsity, moving up the ladder from No. 5 singles and No. 2 doubles as a freshman to No. 1 doubles and co-No. 1 singles his junior and senior years. As a senior he was voted All-Big 10, and he recalls some memorable matches with top nationally ranked players. "I remember losing to Mike Leach [of Michigan] 7-5, 7-6 two weeks before he was to become NCAA champion and losing a three-setter

indoors to Ken Flach" [of the Davis Cup and pro doubles pair, Flach and Seguso]. His freshman year he and his partner took second behind Minnesota's Hakan Almstrom and Kent Helgeson at No. 2 doubles.

Ross, whom Ringlien called "one of the solid older influences on my young life who really took me under his wing and showed me the ropes of adolescence," also went on to play tennis in college at Augsburg. Ringlien, describing his pairing with Ross, said, "He intimidated people with his power and bravado, and I filled in with my consistency and experience as needed."

After graduating from college, Ross stuck with tennis, serving for several years as a local tennis pro and stringer with the Northwest Clubs. Armed with a BS in mechanical engineering, Ringlien took a job with IBM in Charlotte, NC (helping design dot matrix printers), but now he designs application software for warehouse management systems. For recreation he mostly played golf after graduation, but he has returned to tennis, competing in a few money tournaments each year in North Carolina.

Finally, Ringlien speaks fondly of his high school tennis years: "I was very fortunate to be in the company of a group of extraordinary older kids and coaches that welcomed me to the team [he joined the tournament team as a seventh grader] and taught me much about tennis and growing up." He also remembers "playing cribbage on the bus rides, lots of matches in rural Minnesota towns on some very hazardous court conditions, hitting over wire nets [Austin], and shoveling courts and practicing indoors on gym floors. In fact, his "Everyman" experiences mirror those of so many young players who have skipped around the courts in Minnesota over the past seventy-five years.

1977—Tom Van Deinse & Doug Luebbe
Winona Cotter

"Tournabout is fair play," so in 1977 the team that lost to the McGregor twins in the '76 tournament won the title by overcoming the same McGregors in the finals. In what the *1976-1977 MSHSL ANNUAL* called upsets in the team and both individual competitions, Blue Earth beat Minnetonka in team play, Kevin Smith of Hopkins Lindbergh took the singles, and Tom Van Deinse and Doug Luebbe of Winona Cotter captured the doubles crown. Here's what the *ANNUAL* said about these contests: "Perhaps the only thing more upsetting would be ranking the degree of upsets. The doubles victory by Luebbe and Van Deinse, both starters on Cotter's state championship basketball team, was undoubtedly the mildest" ("Blue Earth Wins Boys Tennis Team Title"). I expect they ranked this as the mildest upset because in '76 the Cotter pair lost to the McGregors in a tough three-set match in the quarters and the McGregors were once the top-ranked 16-and-under doubles team in the NWTA.

Determined to avenge their 1976 loss, Van Deinse said, "I remember spending hours and hours and hours practicing tennis. We even shoveled off the courts late in the fall and early in the spring to practice more tennis." Their efforts paid off and in '77 the Cotter boys, Region 1 champions for the second year in a row, waltzed through their first three matches, winning each in straight sets: over Jim Scipioni and Stupca of Virginia; Irv Neumann and Tom Groff of North St. Paul;

Doug Luebbe (Left) & Tom Van Deinse

and a strong duo from team champion Blue Earth in the semis, 1980 Class A singles champion Gregg Anderson and his '79 championship doubles partner Thane Deleon. The final match was a donnybrook, and in the end just two games separated the Winona team from the McGregors, as they prevailed 7-6, 6-7, 6-4. This was the second doubles win in a row for a team from Region 1 and another unlucky finish for the McGregors.

Not surprisingly, the Cotter lads considered this win the highlight of their high school tennis careers. Luebbe remarked, "Beating the McGregors was the highlight for me. After losing the year before [to the McGregors], though we both felt like we could have won that match, we were respectful of their talent but looked forward to the

challenge. I remember thinking, after we split sets, that we could lose again." Van Deinse also called it a memorable moment for him, "especially since that year we had won the small school state basketball championship as well. Following that basketball championship we made the *Winona Daily News* headline, were greeted back to town with a miles-long parade, and were named honorary ambassadors for the city. Following our tennis championship we received a three-inch column write-up hidden somewhere in the sports section. We were not offended by this lack of acknowledgement, but we found it interesting." Ah, the fate of the so-called minor sports.

While Van Deinse and Luebbe rarely competed in NWTA Section tournaments (Van Deinse felt that "there was enough good-to-great competition in Winona and I could play for free" and he also said his parents "couldn't afford to send us nine kids on the junior tournament circuit on my dad's teacher salary"), they were excellent high school players who continued in tennis after graduating from high school.

Luebbe lettered four years in both basketball and tennis at St. Mary's College in Winona. And all four years he played No. 1 singles on a tennis team he called "slightly above average." Van Deinse attended Winona State College for one year and said of his tennis, "It was not memorable except for one good post-season upset playing doubles with Winona High grad Randy Koehler" (whom Luebbe called one of the top guys he played in high school).

After that one year at Winona State, Van Deinse transferred to the U of M where he focused on his studies in math and philosophy of science. Though he no longer competed in college tennis, he taught at John Gardiner's Tennis Camps in Sun Valley, ID. In addition, he said, "I was fortunate enough to play some exhibiiton tennis with and against Ken Rosewall and met or taught countless others in the rich and famous set." He stayed at Gardiner's for five years, teaching "what I was told to teach; but as I gained confidence I started to think about how I actually play and really became a stroke technician." He sees what beautiful strokes his five children have and regrets that he had not learned good strokes and gotten a bit more serious about tennis when he was younger.

But math was also a passion, and even while he worked as a tennis pro at the Owatonna Indoor Club (later in his career), he was editing Bertrand Russell's *Principia Mathematica*. He also worked at different tennis camps in Minnesota, Wisconsin, and Iowa, and in the summers he served as a pro in Michigan. And though he still loves to play the game, he said, "I love to teach tennis maybe more—I know I'm a better teacher than player."

So today he lives in Michigan and serves as the CEO of the Grand Traverse Bay YMCA, a converted older tennis facility. In addition, he still finds time to teach tennis, with help from his two sons.

As for Luebbe's adult life, right after college he began working at IBM in Rochester as a software engineer, then moved into management to work in the development lab as a middle manager. He has three children and still plays tennis, mostly for exercise with his family. His oldest daughter, Lauren, played on three of Rochester Lourdes' state championship girls' teams and was runner-up in doubles in 2002.

Both Van Deinse and Luebbe will be remembered as all-around athletes (Luebbe played football, basketball, and tennis, and Van Deinse basketball and tennis) who helped Cotter win the 1977 basketball title, finish second in region tennis in '77, and take home a medal in the individual tournament. Luebbe is also a member of the Cotter Sports Hall of Fame. (For more on these two champions, see Chapter Ten.)

1978—Greg & Jeff Carlson
Madison

Surprisingly, for the third straight year, a team from outstate Minnesota captured the doubles title, even though Edina East won the team and singles championships (Brian

Johnson). That 1978 team was the brother combination of senior Greg and junior Jeff Carlson of Madison. Region 3 champions and three-time state entrants in doubles, the brothers had also played a major role in Madison's march to the team finals in '75. Their togetherness paid off this year, for the pair breezed through the competition, winning all four matches in straight sets. Because they were region champions, the Madison boys had a first-round bye, then opened play with a win over Dave Johnson and Rob Eidem of Fridley. Then in straight sets they knocked off three very strong pairs, future singles champion Bob Bateman (a ninth grader) and senior Tom Szarzynski of Edina East; the eventual third-place doubles winners from Coon Rapids (seniors Dave Peden and Daryl Randall); and Blue Earth's '79 Class A champions, sophomore Gregg Anderson and junior Thane Deleon. With sweat dripping off their bodies on a 90-degree day, the Carlsons savored their well-earned 6-3, 7-5 triumph over the Blue Earth pair.

Both Greg and Jeff played varsity tennis since their seventh-grade years, and Jeff remembers the pride he took in beating older players that first year, many of whom were seniors who didn't take kindly to losing to a junior high munchkin. He also spoke fondly of the years he and his teammates made the trek to Minneapolis to participate in the State Tournament: "Playing in the State Tournament

Jeff (Left) & Greg Carlson

was always a blast. We would get to stay at the Curtis Hotel. Being from such a small school and playing in one class and beating all of the large schools was a great feeling" (this was the last year, until a short run from 1983 to '86, that there would be just one class in tennis competition).

Both Greg and Jeff participated all six years of their careers at State, either as members of the Madison team or as individuals. Jeff partnered with Greg three years in doubles and in 1979 he made it in singles. Greg played in the tournament for five years in doubles (two years with brother Barry and his last three with Jeff).

As for Madison coach Jolly Carlson, he took pride in knowing that this doubles title (at that time) was a Minnesota record for brothers and a father-coach from the smallest school (87 students in the 1978 senior class). (For more on the Carlson brothers and their father, see Chapter Ten.)

1979—Ben Ziegler & Dan Shannon
Minnetonka—Class AA

Gregg Anderson & Thane DeLeon
Blue Earth—Class A

A new day in state tennis dawned in 1979, as the MSHSL separated the big cats from the small cats, dividing them up into Class AA and Class A schools. In the large-school competition, Lake Conference power Edina East once again won the team title, East's Brian Johnson repeated as singles champion, and Minnetonka's Ben Ziegler and Dan Shannon took the doubles title.

During the year Shannon had played No. 2 singles (behind John Wheaton) and Ziegler had played mostly No. 1 doubles, so they had not played much doubles together in the spring season. And though Ziegler was not a ranked player, Shannon had been a very successful summer tournament player. For example, he was ranked in the NWTA every year from the 12s to the 16s, reaching a position as high as No. 2 in 14 and 16 singles and No. 1 in 16 doubles (with Pat Rost of Sioux Falls).

Though Shannon and Ziegler had one three-set

match of the four they won to secure the title, (a 6-7, 6-1, 6-1 win over Scott Sarkela and Jack Bowe of Grand Rapids in the quarters), the other three were decisive straight-set matches, the first over Jeff Brecht and Mike Borer of Anoka. After that quarterfinal three-setter, in the semis they defeated seventh-grade phenom Casey Merickel and his partner Tony Tillemans from St. Cloud Apollo, then dispatched Lake Conference foes John Hobson and Brian Lew of Edina West in the finals (6-1, 6-3).

Shannon for a number of years was a top local USPTA pro teacher and the director of tennis at the new Fort Snelling Club, but he has recently moved to Montana.

The Class A doubles title went to junior Gregg Anderson and senior Thane Deleon of Blue Earth, the 1978 runners-up. Like Shannon and Ziegler, the Blue Earth pair had only one close match, defeating Chuck Ankeyny and

Ben Ziegler (Left) & Dan Shannon

Dave Meyers of Blake in the semis 6-1, 4-6, 6-2. Then in the finals they romped over Jeff Stueven (a 1980 Class A doubles champion) and John Chesier of Pipestone 6-1, 6-4. The first day of the tournament they handled two foes without any trouble, Pat Doud and Mark Moffett of Staples and Monty Flinsch and Chris Munholland of SPA.

Both Anderson and Deleon were stalwarts on the 1977 Blue Earth state team champions, Anderson holding down the No. 1 singles spot as a freshman and Deleon the No. 3 singles position. Gregg was a crafty lefthander described by his coach, Hal Schroeder, as "a very steady player who hit a nice twist serve." Citing as evidence a net skimmer that cost Gregg the second set in a 5-4 tiebreaker in the singles championship his senior year, Schroeder said, "Gregg never got discouraged." (For more on Anderson, see Chapters Five and Ten.)

Of DeLeon Coach Schroeder said, "He was small in stature—about five foot seven—but he had beautiful strokes and a good attitude. He, too, never gave up." DeLeon was also a very artistic young man, even designing the high school yearbook cover his senior year. Today he makes jewelry and lives in Arizona.

1980s

1980—Tom Shustarich & Mark Maroste
Virginia—AA

Jeff Stueven (Left) & Brad Sorenson

Jeff Stueven & Brad Sorenson
Pipestone—A

In 1980 two teams from outstate schools claimed the doubles titles: Tom Shustarich and Mark Maroste from Virginia in Class AA and Jeff Stueven and Brad Sorenson of Pipestone in Class A. This would be the first time both doubles winners came from outstate schools, something that would take place only two other times in the history of

Tom Shustarich (Left) & Mark Maroste

two-class competition. Moreover, the victory by Shustarich and Maroste was the first singles or doubles title won by players from northern Minnesota schools since John Wirtanen and Jim Miller won the '61 doubles title and a team championship for Coleraine.

For Shustarich and Maroste, just juniors, the road to the championship was bumpy until they reached the finals, where they trounced Burnsville's Rick Lacher and Doug Elsass 6-3, 6-0. Two of their first three matches went the distance (three sets) and their quarterfinal match was a dogfight against Thief River Falls' Bill Jury and Paul Copperang. In the first round the Virginia lads outlasted brothers Randy and Mark Covin of St. Louis Park 6-4, 4-6, 6-4; defeated Jury and Copperang in the quarters 7-6, 6-4; then came from behind to knock off Kevin Gorman and Doug Robertson of Rochester Mayo 4-6, 7-5, 6-2 in the semis.

This was a well-earned championship for two guys who felt more at home on an ice rink than on a tennis court. Both became big-time Division 1 hockey players, Maroste playing collegiately at Michigan Tech (and professionally for several years in Germany) and Shustarich playing college hockey at Princeton. In a *Minneapolis Tribune* article by Roman Augustoviz, Virginia head coach John Juehrs said he "considers Shustarich and Maroste athletes first, tennis players second. They play football, hockey, and tennis. Shustarich was the quarterback on the football team and the leading scorer on the hockey team. And when you face fourth down and half a foot, you learn to cope with pressure" (June 1, 1980).

And though hockey and football may have been their bread and butter sports, they were good tennis players as well. Future Virginia coach Jim Prittinen called Maroste (who began playing tennis with a beat-up racket he scrounged from a garbage can) "the best natural athlete I've worked with." Also, said Prittinen, he was "a flashy guy who put points away." Complementing him, according to Prittinen, was Shustarich, "a solid player who was very steady." Both played summer tournaments, and while neither achieved elite status in singles (Maroste topped out at No. 14 in the 16-and-under singles and Shustarich at No. 23), they earned the No. 1 NWTA ranking their final year in 16-and-under doubles and a No. 4 ranking in the 18 doubles.

So even though they focused more on hockey and football, their state doubles win was not a huge surprise given their success in summer tournament play and given their natural athletic ability. Unfortunately for them, they were not able to defend their title the next year; for they lost to Shawn Bresnahan and Ken Dahlquist of St. Cloud Tech in the first round. Prittinen noted, however, that Maroste played much of the year with a broken hand, so they were not at full strength for the 1981 tournament.

Maroste served for a time as an assistant hockey coach at his alma mater, Michigan Tech, and Shustarich is an engineer in Minneapolis.

The road to the title for the Class A champions (Stueven and Sorenson) was a smoother one, for they polished off all four of their opponents in straight sets. Their first victims were Chris Lund and Dan Freedland of Minnehaha Academy, then they disposed of Richard Kyle and Charlie Stringer of St. Paul Academy in the quarters. On the final day they defeated Jim Finc and Greg Panyan of Gilbert in the semis and clinched the title with a tougher 7-6, 6-4 victory in the finals over senior Mark Warrington and junior Ryan Knee, two key players from Blue Earth's 1980 championship team.

Stueven (a senior) had finished second in doubles in 1979 (with John Chesier) and Sorenson, just a sophomore, performed well in singles his last two years, finishing third as a junior after losing in the semis to '81 champion Jakob Victorin and to runner-up Scott Duncan of Blake in the quarters his senior year. This championship would be the only one for Pipestone and longtime coach Jerry Hutchinson, who called Sorenson "the best player we ever had in Pipestone."

After graduation in 1982, Sorenson went to Gustavus to continue his tennis career. He helped the Gusties finish fifth in the '86 NCAA Division 3 team tournament his senior year, a year he also won the No. 4 MIAC singles and No. 2 doubles titles (with Riley Horan of Rochester). But he was also a key member of the 1983-85 Gustavus teams that finished fifth, second, and seventh respectively in the NCAA national tournament. As a freshman he played No. 1 doubles with Horan, his sophomore year he played No. 2 doubles with Marc Miller, and his junior year he held down the No. 3 singles and No. 1 doubles spots (partnering with Mark Kruger of Minnetonka). Today he works as a financial planner in the Twin Cities area.

As for Stueven, he played tennis at Moorhead State U and earned a degree in engineering.

1981—Bob Bordewick & Jeff Ecklund
Edina East—AA

Ryan Knee & Steve Beckendorf
Blue Earth—A

If tennis wasn't such a gentlemanly sport one could imagine seeing youthful Edina fans wielding brooms and chanting "Sweep! Sweep!" during the 1981 tournament. For Edina East did indeed sweep aside the opposition and take the team, singles (Bob Bateman), and doubles titles (Bob Bordewick and Jeff Ecklund). Seniors Bordewick and Edklund, the Nos. 2 and 3 singles players on East's championship squad, teamed up during the individual tournament and won three matches in regional play and four more at State. This short run of just seven matches earned them the Class AA doubles title.

At State they got off to a slow start, losing a set in each of their first two matches and squeaking out tie-breakers in the first sets. First up was the team of juniors Paul Masse and Gavin O'Duffy of Rochester Mayo, whom the East pair defeated 7-6, 3-6, 6-3. Next they knocked off senior Rick Erdahl and his junior partner Chris Flannery of Minneapolis Washburn 7-6, 4-6, 6-2 in the quarters; then in the semis they defeated Anoka seniors Doug Marker and Bill Ervin 6-1, 6-2. Continuing to click on all cylinders in the final, Bordewic and Ecklund outplayed junior Peter Lilleberg and senior Dave Pahos of Henry Sibley, trouncing them 6-2, 6-1 to complete the Edina East sweep.

And while they were not disappointed to take home the top prize in doubles, both felt that it was a bit like being selected in the tenth round of the NFL draft—nice to be chosen but with not as much recognition. Ecklund, in a *Minneapolis Star* article titled "Edina Doubles Titlists Unimpressed with Win," said, "The way I look at it, it's just doubles. I would never watch the finals of a doubles match. It's boring. We were just here for the ride" (June 7, 1981). Bordewick added, "Yah, a free ride. People forget about the doubles champions by Tuesday [this was Saturday]. But in singles, everyone knows who won that for a couple of years. I don't remember who won the doubles last year... But I remember the singles champion—Chris Combs (of Edina West)" (June 7, 1981).

In a June 8, 1981, *Minneapolis Tribune* article, Bordewic tempered his criticism of doubles after further reflection: "'You can beat a guy pretty bad in singles but then he can team up with another mediocre player and they'll beat you. Doubles evens things out a little.' Then Bordewick paused and admitted, 'Yeah, it was fun.'"

Though Ecklund was not a top-ranked junior player during summer NWTA play, Bordewic was, earning a ranking as high as No. 4 in the 16-and-under singles and No. 1 in 18 doubles with Mark Covin of Minneapolis, a year in which they also won the Sectional doubles championship.

Perhaps Bordewick's success in singles during the summer made him covet that title more, but not so the 1981 Class A champions. Blue Earth's Ryan Knee and Steve Beckendorf were delighted to win their doubles title. According to the aforementioned June 7 article in the *Minneapolis Star*, after they defeated Pine City seniors Tim Werner and Wayne Hagstrom in the finals 6-1, 4-6, 6-4, "Beckendorf threw his racket in the air and he and Knee cheered." Knee, a senior, then said, "I'm sure I'd rather win the singles but hey, this is just as good. I finished third in singles last year [actually he and partner Mark Warrington took second in the doubles] and got a bronze medal [silver]. Third [second] wasn't good enough. I prefer gold. Bronze is kind of an ugly color." Beckendorf, just a sophomore, chimed in, "It's a state title. And we'll have our pictures in the (State High School League) yearbook. That's good enough for me" (June 7, 1981).

Except for that tight three-setter in the finals, the lads from Blue Earth defeated their first three opponents in straight sets, winning over eighth graders Billy Nichols and Scott Worrel of Pine City in round one, juniors Steve Youngs and Jon Jorgenson of Montevideo in round two; and senior Matt Ravden and his junior partner Matt Bellis of SPA in the semis.

This odd couple pairing of Beckendorf (a youngster and just a No. 2 doubles player during the season) and Knee (a senior and Blue Earth's No. 1 singles player) worked out smashingly for the Bucs. Said Coach Hal Schroeder about his champions, "Steve [Beckendorf] hit the ball hard and had a good serve and Ryan [Knee] was one of our most improved players." Schroeder took great pride in watching Knee develop, for "he had no background in tennis when he came to Blue Earth in sixth grade." Though not ranked in NWTA singles, Knee and Beckendorf showed some potential when they earned a No. 10 doubles ranking in Knee's final year in the 18s.

Both lads played some tennis in college, Knee at Montana and Beckendorf at Gustavus. And, according to coach Schroeder, Knee is now a professor at the U of M and Beckendorf lives in California.

1982—Mark Schoening & Ross Erickson
Edina East-AA

Steve Beckendorf & Myles Anderson
Blue Earth-A

The phrase "apples and oranges" is often used to describe things that are very different, so this year there were "apples and oranges" doubles champions. One team, the "apples" from Edina East, was made up of two guys who had played singles all year—senior Mark Schoening at No. 1 and junior Ross Erickson at No. 3—and the other (the "oranges") was made up of two underclassmen who had played No. 1 doubles most of the year, junior Steve Beckendorf (the 1981 champion) and ninth grader Myles Anderson of Blue Earth. In addition, their paths to the finals differed slightly in that the Edina pair encountered great resistance in their first match, struggling in three sets to defeat sophomores Robbie Silas and Mark Kasner of Hibbing 7-5, 4-6, 6-3. Meanwhile, Beckendorf and Anderson cruised to a 6-1, 6-0 first-round win over Ada junior Mark Larsen and his senior partner Lisa Josephson (only the second girl, after Ann Henricksson, to participate in the boys' tournament).

The next two rounds saw both teams advance with straight-set wins. In Class AA Schoening and Erickson knocked off senior Brenden O'Duffy and sophomore Michael Gorman of Rochester Mayo in the quarters; then in the semis they defeated the brothers Paul (a junior) and Scott Greenhaw (a senior) of Hutchinson. Meanwhile, on the Class A front, the Blue Earth lads took out the team of junior John Hovren and his senior partner Dan Toop of Glenwood/Villard in the quarters; they followed that up with a semifinal win over juniors Barry Nordstrom and Jeff Goldenberg of Blake.

Both teams encountered stiff resistance in the finals, however, Schoening and Erickson from Austin's No. 2 and 3 singles players, senior Kevin Arnold and sophomore Steve Gardner, who had paired up for a run at doubles after teammate Scott Barber, the Packers' No. 1 player, decided to play singles. Anderson and Beckendorf had to

fend off another challenge from a Blake team, this time the tandem of sophomores Tom Price and Walter Berry. Though both final matches went three sets, the difference in these matches was that the Blue Earth boys had to claw their way back into the contest after losing the first set, while the Edina boys won their first set. So the Blue Earth team prevailed 3-6, 6-2, 6-4, and the Edina duo won 6-4, 0-6, 7-5. By the way, both defeated players from the respective state team champions: Austin in Class AA and Blake in Class A. Erickson had also been a member of the 1980 Edina West championship squad.

Despite those "apples" and "oranges" differences between the two champions, both showed grit and determination and both took home first-place medals. For Edina it was their ninth doubles championship and for Blue Earth it was their third, and second in a row for the hard-hitting Beckendorf, who became just the fifth player to win with two different partners.

All four of these champions played NWTA tournaments, Erickson reaching a high ranking of No. 8 in singles in the 14-and-unders and a No. 4 ranking in 14 doubles with partner Ron Skanse. He and Schoening also played together in the summer, once ranking No. 8 in doubles in the 16s. Both chose to play doubles this year because, as Schoening noted in an article by Howard Sinker in the *Minneapolis Tribune*, "advancing to state play [in singles] would otherwise have been impossible" (June 13, 1982). Making it impossible were two formidable adversaries, that year's state champion, Darryl Laddin, and runner-up David Wheaton. With Schoening gone, Erickson teamed up in 1983 with a different partner, fellow senior David Cote. Alas for them, they bumped into the Anderson brothers from Blue Earth in the round of 16 and lost.

Following his graduation from Edina, Erickson had a successful college tennis career at Carleton, beginning at No. 6 singles and No. 3 doubles his first year and moving up the ladder to No. 3 singles and No. 2 doubles his senior year. Coach Bob Bonner said of Erickson, "He was a very strong player at No. 6 singles on a team that beat Gustavus at nationals in 1985 and finished sixth in the tournament."

Erickson lives in the Twin Cities and has continued to distinguish himself as a player (reaching a ranking as high as No. 2 in 35-and-over singles in 2002) and as a coach of adult tennis league teams.

Beckendorf had been ranked in doubles, as mentioned earlier, and he was also ranked No. 29 in singles one year in the 16s. His partner, Anderson, was one of the best doubles players ever to play Minnesota high school tennis, and he was always a top-ranked junior doubles player in the Section. In high school he played doubles almost exclusively, working his way up from No. 3 doubles as a seventh grader to No. 1 doubles as a ninth grader, and winning 203 matches in his six-year career.

In 1983 Beckendorf teamed up with junior Mike Fischer but lost early in the tournament, and Myles Anderson paired up with his seventh grade brother Roger and they finished third. (For more on Myles Anderson, see Chapter Ten.)

1983—Dave Nelson & Shawn Bresnahan
St. Cloud Tech

After a four-year run of two-class play, boys' tennis reverted to a one-class format again in 1983 because there weren't enough schools to warrant two classes. It would be more difficult to win a title this year, in part because the draw was also larger (24 teams), so predictably the doubles

Shawn Bresnahan (Left) & Dave Nelson

champions came from a big-school, team champion St. Cloud Tech. This was the senior duo of No. 1 singles player Dave Nelson and No. 1 doubles player Shawn Bresnahan, who swept all four of their opponents in straight sets to take back to St. Cloud the school's first tennis title in singles or doubles play.

Following a first-round bye, the Tigers' pair defeated a team from Blake (senior Barry Nordstrom and junior Shekhar Sane). In the quarters they bumped off the Hibbing pair of senior Mike Nettell and his junior partner, Jeff Lipovetz; then they took care of the Anderson boys from Blue Earth (sophomore Myles and seventh grader Roger) in the semis. The final match provided their stiffest challenge, but the Tech boys nonetheless upended another team from Blake, senior Scott Duncan and his junior partner Tom Price, 7-6, 6-3.

Relatively unknown on the summer tournament circuit, Nelson and Bresnahan were never ranked in doubles and both earned only modest singles rankings which came late in their junior careers (Bresnahan was once No. 9 in the 16s and Nelson No. 15 one year in the 18s).

Of the pair, only Bresnahan played college tennis, at St. Cloud State.

1984—Sean Potter & Todd Schlorf
St. Cloud Tech

Although St. Cloud Tech wasn't able to repeat as team champion this year, two talented youngsters claimed another doubles title for the Tigers. Junior Sean Potter and sophomore Todd Schlorf, Tech's regular-season No. 1 doubles team, outclassed brothers Alfred (a junior) and Sekou (a senior) Bangoura of Coon Rapids in the final 6-2, 6-4. The Bangouras, natives of the west African nation of Guinea, had played singles during the year—Sekou at No. 2 and Alfred at No. 3.

And though this final match didn't tax the Tech lads overmuch, they labored long in the vineyard to get to the finals, particularly in their first-round and semifinal matches. For example, it took three sets to escape in their opening match, a 6-7, 7-5, 6-3 win over White Bear Lake seniors Kai Thierhoff and Thomas Szigat. Their second match on Friday was easier, a 6-2, 6-2 win over Peter

Hart (a junior) and Brad Ward (a sophomore) of SPA; but on Saturday they struggled in the semis against Jeff Lipovetz (a senior) and Mike Vidmar (a junior) of Hibbing, the eventual third-place winners. This time, however, Potter and Schlorf won the first set, but it took three sets to put the Hibbing duo on the canvas (6-3, 5-7, 6-1).

and surprisingly, given Tech's status as a dynasty team, theirs would be only the second (and the last) individual championship earned by Tech players.

It must be added that the Tech lads set themselves up for this title by honing their skills in summer NWTA tournaments. Schlorf was the more successful of the two,

Todd Schlorf (Left) & Sean Potter

This doubles triumph was the *piece de resistance* for a St. Cloud Tech team that had feasted on its opponents all year. And though the Bears from Blake nipped the Tigers in the team final 3-2, all six of Tech's individual tournament entrants clawed their way into the state individual tournament. Schlorf's brother Jay (a senior) and his partner Eric Wolfe (a junior) won a round before losing to the Bangouras, and singles players Pat Dunn (a senior) and John Lauerman (a junior) made it in singles. Dunn, Tech's No. 1 player, lost in the first round to senior Mark Maertens of Brooklyn Center, but Lauerman advanced to the quarters, where he lost to Apple Valley senior Matt Boos. In the end, however, it was the Potter-Schlorf duo that came through,

earning his first singles ranking in the 10-and-unders and sitting as high as No. 2 in singles (in the 14s). On the other hand, while Potter also competed in singles, his highest ranking was just a No. 22 in the 14s. Both were dynamite doubles players, with Potter once ranking as high as third in 18-and-under doubles with his St. Cloud teammate Jay Schlorf.

But it was Todd Schlorf who excelled in doubles. That comment about the best doubles team in the world being John McEnroe and anybody else comes to mind again, for on the Minnesota scene the same could be said of the two youngest Anderson brothers, Myles and Roger. But it could also be said of Schlorf, for he earned No. 1 rankings with his brother Jay (in the 14s and 16s), with teammate Dave Jussila (in the 16s and 18s) and once with Chris Boily in the 14s, a year in which they also won the Sectional doubles. And, in the two years he and Jussila played together, they also won 18-and-under Sectional doubles titles.

After graduating from Tech, Schlorf enrolled at nearby St. John's where he was a standout in MIAC tennis. Today he lives in Texas and works for Banker's Systems. He has kept up his tennis, and is in fact a highly ranked adult player in the Lone Star State. Todd's brother Jay (a senior) also played college tennis, first at St. Cloud State and later with his brother at St. John's, and he was for many years a part-owner of the former Augusta Tennis Club in St. Cloud. (For more on these St. Cloud players, see Chapter Nine.)

1985—Myles & Roger Anderson
Blue Earth

In another of those "feel good" stories, a team from outstate (and from a Class A-size school to boot) won the doubles title this year. However, in some respects it should not have surprised Minnesota tennis fans, for it was won by the two youngest of the Anderson boys from Blue Earth, senior Myles and ninth grader Roger. Almost from the time they were out of the crib, they had been groomed by their father and coach, Chuck, to be champions. Myles claims he started playing at age four and his earliest memories are "of playing tennis in the living room with my dad tossing little sponge balls, whiffle balls, shuttlecocks, and wadded-up socks or anything that could be tossed and hit with a tiny racket that just fit into my hand. We tried to hit it all the way across the living room into the hutch, trying to hit trophies, pictures, or whatever else was in there." One has to wonder how their mother, Ruth Anderson, put up with all this rough activity in the house.

And like Todd Schlorf from St. Cloud, they were extraordinary doubles players who could make other players better. So playing together they were a formidable team that rolled through each of their first three opponents in straight sets until they met up with the defending champions (Potter, now a senior, and Schlorf, a junior) in the finals. By virtue of winning the region title, the Blue Earth lads earned a bye in the first round. So in their first match in the round of 16 they trounced Eden Prairie senior Matt Patterson and junior Joel Severson; then in the quarters they had a harder time of it but still prevailed in straight sets (7-5, 6-3) over last year's third-place winners, seniors Mark Kasner and Mike Vidmar of Hibbing. Next up, in the semis, was the team of senior Tim Jachymonski and junior Jon Dean of Fridley. They, too, fell in straight sets to the Andersons.

Also taking their first three matches in straight sets, Potter and Schlorf were primed to defend their title against the upstarts from Blue Earth. Oddsmakers no doubt favored them and it was an extremely hot day (95 degrees), but after taking the first set 6-3 the Anderson boys gained confidence, only to see the Tech lads storm back to even things up (6-4). This set up a third set which had all the

Roger (Left) & Myles Anderson

drama of a tense murder mystery, with the Andersons solving the case in a nailbiting tiebreaker (7-4). Final score 6-3, 4-6, 7-6 in favor of the Andersons.

About the match Potter told *Minneapolis Star and Tribune* writer Tom Briere, "The Andersons beat us on their lobs; they had us on the defensive going back all day to retrieve those lobs" ("Underdogs Win State Tennis Titles," June 9, 1985).

As for the Andersons, Myles said, "we tried to keep our original shots low." In addition, deferring to his talented younger brother, Myles also said, "I didn't carry him. He carried me today. Yes, honestly" (June 9, 1985).

Roger, in an interview with me, said of the match,

I remember playing on the last court on the first tier at 98th Street [Racquet Club] with what I vaguely recall as a large, boisterous crowd. I say vaguely because all I truly remember is seeing my brother, my opponents, and the court. I remember it as being a very close, well-played, and competitive match either team could have won. I've been asked what I consider to be my greatest sports thrill. I always respond, winning the State Tournament with my brother in 1985.

No strangers to the spotlight, the brothers had paired up in 1983 when Roger was just a seventh grader to upset '82 champion Ross Erickson and his partner David Cote of Edina in the first round and then take third in the tournament. When asked about this experience, Roger replied,

> It was the classic story of two young kids who just didn't know any better. I don't think either of us really paid any attention to the fact we were playing in the State Tournament against people who were older and better. We were just out there playing tennis, and at the time we were real used to winning doubles matches together. But we arrived at the match with our bags packed in the car so we could leave for a tournament in Sioux Falls, SD, which we had been entered in under the assumption we'd be out of the tournament by the weekend. In a way, this took off any pressure we might have felt.

And though this 1985 title was Myles' swan song (after winning two doubles titles and finishing third another year), Roger had more worlds to conquer. It also marked the end of a fabulous junior career in doubles for Myles, a career that saw him ranked No. 1 three times (with teammate Mike Fischer in the 14s and with brother Roger in the 16s and 18s) and saw him ranked every other year with multiple partners such as Tom Trondson of Mounds View and Chris Holden of Northfield. He also won two Sectional doubles titles, one with Fischer and one with brother Roger.

Myles, too, counts winning State with Roger and playing with his brothers as highlights of his high school years: "I only wish we had been closer in age so all four of us could have played together at the same time." His coach, Hal Schroeder, said of him, "Myles was a very good

doubles player, one of the smartest doubles players I've ever seen. He knew where the ball was going and where to place it. You could put anybody with him and he'd bring up that person's ability." (For more on Roger Anderson's career, see Chapter Five and for more on both Myles and Roger, see Chapters Nine and Ten.)

1986—Guy Carteng & Mike Husebo
Edina

In what would be the final year of single-class competition, a true doubles team from Edina, senior Guy Carteng and sophomore Mike Husebo, captured the title. Carteng and Husebo, the No. 1 doubles team on an outstanding Hornets' squad, took no prisoners en route to their championship, winning all four matches in straight sets. Their first victims were junior Barry Hutchinson (son of coach Jerry Hutchinson) and sophomore Kris Kluis from Pipestone. In the quarters the Edina pair vanquished Anoka seniors Bill Carlson and Derrick Johnson.

Then, in the semis, Carteng and Husebo dispatched the team of senior Tom Cieslukowski and sophomore Dan James of Northfield, the eventual third-place winners. And in the finals they trounced a pair from Robbinsdale Cooper who had to win four matches to advance, senior John Andraschko and junior Craig Swanson 6-3, 6-0. (Once again the winning region teams, including Husebo and Carteng, earned byes because they won region titles.)

Clearly the best team in the field, the left-handed Husebo's clever shot-making and Carteng's hard hitting

Guy Carteng (Left) & Mike Husebo

made them a "human buzz saw doubles team" which carved up its opponents. Though both played singles (Carteng held down the No. 3 position in 1984 and Husebo No. 3 in '85 and No. 2 in '88), they excelled in doubles and so this triumph was not unexpected. Both also earned acclaim during summer tournament play in singles, Carteng reaching a ranking as high as No. 5 in the 14-and-unders and Husebo No. 6 in the 18s. And though Husebo was never ranked in doubles, he teamed with two partners (John Trondson in the 18s and Mike Terwilliger in the 16s) to win Sectional titles. Carteng was ranked just once in doubles (No. 3 with Chris Michaelson in the 14s).

An underclassman in 1986, Husebo would advance to the semis in doubles as a junior the next year (finishing fourth with partner Tom Murphy) and nearly make it to State his senior year in singles competition. During the '88 season he played No. 2 singles behind Mike Terwilliger on that powerhouse championship team. His coach that year, Steve Paulsen, said of Husebo, "He was really aggressive, tenacious. In doubles he was all about attacking and coming to net; he liked to chip and charge."

After graduation Husebo attended Western Kentucky U for a time and also played tennis there. He then transferred to the U of M but did not play tennis. After he left college he worked as a local tennis pro, most recently during the summer at Oak Ridge Country Club in Hopkins and at the Northwest clubs the rest of the year. I was not able to track down any information about Husebo's partner Carteng.

1987—Steve Danielson & Paul Ezerski
Eden Prairie-AA

Roger Anderson & Jamie Schmitgen
Blue Earth-A

Back to two-classes and an even 16-draw in 1987, the doubles competition was fierce in both classes. Emerging from the scrums were the teams of seniors Steve Danielson and Paul Ezerski of Eden Prairie in Class AA and (who

else?) another Anderson from Blue Earth in Class A. This Anderson was Roger, the '85 doubles champion and the last of the clan, and his partner, Jamie Schmitgen.

Proving once again that it's difficult to predict the outcome in doubles, the team of Danielson and Ezerski upset the favorites from Edina in the semis and went on to claim the Class AA title. Though they finished first in Region 2 competition, they had lost to Edina's Husebo and Tom Murphy during the year in straight sets (6-3, 6-3); and there were other imposing teams in the other half of the draw such as seniors J. P. Parenteau and Matt Brodahl of Minnetonka and juniors Dan James and Doug Cowles of Northfield. Taking care of business on the first day, the Eden Prairie duo dispatched juniors David Ouyang and Paul Solberg of White Bear Lake and Hastings' senior Rob Judge and his junior mate Mark Horsch, defeating both in straight sets.

This win set up a rematch with Husebo (a junior and a member of the 1986 doubles championship team) and Murphy (a senior). Given that the Edina pair had won in straight sets in that earlier match, it's not surprising that they were confident. In a June 6, 1987 *Star Tribune* article by Ralph Thornton, Husebo said, "I'm less nervous than last year... Tom [Murphy] and I played just so-so at the start of the season, but his serve and return are really good now. I think we have a good shot at it." In addition, the Edina pair had played doubles all year, anchoring the No. 1 spot; Danielson (No. 2) and Ezerski (No. 3) had played mostly singles.

Nevertheless, the lads from this fast-growing western suburb reversed that earlier result, beating Husebo and Murphy in straight sets 6-3, 7-5; then they came from a set down to beat Parenteau and Brodahl in the finals 4-6, 6-4, 6-4. Down 3-1 in the third set as well, Danielson and Ezerski broke serve, held serve, then broke back again.

This was Eden Prairie's first tennis championship, and coach Rich Strohkirch was understandably proud of his players: "These guys have worked real hard ... Steve [Danielson] won his 100th game [match] for the school during this State Tournament, a record. He and Paul [Ezerski] are a couple of real tennis players, believe me" (*Star Tribune*, Ralph Thornton, June 7, 1987). They held down the No. 1 doubles spot during the year, so theirs was one of those rare titles won by doubles specialists. And both, according to coach Strohkirch, played only tennis in high school. According to Strohkirch, Danielson went on to play one year of tennis at St. Cloud State but Ezerski did not compete, instead concentrating on becoming an engineer.

All things considered, 1987 was a good year for Eden Prairie, for the team finished fourth and their No. 1 player, ninth-grade star J. P. Demetriou, took third in the singles tournament. And for Danielson and Ezerski, their victory was special, almost a Cinderella story, for neither of them had ever been highly-ranked junior singles players (Ezerski was ranked only once—No 24 in the 18s, and Danielson was just ranked alphabetically twice in the 16s) and neither had ever been ranked in doubles. In contrast, all six of the other semifinal doubles players had been highly ranked in both singles and doubles. In fact, James from Northfield had been ranked No. 1 three times in doubles (in the 14s, 16s, and 18s with Roger Anderson).

In Class A a pair from team runner-up Blue Earth won the prize, juniors Anderson and Schmitgen. Though no slouch in doubles, Schmitgen would be the first to admit that he was lucky to have Anderson as his partner, for he (Anderson) might go down as the greatest junior doubles player in Minnesota tennis history. Like his brother Myles and St. Cloud Tech's Todd Schlorf, he could lift his partner to the heights. For example, he and his brother took third at State in 1983 and won the one-class title in '85, and in summer NWTA play he was a dominant doubles player who ranked at or near the top in every age category. In his first year in the 12-and-unders he and Myles were ranked No. 5 the first year and No. 7 the second year. The next year, still in the 12s, he was ranked No. 3 with Chris Boily. One year in the 12s he and partner Tom Trondson of Mounds View won the Sectional doubles title. And in his last year in the 12-and-unders, he and his brother Myles were ranked No. 7 in 14-and-under doubles. But the next year he really began to hit his stride in doubles, for he and Myles were ranked No. 1 in the 16s and he and Ripper Hatch of Edina were No. 1 in the 14s. In addition, he and those two partners were the Sectional champions that year (1983). His second year in the 14s he and Dan James were No. 1, then he and Hatch were No. 1 his first year in the 16s (and Sectional champions again) and he and Myles

were again No. 1 (this time in the 18s). With James he earned the No. 1 ranking again in his second year in the 16s, and he closed out his junior career in doubles with another No. 1 ranking in the 18s, again partnering with James and again winning the Sectional championship.

So it was no surprise that he and Schmitgen took home the doubles trophy and won all three of their matches in straight sets. For starters they dispatched juniors Todd Kreibich and Cory Sondrol of Crookston with ease but then they worked up a sweat in the semis against a very strong team from New London-Spicer, brothers Andrew (a sophomore) and Jamy Fernelius (a junior). They won in a closely contested 7-6, 7-5 match. The final against Blake senior D. Jackson and his partner Scott Gage, a junior, found the Blue Earth boys prevailing 6-0, 6-4.

There was some doubt that this pairing (of Anderson and Schmitgen) would even take place, for, according to a June 7, 1987, *Star Tribune* article by Ralph Thornton, "Schmitgen, who fractured and dislocated his right shoulder wrestling in January, only picked up his racket again in mid-March." Coach Hal Schroeder praised Schmitgen's work habits and also said, "He and Roger [Anderson] were very good friends who practiced on their own together. Roger really helped Jamie with his tennis." Anderson called this a memorable tournament "because I was able to play with my best friend in high school [Schmitgen]." With characteristic modesty he also said, "I had made something of a name for myself via USTA tournaments and previous State Tournaments, but Jamie was largely an unknown quantity outside of southern Minnesota since he only played during the high school season and sparingly during the summer. As a result, people who didn't know how good he was would refer to us as Anderson and his partner as they didn't know his name. To this day I never miss a chance to introduce him as 'and partner.'"

Schmitgen returned the praise, saying of Anderson, "I couldn't have had a better partner than Roger. He hasn't lost a match all year" (June 7, 1987). Unfortunately for him, Roger played singles his senior year and so he (Schmitgen) had to find a different partner. He and his 1988 partner, Troy Thompson, advanced to State but finished just fourth, losing to teammates Paul Schroeder and Layne McCleary.

Schmitgen played some college tennis after high school (at Mankato State) and today he lives in Rochester and works in the human resources department at the Mayo Clinic.

1988—Charlie Eifrig & Jason Nasby
Edina-AA

Tom Stender & Steve Roach
Duluth Marshall-A

Perhaps the most compelling narrative coming out of the 1988 doubles competition was the story of the dogged and determined champions from Class A, Duluth Marshall seniors Tom Stender and Steve Roach. Theirs was a partnership that endured longer than many marriages, for, according to Roach, in an article by Wayne Washington in the *Star Tribune*, "we've been playing doubles since we were 8 years old" ("Old Friends from Duluth Marshall Take Class A Doubles," June 12, 1988). And while they had played doubles together all those years, they were only ranked once in NWTA summer play (No. 10 in the 16s, though Stender was also ranked as high as No. 5 with Sean Hill, a future National Hockey League defenseman, in the 14s). So their triumph was not exactly expected. In addition, northern schools rarely produced champions (theirs was just the fourth up to this point) and neither had been highly ranked singles players. Roach, the son of longtime U of MN-Duluth tennis coach Don "Doc" Roach, was never ranked in singles (though he played a good many junior tournaments). Stender, on the other hand, was often ranked, usually between No. 13 and the unexceptional "alphabetical" list. His highest ranking was No. 5 in 10-and-under singles one year.

But they were determined to succeed and so they swept through the 8-player draw to claim the first tennis title of any kind for Duluth Marshall. In the first round they upended seniors Scott Diede and Todd Bergeson from St. Peter in two sets, then outdueled the Blue Earth-Frost-Winnebago duo of 1987 doubles champion Schmitgen (now a senior) and junior Troy Thompson in a three-set slugfest 5-7, 6-3, 7-6. Waiting for them in the finals was the No. 1 doubles team from New London-Spicer, senior Jamy Fernelius and junior Jeff Gilson. But they were no match for the Duluth Marshall lads who defeated them 6-3, 6-3.

In the end they made this marriage work with healthy doses of positive support. As Roach said, in the article by Washington, "It's always positive when we're playing with each other." Stender added that even in tight matches they "never get frustrated with each other" and that "we help each other out there. We don't get on each other" (June 12, 1988). Sounds like good advice for all soon-to-be-married couples.

Current Duluth Marshall coach Kurt Bartell remembers both Stender and Roach from his days of coaching them when they were juniors. Of Stender he said, "He was a very good competitor, and with him there were no lapses or let-ups on the court." And Bartell noted that Roach "had a high first serve percentage and returned well." Agreeing that theirs was an unexpected win, he said, "They just got hot that one weekend." Finally, Bartell said of their games, "Stender and Roach had a lot of personality and they were entertaining to watch."

Former Northfield standout and current Duluth East coach Mark Welinski also coached Stender and Roach during their growing-up-in-tennis years, often hauling them around to tournaments. He said of them, "They were two of the many youngsters who spent many hours hitting at the Longview Tennis Club in Duluth."

After graduation, Stender attended Montana State U for one year, then transferred to St. Thomas College to play tennis for coach Mark Hayday. Now an insurance salesman, he lives in the home in which he grew up in Duluth.

According to Welinski, Roach enrolled at the U of MN-Duluth to play tennis for his father after high school. At UMD he had a very successful career, winning eight Northern Sun Interscholastic Conference titles: four at No. 1 doubles and four in either No. 5 or 6 singles. As a result of his tennis exploits, he was elected to the UMD Sports Hall of Fame. Roach is today a mortgage broker.

Perhaps less surprising, the Class AA champions, senior Charlie Eifrig and junior Jason Nasby, came from team titlist Edina. During the year they anchored Edina's doubles, giving the Hornets a certain point at the No. 1

spot, and for years they had made a splash on the Minnesota tennis scene. Nasby, something of a journeyman who began his tennis career at Northfield before enrolling at Minnehaha Academy and finally Edina, had already been a member of three state championship teams (Minnehaha in 1986 and Edina in '87 and this year). In addition, as a summer tournament player he had excelled in both singles and doubles, ranking as high as No. 4 in singles (in the 14s) and often in the top ten. As a doubles player he earned No. 3 rankings twice with Doug Cowles of Northfield (once in the 12s and once in the 14s), and he and Eifrig finished No. 2 in the 18-and-under doubles one year. Eifrig had been ranked twice in singles, but only as high as No. 23 in 18 singles, and that No. 2 spot with Nasby was his only appearance in the doubles rankings.

To secure their state doubles title, Nasby and Eifrig overcame four worthy opponents, defeating each in straight sets. First they upended a pair from Cretin-Derham Hall, junior Brian Alexander and senior Brian McDonagh. Then they knocked off senior Kevin Jansen and sophomore Shane Abraham of Owatonna in the quarters before taking out a team from Mounds View in the semis, senior John Trondson (son of 1950-51 doubles champion Ron Trondson from Rochester) and sophomore Derek Howe. Finally, they finished the job with a 6-4, 6-2 win over juniors Chris Thompson and Jon Lobland of Rochester Mayo.

Though Nasby would once again play a key role in Edina's success his senior year, as a member of the Hornets' 1989 first doubles team, he and senior teammate Peter Erickson lost to the eventual doubles runners-up from St. Cloud Tech, seniors Wade Bresnahan and Dan O'Shea, in the first round of the individual tournament.

About his 1988 doubles champions, first-year coach Steve Paulsen said, "Nasby was built like a rock and had pretty solid groundstrokes. He was a straight-up, no-nonsense player, not very flashy." Paulsen called Eifrig "a fun-loving, happy-go-lucky guy."

Nasby, like his coach, grew up in Northfield. He earned his first varsity tennis letter as a seventh grader on a team your author coached, playing mostly doubles but even an occasional singles match and finishing with a 9-4 record. He began hitting with his parents and sister Jill (a top Northfield girls' player) at age 10 on a private court near his home, then his mother drove him to 98th Street Racquet Club for STP practices and lessons with Ron York. His parents moved to Edina the next year and he completed his high school tennis career at Minnehaha Academy and Edina.

His freshman year at Minnehaha he played No. 3 singles and lost just one match, as a sophomore at Edina he rotated between Nos. 3 and 4 singles and again lost only one match, his junior year he and Eifrig were undefeated and won that state doubles title, and his senior year he again played No. 1 doubles and lost just one match, that in the State Tournament. So, including his four losses at Northfield, Nasby lost just seven matches in his five-year high school career.

While he rightly credits York for helping him develop his game, he also noted the important role that Mark Halvorson played in his early success. Mark, a former Northfield player and a national ski champion at the U of Utah, coached Jason and other top Northfield players and transported them to tournaments one summer. Nasby also spent two second semester sessions (when he was 14 and 15 years old) at the Bollettieri Tennis Academy in Florida going to school, hitting with top players, riding the bus with the likes of Andre Agassi and Jim Courier, and rooming with five exceptional tennis players from different foreign countries. All these opportunities, he claims, would not have been possible without the great support he received from his parents, Jim and JoAnn.

Regarding his memories of high school tennis, Jason said one of the two biggest highlights was Minnehaha's upset of Edina in the State Tournament in 1986 (the other was his doubles championship in '88). Said he about that magical year at Minnehaha, "We [Minnehaha] knew we had a good team with talent and depth but never expected to win the state title. We were the underdog and just kept winning." As for the doubles title, he said, "I was always an impatient player, so doubles and the fast pace was perfect for me." He and Eifrig made an excellent team, with Nasby on the forehand side and Eifrig on the backhand side. Both also had solid serves.

After graduating from Edina in 1989, Nasby enrolled at the U of WI, following his doubles partner Eifrig who had enrolled the year before. Though he had hung up his tennis rackets, he decided to give football a try. A good athlete who had played wide receiver on the varsity football team his senior year at Edina, he walked on for the Badgers. He played just one year, then decided to concentrate on his studies, graduating in '94 with a BA in communications. Now back in Edina, he is a salesman and principal owner of a manufacturer's representative firm which sells products to retailers such as Target and Amazon.com.

As for Eifrig, he and Nasby grew up on the STP courts together. Nasby called him "a gifted athlete and an extremely competitive person. He was also very smart and had a good head for the game." Nasby also said about his former partner, "His game was all-around solid. He was very quick, he hit very low shots, and he had a good net game."

As mentioned earlier, Eifrig also attended the U of WI, and he too gave up tennis at that point. He graduated from the U of WI and went to medical school at the U of NC. A specialist in retinal eye surgery, he makes his home in the Tar Heel State.

1989—Paul Jeffries & Ricardo Derbez
Moorhead—AA

Tom Fenton & Dave Huhner
Litchfield-A

Though it does not always hold true to form, I have maintained that two top singles players, when joined at the hip for doubles, will usually beat a pair that specialized in doubles during the year. Most often these singles guys are better athletes and they are usually more skilled tennis players. And often they have had success playing doubles with other top players in the summer, so if they can survive those first matches when they are getting used to doubles again (and each other) they will usually do well.

Such was the case this year, for both championship doubles teams were composed of No. 1 and 2 singles players from their teams. In Class AA it was a Moorhead team made up of gifted ninth grader Paul Jeffries and foreign exhange student Ricardo Derbez from Mexico. Neither

had played doubles during the season and only joined up for sub-region compettion. Seniors Tom Fenton and Dave Huhner of Litchfield, the Class A champions, had played some doubles during the year. Said Fenton, in an article by Bob Schranck in the *Star Tribune*, "We usually played a couple of sets of doubles, against coach John Carlson and one of the city's tennis players, Mike Miller" (June 11, 1989).

First up, the Class AA champs from Moorhead. They opened tournament play with a 6-4, 6-0 win over senior Todd Starrett and ninth grader Jon Docken from Hutchinson, then took care of sophomore Dave Edelman and junior Charlie Ackerman of Mounds View in the quarters by an identical 6-4, 6-0 score. As with Fenton and Huhner, they played the role of comeback kids, particularly in the semis and finals when they lost the first sets. Against Edina senior Scott Campbell and his junior partner Ben Friswold in the semis the Moorhead lads were down 6-4, 2-0 before launching their comeback. At that point in the match, Jeffries said, "Coaches Dan Radtke and Dave Drenth told us to play our game and not worry about what they [Campbell and Friswold] were doing" (June 11, 1989). So rally they did, winning 13 of the last 16 games and the match 4-6, 7-5, 6-0. In the finals they also dropped the first set 6-4 before overcoming a very strong pair from St. Cloud Tech, seniors Wade Bresnahan (brother of 1983 doubles champion Shawn) and Dan O'Shea. The score was 4-6, 6-3, 6-3. This victory gave Moorhead its only tennis championship, and Derbez became the only foreign exchange student to claim a state doubles title.

As for Fenton and Huhner, they too were giving their fans anxiety attacks in their first two matches, coming back after dropping first sets. In the quarters (again the Class A field was just an 8-draw) they bumped sophomores Tony Baisley and John Schmid of Winona Cotter 4-6, 6-3, 6-3, then once again struggled early before overcoming Staples-Motley's talented ninth grader David Joerger and his partner, junior Greg Borstad, 4-6, 6-2, 6-3.

After this semifinal match, Fenton told *Star Tribune* writer Schranck, "We're slow starters. We played three sets in both the quarters and semifinals Friday, losing the first set each time. We weren't going to do that today" (June 11, 1989). Sure enough, they did not lose the first set; however, they started slowly again, against seniors Steve Rist and Bill Schleter of Long Prairie. Schranck noted, "They didn't start like champions; however, trailing 2-5 and down 40-love, Fenton and Huhner fought off three set points to turn the momentum and win that game and the next four." Fenton, the Dragons No. 1 singles player during the year, blamed himself for this slow start, saying, "My returns started off shaky. Then they started to click and our intensity picked up" (June 11, 1989). Their tuned-up play brought them the doubles title (7-5, 6-2), and the school's second championship to go along with the team title they helped the Dragons win. These were the first tennis titles for the school.

Surprisingly, neither Fenton nor Huhner had ever been highly ranked Northern Section players (only Fenton had a ranking, and that was an aphabetical ranking in the 16s once).

Of these four 1989 champions, Derbez returned to his south-of-the- border home in Monterey, Mexico; Fenton headed off to St. Cloud State; and the six-foot-six-inch Huhner enrolled at Hamline. Fenton continued with tennis at St. Cloud (for three years), and he stayed in the Granite City after college, where he works in sales for Regent Communications. Huhner did not play tennis at Hamline, instead focusing on basketball for just two years. He, too, stayed in Minnesota, settling in Willmar where he is a chiropractor.

Jeffries, one of the best state high school players not to win a singles title, had an outstanding junior tournament career. For example, he was ranked No. 1 in 10-, 12-, and 14-and-under singles and four other times he was No. 2 in singles. And four times he and his partners (Jon Docken in the 10s, 12s, and 14s and Tom Danford in the 18s) were ranked No. 1 in doubles. In addition, twice he won the Sectional doubles, in the 14s with Docken and the 18s with Danford. Endorsed by the NWTA to play national tournaments, Jeffries competed well on the national scene as well.

One reason he did not win a high school singles title is that he did not compete in high school tennis after 1989. Instead, at the invitation of NWTA tennis director Debbie Gavin from Fargo, ND, Jeffries moved with her family to California to live during the spring of his sophomore

year. He continued to do this his last two years of high school, attending school in Escondido and training at the San Diego Tennis and Racquet Club to prepare himself for summer tournament play.

Also a skilled soccer player, Jeffries gave up high school tennis when he enrolled at Fargo South High School his junior year. He said, "They had tennis and soccer in the fall, and since North Dakota tennis wasn't as strong as Minnesota tennis, I chose soccer. Besides, I was burned out from summer tennis." So he attended school in North Dakota until the spring his last two years, then moved back to California to train in tennis.

After graduation he walked on at the U of KS and was redshirted his first year. A new coach came the next year, so he transferred to Gustavus in the fall of 1993. As a Gustie tennis player he earned all-American status in doubles two years (1994 and '96). In '94 he reached the NCAA quarters in doubles (with Mounds View's Ryan Howe) and he also won four individual MIAC championships: two in singles (at No. 2 in '95 and No. 3 in '96) and two with Todd Bowlby in doubles, the second at No. 1. He and Bowlby captured the ITA Rolex Midwest Regional doubles title in '95 as well.

Coach Steve Wilkinson said of Jeffries, "He was very adept at doubles and knew how to position himself." One of his partners was state singles champion Bowlby. Bowlby had not played much doubles before he came to Gustavus. So, said Wilkinson, "Paul taught Todd how to play doubles." Since his graduation in 1996 he lived in Arizona and Minneapolis and today works as a sales manager for the Gallo Wine Division in Fargo. He still plays tennis; in fact, his USTA league team (made up of former Gustavus players) won the Section title in 2004.

1990s

1990—Jon Docken & Dan Carlson
Hutchinson-AA

Layne McCleary & Eric Lawatsch
Blue Earth-A

For the first time since 1984, Edina did not take home a team, singles, or doubles title. Instead Mounds View took the Class AA team championship, Eden Prairie the singles (J. P. Demetriou), and Hutchinson the doubles (Jon Docken and Dan Carlson). Carlson, a senior, and Docken, a sophomore, held down the Nos. 1 and 2 singles positions during the regular season, then teamed up for individual tournament competition. After winning the region title, Carlson and Docken opened state play with a straight-set win over seniors Fausto Lima and Bryan Barton of Blake. In the quarters they labored against junior Dave Edelman and senior Charles Ackerman of Mounds View but prevailed 6-7, 7-5, 6-2; then in the semis on Saturday they tripped up Hibbing seniors Paul Wojciak and Marcus Karki. And in a very competitive final, they defeated Edina senior Michael Arvidson and his sophomore teammate Tom Danford 6-4, 4-6, 6-4. This would be Hutchinson's only tennis title.

The son of coach Geoff Docken, Jon Docken had a very successful career at Hutchinson, advancing to state competition twice in doubles, once in singles, and twice as a team member. Moreover, he did very well on the summer tournament circuit. As mentioned earlier in the report on 1989 champion Paul Jeffries, he and his Moorhead

Dan Carlson (Left) & Jon Docken

partner were the top-ranked doubles team in their age bracket three times. In addition, he was ranked in singles nearly every year, achieving his highest ranking in the 10-and-unders (No. 6). Carlson's accomplishments were more modest, and, like Docken, his best rankings were earned earlier in his junior tennis career: No. 2 in the 12-and-under doubles with Brian McCormick and a No. 10 in the 10-and-under singles.

Coach Docken praised his doubles champions, saying of Carlson, "He was a strong competitor with a good serve and good groundstrokes. In doubles he had a knack for poaching at the right time." About his son he said, "He had played doubles since he was 10 and had a good cross-court return and an excellent, way-above-average down-the-line return. He was also very good at volleying and and had above-average groundstrokes."

Also an outstanding hockey player in high school, Jon Docken attended Bottineau College in North Dakota to play that sport. After a year there he transferred to Winona State to study computers. Today he works as a chemical sales person for UNIVAR in Prior Lake.

Carlson, whose brother Jon is the very successful Gustavus women's tennis coach, played tennis for the Gusties and had a solid college career. For example, he was the 1993 and '94 MIAC No. 1 doubles champion (with Ryan Howe the first year and Jeff Ross the second), the No. 3 singles champion in '93, and the ITA Rolex Midwest Regional doubles champion in '93 (with Ross). He lives in Plymouth today and is active as a local tennis coach. Carlson has coached the USTA Zone team for five years and is also serving as a representative on the Northern Section Junior Tennis Council. For his work on behalf of junior tennis, he was voted the Ward C. Burton Junior Development Award winner in 2002.

The Class A doubles title went to a pair from another outstate school, albeit perennial power Blue Earth (now Blue Earth-Frost-Winnebago-Delavan). This was the team of senior Layne McCleary (who had finished third and fourth in two previous doubles appearances with different partners) and junior Eric Lawatsch. Once again there were just eight doubles teams entered, so the Bucs' duo had to win just three matches. Their first opponents were conference rivals Jim Riley (a senior) and Mark Milbrath (a ninth grader) from St. Peter, and this Saints' pair gave the Blue Earth lads all they wanted before falling 7-5, 3-6, 6-4. In the semis they defeated juniors Jay Monson and Brian Krousey from Long Prairie, then met another team from southern Minnesota in the finals (sophomore Brad Hested and junior Cory Kallheim from Fairmont). With bookend 7-5 set scores the lads from Blue Earth earned the school's sixth doubles title.

Except that opponents have come to expect stiff competition from Blue Earth players over the years, this win for McCleary and Lawatsch was unexpected in at least one respect: neither came into the tournament with a sterling junior resume. Neither had competed very much in summer competitions and Lawatsch was the only one to earn an NWTA ranking, and that was just once in 18 singles (No. 47).

However, both were stalwarts on Blue Earth's teams over the years, both participating at the varsity level for five years and particularly playing key roles on the Bucs' 1988 championship team. And this year they had taken turns occupying that coveted No. 1 singles position. Coach Hal Schroeder said of McCleary, "Layne was a very hard hitter." Schroeder also noted that he has continued in tennis, and he now makes it his career. After graduation he played one year at Gustavus, then helped coach Blue Earth for three years before earning his USPTA certification. From 1994-2000 he taught tennis at the Top-Notch Resort and Spa in Stowe, VT, before moving back to Minnesota. In 2000 he became the tennis director at the White Bear Lake Racquet Club and since '03 has been the general manager of the club.

His senior year Lawatsch played No. 1 singles for the Bucs and once again advanced to State, this time in singles. He gave a good account of himself, finishing fourth in a tough draw that featured two-time champion Tim George (whom he lost to in the semis) and 1992 winner, David Joerger. Of Lawatsch, Schroeder said, "Eric was also a fine player who was very consistent and mentally tough." Some of that mental toughness may have come from his experience as a football player, for Lawatsch was good enough at that sport to give it a try at Iowa State after he graduated from Blue Earth High School. However, he stayed just one year at Iowa State before transferring to the U of M. Lawatsch graduated in 1995, then, after working for three years he enrolled in medical school in '98. He finished his training in 2007 and today works as a doctor in Neenah, WI. Though he did not play tennis in college, he has played some USTA league tennis.

1991—Stewart Barry & Fergus Weir
Blake-AA

Brian Bakke & J. P. McDonald
East Grand Forks-A

In a dominating performance befitting their status as a dynasty team, Blake very nearly pulled off a clean sweep in 1991, a year in which the Bears "played up" in Class AA. They won the team championship, No. 1 player Chris Laitala finished second in singles, and the team of seniors Stewart Barry and Fergus Weir captured the doubles title. Luckily for East Grand Forks seniors Brian Bakke and J. P. McDonald, there were no Blake players waiting for them in the Class A draw, so they won the small-school doubles.

As standout performers on Blake's ultra-competitive Class AA teams the past four years, Barry and Weir were eager to show off their skills in doubles. Both played singles in the team tournament (though Weir had played doubles during the regular season) and Barry had played singles all four of his years on the varsity squad, the last three at No. 2 singles behind Laitala. So their pairing, essentially that of a doubles player (Weir) and an accomplished singles player who had once been ranked No. 1 in the 10-and-unders and No. 2 in the 12s (Barry), might have seemed a bit odd to an unenlightened tennis fan. However, Barry had demonstrated his prowess in doubles during summer

NWTA tournament play over the years. For example, he and Laitala were ranked No. 1 in 12-and-under doubles (a year in which they also won the Sectional title) and he and Weir had played together often. Once each in the 16s and 18s they were ranked No. 2 in doubles, so they knew how to play together. In addition, though Weir had never been ranked higher than No. 23 in summer singles play, he had held down doubles positions for coach John Hatch since his ninth-grade year.

So they were confident they could do well, and do well they did, sweeping aside all four of their opponents without losing a set. In the first round they defeated a pair of juniors from White Bear Lake (Brad Davis and Ryan Armstrong). Next to fall were seniors Jason Sirek and Andy Larson of Cretin-Derham Hall. And in their Saturday semifinal match at 98th Street Racquet Club they ousted Bloomington Jefferson seniors Brian Doner and Jon Hagele. Having not given up more than three games in any previous set, Barry and Weir were nevertheless prepared to dig deep in the first set of their final match with seniors Chris Rovn and Brad Olson of Robbinsdale Armstrong. And dig deep they did, struggling in a first set tiebreaker but prevailing 7-6 (8-6) before wrapping things up with a snappy 6-1 second set win. Remarkably, given Blake's success over the years, this was the first doubles title for a Bears' team.

Fergus Weir (Left) & Stewart Barry

Future Blake coach Ted Warner remembers getting Barry started in tennis at Woodhill Country Club. Warner described him as a player who "was very solid off the ground. He had soft hands so he could place angles and he had spin."

Meanwhile, over at Eden Prairie High School in Class A, now with a full 16-draw, the East Grand Forks boys cruised through their first two matches before experiencing a speed bump in the semis. Their first victims were Fairmont's Joel Sagedahl and Chris Scott (a senior and junior respectively). Next they took out the team of junior Kevin Josephson and senior Chad Erdman of Lac Qui Parle Valley.

Then came the speed bump in the persons of Rochester Lourdes' seniors Mark Morrey and Terry Aney. After dropping the first set 6-4, Bakke and McDonald rallied for a 4-6, 6-0, 6-3 victory. And in the final they prevailed once more in straight sets (6-4, 6-2), this time over an exhausted duo from Staples-Motley, seniors Matt Peterson and Tim Goeden. As if Peterson and Goeden weren't already tired from playing three team matches on Wednesday and Thursday—helping the Cardinals win a state team title, their three previous doubles matches on Friday and Saturday must have left them totally drained of energy. For each of those matches went three sets and two included 18-point tie-breakers.

The champions, Bakke and McDonald, returned to their Red River Valley home town with the school's only tennis title of any kind, a title that perhaps few in Minnesota tennis circles could have predicted, for East Grand Forks was not a household name in tennis. However, the school, led by sophomore McDonald at No. 1 singles, had finished fourth at State in 1989. Moreover, neither McDonald nor Bakke had done much in NWTA section play to hint that they would win a state championship. Bakke was never ranked in the Section and McDonald's best rankings were a No. 4 in the 14-and-under doubles (with Tim Bohland) and a No. 27 in 16 singles.

Described by Staples-Motley coach Joe Joerger as "a strong, raw-boned kid and a big right-hander with a booming serve," McDonald went to Chapman U in California to play tennis after high school. Of Bakke, Joerger said, "He was a wrestler as well, so he was strong as a little bull. He was also very quick." Both, according to Joerger, were well-schooled tennis players.

1992–Tom Danford & Scott Riley
Edina–AA

Mark Haglin & David Cizek
Staples Area-A

During a tournament in which the Class AA results were as predictable as trout rising to feed on a hatch of caddis flies in June, Edina swept everything (even to the point of seeing its top two players face off in the singles final). Not so the Class A tournament, for a school whose team did not even make it through the section tournament (Staples Area) claimed both the singles and doubles titles. Not since True Team play began in 1973 had both the singles and doubles champions come from a team that hadn't qualified for State, and it would not happen again.

So how did these lads from Staples Area (singles player David Joerger and the doubles team of Mark Haglin and David Cizek) pull off this stunning performance? Perhaps most importantly, these were talented and seasoned seniors who had cut their teeth on state tournament competition as members of the Cardinals' 1990 and '91 state championship teams. (For more about Joerger, see Chapter Five.)

And though Haglin and Cizek had played singles during the year, their strengths were enhanced as a doubles team. In an article by Judd Zulgad titled "Staples Area Makes Clean Sweep," coach Joe Joerger said of their play, "Dave [Cizek] has a great serve and he's a power player, and Mark [Haglin] has a steadying influence" (*Star Tribune*, June 7, 1992). Their complementary styles led them to four wins, the first a nail-biter over senior Chad Gruszka and junior Eric Bialke of Sartell 6-7, 6-4, 6-4. In the quarters they defeated senior Andy Peterson and junior Casey Groves of Virginia, then on Saturday they bumped brothers Paul (a senior) and Matt Drawz (a sophomore) of Breck School. In the finals the boys from Staples fended off a second-set challenge from juniors Aaron Wachlarowicz and Brian Rousstang of Sauk Centre before winning 6-1, 6-4.

For Joerger, the singles titlist, and Haglin and Cizek—and to a lesser extent their teammates and coach—winning these two individual titles was redemption for the disappointment of losing to East Grand Forks in Section 8 team play. Acknowledging, in the article by Zulgad, that "we always put emphasis on the team," coach Joerger nonetheless said of his players' individual performances, "It's a dream come true to win both finals." Haglin added, "I don't know if these wins make up for the team [loss], but it sure feels great." As for Cizek, he too was delighted to win but also a bit surprised: "Last week we were horrible in practice, but we played well enough in the (State) Tournament" (June 7, 1992).

Scott Riley (Left) & Tom Danford

Over at 98th Street Racquet Club, another veteran duo rolled to victory in the Class AA tournament, Tom Danford and Scott Riley of Edina. Riley, who with partner Adam Lofthagen had won a key point for Edina in the team final against St. Cloud Tech, had played No. 1 doubles with Lofthagen for two years. Danford, on the other hand, had played No. 3 singles during the season, so he and Riley paired up for the first time in subsection play. And like the pairing of Haglin and Cizek, their bonding proved serendipitous.

Though they had a titanic struggle in the finals, they moved through the first three rounds of the draw with straight-set wins. In the first round they defeated seniors

Jason Gerhardt and Troy Diekman of Austin 6-4, 7-6, and in round two they took out senior Justin Seim and sophomore Dave Parker of Stillwater 7-6, 6-4. These were competetive matches which toughened them up for the final day's play, and in the semis they showed no mercy to brothers Mark (a senior) and Mike (a junior) Chaly from Minneapolis South, blanking them 6-0, 6-0. But in that final against a Lake Conference pair from Hopkins, they would need all the moxie they could muster.

Described as a nail-biter by *Star Tribune* writer Brian Wicker, the match came down to a third-set tiebreaker "as seniors Scott Riley and Tom Danford survived seven match points to edge Shai Ingber [a sophomore] and Luke Johnson [a junior] of Hopkins 5-7, 6-2, 7-6 (9-7)" (June 7, 1992). There was added incentive for the Edina lads, for they had lost in the section finals to this same Hopkins pair 7-5, 2-6, 6-2.

Riley, son of longtime NWTA Board of Directors member and USTA/Northern Section President's Award Winner Dick Riley, was, according to coach Steve Paulsen, "tall and intimidating at net." Paulsen also said of him, "He was a big boomer, a very aggressive player with a big serve and forehand." His partner Danford agreed, saying of his six-foot-five-inch partner, "He had a fabulous serve." Danford complemented Riley's "put-away game" with a tenacious, never-say-die style and his own strong serve and volley game. Riley, who played mostly doubles in high school, went to college at the U of KS and tried out for but did not make the tennis team. He's now back in the Twin Cities, working for Comcast and living in Hopkins.

Of Danford, Paulsen said, "He was a workaholic and a warrior on the court." And he was also a very successful junior player, especially in doubles. Twice ranked No. 1 (in the 16s with David Joerger and in the 18s with Paul Jeffries in a year they won the Sectional doubles), he was also ranked No. 2 three times with Edina mates Tommy Moe (in the 12s and 14s) and Riley (in the 18s). His highest singles ranking was No. 6 in the 18-and-unders. Riley, on the other hand, was never ranked higher than No. 39 in singles (in the 18s), but he did earn that No. 2 ranking with Danford in 18 doubles.

After graduating from Edina, Danford enrolled at Miami U in Ohio where he played tennis for two years until the university dropped its tennis program in order to comply with Title IX mandates for parity in sports for men and women. During those two years he played Nos. 5 singles and 3 doubles. An English major with an emphasis on philology, Danford graduated in 1996 and moved to Los Angeles to work in the entertainment industry. During his ten years there he worked as an artist and actor, then owned and operated his own music records company. When the Internet side of the business began to fail, he left Los Angeles and moved to Florida where he sold health insurancce for a time. Soon he tired of life in Florida, and, like so many former Minnesota tennis players, returned to his roots. Now he's an actor doing commercials and theater in the Metro area. For example, he's done a good deal of work at Brave New Workshop and he's studied at the Guthrie. He says he also did some tennis coaching in the summer, but he hasn't played in quite some time.

He has fond memories of the Edina teams he played for, especially of the good chemistry exhibited by the 1992 championship team which swept team, singles, and doubles titles. And Danford played a prominent role on the '89 championship team as well, holding down a No. 2 doubles spot his freshman year. His sophomore year he played No. 1 doubles and his junior year he played No. 2 singles behind Scott Sanderson.

As for Haglin and Cizek, their triumph was all the more remarkable, considering that they were never ranked in NWTA summer play and that they had never played together before the subsection tournament. However, according to coach Joerger, "They were good athletes (both played basketball) and they complemented each other. Cizek was a sparky guy who hit hard and Haglin was solid player who didn't make mistakes." In addition, said Joerger, "Haglin had great placement and was a very good thinker, while Cizek had a very good serve. He [Cizek] admired Agassi and so he hit the ball really hard. He didn't have much finesse."

Cizek attended Moorhead State U for a short time, then dropped out after he "got the business bug," Joerger noted. He ran a pizza franchise for a few years and now runs a TCBY store. Haglin attended Gustavus, but neither he nor Cizek played college tennis.

1993—Aaron Dvorak & Ben Bartels
Bloomington Jefferson—AA

Trace Fielding & Matt Drawz
Breck-A

"Sharing the wealth" might be an appropriate adage to describe the 1993 tournament, for in both classes the team and individual champions came from different schools. In Class AA Wayzata won the team title and players from Edina (Marcelo Borrelli) and Bloomington Jefferson (Aaron Dvorak and Ben Bartels) won the singles and doubles. In Class A St. Paul Academy won the team title, Blake's Robert Keith the singles, and Breck's Trace Fielding and Matt Drawz the doubles.

One could also argue that "youth will be served" could have been a suitable motto for the doubles champions, for in both cases the winning pair featured a talented youngster. In Class AA it was ninth grader Dvorak and in Class A it was eighth grader Fielding. Drawz, still an underclassman (a junior), had taken third in 1992 with his brother Paul.

Let's look at the small-school side first. Fielding and Drawz had no trouble with a team from Waseca in the first round, blitzing seniors Jeff Denz and Nate Manthe. In the 1:00 PM match the first day they struggled against junior Mike Emmerich and sophomore Eric Premo of Foley (coach Mike Premo's son), winning in three sets 2-6, 6-4, 6-2; then in the semis on Friday they dispatched Crookston seniors Paul Johnson and Steve Sims in straight sets. In the finals they defeated the unlucky pair of seniors Aaron Wachlarowicz and Brian Rousslang of Sauk Centre, also last year's runner-up team. It was a tight match but the Breck pair won 7-5, 7-5. This was the first of five doubles titles, including a repeat performance by Fielding and Drawz in 1994, that Breck would win

In an article in the *Star Tribune* by Heath Smith, Drawz spoke candidly about his state tournament partners the past two years. "With his brother Paul [his 1992 partner] listening in, Matt Drawz explained why he was going home this time with a first-place medal. 'The difference between [Fielding] and my brother is that this kid is 10 times better'" (June 12, 1993). By winning

the championship, "this kid" became the youngest state champion in Minnesota tennis history. (For more on Fielding's high school career, see Chapter Five.)

As for Drawz's tennis ability, he had a fine high school career but only appeared in the NWTA summer rankings in the 16s: at Nos. 16 and 61 in singles and once at No. 16 in doubles.

Turning to the Class AA scene, Dvorak and Bartels (a senior) won all four of their matches in straight sets, beginning their run to the championship by bumping a pair from Eagan (senior Kyle Freske and sophomore Chris Goodwin). Next they took out seniors Andy Peterson and Casey Groves of Virginia, losers in the first round of the Class A tournament last year. In the semifinal match on Friday Dvorak and Bartels defeated Stillwater seniors Brent Batchelor and Rick Slachta, and in the finals they upended Blaine juniors Craig Gordon and Troy Schakle 6-3, 6-3.

Though both were solid singles players, Dvorak (the No. 2 singles player) and Bartels (the No. 1 player) chose to pair up in doubles because they wanted to avoid Edina's Borrelli, the eventual 1993 singles champion. After their finals match Dvorak remarked, in an article by *Star Tribune* writer Jeff Shelman, that the pairing of opposites worked well for them. "We are both steady players," he said. "We also have a good combination. I have good returns and finesse shots while Ben has a big serve and big volleys" (June 12, 1993).

This was the first tennis title for Bloomington Jefferson; they would go on to win two team championships, one more doubles title, and three singles titles (all in the '90s). Both Dvorak and Bartels were key players in Jefferson's rise to power in this decade, for both were on the roster of the Jaguars' 1991 state tournament team and Dvorak also played No. 2 singles (behind two-time state singles champion Matt Peplinski) on Jefferson's 1994 and '96 state championship teams. An injury kept him from making it back to the individual tournament in '96, and in other years he simply couldn't get out of a very tough region. One major obstacle was his teammate Peplinski, but there were other top foes to contend with such as Hopkins' Shai Ingber and Edina's Derek Brandt.

Despite this relatively disappointing individual state tournament history, Dvorak had an extraordinarily successful junior career. In singles he was ranked No. 1 twice (once in the 12s and once in the 18s, and never ranked lower than No. 5). In fact, the year he was No. 1 in the 12s he won the Section title and, playing up, also finished No. 3 in the 14s. In doubles he had perhaps the best career in Minnesota junior tennis, ranking No. 1 six times and five times winning Section doubles titles (twice with Justin Wismer—in the 14s and 18s, twice with Trace Fielding—in the 12s and 14s, and once with Shai Ingber—in the 12s). He often played up in an age division (with success), and he competed in national tournaments as well—earning a ranking as high as No. 135 in the 16s. He must be included in that pantheon of Minnesota players who could have but did not win a state singles title.

His high school coach, Tom Saterdalen, said of him, "He was very good as a young kid. He had a 24-1 record at No. 4 singles on our team as a seventh grader. His biggest strength was his focus; for someone so young he could stay on task, and he just didn't make any errors." And this championship, just the sixth Minnesota state title for a ninth grader, came early in his career. The other ninth-grade doubles winners were Andy Ringlien of Northfield in 1976, Roger Anderson of Blue Earth in '85, and Paul Jeffries of Moorhead in '89. In singles David Wheaton won in '84 and Chris Laitala in '88.

After graduation from Jefferson he walked on at the U of M but did not make the tennis team. One reason might have been his lack of size, for he was not very tall. According to Saterdalen, Dvorak works in the business world today and does some occasional tennis teaching at Interlachen Country Club.

As for Bartels, he played on the Jefferson varsity for five years and held down the No. 1 singles spot this year. Saterdalen echoed Dvorak's comments about him, "He was a great serve and volleyer, and so Dvorak would set him up and Ben would put them away." Bartels had a solid junior career, though not at the level of Dvorak's, earning a No. 6 singles ranking his last year in the 18-and-unders and rankings between Nos. 10-13 in doubles. And he, too, tried tennis in college, accepting a scholarship to Iowa State. But the Cyclones dropped their tennis program after his freshman year, so he only played just one year at Ames.

1994—Matt Berg & Jon Schibel
Virginia-AA

Matt Drawz & Trace Fielding
Breck-A

In what proved to be a tournament of contrasts, an unlikely pair from Virginia emerged as doubles champions from a wide-open field in Class AA, while the Class A champions were repeat winners. Just the fifth doubles champions from northeastern Minnesota, Virginia juniors Matt Berg and Jon Schibel were the second team from this iron mining town to claim the title (Tom Shustarich and Mark Maroste being the other). Repeating in Class A was the Breck team of Matt Drawz and Trace Fielding.

There were the obvious contrasts such as public school/private school players, outstate northern school/

Jon Schibel (Left) & Matt Berg

Metro-area school, first-time winners/repeat winners; but there were also contrasts within each team. Both featured a Mutt and Jeff combination: Virginia's Berg was five foot nine and his partner Schibel was six foot one, and Breck featured the the five foot ten Drawz and the six foot three Fielding. Also, Berg was a lefty and Schibel a righty. And, according to former Virginia coach Jim Prittinen, they melded their contrasting strengths: "Matt [Berg] was a lefty who played the deuce court and had a lazer-like return. He was so quick, while Jon [Schibel] played a very athletic, physical game, always moving forward and banging the ball."

In the Class AA tournament at 98th Street Racquet Club, the Virginia soldiers began their march to the title by defeating a pair from Bloomington Jefferson's championship team, eighth grader Phil Woo and senior Jeff Heil 6-4, 7-6, then prevailed after a first-set struggle against senior Trevor Johnson and junior Trevor Marohl of Fergus Falls 4-6, 6-2, 6-0. In the semis on Friday they demolished the eventual third-place winners, seniors Thad Arnold and Neil Knutson of Austin 6-0, 6-1; and in the finals they defeated an exhausted Ben Swanson (a senior) and David Jankowski (a junior) from Apple Valley 6-4, 6-2. Swanson and Jankowski had labored for three hours and ten minutes to win their semifinal match in three sets.

Unfortunately for Berg and Schibel, they were not able to repeat in 1995, losing in the region tourney.

Both were all-around athletes who eschewed the tournament tennis route; but though Schibel honed his basketball skills and Berg his hockey skills in the summer, both found time to play tennis with their teammates on a private court near Lake Vermilion. One contrast that speaks well of the unheralded Virginia pair is that neither of them had ever been ranked in summer NWTA tournament play. They were this year's unknown soldiers of Minnesota tennis, while Drawz (and particularly Fielding) were the decorated tennis war heroes of junior tennis. (For their rankings, see Chapter Five for Fielding's results and the 1993 doubles report for more on Drawz.)

After graduation in 1995, Berg enrolled at St. Scholastica in Duluth, where he played both tennis and hockey. Schibel went to the U of WI-Madison but did not play sports. Today they both work as physical therapists.

As for Breck's pair, theirs was a marriage of youth and age (Fielding was a ninth grader and Drawz a senior) and power and steadiness. In a June 11, 1994, *Star Tribune* article by Roman Augustoviz, Drawz said about their strengths, "He's [Fielding] the power guy on the court and I keep everything under control" (June 11, 1994).

Over at Eden Prairie High School, the Class A champions cruised through the draw without dropping a set. They began play with a win over sophomores Chris Blank

and Darin Rieland of Sauk Centre, then bumped seniors Darin Hoepner and Eric Schutz of Granite Falls-Clarkfield. Their semifinal opponents were two more sophomores, Scott Holmes and Troy Pilger of Farmington, whom they defeated 6-3, 6-0. And in the finals Drawz and Fielding defeated the formidable team of future doubles champions Jake Wert (a junior) and Justin Wismer (a sophomore) of team champion Blake 6-4, 6-2. The Breck duo became just the fifth doubles team to win back-to-back titles, the last being Jim Mitchell and Dave Mathews of Edina in 1967-68.

In addition, the relationship between Drawz and Fielding, though for tennis only during the individual tournament, went back a long ways. The *Star Tribune* article by Augustoviz noted that their relationship had "complicated roots. Drawz, as a freshman, played doubles with Fielding's older brother, Bill. 'We were one set away from State,' Matt Drawz said. 'My brother also dated [Fielding's] sister, so we've known each other for a long time'" (June 11, 1994). Now a senior, Drawz had to be content with his memories of three outstanding performances at State in doubles; but for Fielding there was more glory the next year—in singles.

1995—Cullen Flaherty & Matt Lundmark
Duluth East-AA

Jake Wert & Justin Wismer
Blake-A

Was it the immortal Yogi Berra who said it was "déjà vu all over again"? Well, the 1995 doubles tournament seemed like déjà vu, for once again a team from northeastern Minnesota won the Class AA title and a private school duo took the Class A championship. For just the sixth time the AA winners came from the Arrowhead region, juniors Cullen Flaherty and Matt Lundmark of Duluth East. The Class A winners came from Blake (senior Jake Wert and junior Justin Wismer).

Relative unknowns, Flaherty and Lundmark won each of their matches in two sets, beginning with a modest 6-1, 7-5 win over the Chaska pair of senior Scott Hace and junior Dan Benham. Then they defeated seniors Ryan Hill and David Janikowski of Apple Valley in the quarters and overcame a strong Red Wing team made up of juniors Paul Riedner and Jason Fregien in the semis. In the finals they whipped a Lake Conference pair from Wayzata, seniors Matt Coyle and Corey Ehlen, 6-4, 6-1. Quite a performance for the lads from Duluth—not one set given up and only three competitive sets in four matches.

Meanwhile, in Class A competition, Wert and Wismer defeated junior Mike Prosen and seventh grader Kyle Hawley of Eveleth-Gilbert in the first round 6-2, 6-1. In the second round they easily disposed of senior John Carroll and junior Mark Olson of Winona Cotter by the almost identical but reversed score of 6-1, 6-2. Up next for the Blake pair was a young but formidable team from Breck, ninth graders Reven Stephens and Ryan Burnett. Final score 7-6, 6-2 in favor of Wert and Wismer. Then in the finals the Bears' duo smashed their way to a 6-1, 7-6 win over Staples-Motley senior Blaine Joerger

Matt Lundmark (Left) & Cullen Flaherty

and his partner, junior Mike Rollins. In something of an anomaly, both teams won titles without giving up a set.

Just as with last year's winners, the Class A team members were more well known in state tennis circles than the Class AA Duluth duo, so the Blake lads triumph was less surprising. Wismer and Wert were the doubles runners-up in 1994 and Wismer would finish second in singles in '96. In addition, though Wert was only ranked once in the Section (at No. 21 in the Challenger 1 16 singles, Wismer was one of the top junior players nearly every year, reaching the No. 1 position in the 14-and-Under Open Singles one year and earning four other top 4 singles rankings. And in doubles he was ranked No. 1 four times (once with Matt Peplinski and three times with Aaron Dvorak). He and Dvorak also won the 14-and-under Sectional doubles one year and Wismer had some success in

national tournaments as well, ranking No. 149 one year in the 14s.

First-year Blake coach Ted Warner had predicted great things for Wismer, whom he started in tennis when Wismer was a 10-year-old. Warner said of his game, "He had fabulous groundstrokes, and he was a very smart player who had a good all-around game. He was also a great competitor." Wert was primarily a doubles player in high school and, according to Warner, "had a good return of serve and an excellent serve-and-volley game." Neither played college tennis, Wismer attending Augsburg and then the U of M and Wert heading east to school. According to Coach Warner, Wismer lives in California today.

On the other hand, the Duluth pair enjoyed modest success in summer tournament play. Flaherty was ranked just once in doubles (No. 4 in the 16s with George Grombacher) and just once in singles (at No. 25 in the 16-and-under Challenger 1 division). Lundmark had more success in singles, several times earning a high ranking in the Challenger 1 division (once No. 2 in the 18s), and in doubles he was ranked just once in the open category (No. 6 in the 18s). Both had participated on the Duluth East varsity team since ninth grade and were members of the Greyhounds' 1993 state tournament team.

Former Duluth East coach Kurt Bartell noted that Flaherty and Lundmark caught fire during their 1995 tournament run, rolling through the draw like a combine through a wheat field. Both, said Bartell, "were mentally tough and focused, not easily excited or shaken." He added that Flaherty was a talented athlete who had played on a state championship hockey team. "He was a physically strong player with good hands and quickness—an efficient volleyer," Bartell said. About Lundmark, Bartell said, "He was an excellent volleyer and returner who made very few unforced errors. He was very steady and he made you beat him." Both played singles during the year (Flaherty at No. 1 and Lundmark at No. 2), but only Flaherty made it to State in singles—in 1994, his sophomore year. Paired together again in '96, and prepared to defend their title, they returned to State but were unable to deliver another championship. Instead they lost in the quarters to Mounds View juniors David Thawley and Carl Wahlstrand, who took third.

Flaherty did not play college tennis, but Lundmark had a notable career at Gustavus, earning All-American Division 3 honors in 1999 and 2000 and reaching the national singles quarterfinals and doubles semis (with Ryan Dussault) in '99 and the national doubles finals with Mike Hom in '00. In addition, he and two different partners (Dussault in '98 and Hom in '99) won ITA Midwest Regional doubles titles, he won three MIAC doubles titles with three different partners, and he also won two No. 1 MIAC singles titles, in '99 and '00. He's most proud of the fact that he led the Gusties to a runner-up finish in the 2000 team tournament.

1996—Chuck Schultz & Jeff Hahn
Eden Prairie-AA

Troy Kleven & Jake Olson
Crookston-A

Except for the Class A doubles title won by a pair from Crookston, the other five tennis tournaments went to Metro area schools; and all three in Class AA were claimed by Lake Conference schools. These champions were Bloomington Jefferson and Blake in team play, Jefferson (Matt Peplinski) and Minnehaha Academy (Rob Warn) in singles, and Eden Prairie in Class AA doubles. When Eden Prairie's Chuck

Schultz and Jeff Hahn hoisted up their doubles championship medals, they completed a blitzkreig in which Lake Conference players not only took the team title but finished 1-2 in both singles and doubles.

In fact, had the previously undefeated (30-0) No. 1 doubles team of sophomores Ryan Edlefsen and Phil Woo been able to win the doubles, Jefferson would have claimed all three titles. Alas for them, some inspired play by the Eden Prairie pair (senior Hahn and ninth grader Schultz) gave the Eagles their first doubles championship. In round 1 they had to overcome a future state singles titlist (ninth grader Eric Butorac) and his Rochester John Marshall partner, senior Camilo Leos. The score was 7-5, 6-3. They won their next two matches easily, a quarterfinal with seniors Tyler Peterson and Jeff Skubic of Virginia and a semifinal encounter with juniors Ford Rolfsrud and Tony Schmidt of Mankato East. But their biggest obstacle loomed in the finals, their Lake Conference rivals from Jefferson who had beaten them in three sets in the section final.

Given that their first duel with Woo and Edlefsen extended to three sets, it was no surprise that this final match of the season also went the distance. This time, however, Schultz and Hahn prevailed in a come-from-behind 3-6, 6-4, 6-2 battle. It was sweet revenge for the Eden Prairie boys and Hahn told *Star Tribune* writer Nolan Zavoral, "We've been talking for months about doing this, planning all year" (June 8, 1996). And though they lost

Jake Olson (Left) & Troy Kleven

the first set and were on the ropes in the second set, they did not get discouraged. Edlefsen commented, from the losing side's perspective, that "we had a lot of second chances in the second set. I thought we had the match, but we let them up, and they took over. They kept the momentum going into the third set" (June 8, 1996).

Coach Rich Strohkirch remembers that Schultz and Hahn won by "outserving their opponents, attacking them, and volleying well." Of Hahn's game, Strohkirch said, "He was quick on his feet and was a great net attacker." Schultz, who played No. 1 singles from eighth to twelfth grade for the Eagles, was, according to Strohkirch, "a huge server who had a perfect game overall." For Schultz, just the sixth ninth grader to win a doubles title, this would be his only trip to the victory stand.

In the Class A tournament at Eden Prairie High School, Crookston's youthful duo of junior Troy Kleven and sophomore Jake Olson worked through the draw to win the school's first tennis championship. Their first victims, who fell 7-5, 7-5, were senior Thor Nelson and junior Damien Hoffman from Minnewaska Area. Next came senior Travis Keeling and junior Duane Johnson of Duluth Marshall, who extended the Crookston lads to three sets but fell 4-6, 7-5, 6-3. Then in the semis Kleven and Olson once again came from behind to defeat sophomores Jon Simmons and Tom Pohlad from Breck by the same 4-6, 7-5, 6-3 score. Their finals opponents, from powerhouse private school Blake, were Ross Greenstein (an eighth grader) and Blake Baratz (a sophomore). Both were formidable singles players (Greenstein would win the 1997 singles title as a ninth grader and Baratz would finish fourth in '97 and second in '98 in singles). (For more on Greenstein, see Chapter Five.)

Perhaps the Blake lads were a bit overconfident, as noted in the June 8 *Star Tribune* article by Zavoral: "They took us by surprise," said Greenstein. "We thought we could control the match, but they snuck up on us." After again losing the first set—this one in a tiebreaker, Olson and Kleven stormed back to win the final two sets and the match by a score of 6-7, 6-3, 6-4. Said Olson, "We got into a zone that third set. Every match we seem to lose the first set, but the more we play, the more we get into it." For their part the Blake players were gracious losers,

Greenstein saying, "They played well. They deserved it" (June 8, 1996). One might argue that these Crookston boys earned their title more than any other team in state history, for in three of four matches they had to come back from first-set losses and all told they played an exhausting 118 games, a doubles record.

There will be more about Olson and Kleven, for they came back in 1997 to win their second doubles title. Of the Class AA winners, Hahn was not a top Minnesota junior tennis player, appearing just twice in the summer rankings (at Nos. 26 and 9 in the Challenger 118-and-Under Singles). He did go on to play four years of college tennis, however, at St. Thomas.

Schultz, on the other hand, was a standout in both singles and doubles. From the time he began playing tournaments he was ranked at or near the top. For instance, in singles he was No. 1 three times (once each in the 10s, 12s, and 14s) and he won Sectional singles championships twice (in the 12s and 14s). In doubles his pedigree was nearly as solid, for he was ranked No. 1 once (in the 12s) and No. 2 twice, each time, ironically, with his 1996 doubles finals opponent, Woo. He and Woo also won the 12-and-under Sectional title, a title Schultz would win again with Woo (in the 18s) and with Jason Gonzaga of Eau Claire, WI (in the 16s). Often endorsed from the Section for national tournament play, Schultz earned rankings as high as No. 129 in the 14-and-under singles division and No. 20 in the 14-and-under doubles (again with Woo). Also a football player in high school, Schultz did not play college tennis.

1997—David Hippee & Andrew Calof
Wayzata-AA

Troy Kleven & Jake Olson
Crookston-A

Like old wines that get better with age, the Class A champions from Crookston improved with experience and captured their second-straight doubles title, while the Class AA champions came from a city on the shores of Lake Minnetonka, Wayzata. The lads from the Red River were

Crookston's No. 1 and 2 players, Troy Kleven and Jake Olson, and the Wayzata team was that of David Hippee and Andrew Calof.

First, let's look at the repeat champions and their road to the title. Kleven, a senior, and Olson, a junior, advanced to the finals with a straight-set win over senior Jeremy Robinson and junior Peter Zellman of Redwood Valley in the first round and a tough three-setter against seniors Jay Zabel and Jared Bly of Blue Earth Area in the quarters (6-4, 1-6, 7-6). The Blue Earth boys almost pulled off an upset, but Kleven and Olson won the final set tiebreaker in an 8-6 squeaker. Their semifinal opponents were seniors Duane Johnson and Tom Valentini of Duluth Marshall, whom they dispatched 6-4, 6-2. And in what proved to be one of the most dominating performances ever in a doubles final, Kleven and Olson demolished a very good tandem from Blake, future state singles champion Drew Zamansky (a sophomore) and his partner Chris Laurey (a senior) by a double bagel score (6-0, 6-0). Crookston coach Mike Geffre said, "It was like a clinic in doubles." Geffre also recalls Blake coach Ted Warner consoling his lads, saying, "You know, guys, they don't put the score on your second-place medals."

Calling them "the two best kids I coached," Geffre then commented about their respective strengths: "Olson was a phenomenal athlete who was quick and strong. He was also a fierce competitor who did not want to lose

David Hippee (Left) & Andrew Calof

a point. Kleven, a lefty, was also a good athlete who had great hands." Both played other sports as well, Olson football and wrestling and Kleven hockey.

Olson (finally the No. 1 player in 1988 after occupying the No. 2 spot behind Kleven for the previous two years) had played on the varsity since eighth grade. In his final year of competition he finished fourth in the Class A singles tournament, concluding his career with the most wins in Crookston history: 133.

What's perhaps most remarkable about their success at State is that they didn't really spend much time honing their games in summer tournament play. Kleven was never a ranked player and Olson showed up just once in the rankings (at No. 25 in the Challenger 1 16-and-Under Singles).

Both went on to play sports in college, Olson football and tennis at Concordia-Moorhead and Kleven hockey and tennis at Hamline. Kleven's college tennis story reveals as much about his unassuming nature as his tennis ability. Looking for something to do in the spring of his first year at Hamline, he tried out for tennis. His coach wasn't aware of his tennis background and Kleven didn't tell him. So, according to Geffre, the Hamline coach said, "Here's a list of guys—go play them." In a week and a half he had beaten every player on the team and advanced to the No. 1 singles spot. Olson also played No. 1 singles—at Concordia—so he and Kleven often battled each other during MIAC play. Today Olson teaches in Delano and serves as an assistant girls' tennis coach.

In the Class AA tournament the winning team was comprised of a talented underclassman (ninth grader David Hippee) and a senior, Andrew Calof. Given that Wayzata had emerged from the Section 6 scrum and that they had finished second in the team tournament, it wasn't surprising that these two won the doubles. It wasn't easy, however, for they had to overcome the disappointment of losing a heartbreaking team final to Stillwater (4-3) and a marathon quarterfinal match with senior Derek Johnson and sophomore Steve Solberg of Fridley on Thursday. Calof said about their first two matches, a 6-3, 6-3 win over junior Dave Vidmar and sophomore John Ryan of Hibbing-Chisholm and that 6-1, 6-7 (7-4), 7-6 (7-2) quarterfinal victory over

Johnson and Solberg, "Those were the hardest matches. We just wanted to make it to Friday [to the semis] (*Star Tribune*," Joy Spencer, June 7, 1997).

Make it to Friday they did, and as writer Joy Spencer noted in that June 7 article, "They said that match [against Fridley] motivated them as they cruised through their semifinal match 6-0, 6-0 and their final match 6-1, 6-2." Their opponents in the semis were seniors Mike O'Brien and Andy Horton of Elk River and their finals opponents were section foes, senior Andy Finn and junior Ned Spector of Hopkins.

After the last match, Calof said, "It's a good way to end my high school life, but David [Hippee] gets to come back for three more years" (June 7, 1997). Unfortunately, after becoming just the seventh ninth grader to win a doubles title, Hippee could not top this feat in his final three years, though he did lead Wayzata to the team title his junior year (1999) and finished second twice in the individual tournament—once in doubles and once in singles. His sophomore year he and partner Trey Graft (also a sophomore) lost to Bloomington Jefferson's Phil Woo and Rory Theis in the doubles final (for more on this match see the 1998 report in this chapter). And his junior year he couldn't make it out of Section 6 in singles, losing in the semis in '99 to Eden Prairie's Chuck Schultz. This was a big upset, since Hippee had been ranked No. 2 behind D. J. Geatz in the Metro area.

Finally, he earned another trip to the state individual tournament his senior year, though not as the section singles champion. Here's how *Star Tribune* writer Jim Paulsen described Hippee's year after he lost in the section finals to eventual champion Justin Gaard of Edina 6-4, 6-4. "He didn't do it [make State] exactly the way he'd envisioned, but he made it" (June 6, 2000). With D. J. Geatz suspended for the season, Hippee had been ranked No. 1 in Class AA and, according to Paulsen, had "demolished opponents, losing just one set during the regular season" (June 6, 2000). So expectations were high and Hippee said he felt the pressure. Once he made it to State he played well, advancing to the finals. However, he lost again to Gaard and had to settle for a runner-up finish. His coach, Roger Lipelt, said that Hippee had never lost to Gaard before but ironically had lost to him three times this

year (in a section team match and in both the section and state singles finals).

Still, Hippee had earned praise for a superb high school career in which he won a doubles title and helped his school win a team championship. Lipelt praised him as "a really dedicated player who quit basketball after his ninth-grade year to concentrate on tennis." He called him "a marvelous athlete who had a huge topspin forehand, a lot of power, and awesome putaway shots." Assistant coach Dan Nabedrick called Hippee "a terrific player who was fiercely competitive." Two-time singles champion Justin Gaard of Edina, who lost to Hippee so many times as a junior player, said Hippee was tough "because his lefty serve was difficult to deal with." And Greg Wicklund, who worked with Hippee, praised his "nice lefty serve" but also mentioned that he improved a great deal each year.

In addition, he had great success in summer tournament play. For example, he was ranked four times in the top ten in singles (with a high of No. 2 in the 16s) and he was twice ranked No. 2 in doubles, one of those years winning the Sectional title with Eric Butorac. In addition, he was often endorsed to play national tournaments and earned rankings in the 100s. Hippee continued his tennis career at the U of WI, playing all four years for the Badgers, often at No. 1 or 2 singles.

As for Calof, he too had a solid junior career, especially in doubles, for he was ranked No. 2 and then 4 in the 18-and-unders when Section players were ranked individually instead of as teams. In singles his highest ranking was No. 12 in the Open 12s, but he was often ranked high in the Challenger 1 division as well (even No. 1 in the 18s).

Coach Lipelt remembered him as "a really steady player" and Nabedrick said of Calof, "He wasn't a big kid, but he was a great athlete—a really solid player." Nabedrick, who gave Calof his first tennis lesson, said that he didn't come from a tennis background. "He got the most out of his game," but more importantly, according to Nabedrick, "he was just a great guy." After high school he too enrolled at the U of WI but did not go out for tennis or hockey (another sport he had played in high school). Instead, he focused on film studies and business and today works for Miramax in Los Angeles

1998—Phil Woo & Rory Theis
Bloomington Jefferson—AA

Phillip Johnson & Jarett Cascino
Rochester Lourdes-A

Results in the 1998 tournament were almost as predictable as the backhand lob I always hit when I'm pinned behind the baseline, for once again Lake Conference schools won all three Class AA titles and private/parochial schools the Class A championships. I say almost as predictable, because while Edina (No. 1 all year) won the team title and the singles (Cesar Vargas), they did not sweep. Instead, the doubles was a replay of the Section 6 final between Lake Conference foes Bloomington Jefferson and Wayzata. The result was a victory for the Jaguars' pair of Phil Woo and Rory Theis over Wayzata's super sophomores, Hippee and Trey Graft.

In Class A, champion Breck won the team title and the singles (Reven Stephens) and took third in the doubles. And though Rochester Lourdes, a parochial school with a storied history in girls' tennis, had never before won a doubles championship, the winners, considered one of the favorites, came from that school (Phillip Johnson and Jarett Cascino). Johnson, a junior, was a member of Lourdes' 1995 state tournament team and had participated in the state singles draw since his eighth-grade year (1995-97). Ninth grader Cascino was a rising star who would win the state singles title in 2001.

We'll have more to say about Johnson and Cascino in the report on the 1999 tournament, but this year they began their quest with a win over seniors Jeremy Peterson and Robbie Gerdts of Blue Earth Area. Next they dispatched seniors Ryan Melsa and Justin Buchmeier of Crookston, then in the semis on Friday at 98th Street Racquet Club they knocked off the pair from Breck who finished third, seniors Ryan Burnet and Matt Schellhas. And in the finals they defeated an up-and-coming pair from Litchfield, coach John Carlson's son Alex and his partner Chris Patten, both sophomores. (These lads, Carlson and Patten, would stick together their final two years as well, and their loyalty would reward them with a championship in 2000.)

Though Johnson and Cascino had only played together for two weeks (during the year they played Nos. 1 and 2 singles respectively), they dominated the field without losing a set. Against Carlson and Patten in the finals, they carved out a neat 6-2, 6-2 win. Perhaps that previous state tournament experience gave them an edge (Cascino played doubles with Mike Gander in 1997 and Johnson made it to State in singles the past three years). Continuing the pattern of underclassmen winning state doubles titles, Cascino's was the eighth in Minnesota history and the fifth won by a ninth-grade doubles player this decade.

On the Class AA side, in matches played at Eden Prairie High School, Jefferson's Woo and Theis (a senior and sophomore respectively) opened tournament play with a victory over sophomore Titus Christianson and senior Adam Derosier of Fergus Falls. Their quarterfinal opponents, seniors Drew Gerkey and Trevor Larson of Stillwater Area, were also no match for Woo and Theis. Up next was a pair from Red Wing's runner-up team, senior Jesse Plote and junior C. J. Peterson, and they, too, fell in straight sets to the Jaguars' pair. And in that rematch of the Section 6 final, Jefferson's deadly combination of a No. 2 singles player (Woo) and a No. 3 singles player (Theis) won the first set 6-4 against Hippee and Graft, then clawed their way back from a 3-1 deficit to also take the second set (and the match) 6-4. This was the second doubles title for Jefferson, and its last. It was also another year in which both champions blasted through the draw without dropping a set.

For Woo this doubles title was a sweet way to end an exceptional high school career in which he played in the shadow of Jefferson stalwarts Matt Peplinski, Aaron Dvorak, and Ryan Edlefsen (all of whom won state titles before he won his). He made his first appearance at State as an eighth grader and a member of that 1994 state championship team (playing No. 4 singles), then as a sophomore in '96 he and Edlefsen finished second in the doubles tournament. In '97 he did not make it to State. His coach, Tom Saterdalen, said of Woo, "He was a really good athlete and a really upbeat guy."

In another respect Woo seemed predestined to win a state doubles title (though it came later than perhaps anticipated), for he had shown great promise as a junior player from an early age. For instance, he and summer partner Chuck Schultz won two Sectional doubles titles (in the 14s and the 18s) and they were also ranked No. 2 or 3 every year they played together. In addition, Woo was an outstanding singles player who was never ranked lower than No. 10 in his age group and twice was No. 2 (in the 14s and 16s) and once No. 1 (in the 18s). And he frequently played national tournaments in the summers, earning rankings in the mid to high 100s on several occasions, including a ranking of No. 158 in the 14s. Always a gentleman on the court, Woo won the 1993 NWTA Junior Sportsmanship Award.

Like the previous year's winners from Wayzata (Hippee and Calof), Woo also enrolled at the U of WI-Madison. He played tennis there, but his size (he was short) limited him. Today he works in business and lives in Hawaii.

Theis, on the other hand, was never ranked in doubles but earned decent rankings in singles, culminating in a No. 9 placing in the 16-and-Under Open category. And though he was the No. 1 singles player for the Jaguars his last two years, Theis could not advance to State from a section that had too many talented players. Coach Saterdalen, in assessing Theis's game, said, "He was a good volleyer who was also very quick and had good feet." Theis left the state to attend school out east but did not continue with his tennis, according to Saterdalen.

1999—Brad Anderson & Jon Seltzer
Edina-AA

Phillip Johnson & Jarett Cascino
Rochester Lourdes-A

If the 1999 State Tournament was a concert, the doubles winners played a strong final number and an encore after Wayzata opened play with a team victory (the overture) and Eric Butorac won the singles (an outstanding concerto).

Phillip Johnson (Left) & Jarett Cascino

The final symphony, heralding the arrival of three straight Edina champions—and four of the next five—was played by Brad Anderson and Jon Seltzer. And the encore was sweet music for the Class A duo from Rochester Lourdes, senior Phillip Johnson and sophomore Jarett Cascino, who repeated as champions.

Seltzer, who as an eighth grader had helped Stillwater win the 1996 team title, moved to Edina as a sophomore and assumed a key role as a No. 1 doubles player (with Anderson) on the Hornets' '98 team champions. Now a junior, he teamed up with Anderson (also a junior) for a run at the doubles title. With the somber notes of Edina's 4-3 section final loss to Wayzata still lingering in their ears, Seltzer and Anderson were determined to get Edina back on pitch. So they opened with a very competitive 6-2, 2-6, 6-2 win over seniors Luke Wendlandt and Adam Himle of Hutchinson. In their next two matches at 98th Street they first took care of senior John Ryan and junior Kasey Conda of Hibbing-Chisholm and then seniors Ed Edson and Shimul Chowdhury of Rochester John Marshall, both of whom fell by the same 6-2, 6-4 score. The finals matchup was one that can't always be guaranteed, one between the two co-favorites. But this year it came to pass, so Red Wing seniors C. J. Peterson (a third-place doubles winner last year) and his new partner Cam Goetz fought their way through the draw. As so often happens this was an encounter matching doubles players who had played solo all year; but Anderson and Seltzer (Edina's No. 2 and 3 singles players) made the best duet and won convincingly 6-4, 6-3.

Though Anderson admitted that "my game has always been a little inconsistent," in part because "I tried to go for big serves and groundstrokes," he and Seltzer made a good combination because Seltzer was very steady and he (Anderson) got to the net as often as possible to put points away quickly. In addition, said Anderson, "the fact that we played junior tennis together in USTA tournaments gave us a solid comfort level in how we reacted on the court."

In an article by *Star Tribune* writer Jim Paulsen, a happy Anderson said after the match, "Sure, it would be nice to win the singles, because that's where all the best players are. But there are still a lot of great players in doubles and it's a state championship" (June 5, 1999). Both lads had another year left and Anderson again played No. 2 singles and Seltzer No. 3 on an Edina team that captured the 2000 championship, and Seltzer won his second individual title (another doubles with younger brother Charlie). (For more on the Seltzers, see the report on the 2000 doubles tournament.)

Anderson considered his team's 2000 win the highlight of his high school career: "We had been going back and forth with Wayzata the previous two years and they got the better of us in 1999, so we got redemption in 2000 when we beat them 5-2."

With respect to his development as a player, Anderson had worked hard to improve his game, in part by playing junior tournaments in the summer. This hard work saw him advance through the Challenger 1 division to earn rankings as high as No. 6 in the Open 18 Singles division. In doubles he was once ranked No. 1 in points (in the 14-and-unders), and he also earned some national rankings (the highest being a No. 172 in the 14s). Anderson's high school coach, Gary Aasen, praised him as "a rock solid team tennis player who did great in team play. For instance, twice in 2000 he beat Trey Craft from Wayzata." Aasen also noted that Anderson lost a tough section singles match to Wayzata's David Hippee, just missing a chance to play in the state singles tournament that same year. "He finished his senior year with a 20-1 singles record and a 76-14 overall record," Aasen

commented. Aasen also said of Anderson, "He took a long time to mature, eventually developing a huge serve. He was super aggressive on the court."

Enrolling at Boston College after graduation, Anderson became a first-rate college tennis player. After beginning his career at No. 3 singles and No. 2 doubles his freshman year, he then played No. 1 doubles and Nos. 1 and 2 singles his sophomore and junior years. One year he even competed well in a match against future top-ten pro James Blake, then playing at Harvard. Coach Aasen said of Anderson's post-high school play, "He really blossomed in college. He might have played better D1 tennis than all of them [his former Edina players] and he's someone I'd put on my all-Edina team." Anderson did not play his senior year because, he said, "I was having too much fun in college."

After graduating in 2004 with majors in finance and marketing, he moved back to Minneapolis, where he works for an investment and banking firm specializing in mergers and acquisitions.

Once again held at Eden Prairie High School, the Class A tournament gave Rochester Lourdes aces Johnson and Cascino a chance for an encore. And what an encore it was, one that showcased their talent and produced four solid wins and a second-straight championship. Their opening notes produced a convincing win over senior Zach Pettus and ninth grader Peter Stenson of St. Paul Academy and Summit School. In the quarters they knocked out seniors Chris Myrold and Ben Meier of Crookston, and in the 8 AM Friday semis they defeated a veteran team of juniors, the 1998 doubles runners-up from Litchfield, Alex Carlson and Chris Patten 7-5, 6-3. Then they finished with a crashing crescendo, a 6-3, 6-3 win over St. Peter senior Troy Brovold and sophomore Johann Liljengren, son of coach Peter Liljengren. This was a terrific final day performance against two very good doubles teams, one of which would go on to win the 2000 title (Carlson and Patten).

Cascino did not often appear in the summer NWTA junior doubles rankings (his highest ranking was No. 10 in points in the 14s), but he was a skilled singles player who eventually won the 2001 state singles title. (For more on Cascino, see Chapter Five.) Johnson, on the other hand, had a more distinguished junior career in doubles. Once ranked No. 1 (in the 16s), he also won three Sectional doubles titles (two with Eric Butorac in the 16s and 18s, and one with Red Wing's Jesse Plote, also in the 18s). His highest singles ranking was No. 6 in the Challenger 1 division. Johnson completed his high school career this year and went on to play one fall season of tennis at Gustavus, reaching the semis of the 2000 fall Midwest Regional doubles. However, he transferred to the U of M after his freshman year for financial reasons and did not continue in tennis. Johnson earned a degree in chemistry and is today in graduate school studying that subject.

2000s

2000–Jon & Charlie Seltzer
Edina-AA

Alex Carlson & Chris Patten
Litchfield-A

Brotherly love! That had to be the story line for this year's doubles tournament, for three of the best teams were brother combinations, and one pair won the Class AA title. Edina's Jon and Charlie Seltzer became just the fifth brother duo to win the championship, the last was Blue Earth's Myles and Roger Anderson in 1985. The other brother pairs were Minneapolis South's Danny and Mikey Kantar (who finished fourth in Class AA) and Winona Cotter's John and Brian Thomas (the Class A runners-up).

Amazingly, the Seltzers, who played No. 3 (Jon) and 4 (Charlie) singles during the year, had never played an organized doubles match before joining forces for the section meet. Nonetheless, they played beautifully together, much like well-choreographed ballet dancers performaing a pas de deux. The first victims of these Section 6 champions were Mounds View's Mike Wendland (a senior) and Tom Ahlstrom (a sophomore). Next they bumped off seniors Jesse Jagunich and Kasey Conda of Hibbing-Chisholm. Then in the semis it was brothers against brothers, the Seltzers against the Kantars, senior Danny and sophomore Mikey. The result was another straight-set win that propelled the Seltzers into the finals.

And for the second year in a row it was an Edina-Red Wing matchup, but this year the teams were different. Senior Jon Seltzer had a new partner, his ninth-grade brother Charlie. Junior Cam Goetz also hooked up with a different sidekick, senior Adam Witt. Goetz's 1999 partner, C. J. Peterson, had graduated, and Jon Seltzer's partner Brad Anderson played singles this year. Completing

Charlie (Left) & Jon Seltzer

Alex Carlson (Left) & Chris Patten

what *Star Tribune* writer Jim Paulsen called "a dominating performance," the Seltzers defeated the Red Wing lads in straight sets, 6-3, 6-4 (June 10, 2000).

After the match Jon Seltzer told Paulsen, "This [the doubles title] has been our goal since the first day of the season. We knew it would be fun to win one together. We haven't played together officially, but we've hit with each other so many times that we know each other very well." Comparing this year's match to last year's final which Red Wing also lost to Edina, Goetz said, "I thought last year we had a better chance to win. They were just too good for us today" (June 10, 2000).

For Jon Seltzer this was a fitting end to an illustrious career that saw him make his first appearance on the state tournament stage as an eighth grader on Stillwater's 1997 championship team. He also helped Edina win two team titles and joined an elite group of two-time doubles champions. And while he did not appear in the summer junior rankings as often as his younger brother Charlie, he did well early in his career, achieving No. 5 singles rankings in the Open 14s and 16s and a No. 2 ranking (on points) in the 14-and-under doubles. He also played national tournaments, earning a ranking of No. 170 in the 14s one year. Also a hockey player in high school, Jon was, according to Coach Gary Aasen, "competitive as all get out—he hated to lose." In addition, Aasen said, "He earned everything on the court through practice; he was one of the better guys on court in terms of time and discipline." Aasen considered him an all-around player who didn't have one great shot and a superb doubles player who poached very well.

Jon Seltzer graduated from the U of WI-Madison and today lives and works in North Carolina. He did not play tennis in college.

Though Seltzer's brother Charlie won just this one state title (the ninth doubles title by a ninth grader), he had a storied junior career which saw him reach the No. 1 Open singles position in his age group three times (twice in the 16s and once in the 14s) and win two Sectional titles (once in the 12s and once in the 16s). In addition, he finished third in the 18 Open Singles, won the Sectional 12-and-Under Doubles with Rochester's Zach Smith, and earned several national rankings, including No. 119 in the 14 singles division.

Surprisingly, with three more years of competition remaining, he did not achieve his goal of winning a singles title, although he helped Edina win two more team titles his junior and senior years (2002-03). His sophomore year he did not make it to the state individual tourney, but his last two years he competed well in the singles draw, finishing fourth as a junior and runner-up his senior year. Both times he lost to Eden Prairie's Nick Edlefsen in straight sets.

A five-year letterwinner at Edina and the No. 1 singles player his last two years, Charlie Seltzer was a little guy who, according to coach Aasen, "won through patience, discipline, and consistency." Aasen also said, "He was not really a doubles player but was a scrappy singles player who worked very hard."

After graduating from Edina in 2003, Charlie Seltzer enrolled at the U of Richmond, where he also played tennis.

What about the Class A tournament featuring the Thomas brothers, senior John and junior Brian? Well, they lost in the finals to Litchfield seniors Alex Carlson and Chris Patten, the 1998 runners-up and '99 third-place team. It's unusual to see doubles teams stick together for more than than two years, but Carlson and Patten played together for three years and their patience paid dividends. They opened the tournament with a 6-1, 6-1 drubbing of junior Mu Huang and ninth grader Brock Lauritsen of Montevideo, then the Dragons' duo took out senior Willy Leaf and sophomore Jared Novotny of Winona Cotter 6-3, 6-1. In the semis they struggled in the second set against senior John Schollmeier and his sophomore partner Josh Malwitz of Blue Earth Area, but they pulled out a 6-3, 7-6 win to set up their match with the Thomas brothers. Their 6-0, 6-0 win over the Winona Cotter brothers (just the second double bagel score in a state final match) gave Litchfield its second doubles title and the first since 1989. In addition, this was another year in which both the Class A and AA winners won all four matches in straight sets.

But perhaps what was most remarkable about their victory is that for the most part the Litchfield boys were just seasonal tennis players. Carlson was a football and basketball star, and both he and Patten were key members of Litchfield's 2000 Class A state championship basketball team coached by Carlson's father, John, also the tennis coach. Neither played tennis in the summer; in fact, neither appear in any NWTA rankings at any level of play or in any age bracket.

However, Alex Carlson grew up around tennis, often hitting on the Augusta Racquet Club courts in St. Cloud where his father served as tennis director. Because he chose to diversify and play three sports, Carlson was encouraged by his father/coach to become a serve-and-volley player. This advice served him well in doubles, but he also competed well in singles, playing No. 1 for the Dragons for five years.

After high school he enrolled at St. Cloud State, where he majored in physical education, following in the footsteps of both his parents. He did not play tennis at St. Cloud, but he was a four-year starter at point guard in basketball for the Huskies. Today he teaches at Sartell, coaches the boys' tennis team, and serves as an assistant boys' basketball coach. On a side note, his younger brother, John, himself a good high school tennis player, is a tight end on the Notre Dame football team.

Patten played No. 2 singles, and coach Carlson said of his game, "Chris had fantastic hand-eye coordination. He was also very, very quick and was a fierce competitor who hated to lose." Carlson added that his son also hated to lose and was an excellent competitor as well. Patten went to college at the U of MN-Duluth but did not play sports, though he coached the Duluth East High School team one year. Today he works as a chiropractor. (For more on the Carlson family, see Chapter Ten.)

2001—Roy Bryan & Gavin Lee
Edina-AA

Jake Brenk & Brandon Fenn
Breck-A

In yet another year in which Metro schools claimed all three Class AA titles and private/parochial schools took home the prizes in Class A, a pair of Hornets from Edina put a sting on the AA doubles teams and a team from Breck captured the school's third small-school championship.

Oh, yes, Breck also won the team title but Edina, which also won the singles (Justin Gaard), surrendered the team trophy to Minneapolis South. And Rochester Lourdes' Jarett Cascino won the singles in Class A.

Back to the doubles, that buzzing pair from Edina was made up of juniors Roy Bryan and Gavin Lee. In winning the third doubles title in a row for their school, Bryan and Lee began play with a win over seniors Dan Sheldon and Andy Rock of Elk River Area. Next they defeated seniors Skylar Kangas and Chris Kearney of Hibbing-Chisholm. To get to the finals they had to overcome next year's champions, juniors Mikey Kantar and Sion Wilkins of team champion Minneapolis South. The score was 7-6, 6-3 in

Roy Bryan (Left) & Gavin Lee

favor of Bryan and Lee. Then, in an all-Lake Conference dogfight which saw them often playing from behind, the Edina lads overcame junior Amir Mirheydar and ninth grader Albin Hubscher of Wayzata 4-6, 6-2, 6-4. Down 4-1 in the third set, the Hornets buzzed back and won five straight games.

Many years the winning doubles teams consist of singles players who join up for tournament play, believing they have a better shot at a title. Not so with this Edina pair. In a June 9, 2001, article in the *Star Tribune*, staff writer Jim Paulsen said, "Roy Bryan and Gavin Lee pulled off what has become an increasingly rare occurrence in state competition: winning the doubles championship as season-long teammates… Bryan and Lee have been playing together since ninth grade and comprised Edina's top doubles team all season." A euphoric Bryan exclaimed after the match, "It's a huge deal. We didn't expect to do this well, but one thing we have is good chemistry" (June 9, 2001). This good chemistry continued for one more year, and in 2002 Bryan and Lee (still anchoring the No. 1 doubles spot in the lineup) helped Edina reclaim the state team title it gave up this year. However, in attempting to repeat as doubles champions, they ran into a team with a stronger mix, the Minneapolis South boys they defeated in the semis in 2001.

Still, with their first-place medals in hand, Bryan and Lee had reason to be proud, in part because they had not been highly ranked junior players. Lee was never ranked and Bryan only earned some Challenger 1 alphabetical rankings as a very young tournament player and was not ranked in the 16s or 18s. His coach, Gary Aasen, said that may have been because he also played "a ton of hockey." Nevertheless, he was a very successful high school tennis player who, according to Aasen, "was a tennis-mature player. Practice was all business for him, and he was a good doubles player who had great hands."

After graduation from Edina, Bryan enrolled at Gustavus where he carved out an outstanding academic and tennis career. Academically, for example, he earned a 3.90 G.P.A. with a biology major, was named to the 2006 ESPN The Magazine Academic All-American At-Large Team, and was awarded a $7,500 NCAA postgraduate scholarship (one of only 58 individuals to be so honored among all NCAA athletes).

As for his college tennis, after losing seventy-five pounds his freshman year in order to become a top singles player, he gradually worked his way into the Gustavus lineup. For example, as a junior he played No. 5 singles and No. 3 doubles, with his brother Andy as partner. And as co-captain of the 2006 team, he helped the Gusties take third-place at nationals, win an 18th-straight MIAC Conference title, and claim the national Division 3 indoor team title. He held down No. 5 singles and No. 2 doubles spots in the lineup that year, winning conference titles in singles and doubles (again with his brother as his partner).

Bryan's partner Lee came from a tennis family; his father played and his sister competed for the Edina girls' team. Coach Aasen said of him, "He was a good team player and practice performer who was very serious about his tennis." A doubles specialist in high school, he was, said Aasen, "not a big guy and he did not have an overpowering serve, but he really learned how to play doubles."

After graduation he followed Bryan to Gustavus, but he chose to concentrate on academics and transferred to the U of M after his freshman year. Tennis is still in his blood, however, for in 2005 (while still a student at the U) he coached the Benilde boys' team. And he's also done some tennis teaching at the Minikahda Club in the summers.

The 2001 Class A doubles champions were the Breck duo of senior Jake Brenk and sophomore Brandon Fenn. And though this team was more the norm (Fenn was a singles player), it still included a doubles specialist in Brenk. Both were winners in Breck's 4-3 triumph over Blake in the team championship, Fenn at No. 1 singles and Brenk at No. 1 doubles (with partner Chris Pohlad-one of three grandsons of Twins' owner Carl Pohlad who played for Breck).

First up for the Mustangs' duo in the individual tournament was a team from Blue Earth Area (senior Willie Richards and junior Brett Zabel) whom they handled with ease. In their second Thursday match they also won in straight sets, defeating senior John Redgrave and junior Jon Lebedoff of Blake. And in the semis on Friday they rebounded from a first-set loss to defeat seniors Bob Anglin and Luke Grandlund of Staples-Motley 2-6, 6-3, 6-3. They wrapped up a good day's work with a well-earned 6-1, 6-7 (7-5), 7-6 (7-4) triumph over senior Tony Rukavina and junior Jared Novotny of Winona Cotter in the finals.

Brenk, who transferred from Detroit Lakes his sophomore year, had played in the 2000 doubles tournament (with Chris Pohlad's brother Joe) but lost in the first round. It's not surprising that he did well in doubles, for as a junior player he had greater success playing with a partner, earning a ranking as high as No. 7 in the 14-and-under doubles in points. Seconding this view about his doubles prowess, his high school coach (Katie Queenan) said of Brenk's doubles play, "He was a fantastic athlete who had incredible hands. He had a really great doubles sense and he was also a great competitor." And even though he didn't play much tennis until the spring season (he also played hockey), Queenan said that he was "a clutch player who rose to the occasion."

The following year Brenk went to MN State U-Mankato, where he played hockey but no tennis. Fenn would return to Breck with two more opportunities to win a state title.

2002—Mikey Kantar & Sion Wilkins
Minneapolis South-AA

Brandon Fenn & Alex Clark
Breck-A

Even though there is the compelling story of Breck's Brandon Fenn winning his second Class A doubles title, top billing this year must go to the tale of the remarkable triumph of seniors Mikey Kantar and Sion Wilkins of Minneapolis South. Both were products of public parks' urban

Mikey Kantar (Left) & Sion Wilkins

tennis programs, and both were members of the only city school team to win a state title since True Team play began in 1973.

Though both of their tennis and life stories are noteworthy, Wilkins' might be the most engaging. According to a June 7, 2000, *Star Tribune* article by Jim Paulsen, Wilkins is the son of Native American parents (he is "half-Navajo and half-Lumbee—a tribe in North Carolina") and he "picked up tennis three years ago while his family was living in Arizona [when he was a seventh grader]." He credited his athletic father for introducing him to different sports but especially tennis: "I started playing tennis and I really liked it." He liked it so much that he began promoting the sport within the Native American community, putting on tennis clinics at the American Indian Center in South Minneapolis and working with a program called "Standing Tall Tennis." In this latter program he gave summer clinics out west, even on reservations in Minnesota and South Dakota. Said Wilkins about his volunteer efforts, "I want to be a role model for Native Americans. I want to expose them to tennis. Basketball is popular with Native Americans, tennis isn't. But I think if I can bring it to their attention and get them to try it, they might get hooked" (June 7, 2000).

Wilkins' story is also unique because he was home schooled and was playing organized sports for the first

Brandon Fenn (Left) & Alex Clark

time, so one might assume that he would have had a difficult time fitting in with his teammates. Not so, according to South coach, George Beske: "The guys on the team just love him. He's really become a member of the team" (June 7, 2000).

Playing No. 2 singles in 2000, behind Tim Klein, Wilkins helped his South squad take third in the team tournament. And in an extraordinary show of force, he and three of his teammates advanced to State in individual play: Wilkins and Klein and brothers Danny and Mikey Kantar in doubles. Though none would win a title (the Kantars finished fourth), their success gave them confidence for the upcoming year, the best in South history.

With the addition of superstar D. J. Geatz, the Tigers blitzed through the state tournament field in 2001 with the loss of just one point in each of their three matches and secured the first team title for a city school since Minneapolis Marshall won a pre-True Team championship in 1958. (For more on South's team title, see Chapter Eight.) Wilkins, playing No. 3 singles behind Geatz and Klein, and Kantar (at No. 1 doubles) won all three of their team matches. In addition, they teamed up for a run at the doubles title, coming up just short in a disappointing 7-6, 6-3 loss to the eventual champions (Bryan and Lee of Edina) in the semis.

However, they won their third-place match, giving them incentive (and a bit of momentum) to try again in 2002 even though both played singles during the year (rotating between Nos. 2 and 3). Expected to compete for the team title, the Tigers were declawed in the first round by Mounds View 4-3, in part because No. 1 player Geatz was unable to play due to an injury. This loss nonetheless did not deter seniors Wilkins and Kantar.

Clearly the best team in the field, they began their quest for the doubles title with a 6-0, 6-0 win over seniors Brandon Simms and Sam Donner of Lakeville. In the next round they got the matchup they had dreamed about all year against the team that knocked them out last year, 2001 champions Bryan and Lee. This time the result would be very different, as Wilkins and Kantar dominated the Hornets' senior duo 6-4, 6-1. With this win secured, they stormed through the next two rounds, first taking care of juniors Andy Spilseth and Ross Devor of Orono 6-2, 6-1,

then blasting seniors Tom Ahlstrom and Andrew Tulloch of Mounds View in the finals 6-1, 6-2. In what was one of the most dominant performanes in recent years, Kantar and Wilkins lost just 11 games in their four matches.

After securing the title, Wilkins, commenting to *Star Tribune* writer Paulson about their determination to win this year, said, "We said we were going to play together again right after we lost in the semifinals last year. We knew we were good enough to win it. Winning as a team last year was a great feeling, but this is pretty sweet, too" (June 8, 2002). Their victory, and Geatz's miraculous return-from-injury singles title, gave South the first city-school sweep of individual state titles since 1948 when Edmund "Chiefie" Gould of Southwest won the singles and teamed with William Moses to take the doubles.

As for Kantar, the son of a South High ceramics teacher, he got started playing tennis with his older brother Danny in the Minneapolis Urban Tennis Program. Originally more interested in baseball, both opted for tennis after Danny was forced to choose between varsity tennis and freshman baseball. This no-brainer decision led to a four-year varsity tennis career for each of the brothers and two years in which they played doubles together. When Danny was a junior and Mikey a ninth grader, they played No. 2 doubles; then in 2000 they played No. 1 doubles and paired up for the individual tournament, finishing fourth after losing a battle of the brothers in the semis to the Seltzers of Edina. Early in his junior year Mikey played singles, but an injury soon forced him to take a doubles spot, where he and senior Andy Born anchored the No. 1 position for South's 2001 championship team.

Though Kantar and Wilkins credit the Urban Tennis Program for jump-starting their careers, they also benefitted from training in the STP program at various clubs and from playing junior tournaments in the summer. While both had relatively short junior careers, their stars burned brightly. For Wilkins it was one NWTA ranking, a No. 2 in 18-and-under singles, and two national rankings (his highest at No. 215 in the 16s); and for Kantar it was a No. 5 in 16 singles and a No. 8 in 18 singles. In addition, Kantar won a prestigious prize, the 2001 Bill Talbert Junior Sportsmanship Award. As a result he attended the National Tennis Hall of Fame presentation at Newport, RI, where, he said, "I met Pam Shriver and Mats Wilander." In addition, in 2001 he was the national winner of the Arthur Ashe Essay Contest.

Kantar, Wilkins, and Geatz then became key members of the U of M men's tennis team. Geatz was the No. 1 player in 2006, Kantar played Nos. 2 and 3 doubles and some No. 6 singles, and Wilkins played Nos. 1 and 2 doubles and some Nos. 5-7 singles. This must be some kind of modern-day record: three players from one high school team participating on Minnesota's only Division I varsity squad. Still, as Kantar said, maybe this isn't so surprising, given what he called "the great team atmosphere and energy we had at South. From four years in high school we had 10 guys play college tennis." He also said that winning the team title in 2001 "was an unbelievable experience. Almost everyone on the team had grown up in public parks tennis—it was very unique."

But winning the doubles his senior year was sweet as well, Kantar noted. He called his teammate Wilkins "a great partner who is unbelievably smooth and calm. If you wanted to teach someone to play, you would watch him." As for his own game, he said, "I had a big serve and I was athletic." Perhaps as a tribute to his partner, Kantar took classes in Native American studies at the U, graduating with a minor in that discipline and a major in applied plant science. Wilkins, a 2007 graduate, had a major in sports management and a minor in Native American Studies.

While the Class A doubles final may not have generated the buzz the Kantar-Wilkins story generated, it was worthy of more attention than the one line it received in the *Star Tribune*. For one thing it produced a much more competitive final match than the Class AA final, a dynamite three-setter that featured a competitive first set (6-4) and two tiebreakers. In addition, it was the second title for Brandon Fenn, who would go on to complete a historic three-peat in 2003. And finally, the winning team from Breck (Fenn and senior Alex Clark) had to defeat a very strong pair from Blake's state championship team, seniors Jon Lebedoff and Ben Crane.

Fenn and Clark began play with an agonizing 6-7, 7-5, 7-6 win over juniors Blake Berquist and David Lindsay of St. Paul Academy and Summit School. They lost the first set tiebreaker 7-5 and won the last set tiebreaker by the same score, so if one or two points had gone the other way there would have been a different champion this year. Not quite a Houdini-esque escape, but close. Then they had an easier time with senior Mark Dollerschell and junior John Carlson of Litchfield in the quarters, winning 6-2, 6-3.

In the semis they tuned up for another marathon match (the final against Lebedoff and Crane) by defeating Blue Earth Area seniors Blake Duden and Josh Malwitz 6-2, 6-3. The final was a matchup of Breck's No. 1 and 2 singles players (Fenn and Clark) and a No. 3 singles player (Crane) and No. 1 doubles player (Lebedoff). Both seniors (and co-captains of the Blake squad), they helped the Bears overpower three opponents en route to the 2002 team title. So this final blue ribbon matchup produced a blue ribbon result, a 6-4, 6-7 (7-3), 7-6 (7-4) win for Fenn and Clark.

For Clark, who appeared just once in the NWTA summer rankings (alphabetically in both the 12-and-under Challenger 1 Singles and Open Doubles), this match would mark an end to a career that also included participation on two Breck tournament teams. On that 2001 championship team, as he did this year, he held down the No. 2 singles position behind Fenn. Coach Queenan described him as "more of a singles player, a tough competitor who had a good serve." However, she said, "He got better in doubles by playing with Brandon [Fenn], and he could set Brandon up at the net."

Also a football player in high school, he enrolled at Lawrence U in Appleton, WI, with a goal of playing football there. Clark transferred to the U of WI-Madison after a year and gave tennis a try, but he was cut from the squad. As for Fenn, he had some unfinished high school tennis business to take care of in 2003.

2003—Andrew Bryan & Scott Leininger
Edina-AA

Brandon Fenn & Collin Taft-McPhee
Breck-A

In this historic 75th year of Minnesota state tournament competition, there were some predictable stories and also some surprises. Perhaps it was fitting that the team titles went to dynasty teams Edina and Blake and that a doubles pair from one of those schools (Edina) and a singles player from the other (Blake) won an individual title. And it wasn't so surprising that the other two titles came from Eden Prairie in Class AA singles and Breck in Class A doubles, thus ensuring another Metro-area sweep of all six titles. This was not the first year Metro players had dominated play; in fact, it had occurred just ten years earlier (1993).

So those Edina and Blake team titles were not surprising, for they were experienced squads which had won the 2002 titles. Nor was it surprising that Eden Prairie's Nick Edlefsen and Blake's Grady Newman claimed singles championships, for both were pre-tournament favorites.

But doubles is harder to predict, and so the surprises came from those tournaments. The first surprise was a second triumph by a Bryan brother, not one of the Bryan brothers of U.S. Davis Cup fame but another Edina Bryan. His name was Andrew and he was the sibling of 2001 doubles champion Roy. A second surprise was yet another title for Breck's Brandon Fenn, his third and a state record. There have been seven championships in which the same partners repeated and several in which a player won a second title with a different partner, but never has anyone won three doubles titles with three different partners.

So this is the lead doubles story of 2003, the triumph of Breck senior Fenn and his newest partner, junior Collin Taft-McPhee. An article by *Star Tribune* columnist Jim Paulsen described how the two came to play together: "As was the case with his previous teammates, Taft-McPhee became Fenn's doubes partner the day before sections started" (June 7, 2003). Paulsen added, "Fenn had played

Scott Leininger (Left) coach Gary Aasen & Andrew Bryan

singles the entire season, while Taft-McPhee had bounced around between singles and doubles. They played a practice match together before teaming up to win." Normally such inadequate preparation would spell disaster, but not so for the charmed Fenn and his understandably uneasy partner Taft-McPhee. "People told me he was going to ask me to play doubles with him, and I got nervous about it," said Taft-McPhee. "What if I was the one who screwed this up for him?" (June 7, 2003).

He needn't have worried, for with his experienced partner leading the way, the duo made it look easy, taking all four matches in straight sets. First they polished off sophomore Dusty Antoine and junior Patrick Bennett of Luverne, and in the quarterfinals they defeated senior Casey O'Donnell and junior Daniel Bacigalupi of Pine City. In the semis on Friday they fended off the eventual third-place winners from Rochester Lourdes, senior Brian Welch and junior Nick Pearson. Then, in another Breck-Blake final, Fenn and Taft-McPhee took the title with a 6-3, 7-6 (7-3) win over sophomore Dylan Cater and ninth grader Nick Lebedoff (brother of last year's finalist Jon). So this final doubles title for Fenn was the easiest of his three.

When the final match ended, Fenn was asked to comment about his historic accomplishment. In an unassuming manner he replied, "It's just one of many things you achieve in life. I don't think it's that huge of a deal. There are a lot of players who've been out here and have done a lot bigger things than me." But, after reflecting on his performance, he said, "it is a good achievement, and to do it with three different people says I'm mentally tough" (*Star Tribune*, June 7, 2003).

Though he excelled in singles as well (he was, after all, Breck's No. 1 player for two years and earned a No. 5 NWTA ranking in the 12-and-under singles and a No. 8 in the 14s), he set a standard in doubles that may never be equaled. Fenn admitted, in an earlier article by Paulsen, that "my game is more suited in doubles" (*Star Tribune*, June 6, 2003). He added, "I love to come to the net and I love to play with a teammate. Doubles is more fun." Breck coach Reven Stephens, the 1998 singles champion, said of his star player's leadership abilities in doubles, "He's our team leader, no question. He's a great competitor and that really helps whoever he's playing with." Stephens also said that he worked very hard on the court and that "he had a lot of things going on academically. He was a really smart kid who was into the sciences" (June 6, 2003). One of his summer opponents, 2002 doubles champion Mikey Kantar, said of Fenn, "He was a solid player who did everything well. He didn't hit the ball hard, but he had no real weaknesses. And he had a good return of serve."

His previous coach, Katie Queenan, called Fenn "an extremely tough competitor who could pick apart an opponent's weaknesses in singles." But, she said, it was "his great hands, great agility, and great poaching ability that made him the best doubles player I ever coached. He was all over the net." She also noted that except for his sophomore year, when Brenk was an equal partner, Fenn was the backbone of the 2002 and '03 doubles teams.

With his name now mentioned in the same breath as the only other three-time state champions (singles champions Dave Healey and Chuck Darley of Rochester), Fenn graduated from Breck and went on to Dartmouth, where he played just one year of tennis. Taft-McPhee had another year of high school competition left, so he paired up for doubles again in 2004, with Alex Gundry. Unfortunately for him, he and Gundry lost in the first round at State. A good high school athlete who also played soccer, Taft-McPhee went to school at Yale to get his college education.

Over in Class AA there was also some high quality tennis being played, even though this year it did not get the press coverage given, understandably, to Fenn's exploits. Still, the Bryan brothers' story gave fans a chance to witness another historic event, for Andrew (Andy) Bryan of Edina joined older brother Roy as only the third brother combination to claim doubles titles with partners other than each other (the other two were Franz and Bill Jevne of Edina and Myles and Roger Anderson of Blue Earth, who also won one together). Andy—the youngest Bryan and just a junior—had been a prominent player on Edina's championship teams in 2002 and this year, both years holding down the No. 3 singles spot. And though Edina did not win the '01 title, he participated on that team and must have taken great pleasure in watching his elder brother win the doubles title that year.

But 2003 was his year. Roy had graduated in '02, so Andy paired up with Scott Leininger, this year's No. 4 singles and sometimes No. 1 doubles player. Bryan and Leininger, a senior, began their drive to the title with an easy victory over junior Jono Martin and sophomore Nick Crnkovich of Mounds View. In the second match on the opening day of the tournament they defeated senior Rob Trousdale and junior Josh Tomashek of Rochester Mayo, but not without some difficulty, for it took them three sets to overcome the Spartans' lads 6-1, 2-6, 6-2. In the semis on Friday Bryan and Leininger tripped up Orono seniors Ross Davor and Andy Spilseth, a team that had lost just two matches in the past two years, 6-4, 6-4. And in a dominating performance, they claimed the title with a 6-0, 6-2 win over section foes Jon Reed (a senior) and Jamie Rowland (a junior) from Wayzata.

Bryan confessed to some ambivalence about his doubles accomplishments, expressing a greater desire to win the singles and an envy of NHL hockey stars. Said he, in that June 7 article by Paulsen, "Right now, what I really want is to win singles. Every year, I say that I should dedicate myself to playing tennis year-round. But then fall rolls around and I change my mind and start thinking about playing hockey" (*Star Tribune*).

For the most part eschewing summer tournament play (he was ranked only twice, alphabetically in the 10s and 12s Challenger 1 Singles), Bryan employed his considerable athletic skills to good effect in tennis, almost in fact winning that singles title he coveted his senior year. Alas, his teammate Chris Sherman denied him and claimed the 2004 championship. But Bryan would discover his inner tennis self at Gustavus (with help from coach Steve Wilkinson), where he helped the Gusties finish fourth in '05 and third in '06 in the NCAA Division 3 team tournaments.

Individually (in his first two years) he won No. 4 MIAC singles titles in 2005 and '06, and then, with his brother Roy, shared the glory of a No. 3 MIAC doubles championship in '05 and a No. 2 title in '06. Academically, as did his brother, he earned the prestigious ITA Scholar-Athlete Award in '06.

Reminiscing about the younger Bryan's high school career, which included playing varsity hockey, Coach Gary Aasen said, "He was the loosest guy I've seen on the court ever." Aasen said about his game that "he had good hands and he was a great returner. He was mentally tough." Overall he had one of the great Edina individual records during his four years on the varsity. According to Aasen, at one time he had a record of 87-0, and he finished with a record of 94-9. His junior year, the year he won the doubles, he lost just one set all year and compiled a 32-0 record.

Bryan's teammate Leininger had transferred to Edina as a junior, coming from the Chicago area where he had played junior tennis. Aasen remembers him as "a big guy with a big serve who went for everything on every shot." He called him "unpredictable," in part because he hit the same first serve no matter what the score was. But, said Aasen, "I couldn't believe how many times he got out of trouble with a big shot. He had an uncanny ability to play well in big matches." This ability carried him to a 28-2 record his senior year and a two-year record of 46-3.

Girls Playing on Boys' Teams

Displayed in an art gallery in Cheltenham, England, is a painting, titled *The Tennis Party, 1900*, about a social tennis match. In it we see a man dressed in long white pants and shirt positioned in the ad side on a manicured lawn tennis court somewhere in England. His doubles partner, also dressed in white tennis clothing, has apparently returned a serve. On the other side of the net their opponents are aligned in an "I formation" in the middle of the court as they attempt to make a reply.

"I am all the daughters of my father's house, and all the brothers too."
—Twelfth Night

Though there are other figures in the painting on both sides of the court, what's most intriguing is the fact that the person returning the serve, one of the players on the other side of the net, and the two seated figures in the foreground of the picture wear dresses and bonnets. Of course they are women, two of whom play tennis while the seated figures have played or are waiting to play. Moreover, the two women players, unlike their male partners who are fixed in static poses on the court, are both in action postures, with the returner's racket arm extended forward and her female opponent crossing in front of her male partner with her right leg raised up as if running or jumping.

While it was not usual for women to participate with men in sporting events in turn-of-the-century England, it was common for men and women (albeit mostly upper-class men and women) to smack serves and groundstrokes at one another on grass courts all over the country, mostly in friendly mixed doubles competitions. And this was also common in many other parts of the world, including the United States.

In fact, according to Bud Collins' *Tennis Encyclopedia*, the United States was the first country to inaugurate mixed doubles competition in the national championships, beginning in 1892. In that first competition the team of Mabel Cahill/Clarence Hobart defeated Elisabeth Moore/Rod Beach in the finals 5-7, 6-1, 6-4 (Collins 1998, 592). Wimbledon did not introduce mixed doubles play until 1913. From its modern beginnings in England in 1874, tennis has given women a chance to play for the same reasons that men have done so: for vigorous exercise, for the thrill of competition, for a mental challenge, and for the camaraderie of the doubles game. And if a woman had good stroke mechanics and a feel for the game, she could compete with the stronger men and often beat them.

Peg Brenden
St. Cloud Tech

It was the knowledge that she could compete with the boys who played on her high school team that impelled a determined young woman from St. Cloud, far from the elegant social tennis entertainments on the lawns of England, to try to break down the male-only-on-boys'-teams rule established by the MSHSL. From the time she inherited her first warped hand-me-down racket from her brother Jerry, which when playing she flipped over in her hand in order to hit a forehand and backhand with the flattest side, Peg Brenden not only played with boys but competed well with them.

She was introduced to tennis by her older sister Sandy and brother-in-law Jim Tool and received her first formal instruction from Hall of Fame coach Mac Doane and his wife, Harriet. By the time she was a senior in 1972, she decided that she wanted a chance to play tennis on a school team.

But there was no high school girls' tennis (though Title IX was written in 1972, the first girls' season was still two years away), so

Peg Brenden

Peg's only chance was to play on the St. Cloud Tech boys' team. She recalls that "I played with these guys all along and knew I could play with them." Peg's confidence was also bolstered because of her No. 1 Section ranking in Girls 18 Singles (in what was then called the Northwestern Lawn Tennis Association), so she chose to initiate a lawsuit against the MSHSL in order to plead her case. "I wrote a letter in the fall of my senior year [1971] to the Minnesota Civil Liberties Union (MCLU) and asked if they would take the case," said Peg, and in the letter she added this poignant postscript, "Please hurry; I am a senior."

Thomas Wexler, a volunteer lawyer for the MCLU, argued the case, cited as *Brenden vs. Independent School District 742*, in front of Judge Miles Lord in Federal District Court in Minneapolis. Joining the suit was a young woman from Hopkins, a skier and cross country runner named Antoinette St. Pierre. The lawsuit was brought forward because high school rules, noted in the 1971-72 *Official Handbook of the MSHSL*, stated that "Girls shall be prohibited from participation in the boys' interscholastic athletic program either as a member of the boys' team or as a member of the girls' team playing the boys' team. The girls' teams shall not accept male members." And in the tennis section of the *Handbook*, on page 306, it said, "Meets are open to boys only."

In an April 6, 1972, article titled "Peggy Brenden Sues St. Cloud District to Play High School Sports," the MCLU argued that it was unconstitutional to deprive these girls of an opportunity to participate and that "the amount expended on the boys' program is grossly disproportionate to the revenues expended on the girls' program" and the MSHSL "rule violates the equal protection clause of the Fourteenth Amendment and the Civil Rights Act" (*St. Cloud Daily Times*). Furthermore, the plaintiffs argued that the regulation "arbitrarily and capriciously discriminates on the basis of sex without regard to the nature of the particular athletic activity involved and that the regulation has no valid education purpose." Legal counsel for the MCLU, R. Michael Wetherbee, also argued that in the past girls had not been allowed to compete with boys because of discrimination, not biological inferiority. He added, "The fact remains that there are now female high school student athletes whose abilities entitle them to be a team member" (*St. Cloud Daily Times*, April 6, 1972).

The defense team argued mainly that girls have inherent physical differences that make it impossible for them to compete with boys on an equal basis because of their smaller physical stature, lesser oxygen-carrying capacity, lower hemoglobin red cell count, smaller heart size, greater possibilities that they might get injured, and more fragile psyches than have the boys (*St. Cloud Daily Times*, April 26, 1972). After almost three weeks of deliberations and considerable testimony from the defense team, U.S. District Judge Miles Lord ruled that Peggy and Antoinette "may take part in certain non-contact sports with boys' teams" (*St. Cloud Daily Times*, May 1, 1972). Judge Lord said the decision is limited to these two girls "who are able to compete because there is no showing that it would injure them or the boys with whom they play" and because physiological differences do not apply in these cases. "They [Peggy and Antoinette] are fully capable to compete" (May 1, 1972), so he ordered their school principals to certify them as eligible to compete on the boys' teams.

For Peg this was a bittersweet victory, coming as it did May first, near the end of the last season of her eligibility to play high school tennis. And though she had received many positive phone calls during the drawn-out legal proceedings, she was not always aware that her mother had fielded many nasty phone calls, too. Nevertheless, she was delighted to finally gain a place on the team and to be able to compete, her first opportunity coming in a Saturday match against Coon Rapids. Playing No. 3 singles, she lost a 9-7, 7-5 match to Steve Krause, a young man, now also a part of Minnesota tennis lore, who told *Minneapolis Tribune* writer Jim Wells that at times "his legs were so wobbly that he had trouble standing" (May 7, 1972). Though Peg appeared more relaxed than did Steve, there was great pressure on her as well, for she was carrying the banner for young girls all over the state who aspired to the same goals she had set for herself. Peg commented that her only regret about the match was that she felt she should have gone to the net more.

As for Krause, he was gracious and complimentary after the match, saying, "She's good. She was a little more consistent than I was today... I really hope she keeps playing. She earned the right to. I know I'll root for her." Oh, yes, Tech, a very strong team led by Grant Helgeson and Jeff Schwanberg, won the match 4-1. Coon Rapids coach Bob Pivec said of Brenden, "There's no doubt about it, she's good. I think she's better than half the first singles players we've played against this year. She really has good fundamentals. She could certainly make my team" (*Minneapolis Tribune*, May 7, 1972).

Continuing to play under the cloud of a challenge to Judge Lord's ruling, initiated allegedly by the MSHSL to affirm their commitment to develop a strong interscholastic program for girls, Peg played five singles matches during that glorious season but was not selected to play in the upcoming state tournament competition. In part because she was such a good player, she remembers being fully accepted by her teammates. But she especially remembers the joy she felt when she received her first team warmup jacket, with its bright orange color, black racing stripes, and the words "Tech Tigers" on the back. She says she was so excited that she slept in it for a couple of nights. She also remembers how much she loved the competition, the pressure of a match, and "the sense of physical and mental exhaustion after a match," the same things her male teammates and opponents no doubt valued.

Hall of Fame coach Bud Schmid of Brainerd shared the following memories about Peg. When Brainerd played Tech that year, Peg defeated Bud's No. 3 player and the Brainerd player was so upset that he vowed never to play a girl again. Bud also recalls that "this fine young lady was a counselor at our tennis camp at Lake Hubert for two summers while she was a college student."

After high school Brenden majored in accounting at Luther College, where she played No. 1 singles and doubles all four years on the women's team; won tournaments at the U of M, Luther, and Carleton; and competed in the AIAW National College Championships. She was finally happy to be an integral part of an excellent tennis program for women under an outstanding female coach, Sue Oertel.

After completing her undergraduate studies at Luther in 1976, Peg earned a law degree from the U of M, worked as a general practice lawyer for six years, and for over twenty years has been a Worker's Compensation Judge for the state of Minnesota. She admits that her high school experience, one which saw her questioning authority in a positive way, probably inspired her to pursue a career in the legal profession. In honor of her college tennis and career successes, Brenden was the first recipient (in 1994) of the Rolex Achievement Award administered by the Intercollegiate Tennis Association (ITA).

As for her tennis ability, she was elected to the Northern Section USTA Hall of Fame in 2004, validating her many important on-court accomplishments. These included rankings as the No. 1 Girls 18 Singles player and No. 4 Women's Open Singles player in 1971, Section Women's Singles runner-up in '77, No. 1 rankings in Women's Doubles (with Jamie Young) in '82 and '83, a five-time winner of the First Bank Plaza Tournament, and four top-four Women's Singles rankings in the Section.

In addition, she is a member of her high school and college halls of fame, she has coached tennis—serving as co-coach at Augsburg College and as an assistant women's coach at the U of M under Elie Peden (from 1977-79)—and she is on the board of directors of the St. Paul Urban Tennis Program. She is also the past chair and a member of the advisory board of the Pine Tree Apple Tennis Classic, a charity mixed doubles tournament featuring many of the top-ranked adult tennis players in the Northern Section. Of all her tennis accomplishments, however, Peg said, "The athletic accomplishment I'm most proud of is earning my high school letter." She also valued the opportunity to be a member of the only high school tennis team at that time in St. Cloud, relishing the little things like trading food from snack lunches on the way to meets and sharing stories—only slightly embellished—of match highlights.

Peg's season in the sun was relatively short, but she helped lay the foundation for other girls such as Jody Nolen, Peggy Chutich, Marnie Wheaton, and Ann Henricksson, and she helped establish the framework for girls' tennis competition in Minnesota which began in 1974.

Jody Nolen
Litchfield

There were of course other schools that permitted girls to play on boys' teams before 1974, but one which stands out is the Litchfield team coached by Greg Mathews and featuring Jody Nolen, daughter of celebrated doctor and author William Nolen (*The Making of a Surgeon*). Jody grew up playing tennis with her father, brother Billy, and other boys in Litchfield, so she knew she could compete with boys. Coach Mathews, a social studies teacher and dedicated supporter of civil rights issues, had been raised in inner city St. Paul; so he supported Jody when she asked if she could try out for the team her sophomore year, 1970. (For more on Mathews, see Chapter Three.)

Though some coaches were upset about having their players compete against a girl (asking, for example, "What happens if she wins?"), Greg had no such reservations, viewing the situation as a human rights issue. When, for instance, coaches objected to having Jody play their boy, Greg would respond, "He's playing a human being." For two years she played only in exhibition contests when opposing coaches agreed to a match, so, as in Peg Brenden's case, 1972 was her final opportunity to play varsity tennis.

Peg Brenden's lawsuit, and Dr. Nolen's threats to institute legal action if his daughter were denied a chance to play, had given her the opening she needed. Playing third singles or first doubles her senior year, Jody won most of her matches despite having to endure snide, rude, and often sexist comments from fans and even other coaches, comments that, in coach Mathews' words, were "intended to invoke pain." Nonetheless, Jody persevered and won the respect of her teammates who saw her as just another player on the team.

Mathews recalls a particularly memorable match, one of Jody's few losses that fateful year. She was playing first doubles at Alexander Ramsey High School and hundreds of students came out after the final school bell to watch what they must have seen as an aberration—a girl playing against a boy in a competitive interscholastic sporting event. As she took the court, she heard comments such as "Look at her legs, she's so muscular" and "She looks like a man." Despite having to endure taunts and comments such as these, Jody persevered in this and her other matches, always giving a good account of herself on court. Mathews said she was very tough mentally when she took the court. He called her and Peg Brenden "the Jackie Robinsons of girls' tennis."

After she graduated from Litchfield High School, Jody moved out East for college but did not continue with her tennis. Like her father, she became a writer and today lives in the Twin Cities.

1973 was another table-setting year for young women playing tennis in Minnesota, coming just one year before the first girls' tennis tournament, a tournament which came into being because of the 1972 Title IX ruling barring discrimination on the basis of sex and because of the efforts of girls such as Peg Brenden and Jody Nolen. It is also worth noting that the establishment of this federal law reinforced and facilitated the increasing efforts of the MSHSL to offer expanded athletic opportunities for girls. Dorothy McIntyre, newly appointed as executive director of Girls Sports, led the way as state tournaments for girls in every sport were added one by one, with tennis in 1974. Their legacy was to provide opportunities that Mary Jo Kane (currently the director of the Tucker Center for Research on Girls and Women in Sport) described in a March 18, 2004, article in the *Star Tribune*: "Young girls all over the country today grow up with a sense of entitlement to sports. They have better coaching... They have better nutrition... They have better facilities" (Herón Marquez Estrada).

Margaret "Peggy" Chutich
Anoka

Another pioneering young woman was Margaret "Peggy" Chutich, who played for coach Ken Peterson at Anoka and who later finished second in the singles competition at the first girls' State Tournament (losing to Mary Prebil of St. Cloud Cathedral) and then became the second girls' state champion in 1975 by reversing the '74 result in the finals against Prebil.

Her mother played tennis and so Peggy was introduced to the game at an early age, beginning tournament play when she was eleven and eventually competing in some national tournaments. She played on the boys' team in junior high school, then in the spring of her sophomore

year (1973) she earned a spot on the boys' varsity team, playing No. 2 singles behind her brother Mike and ahead of No. 3 singles player Charlie Weaver Jr. (her then boyfriend and now executive director of the Minnesota Business Partnership and former chief of staff for Governor Tim Pawlenty). By any measure her season with the boys was extremely successful. The Anoka team won 16 out of 20 matches and she compiled a record of 18 wins and 6 losses. In part because she made significant contributions to the team, "most of the boys were very supportive and I did feel very accepted by them," said Peggy.

However, not all of her opponents were as accepting. She remembers that "boys who were confident and good players accepted me [Peggy cited an opponent from Coon Rapids, for example], but some guys couldn't cope with it and were beside themselves that they could lose to a girl." Her most memorable moment was a dramatic three-set match with Coon Rapids that, despite leg cramps, Peggy won to secure a 3-2 triumph for her team. When she boarded the bus after the match, she was greeted as a hero(ine); and Charlie Weaver Sr. later presented her with a bouquet of roses. And though she and her brother lost in the region doubles final in the individual tournament, just missing by an eyelash a chance to play in the boys' State Tournament, and at times there was a great deal of pressure on her, she still treasures the experience of playing on the boys' team. She especially liked the underdog role of playing against taller opponents who often had bigger serves, so as a result she had to become a more consistent player.

Of her high school coach, Ken Peterson, she said, "He was a very supportive coach and was really good for my game." She will never forget the team's final touching gesture, flowers and a note from the boys and Coach Peterson thanking her for a great season and inviting her back the next year. History intervened, and instead Peggy would go on to compete against girls, playing on the Anoka girls' tennis team in the fall of 1974.

After high school she walked on as a point guard for the Stanford U basketball team, but tennis was in her blood so she transferred to the U of M to play her last three years, bringing her strong serve and volley game with her and ultimately securing the No. 1 doubles position (partnering with Patty Moran to take second in the Big Ten her sophomore year) and rising up the ladder to play No. 2 singles her senior year. With her degree and a history major in hand, Peggy then earned a law degree and today works for the attorney general's office. Oh, yes, she still plays tennis once a week with none other than Peg Brenden, her trailblazing compatriot.

Marnie Wheaton
Minnetonka

Two other young women who played on boys' teams in those pre-Title IX years were arguably two of the greatest women players in Minnesota history: Marnie Wheaton and Ann Henricksson. Marnie, the only daughter in the illustrious tennis-playing Wheaton family (see Chapter Ten.) began playing the game at age ten with her younger brother Mark on the Deephaven Beach court near her home in Cottagewood. Taught by her grandfather, a self-

Marnie Wheaton

made man and self-taught tennis coach who wanted his grandchildren to take up a lifetime sport, she began playing tournaments at age twelve, traveling with her supportive parents, Bruce and Mary Jane, to Duluth, Sioux Falls, and Rochester.

Then, in her senior year in high school, Marnie had her chance to make history, joining brother Mark on the powerful Minnetonka boys' team that won the 1974 State Tennis Tournament. Though she did not participate in state competition that year, she considers the opportunity to be a part of a team at the State Tournament, albeit as an alternate, one of her most memorable tennis experiences. During the season she played mostly No. 3 singles or No. 2 doubles, winning most of the eight matches she played. According to Marnie she was, in her words, "doing what I was allowed to do. If necessary, my dad was prepared to go to court to give me a chance to play."

She has only fond memories of her season with the boys—especially of playing with her brother Mark and traveling in the bus with the baseball team to meets. None of her opponents gave her any problems. She said, "Most of the people I played were really cool about it." Marnie also enjoyed playing for Coach Gary Peterson, whom she called "a good coach and a humble man."

After high school she attended the U of AZ, where she played tennis for one-half year before transferring to Minnesota to play for (who else?) Elie Peden, whom Marnie described as an excellent coach. Playing the No. 1 singles spot her last two years, Marnie won both the singles and doubles at the AIAW Regionals hosted by Carleton College her senior year. In addition, she won the No. 3 singles title in the Big Ten in 1976 and the Gophers won the Big Ten team title in '79. For her accomplishments on the tennis court she was voted tennis Athlete of the Year, and later elected into the U of M Athletic Hall of Fame.

She graduated from the U with a physical education/coaching major and a broadcasting minor, then did some post-graduate work in broadcasting at Northwestern College in Roseville.

Next, she taught physical education for several years at younger brother David's private prep school in Florida, also coaching tennis, basketball, and volleyball there. She then spent two years teaching physical education part-time at Stanford. For over twenty years, however, she has worked as a flight attendant for Northwest Airlines; and now she has joined brothers John and David as a part-time tennis instructor at the Wayzata Country Club.

Back on the tennis courts in Minnesota, Marnie carved out one of the most successful amateur tennis careers in state history, winning the Women's 30 Singles championship at the National Public Parks tournament in 1985 and earning No. 1 rankings in the Women's Open Singles category of the Northwestern Section in 1977, '79, '81, and '82. In addition, she was ranked No. 1 in doubles for four years in the '80s with three different partners: Meg Horan, Leslie Larm, and Jamie Young. And it must also have been great fun for her to play with her then ten-year-old brother David to gain the No. 1 ranking in Mixed Doubles in 1979. Finally, she won Section Women's Singles titles in 1980 and '83; took the doubles title in '80, '81, and '85; and held the No. 2 Women's Singles ranking from 1983-86. These accomplishments earned her a place in the USTA/Northern Section Hall of Fame.

Ann Henricksson
Mahtomedi

A fourteen-year tennis pro with wins over top-ten players such as Pam Shriver, Wendy Turnbull, and Hana Mandlikova, our final pioneer is Ann Henricksson of Mahtomedi, whose successful junior and college tennis experience established the foundation for a distinguished professional career. Ranked as high as No. 33 in the world, Henricksson won three tour doubles titles and lost three times in singles finals (once to Steffi Graf and another time to Martina Navratilova).

Ann's tennis career began on the backboard of her aunt's tennis court in Mahtomedi when she was nine, and she remembers her first 10-and-under tournament, the Aquatennial in Minneapolis. According to Ann, "I got hooked and never stopped playing tournaments."

Henricksson secured her niche in this history in the spring of 1974, for it was in that season that she became the first of just two girls to participate in the boys' State Tournament. She was only a ninth grader when she and her partner Rog Brian advanced to State, where they lost

to a team from Rochester Mayo (Jamie Bastron and Fred Siekert) 6-1, 6-4 in the opening round. Thus relegated to the consolation bracket, they won two matches (over teams from Moorhead and South St. Paul) before falling to the team of Steve Krahn and Jeff Mash from White Bear Mariner 6-2, 5-7, 6-0 in the consolation finals.

A good showing, indeed, but Ann chose not to participate during the upcoming first fall season of girls' tennis, instead choosing to hone her game by playing national tournaments then and in her final two years of high school. She claims she doesn't remember much from that one year of playing mostly No. 1 doubles on the boys' team, but she did say of her coach, Ken Wharton, that "he was extremely supportive." Henricksson demonstrated her athletic ability that ninth grade year by playing on the boys' basketball team, and she also tried out for the football team.

After graduation from high school she attended Arizona State U for one year, then transferred to UCLA where

Ann Henricksson

she played on a team that won the national women's tennis title her senior year, 1981. This experience was a launching pad for her very successful professional tennis career that lasted from 1981-94.

When she retired from professional tennis, she worked at her sister's restaurant in New York City for a year, served as an assistant tennis coach at the U of California-Berkeley for another year, and directed a USTA Challenger Tournament in Los Gatos, CA, for three years. Now she teaches private tennis lessons at the Stanford Faculty Club in Palo Alto, CA.

While the stories of these five young women are perhaps the most compelling, they are not unique, for there were many other girls who played on boys' teams in the early 1970s, girls such as Cathy Brennan at Minneapolis West and Karen Gibbs at Hopkins. After graduation Gibbs played for the Gustavus Adolphus women's team. She passed away from cancer at age 21 in 1977 and, to honor her memory, Tennis and Life scholarships for junior players are given in her name.

In addition, in my first year of coaching, (1971, the year before Peg Brenden's lawsuit), I was asked by the parents of two young women if their daughters could play on the Northfield boys' team. Since at the time there were no competitive team opportunities for female students, since I thought it was the right thing to do, and since I knew they were capable tennis players, I agreed to let seniors Barb Rossing and Martha Wright join the team. Barb, the sister of our No. 1 player Erik Rossing, was probably the tenth best player on the team. And perhaps because I had a daughter whom I hoped would one day be able to play high school tennis, I had no second thoughts about letting these girls play. No girls asked to play in 1972, but in '73 junior Patti Kimble and senior Nancy Morrison joined the squad for the opportunity to play a few exhibition or "B" squad matches. Nancy was particularly successful, playing mostly Nos. 5 or 6 singles and winning six out of seven matches.

A Parallel Universe— Independent League Tennis

Sue Fischer's Story

Perhaps not as well known is the fact that there were other young women playing on boys' teams during this time in a parallel universe, that of the Minnesota Independent High School League. Not yet affiliated with the MSHSL, this organization (made up of parochial and private schools) was truly "independent" of the League's rules and regulations. Thus it was free to do pretty much what it wanted (within reason, of course), so a number of schools encouraged capable young women to try out for boys' tennis squads. One of the most talented and successful of these girls was Sue Fischer from St. Cloud Cathedral. Fischer had learned to play from St. Cloud's Mr. Tennis, Mac Doane. Then, because she had no one to play with, she hit with her father, Jack. These lessons from Doane and the time she spent on court with her father (including competing together in doubles tournaments), helped her earn the No. 1 singles spot on the Crusaders boys' team in the spring of 1972.

Her dad was also her coach, and she said that for the most part her experiences of playing against boys were positive. However, she recalls that one skeptical and reluctant coach wasn't sure he wanted his No. 1 player to play "a girl." His player, with a more enlightened attitude, said, "I don't care; let's play." Sue said he proceeded to beat her pretty handily.

Fischer played just this one year on the boys' team, for she graduated that spring and went to college at St. Benedict's. But because they had no sports teams for women, she transferred to St. Cloud State after one year there. At St. Cloud she played one year of JV basketball and held the No. 1 singles and doubles positions on the women's tennis team for four years, graduating in 1977 with a major in physical education. For her performance on the tennis courts Fischer was inducted into the St. Cloud State Athletic Hall of Fame in '87, becoming the first modern-day woman athlete so honored by her college.

After graduation she took a job as a middle school physical education teacher and high school coach in Lakeville. (For more information about her coaching career, see Chapter Three.)

Later, in 1983-84, she earned a master's in education from the U of AZ, then changed directions in her life, studying for the bar at William Mitchell College of Law. Today she works as a lawyer in Minneapolis.

Finally, Fischer said that Meg Horan of Rochester Lourdes (a future U. of M player and top-ranked NWLTA adult player) was the best girl playing on a boys' team that she knew of in independent league play.

Other Stories of Note/ Some Final Thoughts

There are no doubt other unsung heroines from this early era in girls' tennis, but I am not aware of them. I do know, however, that there was actually an unofficial high school tournament for girls in the fall of 1947. Eight singles players and two doubles teams were entered, and all the matches were played in one day, August 18. Marilyn French of Rochester defeated Pat Ireland of Wadena (6-3, 6-1) to claim the singles title, and the doubles team of Ann Barstad/Betty Mercer of Detroit Lakes beat the only other doubles entrants (Ella Johnson/Doris Peterson of Proctor) in what must have been a spirited three-set match 6-3, 5-7, 6-4.

In the first official sanctioned girls' State Tournament, held at the Rein Indoor Clubs in St. Paul from October 24-26, 1974, Minnetonka won the team title by clobbering each of its three opponents (Thief River Falls, Madison, and Rochester Lourdes) by 5-0 scores. Some members of that first championship team were Beth Jenkins, Laurie Mueller, Katie Adams, and Cheryl Moran. So even without Marnie Wheaton, who had graduated in the spring, Minnetonka dominated the first girls' State Tournament, then claimed the '75 title as well. As mentioned earlier in this chapter, Mary Prebil of St. Cloud Cathedral beat Peggy Chutich 7-6, 1-6, 7-6 to win the singles title and the team of Linda Glavich/Sheila Robinson of Virginia defeated Beth Jenkins/Laurie Mueller of team champion Minnetonka 6-3, 6-0 for the doubles title.

That first year there were 134 girls' schools fielding teams and 938 individuals playing tennis and, including team players, 86 advanced to the State Tournament. Teams entered in the tournament were Anoka, Blue Earth, Little Falls, Madison, Minnetonka, Rochester Lourdes, Thief River Falls, and Virginia; and there were 16 singles players and 16 doubles teams participating in the individual tournament.

I'm guessing that these pioneers (Brenden, Chutich, Nolen, Wheaton, Henrickson, Brennan, Gibbs, Fischer, Horan, and their less-well-known "sisters") could not have imagined at the time the impact they would have on girls' tennis in Minnesota. For the most part they simply loved the game of tennis and wanted to compete. It wasn't so much that they wanted to play on boys' teams, but it was more a matter of wanting to be part of a program that would challenge them and give each a chance to grow and develop as a person and a tennis player. Clearly the only way they could do that was to join the only "game in town," which was the boys' interscholastic team.

Now they can be pleased that their legacy is secure; for they helped set the table for so many outstanding Minnesota champions, including multiple-singles titlists Kathy Rondano, Anne Lemieux, Lisa Martin, Janet McCutcheon, Ginger Helgeson, Kelly Morrison, Jackie Moe, Kira Gregerson, Gina Suh, Ann Nguyen, Jeanette Clusky, Lauren Patterson, Meagan Tiegs, Natalie Newman, and Whitney Taney. Taney, the daughter of 1971 boys' doubles champion Ted, is arguably the most successful of all these champions. A five-time Class AA state champion (twice in doubles and three times in singles), she finished her incredible high school career without a single loss and a record of 166-0. In fact, since 2002 she compiled a 330-0 combined record in USTA Northern Section and high school matches, thus earning the mantle of "most decorated player in the history of the USTA Northern" (*USTA Magazine*, January/February 2007). In addition, in 2007 she was named the top girls' high school player in the nation.

But it was not just for such elite players that these pioneer women blazed a path, it was also for girls like my daughter Heather, who played No. 1 singles at Northfield and went on to play four years at Beloit College, and all other young women who have been given the opportunity to play this wonderful game. As with all who take risks for a cause, their efforts did not come without costs to them, but tennis in Minnesota is much richer for their trailblazing efforts.

Dark Horse Teams

*I*f you grew up in a small town far from the bright lights of Minneapolis and St. Paul (in my case in Sherburn, MN, population 1,200), and if you dreamed of making the impossible shot that won the state basketball tournament for your team, you can identify with the "dark horses" that on occasion captured the imagination of state tennis fans. Call them what you will (little giants, Davids overcoming Goliaths, Cinderellas, little engines that could, or underdogs), there's no denying that they surprised the tennis big boys just as my hometown team in 1970 stunned the big schools and won the state basketball title before multi-class play began in 1971.

"We are such stuff as dreams are made on."

—The Tempest

With one exception (Minneapolis South) the individuals and four schools featured in this chapter were unlikely winners, coming as they did from small towns with no tennis traditions such as St. James and Greenway of Coleraine, and one small private school whose tennis teams flourished for a few short years because it had a cadre of talented players (Minnehaha Academy). As I pondered what to call these upset winners, the phrase "dark horses" seemed appropriate. For the most part they came out of nowhere to win and they defied the odds. Brewer's *Dictionary of Phrase and Fable* describes "dark horse" as "a racing term for a horse of good pretensions, but of which nothing is positively known by the general public. Its merits are kept dark from betters and book-makers" (332). It's the classic tale such as that of Seabiscuit, a horse which, despite its small stature and unknown merits, captured the imagination of, and inspired confidence in, a beleaguered populace in the midst of the Great Depression. Seabiscuit's story brought tears to the eyes and tugged at the heartstrings of a down-and-out population that desperately needed a lift and something to take their minds off the grinding poverty of the period. Now I make no such claims about these Minnesota tennis teams and players, but for those of us who coached outstate or played mostly in anonymity away from the centers of tennis in Rochester or the Twin Cities, there was satisfaction in the triumphs of these "dark horses," a feeling of, "Yes, they did it against all odds."

So who are these "dark horses" and why have I chosen to tell the stories of these "dreamers?" First, I am excluding Class A winners because they have competed against schools their own size, though there is a temptation to include the small northern school of Staples-Motley (with a town population of 3,500 or so), which won consecutive Class A titles in 1990-91. However, I have not included them because those were two years when traditional Class A power Blake opted to play in Class AA and even won the big school title in 1991. In addition, I have excluded all Minneapolis and St. Paul schools from 1929-60 because, with the exception of Rochester in the '50s, the power in tennis resided in the Metro area. Of course, it's tempting to focus on the 1946 doubles team of Jack Thommen and Edmund "Chiefie" Gould, which won a team title for Minneapolis Southwest by claiming the doubles championship. But after Thommen and Gould, there simply weren't any other skilled tennis players on the Southwest team. Thommen said, "we won only one of ten dual meets during the season." So with the exception of Minneapolis South in 2001, I have not included any Metro area (or big school) teams in this sketch. One might make a case for Austin, which won two state titles (in 1969 before True Team play began and one in '82), but Austin is a Class AA school and it had a successful and rich tennis tradition under Hall of Fame coach Keith Paulson. It was one of the top teams in Region I during his tenure, making four appearances at State during the True Team era.

What, then, qualifies as a "dark horse" team? For starters the team or players have to have hailed from a small town or school, again, except for South. Secondly, they must have won a team championship in competition with larger schools during the days of single-class play or later in Class AA play. Third, the players must have surprised the field by upsetting the favorites and, particularly

in the case of teams such as Minnehaha Academy and Minneapolis South, must have come from schools that had not previously had long and successful tennis traditions. Readers will note that I also chose schools to represent four different constituencies: the small school (St. James), a northern school (Greenway), a private/parochial school (Minnehaha Academy), and an urban school (Minneapolis South).

St. James
Small-School Champion (1954)

We begin with the south central Minnesota community of St. James (population 4,400), a sleepy farming town located on the banks of the Watonwan River. The Watonwan county seat, it was a community with a strong sports tradition. For example, amateur baseball thrived there in the summer; in fact, in the 1950s and early '60s the town supported a semi-pro team in the Western Minnesota baseball league. And the high school had often fielded competitive football, basketball, and baseball teams. But tennis—never. At least not until 1954 when four outstanding athletes led the team to a stunning upset over powerhouse Rochester in the State Tournament on the strength of a doubles championship won by seniors Gerald Kintzi and Dave Anderson and two singles wins by sophomore Mark Anderson, Dave's brother. (The fourth St. James player, senior John Jackson, lost to a Rochester player, 1955 doubles champion Roger Riege, in the first round.) With nine points in the doubles (three points for each of three wins) and four points in singles (two points for each win), the Saints earned thirteen points to edge previously undefeated and top-ranked Rochester by one point.

In at least one respect it was not surprising that St. James captured the 1954 title, for the 1953-54 school year had been one of glorious success on the playing fields and in the gyms of Minnesota for the Saints. The undefeated football team, made up in part of those four aforementioned tennis players and another named Bill Yock, blanked seven of its nine opponents on the way to the mythical No. 1 state ranking accorded the team by the *Minneapolis Morning Tribune*. The basketball team won the district and region and participated in the State Tournament, the baseball team won the district championship, the track team took fourth in the State, and the tennis team capped off this miracle year with a state championship.

In other respects, however, this tennis coup was most surprising; for the Saints' netmen were relatively unknown outside of southern Minnesota and they had lost decisively in a dual meet with Rochester that year. In addition, they learned the game without any coaching to speak of. For example, Mark Anderson said, "I never had a lesson until after my State loss to Healey [Rochester three-time singles champion Dave] my junior year when U of M coach Phil Brain gave me a 10-15-minute lesson on my backhand." Doubles champion Kintzi remembers that he "started playing with my sister's husband when we were in fourth or fifth grade" and that "there were no lessons for me or my teammates in high school." He, like the others, learned the game while playing it, though Kintzi, then just a ninth grader, also received an unexpected mini-lesson once after a match in Mankato when he and his teammates waited for their coach to pick them up. "The Mankato coach worked with me for one-half hour after the match. I learned as much in that half hour as I learned in all my years. He taught me what was right and really gave me a lot of pointers," Kintzi said. This was a particularly selfless act on the part of the Mankato coach, for Kintzi was one of Mankato's prime competitors.

And as it was for many schools in these earlier days of Minnesota tennis, most coaches were not tennis players.

(1st row Left to Right) Mark Anderson, Gerry Kintzi;
(2nd row Left to Right) Bill Yock, Dave Anderson, & John Jackson.

Kintzi recalls that his first coach in seventh and eighth grade was Dick Weech, who had played some tennis but never competitively. Then in ninth grade his coach was a man named Root, who essentially just drove the team to meets. Finally, in grades 10-12, Athletic Director Ab Strommen took over. Kintzi said of him, "He was an excellent coach who was very well organized but not a tennis player." Mark Anderson said of Strommen, "He got to be quite knowledgeable about tennis by reading books, watching the game, and learning from other coaches." For Anderson he became more than just his coach: "He was kind of my mentor and role model."

So the St. James players began with a coaching deficit, and they also had but two cement courts at the high school, at least until the Anderson brothers' uncle got elected to the school board and persuaded the board to build two asphalt courts over the existing concrete courts. Trouble was, the courts were built by a road construction crew, so, according to Mark Anderson, "there were huge stones in them and there were always bad bounces." In addition, there was not enough room behind the baselines or on the sidelines. Furthermore, the only other court in town was another rough asphalt one by the grade school.

Nevertheless, these lads took a liking to the game and, because they were such good athletes, played it superbly. The two Anderson brothers and Kintzi played six years of varsity tennis, lettering each year, and the Saints dominated the South Central Conference which at that time included Fairmont, Blue Earth, Waseca, St. Peter, New Ulm, and St. James. In fact, Kintzi recalls losing only to Rochester and Mankato in his last three years. This despite the fact that each of these four guys (the two Andersons, Jackson, and Kintzi) played baseball (and tennis) during a time when it was possible to play both sports in the spring.

During their careers Kintzi made it to State his last two years (his junior year in singles), Dave Anderson made it one other time, and younger brother Mark arguably had the best career of them all. He won the Region 2 singles title three years in a row, losing in the semis his sophomore year at State to the unbeatable Healey 6-2, 6-1, then in the semis again to Chauncey Riggs of Duluth Central his junior year (11-9, 6-2), and in the finals his senior year to champion Charles Hawke of Minneapolis Central in a tremendous 5-7, 6-4, 9-7 dogfight. This loss to Hawke was his only one that year (1956).

But getting back to that magical year of 1954, when the dark horse nipped the favorite Rochester at the finish line, it all began with the decision of Kintzi and Dave Anderson to play doubles, putting Mark Anderson and Jackson in singles. After sweeping aside the competition in district and regional play, Kintzi and Anderson won all three matches at State in straight sets (see Chapter Six for more on their exploits). And though Jackson lost his match, Mark Anderson came through with two huge wins that garnered four crucial points for the Saints. He defeated Steve Hilding of Duluth East 6-1, 6-1 and then came from behind to defeat Neil Gould of Minneapolis Washburn 2-6, 6-1, 6-1 before falling to Healey.

And so this win seemed more legitimate than some before True Team play was instituted in 1973, when team trophies could be won by just a doubles team or even a singles player, because St. James took four participants to the State Tournament, three of whom won points for the team.

After graduation Kintzi, a star halfback on the Saints' football team, attended the U of M for a year on a football scholarship, then transferred to Mankato State U for his final three years. He did not play tennis in college. Today he lives in retirement in Belmont, IA, where he completed his thirty-nine-year education career as a business education teacher. During his years at Belmont he coached football, basketball, wrestling, and even track; he also served as athletic director for thirty years. Most of those years he was an assistant coach, but he was the head football coach one year and for several years served as the head wrestling coach.

Dave Anderson played one year of tennis at the U of M before deciding to focus on his medical school studies. Today he lives and works as a dermatologist in St. Paul, still active in his profession after forty years. He said that he often played some tennis at the White Bear Racquet Club but now plays only golf.

Dave's younger brother Mark attended Gustavus Adolphus College and played on a six-man tennis team with five guys from St. Peter (two Lawson brothers, Don Palmer, Dale Gustafson, and Bob Adolphson). Mostly holding down the No. 1 singles spot at Gustavus, he recalled playing conference meets against Minnesota legends John Desmond and Jack Roach. He said of those years, "We drove ourselves to the matches and we had no coaching—though in name our coach was a physics prof." When he completed his BS degree at Gustavus in science, he earned his DDS in dentistry at the U of M and worked for forty years as a dentist in Golden Valley while also teaching (for twenty-nine years) at the U Dental School. He has continued to play tennis in retirement, competing often with about twenty friends, in the winter in Arizona. His tennis accomplishments at Gustavus were noticed by Coach Steve Wilkinson, who in 2001 honored him and his teammates for significant contributions to Gustavus tennis and life.

The other key member of that Saints miracle team, John Jackson, graduated from the U of M as well and today works as a lawyer in Des Moines, IA. And though he did not participate at the U, he has kept up his competitive tennis-playing as an adult.

Another member of that team, Bill Yock, is a dentist who did not stray far from home; for he came back to St. James to take over his father's dentistry practice.

Kintzi, who expressed some regret that he didn't reach his full potential because "I never had a coach," nonetheless spoke fondly of his tennis experiences in St. James and of the friends he made. He said, "We were real close and still are." Mark Anderson relished playing against good players, but he also lamented that this usually didn't happen until region or state competition. "Except for the St. Peter players in the conference, there was no one to play against in our small town and we didn't have the coaching or the facilities."

So how did this small school in southern Minnesota rise to the top of the state high school tennis scene? Perhaps there's really no good explanation other than the fact that these were just talented athletes who happened to be born at the same time and in the same town. It's likely these players would say that there was a certain amount of serendipity or karma involved as well, for they needed to win the doubles, they needed Mark Anderson to pick up some points, and they needed the points to be scattered among other teams. Maybe the stars were simply aligned in the heavens in the right way that year, or maybe

it can't be explained any more than one can explain why Beethoven (the second of eight children born to a humble chambermaid) or Caruso (the eighteenth child born in a poor Italian family) emerged to grace the world with their musical gifts.

In any case St. James would never again earn a place in the State Tournament and never produce another state singles or doubles champion. For many years the Saints had to contend with state power Blue Earth, and while they have produced decent teams the past few years under coach Les Zellmann, the girls' teams have been more successful. Sadly, the glory year of 1954 is a fading memory for most people in this small town.

Greenway of Coleraine
Northern MN School Champion (1961)

In one of the most remarkable stories in the history of Minnesota boys' high school tennis, a doubles team from a small community on the Iron Range came to the Twin Cities in 1961 and swept through the competition, earning a doubles title for themselves and also securing a team championship for their school. The school was Greenway of Coleraine (a consolidated high school located in Coleraine made up of the communities of Bovey, Calumet, Coleraine, Marble, Taconite, and other small villages (with a total population just over 3,000).

And the players were Jim Miller and John Wirtanen. Their three victories—and a bye which earned them three points because they won their first match after the bye—gave them and the school twelve points, one more than second-place St. Paul Central. This was only the second team victory by a northern Minnesota school (Duluth Central won in 1949), and it would be the last, even though there would be many other strong area teams from large schools such as Duluth East, Hibbing, Thief River Falls, and Virginia. It would also be just the second doubles title won by a northern school in big-school competition; the first was won by Duluth Central's John Nutting and Bruce Dikson (the year Central also took that team title), and the next did not come until almost twenty years later when Tom Shustarich and Mark Maroste of Virginia won the '80 Class AA doubles title.

One must ask, "How could a small Iron Range school like this win a state championship?" especially since the town in which it was located, Coleraine (population 1,067), is but a dot on the map, a drive-through village between Hibbing and Grand Rapids on U.S. Highway 169 and a town located in the midst of a hockey-mad region. The triumph of Miller and Wirtanen seems, in retrospect, almost as miraculous as that of a man surviving five days in the desert without water. For starters, the school had only fielded a varsity tennis team for three years. Secondly, Miller and Wirtanen had few quality hitting partners (other than their coach) to help them improve their games. Third, in 1959 there were only two high school courts in Coleraine (and two in nearby Bovey), and those two courts in Coleraine were concrete on top of a surface previously used as a skating rink, according to Miller. In fact, he recalls that his father painted the lines on the courts some time in the '50s. Fourth, while Miller—who received his first racket from his grandmother when he was ten—had been playing for a few years, Wirtanen didn't begin playing tennis until he was a ninth grader. And finally, playing as they did against mostly inferior competition and in relative isolation from the center of the Minnesota tennis universe made their win even more remarkable. Miller noted that the championship match against Ronald Jarvis and Dennis LeBarron of Austin was the first he and Wirtanen had ever played in front of a good-sized audience.

Against all odds and despite these obvious impediments, Miller and Wirtanen won the prize, thanks in large part to the arrival in Greenway of one Paul Bouchard, a Lewiston, Maine, native who had won the state doubles championship and finished second in singles his junior year (1952). Bouchard noted that his school, St. Dominic High, also won the team championship that year and that he captured the singles championship his senior year ('53).

Journeying west to the banks of the Mississippi River after high school, he attended St. Cloud State where, in 1957, he won the conference singles title and the doubles championship with teammate Dick Strand from St. Cloud. During his time at St. Cloud, Bouchard also served as student-coach of teams that won the conference championship in 1957 and finished as runner-up in '58.

Also a hockey player at St. Cloud, Bouchard came to Coleraine to teach French and business and to coach junior high hockey; but fortunately for Miller and Wirtanen, he also brought his tennis talents with him as the first coach in the newly minted Coleraine tennis program in 1959. Miller said of him, "The tennis playing improved greatly when Paul Bouchard became the high school coach. He was young [23] and personable and he knew how to play and coach tennis. He organized a summer tennis league when I was in high school and it helped the overall quality of tennis." Bouchard modestly credited the players for dedicating themselves during that summer of '59 while he attended summer school at the U of ND, saying, "The players followed a schedule of weekly play that I had set up and that really seemed to help. Good results showed up the following spring" ['60].

Bouchard knew the team needed better competition, so in 1960 he scheduled a meet at Greenway with reigning state champion Stillwater, a hotly contested match Greenway lost 4-3. And later in that magical year

(Left to Right) **John Wirtanen, coach Paul Bouchard, & Jim Miller**

of '61, Bouchard scheduled a pre-tournament warmup match with a Minneapolis North doubles team that eventually took fourth in the tournament. A wide-eyed Miller, who remembers this as his first trip to the Cities, said of this tuneup match just two days before the tournament, "We were impressed by the quality of the play." Bouchard said of this match, "John and Jim lost the first set 6-1, then came back and won. I told them that's what you'll be up against in the tourney."

In addition to scheduling some tougher competition for his team, Bouchard also made the strategic decision to pair his No. 1 and 2 players (who had rotated back and forth at those spots during the year) in doubles, knowing they would have a difficult time beating Hibbing's two outstanding singles players (Ron Keith and Dennis Chez) and that this would give them a good chance to advance in the upcoming tournaments. The two had played some matches together during the year, so this was a wise move. Miller and Wirtanen won the doubles at the district tournament in Hibbing and in the Region 7 tournament at Duluth. Then, at the State Tournament on the U of M 4th Street courts, Miller (a senior) and Wirtanen (a junior) defeated a skilled team from Minneapolis Roosevelt (Charles Berry and Len Bjeldanes) in the quarters 3-6, 8-6, 7-5. This win earned them six points, three for this match and three for a first-round bye. Miller clearly recalls the match as a tussle that they "won in a third-set squeaker. They had several match points against us but we survived and held on to win."

Next they played the aforementioned team from Minneapolis North (Gilbert Rozman and Jules Beck) in the semis, beating them 6-4, 6-4. In the finals the Greenway pair overcame a slow start to upend Austin's Jarvis and LeBarron 4-6, 6-2, 6-3. Astounded that they had captured a state team title for their school, the two euphoric lads traipsed over to Memorial Stadium, where the state track meet was taking place. Miller said, "We went over there to find the members of the Greenway track team. We wanted to share the news and show them the trophy. Then the public address announcer declared us as the state tennis champions. The most amazing thing had happened."

Indeed it was an amazing thing, in part because they had to come from behind to win two of their matches, but it's fair to say that it also happened because of the League's quirky scoring system, which assigned three points for a doubles win and three for a first-round bye if a team won its next match. Greenway had also been the darkest of the "dark horses" entering the tournament, and certainly unknowns Miller and Wirtanen were not given consideration to win the doubles title. As for the pre-tournament favorites, they were powerful city schools like Minneapolis Roosevelt and St. Paul Central (which took second). But under the scoring system used then, the Greenway duo fairly earned their twelve points and the team title in a tournament in which, as Miller noted, "the points were scattered." And unlike that 1946 team from Minneapolis Southwest that won a team title with a 1-9 season record; Greenway had a solid team and a successful season, winning 8 dual meets, losing 0, and tying 1 (a rained-out 3-3 match with Hibbing). And most of these 8 wins were against bigger schools such as Cloquet, Virginia, Duluth, and Hibbing (which Greenway defeated 3-2 in the last match of the year).

Other members of the team were Tom Dunstan, Jack Stebe, Dave Olds, Rennie Huerd, Tom Holland, and Tom Kingston. Miller also mentioned two other players, 1960 graduates Tom McWaters and Dan Falardou, who helped build the '61 team.

Bouchard left Greenway following the 1961 season, after just three years there, to take a teaching and coaching job at the new Brooklyn Center High School, but he had put the school on the tennis map and helped establish a good program there. In '62, with industrial arts teacher Morse Ridgeway as coach, Greenway had another successful season with Wirtanen leading the way.

As for Wirtanen, his is one of our sport's most tragic stories. After graduation he joined teammate Miller on a very strong Hamline MIAC tennis team, and for three years he was a stalwart on teams which won two championships. In 1964 he won the consolation singles title, and in Miller's last year ('65) the two paired up again in the conference tournament. Seeded No. 1, they were upset in the first round and had to settle for a consolation championship. After the '65 season ended, Wirtanen was diagnosed with cancer and was unable to return to Hamline for his senior year. He died on September 7, 1966, at age 22.

Miller said, "It was tragic and very sad." He continued, "When he died a large number of people from the college went to his funeral in Coleraine. He was mourned by a lot of people in Coleraine and Bovey and the other range towns that made up Greenway High School's population. After the funeral his mother gave one of his tennis rackets to me. I still have it, a Spaulding in a wooden frame."

The son of a Coleraine hardware and appliance store owner, Wirtanen was, according to Miller, "very bright (he was class salutatorian in 1962) and funny. We had many good times together, especially in college." Miller also said that Wirtanen played basketball, bowled, and participated in both the high school band and orchestra. In addition, according to Miller, he played "saxophone in a group called the 'Sassy Seven' that played in pep fests and talent shows." Miller's sister Sylvia, who was Wirtanen's age, remembered him as "quite funny and possessed of a photographic memory." She remembers one incident as an example of his intelligence: "We were in a history class in high school and we found out as we walked in that there would be a quiz. John hadn't read the assignment—and I don't think many of us had. He flipped through the pages quickly in the brief moments before we had to put the books away. And he got all the questions right on the quiz."

Though he has been gone for over forty years, he is still remembered, in particular for the scorebook bearing his name that has been used by nearly all Minnesota tennis coaches for these many years since his death.

Wirtanen's worthy partner, Miller, went off to Hamline with an academic scholarship in the fall of 1961, a year before Wirtanen joined him. In the spring of '62 Miller became a member of the tennis team, and some of Miller's teammates that first year at Hamline included '61 state singles champion Bob Gustafson from St. Paul Wilson, future Hopkins coach Tom Hutton, and Stillwater's Charlie Huss (third-place singles finisher in '60). In '64, a year Hamline won the MIAC team title, Gustafson won the singles championship and Miller and his partner Richard Stebbins won the doubles. Miller graduated in '65 with a BA in mathematics and worked in the computer industry most of his adult life as an operating system programmer and developer, first at Univac and currently at Cray, Inc.

He continues to play tennis, though today he mostly limits his court time to doubles. He said about his tennis, "It has been a large part of my life for the last forty-five years. I have played in adult singles tournaments and socially, but mainly for the competitive spirit of the game. I am now a member of a USTA Senior Mens 4.0 team. In 2005 I competed at the national tournament in Palm Springs, representing the Lilydale Club in St. Paul." The irony of this could not have been lost on the small town lad who once marveled at the bright lights of Minneapolis, which he first saw as a senior in high school.

As for Coach Bouchard, he remembers his star proteges well, saying,

> John and Jim were both excellent students. Both were very easy to work with and would always attempt any suggestions that you gave them—very coachable indeed! Also, they were well respected by their teammates. Both took charge of the summer program that I set up and were able to get the other players to participate. I think this had a lot to do with the team's success as well as their own. As far as playing doubles together, they would complement each other very well. They would never blame or get down on one another. If one got down, the other would just pick up his game, just like good doubles players should do.

Bouchard, who stayed in the Land of 10,000 Lakes because he married a native Minnesotan, taught three years at Greenway and twenty-nine at Brooklyn Center High School. He also coached hockey for eighteen years in addition to coaching tennis for twelve years (two as St. Cloud student-coach, three at Greenway, and seven at Brooklyn Center). For many years he was a member of the Northwest Tennis Club in St. Louis Park, winning numerous singles round robin tournaments as well as some annual club tournaments. Now living in retirement in Georgia, he plays tennis three times a week and some golf as well.

Tennis coaches owe him a great debt, for he created the *Wirtanen Tennis Scorebook*. Named in memory of Wirtanen, it's a well-known and well-used scorebook with a familiar hardbound, green cover. About this scorebook, Bouchard said, "Several thousand copies are still sold annually. My daughter is handling this publication along with two other publications of mine, *Tennis Drills and Skills* and *Tennis for the Coach, Teacher, and Player*. These two were published in the 1970s."

So that's the Greenway story, a tale of beating the odds due to the inspired play of two young men and a canny coach.

Why the Next Two Teams?

Minnehaha Academy & Minneapolis South

One might legitimately question why this chapter includes stories about two Metro-area teams: Minnehaha Academy and Minneapolis South. After all, players from both teams had access to the best coaching and indoor facilities, both played challenging schedules, and both played in an era of open enrollment. And yes, both teams benefited from this open enrollment policy, a policy which saw some players—like the hired gunslingers of the Wild West—move from one school to another in order to play on better teams.

That said, there are good reasons for telling the unique stories of these two teams. First, Minnehaha, a small school associated with the Evangelical Covenant Church, is known for its academics and a strong emphasis on religious education. With a student body population of 551 in grades 7-12 that year (1986), Minnehaha had never before won a state championship in MSHSL competition in any sport, though it had always competed well in independent-school athletics. And except for some later successes, Rob Warn's Class A singles title in '96 and a fourth-place team finish in the Class A tourney in 2002 under the direction of coach Mark Norlander, it had no particular bragging rights in tennis. For years it had played in the shadows of the bigger schools and independent school tennis nemesis Blake. Also, though the '86 championship team had a strong lineup led by Jason Hall and Ryan Skanse, until some talented young players

enrolled in the fall of '85 it was unlikely that Minnehaha would have won the state team title.

Another reason to include their story is that their victory was achieved against the big boys (including Edina) in the final year of single-class competition. It reminded me again of my hometown high school's triumph in the last year before the class system was put in place in basketball (Sherburn in 1970). Finally, a doubles team or singles player did not win this title; rather, it was a team championship earned in head-to-head combat against tennis powers SPA, Edina, and Stillwater.

The 2001 champion Minneapolis South Tigers were in a different pot of stew, a Metro team which had been successful for a number of years in city league competition and had made four previous appearances in the State Tournament, three of which produced consolation championships and another in '00 which produced a third-place finish. So in some respects one could argue that South was a tiger just needing to sharpen its claws a bit more before staking out prime territory. And that would be true, for the addition of big tiger D. J. Geatz gave them the extra advantage they needed to win it all. But one would then be forgetting that this team championship was the only title won by a city school since the True Team format was adopted in '73 and the first since John Desmond and Don Cooper took the doubles title, leading Minneapolis Marshall to one of those put-an-asterisk-on-it championships in '58.

And before that, except for Minneapolis Southwest's title in 1952 (again won by a doubles team, Tom LaMott and Greg Heimark), one needed to go back to the glory days of Minneapolis and St. Paul tennis in the 1930s and '40s. City teams in those days dominated before Rochester began its run in the '50s and before tennis powers began springing up from suburban soil in the '60s. And South had produced just one individual state champion, Walter Monson, in the first year of State competition in 1929. This would change in 2002 when South, actually the favorite to win the team title that year, took both the singles (D. J. Geatz) and doubles titles (Mikey Kantar and Sion Wilkins). City schools had simply not been able to compete with the Edinas of the tennis world until South, also benefiting from inner city programs established by coaches and patrons such as Jack Thommen, Nick Pappas, Lach Reed, John King, Fred King, and others, cut a swath through the field in 2001. In fact, a chip-on-their-shoulders attitude and an identity as a ghetto tennis team inspired the Tigers during this decade-long run which began in '92 and ended with a 4-3 first-round loss to Mounds View in the '02 State Tournament. So I rest my case for these two teams, expecting it to offend some, maybe supporters of small schools like Madison and Blue Earth, for instance. But Madison did not win a team title (for more about their story see Chapter Ten) and Blue Earth, though it did win one title against the big schools (in 1977), also claimed two titles in Class A competition and so dominated Region 2 that I have included its story in Chapter Nine on dynasty teams.

Minnehaha Academy
Private School Champion (1986)

So here's the story of Minnehaha Academy, the "little school that could" coached by Forrest Dahl. Though it had a population of less than 100 students per grade, the Indians dominated three big-school opponents on the way to the championship of the 58th annual tournament.

In many respects this 1986 championship was perhaps the most serendipitous one in state tennis history, for without the addition of three talented players it would have been very difficult if not impossible for Minnehaha to defeat powerful teams such as Edina and Blake that year. Coach Dahl, talking about the "Christmas presents" he received, said, "The 1985-86 school year held three surprises for me. The first was hearing from Jason Hall and Ryan Skanse [Minnehaha's No. 1 and 2 players] that a player named Jason Nasby had moved into the Twin Cities area [from Northfield] and they considered him a very good tennis player who had enrolled as a Minnehaha student. The other two surprises showed up at the spring organizational meeting, two other ranked players named Steve Calhoun and Brandon Maki. Now, with Cory Cardenas, that gave us six ranked players on one team." In fact, Hall was ranked No. 1 in the NWTA in the 18s (and No. 128 in the nation) and Skanse No. 3 in the 18s, Nasby No. 9 and Cardenas No. 19 in the 16s, and Maki No. 11 and

Calhoun No. 25 in the 14s. Surely having this many ranked players must have been a first for such a small school. And though Edina was still the team to beat at the beginning of the year, the addition of these three players gave Minnehaha the muscle needed to challenge the "big boys."

As much as Coach Dahl savored this championship, he also remembers the great joy he and his charges experienced in beating powerhouse Blake for the first time in school history. He said, "Over the years we had always fielded good tennis teams but had never once beaten Blake in a dual match, and because they were in our conference and our section, this was a big problem." Hoping 1986 would be different, Dahl recalls that "late in the spring we hosted Blake and according to my scorebook from that day it was 67 degrees and windy. We played a 7-point match and with the singles lineup of Hall, Skanse, Nasby, and Cardenas, we swept 4 points in singles and lost 3 points in doubles. We had beaten Blake for the first time." And even though Minnehaha lost a dual to St. Cloud Tech (4-3) that same day during an 8-team tournament competition, he noted that his team had won the first three singles against Blake and Northfield and the No. 1 and 3 singles and No. 1 doubles against Tech and that State Tournament play would be in 5-point and not 7-point matches, thus giving them an edge.

Dahl's lads would not disappoint, dominating its first three Region 4 opponents (each by 5-0 scores) before tangling once more with Blake. Despite losing both doubles, Minnehaha once again came out on top by virtue of three singles wins from its top players Hall, Skanse, and Nasby. So the Indians (now called the Redhawks) made it to State for the first time as a team.

At the State Tournament Minnehaha swept aside SPA 5-0 in the first round, then geared up for a semifinal battle with Edina, the preseason favorite and a very dangerous opponent. Dahl also felt Edina was still the favorite, even though Minnehaha was ranked No. 1 in the final coaches' poll. He said, as far as he was concerned, "That gave us the advantage of less pressure. Our advantage was to face them in the semis while they may have looked ahead to their finals' opponent. Some of their players told some of our players about the state championship party that apparently they already had planned. This only inspired my players all the more to play the role of spoilers."

A June 6, 1986, article in the *Minneapolis Star and Tribune*, titled "Minnehaha Captures Tennis Title," also spoke of Minnehaha's underdog status, noting that its championship victory (over Stillwater 5-0) was less surprising than its 4-1 win over Edina. After the semifinal, No. 1 player Jason Hall, quoted in the aforementioned article by Jim Gilbert, said, "I think our team and Edina are the top two teams in the state. We were definite underdogs. I think Edina thought they'd win the two doubles matches for sure, and that at least one of their singles guys would come through."

Edina's lineup included the likes of junior Paul

guy is No. 1 in the state." That player of course was Terwilliger, who had beaten teammate Odland in the region singles final. Skanse, after losing the first set to Terwilliger 6-1, observed in that same June 6 article, "He toyed with me. He wasn't missing anything and I was missing everything" (*Minneapolis Star and Tribune*). But Skanse, a junior, quickly turned the match around and secured a hard-earned point for the Indians by taking the last two sets 6-2, 6-3. Then, when third singles player Nasby rallied after losing the first set 7-5 to Michaelson and won the last two sets by a score nearly identical to Skanses (6-3, 6-2), Minnehaha had the third point it needed. Edina won the No. 1 doubles over Cory Cardenas and Brandon Maki,

Minnehaha Academy—1986 State Champions. (Front row, L to R) Cory Cardenas, Steve Calhoun, Jason Hall, Jason Nasby, Ryan Skanse. (Back row) Coach Forrest Dahl, Mark Wanous, Chris Pope, Brandon Maki, & Jim Kuehn.

Odland (1985 and '87 singles champion), talented ninth grader Mike Terwilliger ('89 singles champion), No. 3 singles player Chris Michaelson (ranked No. 9 in boys' 18s), and '86 doubles champions Mike Husebo and Guy Carteng; so Minnehaha's lads had to overcome some gifted players in addition to the Edina mystique. Adding to the difficulty, Hall had lost two previous times to Odland, including in last year's singles final. Nevertheless, he made quick work of his opponent, beating Odland 6-2, 6-3. Hall, in an interview with Gilbert, said of this match, "I knew he was kind of down. He's not playing real well at the net. I went out really psyched. But I thought Ryan Skanse had the toughest match, because their No. 2

but Steve Calhoun and Jim Kuehn took second doubles, making the final score 4-1.

During the lunch break after the Edina match, before the finals with Stillwater, Coach Dahl tried to settle his players down and warn them about not getting overconfident or having a letdown. He said,

> I could see some sports reporters headed our way so I told the team we'd be leaving to eat at a local restaurant. I wanted them to maintain focus and not be distracted by reporters, family, or old nemeses who were milling around in shock [Edina]. We tried to keep focus [at the restaurant] by discussing Stillwater's lineup, each guy

giving information from any experiences they had playing any of Stillwater's lineup before. That is one thing that did set this team apart from others I had coached. There was a great deal of team thinking, lots of advice-sharing on how to play opponents.

This tactic obviously paid off for, free of distractions and confident they would win, the Indians took the court. Remarked Dahl, in that June 6 article, "We were pumped up because everyone assumed that Edina would win the tournament. Except us." Jim Gilbert recounted Minnehaha's 5-0 triumph in the finals thus: "When Cory Cardenas and Brandon Maki won their doubles match yesterday, it gave the school a 5-0 sweep over Stillwater and the first state championship in its history. Minnehaha... left no doubt who had the best tennis team yesterday... The Indians allowed only the two doubles matches to go as far as three sets. Jason Hall, Ryan Skanse, and Jason Nasby each recorded two-set sweeps in singles" (June 6, 1986). With this victory, the Indians completed the year with a 16-2 dual meet record.

And so it was Minnehaha Academy and not Edina that celebrated, but this would be but a one-year celebration. For though Minnehaha would field a strong team the following year, they would lose key players Hall, Nasby, Calhoun, and Maki. After winning the 1986 singles title, Hall moved on to the U of M, where he became a key member of a team that won a Big 10 title in '89. (For more on Hall, see Chapter Five.)

Nasby, having played one year at Northfield and this year at Minnehaha, took his tennis game to Edina, making the Hornets the clear favorite to win the 1987 title (which they did). "Our family moved up here from Northfield," said Nasby. "My parents used to drive me to the Twin Cities six days a week to play tennis. But now I live just a few minutes from Edina High School, and my parents don't like me to have to drive a half-hour to Minnehaha" (June 6, 1986). Calhoun also enrolled at Edina and Maki left Minnehaha to attend school at Bloomington.

Meanwhile, Skanse finished second in the 1987 singles tournament (losing to Edina's Paul Odland). He then completed his schooling at Gustavus where he had an exceptional tennis career. He was a three-time all-American, the '91 NCAA Division 3 doubles champion, '91 singles semifinalist, and '92 singles finalist. His teammate Hall called Skanse, whom he played often in practice and in region showdowns, one of his top opponents because "he was a fierce competitor." Skanse's '87 teammates Cardenas and Jim Kuehn advanced to State in doubles that year but lost in the first round and the team did not advance, losing to Minneapolis Washburn 4-3 in the region finals. As for Nasby, he became a key member of powerhouse Edina teams which won titles in 1987, '88, and '89, and he also won a doubles title in '88 with Charlie Eifrig. (For more on Nasby, see Chapter Six.)

Coach Dahl, who called 1986 "a year to remember," was the other integral component of that Minnehaha team. Jason Hall said of him, "He was a really good person who was good at keeping us motivated and excited about the game. He also taught us that tennis can be a team sport." Himself a tennis player, Dahl grew up in Michigan where he played at Livonia Franklin High School, captaining the team his senior year. In addition, he played first singles at North Park College in Chicago his sophomore year and served as captain his senior year. After graduating from North Park, he served as an assistant coach at the college while attending seminary. A minister in the Evangelical Covenant Church, he has been a religion teacher at Minnehaha since 1979, where he coached the boys' tennis team from 1980-2000.

Resurrection of Tennis in the Twin Cities
Minneapolis South

After high school tennis in the Twin Cities began to decline in the 1950s, it would be over thirty years before it started to ascend again and over forty years before a city team would win a state team title. In fact, this title, won by Minneapolis South in 2001, is the only one captured by a city school since the advent of True Team play in '73. Before South won the consolation championship in '92, the best performance by a city school in the True Team competition was a second-place finish by a '78 Minneapolis Roosevelt team led by Greg Wicklund. So why was this '01 title such a surprise? For starters, the power in tennis had shifted to the suburbs, to new schools like Edina that could afford the best facilities. In addition, these suburban communities often established comprehensive summer recreation tennis programs which served as feeder systems for the high school teams. And suburban conferences could afford junior high programs which gave these youngsters opportunities to receive good coaching and to play matches against other schools, something the city schools did not have. Also, in general most suburban parents had more money than did city parents, so they could afford to pay for private lessons at the new indoor tennis clubs springing up in the suburbs in the late 1960s and early '70s.

Jack Thommen

While an organization to promote urban tennis in Minneapolis had existed since 1952 (it was called Inner City Tennis), it wasn't until the early '70s that some far-sighted individuals set out to resurrect tennis in the Twin Cities by establishing a summer park program. One of those pioneers was '46 doubles champion Jack Thommen, then a community education administrator in the Minneapolis school system, who said, "It's [tennis] a wealthy man's game; let's bring it to the kids in the streets." (For more about Thommen, see Chapter Six.). Another key figure in this venture was Nick Pappas, at that time the president of the NWLTA, who was asked by then U of M coach Joe Walsh to raise money to start a program at Windom Field in northeast Minneapolis. That first year (1970), with Coach Walsh and one of his players (1967-68 singles champion Rob Daugherty), as instructors, ninety kids showed up for lessons on three W.P.A. Depression-era concrete courts with grass growing out of the cracks. With a modest budget of $5,000 provided by the Minneapolis Public Schools Community Education Department that

John (Left) & Fred King

first year, the program has since picked up speed like a snowball rolling down a hill.

Principal lobbyist Thommen persuaded donors such as Douglas Corporation president Douglas Skanse (father of top players Ryan and Rick), Lion's Clubs, Kiwanis Clubs, VFW organizations, and other individuals such as Lach Reed to contribute funds to support the program. Reed, a Northern Section Hall of Fame member whose name now graces the former Nicollet Tennis Center, had been contributing to tennis projects since the early 1950s. From this humble first effort, a tiny snowball, a wide-ranging program was built, thanks in part to the aforementioned pioneers and other committed tennis coaches and patrons.

For example, John King came in on the ground floor that first year and has been involved as a coach or supervisor of inner city summer programs in Minneapolis and St. Paul off and on ever since. A retired former English teacher in the Minneapolis school system, King grew up in St. Paul and played college tennis at St. Thomas from 1961-64. And for many years thereafter, with his booming serve and excellent net game, he has been one of the top doubles players in NWTA adult tennis, even holding a No. 1 ranking in Men's Open Doubles in '72 with Ric Yates. He also holds six other No. 1 doubles rankings with former Simley High School boys' tennis coach Merle Bryan and Fred King (no relation). The latter King, one of John King's favorite doubles partners, is a Rochester native who recently retired after coaching the Sibley High School girls' tennis team for eighteen years. Fred King, also a Northern Section Hall of Fame member and a self-taught tennis player, excelled at track and basketball in high school but did not play competitive tennis until he enrolled at Rochester Junior College. In his one year there he won the conference No. 1 singles title, then transferred to the U of Montana where he took the conference singles crown as a junior. And like John King, he has been a highly ranked doubles player in the Northern Section for years, utilizing his tremendous speed and cat-quick reactions at the net to confound opponents. He was also an excellent singles player who ranked as high as No. 2 in the 35s and 45s, but in doubles he and his usual partner Ric Yates dominated every age group from the 35s on up. All told, Fred has held over twenty-three No. 1 rankings in doubles (also with John King and Tom Boice).

In 1973 Fred joined John King on the inner city summer tennis teaching team, bringing his superb teaching and playing talents with him. And he, too, has remained a fixture in these programs ever since. Together these indefatigable and inseparable partners have committed themselves to teaching tennis to youngsters—black kids, poor white kids, new immigrants such as Hmong and Somali kids—who might not otherwise have a chance to learn the game, and other kids who couldn't afford a membership in an indoor club.

At first, according to John King, the park programs did not operate on an everyday basis. Instead, top local teaching pros such as Wendell Ottum came to the courts once a week or so for an hour or two and gave clinics to kids who showed up. That all changed when Bob Speed, a former Brainerd high school star and top local teaching pro, organized and directed the program in the summer of 1971. Speed came up with the idea of a full-fledged program of scheduled classes with instruction from full-time teachers. King also remembers that Pepsi provided a good deal of the funding the first two years.

Speed stayed just one more year as the director, then John King took over as the organizer in 1973 and, with Fred King, alternated directing the Minneapolis program until '86. For a number of years Nick Pappas ran the south Minneapolis program while John King ran the one in north Minneapolis and Phil Johnson ran the St. Paul program. Others who were involved in leadership roles during these early years were Vern Backes, a teacher from Minneapolis Henry, and Terry Bruestle, a Henry Sibley High School teacher who served as Twin Cities director for three or four years.

Another program that began in the early 1970s as an attempt to help top-level Minnesota junior players, Junior Tennis Champions, later served promising inner city players as well. U of M coach Jerry Noyce developed the idea and local teaching pro Jack Roach persuaded Woodhill Country Club member Carl Hensel and Minikahda member Jack Dow to commit money for court fees for these junior players and money to take them to tournaments. The idea, according to Roach, was "to get people with dollars behind the program in order to provide competition for junior players." Lach Reed even sponsored dances and other fundraisers to help support the program. Some of the better juniors were given opportunities to hit with top players such as former Edina state champion Bob Amis, and Roach then began to arrange competitions between Twin City players and those from clubs in places like Madison, WI. Eventually, tennis patrons such as Reed and Dow gave money to the Inner City Program as well, in part because it was a nonprofit organization and the patrons could get tax write-offs.

Then, in 1990, John and Fred King engineered a great divorce from Minneapolis, hitching themselves to another suitor, St. Paul. And in '94 they broke from the Northwest Patrons to begin to raise funds themselves, establishing the St. Paul Urban Tennis Program. With an initial $1,500 grant from the St. Paul Winter Carnival Tennis Tournament and its director Paul Steinhauser, the program began to resurrect St. Paul tennis. Today it receives roughly $200,000 a year for support from patrons such as the USTA (its biggest sponsor), the City of St. Paul, the Northern Section, Superamerica, and the Fred Wells trust. And, according to an August 2006 article in *TennisLife Magazine*, "it has grown from 150 kids to 3,200 participants in its summer programs." Across the river in Minneapolis, the Inner City Tennis program (directed by Roger Boyer) "has served over 47,000 young people, mostly from the inner city. In 2005, Inner City Tennis served over 4,600 children ages 3-17 and has a group of over 130 volunteers" (August 2006).

So while the first year was but a brief prelude played out on a few dilapidated courts in Minneapolis, now there are full symphonies of tennis being played on public courts all over the Twin Cities and indoors on the courts at the Reed-Sweatt Family Tennis Center (formerly Nicollet Tennis Center) in Minneapolis and at the Fort Snelling Tennis and Learning Center in St. Paul. It's worth noting that these two indoor facilities sprang up because of the efforts of two men in particular, Lach Reed and Fred Wells. An article titled "Lachlan Reed: A Lifetime of Service," noted that Reed "spearheaded a fund-raising campaign to find Inner City Tennis a permanent, year-round home" (*Tennislife Magazine*, August 2004). This year-round home was named the Reed-Sweatt Center, in honor of Reed and his father-in-law, Harold W. Sweatt.

Wells, also a Northern Section Hall of Fame member, and his wife, Ellen, founded and helped finance the Fort Snelling Center. In addition to this philanthropic effort, Wells has since 1994 financed the USTA/Northern Section-sponsored multicultural tennis program. Two individuals who now play a prominent role in the latter program are Tony Stingley, Northern Section multicultural specialist, and former U of M and Chicago Bulls basketball star Trent Tucker, who funds the Trent Tucker Multicultural College Scholarships for deserving youngsters.

Throughout the past thirty-plus years, many other coaches have shown inner city kids how to play tennis on public courts in Minneapolis such as Armitage, Folwell, Kenwood, and Powderhorn and in St. Paul at Macalester College, St. Clair, Edgcumbe, and Martin Luther King. A partial list of these coaches includes the aforementioned Roach—for whom the NWPTA Lifetime Achievement

Ernie Greene

Award is named—Ernie Greene, Percy Hughes, Bucky Olson, Tom Boice, Ric Yates, Dan Shannon, Tunde Abe, Roger Boyer, and Mike Vidmar.

Greene (who died in 2002), a Northern Section Hall of Fame member in whose name a scholarship is given, also ran a tennis program for African American kids at the Martin Luther King Center in St. Paul. Hughes taught in the St. Paul Urban Program with Greene and is now involved with the Minneapolis Inner City Tennis Program. Called "Mr. Tennis in St. Paul" by Fred King, Olson was for many years the only tennis pro working with youngsters in St. Paul. In what Fred King called "his own way and without fanfare," Olson (also deceased) and his St. Thomas College players (he was then the coach) gave lessons in parks all over the city. Boice and Yates are top adult Section players and local teaching pros who have worked in the Twin Cities programs. Shannon, a former Minnetonka High School player, State doubles champion, and like Fred King a Big Sky champion at the U of Montana, for a time managed the Fort Snelling Tennis Center. Abe is a Nigerian transplant and tennis pro at Ft. Snelling who coaches the St. Paul Central girls' team and works with advanced inner city players. He also takes youngsters to national and minority tournaments and has recently been given the task of starting a Nigerian national team. Boyer has directed the Minneapolis inner city programs for many years. Finally, Vidmar, a former Hibbing High School and Macalester College standout player, is the head teaching pro at the Reed-Sweatt Center. On occasion some pro players such as David Wheaton have also guest taught.

In addition, without the support of patrons and other supporters, these programs could not have succeeded. For example, one of the founders of the St. Paul Urban program is Sandy Martin, a top local women's player and another member of the Northern Section Hall of Fame. According to John King, after Martin asked Lach Reed why St. Paul didn't have a program, she coaxed him into contributing $10,000. She has also served on the boards of both the St. Paul and Minneapolis Urban programs. And the Northwest Patrons, under the leadership of individuals such as Jack Dow (for whom the Northern Section Senior Development Award is named), budgeted money for various programs. Others, such as highly ranked senior player Bernie Gunderson, Steve Wilkinson, Jerry Noyce, and the legendary Norm McDonald, pitched in as well. Gunderson, who served on the board of directors for both the Minneapolis and St. Paul programs, also taught the first year in the St. Paul program and was, according to Fred King, "one of the best advocates for kids I've ever known."

In addition, McDonald, longtime Twin Cities Wilson representative, sold rackets at reduced prices to program sponsors who in turn gave them to the kids. Norm and his son Kevin (who often strung rackets for practically nothing) also gave kids rackets and balls. Finally, businesses such as SuperAmerica (which funded a picnic and awards ceremony), General Mills, and Northwestern Banks donated tennis rackets and T-shirts. In addition, according to Fred and John King, Mike Lynne (of Michael Lynne's Tennis Shop) has done a great deal for inner city programs as well. For instance, he also donated tennis balls and strung rackets.

All these efforts have helped inner city kids compete with their suburban and outstate peers and even players on the national level. Also, beginning in the late 1980s and early '90s, city kids began making state tournament appearances on a regular basis. For example, one youngster who played on park courts in Minneapolis, Todd Bowlby, won the 1994 singles championship. (For more on Bowlby, see Chapter Five.)

In addition, Minneapolis teams such as Southwest (1999, 2003), Washburn (1987, 1993-96), and South (1992, 1997-98, 2000-02) advanced to the team tournament and were very competitive there. For example, Southwest finished second and third those two years, Washburn third in 1993-94, and South third in 2000.

Minneapolis South
Urban Tennis Champions (2001)

But it wasn't until 2001 that the modern evolution of city tennis from prey to predator was complete, for that year the Minneapolis South Tigers feasted on three opponents and claimed the state team title. For the first time since Minneapolis Marshall in '58 (a team led by doubles champions John Desmond and Don Cooper) and for the first time since True Team play began in '73, a city school had risen to the top of the tennis food chain. And they did it with a certain inner city swagger and panache. *Star Tribune* writer Jim Paulsen, in a June 7, 2001, article, said this about these South High netmen: "The Tigers have relished their image as tennis outsiders—city kids excelling at a country-club sport—and wear T-shirts reading 'South: Ghetto Tennis.' It's a moniker the entire team rallies around." While their triumph was in at least one respect not surprising (South and Edina were considered the two top teams all year), it was surprising in that the team had come from so far to win this title. Hall of Fame coach George Beske said, "I remember going to the State Tournament in 1980 when Gary Aasen [current Edina coach] was playing for Fridley. I remember thinking then that we have so far to go to get to that level" (June 7, 2001). But over the next few years, thanks in large part to the urban tennis programs described earlier in this chapter, South's fortunes began to rise. Under Beske's leadership (he coached from 1986-2003), the Tigers won twelve Minneapolis City Conference titles, twelve Twin City titles, and six section championships.

At State the team won four consolation trophies, finished third another year, and in 2001 took home the whole bacon. In addition, many South High players advanced to state individual competition and some of them excelled. For instance, in 1992 brothers Mark and Mike Ghaly took third in doubles and the next year Mike finished third in singles, in 2000 brothers Danny and Mikey Kantar finished fourth in doubles, and in the championship year of '01 Mikey Kantar and Sion Wilkins earned a third-place doubles medal. Then, in the year South was expected to repeat its team triumph ('02), D. J. Geatz won the singles championship and Mikey Kantar and Wilkins the doubles title.

become really excited about tennis and becoming very good tennis players." Of course South was not the only team to benefit from the urban program, but it became the poster child for inner city tennis by virtue of this 2001 state championship.

And while the Tigers fielded a strong team in 2000 without him, the addition of D. J. Geatz ('02 singles champion) gave them the marquee No. 1 player which made South a legitimate state contender in '01. In that June 7 *Star Tribune* article, Jim Paulsen said, "Geatz, the talented-yet-enigmatic junior, was clearly the key for the Tigers, his third team in four years. He played for

Minneapolis South—2001 AA State Champions. (Left to right) Sim Priest, Andy Born, coach George Beske, Mark Thorkelson, Chase Hanson, Allen Gleckner, Diego Milan, Max Maliga, Sion Wilkins, Mikey Kantar, C.J. Keen, Tim Klein, Brandon Heath, Sean Keir, D.J Geatz.

Some of the players on the 2001 championship team cut their teeth in the Urban Tennis Program and at least one, No. 2 singles player Tim Klein, acknowledged, in the article by Paulsen, his debt to that program: "It [the ghetto tennis mentality] says a lot about us. We play our home matches at Powderhorn Park and that scares some teams. A lot of us—me and Mikey Kantar and Andy Born and Allen Gleckner—grew up in the Urban Tennis Program and we used to talk about winning the State Tournament. I think it's wonderful that a city team does this" (June 7, 2001). Coach Beske also credited inner city tennis for the team's success and expressed pride in "seeing kids who learned basic tennis in the Minneapolis Urban Tennis Program

Edina's 1998 Class AA championship team as an eighth grader and transferred to Minneapolis Southwest for his freshman and sophomore years before finding an ideal situation at South this year." With Geatz at the top of the lineup, everyone else moved down a notch and thrived in their lower positions. Now with a formidable singles lineup of Geatz, Tim Klein at No. 2, Sion Wilkins at No. 3, and Diego Milan at No. 4; and with a strong doubles lineup of Mikey Kantar/Andy Born, Allen Gleckner/Brandon Heath, Sean Keir/Max Maliga or Chase Hanson, South was nearly invincible. Holding all these trump cards, Coach Beske's netmen thrashed all three of its state tournament opponents by 6-1 scores. After beating

Mankato West in the first round, the Tigers avenged a 7-0 loss in the 2000 tournament and a regular-season loss to defending champion Edina by whipping them, then polished off first-time qualifier Mahtomedi in the finals. With losses only to suburban powers Edina and Eden Prairie, the Tigers completed the season with a sparkling 24-2 record.

After this heady triumph, with Geatz, most of last year's team, and talented ninth grader Danny Wilson in the lineup, the Tigers found themselves in an unaccustomed position as the favorites in 2002. Unfortunately, after they rolled through section challengers, their dream became a nightmare when Geatz went down with an injury the day before the team tournament began. Another article by Paulsen, in the June 5, 2002, *Star Tribune*, recounted how "The Minneapolis South senior and the state's top singles player slipped while practicing in the rain Monday and sprained a ligament in his right knee. The injury kept Geatz from playing for the Tigers in the Class AA team quarterfinals Tuesday." Still, even without Geatz and with a juggled lineup, the Tigers almost pulled off a victory against Mounds View in the first round, losing in a squeaker 4-3. South players displayed a good deal of class after the match, refusing to use Geatz's injury as an excuse. "Mounds View stepped it up," South captain Mikey Kantar said. "We felt we could still win, but they made the shots they had to make" (*Star Tribune*, June 5, 2002). And this loss did not deter them from completing what turned out to be a sensational tournament for the Tigers, for they won their next two team matches to claim the consolation prize (finishing with a 23-3 team record) and swept both the individual prizes (Geatz winning the singles and Wilkins and Mikey Kantar the doubles). This "double" in individual competition was the first for a Minneapolis public school since 1948 when Southwest's Edmund "Chiefie" Gould took the singles and teamed with William Moses to win the doubles. (For more about Geatz, see Chapter Five, and for more on Wilkins and Kantar, see Chapter Six.)

While South's players owed a great debt to their urban tennis teachers and other pros, their high school coach also played a significant role in this triumph of "ghetto" tennis. Though he did not play high school or college tennis (Beske grew up playing with friends on the only court in his hometown of Hector, MN), he studied the game and worked hard to mould competitive teams. One key to South's success, according to Beske, was conditioning, "We tried to work them hard in practice with physically challenging drills. I really think this helped them with their mental game and discipline. Physical conditioning really helped the players more with their discipline as opposed to the improvement physically because most high school athletes are already in fairly good physical shape." Beske also scheduled matches against good teams to "force them [the players] to concentrate," because often the Tigers dominated their city conference rivals. In addition, Beske had players write down their team and individual goals at the beginning of the season and he encouraged them to play in the off season. In addition, he "gave the team plenty of publicity at school and made it a big deal to be on the tennis team." Beske even posted a lineup-announcement board outside his classroom (he taught math) and watched while "other students wandered by the board and stopped to look at the names and other tennis information on the board."

Of course he experienced the usual tennis-coach frustrations such as students with attendance or academic problems, players with attitude issues on court, and players who didn't work hard, but he was often more frustrated when other coaches "thought that all of our players should be perfect all the time while some of their players were acting up on the courts." Maybe it's a perceived double standard, the belief that city kids are somehow less well behaved than their suburban or outstate counterparts.

Beske retired from the boys' coaching position after the 2003 season, but he continues to work as a coordinator for the South Minneapolis Inner City Parks summer tennis program, work he has been doing since 1991. Thus he keeps his hand in a program that has been good to him and the South High Tigers. (For more on Beske, see Chapter Two.) With people like Beske and so many other dedicated tennis coaches and patrons laboring in these urban programs, and with available facilities such as the Reed-Sweatt, Fort Snelling, and now Baseline Tennis Centers, talented players will continue to emerge from the Twin Cities. And maybe it's only a matter of time before a team like South comes out of Minneapolis or St. Paul to capture another state title.

Dynasty Teams

In June of the millennium year 2000 a tennis team from Edina began what would be an extraordinary performance at the State Tournament. Like Sherman's army on its march to the sea during the Civil War, this team demolished all foes standing in its way. First to fall was Fergus Falls on Tuesday, June 6, in a 7-0 rout. Then it was Minneapolis South in the team semifinals, in a 7-0 pasting. And finally the Hornets stung Red Wing 6-1, sending the Wingers off in search of some anti-venom potion. As if this dominant performance wasn't enough, these Edina lads continued their march to the sea by sweeping both individual state titles as well, Justin Gaard taking the singles and brothers Jon and Charlie Seltzer winning the doubles.

"Uneasy lies the head that wears the crown"
—Henry IV

The team triumph was propitious, for it was Edina's 100th state championship since its birth as a Metro ring suburban school in 1949. But perhaps most appropriately, it was won by a tennis team, and tennis teams had won almost 20 percent of those 100 titles (nineteen). Only Duluth Central, with twenty Alpine ski team championships, had won more in boys' competition up to this point. Furthermore, with eighteen girls' titles, it could be argued that tennis was the signature sport for a school that also prided itself on its success in hockey (nine titles), golf (thirteen combined for boys' and girls' teams), and swimming (twelve combined).

The coach of the 2000 team, Gary Aasen, used the possibility of winning the school's 100th title as motivation for his players. In an article in the June 8, 2000, *Star Tribune*, he told staff writer Roman Augustoviz, "We look at the board and see that tennis has won all of those championships, so it's fitting that the 100th should be tennis." Fitting indeed it was for them and fitting for us, since it provides a perfect introduction to this chapter titled "Dynasty Teams." And though there have been other dominant teams since the initial season of 1929, none have stood out like Edina, especially if one defines "dynasty" as the length of time a team reigns or is in power. Since winning its first team title in '59 (in the era before True Team play), teams from Edina have been formidable presences in state competition nearly every year, winning twenty-one championships in those forty-four years from 1959-2003, almost one every other year. In addition, an Edina team finished second four times and third five times; and since '73 Edina teams have advanced to State from Section 6 twenty-one times. Furthermore, Edina players have captured seventeen singles titles and sixteen doubles titles since '59. Is it any wonder that many opponents lose heart when they travel to the Hornets' nest to play a match? For they know of this long tradition of success, and when they arrive at the courts they are confronted with signs that list all the boys and girls team and individual champions. (See photo of these signs on this page.)

So Edina is Minnesota's premier dynasty tennis team, our equivalent of the Boston Celtics or Los Angeles Lakers in professional basketball, the New York Yankees in baseball, or the once-dominant Montreal Canadians in hockey. But are there others worthy of the name "dynasty team," and, if so, how should they, and Edina, be defined? Do they spring up full-blown like Venus from the sea, emerging suddenly and without notice or do they emerge gradually, like a slow-growing oak tree? It's probably more the latter. So with that in mind, here are the criteria used to determine these dynasty teams. They have:

- Won at least three (3) team titles.
- Dominated section competition.
- Maintained ultra-competitive teams over a long period of time.
- Made at least ten state tournament appearances since 1973 (when True Team play began).
- Had stability in coaching.
- Received exceptional support from the community.

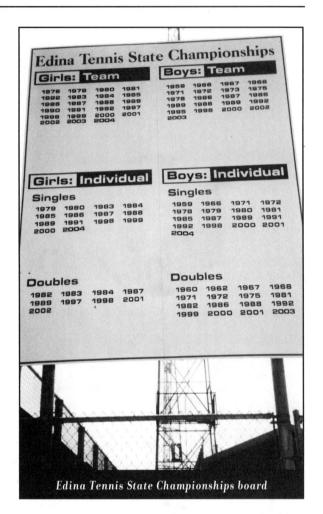

Edina Tennis State Championships board

With these criteria in mind, here are these elite Minnesota teams: Edina, Blake, Rochester, St. Cloud Tech, and the little giant, Blue Earth. Having selected these schools, I know there will be teams left out which deserve consideration. Here are some of those teams, along with the reasons why they were excluded from the elite group.

First of all, a number of teams from the Twin Cities that won championships in the 1930s, '40s, and even '50s deserve to be mentioned. For example, Minneapolis Central won four titles and four other schools, St. Paul Central, Minneapolis Washburn, Minneapolis West, and Minneapolis Southwest, won three. But these all happened before True Team competition began in 1973, when a school could win a championship with only a doubles team or just a singles player. For example, singles champions Myron Lieberman of St. Paul Central in '35 and Brad Pitney of Minneapolis Washburn in '45 earned the only points for their schools and thus earned them state titles. Yes, I know, Rochester is included and they won titles before '73 as well; but they dominated Minnesota tennis from the early 1950s to the mid-60s and they have made six more trips to state between 1973-2003. Other schools which made at least nine state appearances since '73 and merited consideration but were excluded for one or more reasons were the following:

Class AA

Duluth East—a very strong team from Section 7 which made eleven state tourney appearances but never won a state title.

Hibbing/Hibbing-Chisholm—another power from Section 7 which made thirteen state tournament appearances but, as with Duluth East, never won a championship.

Hutchinson—ten State appearances, no titles.

Virginia—Section 7 school that made seven state appearances as a AA school and three as a Class A school. Again, Virginia did not win a championship.

Class A

Crookston—from Section 8. Advanced to State ten times but finished no higher than third.

Litchfield—made nine appearances and won one championship (in 1989).

Winona Cotter—from Section 1, Cotter appeared at State nine times and won one championship (in 1999).

In addition to these teams, others have met some of the benchmarks and won championships and/or dominated for just a few years. One such team was Austin, which won one state title (1969) in the days before True Team competition and one Class AA championship in '82. Under coach Keith Paulson the Packers were always competitive, winning three straight Section 1 titles from 1980-82 and almost always finishing near the top in the tough Big 9 conference.

Another worthy Class AA school was Bloomington Jefferson, which won two state championships under coach Tom Saterdalen (in 1994, '96) and gave Edina all the competition they wanted in the '90s.

Mounds View also deserves a mention for its eight state appearances, one a runner-up finish (to Edina in 1988), a 1990 championship, and consistently strong teams in the late '80s to the present. One must also not overlook Stillwater, which, under the direction of Bill Herzog and then Chuck Anderson, made seven state tourney appearances from 1986-97, finishing as runner-up twice and winning one championship under Anderson (in '97). And Wayzata, like the swift passing of a meteor in the night sky, enjoyed its own brief run in the 1990s, winning two state championships (1993, '99) under coach Roger Lipelt and finishing second in its other three state appearances.

On the Class A side, Staples-Motley won two championships in back-to-back years (1990-91) but made only four trips to State. St. Paul Academy, which advanced to State four times as a Class AA school and eleven times as a Class A school (where it won one championship in 1993), has been a strong team going back to the late 1960s and early '70s when it competed in independent-school competition. Coach Cliff Caine built the program and a succession of coaches kept SPA's strong tradition going. But it won only one title, so based on the important criteria of "having won three titles," it is excluded.

Finally, this team may have the best reason to file a grievance, namely Breck. Though the Mustangs won four Class A championships from 1995-2001, they only advanced to State seven times and they had what one might call a revolving-door coaching situation with at least four different individuals at the helm during those years: John Severn, Louis Gulliou, P. J. Priest, and Katie Queenan (under whom they won two of their four titles). And while they were a dominant Section 3 team during these seven years, theirs was also a brief run.

So that leaves five elite teams that meet most or all of the criteria of dynasty teams mentioned earlier: winning three or more team titles, dominating section competition, being competitive over a long period of time, making ten or more state appearances, having stability in coaching, and receiving exceptional support from the community. These favored five are, once again, Edina, Blake, Rochester, St. Cloud Tech, and Blue Earth.

(For more on the coaches mentioned in this chapter, see Chapters Two and Three. And for more on the state champions from these schools, see Chapters Four, Five, and Six.)

EDINA

At the head of the class, our tennis valedictorian, is Edina, a school that has so thoroughly dominated Minnesota tennis the past forty-four years (in both boys and girls play) that its accomplishments rival those of the best national high school powers. And as if winning a team title almost every other year since 1973 (twenty-one) wasn't enough, Edina has also produced thirteen singles champions who won seventeen titles and fifteen doubles teams which won sixteen titles (Jim Mitchell and Dave Mathews won two together). In perhaps the same way one associates Vienna with music and Florence with art, one associates Edina with tennis. When families move to the Twin Cities area and have sons or daughters who play tennis well, often they will purchase homes in Edina in order to give their children the best opportunities to compete and improve their tennis games. In recent years players have also transferred to Edina to be a part of the Edina tradition and mystique. And when players from visiting teams arrive at the courts for a match and glance up at that daunting list of state team and individual titles posted on a board, they're often beaten before the match begins.

So how did this first-ring suburban school, split for nine years (1973-81) into two high schools, Edina East and West, become the behemoth of Minnesota high school tennis? For starters it has had excellent coaches throughout the years, beginning with first coach Ted Greer in the spring of 1950. Like his successor, John Matlon, Greer is a member of the MN Tennis Coaches Hall of Fame.

Then, under Matlon's direction from 1957-77 the Hornets won fifteen Lake Conference championships, twelve District 18 and Region 5 titles, and eight state championships. A taskmaster who emphasized fundamentals and tactics, his training methods were legendary. Two-time state doubles champion Dave Mathews remembers how Matlon "got us in shape with wrestling

exercises, Hindu pushups, situps, and leg lifts. And we continued to do running and rope-jumping even before the State Tournament." Ted Taney, another state doubles champion, echoed Mathews' views: "He [Matlon] made us work hard and he worked so hard himself." Matlon, in a June 11, 1972, *Minneapolis Tribune* article, said about his philosophy, "These kids have to be in fantastic shape. If they're in shape, they'll be mentally alert... They'll be able to overcome an opponent because of their condition. When an opponent sees a shot that should be a definite point returned, it takes some of the steam out of him. We do a lot of calisthenics, running, and rope-jumping."

He also surrounded himself with capable assistant coaches such as Les Szendrey, who succeeded Matlon in 1978, and he developed a feeder system at the junior high level with top flight coaches such as Greer (who returned after a stint as principal). And despite his reputation for being a taskmaster, he was also a player-friendly coach, according to Szendrey. In support of this view, Mathews said, "He [Matlon] followed us all the way until he died. I received letters from him and he often called."

Following Matlon's path was not easy, but Szendrey became an able successor, serving as the master's assistant for several years and as head coach from 1978-87. A coach who emphasized tactics but also continued Matlon's tradition of focusing on basic fundamentals of the game, Szendrey thought of himself as a "player's coach" as well. During his ten years at the helm the Hornets captured four more state championships.

A young man from Northfield who had stayed home to play college tennis (at St. Olaf), Steve Paulsen took over for Szendrey in 1988. Just twenty-five years old and at the time a teaching pro at the Northwest Club in Richfield, Paulsen became better-known as the longtime coach of another dynasty squad, the Edina girls' team. However, he also inherited an extremely talented boys' team which won the state title his first year of coaching. In his six years as boys' coach, Edina won two more titles.

Then, in 1994, Gary Aasen assumed the mantle as head coach and, like Paulsen, soon led Edina to a championship in just his second year ('95). From this auspicious beginning, Aasen's teams have captured four more team titles, one of which occurred in a year when the Hornets were undefeated (2002). And while Aasen believed in establishing priorities for his players of (1) family, (2) school, and (3) tennis ("They must be honored and stay in that order"), he also continued the tradition of his predecessors of emphasizing fundamentals. Said Aasen, "Even in a short season some fundamental technical work must be done. You'll be rewarded for this in the following season—probably not the current one." Like Paulsen, Aasen was a teaching pro, so he was eminently qualified to provide this technical assistance to his players.

Including Ray Punkris, coach of Edina West's 1980 team champions, there have been just six Edina head coaches since Greer inaugurated the tennis program in 1950. These coaches have led Edina to their twenty-one state titles (15 in the True Team era). And though six were earned in the days when individuals scored points for their team, all those Edina teams were loaded with talent. For example, Edina's first championship team (in 1959) was led by singles champion Keith Butterfield and doubles runners-up (and '60 champions) Andy Goddard and Franz Jevne. The 1967-68 teams were led by Mathews and Mitchell—doubles champions both those years—and singles players Robb Jones (1966 singles champion and '67 singles runner-up) and Ted Warner (consolation singles champion in '68 and singles runner-up in '69). And the 1971-72 teams were made up of players who won the singles and doubles both years: Bob Amis ('71) and Craig Jones ('72) in singles, and Chris Barden and Ted Taney ('71) and Barden and Dixon Dahlberg ('72) in doubles.

So excellent coaching plays a significant role in creating dynasty teams, but even more importantly, there must be good players. One of my former Northfield coaching colleagues used to say, "Jimmy, you aren't going to win unless you have the horses." He's right, of course, and Edina has had its share of thoroughbreds that have kept it in front of the pack since 1959. That was the year Butterfield won five matches on the way to the school's first singles championship. His 10 points and the 9 earned by Jevne and Goddard (who finished second in the doubles) gave the Hornets 19 points and their first team title.

It would be six years before Edina won its next title, and that one had to be shared with North St. Paul in 1966. But once again the Hornets had a dominant player, singles champion Robb Jones. The next year ('67) Edina edged Lake Conference rival Minnetonka 20-15, then in '68 it scraped out a 23-22 victory over Rochester to claim its first undisputed, back-to-back titles. These were two strong teams featuring doubles champions Mathews and Mitchell, but in '67 Robb Jones earned 8 of Edina's 20 points by finishing second to Rochester Mayo's Rob Daugherty. And in '68 Ted Warner earned 3 points to add to the 12 earned by Mathews and Mitchell. Warner's was the deciding point in the Hornet's 23-22 victory over Rochester Mayo. After losing his first-round match to Dan Halvorsen of Owa-

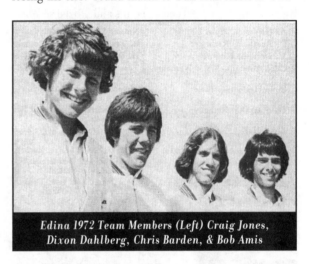

Edina 1972 Team Members (Left) Craig Jones, Dixon Dahlberg, Chris Barden, & Bob Amis

tonna 6-3, 6-2, Warner told *Minneapolis Tribune* writer Nolan Zavoral, "I was really down... All I could think about was that the team needed me in the championship bracket and that I let them down. But my coach (John Matlon) told me to forget the loss and concentrate on future matches" (June 9, 1968). Battling back through the consolation draw, Warner beat Dave Kubes of North St. Paul in his final match to secure the 23rd point for his team.

So these 1967-68 teams were not just one-note wonders that won because a doubles team or a singles player earned all the team's points. In fact, these and most of the Edina teams in the '60s were strong up and down the lineup, for between 1962 and '69 the Hornets won 63-straight Lake Conference dual meets.

After one-point losses to Austin in the state finals in 1969 (12-11) and Robbinsdale Cooper in '70 (16-15), the dynasty shifted into a higher gear, for the teams from 1971-72, it could be argued, were two of the most dominant in state high school history. Loaded with talent, these pre-1973 teams swept both the singles and doubles titles and delivered knockout punches to its competitors. In 1971 the Hornets got revenge on Cooper, the second-place team and 1970 champions, doubling up the score on them (32-16). That year Bob Amis won the singles championship and Craig Jones finished third. Chris Barden and Ted Taney won the doubles.

Then, in the second-most dominant performance at a State Tournament in the days before True Team competition (Rochester had beaten Hibbing 44-12 in 1950), the Hornets once again earned 32 points and blitzed second-place St. Cloud Tech (which had just 12 points). And once again Edina's thoroughbreds raced to the finish line, with Barden winning the doubles—this time with Dixon Dahlberg—and a teammate, Craig Jones, taking the singles. Amis finished third. As in the previous year, the doubles

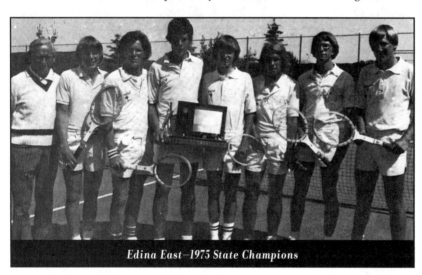

Edina East–1975 State Champions

team earned 15 points, the singles champion 10, and the third-place singles finisher 7.

In the first year of MSHSL True Team play (1973), Edina, led by '72 singles champion Craig Jones, stung Little Falls 5-0 in the first round, scraped by Rochester Mayo 3-2 in the semis, then edged White Bear Lake 3-2 to claim the title. This would be the first of sixteen True Team titles Edina would win, and though the Hornets had a strong squad the next year, Minnetonka won the '74 title. In '75, now as Edina East, the Hornets buzzed through the draw, winning all three matches by 5-0 scores and completing

an undefeated season in which its closest call was a 3-2 win over Minnetonka in a tournament in Austin. The Hornets were led by No. 1 player Greg Swendseen, who finished runner-up in singles to Mark Wheaton, and doubles champions Scott Nesbit and Bill Arnold.

The split into two high schools from 1973-81 diluted the talent in Edina; nonetheless, Edina teams still won state titles in 1978-79 and '81 (East) and '80 (West). Those East teams were led by Brian Johnson (1978-79 singles champion) and Bob Bateman ('81 singles champion) and doubles players such as '81 champions Bob Bordewick and Jeff Ecklund. And West's one great team was led by '80 singles champion Chris Combs.

The 1978 East team upset '77 champion Blue Earth in its first match at State (4-1), then struggled through two 3-2 matches, in the semis against Northfield and in the finals against Minneapolis Roosevelt. I recall, vividly, that my team (Northfield) lost that 3-2 semifinal match after leading 5-1 in the third set at first doubles.

Ninth grader Bob Bateman, a member of that first doubles team, recalls the final match against Roosevelt. "The win over Roosevelt was sweet, but it came at the expense of another of my best friends, Dave Schulze. Wicklund and Schulze, Larson and Ramsey [Mike, future NHL hockey star and now an assistant coach of the Minnesota Wild]. They had a great team. We were lucky we had Brian Johnson leading the way for us or we'd never have beaten them. And we were lucky we had Jim [Nesbit] and Bob [Bordewick] to pull us through in doubles."

No such struggles ensued in 1979, for the Hornets easily captured the Class AA championship in the first year of two-class competition. Called the "Sultan of Class AA" by *Star Tribune* writer Jon Roe, this team expected to win and they played with a bit of a swagger. Wearing shirts with "Sultan 79" emblazoned on them, these confident netmen swept all three opponents (Minneapolis Southwest, Willmar, and Virginia) by 5-0 scores on their way to the title. "We started wearing those shirts last year," said Brian Johnson [1978-79 singles champion], in the article by Roe. "It's kind of a joke. Each guy on this team is a sultan of something; Sultan of the court; Sultan of the round-house swing; Sultan of the double-fault; Sultan of truculency" ("Edina East Wins State Tennis Title 2nd Straight Year," June 3, 1979).

Unfortunately, the shift to a two-class system deprived the Hornets of what might have been their toughest competitor, Class A champion Blake, a 3-2 loser to East during the year. So dominant were the Hornets that they did not lose a set in their three state matches, and though happy with the win, coach Szendrey expressed empathy for strong teams from Region 6, such as Minnetonka and Edina West, that lost to East and did not make the tournament. Knowing that the competition at State would not be as challenging, Szendrey told Roe that "our biggest

Edina East–1978 State Champions

problem in winning the team title was in getting out of the woods—getting out of our regional. Once we were able to do that, my biggest job was in keeping the boys relaxed and not getting overconfident." Noting that his players would have liked a more competitive tournament, Szendrey also said, "It would have meant more to all of us if all of the best players and teams had been here." (*Minneapolis Tribune*, June 3, 1979).

With singles champion Chris Combs leading the way, Edina West won its only boys' tennis title in 1980, beating Thief River Falls 3-2 in the first round, Minneapolis Southwest 4-1 in the semis, and Anoka 3-2 in the finals. Memorable for an incredible weather delay (see Chapter

One), the '80 final came down to the wire, with West's third singles player Dan Moran outlasting Anoka's Jon Staton 6-3 in the third set to clinch the victory. An article in the May 29, 1980, *Minneapolis Tribune* by Howard Sinker reported that "Moran's teammates carried him off the court." After the match, the five foot nine, 135-pound Moran declared, "Wake me when this is over." He also said the delays and crowd didn't bother him.

Another article by Sinker attributed the success of Lake Conference schools such as Edina West to the fact that it "has courts on campus and B-squad and junior high feeder programs. The Cougars [West] can practice at school year 'round because the gymnasium has tennis court boundaries painted on its floor" (*Minneapolis Tribune*, May 31, 1980).

In 1981 the ball was back in Edina East's court, and they proved more than capable of handling it, defeating strong teams from Henry Sibley (3-2), Anoka (5-0), and St. Cloud Tech (3-2). But this had been in many respects a trying year for East and coach Szendrey, for they had to overcome one significant injury and a team "issue." In a June 5, 1981, *Minneapolis Tribune* article, staff writer Howard Sinker noted that the injury was to Bordewick, a senior who missed some time because he "hurt his back when he fell off a mechanical bull in Texas during spring break." The "issue," according to Sinker, had to do with senior Bob Barth, who returned to the lineup after being suspended from school for his part in publishing an "underground" newspaper and being benched by coach Szendrey for leaving town to visit colleges. So the final win over St. Cloud Tech, a team that had beaten East during the year, was achieved in spite of the above-mentioned distractions. The Hornets were led by a strong singles lineup of Batemen at No. 1, Bordewick at No. 2, and Ecklund at No. 3, and the doubles teams of Barth/Charlie Weigel at No. 1 and Mike Bennett/R. J. Matson at No. 2. *Tennis Midwest* publisher Bob Larson's son Cort was an alternate. In the individual competition

Bateman took the state singles crown and Bordewick and Ecklund teamed up to claim the doubles title, thus achieving another sweep for Edina.

After a five-year team drought, Edina put a stranglehold on the competition for three years (1987-89), dominating Minnesota tennis as perhaps no team has done since the advent of True Team play. These were years in which the Hornets' lineups were loaded with all-star talent: Paul Odland (1985 and '87 singles champion), Mike Terwilliger ('89 singles champion), Mike Husebo ('86 doubles champion), Charlie Eifrig and Jason Nasby ('88 doubles titlists), Tom Murphy (fourth in doubles in '87), Scott Campbell and Ben Friswold (fourth in doubles in '89), Peter Erickson (a strong singles player), Jon Eyberg (a key doubles performer), to name the most prominent of them.

It was perhaps fitting that Edina would win the title in 1987, for this was a historic year in state tennis. After a four-year hiatus, when the tournament consisted of just one class, the MSHSL once again (and for good) instituted

Edina–1987 State "AA" Champions

two-class competition. In addition, '87 was the first year 7-point matches were held in the Class AA tournament. So perennial power Edina flexed its muscles, showing off the depth needed to win a title when four points (out of seven) instead of three (out of five) were required and capturing its eleventh championship in the past twenty years. And though the Hornets blew through the competition during the year like a tornado, destroying every opponent in its

path, including Owatonna in the first round at State (a 7-0 win), it had some anxious moments in the state semifinal match with Mounds View, a 6-1 win. "The score doesn't tell the story," said coach Szendrey, in a *Minneapolis Star and Tribune* article. "It was closer than that" (June 5, 1987). Mounds View coach Jon Staton, the unfortunate third singles loser in the critical match in Anoka's 1980 title match with Edina West, agreed with Szendrey. "We could have won it," he said. "Our third doubles lost in three sets, first singles went 7-5 in the third, third singles lost 7-6, 7-5. That's close" (June 5, 1987).

And except for Peter Erickson's 2-6, 6-4, 6-4 win over Brian Boland (current U of Virginia mens' coach) at No. 4 singles, Edina won the other six matches in straight sets over St. Cloud Tech to claim the championship 7-0. Paul Odland won 6-2, 6-2 over Dave Jussila (future Gustavus star) at No. 1 singles; Mike Terwilliger took just forty minutes to defeat his No. 2 singles foe, Donn Robertson; and Jason Nasby polished off Mike Boland at No. 3 singles 6-2, 6-4. All three doubles also won in straight sets: Tom Murphy and Mike Husebo at No. 1, Charlie Eifrig and Tim Duffy at No. 2, and Jon Eyberg and Ben Friswold at No. 3.

A dejected Bill Ritchie, Tech coach, remarked to writer Thornton after the match, "We were shooting for Edina all season. We came in here thinking we could beat them, but they were just too good" (*Minneapolis Star and Tribune*, June 5, 1987). Indeed they were, and with that lineup they might have been the most dominant team in Minnesota history, for they had also demolished their Region 6 opponents and beaten top teams Mounds View, Tech, and Eden Prairie 7-0 during the season. It was also a fitting end to the twenty-nine-year coaching tenure of Szendrey.

Under new leadership in 1988, from first-year coach Steve Paulsen and new No. 1 Player Mike Terwilliger, the Hornets won again; but this victory was not by a team as dominant as the '87 one. With nine of the top ten players returning, coach Staton's undefeated Mounds View team (17-0) came into the tournament as the favorite. So after beating a very strong Blake team in the first round 7-0, then dispatching Hutchinson 6-1, the Mustangs got the revenge match they sought with Edina.

Meanwhile, the Hornets won their first two matches by 7-0 scores (over Roseville Area and St. Cloud Apollo), so they were on a roll that would continue in the final. Since an opening loss to Mounds View, Edina had won eighteen straight matches. Coach Paulsen told *Star Tribune* writer Roman Augustoviz, "In the long run that loss was a real good thing. Mounds View was ranked No. 1 all season long; it took the pressure off us and the guys came in here hungry" (June 10, 1988).

A quick start fueled the Hornets in this final match. "We won six out of seven first sets. But I knew we would come out smoking," remarked Paulsen. "I told the guys that we had to get right on top of them. A point here or there could make a big difference. We started well and closed it out," said the coach (June 10, 1988). Edina's doubles (Eifrig and Nasby, Campbell and Chris Robinson, and Eyberg and Friswold) played especially well, and the Hornets quickly took a 5-1 lead before Mounds View's Brian Benkstein rallied for a three-set win over Peter Erickson to make the final score 5-2. So second-rated Edina completed the year with a 19-1 record and also captured the school's seventh team sports title during the 1987-88 school year, a state record for one year.

The Hornets completed their singular three-peat in 1989 with wins over three formidable opponents: Mounds View (5-2) and St. Cloud Tech again (4-3), and Blake (6-1). These victories gave Edina a 22-0 record for the year and an exalted place in the record books, for this was its fifteenth state title. And even though the Hornets were the top-rated team coming into the tournament, their three opponents did not roll over and play dead just because they were up

against a dynasty team. Mounds View, which would next year win the title it had coveted after four frustrating years (upending Edina in the semis and St. Cloud Tech in the 1990 finals), took two points against Edina. And second-ranked St. Cloud Tech nearly pulled off an upset, falling to the Hornets 4-3 in the semis. Edina's No. 2 singles player, Peter Erickson, who lost the only point in the final match (a 6-1 Edina victory over Blake), won the clinching point against Tech. *Star Tribune* writer Roman Augustoviz said of this match, "His [Erickson's] three-set triumph... gave the Hornets (21-0) a shot at winning their third straight title. Erickson once again beat Brian Boland 5-7, 7-5, 7-5 for the deciding point in the Hornets' 4-3 victory over St. Cloud Tech" (June 9, 1989). This semifinal dogfight with Tech was Edina's closest match of the season, and coach Steve Paulsen was somewhat surprised. "We had beaten them 6-1 before, although a lot of the matches were close.

Edina—1989 State "AA" Champions

Maybe our players underestimated them. But especially in doubles, they played fantastically" (June 9, 1989).

Of Erickson's match against Boland, Paulsen recalled, in the aforementioned article, "Peter is known as a three-set player and I think that gave him the experience to pull it out. He's a gutty player, one you want in a match where one shot here and there can decide it. And Peter made the shot of the tournament, a backhander down the line on the dead run at 4-4 in the third set. If he had missed it, he would have been down 4-5 but, instead, it pulled him to deuce." Erickson (25-2 on the season) called that game a turning point. "He had a lot of chances to hold. But I broke him right there" (June 9, 1989).

Tech co-head coach Jerry Sales was proud of his team, acknowledging that his lads "played as well as we could" and lamenting that "we were just one or two steps away." But he also took consolation in knowing that "a lot of people told me it was one of the greatest tournament matches that they had ever seen. And for us it was the final. We had been rated No. 2, and we showed that's where we belong" (*Star Tribune*, June 9, 1989).

But it was not the final, and Edina still had to dispose of a pesky young Blake team led by sophomore Chris Laitala and a team made up solely of sophomores and juniors. This they did, winning 6-1 by sweeping the doubles and taking three of the four singles. The feature singles match was at No. 1, where senior Terwilliger (who would go on to win his only singles title two days later) upended defending Class AA champion Laitala 6-4, 6-4.

One could make a convincing case that these 1987-89 Edina teams, and the '86 team, were perhaps the greatest in Minnesota boys' tennis history, for had three top-ranked players not moved to Minnehaha Academy in '86, Edina would most likely have had a four-year championship run. Given that strong Lake Conference teams such as Eden Prairie, Minnetonka, and emerging powers such as Bloomington Jefferson stood in their way of even advancing to State, this run was all the more remarkable. And when they got to State they weren't playing cupcakes, for they still had to overcome powers such as St. Cloud Tech, Blake, and Mounds View.

In 1990 the Hornets made it back to the tournament, but Mounds View finally knocked them off en route to its first team championship; so Edina had to settle for third place, its lowest finish since '86.

After fighting its way through Region 6 combatants for seven straight years (1984-90), the Hornets were taken out by Eden Prairie in '91. Yet under the leadership of seniors Scott Sanderson (1991-92 Class AA singles champion) and Tom Danford and Scott Riley ('92 doubles champions) and junior Marcelo Borrelli ('93 Class AA singles champion), Edina captured its sixteenth state title in '92, though not without some controversy and difficulty. The controversy centered on Borrelli, who transferred

from Hill Murray to play his final two years of tennis at Edina. Stillwater coach Bill Herzog criticized the state's open enrollment policy and groused, in an article by Brian Wicker, that "it [open enrollment] really destroyed the tennis season in the state of Minnesota, as far as I'm concerned. Twenty teams had a chance to win it all—until the first of November (when Borelli transferred)" (*Star Tribune*, June 5, 1992). Edina coach Steve Paulsen did not want to be drawn into the argument, though he also had reason to play the "what if?" game. "What if we had Tom Moe and he hadn't had elbow surgery? The doubles teams and the other singles players still have to perform and they proved today they could win it," Paulsen responded. "Moe might have played third or fourth singles, but he missed the entire season" (June 5, 1992).

That "today" match was the semifinal with Stillwater, so the controversy continued on the courts. This also proved to be Edina's most difficult match of the tournament, for they had beaten Duluth East 6-1 in the quarterfinals and then handled St. Cloud Tech 6-1 in the finals. Stubborn Stillwater fought hard, but Edina prevailed 4-3. In the finals Sanderson and the No. 1 doubles team of Adam Lofthagen and Scott Riley quickly won their matches, then Borrelli at No. 2 singles and the No. 2 doubles team of Brett Pauley and John Sauer also won, clinching the title for the Hornets. The top-rated team all year, Edina lived up to its billing and finished the season with a 21-1 record.

Until Stillwater upset Wayzata in the 1997 final, teams from Section 6 won the next four titles. Wayzata captured the '93 title and Bloomington Jefferson won in 1994 and '96. Edina, however, won just one of those championships, that one in '95, a year in which they did not qualify a single player or doubles team for the individual tournament. In that '95 season, after upsetting heavily favored Jefferson in the region finals 4-3, the Hornets, with a lineup made up of relatively unknown players, nonetheless won their three state tournament matches with relative ease. Led by second-year coach Gary Aasen, Edina completed the season with a fine 18-3 record. First they took out Roseville Area 7-0, then knocked off Virginia 5-2 in the semis, and won the title with a 5-2 triumph over St. Cloud Tech, a team they had also beaten 5-2 in an early-season non-conference encounter. In the championship match, singles victories by No. 1 player Eric Koch, No. 2 Derek Brandt, and No. 4 Mike Underwood and the Nos.1 and 2 doubles teams of Marty Senn-Chris Skeffert and Ian Campbell-Erich Schellhas gave the Hornets their five points. Usually an Edina championship team had at least one individual champion on the roster, but this team had none. In fact, only one player from this team ever advanced to play in the individual tournament, 1996 state singles runner-up Derek Brandt.

After this anomalous win in 1995 (anomalous at least for Edina), the Hornets claimed yet another title in '98 with a potent lineup led by '98 singles champion and No. 1 player Cesar Vargas, transfer and eighth-grade phenom D. J. Geatz (2000 singles champion) at No. 2 singles, senior Karl Wilber (future St. Olaf player) at No. 3 singles, and ninth grader Justin Gaard (future two-time singles champion) at No. 4 singles. Having lost just one match during the season, the Hornets came into the tournament as favorites and they did not disappoint. They were so dominant that they lost only one of twenty-one matches during the team competition and only four of forty-five sets. First they stomped on Chaska 7-0 and followed that up with a 7-0 semifinal romp over St. Cloud Tech. In the final they lost only at No. 3 doubles in a 6-1 triumph over a strong Section 1 team from Red Wing.

And as in many other years, the competition at State was not as challenging as that in Section 6, for the Hornets had to avenge a 4-3 regular-season loss to Jefferson in the region finals. In that match D. J. Geatz beat Phil Woo to give the Hornets a 4-3 win over the Jaguars. Nevertheless, coach Aasen was still concerned going into the tournament. In a June 4, 1998, *Star Tribune* article, he told Jim Paulsen, "After coming out of our section, which is so tough, I was a little concerned about getting the guys up to

play in the State Tournament. But they were ready to play." Vargas, a senior foreign exchange student from Mexico, came out firing in the Red Wing match against Jesse Plote and breezed to a 6-1, 6-1 win. He broke Plote in the first game and, "Using a variety of powerful groundstrokes, feathery drop shots and a high-kicking second serve, Vargas was in control the entire match," the *Star Tribune* article noted. Red Wing coach Tom Gillman (a former Breck High School and Stout State player) expressed pride in his team's effort, but he acknowledged "There's no doubt Edina has the best team and deserved to win" (June

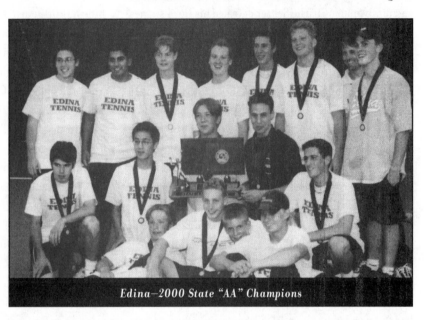
Edina—2000 State "AA" Champions

4, 1998). With those four singles players leading the way and sweeping their three team matches, the Hornets completed the season with a stellar 21-1 record. They also received solid play from the doubles teams of sophomores Jon Seltzer and Brad Anderson (1999 doubles champions) at No. 1, juniors Nick Brandt and Brady Seeman at No. 2, and ninth grader Drew Levin and sophomore Sean Borg at No. 3. Aasen noted that five of these players eventually went on to play Division 1 tennis.

Nineteen and 100 in 2000. These were the relevant numbers defining the Edina champions this year. This nineteenth tennis title was the 100th state championship for the school, and it happened in the first year of the new millennium. Unlike the unheralded 1995 team, this Edina squad resembled the '98 champions in that it had a star-studded lineup led by future two-time singles champion Justin Gaard. The Hornets, stung by '99 champion Wayzata in the '99 Section 6 final, more than made up for that loss by applying huge stings to its three opponents at State in 2000 (as noted on page one of this chapter).

With a potent singles lineup of Gaard (a junior) at No. 1, senior Brad Anderson at No. 2, and 2000 doubles champions and brothers Jon (a senior) and Charlie Seltzer at Nos. 3 and 4, Edina won all four singles matches in the finals against Red Wing in straight sets. All told, these four singles players gave up only 12 games in eight sets; and ninth grader Charlie Seltzer defeated his No. 4 singles opponent 6-0, 6-0. In doubles sophomore Roy Bryan (a 2001 doubles champion) and his first doubles partner, junior Drew Levin, won in three sets; and eighth grader Chris Sherman and sophomore Gavin Lee (Bryan's 2001 partner) won easily at No. 2 doubles. Edina's only loss was at No. 3 doubles, where senior Sean Borg and sophomore Adi Zhuravel were beaten by the undefeated Red Wing team of Adam Witt and Ben Ryan. *Star Tribune* staff writer Jim Paulsen commented about what teams such as Red Wing tried to do to combat Edina's singles strength: "The strategy most teams adopted when they faced Edina was to load up and try to win all three doubles matches, then hope to emerge with a singles point. With Red Wing's depth in doubles, it wasn't out of the question that the Wingers could defeat the Hornets" (June 8, 2000). But it didn't work for Red Wing and it didn't work for other teams either. As Justin Gaard said, "If teams want to stack their doubles, that's fine with us. We'll still probably win the singles. We usually only lose about two games a set" (June 8, 2000). In the South match they did even better than that, losing only 4 of 52 games in their singles matches.

And even though this was a historic victory for the Edina netmen—the school's 100th state title—that accomplishment took second place behind erasing the memory of last year's loss to Wayzata. Coach Aasen said this about his team's motivation this year: "We were aware of that, sure, but I don't think winning the 100th was our main motivation. We wanted to win this more for ourselves" (*Star Tribune*, June 8, 2000). Edina's finals win over Red Wing gave them 18 team victories on the season, against just 1 loss, that to Wayzata 4-3.

With a young team that returned seven of ten starters, it would have been safe to bet on Edina in 2001 to repeat as champions. Unfortunately for the Hornets, they were not able to handle the upstart Minneapolis South Tigers led by former Edina netman D. J. Geatz; so they geared up in '02 for what would be the best season of coach Aasen's tenure. And once again the bad memory of a loss the previous year animated the angry Hornets, that loss a thorough 6-1 drubbing at the hands of '01 champion South.

For a school so proud of its tennis tradition, losing so badly was an embarrassment, as coach Aasen noted in a June 8, 2000, article in the *Star Tribune* by Jim Paulsen: "That just doesn't happen at Edina. It was a wakeup call." So the Hornets, undefeated during the 2002 regular season and favored to win, blew through Henry Sibley in their first state match 7-0. But then they had to rely on their strong singles lineup to squeak through against Mounds View in the semis. The Mustangs won all three doubles, but Edina's singles players sent the Hornets into the finals by taking the four points needed to win the match.

So after this 4-3 scare, the Hornets came out buzzing in the final against Eden Prairie, winning all but the No. 1 singles match (where Charlie Seltzer lost to 2003 singles champion Nick Edlefsen). Despite this not unexpected loss at No. 1 singles, Edina had no trouble with Eden Prairie. Singles players Chris Sherman (a sophomore) at No. 2, senior Adi Zhuravel at No. 3, and sophomore Andy Bryan at No. 4 won in straight sets, as did the doubles teams of Gavin Lee and Roy Bryan at No. 1 (both seniors), junior Scott Leininger and senior Mike Krasno at No. 2, and senior David Shapiro and sophomore Reid Mason at No. 3.

Roy Bryan and Lee, one of the few true doubles teams to win a state individual doubles championship (in 2001), also harked back to that Minneapolis South loss last year as motivation. "I was mad for a long time after that," Bryan said. According to the previous *Star Tribune* article by Paulsen, "Lee kept a copy of the result, given to all team members by Aasen [coach Gary] in a motivational ploy..., in his racquet bag." Said Lee, "Getting the state title back was our whole goal. We knew we were favored, but we could look at that piece of paper and know we weren't defending champions" (June 8, 2002).

Thus the favored team held serve, so to speak, and finished the season with an unblemished 21-0 record. And with topnotch singles players such as Chris Sherman, Charlie Seltzer, and Andy Bryan returning, Edina would be the odds-on favorite for the seventy-fifth state high school tennis championships in 2003. But winning this twenty-first title was not as easy as the pundits imagined it would be. Even coach Aasen had doubts about his '03 team. He admitted, in a June 5, 2003, article by Jim Paulsen, "that he wondered about his team's ability to win another state championship" (*Star Tribune*). Even though they were the unquestioned favorites with high expectations, there were some concerns. "If you would have asked me, in the middle of the season, I would have said I had some doubts," Aasen said. "We showed the potential at times, but I didn't see as many good things as I had in other years." Recognizing that he could rely on his outstanding singles players (Seltzer, Sherman, Bryan, and Leininger), Aasen nonetheless realized that he needed to develop his young doubles teams if the Hornets were to succeed. Fretting about the many unknowns with this year's squad, Aasen said, "We had five new role players to try to fit in" (*Star Tribune*, June 5, 2003).

So to take some of the pressure off the newcomers, Aasen did not mention the State Tournament during the year; instead he set reasonable goals for his team: (1) winning the Edina Invitational, (2) winning the conference title, and (3) improving doubles play. Said he, "We talked about everything except the State Tournament. Didn't bring it up once until we got here" (June 5, 2003).

Ironically, the coach felt that a regular season-ending loss to eventual Class A champion Blake (only the Hornets' second loss) gave his team the confidence it needed. In that June 5 article by Paulsen, Aasen said, "We didn't win, but we competed like gangbusters. That's what I needed to see. I knew then that we would be ready" (*Star Tribune*, June 5, 2003). So with four singles stallions and a rapidly improving doubles lineup, Edina captured the 2003 title, though not without some anxious moments. Right out of the gate they had a tough match against perennial power Mounds View, one of their toughest competitors over the past fifteen years or so. In beating the Mustangs 4-3, Edina needed a stellar performance from its No. 3

singles player, junior Andy Bryan. Playing behind talented teammates Seltzer and Sherman, Bryan had cruised through the year without a loss and often without much opposition. That would change in the Tuesday quarterfinal with Mounds View, for with the match tied at 3-3 and all the pressure on him, Bryan came through. In another *Star Tribune* article, staff writer Jim Paulsen noted that Bryan struggled in his first set against Julian Tokarev, but "he roared through the second by playing textbook serve-and-volley tennis." The result was a 7-5, 6-1 win that sent Edina into the semis on Wednesday. Coach Aasen praised Bryan, saying, "You saw some of those volleys he made. You couldn't play much better than that." Bryan himself seemed a bit surprised at how well he played. With a smile on his face he said, "There were times in that second set when I felt I couldn't do anything wrong" ("Bryan Powers Hornets," June 4, 2003). Edina's points were earned by its four singles players in this crucial match.

Up next was Minneapolis Southwest, whom the Hornets dispatched 5-2—losing only at No. 2 and 3 doubles, then came Section 8 champion Orono in the finals. Again the Hornets prevailed by a 5-2 score, winning all four singles and No. 3 doubles. And once again the Hornets' strong singles players (Seltzer, Sherman, Bryan, and Leininger) won easily, taking every match in straight sets. At No. 3 doubles Tom Brunkow and Robert Sandberg triumphed in straight sets. Commenting about the title, Seltzer, a senior who was a key member of three state championship teams, said, "We knew that we [the singles players] would have to carry things for awhile because we had some inexperience at doubles. We took some pressure off them so they could get their confidence up" (June 4, 2003). The result of this combination, a nearly unbeatable singles lineup and competitive doubles teams, was a 21-2 record and yet another jewel in the crown for Edina, the "Titletown of Tennis" in Minnesota.

How then does one account for such a successful program, one of the most dominant in state high school sports history? What's the recipe and what are the ingredients?

For starters the first ingredient was cordon bleu coaching, starting with first chef/coach Ted Greer. When Edina High School opened in 1949, he was hired to teach math; but he was also asked to start up the tennis and hockey programs. During the first two years (1950-51) there were no high school or public courts in Edina so, according to Greer, "we practiced and played our matches on courts in Minneapolis that no one else used because they were in such bad shape." Greer also noted that until the school built five excellent courts his third year, "all our players were beginners." Soon, Greer said, "We began to get some of the better players but none with tournament experience." His last year ('56) the Hornets tied St. Louis Park for the Lake Conference championship, and so he left the program in good shape for coach Matlon.

Though Matlon had not played tennis as a youngster, he had been a champion wrestler in college, so he knew what it took to train players for competition. In addition, he was blessed to have as his assistant for many years a man who had been a top player in his native Hungary, Les Szendrey. After Matlon retired in 1977, Szendrey took the reins for ten years and Ray Punkris took over at Edina West.

Since 1988 Edina's coaches have been young and successful teaching pros Steve Paulsen and Gary Aasen. It's not surprising that the school eventually hired these two top teaching pros, for many schools have been taking that route the past twenty years or so as more indoor clubs began springing up and more pros became available to coach high school teams. Even during Matlon's latter years and throughout Szendrey's tenure, Edina's players received coaching from their tennis pros to supplement that which they received during the season. The final tallies of championships under these coaches would be Matlon (eight), Szendrey (four), Punkris (one), Paulsen (three), and Aasen (five).

So if coaching is the first ingredient, what's the second? Maybe in Edina it's support from the parents and the community, for once the school began to establish a tennis reputation, more parents began sending their kids to summer tennis camps and paying for indoor court time and lessons in the winter. Some critics might argue that Edina parents could at times be a bit more fanatic in their devotion to their children's tennis lives than they should have been, but there's no denying that the Edina program has enjoyed extraordinary financial and emotional support from the community over the years.

A third ingredient is one that took a few years to develop but is now a huge factor in Edina's success: tradition. It's the Edina mystique that comes from a long history of success. There are the intimidating signs on the tennis courts, the canny coaches, the twenty-one state team titles, and the confident and fundamentally sound players. But there's also a tradition that has enabled the school to attract families with tennis-playing children in this age of open enrollment. For example, the transfers of top players such as Jason Nasby, Marcelo Borrelli, Jon Seltzer, and D. J. Geatz helped the Hornets win state titles but also rankled many of its conference, region, and state tournament foes, not to mention the teams from which they transferred. In addition, that mystique produced what I'll call the "fear factor." In much the same way that a home game might be worth several points to the home team in basketball, so the Edina mystique was probably worth a few points and even sometimes games to Edina because opponents might have thought, "Oh, no, we're playing Edina tomorrow!"

Another ingredient was that of internal competition. These Edina teams had so many talented players that they constantly pushed each other to get better, both in practice and in face-to-face competition. For example, often they had to play each other in district/region (subsection/section) competition in order to advance to the next level of play. And more often than not their challenge matches or mini-competitions in practice were more challenging than matches with players from opposing teams. In addition, competition for positions on the team was always fierce; players who couldn't crack the varsity at Edina would have played up in the lineup of most any other team in the state.

One final ingredient is competition from unexpected sources such as volunteer hitting partners. When I coached at Northfield, I often invited college players from St. Olaf and Carleton, alumni players, and local adult players such as then Carleton mens' coach Bob Bonner and his teaching colleague, Steve Kelly, to hit with our players before region and State play. These volunteers provided excellent sparring partners for our players, and Edina had those same resources available in the form of alumni players. Gary Aasen, noting the important role they played in his team's successes, said, "We always had former players hanging around. Their presence and them hitting with our guys helped carry our teams during the 1998-2003 seasons. They came up every year and beat up on our guys and even went to our team banquets. They had a lot to do with the psyche and chemistry of our teams."

But not many teams had another kind of volunteer, the one who would hang around the courts looking for a game with young, spirited high school players. In Edina's case it was Per Palm, an accomplished player who competed in NWLTA summer tournaments, achieving rankings as high as No. 1 in 60 singles and several No. 2 rankings in the 60s and 70s.

Both Scott Nesbit (1975 doubles champion) and Bob Bateman (1980 singles champion) spoke admiringly of Palm and recalled their impromptu matches with him. Bateman called him "the ideal practice partner for a young tennis player. Mr. Palm was an avid player and very, very consistent. To beat him you had to figure out a way to win because he wasn't going to lose." Nesbit remembers Palm, a Swedish immigrant, as a guy "who would play anybody, any time. He was a court rat. You would hear this pounding on the backboard and then his voice saying, 'Hey, boys, anybody want to play?' He had a horrible serve, but he was very crafty, he hit with lots of spin, and he got tons of balls back. He was a hurdle you had to overcome, like beating my dad for the first time."

Nesbit offered one other reason why those Edina teams in the 1960s and '70s were so successful. "There was not a lot of pressure to get jobs. We weren't mowing lawns or working at a hardware store. Instead we were out playing tennis—it was kind of our job."

In the end the Hornets could be the poster child for Hillary Clinton's mantra, "It takes a village to raise a child." or in this case, a tennis program.

BLAKE

Things were going smoothly during the 1984 State Tournament on the outdoor courts at 98th Street Racquet Club on Tuesday, June 7. Sunny skies greeted the competitors for the 9 AM matches featuring Blake versus Apple Valley and defending champion St. Cloud Tech versus Edina. With the sun beaming down on them, undefeated tournament favorite Tech and the small independent school of Blake warmed up, both advancing to the finals with 4-1 victories. Blake, which had won three previous state titles, but all in the incipient small-school tournaments which were suspended from 1983-86 after just four years of competition (1979-82), was seeking to become just the second Class A school to win a state championship against the big boys.

And things continued to go well for the upstart Bears in the finals against Tech until the sun disappeared and a storm blew in, threatening to spoil the party. When the rains came, Blake's No. 1 and 2 singles players, senior Tom Price and junior Steve Sell had beaten their St. Cloud opponents (senior Pat Dunn and junior John Lauerman) and Tech had won both the doubles in this 5-point match. Eventual 1984 doubles champions, junior Sean Potter and sophomore Todd Schlorf defeated Blake's No. 1 doubles team of seniors Walter Barry and Shekhar Sane; and Tech's No. 2 team of senior Jay Schlorf and junior Eric Wolfe beat Blake's team of junior Bill Schmoker and

Blake–1984 State Champions

ninth grader D. Jackson. So the match, tied 2-2, would be decided by the No. 3 singles match between Blake's junior Ted Bonniwell and Tech's precocious ninth grader, Dave Jussila, a future Gustavus top player.

An article by Tom Briere in the *Minneapolis Star and Tribune* described the drama of this ultimate match between Bonniwell and Jussila, tied at 7-6, 3-6 and at the point when a thunder and lightning storm came through: "the storm hit, chasing the combatants from the outside courts at 98th Street five miles down the road to the indoor courts at the Burnsville Club... The 6-foot-6 Bonniwell took the 11th game in 20 points [breaking Jussila], then held service to close out the limping Jussila in the 12th game" [7-5] (June 8, 1984). Adding to the drama of the weather and the importance of this match was the condition of Jussila's leg. Apparently he had experienced left leg cramps on the ride to Burnsville and was icing his leg in the car. In addition, there was some earlier drama surrounding Blake coach John Hatch and his son Andy, a senior. In the semifinal match between St. Cloud Tech and Edina, Andy played first doubles for the Hornets. One wonders if the coach would have preferred playing against his son's team in the finals. MSHSL tournament manager Orv Bies said, "We've never had so much drama in the State Tournament" (June 8, 1994).

But the climax of the drama was a surprise. Blake had upset Tech and won a state championship against the Goliaths of Minnesota tennis, schools with much larger enrollments than theirs. First they had beaten Hibbing 4-1 in the quarters, then they took out Apple Valley in the semis also by a 4-1 score, and of course they vanquished Tech in that 3-2 tense final, completing their magical season with a 21-3 record.

While Blake had won three previous state tournament titles in Class A, this one was special; for it put them in the company of only one other Class A school which had won the tournament against larger schools, Blue Earth in 1977. (Eventually two other schools would win titles against the big schools, Minnehaha Academy in '86 and Blake again in '91.) In some respects, however, this 1984 victory was no fluke, no dark horse triumph, for Blake had always been able to compete against the bigger schools and coach Hatch even elected to compete against Class

AA schools for several years before finally shifting back to Class A in '92.

All told Blake has won twelve titles (two in AA and ten in A) and has made a total of twenty-three state tournament appearances (two more than Edina) as a team since True Team play began in 1973 (seven appearances in AA and sixteen in A). Clearly, it deserves the label "dynasty team."

But even before Blake became a state power in the late 1970s, it had been a school noted for tennis. For example, the Bears tied St. Paul Academy (SPA) for the team title in the first combined parochial/private Minnesota Independent High School League (MIHSL) tournament in 1968. With Shep Harder beating George Pesar of SPA 7-5, 6-8, 6-3 in singles and John Savage and John Massie of Blake finishing second in doubles to SPA's Tom Wood and Rob Pesar, Blake and SPA each finished with nine points. In '71 the Bears, on the strength of a doubles title won by Peter Moos and Peter Stalland (over Paul Muesing and Dave Kaiser of New Ulm Luther), claimed the outright MISL championship (14-6 over Luther). So that would give them fourteen titles if we added these two to the twelve earned in MSHSL competition.

But there's more. In the mid-to-late-1940s there were some outstanding players from Blake who won championships in the Interscholastic Tournaments held following the State Tournaments. Perhaps the best of these players was Henry Norton Jr., a 1948 Blake graduate who won the Interscholastic singles tournament in 1947 and '48 and finished second in singles in '45 and in doubles in '47 (with partner Henry Adams). Not only did he win these two singles titles, but in doing so he defeated two state high school champions: Pudge Whitcomb in 1947 (6-2, 6-2) and Edmund "Chiefie" Gould in '48 (6-4, 6-3). In addition, in '47 he led Blake to the team Interscholastic tennis title. Top high school players of the era such as '46 doubles champion Jack Thommen and '47 champion Bill Kuross both lauded Norton as one of the toughest players they competed against in the summer.

The No. 1 player his junior and senior years at Blake, Norton recalls that his teams (coached by Prescott Cleveland) were undefeated for three years, beating all the top MSHSL teams during those spring seasons. Unfortunately,

Blake was an independent school and at the time was not permitted to play in MSHSL-sanctioned tournaments, so they had no opportunity to win a State Tournament. Kuross, whom Norton called "the best guy I played in 1948," said that Norton had his own private grass court at home in Deephaven.

Another outstanding player from Blake's early years was Scott Donaldson (mentioned earlier in the profile of Jack Thommen), who also won the Interscholastic Tournament (in 1945) and led Blake to the team title that year, beating his then very young teammate Norton in the final 6-1, 6-0. The next year, though he did not win the singles, he and teammate Bill Taylor defeated the reigning state high school doubles champions Thommen and Gould 6-2, 6-3 to claim the Interscholastic doubles title. Donaldson, by the way, was the son of the owner of the famous Donaldson's Department Store.

And along with the aforementioned Henry Adams, another top Blake player from this era was Fred Boos, who as a sophomore won the final Interscholastic tournament singles title in 1949. This tournament was held in late August at Carleton College in Northfield. Later, another well-known Blake player was Dave Nash, perhaps the most successful adult male NWTA Section player in state history, winner of many national age-group titles.

But all of this was but a prelude of better things to come, for when coach John Hatch took over the reins in 1978, the Bears began what would become a twenty-five-year dynasty. Of course Hatch benefited from the tradition and success of earlier Blake teams which competed in the independent tournaments, and there were fine coaches before him as well. In fact, in what could perhaps be a *Guinness Book of Records* first, all the Blake coaches except current coach Ted Warner were English teachers. First there was Prescott Cleveland in the 1940s, then there was Bill Fisher, and finally Hatch's predecessor Keller Pollock. Even interim one-year coach Darrell McAnnany was a member of Blake's English department.

These coaches were all successful, but it is Hatch we remember as the one who guided Blake during its first glory years as a MSHSL team. During his sixteen years as head coach of the Bears (1978-94 with one year off for a sabbatical), his teams won 285 matches and lost just 49, an average of roughly 18 wins and 3 losses a year. In just his second year ('79) Blake won its first state title—in Class A during the first year of two-class play. Then, to put an exclamation mark on his extraordinary career, the Bears claimed the last of Hatch's seven championships his final year of coaching ('94), again a Class A title. During those sixteen years his teams also advanced to State fifteen times, finishing runners-up twice (once in Class AA) and third place two other times. Only twice did Hatch's teams fail to win a region title, and the year he was on sabbatical ('82) his assistant coach, McAnnany, took over and led the Bears to the Class A title.

Luckily for Blake, Hatch was succeeded by former Edina high school star and teaching pro Ted Warner, who has maintained the high standard of coaching established at Blake. And because he almost always inherited talented players as well, he has led Blake to four more Class A titles.

Thus, with just three coaches in twenty-six years (one of whom served for only a year), the Bears have captured twelve state team titles. So let's have a look at these championship teams, beginning with the 1979 squad that won the Class A title in the inaugural year of two-class

Blake—1979 State "A" Champions

competition. Surprisingly, especially in light of the fact that Blake had the top two singles players in Class A (singles champion Louie McKee and runner-up Tom Ferris), the Bears were only ranked No. 5 in the first coaches' poll. As the year progressed and Blake knocked off all of its Class A opponents, they would eventually move up to No. 1. With just two losses during the year, both 3-2 to Lake Conference powers Minnetonka and Edina East, the Bears entered the State Tournament as the clear favorite.

Had Blake competed in the Class AA tournament this year (won easily by Edina East), they would have given the Hornets their stiffest test. So it's not surprising that they cruised through the Class A draw to win the school's first MSHSL team championship. Led by top-ranked and No. 1 singles player McKee and No. 2 man Ferris, a future Carleton College player, the Bears defeated Staples 5-0 in the first round and pre-season favorite Blue Earth 4-1 in the semis. The win over Blue Earth set up a classic confrontation between teams coached by future Hall of Fame coaches, Cliff Caine of SPA and Hatch. This would be the only time these two coaches would match wits in a state finals match, and Hatch's Bears bested Caine's squad 4-1 to take home the first-place trophy, completing a terrific 19-2 season. Further evidence of Blake's strength as a team came two days later when McKee beat Ferris for the singles title and the Bears' Chuck Ankeyny and Dave Meyers finished third in the doubles competition. Other members of Blake's first championship team were, in alphabetical order, Rob Hudnut, Mark Jacobs, Derek Malmquist, Jay McLaughlin, and Mark Schulze.

After a second-place team finish in 1980 (behind Blue Earth), Blake claimed four state championships in the '80s, including the single-class title in '84 discussed at the beginning of this chapter. Led by No. 1 singles player Scott Card, a junior, in '81 Blake took its second Class A title by romping through the competition with the loss of just one point. First they dispatched Granite Falls 5-0, then they turned the tables on the team that had beaten them in 1980, Blue Earth, in the semis (4-1). In the finals they blanked Wadena 5-0. And though the Bears had been ranked second behind Blue Earth, it proved its mettle by defeating the Bucs handily. In addition, a regular-season 3-2 victory over '81 Class AA champion Edina

East served notice that Blake would be hard to beat. With a strong singles lineup of Card ('81 singles runner-up and '82 champion) at No. 1, senior Mark Jacobs at No. 2, and sophomore Scott Duncan ('82 singles runner-up and '83 doubles runner-up) at No. 3, and excellent doubles teams of senior Chuck Webster and Junior Barry Nordstrom at No. 1 and sophomore Jeff Goldenberg and ninth grader Walter Barry ('82 doubles runner-up) at No. 3, Blake finished the year with a 20-1 record.

After this best-ever season of Coach Hatch's career, he took a well-deserved sabbatical in 1982. However, the Bears were not hibernating; and under the direction of interim coach McAnnany the school won its third Class A state title. With nearly the entire cast returning from the '81 championship team, and with the addition of sophomore Tom Price, Blake once again defeated Wadena in the finals, this time 4-1. Unfortunately for Class A tennis fans, the top two teams did not meet in the final, so No. 1 Blake had to duel No. 2 Blue Earth in the first round, escaping with a 3-2 win. Number 3 singles player Price, 23-0 in singles during the year, won a key match against Blue Earth's Tim Weber and also defeated his No. 3 opponents in the team's semifinal 4-1 win over Pine City (Bill Nichols) and in the final against Wadena (Gary Pundt). Card and Duncan (at Nos. 1 and 2 singles) and Price led the way, but the doubles teams were also very strong: Walter Barry and Barry Nordstrom at No. 1 and Jeff Goldenberg and Shekhar Sane at No. 2.

And once again Blake players showed off their prowess in the individual tournament, as Card beat teammate Duncan in the singles final, Price and Walter Barry took second and Nordstrom and Goldenberg finished fourth in doubles.

Even though Hatch preferred competing against the smaller schools in order to give more kids a chance to compete, he had no choice in 1983, for there weren't enough small schools competing that year for two-class play. Despite having to compete against the big school grizzlies, the Bears more than held their own during this four-year interregnum of one-class play, advancing to State three of these four years. In '83 they finished third, in '85 they lost to champion St. Cloud Tech 3-2 in the first round, and (as described in the beginning of this report) in '84 they won the title. And had the dark horse Minnehaha Academy not stood in its way, Blake would have participated in the '86 tournament as well.

Back in the familiar territory of Class A competition in 1987, the Bears once again staked their claim as the alpha male of small-school tennis, taking home their fifth team trophy under coach Hatch. With just four schools entered in the Class A tournament, a consequence of the low number of small schools fielding tennis teams, Blake defeated a stubborn SPA 3-2 in its first match and perennial rival Blue Earth 4-1 in the finals. And, according to Hatch, the Bears won this title with depth. "We haven't anyone ranked in the top 25," said Hatch, in an article by Ralph Thornton in the June 5, 1987, *Star Tribune.* "Our doubles is strong [seniors Donald Jackson and Scott Diamond at No. 1 and seniors Chris Johnson and Tad Quill at No. 2], and we try to pick up a point in singles here and there. It's a great bunch of kids, but no stars. We're just a bunch of no-names," he said. Thornton begged to differ with Hatch's comment about no-names, saying, "Well, not exactly. Of the winning first doubles combination, Donald Jackson is a grandson of former Pillsbury CEO Robert Keith and partner Scott Diamond calls former Vikings mogul Max Winter 'Grandpa.' Third singles winner Scott Gage [a junior] is a grandson of multi-millionaire Curt Carlson" (June 5, 1987).

Blue Earth competed well but won only the No. 1 singles match in which top-ranked Class A player Roger Anderson beat Blake senior Jay Pearson. Junior James Moulton won his match at No. 2 singles, as did Gage at No. 3 singles and the two doubles teams. In the individual tournament Blake did not have a singles entrant, but Gage and Jackson teamed up and took second in the doubles (behind the champions from Blue Earth, Anderson and Jamie Schmitgen).

For the next four years, in part because he wanted to give his talented young players (such as Chris Laitala, Stewart Barry, Fergus Weir, Dryw Danielson, and

Alan Gilbert, all ninth graders in 1988) the best competition, coach Hatch opted to put his teams back in the cauldron with the big schools again. And each of those years the Bears advanced to State from Region 5AA, earning a runner-up finish in 1989 and, in an unprecedented accomplishment, winning the Big-School title in '91. This was unprecedented because only Blake among "small" schools captured <u>two</u> state titles in competition against larger schools (Blue Earth and Minnehaha Academy each won one).

And though they lost in the first round in both 1988 and '90, in both cases these were losses to top teams: runner-up Mounds View in '88 and Edina in '90 (4-3). In addition, in '88 Blake lost just three matches during the regular season, all 4-3 losses to top teams Edina, Hutchinson, and Robbinsdale Armstrong. So it was not a surprise to tennis aficionados around the state that Blake was a formidable opponent for anyone, and in '91 they proved they could cut down the tall trees in the tennis forest by capturing the Class AA title.

This 1991 team might have been the best of all of coach Hatch's teams, for it had a dynamite lineup which included the likes of No. 1 singles player Chris Laitala ('88 AA singles champion and two-time AA singles runner-up), the '91 doubles champions (seniors Stewart Barry and Fergus Weir), and future two-time class A singles champion Robert Keith. Laitala, Barry, Weir, Alan Gilbert, and Jeff Sell also provided senior leadership on a team which included younger players such as ninth-graders Keith and

Blake—1991 State "AA" Champions

Jon Saliterman and eighth grader Ben Wismer.

Both Blake and St. Cloud Tech proved they were the top teams in Class AA by overwhelming their opponents in the first two rounds and advancing to what promised to be a classic confrontation between a team strong in singles (Blake) and one strong in doubles (Tech). Blake had beaten Duluth East 7-0 and Eden Prairie 6-1, while Tech had methodically disposed of Stillwater and Hastings by 6-1 scores. So Tech knew it had to scrape out a singles win (which it had done in a regular-season match with Blake) and the Bears knew they had to win all four singles matches. In a coaching move that helped Blake hit the jackpot, coach Hatch brought Fergus Weir up from first doubles to play No. 4 singles (behind Laitala, Barry, and Keith); and sure enough, he won one of the crucial four singles points that gave Blake its 4-3 victory. Though Weir had known of this potential lineup switch long age, he told *Star Tribune* writer Brian Wicker that the enormity of the moment nearly overwhelmed him. "It hit me about 10 minutes before I went on court" (June 7, 1991), he said. So while Laitala and Barry won easily at Nos. 1 and 2 singles, both Keith (at No. 3 singles) and Weir lost their first sets, putting them both in quicksand and making Blake's chances look grim. Nevertheless, both pulled themselves out of the muck and onto the high ground, capturing the final two sets and earning Blake its sixth state title. Afterward Weir said, "I've waited four years for this. This is just unbelievable" (June 7, 1991). And that it was, for only four times had a small school toppled the giant redwoods as Blake had just done.

It would also be Blake's last (and Class A's last) championship won against the bigger schools. Opting for a "discretion is the better part of valor" approach, Coach Hatch decided it would be prudent for Blake to compete once again against schools its size in 1992. No doubt the loss of five key seniors from a potent '91 lineup figured into his decision (these included '88 singles champion Laitala and '91 doubles champions Barry and Weir), for his '92 team was a young squad with just one senior on the roster. And though the Bears' top players were mostly eighth to tenth graders, they had no trouble winning the team championship this year, the fifth in Class A and seventh overall for the school. Led by future two-time Class A singles champion Robert Keith, just a sophomore, Blake

rolled over its opponents with a loss of just two of fifteen matches played. First the Bears dispatched Virginia 4-1, trounced Fairmont 5-0 in the semis, then knocked off East Grand Forks 4-1 in the finals. Though Keith was Blake's only entrant in the individual tournament, it had a strong lineup made up of singles players Keith, sophomore Jon Saliterman, and eighth-grader Justin Wismer, and doubles teams made up of ninth grader Jake Wert and junior Dan Moore at No. 1 and ninth grader Ben Wismer and senior Jon Breyer at No. 2.

It had been the favorite to win in 1992 and Blake did not disappoint. But one of the Bears' traditional independent school rivals, SPA (now called St. Paul Academy and Summit School), spoiled its plans for a third straight team title in '93, beating the Bears 3-2 in the semis and winning its first-ever state championship over an outclassed St. Peter squad 5-0.

And though it was deprived of revenge against SPA in the 1994 tournament (SPA was upset by Crookston in the semis), Blake regained its bragging rights as the state's top Class A tennis team by sweeping all three of its opponents (Granite Falls-Clarkfield, Foley, and Crookston) by 5-0 scores. Once again led by state singles champion Robert Keith, now a senior, the Bears lost just one set in these three matches. Remarkably, in the final against Crookston singles players Keith, senior Jon Saliterman, and junior Ben Wismer each won their matches by 6-0, 6-0 scores, double bageling their opponents. And Blake's doubles teams of sophomore Justin Wismer and junior Jake Wert at No. 1 and senior Wonju Kim and the aptly-named eighth grader Blake Baratz at No. 2 didn't take much longer. In fact, from start to finish the entire match lasted just 42 minutes, very likely a record for a state tournament team final.

With a year-end record of 21-2, this would be one of coach Hatch's best teams. And it would also be his last, so he certainly bowed out in style, completing his Hall of Fame career by leading the Bears to their eighth state title and seventh under his tutelage. Some of his players had lobbied him to move up to Class AA for this season, and Hatch was tempted, but, as he told *Star Tribune* writer Rachel Blount, "we're a really good five-point team, and maybe we're not quite as good as a seven-point team" ("Blake Captures Third Class A Title," June 9, 1994). Crookston coach Mike Geffre would not necessarily have agreed with

Hatch, saying of Blake that they are "the best team he has seen in either class this season" (June 9, 1994). One of Blake's 21 wins was against Class AA champion Bloomington Jefferson, but we'll never know how Blake might have fared this year if it had to win seven instead of five points against the bigger schools in Class AA.

So now it was Ted Warner's turn to lead the Bears, and he would be up to the challenge of filling Hatch's shoes. A former top player for Edina, Warner got started in tennis by his mother, JoAnn, who hit with him and eventually sent him to Nicollet Park to play on the backboard. Eventually Warner became an important member of those dominant late-1960s Edina teams, winning the crucial consolation point that gave the Hornets a one-point victory over Rochester in the 1968 tournament. An outstanding basketball player as well, Warner had the good fortune to play on Edina basketball and tennis teams that rang up 69-game winning streaks. And his senior year ('69) he finished second in the singles tournament to Minneapolis West's Tom Brennan.

So he came to Blake with impeccable playing and coaching credentials. Though Blake did not win the title his first year—upstart Breck beat them 3-2 in the 1995 finals to claim its first-ever state championship—the Bears won the '96 title and claimed three more under Warner's guidance (in 2000, '02, and '03).

In that 1996 season Blake captured its ninth title with a hard-fought 3-2 victory over Duluth Marshall. To reach the finals the Bears took out '95 champion Breck in the first round 4-1, then upended a strong team from Crookston 4-1. A June 6, 1996, article in the *Star Tribune* by Roman Augustoviz said of the final match with Duluth Marshall, "The Bears got quick victories at first and third singles from senior Justin Wismer and sophomore Blake Baratz and, with the match score at 2-1, got their deciding point when Phil Lee [a junior] and Benji Hartman [a senior] won 6-3, 6-2 at second doubles." Coach Warner said of his team, "What we try to reinforce with all our guys is that at all five points we have to play as hard as possible. You can't expect everybody to be on. What I really feel good about is that different players came through" (June 6, 1996). Other members of this outstanding team included future state singles champions, eighth grader Ross Greenstein (1997) and ninth grader Drew Zamansky ('99).

Uncharacteristically, Blake then went three years without winning a championship; for strong teams from Breck (1997-98) and Winona Cotter ('99) thwarted their efforts. In '97 the Bears finished second to Breck, losing 4-3 in the first Class A seven-point team competition. In '98 the Bears missed the tournament for the first time since '86, losing to Breck in region competition 4-3 after also losing 7-0 to them during the season. And after upending Breck in the Section 5 finals, Blake entered the '99 draw as one of the favorites, but a young Winona Cotter squad surprised them 5-2 in the finals to claim its first-ever state title. That run of twelve straight state appearances as a team, by the way, is a Minnesota record that might never be broken.

Coming into the 2000 tournament the Bears were cast in the unexpected role of underdog, for they had lost to Breck 4-3 during the year and defending champion Winona Cotter was considered a favorite by many. Nevertheless, Blake surprised the pundits by clawing out a 4-3 win over Cotter in the quarters, cruising 7-0 over Duluth Marshall in the semis, and then turning the tables on Breck in the finals, again winning a close 4-3 match.

Coach Warner must have been tearing his hair out in the Cotter match, for in that contest he had to depend on a freshman to break a three-all tie. With fans and players from both Cotter and Blake looking on, future singles champion Grady Newman and his No. 1 singles opponent, senior John Thomas, were on the hot seat. *Star Tribune* writer Jim Paulsen said of Newman's match, "Win and the Bears advance; lose and be relegated to today's consolation round. Newman did win, rallying from triple-game point to break Thomas in the match's final game" ("Freshman's Big Victory Wins It for Blake," June 7, 2000). His 6-2, 7-5 win gave Blake a 4-3 win and sent the Ramblers, not Blake, into the consolation round. Newman said of the match, "I had no idea that the score was tied. I knew I was the last match and I really wanted to win because I lost in the finals last year. It wasn't until after I'd won and everybody was coming over and patting me on the back that I found out that my match was it." And though Newman's win was the clincher, another important point came from a surprise position, second doubles: "Cotter's Nick Lindholm [a junior] and Jeremy Brickner [a ninth grader] had lost only once all year, but they were handled with relative ease by Blake's Mirza Tabakovic [a senior] and Ben Crane [a sophomore] 6-2, 6-2" (June 7, 2000).

The final against Breck was another anxiety-producer, but for a different reason: Blake had to come from behind in so many matches. In a *Star Tribune* article by Michael Rand, coach Warner said, "I was proud of the kids that came back. We came out nervous, and we were down in matches all over the place" (June 8, 2000). Perhaps, as Warner noted, the nervousness had more to do with the fact that his lads were playing private school rival Breck than that they were in the state finals. So though they started as cold as a mid-January day in Fairbanks, Alaska, they soon warmed to the task. Newman, playing No. 1 singles, rallied from a 3-5 deficit in the first set to defeat Tom Loper 7-5, 6-3. And that same No. 2 doubles team that earned a crucial point against Cotter again came through. "Tabakovic [Mirza] and Crane [Ben] stole the momentum from Breck's court, rallying from a set down to win... and help Blake to a 4-3 victory" (June 8, 2000). The score was 4-6, 6-0, 6-3. The other two points came from singles players Chi Pham (an eighth grader) at No. 1 and Ben Hofkin (a sophomore) at No. 4, but it was Newman's win which once again gave Blake its fourth point and the victory. Breck rallied to win the last two matches (at No. 1 doubles and No. 3 singles), but it was too little, too late.

And though Blake would once again advance to the state team tournament in 2001, its longtime rival Breck stole its thunder, defeating Duluth Marshall 4-3 in the finals. Deprived of its chance to match up with Breck by Marshall (which upset Blake 4-3 in the semis), the Bears had to settle for third place.

Not so in 2002, for with a very strong (but relatively young) lineup of excellent singles players, the Bears returned to their perch atop the Class A tennis world. Opening the tourney with a dominating 7-0 win over Waseca, the Hopkins school followed up with 6-1 victories over Rochester Lourdes in the semis and Virginia in the finals to claim its eleventh state title. Led by senior co-captains Ben Crane and Jon Lebedoff, who reminded their teammates of their upset loss to Duluth Marshall in '01, the Bears were, as Crane told *Star Tribune* writer Jim Paulsen, "a lot more focused this year" (June 5, 2002). Crane (the No. 3 singles player) and his talented singles mates,

sophomore Chi Pham at No. 1, junior Grady Newman at No. 2, and ninth grader Dylan Cater at No. 4, caused Virginia coach Dave Gunderson to go strong in doubles in an effort to thwart the Bears. In a June 6, 2002, *Star Tribune* article, Jim Paulsen noted that "Gunderson juggled his lineup for the Class A team championship match against Blake's powerhouse outfit. He removed sophomores Joe Prebich and Luke Gentilini from their normal positions as the No. 1 and No. 2 singles players, pairing them at No. 1 doubles." Hoping to steal one singles victory and all three doubles, Gunderson's boys won just one point, at first doubles, over Lebedoff and his partner, junior Dan Bretl. In singles Pham won 6-1, 6-0; Newman 6-1, 6-1; Crane 6-0, 6-0 and Cater 6-0, 6-0. Blake's doubles winners were eighth grader Nick Lebedoff and sophomore Zach Olson at No. 2 and junior Michael Stern and senior Ben Hofkin at No. 3.

After the match coach Gunderson sang the praises of Blake: "We lost to a good team. They've got a lot of Division 1 players." Bears' coach Warner called his team the deepest he's had in his eight years at the helm. "When we played AA teams during the year, when we played Mounds View and Eden Prairie, the same thing kept coming back from their coaches: 'I've never seen as deep a team as you've got'," said Warner (June 6, 2002).

With eight of its 2002 tournament players returning, Blake notched yet another team victory in '03, its twelfth overall and tenth in Class A. One measure of the strength of this Bears' squad was the fact that four team members also advanced to state individual competition, where senior Grady Newman won the singles title and sophomore Dylan Cater and partner Nick Lebedoff, a ninth grader, took second in the doubles. Chi Pham was the other Blake singles entrant. With a record of 19-2 coming into the tournament, Blake was heavily favored to defeat its unranked Tri-Metro finals opponent SPA. But first the Bears disposed of Waseca 6-1 and Duluth Marshall 7-0.

An interesting sidelight in this finals matchup was that veteran coach Warner of Blake had at one time given private lessons to SPA coach Matt Schultz, a former SPA player in the 1990s. And though Blake prevailed by a 6-1 score, the match was closer than might have been expected. According to a *Star Tribune* article, again by Paulsen, "St. Paul Academy, however, forced Blake to a third set in five of the seven matches—something the Bears didn't face in a 6-1 victory against St. Paul Academy during the regular season." Coach Warner admitted that "they [SPA] played extremely well, and we gutted some things out." He added, "The hardest thing to do in high school sports is repeat. Everyone's gunning for you" (June 5, 2003).

In the end Blake's experience was too much for the SPA boys. The Bears won all three doubles matches—two in three sets, then clinched the title with Lebedoff's win at No. 4 singles. Pham, a junior, also won at No. 1 singles over junior Sam Salyer 6-3, 6-7, 6-3; and Newman bumped off SPA senior Blake Berquist in straight sets 6-2, 6-2 at No. 2 singles. Winners in doubles were the teams of Dan Bretl and David Baker (both seniors) at No. 1, Zach Olson and Michael Stern (a junior and senior pair at No. 2), and Ryan Rosoff and Blake Nicholson (a ninth grader and a junior at No. 3). Only sophomore Dylan Cater lost (at No. 3 singles), and that too was a three-set match.

So Blake returned to its Hopkins home with its twelfth state title, its fourth under Warner during his nine years as coach. And while we aren't tempted to call them the New York Yankees of Minnesota high school tennis (that appellation is reserved for the Edina Hornets), they have nonetheless set a standard that all Class A schools, and most Class AA schools for that matter, can envy. Since that first Class A championship in 1979, the Bears advanced to the State Tournament every year but two ('86, '98), an astonishing twenty-three out of twenty-five years. In addition, they claimed those twelve state titles, about one every two years; finished second five times (including once as a Class AA team), and finished third three times (once in AA). So when they reached the State Tournament they were almost always in contention for a title. And in most of those years Blake's top players advanced to State in individual competition. The ledger on this score reads as follows: eight singles championships, two doubles championships, eight singles runners-up, and eight doubles runners-up. Truly, with these accomplishments, Blake deserves its place in this pantheon of dynasty teams.

Blake—2003 Class A State Champions

As for reasons why Blake has been so successful in tennis, coach Warner offered these insights. For starters, he said, "For years we've been able to fill out our teams with other three-sport athletes, many coming from very competitive soccer and hockey programs at Blake. However, that's becoming harder now that the school offers more sports and we're losing some to new sports such as lacrosse." Of course the Blake tennis tradition is an important reason why they continue to be successful, but Warner also mentioned a related feature. "Another thing I tried to build in is the expectation that the top kids need to pay back to the younger kids." And, he added, "They've been instilled as co-coaches and leaders so eighth and ninth graders know how much the juniors and seniors have done for them. Some of practice is about 'you' but most is about 'team.' It's all about the group and having fun."

Finally, Blake has been blessed with outstanding coaches such as Warner and Hatch and early coaches such as Prescott Cleveland.

Rochester

When the Mayo brothers, Charles and William, founded a clinic in the southeast Minnesota prairie outpost of Rochester in 1889, they could not have imagined that in the 21st century this clinic/hospital would have 3,000 doctors on staff and 3,000 more being trained; 50,000 allied health personnel; and, according to an article in the September 2006 issue of *Minnesota Monthly* magazine, "way more guys (and a few gals) sweeping the sidewalks and buffing the marble than one would think possible." The clinic is big business, a conglomerate that took in "five billion dollars" last year while treating "513,000 people from across the globe" and performing "500 surgeries a day" (September 2006). An empire which treats royalty and peasants alike, it is perhaps the premier health care provider in the U.S. and maybe the world.

Just as the Mayo brothers could not have envisioned this modern health-care empire, surely they could not have imagined that this sleepy village would also become something of a tennis empire and that their clinic would play a major role in developing the sport in Rochester. In fact, a Mayo doctor, Henry Helmholz, persuaded the clinic to buy the land for what became the Rochester Outdoor Tennis Club on 13th Avenue Northwest. According to Marv Hanenberger (Rochester's "Mr. Tennis"), six clay courts were constructed in 1928 and the first club tournament was held that year. Hanenberger, now in his 90s and living in Green Valley, AZ, recalls those early years at the club as if they were yesterday. "In 1928, when I was fourteen years old, I became the only non-doctor member of the club," he said. Not long after that, he and partner Fred Hargesheimer finished second in the '32 state high school doubles tournament, so his time on the "Mayo" courts, often playing with doctor members, paid off. After graduating from high school, he became the first tennis pro at the club, serving in that role from 1933-35 while trying to earn money to pay for tuition at Rochester Junior College. He remembers rolling the clay courts with a huge cement roller, but since he was too small to handle this job, he hired a football player to do it. Later, he said, the club purchased a power roller.

Marv Hanenberger, Rochester's "Mr. Tennis"

Right after WWII the club converted the clay courts to hardcourts, and many excellent tennis pros taught there in the next decades. For example, Hanenberger said that U of M coach Phil Brain came down on Mondays to give lessons in the late 1940s, and in the early '50s Hughes Davis was the pro. Davis was a former North Carolina state champion and later a high school coach in Illinois, according to Hanenberger. Dave Healey (three-time state singles champion) spoke very highly of Davis, recalling "our sessions together, sitting on the grass, where he would pontificate in his southern drawl. He provided many stories to what he called our 'Junior Davis Cup' team." Healey called him "an outstanding teacher of both the mental and physical aspects of the game."

In the late 1950s a pro from Milwaukee named Swanson worked at the club, and two-time state doubles champion Ron Trondson also taught there a couple of years while his former doubles partner Henry Dison served as the manager. Then, in the early '60s, Mrs. Janet Milliken, a Mayo doctor's wife who had come from the Iowa Country Club in Des Moines, served as the pro. Steve Wilkinson (also from Iowa) worked at the club from 1963-65; and Steve Ehlers and Tim Burke (a Rochester native) also taught there in the late '60s. In the early '70s the 1972 Big Ten No. 1 singles champion from the U of M, Jim Ebbitt, served as the club pro. But from '79 on the head pro has been Tim Butorac, a former Gustavus all-American and father of '99 state Class AA singles champion and touring pro Eric Butorac.

According to Greg Lappin, author of *Tennis Doubles: Winning Strategies for All Levels* and a trailblazer in opening new tennis clubs in Eden Prairie and Rochester, the Rochester Outdoor Club (eventually run by the Park and Recreation Association) was the only club in town until 1969 when the first Rochester Indoor Club opened. Started by a man named Dan Corrigan and owned for many years by Jim and John Horan, it is now owned by ten investors, one of whom is Tim Butorac. Now that it had an indoor club, Rochester provided winter tennis for its citizens, including the many talented junior players living there, and it provided a backup site for tournaments such as region/section high school playoffs in the spring and fall.

Then, in 1993, Lappin came to Rochester after a successful career in the Metro area that included stints as a pro at the Richfield Teaching Center from 1980-85 and as the founder (in '85) and director (from 1985-91) of the Flagship Athletic Club in Eden Prairie. Lappin called himself (and fellow pro Kevin Ylinen) the "grunts and teaching pros for the STP program at Richfield," and, while at Flagship, he helped organize fundraisers for inner city tennis programs and a Pro-Am tournament. But, he says, "I'm most proud of playing a role in the resurgence of Rochester tennis," a resurgence that began when he came to Rochester to help open the state-of-the-art Rochester Athletic Club (RAC) located at 3100 19th Street Northwest. Lappin helped pick the site and he hired the staff for this $12 million facility.

Opened in October 1993, the RAC has become the site for numerous tournaments, including one in the summer on the its outdoor clay courts, and the Section 1 girls' and boys' playoffs. And thanks to pros such as Scott Boyer (the current tennis director) and Kevin Rust, the club has indeed helped put Rochester tennis back on the map. For example, Rust's Rochester Lourdes girls' teams have won eleven straight team championships, six singles titles, and seven doubles championships. In addition, the Lourdes boys' team has made two Class A appearances at State since 1995. And since '96 the Mayo boys' teams have advanced to State nine times, finishing second twice (in 2004 and '05). Moreover, the talent is now spread around to schools other than Mayo and Lourdes. For instance, John Marshall's Eric Butorac won the '99 Class AA singles title and the "new kid on the block," Century, is an emerging power.

But this is now. What about those golden days of Rochester tennis (the 1950s to the early '70s)? Lappin, who is currently the general manager of the RAC, makes the claim that the success of Rochester tennis in those days was due to the efforts of one man, the indefatigable Marv Hanenberger. It's difficult to argue his point, though there were of course many other pros and high school coaches who played important roles in the development of tennis in Rochester, for Hanenberger (affectionately known as "Hanny") was literally a "witness to the creation." He played in the fourth State Tournament sponsored by the MSHSL in 1932, served as an official player-coach of the Rockets his senior year ('32), worked as a teaching pro at the Rochester Outdoor Club from 1933-35 to earn money for college (which, because it cost him his amateur status, made him ineligible to play tennis at the U of M), and returned from WWII service to begin his role as a tennis mentor to Rochester kids.

Generous to a fault with both his time and money, Hanenberger "threw himself into teaching the game to any kid who wanted to learn." In an article in the *Green Valley News and Sun* (AZ) paper titled "Mr. Tennis Still Swinging at 90," Hanenberger told writer Mike Touzeau, "I'd pick out a kid that looked like he had some talent and ask him, 'Do you really want to learn this game'?" (April 16, 2004). Having grown up during the Depression, Hanenberger knew what it meant to struggle to make a living (he started working at age 12 for $3 a week washing windows and later worked for Briese's Clothing Store on weekends and in the summers for nine years), so he was especially generous to kids who could not afford lessons, tournament fees, or other tennis expenses. The article in the Green Valley paper also noted that "he's [Hanenberger] never accepted a dime from any of them, and in fact spent thousands in tournament entry fees, hotel rooms, bus and plane tickets, and court fees for any one of them who needed it to expand their talent and love for the game he cherished" (April 16, 2004).

The results of his efforts produced six Minnesota state singles champions (four of whom won multiple titles) and two doubles champions (one pair winning twice). In addition, he was for a number of years the personal coach for Howard Schoenfield, who won the national 18-and-under junior tournament at Kalamazoo when he was just 17 and once beat John McEnroe in the juniors. Tennis's version of a chameleon, Hanenberger could change his coaching method to suit the player. He said, "I tried to teach whatever way was most natural for the person I worked with. It could have been the continental, eastern, or western grip, it made no difference because I could teach what was most natural for the player." Also a good strategist, Hanenberger emphasized keeping "a cool mind, not making outbursts on the court, and playing by the rules." In all the years he helped his Rochester boys, including taking them to national tournaments at Kalamazoo, MI; California; Louisville, KY; and to many other tournaments, he took great pleasure in seeing them make progress in their games and grow in their dedication to and love for tennis. And he continued to follow their careers in college as well.

Many of his former players still keep in touch with him, recalling with fondness the times Hanny took them to eat at the Hubbell House in Mantorville or even on out-of-town trips. Three-time state singles champion Chuck Darley recalled one of those times, saying, "Marv took us to nationals at Kalamazoo and he fattened me up. I was a scrawny kid."

A top amateur player in his day (when he had time to play tournaments), Hanenberger still plays tennis several days a week; and since his retirement he's continued to coach at Green Valley. For example, while in his 80s he helped coach the local high school boys' and girls' teams which won state titles, and he helps his senior citizen peers with any tennis questions they might have.

As the owner of a popular and prosperous Rochester clothing store called Hanny's, famous for outfitting employees of IBM, doctors from the Mayo Clinic, and a few movie stars, Hanenberger used his money to aid the cause of many charities and especially tennis in Rochester and Minnesota. For example, he gave $100,000 to the U of M tennis program; so the U dedicated a wing of the Baseline Tennis Center as the Marv Hanenberger Tennis Hall of Fame. Also, he helped organize tennis clubs in the southern part of the state so high school players could belong to the USTA and get into organized tournaments. As well, according to the April 16, 2004, article in the *Green Valley News and Sun*, he was honored by the Rochester Outdoor Club in 1972 for "40 years of service to young people, and the junior tournaments, camps, and clinics he created there which are still major events in Rochester." Finally, in 2006 the city of Rochester honored him by naming the Outdoor Tennis Club the Marv Hanenberger Tennis Center. It also honored former players by naming courts after Rochester's State singles champions. When asked what he wanted to do with the rest of his life, Hanenberger said, "Keep playing tennis" (April 16, 2004).

But this chapter is about a dynasty team, and so Rochester is a bit of an anomaly because its team triumphs were earned in the days before True Team play. Nonetheless, under the rules at the time, the Rockets dominated state play from 1950-'65, winning nine championships before Edina began its rise to power. As the unofficial "coach" of many of those individual champions, and since individuals winning singles and doubles titles translated into team titles those days, Hanenberger must be given a great deal of credit for Rochester's team success. There were certainly other factors as well, such as a large population of tennis players from which to find competition.

And, as coach Dick Thatcher noted, "We had wonderful facilities." Bob Gray, 1965 State singles champion, spoke lovingly of those eight courts at the Outdoor Club where he and his mates hung out for hours and played tennis virtually all day: "The ambiance of the Club was great; it had a nice clubhouse and a screened-in porch. It was a second home to us."

In addition to the coaching players received from Hanenberger and other pros at the outdoor club, they were mentored in high school by men such as Merle Davey and Thatcher who were not always tennis coaches but who knew how to deal with teenage boys. And because many of the doctors who came to Rochester to work at the Mayo Clinic were tennis players, there was a trickle-down effect. A good number of them played tennis and so their children took up the game as well (for instance, Chuck Darley and the brothers Daugherty and Brandenburg).

Others didn't play but had the resources to help pay for their children's lessons, and of course the Outdoor Club for many years was basically a club for Mayo doctors. As a result doctors' children (and later all Rochester children) had ready access to summer lessons. Bob Gray said that the Club had a ladder system which allowed juniors to challenge adults who were above them on the ladder. Many of these adults were doctors (often practicing residents from all over the country) who were excellent tennis players, so juniors would call the adults and say, "I'd like to play a challenge match." Often the matches would take place during the doctor's/adult's lunch break, and, according to Gray, "The junior's friends would come to watch, hoping to see the youngster beat the adult." Sometimes, Gray said, "the adults would also help us with our games, give us advice."

In addition, once Rochester became a tennis power, the dynasty factor kicked in. Success breeds success, and so more and more of Rochester's kids took up tennis because they wanted to be a part of that success. Gray talked about how this "dynasty factor" contributed to Rochester's success, saying, "When we practiced at the outdoor club, we always had role models to study and emulate." These former champions, Gray noted, "demonstrated the practice skills needed to succeed and they were dependable and conscientious."

Finally, now that there are two indoor centers, Rochester is once again becoming a tennis power in the section and state, and it's likely schools from the city will continue to make it difficult for other teams in the section to compete with them. The playing field definitely favors schools that have such advantages.

Now let's go back and relive those glory years of Rochester tennis, starting with the Rockets' first state championship in 1950, the initial year the MSHSL recognized a team tennis champion. Merle Davey was the coach and the stars of the team were Don Ranthum, Bob Reid, and cocaptains Henry Dison and Ron Trondson. All just juniors, this fearsome foursome dominated region play (Ranthum and Reid finishing 1-2 in singles and Dison and Trondson winning the doubles) and then state tournament play at the U of M courts. Undefeated coming into the tournament, the boys from Rochester swept through to the semis, where only Reid lost (to '51 champion Vincent Bugliosi of Hibbing). The Rockets wrapped up the title on the first day by earning 6 points (one for each win), 4 more than second-place Hibbing. The final day, with Ranthum winning the singles and Dison and Trondson the doubles, the Rockets had a sweep, earning 9 points to Hibbing and Minneapolis Central's 3 each. Some sources noted that an alternate scoring system was used, one in which Rochester received 44 points and Hibbing 12. In any case, the margin was decisive and the lads from Rochester had earned the first of Rochester's nine titles. Other members of this team who did not participate in the State Tournament were Jim Myrick and Myron Rynerson.

With the fearsome foursome and other good players such as Myrick and Tom Reeves back in 1951, the Rockets defended their title; but it was with a narrower margin of victory. Dison and Trondson defended their doubles title, but Ranthum and Reid both lost to Bugliosi, Ranthum in the semis and Reid in the finals, so the final tally was 42 points for Rochester and 30 for Hibbing. Undefeated in dual meets for four straight seasons, Rochester had what coach Davey described (in an article titled "Rocket Netters Edge Shattuck in Exhibition") as "the toughest [match] the Rockets have had in the past four years, a 5-4 squeaker over Faribault Shattuck" (*Rochester Post-Bulletin*, May 24, 1951). In this meet Dison and Trondson lost their only match during two years of competition.

Suffering the loss of these four lads meant that Rochester had a lean year in 1952, though ninth grader Dave Healey advanced to State in singles and lost in the semis. But when Healey and his compatriots such as sophomores Roger Jackman and Roger Riege and senior captain Jerry Parker entered the picture in '53, Rochester claimed its third title in four years. Healey won the singles, the first of his three straight, and Jackman and Parker took second in the doubles, giving the Rockets 14 points to the 9 earned by runner-up Minneapolis Central. Though Jackman and Parker lost to Mike Dunn and Jack Roach of Minneapolis Central in the finals 6-2, 4-6, 6-0, coach Davey, especially pleased with the efforts of his doubles team, said, "These two boys turned in their top performances of the season in the state doubles competition" (*Rochester Post-Bulletin*, "Rockets Take State Title in

Rochester–1953 State Champions. Roger Riege, Larry Parker, Dave Healey, Roger Jackman, & coach M.S. Davey

Tennis Meet," June 3, 1953).

Healey finished with an unbeaten record and the team captured first place in District 3, Region 1, and Big Nine Conference competition. The only senior on the team was Parker, and the other state tournament team members, Healey, Jackman, and Roger Riege, were just sophomores.

Divine intervention kept the Rockets off the gold medal stand in 1954, for that's the year a team of saints (St. James) dethroned Rochester by the narrowest of margins, 13-12. Healey won his second singles title, but he had to wait until the next year before he could boast of helping the Rockets win another team championship.

With Jackman, Riege, and Healey itching to redeem themselves, the Rockets dominated the field in 1955, earning 17 points while Duluth Central and St. Peter tied for second with just 6 each. Of Rochester's four state entrants, only sophomore Chuck Baker lost, to singles runner-up Chauncey Riggs of Duluth Central in the first round. Healy capped his career by taking his third straight singles championship and Jackman and Riege claimed the doubles title with a 6-0, 6-2 win over Stan Palmer and Bob Adolphson of St. Peter. One other stalwart during the 1952-55 years, according to Healey, was John Strobel.

Despite the loss of its three senior state champions,

Rochester eked out yet another win in 1956, its last in the decade of the '50s, earning 9 points to the 8 won by second-place finishers Minneapolis Central and Duluth East. The heroes this year were junior Chuck Baker and senior Dave Love, who captured the doubles title, thus earning all nine points.

It would be six more years before the Rockets would win a state team title, though the boys in red and black made good showings in 1957 (finishing second) and '59 (taking fourth). Baker was back in '57 for his senior year to defend his doubles title, but he and Dick Ostrom lost in the finals, and in '59 Harold Dirksen finished second in singles. The previous year ('58) Dirksen had paired with Leroy Lidstrom to take third in doubles.

After these relatively lean years by Rochester standards, a whirlwind blew in from Iowa to help the Rockets break the drought. This tempest from the south took the form of one Chuck Darley, and he destroyed everyone in his path for three years. Not only did Darley fell all his opponents, but he led his team to three straight championships. A youthful squad led by sophomore Darley and ninth grader Bob Gray, the 1962 champions garnered 18 points (to second-place St. Paul Central's 13). With a bye in the first round, Darley went on to win four matches to claim the singles title, and Gray also won four, losing to Darley in the finals. Thus, as Rochester's (now John Marshall) only state entries, this dynamic duo accounted for all 18 points, Darley earning 10, including 2 for his first-round bye, and Gray 8. In dual meets the Rockets were not undefeated: they won 6 of 8 matches, but the strength of their two individual stalwarts won the state title for them. During the regular season the Rockets had also received good production from next year's doubles runners-up, Bob Bergstedt and John Lillie, Mark Wood, and Ed Henderson.

The following year (1963) promised to be an even better one for the Rockets, in part because they had a doubles team in the state draw (Bergstedt and Lillie), but also because Darley and Gray were back again. They did not disappoint their fans, earning a staggering 27 points to 12 for the second-place team, more than doubling the score of Minneapolis West, and claiming their second straight 1960s title. An article in the *Rochester Post-Bulletin* titled

"JM Netters Clinch State Title," described the Rockets' dominance thus: "If a vote were taken to shorten the two-day state prep tennis tourney to a one-day affair, John Marshall's Dick Thatcher probably would be the first in line to okay the change. You see, Thatcher's talented Rockets don't need the second day. For the second straight year, JM has wrapped up the team championship before the final day's scheduled matches" (June 8, 1963). With two wins and points from a bye by Darley, three wins from Gray, and two from the doubles team of Bergstedt and Lillie, the Rockets amassed 18 points the first day, enough to stave off any would-be pretenders. Since doubles wins counted 3 points, Bergstedt and Lillie earned 6 points, winning 6-4, 6-0 in the first round and 6-1, 3-6, 6-2 in the quarters (over a stubborn pair from St. James, Gary Fleming and Brad Offerdahl). Darley's six points came from a bye and 6-3, 6-4 and 6-2, 6-2 wins, while Gray's three wins (and also six points) were two straight-setters and 6-2, 4-6, 6-1 quarterfinal victory over the ever-dangerous Paul Krause of St. Louis Park. On the U of M courts the next day, Saturday, the Rockets nearly pulled off a rare triple: team, singles, and doubles championships. Though it was not to be, Darley won two matches and beat Gray in the singles final again and Bergstedt and Lillie took second in the doubles, thus giving the Rockets their 27 points.

With Darley, Gray, Lillie, Dave Daugherty, and Mark Wood returning in 1964, coach Thatcher looked to be sitting on the catbird seat. However, there were dangerous predators out there, most notably the Hornets from Edina-Morningside, led by their top two players Chip Otness and Rob Granger, and the spoiler from St. Louis Park, Krause. Darley sensed this would be a more difficult year, noting in a *Rochester Post-Bulletin* article by Rich Melin that "'people just assume that we (Darley and teammate Gray, the 1-2 finishers the past two years) will get into the finals.' But he's not buying that attitude, working 'as hard as I can to get ready'" (June 4, 1964).

Darley's intuition proved true, for his nearly-invincible mate, Gray, lost in the first round to the spoiler Krause 6-4, 6-4 and the doubles team of Lillie and Wood won just one round before losing to 1965 doubles champions Brian Mahin and Dave Yorks of Minnetonka 7-5, 4-6, 6-2. So with Edina singles players Otness and Granger rolling up 12 points the first day, the Rockets (with 11 points) found themselves behind in the count going into the final day for the first time in three years. Not to worry; Darley dumped Otness in the semis, but in a tough 6-3, 7-5 match, and Granger lost to Hibbing's Dennis Chez.

Rochester—1963 State Champions. Coach Dick Thatcher, Bob Bergstedt, John Lillie, Bob Gray, & Chuck Darley

Then, with the injured Gray finishing with a gutsy performance—winning two consolation matches, and Darley closing out Chez (6-3, 6-0), the Rockets took home their eighth team title and third in a row. The margin was close (17 to Edina's 13) and Rochester's depth was essential.

Calling it "strictly a team victory," Thatcher also said, "we never could have done it without four points from (Bob) Gray in the consolation bracket and three from the doubles team of John Lillie and Mark Wood" (*Rochester Post-Bulletin*, "Darley the Ace, but Depth Earns Eighth JM Title, "June 8, 1964). Thatcher praised Gray's effort in particular, for he was playing with "aching pulled tendons in his upper left arm [he was a lefty] which forced him to resort to an underhand serve on occasion" (June 8, 1964).

With the biggest Rocket now launched on to college (Darley enrolled at the U of CA-Berkeley to play tennis there), and only Gray of the four-man 1964 state tourney team returning, coach Thatcher feared he might have a rebuilding year. But senior Dave Daugherty, his very talented brother Rob (just a freshman), and George Margellos filled in for last year's stalwarts to help JM easily advance to State again in '65. Still, when sophomore Margellos lost in the semis of the region, Thatcher worried that a three-man team might not be strong enough to win State (Gray in singles and the doubles team of the Daugherty brothers had easily advanced by winning region championships). Thatcher told *Rochester Post-Bulletin* writer Gail Anderson, "I think there's a 50-50 chance we can make it." However, Thatcher also said, "if Gray can go all the way and we can get our doubles team at least to the semifinals, we'll be tough to beat" (June 7, 1965).

Tabbing Edina as the team's biggest threat, for they qualified the Nos. 2 and 4 singles players in the state (Chip Otness and Robb Jones), Thatcher felt the draw would be crucial. As it turns out, he needn't have worried. Gray, the No. 1-ranked player in the state all year, entered the tournament with an unblemished 23-0 record and the Daugherty boys were 14-0. All three took care of business. First off, Gray destroyed Jones 6-0, 6-0 in the second round and "then overcame a 4-2 deficit in the second set to beat Paul Krause of St. Louis Park (6-4, 6-4) in the quarterfinals" (Rochester Post-Bulletin, "JM Netters Win Fourth Straight Title, "June 12, 1965). In the semis he routed Merle Karr of Hibbing 6-0, 6-1, then knocked off two-time doubles champion John Brennan of Minneapolis West in the finals 6-3, 6-1.

Meanwhile, the Daughertys were working their way through the draw, first beating the very tough team of Dave Stearns and Dave Woodward of St. Cloud 4-6, 6-1, 6-2. Next they defeated Jim Franham and Dennis Killian of White Bear Lake 6-2, 6-2, and in the semis they knocked off Ken Bartel and Pat Carey of Elk River 6-4, 6-3. Alas, their 17-0 run ended in the finals, for they dropped a hard-fought 5-7, 6-2, 7-5 match to Minnetonka's Brian Mahin and Dave Yorks. But the 9 points they earned, coupled with Gray's 10, were more than enough to give the Rockets their fourth straight state title (a record for consecutive team championships that still stands today). Second place Minnetonka came in with 12 points.

Remarkably, though several of its teams would come close on a number of other occasions, this ninth title would be the final Rochester championship.

Thatcher and his lads could not have known this, so for the moment they were exulting in yet another championship for the school and the community that had spawned so many great players and teams. In an article by Rich Melin, Thatcher called it "the most satisfying one (over the past four years) because we weren't such overpowering premeet favorites" (*Rochester Post-Bulletin*, "Rocket Net Title 'Most Satisfying.'" June 14, 1965). He also gushed about his star player Gray, who finished the season with a 27-0 record: "Gray was outstanding. He made some absolutely fantastic shots." And finally, he said of his tall tree doubles team (Dave Daugherty was six foot seven and Rob six foot two), "Dave and Robert Daugherty are the best doubles team we've had in my four years as coach at JM... Pressure doesn't bother the Daughertys" (June 14, 1965).

While Rochester would not claim another state title, this did not mean they would never be heard from again. Au contraire, for in 1966 JM finished third, then the new school, Rochester Mayo, took third in '67 and second in '68, with two-time state champion Rob Daugherty leading them. In two of those years the Rockets came oh so close to winning, picking up 12 points to the 13 co-champions Edina-Morningside and North St. Paul earned in '66 and once again losing to Edina-Morningside by a nose in '68 (23-22).

The 1966 team relied on just two singles players again, the now six foot four Daugherty (a sophomore and ranked No. 1 in the state) and another sophomore, Bob Brandenburg. Unfortunately for Brandenburg, coach Thatcher's fears about the draw came true, for he drew the No. 3 player in the first round (Dave Stearns of St. Cloud Tech) and lost 6-1, 6-2. Thus consigned to the consolation draw, he could only earn one point for each win. And though Daugherty won three matches and picked up 8 points (including two for a first-round bye), these and Brandenburg's 4 points earned in taking the consolation championship left the Rockets one point short. If Daugherty had beaten Edina's Robb Jones in the final, the Rockets would have claimed the title, but coach Thatcher was proud of his sophomore standouts nonetheless.

And even with Daugherty's first singles title, the 1967 Rockets finished third, with 13 points, behind Minnetonka's 15 and champion Edina's 20. Prospects were brighter in '68 until Bob Brandenburg, now a senior, sustained a knee injury in a district tournament basketball game. Amazingly, however, he made a quick recovery and "was back to 'normal' about three and one-half months ahead of schedule" (*Rochester Post-Bulletin*, "Brandenburg Recovery Boosts Mayo Net Stock," June 6, 1968). So he teamed with Tim Burke (a future Metro-area teaching pro and a stalwart on Mayo teams from 1966-68) and they finished second in state doubles play. Daugherty, as expected, easily captured the singles, giving the Mayo Spartans 22 points. But it wasn't enough to hold off Edina, for Ted Warner captured the Hornets' 23rd (and championship) point by winning the consolation title.

During the following four years Mayo finished fourth in 1969 (mostly on the strength of a second-place doubles finish by senior Steve Yost and sophomore Tony Bianco), out of the running in '70 and '71 (though in '71 Mark Brandenburg and Bianco in doubles and Mark's brother Scott in singles won the region, qualifying for State), and third in '72. In '72 Mark Brandenburg finished fourth in the singles.

Poised to win the first True Team title in 1973, the Spartans fielded an excellent singles lineup of juniors Mark Brandenburg and Fred Siekert, and senior Scott Brandenburg, and doubles teams of junior Chris Bianco and ninth grader Dave McGill and junior James Bastron and senior Bob Ashenmacher. But the tennis gods did not favor them and they finished third, losing a heartbreaking 3-2 semifinal match to eventual champion Edina when Mark Brandenburg cramped up against Craig Jones. Then, in '74 Austin upset Mayo in the region. Brandenburg, however, won his second state singles title and the doubles team of seniors Siekert and Bastron advanced to the semis in the doubles tournament.

So it would be ten years before Mayo would advance to State, for the Spartans took second in the region in 1975, '79, and '82 before breaking through once again in '83. Then another dry spell occurred, and the next state team appearance for Mayo did not occur until 1996. That year the Spartans finished second behind Bloomington

Jefferson, and since then they have made state appearances in 1997, '99 (third place), and 2003. Also, since 1973 only one Class AA Rochester player or doubles team has won an individual championship: Eric Butorac of JM in '99. Kevin Gorman and Doug Robertson of Mayo finished fourth in doubles in '80, Jon Lobland and Chris Thompson of Mayo took second in '88 and third in '89, and Ed Edson and Shimul Chowdhury of John Marshall finished fourth in doubles in '99. And though no Rochester AA team has won State, there is every indication that one may soon tame Minnesota's current top tigers, Edina and Mounds View.

On the Class A front, Rochester Lourdes has made six appearances in the past three decades (1979, '80, '82, '91, '95, and 2002), but its highest finish was third in '02. And though the team has not clasped the golden bowl, singles player Jarret Cascino ('01) and the doubles team of Cascino and Phillip Johnson ('98, '99), won individual titles. In addition, Mark Morrey and Terry Aney finished third in doubles in '91, Cascino took second in singles in '00, Paul Johnson and Haberman finished third in doubles in '02, and Pearson and Brian Welch finished third in '03.

And while the Lourdes' boys have generally acquitted themselves well over the years, their sisters have dominated. Particularly under coach Kevin Rust, the head coach since 1991, Lourdes has become the big gorilla of Class A Minnesota girls' tennis, winning seven state team championships through 2003 and capturing five singles titles (two by Lauren Patterson and three by Megan Tiegs) and six doubles titles in a row from 1998-2003 (three featuring the Tiegs sisters—Megan, Christen, and Rachel—and four featuring the Palen sisters—Lindsay, Alexa, and Alyssa). In the late 1970s and early '80s, Lourdes also fielded strong teams, one of which (the '78 version) won a Class A state title. Also, Marylee Libera won the Class A '81 singles championship.

Finally, there have been many coaches guiding Rochester's successful boys' teams over the years. For Lourdes Chuck Willinghanz was the coach off and on in the 1980s, former Lourdes player Todd Carroll coached from 1987-88, Gordy Ziebart coached a number of years (including during the 1991 and '95 state tournament years), and Kevin Rust guided the Eagles to a state tournament appearance in 2002. Rust, a USPTA pro in Rochester, also coached the Lourdes' boys from 1983-86 and has now been the coach since 2000.

And for the new kid on the block (Century) it has been J. Allen (the first coach there), Joe Boyer, and Scott Boyer, the current coach. JM has had a number of coaches since Mayo opened in 1967, but Al Wold directed the team for many of those late 1960s and '70s years; Craig Sheets took a turn, Paul Bachman coached for two or three years, Dave Edwards held the reins for seven years in the '90s, Joe Boyer coached one year, and now the coach is Josh Heiden.

And starting with Merle Davey in the late 1940s, Mayo has had many outstanding coaches. These include the aforementioned Dick Thatcher in the '60s, Bill Fessler (Mayo's first coach in '67), Terry Strawn (he coached Mayo in 1968-69, '75, and from 1983-85; he is deceased), Bob Riege (also deceased, he coached from 1970-74), Bob Gray (1976-82), Dave Berg ('86), Kevin Rust (1987-90), Les Cookman, and Lorne Grosso (1993-2004), and currently former No. 1 Mayo player Jeff Demeray. Of all the coaches from 1973-2003, the following led Mayo to state tournament appearances: Riege in 1973; Strawn in '83; Grosso in 1996, '97, '99, and 2003. The most successful of these three was Grosso, whose Spartans finished second in '96. Known also as a very successful hockey coach, Grosso was an excellent athlete who became, according to Bob Gray, "a good tennis player."

So that's the story of the Rochester dynasty, one that began in the 1950s and extended through the early '70s, faded a bit in the late '70s and '80s, but has now regained its vitality and promises to remain healthy for years to come. It's a story of a community that owes its existence to that clinic founded many years ago, a clinic that also helped launch the careers of countless young tennis players who put Rochester on the Minnesota tennis map. I suppose it's not an accident that the most successful Rochester boys' tennis program the past forty years has been the one at a school named after the Mayo brothers, for, as noted earlier, many of the youngsters who played for the Mayo Spartans were children of doctors at the clinic.

St. Cloud Tech

If ever a tennis team could be considered the perpetual bridesmaid, it would be St. Cloud Tech. Between 1976-2003 Tech dominated Region/Section 8 play, advancing to State twenty times; yet it won just three titles. On eight occasions it was the bridesmaid, finishing second, and on five other occasions it finished third. So it has been one of the top three teams in Minnesota sixteen of those twenty-eight years.

How then does it qualify as a dynasty team? Well, it won three titles, and like Edina, Blake, Rochester, and Blue Earth it dominated its section opponents. For example, in the decade of the 1980s Tech advanced to State eight times and in the '90s did even better, winning nine of ten section titles. In addition, the Tech Tigers qualified many talented singles players and doubles teams for state individual competition. Perhaps most importantly, however, it had coaching stability, with Bill Ritchie and Jerry Sales at the helm for thirty-one and twenty-three years respectively and assistant Paul Bates taking over in 2002. Both Ritchie and Sales began coaching the Tech varsity team in '71, but they would be the first to admit the debt they owed to their predecessor, Mac Doane, the father of St. Cloud tennis.

Though individual players and doubles teams from St. Cloud Tech had enjoyed success before 1976 (for example, current Minnetonka coach Dave Stearns and his partner Dave Woodward finished fifth in the '65 doubles tournament; Stearns took third in singles in '66; Woodward and Larry Nielsen earned a third-place medal in doubles in '67; Grant Helgeson and Jeff Schwanberg took second in doubles in '72; Helgeson finished third in singles in '73; and Helgeson's brother Kent and partner Jerry Schwanberg, Jeff's brother, finished fifth in the '75 doubles tournament), it wasn't until 1976 that Tech began its long run of successful team play. And remarkably, they won the state championship the first year they competed in the True Team tournament. With two Helgeson brothers at Nos. 1 and 2 singles and Jerry Schwanberg at No. 3 leading the way, Tech defeated three of the top teams in the state: Blue Earth 5-0, Minneapolis Roosevelt 4-1, and

1974 champion Minnetonka 3-2. In what was considered by some a mild upset, the Tigers scratched out a victory over the pre-tourney favorite, Lake Conference power Minnetonka, in the finals. Two matches went to three sets, with Minnetonka winning at No. 2 doubles and Tech taking the crucial No. 1 singles match.

That match featured defending singles champion, undefeated Mark Wheaton of Minnetonka, against Tech's top gun, senior Kent Helgeson. In one of the most thrilling individual state tournament matches in these early years of True Team competition, Helgeson came from behind to defeat his higher-ranked opponent 3-6, 7-5, 6-4 in the deciding match. Tech coach Bill Ritchie had special praise for the play of his No. 1 player, saying, "In the tourney, Kent [Helgeson] showed he had the patience to wait for the good shot and come in behind it and put it away. I didn't know if he'd be able to do that against Wheaton, but he did" (*St. Cloud Daily Times*, "Tigers Reign in Tennis," June 7, 1976). Ritchie also lauded Helgeson's "concentration" and the fact that he "seldom gave away any easy points," but he felt that "the mental toughness required to win four straight games [he was down 5-3 in the second set after losing the first 6-3] like that against Wheaton took a lot out of him" (June 7, 1976). As a result, he lost to Paul Holbach of White Bear Lake in the semis of the individual tournament.

Needing two more points to win the match, the Tigers had gotten them earlier from their singles players. At No. 2 Kent's younger brother Brace, a sophomore, disposed of Bill Kruger 7-5, 7-6 and senior Jerry Schwanberg beat his No. 3 singles foe Glenn Britzius 6-3, 6-1. In doubles Minnetonka's No. 1 and 2 teams prevailed, Mark Smith and Mark Burton defeating Tech's Todd Holes and Paul Wehlage 7-5, 6-1 and 'Tonka's Jim Adams and Steve Stuebner trimming junior Mark Smith and freshman Jon Schwanberg (Jerry's brother) 6-4, 3-6, 6-2. Thus Tech earned its first state team title, an accomplishment considered even more noteworthy because, as noted earlier, it happened in the Tigers' first state team appearance. Tech's only loss of the season was to Coon Rapids, so the Tigers finished the year with a sparkling record of 21-1. Team success usually means individual success, and Tech's singles players especially had gaudy records.

Before entering individual competition, Kent Helgeson had a record of 30-2, Brace Helgeson had an unblemished record of 23-0, and Jerry Schwanberg was 24-1 (June 7, 1976).

It would be seven years before Tech would bring a first-place trophy back to the Granite City. In between they won three other region titles but experienced disappointment at State. In 1977, for instance, Minnetonka exacted a measure of revenge for that '76 upset, defeating the Tigers 4-1 in the semis. And so they had to settle for a third place finish.

From 1978-80, three relatively lean years for St. Cloud Tech tennis, strong teams from Thief River Falls advanced to State from Region 8. Except for another three-year tournament drought from 2000-2002, Tech would never go more than a year without making a state tournament appearance. So in '81 they were back in the Class AA tourney with a strong lineup and a confident team (they had, after all, beaten Edina East in a regular-season match). But after narrowly escaping in their first two matches (3-2 wins over Austin and Hutchinson respectively), the Tigers fell to Edina East 3-2 and had to settle for bridesmaid status. All things considered, this was a good showing for a young lineup that gave promise of better things to come. Tech's top players Dave Nelson and Shawn Bresnahan were sophomores, Ken Dahlquist a junior, and John Lauerman just an eighth grader.

With these four returning in 1982, and with the addition of the Schlorf brothers (Jay and Todd) and Sean Potter, Tech returned to State that year. Unfortunately for them, as good as they were, there was one Class AA team better, Keith Paulson's 24-0 Austin Packers. Tech opened the tournament with a 3-2 win over Hutchinson and then subdued Edina in the semis 4-1, but they were outclassed in the final by Austin 5-0. For the second year in a row the Tigers were bridesmaids.

Not so in 1983, for this even more experienced Tech squad rolled over its three opponents to claim its second state title, this time in the restored one-class tournament. With a strong singles lineup of senior Dave Nelson at No. 1, sophomore John Lauerman at No. 2, and junior Pat Dunn at No. 3 and dynamite doubles teams of senior Shawn Bresnahan and junior Jay Schlorf at No. 1 and sophomore

Sean Potter and ninth grader Todd Schlorf at No. 2, the Tigers lost only two points in three matches. First they blanked St. Thomas Academy 5-0 in the quarters, took out Blake 4-1 in the semis, then defeated Coon Rapids in the finals by the same 4-1 score. In the final match Tech swept the doubles (Bresnahan and Jay Schlorf won 6-3, 6-2 and Potter and Todd Schlorf won 6-2, 6-3) and claimed two of the singles. At No. 2 singles Lauerman defeated Sekou Bangoura 6-3, 6-2 and Dunn knocked off Sekou's brother, Alfred, at No. 3 6-1, 6-2. Only Nelson at No. 1 singles lost (to state singles runner-up Tom Olmscheid), but by a respectable 6-3, 6-4 score.

In an article by Tom Elliott in the *St. Cloud Daily Times*, coach Ritchie called this his most balanced team and said that since early in the year he "had been telling his squad that they were the elite of the state" (June 10, 1983). So it was no surprise that the Granite City boys won, and this championship was particularly gratifying to seniors Nelson and Bresnahan. This was the third straight year Tech had reached the finals, and Bresnahan told Elliott, "We knew this would be the best chance we would ever have. So we knew that we had better go out and get it done." Bresnahan had been on varsity for three years and Nelson for four, and they had, as the article said, been "bridesmaids for the last two [years]." No. 2 doubles player Sean Potter expressed how he and his teammates felt about the wait for Nelson and Bresnahan: "It's about time for these guys. They've been working at it a long time." Coach Ritchie said that in order to avoid "chokes, goof ups, miscues, upsets, or 'glips,' we had a short meeting in my hotel room and I reminded them that they were the front-runners and that they should play like the front-runners they are" (*St. Cloud Daily Times*, June 10, 1983). And that they did, earning the Tigers a well-deserved state championship.

Adding frosting on the cake, Tech's doubles team of Bresnahan and Nelson became the first from their school to win an individual title.

Though the Tigers came into the 1984 tournament as the favorites (they were, after all, the defending champions and had a 16-0 record coming in), they could not fend off upstart Blake, the small school which became just the second Class A school to capture a True Team

championship against the big schools. The score was 3-2, and for the third time Tech played the role of bridesmaid. Perhaps of all its losses in the finals, this might have been the most disappointing because the talent on this team was undeniable. So dominant was Tech that it claimed both singles and doubles spots from Region 8 for state individual tournament play: John Lauerman and Pat Dunn in singles and the doubles teams of Jay Schlorf/Eric Wolfe and Sean Potter/Todd Schlorf (who would win the doubles title this year-1984).

The 1980s was truly the glory decade of St. Cloud tennis, for Tech was one of the top teams in the state each year and its individual players were some of the top competitors in the NWLTA Section: John Lauerman (twice ranked No. 1 in singles), the Schlorf brothers, Dave Jussila, Brian Boland, Sean Potter, Shawn Bresnahan, Dave Nelson, Pat Dunn, to name a few. So it was not surprising that the Tigers performed well at State during this decade, winning two titles, finishing second four times, and taking third place once. But it was at the zenith of its powers in 1985, at the mid-point of the decade. Coming in to the tournament as the favorites (they had, for example, beaten Blake 5-2 during the year), the Tigers upheld their ranking and won their third and, as it turned out, their last state team championship while once again qualifying all six individuals for the singles and doubles tournaments. Tech's No. 1 player, senior John Lauerman, took third in the singles tourney, and sophomore Dave Jussila lost in the first round to Ryan Skanse of Minnehaha Academy. In doubles senior Eric Wolfe and his partner, junior Tim Hobday, won a round before losing to the fourth-place finishers from Fridley (Tim Jachymonski and Jon Dean). And for the third year in a row, a Tech pair advanced to the finals, the defending champions Potter and Todd Schlorf (a senior and junior respectively). Alas, this time they lost to Myles and Roger Anderson of Blue Earth.

The road to this 1985 team championship was a bumpy one, though, for Tech had to claw its way past three difficult teams before they could hoist up the trophy, squeaking by defending champion Blake and powerful Edina by 3-2 scores, and then edging White Bear Lake in the finals 4-1. In that final match, according to Bill Peterson of the *Minneapolis Star and Tribune*, Tech's second doubles team of Mike Andreotti (a basketball player) and Tim Hobday (a hockey player) came back from 4-1 down in the third set to clinch the team win, taking the last five games (June 7, 1985). In addition, Tech singles players Lauerman, Todd Schlorf, and Jussila all won their matches. Tech's only loss was an unexpected one, unbeaten Sean Potter and Eric Wolfe at No. 1 doubles lost for the first time all year, to John Abbott and Gene Carlson 7-6, 6-3.

In an article by Tom Elliott titled "Tech Completes Its March to Title," Tech assistant coach Jerry Sales commented after this loss at No. 1 doubles, "I tell you, I was a little shook when I saw something like that. When a state champion (Potter at doubles in 1984) goes down, your confidence gets put to question, not to mention the kids'" (*St. Cloud Daily Times*, June 7, 1985). But, as the article noted, "Sales' concerns became unwarranted as Andreotti and Hobday came through." Though they had lost in the first two team matches and had split sets with White Bear Lake's Ross Sandison and Tom Hoffman, they gave their teammates a lift with some inspired play. Andreotti, a sophomore whose father Al was the head basketball coach at Tech, said, "We were getting up to the net and putting it away instead of laying [sic] back" (June 7, 1985).

In the end this proved to be an easier match than the 3-2 semifinal win over Edina, which had defeated Tech during the season. An earlier article by Elliott in the *St. Cloud Daily Times* described the pivotal point in that match (a 6-4, 4-6, 6-4 victory by Jussila over Edina's Mike Husebo) in these words: "Jussila went through two racquets in the victory and ended up using teammate Todd Schlorf's racquet to finish off his No. 3 singles match" (June 6, 1985).

After the Tigers finished devouring their three opponents, coach Ritchie reflected on the success his teams had enjoyed for five straight years during which they finished second three times and won two championships. "I don't know why," he said. "But all I know is that we have been able to play championship caliber tennis for five straight years. And that takes some talent... It's just a miracle to get this far this many times" (*St. Cloud Daily Times*, June 6, 1985). Some of their success could also be attributed to good coaching from Ritchie and Sales (and recent St. Cloud State grad Tony Tillemans, whom players credited), but some of it was team chemistry. Sean Potter called this "the closest team I've been on." As evidence, the June 6 article by Elliott noted that the lads played poker the night before their Edina match.

Of the remaining years in this decade (the 1980s), Tech advanced to State in three of them, losing in region competition only in 1988, to crosstown rival St. Cloud Apollo. In '86 the Tigers lost to Edina 5-0 in the first round at State and in '89 they took third by defeating Hibbing 4-3 after losing a tough match to eventual champion Edina in the semis. And even though they finished in that bridesmaid spot again in '87 (losing 7-0 to one of Edina's most dominant teams), the '89 third place team was probably the stronger of these two squads. That '89 team lost a 4-3 heartbreaker to Edina in the semis, and but for a foot injury suffered by Brian Boland the Tigers might have won the championship. Midway through the last set against his No. 2 singles opponent, Peter Erickson, Boland hurt his foot. Erickson won 7-5 in the third, but coach Sales told *Star Tribune* writer Roman Augustoviz, "We don't look at it as an excuse; we [Tech coaches] don't talk excuses" (June 9, 1989).

To borrow words from the famous first line of Dickens' immortal novel *A Tale of Two Cities*, the 1990s "were

Saint Cloud Tech–1985 State Champions

the best of times and the worst of times" for St. Cloud Tech tennis. The best of times occurred in the last week of May, for in nine years in this decade the Tigers won their section and advanced to State. But when they took the courts during the first or second week of June they could not bring home the prize, hence the tag "worst of times." Now no one would say that these state tournament performances were dreadful, for Tech finished runner-up four times in this decade and third three other times. However, there's no denying that the tag of "always a bridesmaid" fit them during the '90s. And maybe bad luck had something to do with it.

In four of the first six years of the 1990s Tech's teams finished second (1990-92 and '95), losing to everyone's nemesis Edina twice and to Blake and Mounds View the other years. In '90 the Tigers advanced to the finals with comparatively easy 7-0 and 6-1 wins over Hastings and Eden Prairie respectively but were beaten by Mounds View 5-2 in the championship match. Tech won two of the doubles, and three of the four singles matches—all of which Mounds View won—were close; so the Tigers had an excellent chance. Coach Ritchie praised Mounds View, in an article in the *Star Tribune*, saying, "They have more talent than we do" (Nolan Zavoral, June 8, 1990). And he expressed pride in his boys: "I can't be disappointed about today. My kids played up to their ability" (June 8, 1990).

However, disappointment might have been the appropriate word to describe the 1991 Tech season, for the Tigers were the team favorite coming into the tournament. And they soon lived up to the hype by mauling their first two opponents 6-1 (Stillwater and Hastings). Standing in the way in the finals was Blake, a team the Tigers had edged 4-3 during the season, so they had confidence they could win. Alas, it was not to be, for the match played out according to form, Blake's strength in singles prevailing over Tech's strength in doubles. The final score was 4-3.

Though Tech once again finished second in 1992, this was not unexpected, for Edina had been the No. 1 team all year and had rarely experienced a challenge. Except for a win at third singles, Tech came out on the short end against the Hornets, losing 6-1.

In 1993 the Tigers lost 6-1 in the first round to eventual champion Wayzata, and in '94 they missed the tourney after having advanced from Section 8 five straight years

and twelve of the previous thirteen years, beginning in '81. Truly, this was a remarkable run that was ended by Fergus Falls. In '95, however, Tech returned with a vengeance, advancing through the draw to the finals once more, where, for the eighth time they had to settle for second best. After bumping Red Wing from the championship bracket 6-1 in the first round, the Tigers squeaked by Stillwater in the semis 4-3. Unfortunately for them, and for so many other teams over the years, superpower Edina was waiting in the wings. The result was a 5-2 win for the Hornets and the last of Tech's bridesmaid finishes. Since the Hornets had defeated St. Cloud by the same 5-2 score during the year, the result was not surprising. Edina won at first, second, and fourth singles and at first and second doubles.

And though Tech advanced to State in each of the final years of the 1990s, they finished third in three of those years. In '96 they beat Buffalo in the first round 7-0, lost to champion Bloomington Jefferson in the semis 5-2, then beat Virginia 4-3 to earn the third-place trophy. This was the first year former assistant coach Paul Bates would serve as co-coach with Ritchie.

With ten lettermen and top young players such as sophomores Kevin Whipple (a future Gustavus star and now the Roseville coach and a White Bear Lake Club teaching pro) and Ajay Prakash leading the way, Tech once again took third place in the 1997 tournament, beating Cretin-Derham Hall 6-1, losing to runner-up Wayzata 5-2, then defeating Rochester Mayo 6-1.

1998 brought the same result, for as in '96 the Tigers won a round (beating Mounds View 6-1) before running into the team that eventually won the title. This year it was again the relentless No. 1-ranked Edina Hornets, who would lose just one of 21 points in three matches. The Tigers, who were ranked fifth, did not win that one point, instead falling 7-0 to Edina before recovering to edge Hibbing/Chisholm 4-3 for yet another third-place finish, their third in a row and fifth overall.

Considered a co-favorite with Wayzata in 1999, in part because of its senior-laden and experienced lineup led by No. 1 player Whipple, Tech suffered an unexpected loss to Minneapolis Southwest in the first round 5-2 and so was bumped into the consolation round where it defeated Mounds View 4-3 before losing the fifth-place match to

Hibbing 5-2. Despite these team setbacks, Whipple (the third-place winner in '97 and '98) performed admirably in the individual tournament, losing to seventh-grader D. J. Geatz in '97, champion Ryan Edlefsen in '98 (both of these matches were in the semis), and to future Gustavus teammate Eric Butorac of Rochester John Marshall in the '99 singles final.

For the next three years the Tigers were inside the cage, forced to watch Section 8 rivals Fergus Falls (2000) and Elk River Area (2001-02) play in the arena they had so often competed in. Finally, now directed by coach Paul Bates, the Tigers once again fielded a strong team and advanced to the State Tournament in 2003. Led by players such as Michael Engdahl (who went on to play at St. Cloud U), Ryan Beduhn, and Chaise VanOverbeke (all juniors), Tech lost its first match to Orono 6-1, defeated Cretin-Derham Hall 4-3, then lost to Rochester Mayo in the consolation final 6-1, thus achieving the same result as in their last appearance in '99.

For some of the same reasons that the other dynasty teams were successful, so these reasons apply to St. Cloud Tech. Parental support and good coaching were of course two factors. About the coaching, retired coach Jerry Sales mentioned that "we (Bill Ritchie and I) frequently met and talked lineups, we had well-planned practices, and we were flexible." He and Ritchie worked well together and they worked hard.

In addition, according to Sales, "We had a wonderful tradition that began with Mac Doane. There was a good city program [started by Doane] that would engender a lot of players, especially in the 1960s and '70s during the tennis boom and even before in the 1950s. The city program gave us a good pool of players and it [to play tennis] was a cool thing to do at the time." And while Sales thought the city program was a major factor in Tech's success, he also noted that "it's about a little bit of luck—when other teams are a bit down and when things have to be open for you."

Finally, he mentioned the advent of the Augusta Tennis Center in the 1970s as an important reason why St. Cloud players had a chance to develop. Until it closed around 1990 it was run successfully by people such as Jay Schlorf (a former Tech star player) and Jack Bowe, with help from others such as Sales.

Blue Earth

How on earth does a small town of about 4,000 people, located over 100 miles from each of Minnesota's two main tennis centers (the Twin Cities and Rochester), become one of the state's tennis powers? Is it the blue/black clay found along the Blue Earth River that was molded into local young tennis stars? Or is it the influence of the Jolly Green Giant, whose mammoth statue hovers over the city and brings its citizens good luck? Or perhaps it's the school's nickname, the Buccaneers, which gives its sports teams a special aggressive nature (though it's hard to imagine one-eyed pirates floating down the Blue Earth River and then slashing their way through cornfields). Or maybe it's because this farm community produces stout youngsters raised on food grown on some of the richest farm land in the world.

It doesn't seem possible that this little tennis oasis in the midst of a racket-sport desert could produce three state team championships (including one earned in competition with the big schools), an almost unthinkable twenty-two region championships, twenty-five South Central Conference championships—including two ten-consecutive runs under coach Hal Schroeder, two state singles champions, and six doubles champions.

In the end, however, it wasn't the clay soil, the Jolly Green Giant statue, the school nickname, or any other hocus pocus that made Blue Earth a tennis dynasty. Instead it was initially the Herculean efforts of one man who built the program, Hall of Fame coach Hal Schroeder. Secondly, while Schroeder was the engineer, he needed some help from the conductors and brakemen to keep the train moving. So while the Bucs were competitive in Schroeder's early years, it wasn't until a family of four talented boys arrived in 1977 that Blue Earth's tennis train began knocking all comers off the tracks. This was of course the Anderson family, so from 1977-88 (the year the youngest Anderson, Roger, graduated) the Bucs won those three team championships, made eleven appearances at State, and won seven of their eight individual titles. Of these eight individual titles, the Anderson boys were a part of six of them (Roger and Gregg won the two singles championships and Greg, Myles, and Roger won four doubles titles).

But there was tennis life at Blue Earth before the Andersons came and after they departed, for the Bucs won eleven other region titles (three before 1977 and eight after '88). Before the Andersons arrived Blue Earth won region championships in 1973, '74, and '76 and the Bucs also had many outstanding players who advanced to State in those years. These included coach Schroeder's first state participants in 1961, Ron Wruchi in singles and Gary German and Steve Ehrich in doubles. Following this breakthrough several doubles teams qualified but did not place at State: Duane Brownlee and John Skaden in '67, Terry Barnes and Dick Gretillat in '68, Mike Sasse and Roger Classon in '69, and Doug Rome and Dick Skaden in '72. Also qualifying in singles were Roger Malwitz in '69 and Wayne Mikkelson, Blue Earth's first three-time conference singles champion, who qualified in '70. That year Mikkelson won a round but then lost to Edina's Bob Amis 6-0, 6-0.

But the Bucs' individual players began to shine in 1973 when Randy Oldenburg and Randy Quint took second in doubles. Then Scott Jacobson, currently the U of Nebraska women's tennis coach, finished second in 1977 and third in '78 in singles. In addition, coach Schroeder's son Mark advanced to State in doubles with Mike Weise in '74 and with Jacobson in '76. Jacobson also paired with Frank Beckendorf in doubles at State in '75.

Blue Earth–1977 State Champions

And after the Andersons left, Blue Earth took home region titles in 1994, '95, '96, '97, '98, '99, 2000, and '01. Moreover, Layne McCleary and Eric Lawatsch won the doubles title in '90, and the Bucs qualified many players for state singles and doubles play during these years. These included coach Schroeder's youngest son, Paul, and McCleary in '89 (fourth in doubles), Lawatsch in '91 (fourth in singles), and Mick Willette-Jay Zabel in '93 and Blake Duden-Josh Malwitz in 2002 (both of whom also finished fourth in doubles).

But clearly Blue Earth's glory years were those in which Schroeder coached and the Anderson brothers performed their magic. Let's recall Blue Earth's three championship years (1977, '80, and '88) and how the Bucs won those titles. First, it should be noted that Blue Earth's dynasty was, like Rome's, not built in a day. Coach Schroeder started the program in 1955, and though he had some strong teams and individual players (as noted earlier) in the 1950s and '60s, it wasn't until '73 (the first year of True Team play) that the Bucs made a splash in the Minnesota tennis pond. That year they won the team consolation championship, and Quint and Oldenburg took second in doubles. In '74 and '76 they made it back to State but did not place, then in '77 the Bucs had their breakthrough year. With a singles lineup of Scott Jacobson at No. 1 singles, Gregg Anderson at No. 2, and Thane DeLeon at No. 3 and a doubles lineup of Scott Weber-Mark Warrington at No. 1 and Pat Fischer-Bill Olivo at No. 2, Blue Earth confounded the pundits and won its first state championship. And this with a lineup of underclassmen: Jacobson and Olivo were the elder statesmen—both were juniors—while the others were sophomores and ninth graders.

The overwhelming pre-meet favorite was Minnetonka, which came into the tournament having lost only to Edina East early in the season. In region play the Skippers avenged that loss and, after winning 3-2 over Minneapolis Roosevelt and 4-1 over St. Cloud Tech in the first two rounds were considered a lock to win the title, at least according to Roosevelt coach Bucky Freeburg, who told *Minneapolis Tribune* writer Bruce Brothers, "I can't see anybody beating them now" (June 10, 1977). Meanwhile, Blue Earth had squeaked by Northfield 3-2 (on the strength of wins at No. 1 and No. 3 singles from Jacobson and DeLeon respectively and at second doubles from Fischer and Olivo) and then Duluth East 3-2 in the semis. In the latter match the same three positions came through for the Bucs.

According to *St. Paul Pioneer Press* writer Jim Wells, a happy but pleasantly surprised Schroeder said, "We never expected to get this far. We thought we had a chance, but most of the city clubs have much more experience than we have" (June 10, 1977). Never mind that Northfield was not a city school, but now the Bucs were up against mighty Minnetonka, a Lake Conference power. Once again the Blue Earth boys prevailed by the thinnest of margins (3-2), winning at No. 1 and 2 singles (Jacobson and Gregg Anderson) and No. 2 doubles (Fischer and Olivo). This victory capped an improbable season in which these fresh-faced lads from Blue Earth won 16 out of 17 dual meets, knocked off three much bigger schools to claim a one-class title, and placed a singles player (Jacobson, who finished second) and a doubles team (Anderson and DeLeon, who took fourth) in individual competition. According to coach Schroeder, Wells said this 1977 championship was secured with three of the biggest upsets in Minnesota sports to that point (June 10, 1977).

With the entire team back in 1978 the Bucs advanced to State with an undefeated record but were bounced out 4-1 in the first round by eventual champion Edina East. And though coach Schroeder entered his team in four top-notch Saturday tournaments during the year (all of which the Bucs won), the lack of competition in the region may have hurt his team. Despite that disappointing loss to Edina East, Blue Earth recovered to win the consolation championship, first beating Henry Sibley 5-0 and then Coon Rapids 4-1. And once again Jacobson (who entered the tournament with a 41-0 record) did well in singles, finishing third, and Anderson (a sophomore) and DeLeon (a junior) took second in doubles.

Toppling the big school giants in 1977 gave Blue Earth (school population just over 300 in grades 10-12)

great pleasure, but in '79 the Bucs crossed swords (rackets) with their small-school peers in the first Class A tournament. They did well, taking third and winning a doubles title (Gregg Anderson and DeLeon); but that year Blake, led by state singles champion Louie McKee, was too strong, defeating the Bucs 4-1 in the semis.

In 1980 the boys from Jolly Green Giant country got their revenge, winning their second state title (this one in Class A) by upending Blake in the finals 3-2. Led by senior Gregg Anderson at No. 1 singles, the Bucs fielded a strong lineup which also included seniors Scott Weber at No. 2 and Mark Warrington at No. 3 singles and doubles teams of ninth grader Steve Beckendorf and senior Troy DeLeon at No. 1 and sophomore Ryan Knee and eighth grader Myles Anderson (Gregg's brother) at No. 2. In its first two matches Blue Earth rolled over Granite Falls and St. Paul Academy (SPA) by 5-0 scores. Then after beating Blake to win the team championship, Gregg Anderson won the singles title and Warrington and Knee finished second in doubles.

Though the Bucs advanced to State each of the next five years (1981-85), they finished no higher than fourth ('81 in Class A and '83 in that year's single-class tournament). Nonetheless, these were excellent Blue Earth teams which always lost to high-powered teams. For example, in '81 the Bucs lost to Blake 4-1 in the semis, in '82 they were tripped up by Blake again (3-2 in the first round), in '83 they lost to Coon Rapids 3-2 in the semis and to Blake 3-2 in the third-place match, in '84 Edina beat them 5-0 in the first round, and in '85 they were defeated by SPA in the first round 3-2. If they had been able to compete in Class A during the 1983-85 years, they might have been able to scrape out another team title. And during those five years the Bucs produced three doubles champions: Knee and Beckendorf in '81, Beckendorf and Myles Anderson in '82, and brothers Myles and Roger Anderson in '85 (this one in the one-class tourney).

1986 marked the end of a remarkable run in which Blue Earth advanced to state ten years in a row (1976-85), for Hutchinson won the Region 2 title in this last year of single-class competition, defeating Blue Earth in the finals. But the Bucs were back in '87 (once again in Class A) and they finished second, losing 4-1 to top-ranked

Blake in the finals. This was the first of four years in which just four squads competed for the team prize (the field expanded to its current eight-team format in '91). And though Blue Earth did not win the team championship in '87, Roger Anderson and Jamie Schmitgen took home the doubles title.

The next year, 1988, the Bucs (now the combined Blue Earth-Frost-Winnebago High School) won the team crown, their third (and final) state title. Their senior leader was Roger Anderson (the last of the clan), but this was a star-studded lineup made up of singles players Anderson, Schmitgen, and Troy Thompson, and the doubles teams of Paul Schroeder-Layne McCleary and Bob Ankeny-Eric Lawatsch. It was a lineup which featured senior leaders (Anderson, Schmitgen, and Ankeny) and talented underclassmen such as McCleary (a sophomore) and Lawatsch (a ninth grader) who together would eventually win a state doubles title in '90. Moreover, five of these seven players qualified for state individual competition that year: Anderson in singles and the doubles teams of Schroeder-McCleary and Schmitgen-Thompson.

In the team tournament the Bucs opened with a 3-2 win over New London-Spicer, then trounced St. Peter in the finals 5-0. The win over St. Peter was especially gratifying, for the Saints had defeated the Bucs 3-2 in the second match of the season, ending (according to the 1988 tournament summary in the 1989 MSHSL tennis tournament program) "a regular-season winning streak by Blue Earth that had reached 111 straight wins over nine years."

After winning the team title, Anderson slashed his way through the singles draw to claim bragging rights as the top Class A player in the state, and Schroeder and McCleary upended their teammates Schmitgen and Thompson to take third in the doubles tournament. Anderson recalls these glorious years with great fondness, remembering particularly "the camaraderie with teammates," especially at the annual breakfast before the Blue Earth Invitational Tournament. "Several players would meet up at the Vienna Bakery for a 'healthy' breakfast of donuts and Dr. Pepper. After eating 2 to 3 donuts and drinking a large Dr. Pepper, we all had stomach aches that would last through mid-morning."

Alas, as in real life, all good things come to an end; so with the graduation of Roger, the Anderson era was over at Blue Earth. Since their arrival in 1977, the four Anderson boys (Chris, Gregg, Myles, and Roger) helped the Bucs win twelve region championships (and its three state titles), and together they won two singles crowns (Gregg and Roger) and four doubles titles (Roger and Myles each claiming two, including one in which they paired up). No team in state tennis history has benefited so much from a family move as Blue Earth, for the Andersons gave the Bucs tremendous doubles play, added depth, and quality at the top of the lineup. Oh, sure; the Bucs had Scott Jacobson, a terrific No. 1 player when the Andersons arrived, but Gregg and Roger Anderson held down that spot for seven years after Jacobson graduated in 1977, Greg from 1978-80 and Roger from 1985-88.

So while the Buccaneers continued to cut down their opponents in region/section play, they were unable to intimidate their opponents at State. Their best performances during these latter years were a consolation championship in 1998 (under coach Jerry Sonich) and third place in 2000 under coach Mick Willette, a former Blue Earth player.

The Schroeder years ended in 1991, and he was succeeded by young Dave Aasen, a talented coach who led the Bucs to state in '94 but tragically lost his life in a car accident on an icy patch of Highway 14 in the fall of '94. Sonich took over in '95, leading Blue Earth to five straight state team appearances, then Willette became the coach when Sonich retired in 2000. Willette in turn was succeeded by current coach, Travis Armstrong. And though Blue Earth has not won a team championship since '88, the memory of those swashbucklers of yore is still fresh in the minds of Bucs' fans.

All in the Family

Ask any high school coach what it was like to coach his/her own children and in most cases the response will be a broad smile and a comment something like "it was one of the great joys of my life." This is not to say that the parent-coach relationship is always smooth sailing—sometimes, for example, the overzealous parent-coach puts too much pressure on the child. But in most cases the opportunity for the parent to coach the child and the child to play for the parent forges a bond stronger than steel and produces indelible memories. Blood is thicker than water, after all. I know I considered it a pleasure to coach my son Chris for four years and to serve as an assistant coach for my daughter Heather's team for one year. So this chapter will focus on that family bond, as revealed especially from the perspective of prominent tennis brothers (and in some cases a sister) who had an enormous impact on Minnesota high school tennis. Most but not all the featured players in these families were coached by a parent; but even in cases where the parents did not coach their children, they were very supportive.

"We few, we happy few, we band of brothers."
—King Henry the Fifth

So who are these well-known tennis families? They are the Andersons of Robbinsdale Cooper/Blue Earth, the Brandenburgs of Rochester, the Brennans of Minneapolis West, the Carlsons of Madison, the Helgesons of St. Cloud, the Joergers of Staples-Motley, the Luebbes and VanDeinses of Winona Cotter, and the Wheatons of Minnetonka. The featured families were chosen for what I call the All-State Family Team on the basis of some or all of the following criteria: (1) at least three brothers who were successful at the

State Tournament, (2) coaching from a parent, (3) participation on a state championship team and/or winning a state singles or doubles title, (4) success in summer tournaments, and (5) other contributions to Minnesota high school tennis. I have done my best to track down families that qualify on the basis of these criteria, but I expect I may have missed some (particularly from the early years of the 1930s and '40s). So I apologize to any who are not profiled. Before telling their stories, however, I have included comments about some I am calling Honorable Mention families.

Honoring Minnesota tennis families is not an original idea; the USTA Northern Section has been doing it since 1976. In fact, many of those recognized by the USTA (such as the Martin, Moe, McGraw, Hatch, Wilkinson, Bob Larson, Riley, Hagen, and Donley families) have been important figures in high school tennis as well. So in the spirit of that 1970s saying "the family that plays together stays together," here are the stories of these families, beginning with the Honorable Mention Families.

Honorable Mention Familes

Going back to the year 1930, the brother team of Robert and Richard Tudor from St. Paul Central captured the second state doubles title, Robert also winning the singles championship.

Another family that produced a state singles champion was that of the Shragowitzes of Minneapolis North. Jim Byrne of the *Minneapolis Morning Tribune*, in an article titled "Shragowitz Family Shows Net Profit," said of them, "In that North High School district the Shragowitz family holds a prominent position in the sports spotlight. Of course, man of the moment is Esser Shragowitz who surprised in prep tennis circles by walking off with the state tennis championship Wednesday at the University [1946]. But his brothers Harry, Babe, and Sam also are good netmen and four good men are enough for any team" (June 3, 1946).

We must also mention the Andersons of St. James, brothers Robert, Dave, and Mark. Dave and Mark were key members of the 1954 small-school team which won the State Tournament (see Chapter Eight). That year Dave and his partner Gerald Kintzi won the doubles title, and Mark distinguished himself in state singles play for three years, finishing second his senior year ('56). And lest we forget the older brother, youngest brother Mark credits Robert (a '49 St. James graduate) for helping launch his tennis career.

A private-school brother trio is that of the Barrys from Blake: Walter, Randall, and Stewart. All were key performers for the Blake Bears, with Walter and Stewart especially distinguishing themselves. As a ninth grader Walter played No. 2 doubles on the 1981 Class A championship team and No. 1 doubles as a senior on the '84 team that won a title when there was only one class. A doubles dynamo, he also teamed with Tom Price to take second in the '82 tournament when he was just a sophomore. His junior year he played No. 3 singles on Blake's state tournament team but did not make it to the individual tournament. His senior year he and Shekhar Sane made it to State in doubles but did not place.

Randall Barry was an alternate on Blake's 1985 state tournament team, and youngest brother Stewart helped the Bears win their second one-class team title in '91 and, with Fergus Weir, also won the doubles championship that same year. Stewart first made an appearance at State his freshman year as the No. 4 singles player on Blake's Class AA team entry in '88, and his sophomore year he played No. 2 singles on Blake's '89 runner-up team (behind Chris Laitala) and participated in the singles tournament as well. As a junior he again played No. 2 singles on Blake's Class A tournament team (again behind Laitala) but did not make it to the individual tournament. In his breakthrough year, '91, he again played No. 2 singles behind Laitala.

The Barry brothers experienced success in summer tournament play as well, Walter once earning a No. 3 singles ranking in 12-and-under singles, Randall a No. 2 doubles ranking in the 12s (with Chris Boily), and Stewart a No. 1 ranking in 10-and-under singles. Stewart also ranked No. 2 in doubles twice, once in the 16s and once in the 18s (both with his state tournament partner Fergus Weir). John Hatch, who coached all three, said they came from a "good, solid family" and that they were "all good team players who played other sports."

Other brother pairs include the following who experienced success in the State Tournament. First, in 1960 Franz Jevne of Edina captured the doubles title with partner Andy Goddard; and in '62 his brother William Jevne paired with Goddard to hoist up another doubles trophy. Brothers Greg and Reid Pederson of Coon Rapids took the '66 doubles crown, and Jay and Todd Schlorf were key performers on St. Cloud Tech's championship teams in the 1980s. Jay held down a No. 1 doubles spot on the '83 team while younger brother Todd played No. 2 doubles that year. Todd then won the '84 doubles title (with Sean Potter), played No. 2 singles for Tech's '85 team champions, and took second in doubles that year. Jon and Charlie Seltzer of Edina won the Class AA doubles in 2000 after Jon had won an earlier championship with partner Brad Anderson in '99. And another pair from Edina were the Bryan brothers, '01 Class AA doubles champion Roy and '03 doubles champion Andrew. But except for the Shragowitz and Anderson families, these champions were composed of just two brothers.

During the seventy-five years of state competition there have also been a number of brothers who were groomsmen and not grooms, perhaps the best being the McGregor twins (Doug and Don, once the No. 1-ranked 16-and-under NWTA doubles team) from Duluth East who lost three-set heartbreakers in the doubles finals in 1976 and '77. Noted Rochester tennis figure Marv Hanenberger and his brother Duane lost doubles finals as well, Marv in 1932 and Duane in '37; and another Rochester pair, two-time singles champion Rob Daugherty and his brother Dave finished second in the '65 doubles tournament. In addition, it's impossible to overlook the Britzius family of Rochester and Minnetonka, for the godfather of this clan, Charles "Chuck" Britzius finished second in the first state singles tournament in 1929 and, with partner Walter Hargesheimer, brought a doubles title home to Rochester that year. His son Dale partnered with Jim Colwell of Minnetonka to take second in the '67 doubles tournament and son Glenn, for many years a top adult player in the Northern Section, was an important member of 'Tonka's '76 runner-up team.

In the coaching fraternity many were privileged to tutor their sons. For example, Hall of Fame coach Keith Paulson's son Dan played No. 1 singles for Austin his senior year and son Tom played doubles on Keith's 1982 championship team. Hal Schroeder's family deserves a mention as well, for his two boys and two daughters were fine performers, Mark playing No. 1 singles in the early 1970s, Paul finishing third in the '88 Class A doubles tournament with partner Layne McCleary and playing on the championship team that year, and daughter Laurie winning the Class A girls' doubles title in '78. So many other coaches and brother combinations graced the high school tennis stage over these seventy-five years, and I'm sorry I can't mention them all, but I salute them nonetheless. Now it's on to the All-State families.

All-State Families

The Andersons of Robbinsdale Cooper/Blue Earth

The first family is the Andersons of Robbinsdale Cooper/ Blue Earth, winners of twelve state team, singles, and doubles championships. Their saga began in the Iron Range town of Virginia where the patriarch of the family was born. It was in this place noted more for hockey than tennis that Chuck Anderson, one of the most colorful and successful coaches in Minnesota history, grew up. He began his tennis-playing career by hitting with a neighbor girl and her friend, the high school coach's daughter, in seventh grade. He played hockey in high school, but Chuck also made a name for himself in tennis as a four-year member of the Virginia team coached by Emil Erickson, the father of one of those girls he first hit with. Playing mostly doubles (which he became a master at coaching), Chuck advanced to State with partner Dan Madich in 1951; and he served as captain his senior year. From Virginia Chuck went to college at Hamline, there to once again play hockey where, he said proudly, "I had the assist record one year." In tennis he played both doubles and singles, winning the No. 5 MIAC singles championship his junior year.

Graduating with an education degree and majors in history and physical education in 1958, Chuck took his first teaching and coaching job at Elk River that fall. As with so many teachers in smaller communities during this time, Chuck was asked to do almost everything except sweep the floors and clean the bathrooms. Despite the fact that he taught health, physical education, geography, history, and driver's education, he still found time to inaugurate both the hockey and tennis programs in this then small town located up U.S. Highway 10 from Anoka.

After five years he left Elk River (in 1963) with a gold watch and memories of successful hockey and tennis teams. His tennis teams, for example, at one time won twenty-three-straight dual meets. Moving south to Robbinsdale Cooper to teach, Chuck also started up the hockey and tennis programs there. It was at this new Lake

Conference school that he would first serve notice to the state tennis powers that his teams would be formidable opponents, for in 1969 they shut out Edina 5-0 and then won the state title the following year ('70). This championship team included twelve players who competed at the college level. Perhaps the most notable of them were Chuck Puleston, who took third in singles that year and went on to play at the U of M; Kevin Ylinen, who, with Tim Butorac, placed second in doubles and played two years at the Naval Academy, then joined Butorac at Gustavus; and Butorac, who became an all-American at Gustavus.

Anderson remained as head coach at Cooper through the 1976 season, then he coached Breck for another eight years, though he still taught at Cooper. Next, he spent nine glorious years as the coach of Edina girls' teams that won 168 straight dual meets and nine consecutive state team titles from 1984-92 and of state champions Ginger Helgeson, Jackie and Jenny Moe, Jennifer Nelson, Megan McCarney, Martha Goldberg, Susan and Cathy Birkeland, and Kari Sanderson (sister ot two-time boys' champion Scott Sanderson). Chuck also took a spring job as coach of the Macalester College men's team in 1980 and stayed with the Scots' tennis program through the '87 year.

And during the summers he could be found sharing his considerable tennis knowledge with youngsters at the Lake Hubert Tennis Camp near Brainerd (which he and Bud and Sue Schmid started in 1973) and tennis clubs such as North Oaks, Golden Valley, and Olympic Hills. In addition, he and his wife, Ruth, chauffeured their four sons to tennis tournaments all over Minnesota and the U.S. for many summers.

Though he retired from teaching at Cooper in 1992, Chuck was not yet ready to put down his tennis racket; for upon the retirement of head coach Bill Herzog in '93, Anderson took the Stillwater boys' coaching job. Perhaps the most well-traveled coach in state history, he continued to accumulate frequent driver miles on his daily spring commutes to Stillwater. Legendary Stillwater football coach George Thole called Chuck "the meandering guru." He spent ten years at Stillwater and added the second boys' team title to his resume, a title earned by virtue of a stunning upset of favored Wayzata in the '97 final which one wag dubbed "the 98th Street Miracle."

Known especially for his ability to coach doubles teams and his innovative teaching techniques, Chuck was a coaching fixture on the Minnesota scene for all or part of six decades (a record that no one is likely to break); in fact, he might be the longest-serving tennis coach in state history. He lived to coach tennis, and he was intending to continue as the Stillwater coach in 2006, but he died unexpectedly in November '05 at age 69.

A master tactician, Chuck always prepared his teams well with a balance of play and drills. Hall of Fame coach Bud Schmid said of Chuck's unique ability, "Chuck Anderson was a master at getting his teams ready to play. He was an innovator of many drills to encourage fun competitive play." In those first few spring practice days, when cold weather and even lingering snowstorms forced teams to practice indoors, Anderson created serving contests, wall ball games, and something he called "tennis bocce ball" (no doubt harking back to his days on the Range) to prepare his players for outdoor play. In his desire to make drills competitive, he originated a two-ball/one-ball drill (sometimes also called twenty-one or bingo) that proved effective for all levels of play, even for tennis mixers involving players of differing abilities. Two players begin play on a court (one has two balls and the other has one) while other players, waiting their turns, have two balls in hand. One of the waiting players replaces one player when that player has no ball left to start play. The game is a progressive twenty-one-point contest in which the first five points begin when one player drops and hits the ball from behind the baseline. Points six to eleven begin with an easy serve that doesn't have to be in but must be over the net, then points twelve to twenty-one begin with a serve that has to be in the service box.

Like E. F. Hutton, an investment company that believed in earning money the old-fashioned way, through hard work, Chuck applied this motto when choosing his lineup. Sure, eventually he might have to make the decision himself, but he took note of how well his boys performed in drills and on Friday he allowed challenge matches with but this one rule, "an incumbent has to be beaten twice before losing his position."

Chuck took pride in the fact that he did something worthwhile for this lifetime sport that for him taught "a lot of life's lessons." He said that the best thing about high school tennis is that "it gives the kids something they can do the rest of their lives and provides instant friends no matter where you go." Chuck was *sui generis*, a Minnesota original who, though he had his share of battles with school administrators, stuck to his principles. And, like Frank Sinatra, he did it his way. This meant co-founding (with Ed Sewell) in 1960 the Pony-Polar Tournament, the oldest invitational tourney in Minnesota, sponsored by Elk River and North St. Paul. Still being played after all these years, it was later called the Early Bird Tournament and is now called the Herzog Tournament, after former Stillwater coach Bill Herzog. His way also earned his teams two boys' state championships and nine girls' state titles. And his way produced many individual entrants in boys' State Tournaments and ten girls' singles and doubles state champions. Finally, his way resurrected a languishing Macalester College men's tennis program (which had been so successful under Cliff Caine in the late 1950s and early '60s) and helped it become competitive once again in the MIAC.

While these accomplishments alone are enough to earn him a spot in the MN Tennis Coaches Hall of Fame some day, perhaps his most enduring legacy will be that as father and coach of four sons who helped Blue Earth become a state tennis power from the mid 1970s to the late '80s. Early in his teaching and coaching career at Cooper, Chuck began playing doubles on Tuesdays and Thursdays with some friends. One of these friends, knowing that Chuck had a young family, asked him one rainy day when their foursome was waiting for the rain to stop so they could play, "How many of these guys have kids?"

Chuck replied, "All of them."

To which the man responded, "How many of them have kids who play tennis?"

"None of them," said Chuck.

"Well, don't you make that same mistake [of neglecting them]," his friend said.

His admonition struck Chuck like a thunderbolt, so from that moment he decided he would spend more time with his kids. "I cut back because I wanted to play with them," he said. As a result, he gave them the greatest gift a father can bestow on his children: his time.

So whether it was outside on local courts; inside at the Minneapolis Tennis Center, Olympic Hills Country Club, North Oaks Country Club (all places where Chuck taught tennis); at the Edina, Cooper, or Stillwater High School courts; on the gym floor at Macalester after college practices; or all over Minnesota on road trips, Chuck played tennis with his sons. Often they played family doubles matches, and often Chuck would partner with one of them in father-son tournaments. Son Gregg, who teamed with his father in several national tournaments, joked, "Each of the four boys drew straws to see who played with Dad." And always the father-coach was teaching his boys, helping them with their strokes, showing them how to exploit an opponent's weaknesses, initiating them into the myriad intricacies and wonders of the doubles game. As a result, three of them won state individual titles and all participated on state championship teams at Blue Earth, but it was Chuck's emphasis on perfecting the doubles game that paid the greatest dividends. All four were good to exceptional doubles players, and Myles and Roger may have been two of the best doubles players in state history—both winning two titles, one as partners in 1985 when Myles was a senior and Roger a ninth grader. As a coach who saw them play many times over the years, including one summer when my son Chris paired up with Myles for tournament play, I was always impressed with their doubles intelligence. They simply did not make many unforced errors, they always seemed to make the right shot for the occasion, they covered the court well, and they kept their opponents off balance.

In addition, because they developed a passion for the game, they found other opportunities to play with each other. Youngest brother Roger remembers these days: "I credit the majority of the success I've had in tennis to being able to play with my brothers on a daily basis (or more accurately, they being forced to let me play)." Collectively the boys shared a fanatic devotion to the game that might be unparalleled in Minnesota tennis history. Roger, too modestly I believe, said, "I've never considered myself to be an overly talented player but a court rat that didn't lack for opportunity to hit a lot of tennis balls with people who were better."

Both Roger and Gregg recall having a racket in their hands even in their very early years. For example, Roger's first memory was of tennis, hitting shuttlecocks in the Anderson living room. "I remember using an old wooden racket, which had been sawed off so short that there was only a head that went immediately into a handle. I remember taking great pleasure in trying to hit whoever was throwing the shuttlecock at the other end of the room." Gregg, eight years Roger's senior, remembers playing against the wall at Cooper High School when he was six years old. And seven-year-old Roger also recalls "intermittently watching my brothers play and hitting on the backboard during the 1977 State Tournament won by Blue Earth and played at the U of M Fourth Street courts.

Once the boys landed at Blue Earth to live with their aunt (parents Chuck and Ruth remained in New Hope), they were privileged to continue playing with each other, both outside of team practice time and as team members during practices. Their careers often overlapped, so, for instance, on both the 1977 and '80 championship teams, two of them were members of the seven-man state tournament lineup. In '77, ninth grader Gregg played second singles and older brother Chris, a sophomore, played some doubles and served as an alternate on the tournament team. And in '80, Gregg's senior year, he played No. 1 singles and seventh grader Myles held down a No. 2 doubles spot.

During this truly remarkable Anderson family saga at Blue Earth, starting in 1977 and ending in '88 when Roger graduated, the Bucs won three state team titles and the boys captured four doubles crowns and two singles championships. And though oldest brother Chris did not win an individual title, he was an integral member of the 1977-79 Blue Earth teams and, like his younger brothers, he too went on to play college tennis, at St. Cloud State. Chris lives in Waite Park and works as a paramedic for North Memorial Ambulance Service. He still plays some tennis, especially with his two daughters and son, all of whom played high school tennis for St. Cloud Apollo. His daughter Aaryn, who graduated in 2007, made it to State in doubles two years.

Gregg, who played on both the 1977 and '80 championship teams and won both a singles and doubles state title, went to the U of IN on a tennis scholarship and played mostly Nos. 5 or 6 singles and No. 2 doubles. His sophomore year he was runner-up at No. 6 singles in the Big Ten Tournament. He also played the pro satellite circuit for two summers (stringing rackets for pin money and living out of a Volkswagon camper), and served as an assistant coach at Indiana while completing his MBA (in marketing and finance). After a three and one-half year overseas assignment for General Motors in Thailand and Singapore, he continues to work for GM in Detroit. He is pleased that two of his three children play tennis. Gregg considers it a great privilege that he was able to play on championship teams with his brothers Chris and Myles.

Third brother Myles, whose 203 high school wins might be the second most in Minnesota high school boys' tennis history, played on the 1980 championship team and also won two state individual titles, both in doubles. In fact, some observers felt that the doubles final his senior year, when he was paired with ninth-grade brother Roger, may have been the most exciting match of the '85 tournament. This was a particularly gratifying victory, in part because it was earned during a season in which the tournament was single class and because the boys defeated the defending champions from St. Cloud Tech, Sean Potter and Todd Schlorf, in a grueling three-set match played on a sweltering 100-degree day: 6-3, 4-6, 7-6.

Myles also moved on to play tennis in college, first at North Hennepin Community College (1988-90) where he qualified for Nationals in both singles and doubles. During those two years he played Nos. 1 or 2 singles and No. 1 doubles (with '86 state doubles runner-up John Andrashco of Robbinsdale Cooper). Then he finished his college tennis career at St. Cloud State, playing anywhere from Nos. 1 to 3 singles and No. 1 doubles. Both years he was a conference doubles champion.

After graduation he coached the boys' team at Columbia Heights from 1994-96, and he still does some tennis teaching in the summer and plays league tennis with his college partner Andrashco. He makes his living as an associate treasurer in cash management for United Health.

But it was younger brother Roger who outdid them all, winning 216 matches in high school, the most in Minnesota history. He won three individual state titles (two in doubles and one in singles) and led the Blue Earth Bucs

to a team title in 1988. Perhaps most remarkably, he lost only a handful of matches in his six-year career as a varsity performer. After graduating in '88, Roger went to the U of M to play for Coach Dave Geatz, cracking the lineup his last three years and serving as co-captain his final year. Of these years he said, "We were fortunate to win three Big 10 titles during my playing time (although the first was when he was a redshirt freshman) with the last two on teams that went undefeated in the Big 10."

Roger obtained a degree with honors from the U of M in electrical engineering with minors in mathematics and management, then attended medical school at Tulane U in New Orleans under the army's Health Professions Scholarship Program. Before attending medical school he also worked as an assistant tennis coach at the U of M from 1994-96 and taught tennis for two years. After leaving Tulane he completed an internship at the Madigan Army Medical Center in Tacoma, WA; served a one-year tour as a flight surgeon in Korea; spent a year in an ophthalmology residency at the Madigan Army Medical Center; received a prestigious Glaucoma Fellowship in Miami, FL; and now is a board-certified ophthalmologist at Fort Hood, TX.

Parents Chuck and Ruth took pride in their sons' tennis accomplishments, which were earned without their ever having taken private lessons; but they were equally proud of the fact that all graduated from college without asking for a dime from them. In fact, the four have a total of eight degrees. Chuck also noted that while the boys had their normal disagreements while growing up, they never fought and always supported one another when they played doubles together. All told, the boys won an astonishing 667 matches in twelve years. Myles won 203 (all but 3 in doubles), Gregg 169 (including 69 in a row), Chris 79 in just three years of competition, and Roger 216 (with only 11 losses). Roger also won 76 matches in a row. This record is not likely to be surpassed and "is quite possibly a national record for four brothers," as Gregg Wong noted in a June 11, 1988, article in the *St. Paul Pioneer Press* titled "Anderson Era Ends at Blue Earth." (For more about this extraordinary Minnesota tennis family, see Chapters Five, Six, and Nine.)

The Brandenburgs of Rochester

In southeast Minnesota were the Brandenburgs: two-time singles champion Mark; oldest brother Rob, who, with Tim Burke (now a Twin Cities tennis pro) finished second in the 1968 doubles tournament; and Scott, the No. 3 singles player on a powerful '73 Mayo team and an integral member of Mayo's very strong early '70s teams. Theirs was another of our Blue Ribbon tennis families, in part because they had so much in common with so many of the other All-State families. To begin with, their father was an excellent player who won the North Dakota state singles title in 1936. And their mother, who was, according to middle son Scott, "very supportive in our tennis upbringing," still plays quite well even in her 80s. Like all the children of these other stellar tennis families, the three Brandenburg boys had in-house hitting companions and, like most of them, from the time they began playing (variously from ages 7-9), they also received excellent coaching from the likes of Steve Wilkinson and Marv Hanenburger.

And like these other children, they played a great deal of tennis. According to Scott, "Our summers revolved around tennis and tournaments. Every day we had lessons, every weekend we had tournaments—many in Iowa and a lot in the Twin Cities." As a result they all became outstanding tennis players, but because they were also exceptional athletes they did not focus solely on tennis. Rob and Mark excelled in basketball and, as Scott said of himself, "I got heavily involved in football, for which I received several scholarships" (though he would only play tennis in college). This makes youngest son Mark's accomplishment of winning two singles titles all the more remarkable, for almost all champions today play only tennis the year round.

As for their tennis skills Scott said, "My tennis game was based on my legs. I didn't have a particular strength—no huge serve or big backhand—rather, I ran my butt off and chased everything down. I was aggressive at the net, however." Scott said of his brothers' tennis skills, "Rob had a good groundstroke game but Mark had the full package—serve, volley, groundstrokes."

After high school all three played tennis in college,

Rob just intramurals (he was a champion at Michigan State) and Scott at North Dakota State where he captained the team and played No. 3 singles and No. 1 doubles.

Following a stint as the director of a U.S. Junior Tennis League program in the Fargo-Moorhead area, a pilot program that won a national achievement award, Scott works as a senior associate for Coldwell Banker in Fargo, ND.

Rob Brandenburg was a cardiologist at Abbott Northwestern Hospital who lived in Orono and Mark works as a certified life and business coach.

Regrettably, Rob died of a heart attack in 2002 after suffering for years from a rare form of Parkinsons, but before his death Scott often played tennis with him. "I had many matches with Rob later in our tennis life and still only rarely beat him, until his illness slowed him down." Scott said he also played Mark last summer [2005] and "his game is still fantastic, particularly for a near 50-year-old." (For more about Mark Brandenburg, see Chapter Four.)

The Brennans of Minneapolis West

"Serendipity," a lovely word that describes the sometimes fortunate discoveries made accidentally on our journeys through life, fits the next All-State tennis family perfectly, the Brennans of Minneapolis. And since the Brennans are Irish, maybe we should also call this particular discovery the luck of the Irish. Call it what you will, it is not likely there would have been such a tennis-playing family had tech sergeant Dan Brennan not met a British army captain named Helen Harmsworth while he was stationed in England during WWII. Born in Africa, she had moved to England at age four with her father, an official with the British government. The daughter of Lord and Lady Harmsworth, this spunky young woman's war-time job was shooting down German buzz bombs. Their romance was a "love game" that ended in a marriage that eventually produced four tennis-playing children who became formidable competitors for the Minneapolis West Cowboys throughout the 1960s and '70s.

Helen (Harmsworth) Brennan, who grew up with a tennis racket in her hand, was an accomplished tennis player who had, according to second son Tom, "good hand-eye coordination." So she taught her husband, a hard-charging, Type A guy who needed an outlet like tennis for his energy, to play the game. And in a sort of family domino-effect, first she and then later her husband taught the children how to play the game. Both Helen and Dan also became top-ranked adult players in the NWLTA Section, and Dan also played mixed doubles with Helen and father-son doubles with his sons. The family lived in the Kenwood area of Minneapolis and the parents introduced their children to tennis at the Minneapolis Tennis Club (MTC), where they were members.

Oldest son John remembers those early years with great fondness, recalling, "We spent our weekends at the MTC and we had a wonderful time playing there on the clay courts." Youngest son Mike said, "My friend Mark Nammacher (third-place state singles finisher in 1975) and I rode our bikes down there [to the MTC] and played all the time from morning to night." State singles champion Tom ('69), the second son, remembers "being four years old and waiting at the club for Mom and Dad to finish their matches so I could hit with them." In fact, Tom (and to a lesser extent Mike) claims that he spent most of his formative tennis years hanging out at the MTC at the Parade Grounds "until I was about 14."

Now it would not be fair to say that the Brennans learned everything they needed to know about tennis from their parents, for John said that he took lessons for four or five years from Frank Voigt, beginning at age 13, and then with Bill Kuross. He recalls one memorable experience during the time he worked with Kuross: "Kuross brought Ken Rosewall to the Kenwood Park Tennis Courts... Later, Bucky [Zimmerman-1963-64 doubles champion with John] and I were ballboys for Laver, Gonzalez, and Rosewall when they played an exhibition at the Minneapolis Auditorium and we got to hit with Rosewall." And though he was only 11 years old at the time—the year was 1961—Tom also remembers being a ball boy for some of those exhibition matches at the Auditorium featuring the "Handsome Eight" pro tennis players such as Jack Kramer, Pancho Segura, Tony Roche, Butch Buchholz, Bobby Riggs, and the aforementioned Laver, Gonzalez, and Rosewall. John also said he hit with Kramer on one of those occasions.

Tom also took lessons from Voigt from the ages of 9 to 11 and from Kuross in the summers from 1962-64, and youngest son Mike recalls (as did John and Tom) taking the bus to play at the Nicollet courts in the summers. Mike credits the Junior Champions Program for helping him develop his game even more. "When I was in junior high we played a pro and one of our peers once a week," he remarked. But it was Jack Roach who perhaps made the biggest impact on his tennis game: "Jack taught me a lot during the 10-15 lessons I had one summer. He really taught me how to hit a flat serve, for example."

And though this is primarily a story about the three Brennan boys, it has other compelling plot lines. For instance, the youngest child, Cathy, was also an excellent player who, like so many young women of her era, did not have a team of her female peers to play on. So she played on the Minneapolis West boys' team for three years. The eldest of the five Brennan children, Diana, did not play much tennis as a youngster, though she played later as an adult.

Mother Helen's role in this drama has been chronicled earlier in this profile, but there is much more to be said about the patriarch of the family, Dan Brennan. Described by John Brennan's doubles partner Zimmerman as a "volatile, Hemingway-esque character and a dominating father," he was an ambitious taskmaster who was driven by demons to seek perfection for himself and his children. In fact, according to his son Mike, he enlisted in the Canadian Air Force after spending a month with Ernest Hemingway who told him, "You have to go to war in order to learn to write." After serving with distinction in WWII (he earned a silver star and a purple heart), Brennan came back to the U.S. and took up tennis (after being taught by his wife) with an almost manic compulsion. Soon he began competing at his club and in tournaments, and then he began teaching his children. While oldest son John admits that "the reason we all played tennis was because of my mother," all three brothers credited their father for helping them discover the competitive drive needed to succeed on the courts. Tom said, "Dad taught us early on how to prepare for matches, even two hours before a tournament. He used to play a set with me before the first match of a tournament and before the finals." Though he had an unorthodox playing style, according to Tom, he was a gritty competitor.

There was an element of fear in this father-son relationship as well, for Dan expected his children to excel and he pushed them hard. Mike, recalling his own anxiety about this relationship, said, "We worried about what we would tell Dad if we didn't win the tournament. We had better do well because that was our ticket to college." The Brennans had invested a good deal of money, including tournament fees and expenses, on their children's tennis and they expected good results. Tom continues with this refrain: "We were all striving for rankings so colleges would notice us. My father would give me two weeks off to be a kid."

Father Dan's approach paid off, for all three boys were highly ranked juniors; and two of the three won state titles, Tom in singles and John in doubles. In NWLTA summer play, John was ranked No. 1 in the Section in both the 13-and-under and 15-and-under divisions and No. 2 in the 18-and-unders. In addition, he and his high school teammate/doubles partner Zimmerman were No. 1 in doubles for two years. Tom was ranked No. 1 in the 14s, 16s, and 18s and also achieved a national ranking of No. 40 in the 18-and-unders in 1968.

And youngest son Mike earned high rankings from the time he began playing in the 12-and-unders, achieving a No. 2 ranking three times, twice behind two-time state champion Mark Brandenburg (once in the 14s and once in the 16s) and once behind Grant Helgeson (his second year in the 16s). With his Minneapolis West teammate Nammacher he was also ranked No. 1 in doubles once in the 16s. 1975 doubles champion Scott Nesbit said of Mike, "He was like a moose, a big guy with a one-handed slice backhand. A very stylish player."

In addition to being a ranked senior player, father Dan was variously a newspaper reporter for the *Minneapolis Star and Tribune*, a press secretary for Hubert Humphrey when Humphrey was mayor of Minneapolis, and a novelist. A prolific writer, he penned twenty-five novels, including one son Tom claims was about him. It must not have been a flattering portrait, for it was called, tellingly, *Double Fault*. One last story may serve to illustrate the ultra-competitive nature of Dan Brennan, this larger-than-life character. It's a story Tom tells. "At age 11 my father put me on a train for Peoria, Illinois, to play in a national junior clay court tournament. I lost in the semifinals," he recalls, "and when I came back my father was furious. He said, 'I didn't send you all the way to Illinois to lose.'"

Perhaps less well known about the elder Brennan is the fact that he helped inaugurate the first indoor tennis club in Minnesota, renting the roller rink in St. Louis Park and setting up courts over the concrete floor of the rink. This took place in the early 1960s before the advent of indoor clubs in the Metro area, and son Mike said that the courts, though "glazed over and very fast," were booked all the time.

Finally, since the exploits of John and Tom are covered in Chapters Five and Six, it is appropriate to say more about Mike here. Very successful in Minneapolis conference play, Mike twice won the City singles championship and finished second to his teammate Nammacher another year. And though he was not as successful in high school as his older brothers (he usually lost in region play to Lake Conference opponents such as Craig Jones from Edina and Steve Benson from Bloomington), he had a very successful college career. After attending boarding school at Berkshire in western Massachusetts for a year following his high school graduation from West, Mike was recruited to play hockey at Division 2 Lake Forest College in Chicago. Here he played just two years of varsity hockey, but it was in tennis that he excelled. Playing No. 1 singles and doubles all four years, he won the conference singles title two of those four years (splitting them with old Edina High School foe Greg Swendseen from Carleton). During his time at Lake Forest the Foresters played Division 1 schools such as Marquette and DePaul; and his senior year he advanced to the Division 2 championships where he lost in the first round in three sets. In addition to this time on the courts at Lake Forest, he taught tennis at the Cold Spring Harbor Tennis Club on Long Island (as his brothers had done before him) for several years during the summers after high school.

With degrees in city planning and psychology, Mike left Lake Forest in 1979 for a job as a floor trader on the

Chicago Board Options Exchange, a job he held for eighteen years. At night for several years he also taught tennis at the Midtown Tennis Club to supplement his income. For a time he held a No. 2 ranking in "B" level national tournaments in squash as well. Now he works as a project manager building high-end single family homes on the North Shore of Chicago. And he has taken up tennis again after a hiatus of several years. He said, "I'm loving it. I play in a doubles group with ex-college players and some satellite players."

So while the Brennan family story began with a serendipitous meeting between a tennis-playing British woman and a "Yank," it would not have been much of a tale if it hadn't also included a family commitment to tennis, some natural athletic talent on the part of the children, and a great deal of hard work.

The Carlsons of Madison

The Latin saying *parvis e glandibus quercus* (*Bartlett's Familiar Quotations*, 119) seems appropriate in describing this next tennis family, for from one little acorn tall and mighty oaks (five tennis-playing children) grew up in the fertile soil of western Minnesota. The little acorn was Robert "Jolly" Carlson, called the smallest and youngest (he was then a sophomore) prep high school champion in America by the New York Times in 1939. Carlson, not quite five feet tall at the time, grew up in South Dakota but made his mark as a tennis coach in the tiny border town of Madison, MN. From that fateful moment in the summer of 1957, when he chose to conduct the summer recreation program (which included tennis) instead of teach driver's education, until he retired in 1990, Jolly Carlson lived out his dream of coaching. "Since I was knee high to a grasshopper, the only thing I ever wanted to do was coach," he said. For more about this little acorn who himself became a mighty oak in the state tennis world, read his profile in Chapter Two. But what of his progeny, the mighty oaks who helped put Madison on the Minnesota tennis map?

There were four boys and a girl, and they all contributed to the remarkable success of their father's teams throughout the decades of the 1970s and early '80s. Of the boys, the two youngest (Greg and Jeff) competed in six State Tournaments, winning the doubles title in '78. (For more about their doubles championship, see Chapter Six.) Barry, the oldest, competed in four State Tourneys, two in singles and two in doubles; and the second son, Gary, played in five. Daughter Kristin, the youngest of Jolly and Carol Carlson's children, lettered for six years, played as a ninth grader on a team that finished fourth in the State Tournament, and advanced to State individual competition four times.

Though none of the boys (or Kristin) would win a singles title, Gary advanced to the singles tournament his last three years (1974-76) but had the misfortune of running into Paul Holbach from White Bear Lake (a top player who finished second to Mark Wheaton in '76) each of those years. As a sophomore and junior he was bounced out by Holbach in the first round, and as a senior he lost to him in the quarters. Despite these losses, he did very well in state tournament play, advancing to the individual tournament five straight years and making important contributions on Madison's three straight team entries. His sophomore and junior years he finished runner-up in the consolation bracket.

And after youngest brother Jeff won the 1978 doubles title with brother Greg, he had the bad luck to draw champion Louie McKee of Blake in the first round of the Class A singles tournament in '79, his senior year. In the two years prior to winning the doubles, he and Greg also advanced to State, falling in the quarters to pairs from St. Cloud Tech on both occasions. In what is likely the most remarkable brother-brother doubles-team record in state tennis history, Greg Carlson advanced to State five times, twice with older sibling Barry (in 1974 and '75) and three times with Jeff (1976-78).

In addition to their accomplishments in the individual tournament, the boys led Madison to four state team tournament appearances (three when there was just a single-class tourney and one in Class A). In 1975, with the brothers making up four-sevenths of a very strong team, they led unheralded Madison to the finals where the little giant lost to powerhouse Edina.

Their success in high school resulted in part from

their play in the juniors, for the boys all played in summer tournaments and three of the four earned high rankings in the Section throughout the 1970s. Though Barry was not ranked in the Section, he was ranked No. 7 by the high school coaches before his senior year and he and Gary won the consolation doubles title in '73. He also made it to State in singles in '72 but lost in the first round; and in 1974

Barry (2nd from left), Gary (4th from left), Greg (5th from Left) & Jeff Carlson (far right)

and '75 he and Greg teamed up and made it to State, losing in the first round in '74 and winning a round in '75.

Second son Gary was ranked as high as No. 5 in boys 14 singles and No. 2 in boys 14 and 16 doubles, pairing with future U of M star Mike Trautner from South Dakota. They earned this No. 2 ranking in their second year of boys 14s and also in their first year of boys 16s.

And third son Greg was ranked as high as No. 2 in boys 14 singles the same year (1974). In a preview of things to come, he and brother Jeff were ranked No. 1 in boys 14 doubles. In Greg's first year in the 14s he was also ranked No. 1 in doubles (with John Stauffer of Fargo, ND).

Youngest brother Jeff, arguably the most successful of the Carlson brothers, was ranked as high as No. 1 in singles in the 12s; but he also earned singles rankings of No. 3 in his first year in the 12s and his first year in the 14s, No. 4 in his last year in the 14s, No. 3 in the16s, and No. 11 in his last year in the 18s. In addition, he was a superb doubles player who earned rankings with a variety of top players from his era: No. 1 with Brace Helgeson in his first year of the 12-and-unders and No. 3 with Jay Lauer of Sioux Falls that year, No. 1 with 1976 doubles

champion Andy Ringlien in his last year of the 12 doubles, and No. 1 with his brother Greg the next year.

Given that the Carlson kids had no access to indoor courts and that they did not take lessons from tennis pros, their success was all the more remarkable. Why then were they able to compete and more often than not overcome opponents who had been given these advantages? First, and perhaps foremost, they had their own coach right at home, their dad, a man who knew the game and knew how to teach it. Secondly, like fish growing up in a pond, they grew up with their own tennis courts nearby. Oldest brother Barry talks about "walking out the front door and banging the ball against the board my dad put up on the courts across the street from our house." Barry recalls that the board had white dots painted above the net line and that he and his siblings practiced hitting those dots. Later, when the boys helped their dad teach summer lessons, the "students" enjoyed hitting on this board. According to Barry, "If you got ten in a row against the board, above the line, you received a bubble gum; then after winning the gum you could move up to a Tootsie Pop for twenty-five in a row, a can of pop for fifty in a row, and a malt at the local DQ if you ever made it to 100!"

In addition, they became good players because Jolly knew how important it was to enter them into the pressure cooker of junior tennis tournaments in the summer. All four boys (and sister Kristin) became successful junior players (as noted earlier), and they all recall the great experiences they had in traveling around the summer circuit (often with Dad or Mom) and making friends with top players from all over the region. Jeff played his first tournament at age 8 and by age 10 was traveling to Sioux Falls, Aberdeen, Duluth, Rochester, St. Cloud, and the Twin Cities. He said of these experiences, "All of the tournaments provided housing with families in the communities. It was a great way for us to learn how to be appreciative and to 'mind our manners.' Tournament entry fees were $1.50 for singles and $2 per doubles team."

Barry remembers getting to know families such as

the Wheatons, Helgesons, Burtons, and Trautners. "Mike Trautner, Gary's doubles partner, would always spend a week with us and Gary a week with the Trautners," he said. When Jeff was 12 and ranked No. 1 in the Section, he played in Knoxville, TN, and recalls a brief encounter with Chris Evert's brother John. He "borrowed a quarter from me there and has never paid me back!" At age 16 he was the only Carlson boy still playing tournaments, so he often had to hitchhike. Imagine parents letting their children do that today!

The success of the Carlsons is even more striking when one considers that they never played tennis in the winter, mainly because there were no indoor courts near Madison. Instead, in Barry's words, "All of us on the team were three or four sport players, so tennis happened in the spring and summer. We played basketball to get ready for tennis, we played football or cross country to get ready for basketball." Second son Gary said, "I played football or ran cross country in the fall and played basketball into March. In the summer I played more golf than tennis as well as some baseball and basketball." Jeff also recollected that he and his brothers played golf in August and that the tennis team could beat the golf team in golf. So they were good athletes as well, but perhaps the most important factor in their tennis success (as in the case with all these tennis families) was that they all had built-in hitting partners right in their own house.

Unfortunately, they were never able to play with their father because his health problems made it impossible for him to exercise vigorously, so they had to rely on each other. Of course Jolly threw balls to them in practice, but they valued more the lessons about life and tennis he taught them. Son Greg said of these lessons, "My dad was from the old school. You practiced hard, played hard, and played honestly." All four boys recall that their dad was a stern disciplinarian who had no tolerance for misbehavior on the court, including offensive language. Barry recalls being pulled off the court by his dad when he once said damn. This was an episode that was so vivid in his memory because both Jolly and Carol had instilled in all five children the importance of controlling one's language in all situations. Barry said that Jolly also "required us to always have our shirts tucked in and everyone to be in uniform—you played how you looked and felt." And Jeff remembers

being reprimanded after a match for telling an opponent to "Shut up!" when the opponent clapped after he [Jeff] missed an easy backhand volley.

And though she herself did not play much tennis, the woman who was known in Madison as "Mom Tennis," mother Carol Carlson, played an important role in the development of her childrens' games. According to Barry, "She spent many years as Dad's assistant coach, sometimes officially and at other times unofficially. She would travel with the team because sometimes our JV was at one place and the varsity at another; she then drove the JV team and served as their coach."

This early training in both the physical and mental aspects of the game paid rich dividends for the boys and their Madison team. All four played six years of varsity tennis, Jeff and Greg won that doubles title in 1978, and of course little David—Madison—reached the finals of the '75 team tournament. Though they lost to Goliath (Edina) by a 5-0 score, the boys remember the magic of that tournament experience. Barry, a senior, recalls how his dad moved him from No. 1 doubles to No. 1 singles for the tournament (he and singles teammates Ross Lund and brother Gary were all even in ability) and split brothers Greg and Jeff to strengthen the doubles. This paid off especially in the semifinal match with Coon Rapids, for Madison eked out a 3-2 win on the strength of wins at No. 1 doubles and Nos. 2 and 3 singles.

An article in the June 5, 1975, *Minneapolis Tribune* titled "Coach Is Like Expectant Father As Son Puts Team in State Finals," described the clinching No. 1 doubles match won by Jolly's son Greg, a ninth grader, and his partner Pete Kraemer: "Coach Jolly Carlson couldn't stand to watch. 'Might nerve the boys,' he said. 'And I get a bit nervous, too!'" Here's how Greg (in that same article) described the dramatic ending to that match: "It was a tie-breaker in the third set and I was serving for the match at 4-3. Pete dinked the ball and we won. The entire crowd was watching the match and several team members scaled the fence to begin the celebration. As a stoic Norwegian not wanting to show emotion, I started crying and hyperventilating. So I had to be taken to the emergency room—I was stiff as a board."

And though Madison lost in the finals, the little town gave the team a post-tournament reception befitting what Barry called Super Bowl winners. "The town came out to meet us with firetrucks, lights flashing, and we got driven around town in the firetrucks." Greg said that there was also a big party at the gym and that each team member was given Peavey hats from a local department store and shirts with "Madison" emblazoned on them.

Before advancing to the region and State Tournament in these heady years, Madison had to defeat a strong Montevideo team coached by Windy Block, which they did for eighteen years in a row. Greg especially remembers the four Hagberg boys (another good tennis family) and one of them in particular, his sometime summer doubles partner. He was Neil Hagberg, today one-half of the well-known singing duo, Neil and Leandra.

Perhaps more than any of these famous Minnesota tennis families, in part because they came from such a small, rural, town, the Carlsons best represent the community/family culture which produces champions. Greg compared their tennis family to that of "farm families working in the fields together. You spend a lot of time with players and it's not that often that a seventh grader can be on a level playing field with a tenth grader. We have the same interests, the same objective."

In addition, because they traveled to meets in cars, they developed close relationships with their teammates and shared memories such as the following near disaster. Coming home from a meet in Montevideo, Coach Carlson was driving through Lac Qui Parle Village when four horses came galloping out of a gate and ran in front of the car. Jolly said, "I swerved just in time and the horses missed the driver's side by inches."

From the westernmost border of the state, all five Carlson children moved to southeast Minnesota for their schooling, to St. Olaf College in Northfield, a town that four of the five now call home. Barry, recruited by then coach Chuck Lunder, was the first and for seven years in a row one of the Carlsons captained the Ole team. All were successful performers on strong teams that unfortunately had to compete with national powerhouse Gustavus, but most years they finished second in the conference.

Barry played mostly Nos. 5 or 6 singles and Nos. 2 or 3 doubles. Gary played one year at the Air Force Academy (Nos. 5-6 singles and No. 3 doubles), then transferred to

St. Olaf for his sophomore year to join Barry. As an Ole he played No. 2 singles his sophomore year and No. 3 singles his junior and senior years. He and No. 1 doubles partner Dan Anderson from Austin finished second to national champions John Mattke and Paul Holbach of Gustavus two of those years.

Greg played variously from Nos. 4-6 singles and Nos. 2 to 3 doubles; and Jeff played No. 4 singles as a freshman, No. 1 as a sophomore, and No. 2 (behind current Edina girls coach Steve Paulsen from Northfield) as a junior and senior. As a senior Jeff compiled a 36-6 record, beating several nationally ranked players and qualifying for nationals. He and Steve lost a three-set match to the No. 2 seeds at No. 1 doubles that year. His senior year he was also ranked No. 31 in singles and No. 11 in doubles (with Paulsen) in Division 3.

Daughter Kristin, limited to two years of competition because of the demands of her nursing studies, played two years at St. Olaf. Her senior year she lost only one match in the conference.

After graduating from St. Olaf three of the Carlson boys entered the business world; in fact, Greg, Jeff, and sister Kristin's husband (Justin Stets) today run a financial planning and investment advising service with offices in Northfield and Hastings. After twenty-three years with Lutheran Brotherhood, Barry now works at St. Olaf in the development office, and Gary is a physician in Northfield. Kristin, a nurse practitioner, is an assistant girls' tennis coach at Northfield High School and at St. Olaf. Jeff also coaches tennis, as an assistant boys' coach at Hastings.

All still play tennis and, thanks to their mother's gift in her husband's memory, all the grandchildren have attended Steve Wilkinson's *Tennis and Life* camps for several summers. Perhaps because he remembered those spartan years of chipping ice off the three Madison courts and hitting against a brick gym wall in early spring, Jeff treated himself to a clay court on his property in Hastings. According to Barry, "Each year Jeff has a 'tennis day' that starts with the kids all playing tennis and tennis games with the parents giving instruction. The day is capped with a match of Barry/Gary taking on Jeff/Greg, Minnesota state high school champions. It is always a close match but Greg and Jeff have won all but two times over the last twenty-some years."

All this attention to tennis has paid off, for the little Carlsons (and the Stets, Kristin's children) have kept the Carlson legacy alive. In 2005-06, for example, there were four Carlson girls and one boy on the Northfield varsity teams and younger ones waiting in the wings.

The Helgesons of St. Cloud

On the cover of a 2003 tourist brochure titled "Norway—Facts and Information" is a color photo of two blond hikers resting on a rock after, one presumes, a strenuous hike in the fjord countryside. They are gazing down at the famous Geirangerfjord, its deep blue waters bisecting steep rock cliffs painted a verdant green at the lower elevations and a snow-capped white at the top. It struck me that the Norwegian Tourist Office could just as well have used any of the three St. Cloud Helgeson boys or their sister in that picture, for with their blond locks, fair skin, and blue eyes, they look more Nordic than most native Norwegians. To be sure there have been many Minnesota tennis players named Nelson, Swenson, Halverson (and the Andersons and Carlsons in this chapter), but if ever a state tennis family represented our Scandinavian ancestors, it was the Helgesons. You doubters need only take a look at the family photo in this chapter to see what I mean. If they had been raised in Norway, these sturdy youngsters could just as easily have mastered Holmenkollen Hill in Oslo; but it was our good fortune that they were brought up in St. Cloud and chose to focus more on competitive tennis than skiing (though all were skiers as well).

These precocious tennis players, like others profiled in this chapter, had a parent or relative who introduced them to the game and encouraged them throughout their junior tennis-playing years. In the case of the Helgesons it was father Jerry, a former NBC and all-opponent member of the all-American football team in 1953 (he was a middle linebacker) and Big Ten discus champion at the U of M. Jerry was also an enthusiastic and skilled 6-handicap golfer and of course, a tennis player. Youngest son Brace said that his father decided that golf took too much time and didn't keep you in shape for all the

time invested, so "my father made a somewhat sudden decision to quit golf around the time I was seven years old and turn all of his energies into tennis."

Tennis soon became the family's passion, especially after they moved into a new house at the St. Cloud Country Club. Oldest son Grant, describing this new home, said, "It overlooked the 16th hole at the Country Club and had a racquetball court in the basement and a tennis court in the front yard." Except for a few families such as the Schwanbergs, there weren't many hitting partners for the Helge-

Helgeson Family. (Boys) Brace, Kent, & Grant. (Parents) Jerry & Ann.

son clan in St. Cloud, so from the time they were eight or nine years old they honed their skills by hitting with one another on the family court. And on the days when they just wanted to be alone with a ball and a racket, they hit on the backboard their father added on this home court. Grant remembers his father hitting balls to him when he was eight, and Kent credits Hall of Fame coach Mac Doane for jump-starting their careers. "Mac Doane," whom Kent called the Norm McDonald of St. Cloud, "started us off. He sold rackets, balls, and other tennis equipment; and he also strung rackets for us."

There were no indoor courts in St. Cloud at the time, so these blond Vikings needed to make voyages to other places before they could begin to conquer the Minnesota tennis world. Kent talks about getting up at 5 AM and driving to nearby St. John's U in the winter to play. He said, "A man we called 'Walrus' drove us in an old Datsun (with the defrost on full blast on frigid days) so we could play on their taped-off wood courts before classes began." He also recalls meeting then tennis pro, former St. Cloud star, and current Minnetonka coach Dave Stearns at "a little club in Albertville" for hitting sessions. Brace mentioned that Stearns also came to their house to give occasional lessons on the Helgeson court.

Even so, father Jerry soon realized that his charges needed more "schooling," so for four years he sent them to the Ramey Tennis School on the campus of Carleton College in Northfield for four weeks each summer. This was about the time all three boys began to hit the tournament circuit, and all would achieve high rankings in the Section. For example, Grant was ranked No. 1 in Boys 16 Singles for the 1972 season and No. 1 in Boys 18 Doubles (with Mark Brandenburg) in '73. Middle son Kent was ranked No. 1 for two years in 14 doubles (each time with Mark Wheaton), and he was twice ranked No. 3 in singles, once in the 14s and once in the 16s. Brace, arguably the most successful tournament player among the boys, was ranked No. 1 his second year in 12 singles and doubles (partnering with Jeff Carlson), No. 1 his second year in 14 singles, No. 4 his first year in 18 singles, and No. 1 his final year of 18 doubles (with Louie McKee).

During the high school tennis seasons, as it became more and more difficult for the boys to find good competition in their school meets, Coach Bill Ritchie allowed them to drive to the Twin Cities for practice matches with top Metro-area players. Brace describes these forays thus: "I'll always remember driving down to the Twin Cities, with my brother Kent, four out of the five years I played, in order to get competitive matches. We either hit with each other or we jumped in the car and headed to the Twin Cities twice a week."

All this hard work paid off, for St. Cloud Tech won its first state team tennis championship in the bicentennial year of 1976. Unfortunately, Grant was dropped from the tennis team his senior year for skipping school and had graduated in '74; so senior Kent and sophomore Brace, playing Nos. 1 and 2 singles respectively, led the way to a thrilling victory. Flashing their blond locks and brandishing their rackets like swords, these two Norsemen won two of the matches that helped St. Cloud earn a 3-2 upset of Lake Conference power Minnetonka. Kent's was the most dramatic match because he upended '75 state champion Mark Wheaton, slashing his way back from a 6-2, 5-1 deficit to win 6 games in a row in the second set and then closing out the third set 6-1. His was the final match and he had to beat Wheaton in order for St. Cloud to win. Both doubles teams (Jon Schwanberg and Todd Holes at No. 1 and Paul Wehlage and Mark Smith at No. 2) had already lost and Jerry Schwanberg had won at No. 3 singles. Meanwhile, Brace had won his first set and was up 5-2 in the second against Mark Burton when, in his words, "I coasted for a few games while I kept an eye on Kent's match next door which was starting to heat up because Kent started making some incredible shots and started one of the greatest comebacks in state high school history." Wheaton [Kent's opponent] was undefeated that year and an overwhelming favorite to win the individual title for a second year and to lead his team to a state championship. Although Brace eventually won his second set 7-5, he remembers that his Dad upbraided him "about what I was putting at risk."

Both brothers will never forget the euphoria they experienced and the reception they received from the citizens of St. Cloud after the match: a fire engine and police escort into town, about 1,000 people cheering them in the school gym, and a party at the Helgeson house. Brace, recalling this memorable party, said, "My father and mother, Ann, and some of the other parents threw a big celebration that evening at our house on that very tennis court that he had built years before where the seeds of our tennis careers would be planted."

Though none of the boys won a state singles or doubles title, Grant finished third in the 1973 singles tournament as a junior and he and partner Jeff Schwanberg were the doubles runners-up in '72; Kent took third place in the '76 singles tournament; and Brace finished fifth in the doubles in '75 and third in the doubles in '76, both times with Jerry Schwanberg. Brace unfortunately lost in the quarters of the singles tourney his junior year ('77) to runner-up Scott Jacobson of Blue Earth, then he lost in the round of 16 his senior year to '77 champion Kevin Smith (whom he had beaten earlier in the year) in an agonizing three and one-half hour battle 7-6, 5-7, 7-6. According to Brace, "Jerry Noyce called it the best high school match he had ever watched, which, coming from Jerry Noyce meant a lot to me." Since he had only lost one match that year (an upset loss to Steve Brandt of Mounds View in the region finals), he was confident he would win the singles title; so of course he was heartbroken when he lost to Smith.

Thus it was left to the youngest of the Helgeson blonds, sister Ginger, to win individual state titles. That she did and more, leading her Edina team to four state titles and becoming the first three-time Minnesota girls champion (1983-85). (In Class A Kira Gregerson of St. Paul Academy (SPA) won four titles, Gina Suh of SPA won five, and Megan Tiegs of Rochester Lourdes three; and in Class AA Anh Nguyen of Bloomington Jefferson tied Suh for the most singles titles in state history for boys' and girls' tennis with five). Ginger's brother Brace coached her after he graduated from college, and he followed her very successful college and pro career with justifiable pride. At Pepperdine U she was a three-time all-American, won the National Hardcourt Tournament in Minnesota her senior year, and as a pro earned a ranking as high as 29th in the world and 20th in earnings one year. She held singles wins over Martina Navratilova and Conchita Martinez (after Martinez won Wimbledon in 1994) and a doubles win over Monica Seles, to name just three of the top pros she defeated during her eight-year career. With Jeanne Arth and Ann Henricksson she shares the honor of being Minnesota's greatest women professional players.

But she was not the only family member who excelled at the next levels in tennis. After what he described "as a year in Alaska finding my soul," Grant played one year at North Idaho Junior College, enrolled at the U of M the next year—where he played No. 1 doubles with Mark Brandenburg and No. 2 singles—then transferred to Arizona State

U (ASU) where he played three years as a self-described "small fish in a huge ocean at ASU."

Brother Kent matriculated at Mesa Junior College in Arizona for two years, where he finished third in singles in the national tournament his second year. Then, after joining brother Grant at ASU (for one semester), he received a scholarship from Jerry Noyce and packed his bags to return home (to the U of M). During his two years at the U he played No. 1 singles and doubles on a team of "individuals that played together" and won the Big Ten title in 1981, the first since 1933 for the Gophers. He and partner Mike Trautner, ranked in the top five in doubles in the country, beat Michigan's top team of Rick Leach and Mike Horwitch in the semis but lost in the finals. In '80 he and Hakan Almstrom won the No. 2 Big Ten doubles title, and in his senior year ('81) Kent earned All-Big Ten honors and served as co-captain of the Gophers (with Trautner). Like his sister Ginger and brother Brace, Kent got a taste of pro tennis, playing three Penn Circuit, Missouri Valley tournaments between his sophomore and junior years and after his senior year.

Youngest brother Brace got a full-ride tennis scholarship to Lamar U in Texas, where he played between Nos. 1-3 singles and Nos. 1-2 doubles for two years. He had taken off the first half of his second year at Lamar to play on the Nike Professional Tour with Mark Brandenburg, an experience that he called "very sobering—lots of cheating and cutthroat competition." So he left the tour, finished the season at Lamar, and came back to Minnesota to play the summer circuit. He fondly recalls his success in the Minikahda Tournament that summer: "After winning the qualifying tournament [beating Steve Wilkinson, among others], I played Nick Saviano in the main draw of eight. He was ranked 19 in the world at the time. I lost 6-3, 6-3 and afterward Jerry Noyce offered me a scholarship." And though as a transfer he had to sit out a year and did not play with Kent, he watched Kent and his future team claim that Big Ten title in 1981. His junior year ('82) he won the No. 3 Big Ten doubles title (with Peter Kolaric), lost to all-American Ernie Fernandez of Ohio State in the No. 1 singles semis, and earned All-Big Ten honors. Then, his senior year ('83), he won the No. 6 Big Ten singles championship.

So though they left home to play tennis after high school, these homeboy Vikings came back to their roots to play college tennis. Today, however, only one remains in the state, Brace. He has been selling homes for over twenty years for Coldwell Banker in Eden Prairie. On the health front, it's worth mentioning that he, like Lance Armstrong, survived a bout with testicular cancer. In fact, he used the same doctor Armstrong used.

The second of the Helgesons, Kent, has three boys who were highly ranked junior players (one of whom was ranked No. 1 in the country in 18 singles in 2003), and he works in Overland Park, KS, as a money manager for the Mason James Management Company. Oldest sibling Grant and his wife, Laurie, parents of two children, play tennis together and in fact were the only husband and wife team to participate in the 4.5 USTA National Mixed Doubles Tournament a few years ago. As a student at ASU Grant started a small tennis teaching business in which he gave lessons to people who had their own tennis courts. This business helped him survive after college while he began to establish himself in real estate sales. It also helped him get to know people in the Scottsdale area, and many of them helped him launch what is today a successful real estate career in the area.

All three brothers were key figures on the Minnesota high school tennis scene, and though they certainly have some regrets (Brace not winning the singles title his senior year and Grant regretting that in his senior year "I started hanging out with the wrong kind of crowd and didn't focus on my tennis," for instance), they have wonderful memories of those years. All three began their varsity careers as eighth graders and all recalled the friendships and team camaraderie they developed with their St. Cloud mates. Grant also enjoyed "traveling around Minnesota and meeting different tennis coaches and players." And all were formidable competitors who were often feared by their opponents (in part because they were intense and had big serves and aggressive games), perhaps in the same way that Europeans feared the marauding Vikings from Norway. Edina's Bill Arnold (1975 doubles champion) said about the Helgesons, "These were players that scared me... any Helgeson. I think Kent and Brace would eat raw zebra meat before a match." All were also all-around athletes; Kent, for instance, was an all-State linebacker in football at Tech and all were accomplished downhill skiers.

Unlike a Minnesota football team with a Scandinavian name, these Vikings helped their school team win one Super Bowl, a 1976 team tennis championship. (For more on the Helgesons, see Chapter Nine.)

The Joergers of Staples-Motley

From west-central Minnesota we have the Joerger family of Staples-Motley, coach Joe and tennis-playing sons David, Blaine, and Jeff. Under their father's direction the Cardinals' teams made four appearances at State, winning Class A titles in 1990 and '91, and his son David won the '92 singles championship. In addition, Joerger coached the '92 doubles champions (Mark Haglin and David Cizek) and several of his other players performed well at State. These included son David's second place finish in singles in '91 and son Blaine's second-place showing in the '95 Class A doubles tournament (with partner Mike Rollins).

Coach Joe Joerger & 1990 Class A Team Champions, Staples-Motley

Coach Joerger's third son, Jeff, though not as successful as his older brothers, nevertheless made it to State in doubles as a junior in 1996, losing in the first round.

According to father Joe, Jeff took up tennis a bit later than David and Blaine (both of whom began playing at age 10) and was not quite as committed as they were. And while David achieved the greatest success, Blaine was no slouch as a junior player, ranking as high as Nos. 6 and 3 in his two years as a 10-and-under player.

Father Joe has two other children, whom he calls his "second shift," but neither of them play on a high school tennis team. Both attend a school that does not offer the sport of tennis, Henning High School, so they have concentrated on other sports. Daughter Becky plays basketball and runs cross country and is planning to work in the medical field when she graduates in 2008. The youngest Joerger, and fourth son, is William—a football and basketball player. Both, according to Joe Joerger, "just hit the tennis ball around every once in a while."

(For more on the Joergers, see the profile of coach Joe Joerger in Chapter Three and the one on David Joerger in Chapter Five.)

The Luebbes & VanDeinses of Winona Cotter

I remember all too well the Luebbe and Van Deinse brothers from Winona Cotter. In 1977, when my Northfield team defeated Cotter in the Region I team final 3-2, three of their seven players were Luebbes and two were Van Deinses. And that year Doug Luebbe and Tom VanDeinse won the state doubles title over the McGregor twins of Duluth East.

These lads were fixtures on Cotter teams for well over a decade, the last of the Luebbe brothers, Derek, leading the Ramblers to a runner-up Class A team finish in 1989 and also taking home a third-place singles medal that year. As with so many talented outstate players, the Cotter boys were relatively unknown outside their geographic area, far southeast Minnesota. One reason is that Winona is 118 miles from the Metro area, but in addition Cotter rarely played schools from outside the area and almost all its top players chose not to compete in NWLTA summer tournaments in the Twin Cities. Instead they often played in Winona, Rochester, Mankato, Austin, and southwest

Wisconsin in the summers. Consequently, they were rarely ranked in the Section.

The oldest of the Luebbe brothers, 1977 state doubles champion Doug, also commented that they didn't need to travel very far for good coaching or for hitting partners. "We had some great instructors such as Bill VanDeinse, a former Gustie who taught for many years in Winona, as well as Mark Peterson—who had played at Notre Dame," said Luebbe. "In addition," he noted, "there was lots of good competition in Winona at the time including my brother Dave and the older VanDeinse brothers Bill, Paul, and Tom." Sometimes we'd have lessons for four hours and then play another hour or two afterward."

Though Doug Luebbe and Tom VanDeinse were the only brothers to win a state title, Doug's youngest brother, Derek, was a forceful region presence for many years and both families combined sent eleven tennis-playing sons to Cotter, very likely a record for one team in Minnesota. Three Luebbes, as mentioned earlier, were members of Cotter's 1977 Region I runner-up team (senior Doug played No. 1 singles, junior Dave No. 3 singles, and sophomore Dan No. 2 doubles). All played four years on the varsity, as did Dennis and Dean. The youngest Luebbe sibling, Derek, played five years on varsity. All the Luebbes, readers will note, have have first names beginning with the letter D.

His senior year in high school Dave Luebbe advanced to State in singles but lost to Mel Chez of Hibbing in the first round. He continued his playing career at Bemidji State College, and brother Doug played at St. Mary's College in Winona. According to Doug, Dave "continues to play tennis and runs the Teton Pines Tennis Center in Jackson Hole, WY. He has been there for over twenty years." Youngest brother Derek went to Valparaiso U to play Division 1 tennis. (For more about Doug Luebbe and Tom VanDeinse, see Chapter Six.)

As for the five VanDeinse boys, middle son Tom was the only one to win a MSHSL-sponsored title, though oldest brother Bill (affectionately called "Will") won two Catholic School titles before Cotter began competing in the public-school arena. Tom claims that both his older brothers (Bill and Paul) were better players but that he excelled because of his athletic ability.

Tom, remembering how this family of five boys and four girls got started playing tennis, recounted, "When I was three years old, I very distinctly remember my dad driving all nine of us kids by a fenced area in a big park in Winona. These were the Winona Park and Rec tennis courts. My dad was actually driving us by a house that we were about to purchase right behind these tennis courts. Fortunately for us, the previous owner had left some old racquets in the basement (with steel strings), and worm-eaten white tennis balls were easy enough to find in the surrounding woods." Thus, in this fateful event, began the tennis careers of the VanDeinse boys, who soon began gathering with neighborhood kids for "pick-up" games of tennis and other sports at their backyard park. Tom, who rhapsodized about these "good old days," said, "In the '70s a common phrase heard around the park was 'I'll play you for the court.' Wood racquets. White balls in pressurized cans you opened with a key like a can of spam. Remember spinning the racquet for 'rough or smooth?' Those were the days!"

But the VanDeinses also took tennis lessons at the "Park Courts" in Winona from excellent teachers such as Pat O'Day and Pat Sherman ("a skilled player who developed tennis elbow in her right arm and then taught herself to play with her left arm"). In these lessons, Tom recalls, we "learned how to score, how to bounce a ball up and down 100 times, and what 'down-the-line' and 'cross court' meant, that tennis is a 'game of inches,' and that it's important to 'just get the ball in'." Mostly, however, he remembers playing a great deal of tennis, "first one to 100 points, best-of-15 sets, and round robins with whoever showed up." And, like the Luebbes, the VanDeinse boys didn't need to call up a friend to come and hit with them; instead they could just roust one of their brothers out of bed and say, "Let's go hit."

All the brothers ended up doing some tennis coaching; in fact, Tom said that at one time or another he had taught with all of them. Oldest brother Bill played some tournament tennis after finishing his college career at Gustavus, thanks to a benevolent aunt who, according to Tom, felt a need to do "penance for the time when he [Bill] broke his arm on a slide while she was supposed to be watching him." Of his other three brothers, Tom said,

"Paul was better than me but was never able to go as far as he could have. Jim and Jon [the two youngest brothers] were progressively less serious about tennis but did OK."

The Wheatons of Minnetonka

Some readers of a certain age may remember rushing home from school in order to settle down on the couch to listen to popular serialized radio shows in the days before TV. One such show, enticing us with its opening call of "Jack Armstrong, Jack Armstrong, the All-American Boy," aired from 1933-50. A show that was phenomenally popular with children, it featured a high school boy (Jack Armstrong) and his friends from fictitious Hudson High School, Billy and Betty Fairchild, and their Uncle Jim. In some of the most outrageous plots ever concocted, according to a Web site titled "Sounds from the Past—Jack Armstrong," the programs focused on this merry crew in their global "pursuit of criminals, intrigue, and adventure" (Chris Plunkett, May 19, 2003). Sponsored by the breakfast cereal Wheaties, the show also offered gift promotions that were wildly successful. "For ten cents and a couple box tops, children would send away for Jack Armstrong 'shooting planes, dragon eye rings, pedometers, Egyptian whistling code rings, flashlights, compasses, oriental stamps,' and many other exciting and valuable premiums." These sales gimmicks were so effective that following the first promotional offer it was rumored "that the nation's supply of Wheaties was interrupted for months" (Web site, May 19, 2003).

So where am I going with this blast from the past? Well, Jack Armstrong was a teenaged super-athlete, the show was sponsored by Wheaties, ... Hm! Here in Minnesota we had a famous tennis family of teenaged super-athletes, one of whom was featured on a Wheaties box; and the tag of all-American boy (and girl) could be applied to all four of these siblings from Minnetonka. To be sure they did not catch cattle rustlers in Arizona, chase bandits across polar ice floes, hunt down pirates in Zanzibar, nab Nazi spies, or trek across the Andes. But their adventures on the tennis courts, here in Minnesota and across the globe, were just as memorable to those who saw them play.

(Left to Right) Grandfather Hessey, father Bruce, Marnie, mother Mary Jane, David, Mark, & John Wheaton

So why not call them, the Wheatons, our all-American tennis family?

Their story began on the Deephaven beach court near their home, where grandfather John Hessey (described by oldest child, Marnie, as "old-school") taught them the proper tennis technique, which he studied extensively in books, articles, and his own imagination. Hessey's grandson, Mark, recalls these early lessons when he was eight or nine years old:

> In his [Grandfather Hessey's] community tennis classes he taught the fundamentals of strokes. He'd go down the baseline and make sure we had the grip right—no extreme Western forehand grips, just Continental and Eastern forehand—then we'd do "dry" swings. He'd also show us different spins, for a topspin forehand and a slice backhand. He also taught me the different serves: the slice, the flat, and, his favorite, the American twist serve. He'd hit balls to us with his metal frame, wire string racket called the Dayton "Lone Eagle." He often said to me, "Make the other guy miss" and "Hit it where he ain't," advice which I followed to a T in my early junior days before I got big enough to play more aggressively.

Hessey was a self-taught tennis player and an extraordinarily fit man who swam a mile a day into his 80s, lifted weights, and played golf up to age 100, two years before he died at 102. Youngest sibling David did not receive much coaching from his grandfather, for when he began to play tennis, mother Mary Jane (Hessey's daughter) did some coaching and both she and father Bruce chauffeured daughter Marnie and the boys to tournaments. Third sibling John said, "I was the 'tag along' brother to Marnie and Mark, and since they were playing tournaments in their teens it was natural for me, as a nine- or ten-year-old, to take up the game. I was watching the older kids play and it inspired me to give it a try. I have fond memories of hitting against the backboard at the Lafayette Club in Orono or the club in Duluth. I also remember hitting with John McEnroe's little brother Patrick (three or four years old at the time), in Chattanooga, TN, where our older brothers were competing in the boys' 12 nationals."

Like a big bear in a soggy forest, the Wheatons left

enormous footprints on the Minnesota high school and college tennis landscape. The results of their early training (and an insistence on "perfect technique" by their grandfather) are noted in other chapters in this book, but here are some of them again. Marnie was a member of the 1974 Minnetonka boys' championship team, earned top rankings as a junior (No. 1 in doubles with Ann Henricksson and No. 2 in singles her second year in the 18s, for example), played four years at the U of M, and was one of the top adult women players in the Section for over ten years.

Mark won three state individual championships: two in singles and one in doubles. He was also ranked No. 1 or 2 in singles and No. 1 in doubles as a junior player for many years, he helped Minnetonka win its first and only boys' team championship in 1974, and he competed in college, like Marnie, at the U of M, winning the No. 3 doubles title in the Big Ten tournament. (For more about Mark's career, see Chapter Four.)

And though he didn't win as much hardware or earn as much acclaim as his siblings, brother John was a top player as well. As a junior he was ranked as high as No. 5 (in the 12s) and No. 6 (in the 18s) in singles and No. 2 in doubles (in the 18s) with teammate Glenn Britzius. In high school he and Britzius advanced to the quarters in the doubles draw at State his junior year (1978), he played first doubles on Minnetonka's '77 state runner-up team, and as a senior he played No. 1 singles. Of his high school years John remembers tough matches he had with the likes of John Gotschall from Edina East and Chris Combs from Edina West, but he also reminisced about the "great fun and relationships we had—for instance, water skiing with Glenn Britzius right before a match (in 1978) proved to be a bad idea. Our muscles were tight as drums and we could barely hit the ball. Other highlights included playing against Mike Ramsey (future Olympic and pro hockey player who was an outstanding athlete) and Coach Peterson chewing us out for reckless driving on our way back from a match in Mankato."

Youngest sibling David's exploits are described in Chapter Five, but it is worth noting here that he was the No. 1-ranked 12-and-under singles player in the NWTA when he was only nine years old, a ranking he would hold in the 12s for three more years until he left the state to play on the national scene in the summers. He was eventually ranked No. 6 in the world at age 18 after winning the 1987 U.S. Open Junior title in a draw which included Pete Sampras, Jim Courier, and Michael Chang.

Like Jack Armstrong, each of the Wheatons could be considered an all-American boy/girl who grew up in an all-American family. A close-knit family with a strong religious faith, they were raised in the charming village of Cottagewood in Deephaven, on the shores of Carson's Bay on Lake Minnetonka. Here they could walk to the local grocery store for a Fudgsickle, jump in the lake for a swim, ice skate in the winter, and, of course, play tennis on the two Cottagewood courts just a block from their house. So often did they play on these courts in the 1970s and '80s that the morning after Halloween one year they arrived at the courts to play and found that the court surface was spray-painted "Wheaton Memorial Courts" in huge white letters, possibly by a neighborhood kid playing a prank or by someone who got tired of waiting for them to get off the courts.

Their parents supported and encouraged them in tennis throughout the years, Mary Jane serving as their early coach (especially to David), motivator, and mentor, while also setting up practices. She also made sure that her four young tennis players practiced a good deal among themselves and with other good local players, and she also sacrificed her spare time by making meals on the fly and driving her children to courts both near and far.

Father Bruce was a willing helper, provider, and encourager who drove them to tournaments and provided behind-the-scenes advice and a rational plan for picking tournaments to play, colleges to attend, and professional contracts and agencies David should select. Bruce also took vacation time to travel to tournaments with his children. And, according to Mark, "It was an unspoken expectation that we would try our hardest in every match and never act in a way which would dishonor God or the family name. They [the parents] always put schoolwork first and wouldn't allow tennis to come before getting a good education."

In addition, Bruce and Mary Jane made many other sacrifices for their children. For example, in 1985 they moved to Florida so David could train at the Bolletierri

Tennis Academy in Bradenton. For three years they rented a place in Florida for part of the year in order to support David's dream of becoming a tennis professional. Fortunately they kept their place in Cottagewood and they still live in the house they have called home for thirty-four years. Today all four children live in the Minnetonka area, almost within shouting distance of their parents. But the closeness of this family cannot be measured by proximity alone; it is perhaps best represented in the ways each of them assisted youngest child David in his rise to the highest levels of pro tennis.

We've already mentioned the parents' move to Florida so David could train at the Bolletierri Academy, but brother Mark traveled with and coached David, who left Stanford after leading the Cardinal to the NCAA team title his freshman year (1988). With Mark's help David moved up in the rankings from No. 800 to the top 100 in one year. About this experience Mark said, "That first year I coached David full-time and after that I did it part time during my residency." Mark recalls how special this experience was for both of them but especially for 19-year-old David, traveling with his surfboard to places like Hawaii where he won a Masters Satellite tournament and Brasilia where he won a Challenger tournament and defeated the No. 34 player in the world (Luiz Mattar). Mark called these "the simple and innocent days when we drove scooters and looked for surf before we looked for the practice courts or found a modest hotel or family we could stay with."

Soon, said Mark, came "the days of huge crowds at Grand Slam events, big prize money, contracts, courtesy cars, signing autographs, and intense pressure"; but that first year was most memorable. Once David became successful on the pro tour, Mark continued to travel with and coach him, taking vacation time to join him at Wimbledon, the U.S. Open, and other venues.

Brother John also traveled with David on the junior circuit and later served as his agent, negotiating and managing his endorsement deals, his special appearances, and his tournament scheduling. After spending three years at Moody Bible Institute, playing one year of tennis at the U of M, and then receiving a law degree from Pepperdine University, John worked for the renowned International Management Group (IMG) for ten years as David's agent. During this time he also functioned as an IMG rep on certain occasions for other pro tennis players such as Jim Courier and Monica Seles and for events such as the First Banks Cup and the American Cup at Target Center. In addition, he served as an associate director at the Bolletierri Tennis Academy for one year and ran the Wheaton Tennis Academy at the Decathlon Club for six years until a fire shut down the club (and the Academy) in 2000. In '06 John was hired as director of tennis at the Wayzata Country Club and David joined him as Touring Tennis Professional.

Throughout the years Marnie provided big-sister advice for her kid brother and traveling companionship for David when Mark or John weren't available. In addition, she was not afraid to give David her insights to help him perform better. (For more about Marnie, see Chapter Seven.)

Just a few minutes walk down the road from where Bruce and Mary Jane Wheaton still reside on Cottagewood Avenue, Marnie, Mark, and John each live—and David lives ten minutes away. Marnie works as a flight attendant for Northwest Airlines, Mark is a physician, and John is a professor at Crown College in St. Bonifacius.

David has his own radio show, addressing current events, culture, and faith; speaks to various organizations; and has written a book released in 2005 titled *University of Destruction*," a book which gives Christian students going to college a spiritual game plan to combat the potentially destructive influences they might face. He remains involved in tennis, giving exhibitions and clinics, playing in over-35 mens' doubles events at Wimbledon and the U.S. Open, and writing feature articles for the *Star Tribune* on each of the four Grand Slam tournaments. In addition, he currently serves on the USTA Board of Directors. In 2005 he also served as the interim U of M men's tennis coach and that same year joined his sister, Marnie, as a member of the USTA/Northern Section Tennis Hall of Fame.

So why do we call the Wheatons an all-American family? For starters there are three generations of tennis players and coaches in the family, beginning with grandfather Hessey. There is mother Mary Jane, who prodded and encouraged her children, and father Bruce (he really did eat Wheaties long before Mark was pictured on the box) who guided them all with calm and reason. There is Marnie, the all-American girl who today flies the friendly skies as a flight attendant. Then there's physician Mark, who epitomized the spirit of that original all-American boy, Jack Armstrong. And there's John, a professor at Crown College and director of the Honors Program there.

The fourth Wheaton, and third all-American boy, is David, the state champion, top-ranked pro player, talk-radio host, part-time journalist, World Team Tennis performer, Wimbledon 35-and-over doubles champion, and now published author. But perhaps there is no better evidence of his all-American status than these facts: 1988 college tennis all-American at Stanford, member of the '93 U.S. Davis Cup team, U.S. Olympic Committee "Athlete of the Year—Tennis" in '87, and an honor bestowed by Minnesota governor Arnie Carlson in '91, "David Wheaton Day." An all-American in every sense of the term, he even chose the symbolic date of July 4th to launch his pro tennis career and wore a stars-and-stripes headband to show his support for U.S. troops during the Gulf War. That signature headband became his trademark and he wore it almost his entire career. Finally, this was a family that practiced together and even played tournaments together (father-son, mother-daughter, and mother-son).

Jack Armstrong, you have nothing on this all-American family. (For more about David, see Chapter Five.)

Appendix A

MSHSL Team
Tennis Champions

Note:

The MSHSL did not officially recognize a team champion until 1950, but starting in 1934 team standings were kept and included in the MSHSL yearbook. Newspaper articles from this early period refer to team "state champions." The following listing includes the team champion and the runnerup for each year.

YEAR	TEAM CHAMPION	TEAM RUNNER-UP
1934	Minneapolis Central—11 points	*Proctor—8 points*
1935	St. Paul Central—8 points	*Minneapolis Roosevelt—7 points*
1936	St. Paul Central—7 points Minneapolis Roosevelt—7 points	*University High—6 points*
1937	Minneapolis Central—10 points	*Proctor—7 points*
1938	Minneapolis Washburn—9 points	*Minneapolis West—8 points*

YEAR	TEAM CHAMPION	TEAM RUNNER-UP
1939	Minneapolis Central—11 points	Minneapolis West—8 points
1940	Minneapolis West—13 points	Hibbing—9 points
1941	St. Paul Central—10 points	Minneapolis West—7 points
1942	Minneapolis West—13 points	Minneapolis South—6 points
1943	Minneapolis West—13 points	Minneapolis Washburn—6 points
1944	Minneapolis Washburn—12 points	Minneapolis Roosevelt—5 points Minneapolis Central—5 points & Cloquet—5
1945	Minneapolis Washburn—7 points	Minneapolis Southwest—6 points
1946	Minneapolis Southwest—12 points	Minneapolis North—7 points
1947	Winona—5 points	Minneapolis Washburn—4 points
1948	Minneapolis Southwest—7 points	University High—3 points
1949	Duluth Central—9 points	Minneapolis North—8 points
1950	Rochester—44 points	Hibbing—12 points
1951	Rochester—42 points	Hibbing—30 points
1952	Minneapolis Southwest—9 points	Minneapolis Washburn—8 points
1953	Rochester—14 points	Minneapolis Central—9 points
1954	St. James—13 points	Rochester—12 points
1955	Rochester—17 points	Duluth Central—6 points St. Peter—6 points
1956	Rochester—9 points	Duluth East—8 points & Minneapolis Central—8 points
1957	Minneapolis Central—15 points	Rochester—10 points
1958	Minneapolis Marshall—12 points	St. Paul Monroe—11 points
1959	Edina—19 points	Faribault—14 points
1960	Stillwater—13 points	Edina—12 points
1961	Greenway of Coleraine—12 points	St. Paul Central—11 points
1962	Rochester—18 points	St. Paul Central—13 points
1963	Rochester—27 points	Minneapolis West—12 points

YEAR	TEAM CHAMPION	TEAM RUNNER-UP
1964	Rochester—17 points	Edina—13 points
1965	Rochester—19 points	Minnetonka—12 points
1966	North St. Paul—13 points & Edina—13 points	Rochester Mayo—12 points & Coon Rapids—12 points
1967	Edina—20 points	Minnetonka—15 points
1968	Edina—23 points	Rochester Mayo—22 points
1969	Austin—12 points	Edina—11 points
1970	Robbinsdale Cooper—16 points	Edina—15 points
1971	Edina—32 points	Robbinsdale Cooper—16 points
1972	Edina—32 points	St. Cloud Tech—12 points
1973	Edina East (First True Team Tourney)	White Bear Lake
1974	Minnetonka	White Bear Lake
1975	Edina East	Madison
1976	St. Cloud Tech	Minnetonka
1977	Blue Earth	Minnetonka
1978	Edina East	Minneapolis Roosevelt
1979	AA Edina East A Blake	Virginia St. Paul Academy
1980	AA Edina West A Blue Earth	Anoka Blake
1981	AA Edina East A Blake	St. Cloud Tech Wadena
1982	AA Austin A Blake	St. Cloud Tech Wadena
1983	St. Cloud Tech	Coon Rapids
1984	Blake	St. Cloud Tech
1985	St. Cloud Tech	White Bear Lake
1986	Minnehaha Academy	Stillwater
1987	AA Edina A Blake	St. Cloud Tech Blue Earth
1988	AA Edina A Blue Earth Area	Mounds View St. Peter

YEAR	TEAM CHAMPION	TEAM RUNNER-UP
1989	AA Edina A Litchfield	*Blake* *Winona Cotter*
1990	AA Mounds View A Staples/Motley	*St. Cloud Tech* *Orono*
1991	AA Blake A Staples/Motley	*St. Cloud Tech* *Orono*
1992	AA Edina A Blake	*St. Cloud Tech* *East Grand Forks*
1993	AA Wayzata A St. Paul Academy	*Stillwater* *St. Peter*
1994	AA Bloomington Jefferson A Blake	*Blaine* *Crookston*
1995	AA Edina A Breck	*St. Cloud Tech* *Blake*
1996	AA Bloomington Jefferson A Blake	*Rochester Mayo* *Duluth Marshall*
1997	AA Stillwater A Breck	*Wayzata* *Blake*
1998	AA Edina A Breck	*Red Wing* *Winona Cotter*
1999	AA Wayzata A Winona Cotter	*Minneapolis Southwest* *Blake*
2000	AA Edina A Blake	*Red Wing* *Breck*
2001	AA Minneapolis South A Breck	*Mahtomedi* *Duluth Marshall*
2002	AA Edina A Blake	*Eden Prairie* *Vlirginia*
2003	Edina Blake	*Orono* *St. Paul Academy*

Appendix B

State Tennis Team Participants
(Class AA) 1973-2003

Note:

The following abbreviations: **ch.** for champion, **r-up** for runner-up, **3rd pl.** for third place, and **cons. ch.** for consolation champion.

* See Class A Participants for more on these teams.

ANOKA 1980 (r-up), 1981 (3rd pl.), 1982, 2000

AUSTIN 1974 (3RD pl.), 1980, 1981, 1982 (ch.), 1994 (cons. ch.)

APPLE VALLEY 1984, 1990, 1991, 1992, 1993

BEMIDJI 1973, 1974

*BLAKE 1983 (3RD pl.), 1984 (ch.), 1985, 1988, 1989 (r-up), 1990, 1991 (ch.)

*BLUE EARTH 1973 (cons. ch.), 1974, 1976, 1977 (ch.), 1978 (cons. ch.), 1983, 1984, 1985

BLOOMINGTON JEFFERSON 1991, 1994 (ch.), 1996 (ch.)

BLAINE 1994 (r-up)

BRAINERD 1975

BUFFALO 1996

BURNSVILLE 1979, 1989

COON RAPIDS 1975 (3rd pl.), 1976, 1977, 1978, 1983 (r-up), 1984

CHASKA 1998, 2000

CRETIN-DERHAM HALL 1997, 1998, 2001, 2003

DULUTH EAST 1973, 1976 (cons. ch.), 1977, 1982, 1986, 1987, 1991, 1992, 1993, 2002, 2003

ELK RIVER AREA 2001, 2002

EDEN PRAIRIE 1987, 1990, 1991, 2002 (r-up)

EDINA 1982, 1984 (3ᴿᴰ pl.), 1985 (3rd pl.), 1986 (3rd pl.), 1987 (ch.),1988 (ch.), 1989 (ch.), 1990 (3rd pl.), 1992 (ch.), 1995 (ch.),1998 (ch.), 2000 (ch.), 2001 (3rd pl.), 2002 (ch.), 2003 (ch.)

EDINA EAST 1973 (ch.), 1975 (ch.), 1978 (ch.), 1979 (ch.), 1981 (ch.)

EDINA WEST 1980 (ch.)

FERGUS FALLS 1994, 2000

FRIDLEY 1981, 1982

HASTINGS 1976, 1987, 1989, 1990, 1991, 1992

HENRY SIBLEY 1978, 1979, 1980 (3rd pl.), 1981` 1999, 2000, 2001, 2002

HIBBING 1974, 1981, 1983, 1984, 1985, 1988, 1989, 1990

HIBBING/CHISHOLM 1997, 1998, 1999 (cons. ch.), 2000 (cons. ch.),2001

HUTCHINSON 1980, 1981, 1982, 1986, 1988, 1989, 1993, 1994, 1997,1999

IRONDALE, 1979

LITTLE FALLS 1973

*MADISON 1973, 1974 (cons. ch.), 1975 (r-up)

MAHTOMEDI 2001 (r-up)

MANKATO WEST 1992, 1995, 2001

MINNEAPOLIS ROOSEVELT 1976, 1977 (cons. ch.), 1978 (r-up)

MINNEAPOLIS SOUTH 1992 (cons. ch.), 1997 (cons. ch.), 1998 (cons. ch.), 2000 (3rd pl.), 2001 (ch.), 2002 (cons. ch.)

MINNEAPOLIS SOUTHWEST 1979, 1980, 1999 (r-up), 2003 (3rd. pl.)

MINNEAPOLIS WASHBURN 1987, 1993 (3rd pl.), 1994 (3rd pl.),1995 (cons. ch.), 1996

*MINNEHAHA ACADEMY 1986 (champ.)

MINNETONKA 1974 (champ.), 1976 (r-up), 1977 (r-up)

MOORHEAD 1974

MOUNDS VIEW 1987 (3rd pl.), 1988 (r-up), 1989, 1990 (champ.), 1998, 1999, 2002 (3rd pl.), 2003

NORTHFIELD 1975 (cons. ch.), 1977, 1978 (3rd pl.), 1985, 1986

*ORONO 2003 (r-up)

OWATONNA 1987

*PIPESTONE 1975

RAMSEY (ALEXANDER) 1977

RED WING 1995, 1998 (r-up), 2000 (r-up), 2001 (cons. ch.)

ROCHESTER MAYO 1973 (3rd pl.), 1983, 1996 (r-up.), 1997, 1999 (3rd pl.), 2003 (cons. ch.)

ROSEVILLE AREA 1988, 1993, 1994, 1995, 1996

ST. CLOUD TECH 1976 (champ.), 1977 (3rd pl.), 1981 (r-up), 1982 (r-up), 1983 (ch.), 1984 (r-up), 1985 (ch.), 1986, 1987 (r-up), 1989 (3rd pl.), 1990 (r-up), 1991 (r-up), 1992 (r-up), 1993, 1995 (r-up), 1996 (3rd pl.), 1997 (3rd pl.), 1998 (3rd pl.), 1999, 2003

ST. LOUIS PARK 1983

*SAINT PAUL ACADEMY 1976 (3rd pl.), 1984, 1985, 1986.

ST. THOMAS ACADEMY 1982 (3rd pl.), 1983

ST. CLOUD APOLLO 1988 (3rd pl.)

STILLWATER/STILLWATER AREA 1986 (r-up), 1991 (cons. ch.), 1992 (3rd pl.), 1993 (r-up), 1995 (3rd pl.), 1996, 1997 (ch.)

THIEF RIVER FALLS 1975, 1978, 1979, 1980

*VIRGINIA 1975, 1978, 1979 (r-up), 1980, 1994, 1995, 1996

WAYZATA 1993 (champ.), 1997 (r-up), 1999 (ch.)

WHITE BEAR LAKE 1973 (r-up), 1974 (r-up), 1985 (r-up)

WILLMAR 1979 (3rd pl.)

WINONA 1988, 2002

State Tennis Team Participants (Class A) 1979-82 & 1987-2003)

* See Class AA Participants for more on these teams.

ACADEMY OF THE HOLY ANGELS 1996

BENSON/KERKHOVEN-MURDOCK-SUNBURG 1992, 1993, 1995, 2000

*BLAKE/THE BLAKE SCHOOL 1979 (ch.), 1980 (r-up), 1981 (ch.), 1982 (ch.), 1987 (ch.), 1992 (ch.), 1993 (3rd pl.), 1994 (ch.), 1995 (R-up), 1996 (ch.), 1997 (r-up), 1999 (r-up), 2000 (ch.), 2001 (3rd pl.), 2002 (ch.), 2003 (ch.)

*BLUE EARTH, BLUE EARTH-FROST-WINNEBAGO, BLUE EARTH AREA 1979 (3rd pl.), 1980 (ch.), 1981, 1982, 1987 (r-up),1988 (ch.), 1994, 1995, 1996, 1997, 1998 (cons. ch.), 1999, 2000 (3rd pl.), 2001

BRECK SCHOOL 1989 (3rd pl.), 1995 (ch.), 1996, 1997 (ch.), 1998 (ch.), 2000 (r-up), 2001 (ch.)

CHISAGO LAKES 1992

CROOKSTON 1988, 1993, 1994 (r-up), 1995 (3rd pl.), 1996 (3rd pl.), 1997, 1998 (3rd pl.), 2000, 2001, 2003

DULUTH MARSHALL 1995 (cons. ch.), 1996 (r-up), 1997 (3rd pl.), 2000, 2001 (r-up), 2003 (3rd pl.)

EAST GRAND FORKS 1989, 1992 (r-up), 2002

FAIRMONT 1990 (3rd pl.), 1991 (3rd pl.), 1992 (3rd pl.)

FOLEY 1994

GILBERT 1979, 1980

GRANITE FALLS, GRANITE FALLS-CLARKFIELD, YELLOW MEDICINE EAST 1980, 1981, 1991 (cons. ch.), 1994 (cons. ch.), 1999, 2002

LITCHFIELD 1989 (ch.), 1991, 1997, 1998, 1999, 2000, 2001, 2002 (cons. ch.), 2003

*MADISON 1979

*MINNEHAHA ACADEMY 2002

MONTEVIDEO 1982 (3rd pl.), 1996, 1997, 1998, 2001

MOUNDS PARK ACADEMY 2003

NEW LONDON-SPICER 1998 (3rd pl.), 1995, 1996

*ORONO, ORONO-LONG LAKE 1990 (r-up), 1991 (R-up)

PARK RAPIDS AREA 1999

PINE CITY 1981 (3rd pl.), 1982, 1990, 1993, 1998, 1999 (cons. ch.)

*PIPESTONE AREA 2003

ROCHESTER LOURDES 1979, 1980, 1982, 1991, 1995, 2002 (3rd pl.)

ROSEAU 1979, 1980

ST. CLOUD CATHEDRAL 1992, 1993, 1994

*ST. PAUL ACADEMY, ST. PAUL ACADEMY AND SUMMIT SCHOOL 1979 (r-up), 1980 (3rd pl.), 1981,
        1982, 1987 (3rd pl.), 1991, 1993 (ch.), 1994 (3rd pl.), 1998, 1999 (3rd pl.), 2003 (r-up)

ST. PETER 1988 (r-up), 1993 (r-up)

STAPLES, STAPLES-MOTLEY 1979, 1987, 1990 (ch.), 1991 (ch.)

*VIRGINIA 1991, 1992 (cons. ch.), 2002 (r-up)

WADENA 1980, 1981 (r-up), 1982 (r-up)

WASECA 2002, 2003 (cons. ch.)

WAUBUN 1981, 1982

WINONA COTTER 1989 (r-up), 1992, 1993, 1994, 1997 (cons. ch.), 1998 (r-up), 1999 (ch.), 2000
        (cons. ch.), 2001 (cons. ch.)

* See Class A Participants for more on these teams.

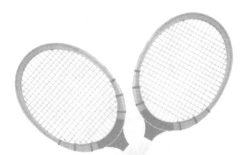

Appendix C
Historic Draw Sheets

1929 SINGLES DRAW—First State Tournament

Bye
J. Halverson (Proctor)
— Halverson

R. Putnam (Red Wing)
Bye
— Putnam

Halverson (7-5, 6-2)

P. Wilcox (Mt. Lake)
N. Wilkins (Red Wing)
— Wilkins (6-1, 6-2)

R. Campbell (W. Bear. Lk.)
W. Monson (Mpls. South)
— Monson (6-4, 6-1)

Monson (6-1, 6-0)

Monson (6-1, 3-6, 6-4)

Bye
A. Hargesheimer (Roch.)
— Hargesheimer

C. Roslyn (W. Bear. Lk.)
Bye
— Roslyn

Hargesheimer (6-2, 7-5)

Bye
R. Wilcox (Mt. Lake)
— R. Wilcox

Charles Britzius (Roch.)
Bye
— Britzius

Britzius (7-5, 6-2)

Britzius (7-5, 6-2)

Monson
(8-6, 4-6, 7-5, 6-4)

1929 DOUBLES DRAW—First State Tournament

Cool and Watson
(Mpls. West)

White Bear Lake
(5-7, 6-1, 6-2)

Roslyn and Campbell
(White Bear Lake)

White Bear Lake
(7-5, 6-2)

Spurbeck and Brophy
(Proctor)

Proctor
(6-2, 6-1)

Putnam and Wilkins
(Red Wing)

Rochester
(6-3, 6-3, 6-4)

Bye

Mt. Lake

R.Wilcox and P. Wilcox
(Mt. Lake)

Rochester
(6-3, 6-4)

Hargesheimer and Britzius
(Rochester)

Rochester

Bye

1973—First TRUE TEAM Tournament

Rochester Mayo

Mayo (4-1)

Blue Earth

Edina East (3-2)

Edina East

Edina East (5-0)

Little Falls

Edina East (3-2)
(Champions)

Madison

Bemidji (3-2)

Bemidji

Wh. Bear Lk. (4-1)

White Bear Lake

Wh. Bear Lk. (4-1)

Duluth East

Edina East 1973 Team—State Champions

Third-Place Match

Mayo

Mayo (4-1)

Bemidji

Consolation Rounds

Blue Earth

Blue Earth (5-0)

Little Falls

Blue Earth (3-2)
(Cons. Champions)

Madison

Duluth East (4-1)

Duluth East

Appendix D
Presidents of the MN State H. S. Boys' Tennis Coaches Assoc.

2004-06 Les Zellman—St. James
2002-04 John Eberhart—Pine City
2001-02 George Beske—Minneapolis South
1999-01 Naomi Hagestuen—Eastview
1997-99 Mike Remington—Eagan
1996-97 Jane Kjos—Benson
1995-96 Loren Dunham—Fairmont
1993-95 Rich Strohkirch—Eden Prairie
1992-93 Mike Premo—Foley
1990-92 Ken Anderson—Irondale
1989-90 Don Wojciechowski—Spring Lake Park
1988-89 Dennis Flesner—Little Falls
1987-88 Jerry Sales—St. Cloud Tech
1986-87 Gary Plank—Duluth Central
1985-86 Keith Paulson—Austin
1984-85 John Eberhart—Pine City
1983-84 Milt Verant—Hibbing

1982-83 Ken Peterson—Anoka
1981-82 Jolly Carlson—Madison
1979-81 Bill Ritchie—St. Cloud Tech
1978-79 Lyle Steffenson—Hastings
1977-78 Ken Peterson—Anoka
1976-77 Jim Holden—Northfield
1974-76 Bruce Getchell—White Bear Lake
1973-74 Tom Byrne—Owatonna
1972-73 Bud Schmid—Brainerd
1971-72 Ed Sewell—North St. Paul
1970-71 Glenn Ray—Minneapolis Edison
1968-70 John Matlon—Edina
1963-64 Dick Thatcher—Rochester

Appendix E

BOYS' COACHES
Listed by Region/Section

Following are the names of other prominent coaches I am familiar with. Most coached for many years and some led their teams to the State Tournament. (Note: their state tournament appearances are listed in parentheses.)

Region/Section 1

1. Paul Andrejewski—Waseca (affectionately called "Mr. A" by his players)
2. Joe Boyer—Rochester Century, Rochester John Marshall, Virginia (1995, '96)
3. Jerry Childs—Red Wing
4. Gary Eagan—New Prague
5. Dave Edwards—Mankato West (1992), Rochester John Marshall. Edwards was '99 Class AA singles champion Eric Butorac's coach.
6. Mark Ensrud—Northfield
7. Lorne Grosso—Rochester Mayo (1996, '97, '99, 2003). Grosso was voted MN Boys' Tennis Coach of the Year in '97.
8. Orrin Jirele—Albert Lea
9. Joe Joran—Apple Valley (1984, '90)
10. Bret Joyce—Stewartville. Joyce started the abbreviated Stewartville program. The school no longer has a boys' tennis program.
11. Jack Knotz—Faribault
12. Curt Matejcek—Owatonna. Matejcek is a former Owatonna High School and Mankato State player and assistant to the retired Ron Phillips.

13. Jack Olwell—Farmington. Still coaching both the boys and girls teams, Olwell began coaching the boys' team in 1981.
14. Ron Phillips—Owatonna (1987)
15. George Pulchinski—Austin Pacelli
16. J. Paul Richards—Winona (1988)
17. Kevin Rust—Rochester Mayo, Rochester Lourdes (Class A—2002). Better known as the coach of Lourdes' dynasty girls' teams, Rust is a teaching pro at the Rochester Athletic Club. He has won two major Northern Section awards for coaching: the Ward C. Burton Junior Development Award in 1999 and the Frank Voigt Pro of the Year Award in 2005.
18. Chuck Willinghanz—Rochester Lourdes (1979, '80, '82)
19. Al Wold—Rochester John Marshall. Also a successful basketball coach whose teams won state titles in Faribault and Rochester, Wold served for many years as Region 1 tournament manager.

Region/Section 2

1. Bruce Arlt—St. Peter (Class A—1988, '93)
2. Scott Berg—Chaska (1988, 2000)
3. Ross Bettin—Martin County West
4. Jerry Carlson—Hutchinson
5. Bill Cauchy—Hutchinson (1980, '81, '82)
6. Janet Dickinson—LeSueur
7. Gil Idso—Willmar (1979). Idso started the Willmar boys' program and coached for 26 years.
8. Peter Liljengren—St. Peter
9. Jim Miller—Prior Lake. Miller is another of those individuals who served as the first coach of his school's tennis team. In his case he started the boys program in 1974 and the girls in '76. Retired in 2006, he coached the boys for 32 years and the girls for 30 years.
10. Joe Poncin—New Ulm. Joe, who began at New Ulm in 1972, is still coaching.
11. Jim Sand—United South Central (formerly Wells)
12. Elton Schoenrock—Mankato West
13. Jerry Sonich—Blue Earth (1995, '96, '97, '98,

'99). Hal Schroeder's long-time assistant coach, Sonich led the Bucs to five straight state tournament appearances and a consolation championship in '98.
14. Dave Svingen—Luverne (coached for over 30 years)
15. Marlene Swanson—Worthington
16. Bruce Wessman—Waseca (2003)
17. Gordy Ziebart—Rochester Lourdes

Region/Section 3

1. Winthrop "Windy" Block—Montevideo (Class A—1982). Block served as treasurer for the boys' tennis coaches association for a time, and his boys always competed well against those excellent Madison teams coached by Jolly Carlson.
2. Dave Hegna—Glenwood (now Minnewaska Area)
3. Conrad Hoff—St. Paul Johnson. For many years Hoff managed the State Tournament when it was held at the U of M courts.
4. John Howard—MACCRAY. Howard's is a remarkable story of overcoming adversity, for he survived a serious car accident to return to teaching and coaching. In addition, according to Willmar coach Hal Miller, "There is hardly anyone who has spent more time and money on tennis, even at times buying his own tennis balls. He's given his heart and soul to MAC-CRAY's tennis program."
5. Mark Johnson—Montevideo (Class A—1996, '97, '98, 2001)
6. Gordon Kasel—Granite Falls (Class A—1980, '81, '91, '94, '99, 2002). Kasel was voted by his peers as MN Boys' Tennis Coach of the Year in '01.
7. Charlie Keifenheim—Buffalo.
8. Randy Muetzel—Cretin-Derham Hall (1997, '98, 2001, 2003)
9. Dave Poehler—Tartan
10. Harvey Shaw—Redwood Falls
11. Cal Sorenson—South St. Paul
12. Elmer Vanderah—Henry Sibley (1978, '79, '80, '81)

Region/Section 4

1. Chuck Anderson—Robbinsdale Cooper, Breck, Stillwater (1995, '96, '97). Anderson led both Stillwater ('97) and Cooper ('70) to team championships. (For more on him, see Chapter Ten.)
2. Ken Anderson—Irondale. Ken served as president of the boys' coaches association from 1990-1992.
3. Forrest Dahl—Minnehaha Academy. Dahl coached the 1986 state champion Minnehaha team. (For more on Dahl, see Chapter eight.)
4. Dick Hemberger—Park-Cottage Grove
5. Bill Herzog—Stillwater (1986, '91, '92, '93). He was voted Class AA MN Boys' Tennis Coach of the Year in 1993.
6. Doug Niska—North St. Paul
7. Maurice "Morrie" Roberg—Fridley
8. Bob Sack—St. Anthony
9. Mel Smith—St. Paul Academy (Class A—1991, '93). Smith coached SPA to the 1993 title.
10. Greg Warhol—Centennial

Region/Section 5

1. Jim Barry—Minneapolis Southwest (1980)
2. Ray Carlson—Minneapolis North
3. Clayton "Bucky" Freeberg—Minneapolis Roosevelt (1976, '77, '78), Minneapolis Southwest. George Beske of South recounts that Freeberg's biggest coup was persuading Greg Wicklund to quit baseball and come out for tennis. Wicklund said of his high school coach, "He knew the game and helped me with my slice backhand and kick serve."
4. Carl Gustafson—Minneapolis West
5. Ed Nagle—Minneapolis Central
6. Glen Ray—Minneapolis Edison. Ray was the second president of the boys' tennis coaches association (1970-71).
7. Jack Roach—Minneapolis Edison, Kellogg, and Aitkin. (For a profile on Roach, see Chapter Six.)
8. Mike Sack—St. Anthony, Holy Angels (Class A—1996 in Section 1)

Region/Section 6

1. Dale Anderson—Hopkins Lindbergh, Hopkins
2. Paul Bates—St. Cloud Tech. Bates replaced Hall of Famers Bill Ritchie and Jerry Sales.
3. Steve Begich—Richfield.
4. Ed Bolger—Long Prairie
5. Harold "Butch" Derksen—Robbinsdale Armstrong
6. Rick Engelstad—Pine City. Though Rick is starting just his sixth year as the Pine City boys' coach, he assisted John Eberhart for many years and has been very active in the tennis coaches association. He has been a section representative and he serves as treasurer of the association and as director for the very successful spring coaching clinics held at the White Bear Lake Racquet Club.
7. Dennis Flesner—Osakis, Little Falls. Flesner served as president of the boys' tennis coaches association during the 1988-89 school year.
8. Tom Frederich—Robbinsdale Armstrong
9. Don Gerlach—Burnsville
10. George Henke—Deephaven (one of the Lake Conference pioneer coaches)
11. Marv Hartung—Bloomington Kennedy
12. Larry Hodgson—New York Mills
13. Tom Hutton—Hopkins Eisenhower, Hopkins. Though Hutton is perhaps better known for his successful basketball teams, he was a top player on MIAC championship Hamline U teams in the 1960s and has coached good tennis teams at Hopkins.
14. Paul Jorgenson—Osakis. Coached Osakis from 1963-67 and from 1970-82.
15. Mark Muntifering—St. Cloud Apollo

16. Ray Punkris—Edina West (1980). For more on Punkris, see Chapter Nine.)
17. Mac Redmond—Bloomington Jefferson
18. Dave Reier—St. Louis Park (1983)
19. Ellis Scheevel—St. Cloud Cathedral (Class A—1992, '93, '94)
20. Dave Stearns—Minnetonka. Dave is a former St. Cloud star player.
21. Mel Undlin—Sauk Centre. Undlin coached for a number of years until Sauk Centre dropped its boys' program.
22. Jim Walsh—Osakis
23. Joe White—Bloomington. White was the coach of the first tennis team in the new Bloomington High School in the spring of 1951. A biology teacher, White taught in the Bloomington system until 1985. He died in 2004.

Region/Section 7

1. Jim Alstad—Grand Rapids
2. Paul Bouchard—Greenway of Coleraine/Brooklyn Center. Bouchard was the coach of the 1961 championship Greenway team and author of the *Wirtanen Scorebook*. (For more on him, see Chapter Eight.)
3. Bill and Shirley Brunsdale—Mahnomen
4. Emil Erickson—Virginia. Erickson was Chuck Anderson's high school coach, and he also started up the tennis program at Mesabi Community College. Former Virginia coach Jim Prittinen reported that Erickson often rode his bike to the courts to play with willing youngsters and he continued to play tennis well into his 80s.
5. Mike Guzzo—Silver Bay
6. Lou Janesich—Grand Rapids. 2005 Class AA Boys' Coach of the Year.
7. Michael Krebsbach—Virginia (1991, '92-Class A and 1994-Class AA)
8. Phil Lahti—Duluth East (1987). Though Lahti only coached one year at East, he is included because for 12 years he ran the indoor club at Duluth and coached nearly all the top Duluth players, including Eric Donley and his three

talented sisters. He also coached five East girls' teams into state and today serves as a stringer on the pro tennis circuit.
9. Larry Longmore—Silver Bay.
10. Greg Patchen—Forest Lake
11. Gary Plank—Duluth Central. Plank served as president of the tennis coaches association from 1986-87.
12. Jim Prittinen—Virginia (1979, '80). A dentist by trade, Prittinen has had his hand in Virginia tennis for years, including working to get an indoor tennis center there and serving as a coach on the high school teams.
13. Tom Prosen—Eveleth-Gilbert (Class A—1979, '80). Longtime coach at Eveleth-Gilbert.
14. Lee Stark—Hibbing. A French teacher, Stark coached the Bluejackets from 1958-72
15. Dan Sundberg—Virginia (1975, '78)
16. Jim Turchi—Duluth East (1973, '76, '77)

Region/Section 8

1. Scott Engelstad—Bemidji. Brother of Pine City coach Rick Engelstad, Scott was 2004 Class AA Boys' Tennis Coach of the Year.
2. Bill Figg—Alexandria
3. Ellis Halgrimson—Bemidji (1973, '74)
4. Gary Harris—Detroit Lakes
5. Curt Johnson—Elk River Area (2001, '02). Johnson is a mailman.
6. Randy Klassen—Elk River. He was voted the 2003 MN Boys' Coach of the Year in Class A.
7. Bruce Thompson—Brainerd

OK, that's my list; and it comes with apologies to any I have left out.

Appendix F
Parochial/Private School Results

(Partial Results—Mostly Singles)

1946—McNairy—St. Thomas Academy

1948—Jack McGinnis—DeLaSalle

1949—McGinnis again

1950—Bob Clarkin—St. Thomas Academy (Bucky Olson was his coach)

1951—Clarkin again (described as having "a classy back court game")

1952—Dick Collins—DeLaSalle

1954—Jerry Strang—Cretin (St. Thomas Academy won its fifth straight team title)

1955—Stang again

1957—Phil Muller—DeLaSalle

1958—Larry Haugh—Cretin

1959—Dan Dwyer—St. Thomas Academy. (Bucky Olson still the coach)

1960—Tom Arth (Jeanne Arth's brother)—Cretin. Just a sophomore, he beat Dwyer in the semis after losing to him in the finals in '59.

1961—Ron Meyer—DeLaSalle (beat Arth in the finals)

1962—Meyer over Arth again. (Meyer and Arth met in the finals three years in a row)

1965—Jeff Mork—Benilde

1966—Craig Thornton—Winona Cotter (a freshman)

1967—Tom Paul—Duluth Cathedral

1968—Paul again. Bill VanDeinse and Pat Wadden of Winona Cotter won the doubles. This was the first combined MN Independent School League (MISL) meet.

1970—Bill VanDeinse—Winona Cotter (he defeated Jim Kronschnabel of St. Thomas Academy)

1971—Kronschnabel again. (this time he defeated VanDeinse)

1972—Kronschnabel yet again. Kronschnabel's only high school loss was to VanDeinse in '70—he had a record of 67-1 coming into the tourney. Paul Muesing (future Metro-area pro) and Dave Kaiser of New Ulm Luther won the doubles.

1973—St. Paul Academy (SPA) won the team title.

1974—SPA won this last MISL team championship. Cliff Caine was the coach and there were 22 independent and parochial teams competing.

Appendix G
Media Reporters & Tennis Patrons

Media Reporters

Over the years radio, newspaper, and television reporters have given much-needed recognition to young tennis players. In Northfield, for instance, KYMN radio sponsored a Saturday morning show called Coaches' Corner that featured interviews with Northfield coaches conducted by longtime Northfield businessman, civic booster, radio personality, and sports promoter Dan Freeman.

Unfortunately, until the mid-to-late 1970s there was very little newspaper coverage of high school tennis and most articles were short, factual pieces with no bylines. But when tennis became more popular in the mid-1970s, newspapers began to devote more space to the sport. Therefore, there were many notable writers (and other media personnel) who penned high quality articles. So here is a partial list of some and short profiles of four who were given special awards by the USTA/Northern Section.

Jimmy Byrne (*Minneapolis Star*).

Byrne covered Minnesota prep sports for many years. Because he suffered from cerebral palsy and was unable to drive, he often cadged rides or rode streetcars or buses to events. For his coverage of tennis he was given the Ward C. Burton Award in 1967. Byrne died in 2006 at age 86.

Bob Larson
(*Tennis Midwest* and other tennis publications).

A tireless promoter of high school and college tennis, especially the U of M Gophers, Larson has won numerous awards form the USTA/Northern Section, including the Section's first Media Award in 1997. He also won the USTA/Northern Section President's Award in '79, and he's a member of the Section Hall of Fame. In addition, in '92 he and his wife, Jean, and their two children (Cara and Cort, both former Edina High School players) were voted NWTA Family of the Year. Bob has also served as an NWTA president and delegate and he has served on several USTA committees. In addition, he founded the MN Tennis Hall of Fame in '79 and co-founded the U of M booster club called the Baseline Club. Bob continues to publish (*Tennis News* and *MN Tennis News*), and he's a No. 1 Edina fan.

Bob Larson

Minneapolis Star Tribune writers.

These included, among many others, Roman Augustoviz, Rachel Blount, Tom Briere, Bruce Brothers, Jim Paulsen, Michael Rand, Ralph Thornton, Brian Wicker, Nolan Zavoral, and Judd Zulgad.

Pat Ruff (*Rochester Post-Bulletin*).

Pat is the 2006 NWTA Media Excellence Award winner.

St. Cloud Daily Times writers.

Tom Elliott and Tom Larson.

St. Paul Pioneer Press writers.

Mike Fermoyle, Rick Shefchik, and Jim Wells.

The Sun Newspaper

John Sherman.

Television Supporters

These include Charlie Boone of WCCO radio, Diana Pierce and Belinda Jensen of KARE 11 TV, and Frank Vascellaro of WCCO TV, all of whom have promoted tennis in Minnesota and, as a result, have been selected as USTA/Northern Media Excellence Award winners.

Greg Wicklund (*TennisLife Magazine*).

In addition to his exploits on the court as a top high school (Minneapolis Roosevelt), college (U of M), and adult player and his long and successful career as a USPTA teaching pro in the Metro area, Greg has distinguished himself as a writer. He began by penning a chatty column for Bob Larson's *Tennis Midwest* magazine (called "Service Line") and now writes a very popular column in *TennisLife Magazine* called "Racquet Ramblings." Greg is also the 2005 USTA/Northern Section Media Excellence Award winner.

As a player he got a late start in tennis (at sixteen) because he also played baseball and basketball, but he soon moved into the lineup for Coach Bucky Freeburg's Roosevelt team (No. 2 singles his sophomore year and No. 1 singles his junior and senior years). He credits playing with his mentors (John Desmond, Jerry Pope, Tony Williams, John Shannon, Jack Roach, Dick Martinson, Norm McDonald, Connie Custodio, Ken Boyum, and Dave Petersen) for helping him get better. And though he did not win a state title, he had an outstanding career at the U of M, playing mostly Nos. 4 or 5 singles for Jerry Noyce and winning the No. 5 Big Ten singles title his senior year. In

Greg Wicklund

addition, in the winter of 1983 he tried the pro circuit and earned a ranking of No. 450. He also served as Noyce's assistant coach for six years.

But for most of his career, beginning in 1982, he has taught at 98th Street Racquet Club in the winters and at the Edina Country Club in the summers, working especially with dozens of ranked junior players. Greg has continued to play competitive tennis, and he has been one of the top NWTA adult players for years, earning numerous No. 1 rankings in several age groups and winning several Sectional titles as well.

Greg Wong (*St. Paul Pioneer Press*).

Wong wrote a weekly tennis column for over twenty years and for thirty years covered the boys' and girls' State Tournaments, the U of M teams, local Division 3 programs, and other tennis events. In 1998 he was the second USTA/Northern Media Award winner and in 2003 (at the U.S. Open) he was awarded the USTA Media Excellence Award. He's a former member of the NWTA Board of Directors, a longtime member of the U.S. Tennis Writers Association, and a 1988 recipient of the Northwestern Section Tennis Association Special Award. To cap it off, he was voted into the NWTA Hall of Fame in ' 03. By the way, he's also an avid player.

Tennis Patrons

I would be remiss if I did not also mention the many patrons who have given their money and/or time on behalf of high school tennis in Minnesota, so here are some who deserve consideration.

Ward Burton.

A Minnetonka area resident, Burton contributed greatly to local junior tennis and has an NWTA award named after him: the Ward C. Burton Junior Development Award.

Dan Corrigan.

Corrigan was the owner of several of the first tennis clubs in the Twin Cities: Southdale, the St. Paul Racquet Club, and Eagandale.

Jack Dow.

A founding president of the Northwest Tennis Patrons, Dow is perhaps better known as the founder of the Senior Tennis Players Club. An NWTA Senior Development Award is named after him, he was voted Tennis Pro of the Year in 1983, and he is a Northern Section Hall of Fame member as well.

Skip Gage.

A varsity tennis performer at Northwestern U over 40 years ago and the former CEO of the Carlson Companies, Gage has four years helped support inner city tennis programs.

Mike Lynne.

Owner of a tennis shop in St. Louis Park, Lynne and his wife, Mimzy, have given many gifts of money and tennis equipment, particularly for inner city youngsters. In 2001 they received a special award from the Northern Section.

Jim Murphy.

Murphy is a former men's coach at St. John's U who founded the Tennis Foundation of St. Cloud. He was also a former president of the Northern Section.

Harvey Ratner & Marv Wolfenson

Harvey Ratner and Marv Wolfenson.

The founders and developers of the Northwest Tennis Clubs, Ratner and Wolfenson deserve a great deal of credit for the Minnesota tennis boom in the 1970s and '80s. After opening the Richfield Club in 1968, these two expanded, bought, and built clubs all over the Minneapolis area and, as a result, in 1985 there were a total of thirteen Northwest clubs. These clubs gave local youngsters an opportunity to develop their games in the winter.

Wolfenson was an avid and successful tennis player (for instance, he earned several No. 1 or 2 rankings in the Men's 50 and 55 divisions), and both he and Ratner have been justly honored by the Section for their contributions. There is a community service award named after them, an award they won in 1996, and both are members of the Northern Section Hall of Fame. Wolfenson also won the Ward C. Burton Junior Development Award in '76. They are perhaps best known as the men who brought professional basketball (the Timberwolves) back to Minneapolis, but their hearts were in tennis as well. Ratner died in 2006.

Lach Reed.

Reed donated to so many projects over the years and contributed to the Reed-Sweatt Tennis and Learning Center (formerly the Nicollet Tennis Club now named after him and his father-in-law, Harold Sweatt). In 1952 Reed also founded an important philanthropic organization called the Northwest Tennis Patrons, and his Brackett's Point

Junior Geriatric Tennis Invitational—held on his clay court in Wayzata—has been an important fund raiser for Inner City Tennis, which he also founded in '52. Reed, who won the NWTA President's Award in '82 for these and other efforts on behalf of Minnesota tennis, is also a member of the Northern Section Hall of Fame.

He grew up playing on clay courts in Turkey and played at Andover and Yale as a young man. In addition, he was for many years a top senior player in the Section, earning several No. 1 rankings in both singles and doubles. Reed died at age 90 in 2007.

Fred Wells.

Wells made significant contributions to multicultural tennis programs in the area, including financing the Fort Snelling Tennis and Learning Center which opened in 2002 and establishing (with his wife Ellen) a foundation called the Wells Foundation. Wells, who played tennis and squash, made his money in the grain trading and marketing business.

Fred and Ellen received the Northern Section Special Award in 1998, and Fred received both the Section Community Service Award in '99 and the Unsung Hero Award in 2003. He was also one of six national USTA Community Service Award winners in '00. Wells died in '05 at age 77.

Reference List

Bartlett, John and Justin Kaplan, gen. ed. 1992. *Bartlett's Familiar Quotations* 16th ed. Boston: Little, Brown, and Co.

Brewer, E. Cobham. 1978. *Brewer's Dictionary of Phrase and Fable.* New York: Avenel Books.

Collins, Bud and Zander Hollander, eds. 1998. *Bud Collins' Tennis Encyclopedia.* Detroit: Visible Ink Press.

Kundera, Milan. 1999. *The Book of Laughter and Forgetting.* New York: Harper Collins.

Morris, William, ed. 1969. *American Heritage Dictionary.* Boston: Houghton Mifflin.

Photos & Captions

Photos Courtesy of MSHSL

Photos Courtesy of USTA/Northern

About the Author

A baseball and basketball player as a youngster, Jim Holden was an adult convert to tennis who became a coach before he knew much about the game. Despite this impediment, he accepted the challenge and coached the Northfield high school boys' team for seventeen years. (For an account of his tennis coaching years, see the profile in Chapter Two).

Now retired from a forty-year career in teaching, twenty-nine as a secondary English teacher and eleven as a professor of education at Gustavus Adolphus and St. Olaf Colleges in Minnesota, Holden still takes time to play tennis. In addition, as an avid fly-fisherman he has become acquainted with almost every trout stream in western Wisconsin and southeast Minnesota. He and his wife, Caroline, raised two children, Chris and Heather, both of whom played high school tennis for Northfield and went on to play college tennis. He and Caroline also enjoy traveling, reading, bird watching, walking in the woods, and indulging every whim of their seven lovely grandchildren.